Sara Coleridge Coleridge, Edith Coleridge

Memoir and letters

Sara Coleridge Coleridge, Edith Coleridge

Memoir and letters

ISBN/EAN: 9783337821630

Printed in Europe, USA, Canada, Australia, Japan

Cover: Foto ©ninafisch / pixelio.de

More available books at **www.hansebooks.com**

MEMOIR AND LETTERS

OF

SARA COLERIDGE.

EDITED BY

HER DAUGHTER.

"A Spirit, yet a Woman too."
WORDSWORTH.

NEW YORK:

HARPER & BROTHERS, PUBLISHERS,

FRANKLIN SQUARE.

1874.

MEMOIR AND LETTERS OF

SARA COLERIDGE.

PREFACE.

"Poor is the portrait that one look portrays,
It mocks the face on which we loved to gaze."*

And if this be true of such external resemblances as pictorial art is employed to produce, it is equally true of that unconscious self-portraiture, that revelation of the inner mind, which is contained, in a greater or less degree, in any collection of published letters. The interest which such works are intended to excite is, in the main, biographical, and their object is not merely to preserve and bring to light a number of writings of intrinsic merit and beauty, but still more, perhaps, to present to the reader a record, however imperfect, of the personal characteristics, both moral and intellectual, of the writer.

But how faint and inadequate, if not incorrect, is that image of the departed which can alone be thus reproduced! Even the original correspondence, could it be given entire in all its details (which is, for obvious reasons, impossible), would be but as a mirrored reflection—a selection from the correspondence is but its scattered fragments.

The difficulty which must attend on all such undertakings as that on which I have been engaged, in editing the letters

---

* Lines in "Phantasmion."

of my Mother, is rather increased than diminished by that very quality which constitutes their peculiar charm—I mean their perfect genuineness and life-like reality.

Touching descriptions of personal feeling, acute remarks, and wise reflections occur here in abundance, which seem, to the eye of affection, to be "gems of purest ray serene," the utterances of a heart full of sensibility, and an intellect at once subtle and profound. Yet, severed as they must often be from the context which justified and explained them, these thoughtful comments on the life within and around her may, it is to be feared, either lose their full significance, or assume one that is exaggerated and untrue.

Even those portions of the following collection which seem, at first sight, to be most abstract and elaborate (such as the critical discussions on Art and Poetry, and those which intimate the results of speculative thought and religious inquiry), will be found, on consideration, to be full of personal references, suggested by special occasions, and connected at all points with the realities of life.

The letters of Sara Coleridge were not acts of authorship, but of friendship; we feel, in reading them, that she is not entertaining or instructing a crowd of listeners, but holding quiet converse with some congenial mind. Her share of that converse we are privileged in part to overhear, while the response is borne away by the winds in another direction.

A book composed of epistolary extracts can never be a wholly satisfactory one, because its contents are not only relative and fragmentary, but unauthorized and unrevised. To arrest the passing utterances of the hour, and reveal to the world that which was spoken either in the innermost circle of home affection, or in the outer (but still guarded) circle of social and friendly intercourse, seems almost like a betrayal of confidence, and is a step which can not be taken by survivors without some feelings of hesitation and reluctance. That reluctance is only to be overcome by the sense that, however natural, it is partly founded on delusion — a delusion which leads us to personify "the world," to our imagination, as an obtuse and somewhat hostile individual, who is certain to take things by the wrong handle, and can not be trusted to make the needful allowances and supply the inevitable omissions. Whereas it is a more reasonable, as well as a more comfortable belief, that the only part of the world which is in the least likely to concern itself with such a volume as this, is composed of a number of enlightened and sympathetic persons, who, it is hoped, though strangers to all but the name of Sara Coleridge, may yet derive from her letters some portion of the gratification which they once afforded to those who knew and loved her. And if it be well for us to "think on whatsoever things are true, whatsoever things are pure, whatsoever things are lovely," and to rejoice in "any virtue and any praise," we ought surely to be willing that all who desire it should hear the music of the words in which these things are uttered, and see the light of the life in which they shone.

In conclusion, I have only to offer my respectful and grateful acknowledgments to those who have rendered this memorial possible by their kindness in intrusting me with these treasured records of a friendship long past, yet never past away.

E. C.

Hanwell Rectory, *May* 7, 1873.

CONTENTS.

CHAPTER II.—1834.

CHAPTER III.—1834 (*continued*).

CHAPTER IV.—1835.

CHAPTER V.—1836.

CHAPTER VI.—1837.

CHAPTER VII.—1838.

CHAPTER VIII.—1839.

CHAPTER IX.—1840.

CHAPTER XII.—1844.

CHAPTER XIII.—1845.

CHAPTER XIV.—1846, *January-July.*

CHAPTER XV.—1846, *July–December.*

CHAPTER XVI.—1847, *January - July.*

CHAPTER XVII.—1847, *July – December.*

CHAPTER XVIII.—1848.

CHAPTER XXI.—1849, *July–December.*

what they Might Be.—Remarks of Sir Francis Palgrave on the Resurrection of the Body, and on the Gospel Narratives of the Healing of Demoniacs.—Proposed View of the Miracles in Question does not "Explain them Away."—A Last View of Herne Bay.—Home and Social Duties.—Archbishop Trench on the Miracles. — Associations with Places. — Love and Praise. (396–402.)——IX. Kentish Landscapes.—Scenery of the Lakes. (402.)——X. A Pet Name.—Child-like Playfulness of Aristophanes.—Theological Readings of S. C.—The Miracle of Gadara.—The Origin of Mental Disorders not a Religious, but a Scientific Question. — Language of our Lord on such Occasions that of Parable.—Liability of Animal Natures to Frenzy.—Metaphysical Views of the Early Fathers not held now by any School of Thinkers.—Mr. Coleridge's Letters on Inspiration.—"The Old Curiosity Shop."—Little Nell and Mignon. (403–407.)——XI. Remarks on an Article on "Tennyson, Shelley, and Keats," in the *Edinburgh Review.*—Inferiority of Keats to Shelley in Point of Personal Character.—Connection between Intellectual Earnestness and Moral Elevation.—Perfection of his Poetry within its own Sphere.—Versatility ascribed by the Reviewer to Keats in Contrast to Coleridge. — Classification of her Father's Poems, showing their Variety. (407–411.)——XII. Personal Likeness between Mr. Coleridge and Lord Macaulay. (412.)

CHAPTER XXII.—1850, *January-July.*

I. Chinese Selfishness. — The Irish Famine. — Objects of Charity. — Church Decoration, and the Relief of the Poor.—Butchers' Prices.—Sudden Death of Bishop Coleridge.—The Anglican Formularies a Compromise.—Non-natural Sense put on the Baptismal Service by One Party, and on the Articles and Homilies by Another.—Mystic Theory of Regeneration, Unsupported by Antiquity, Opposed to the Moral Sense, and Contradicted by the Epistle of St. John. (413–419.)——II. Various Occupations of S. C.—Fatigues of Chaperonage.—Barry Cornwall at a Ball.—Waltzing.—Invitation to the Lakes.—Effect of Railway Traveling on her Health.—(419–421.)——III. "Telling" Speeches not always the Best. (421, 422.)——IV. Death of Mrs. Joanna Baillie. (422.)——V. Mr. Carlyle's "Latter-day Pamphlets" compared with his "Chartism."—Ideal Aristocracy.—English Government. (422, 423.)——VI. Home Amusements.—Reasonings of an Anti-Gorham Controversialist.—Holiness the Evidence of Election, not its Ground. (423–425.)——VII. Illness of Mr. Wordsworth. (425.)——VIII. Lives of the Lake Poets.—Presumption of Incompetent Biographers. (425, 426.)—— IX. Hopes of Mr. Wordsworth's Recovery. — His Natural Cheerfulness.—Use of Metaphysical Studies. (427, 428.)——X. A Relapse.

CHAPTER XXIII.—1850, *July–December.*

LETTERS TO MRS. MOORE, MISS FENWICK, AUBREY DE VERE, ESQ., PROFESSOR HENRY REED, REV. EDWARD COLE-RIDGE, MISS MORRIS, EDWARD QUILLINAN, ESQ., HON. MR. JUSTICE COLERIDGE 451–482

CHAPTER XXIV.—1851, *January-July.*

CHAPTER XXV.—1851, *July–December.*

Memoir.

RECOLLECTIONS

OF THE

EARLY LIFE OF SARA COLERIDGE.

WRITTEN BY HERSELF,

In a Letter addressed to her Daughter.

I.

MY DEAREST E——,

I have long wished to give you a little sketch of my life. I once intended to have given it with much particularity, but now *time presses**—my horizon has contracted of late. I must content myself with a brief compendium.

I shall divide my history into childhood, earlier and later; youth, earlier and later; wedded life, ditto; widowhood, ditto; and I shall endeavor to state the chief moral or reflection suggested by each—some maxim which it specially illustrated, or truth which it exemplified, or warning which it suggested.

My father has entered his marriage with my mother, and the births of my three brothers, with some particularity, in a Family Bible, given him, as he also notes, by Joseph Cottle on his marriage; the entry of my birth is in my dear mother's handwriting, and this seems like an omen of our life-long separation, for I never lived with him for more than a few weeks at a time. He lived not much more, indeed, with his other children; but most of their infancy passed under his eye. Alas! more than

---

* This fragment of autobiography was begun during my mother's last illness, eight months before her death.—E. C.

C

any of them I inherited that uneasy health of his, which kept us apart. But I did not mean to begin with—alas! so soon or so early to advert to the great misfortune of both our lives— want of bodily vigor adequate to the ordinary demands of life, even under favorable circumstances.

I was born at Greta Hall, near Keswick, December 22d, 1802. My brother Hartley was then six years and three months, born September 19th, 1796, at Bristol; Derwent, born September 14th, 1800, at Keswick, two years and three months old. My father, Samuel Taylor Coleridge (married at Bristol, October 4th, 1795, to Sarah Fricker, eldest daughter of Mr. Fricker, of Bristol), was now twenty-nine years of age; my mother, thirty-one. Their second child, Berkeley, born at Nether Stowey, May 10th, 1798, died, while my father was in Germany, February 10th, 1799, in consequence of a cold caught after inoculated small-pox, which brought on decline. Mamma used to tell me mother's tales, which, however, were confirmed by my Aunt Lovell, of this infant's noble and lovely style of beauty—his large, soft eyes, of a "London-smoke" color, exquisite complexion, regular features, and goodly size. She said that my father was very proud of him, and one day, when he saw a neighbor approaching his little cottage at Stowey, snatched him away from the nurse half dressed, and with a broad smile of pride and delight, presented him to be admired. In her lively way, she mimicked the tones of satisfaction with which he uttered, "This is my second son." Yet, when the answer was, "Well, this is something like a child," he felt affronted on behalf of his little darling Hartley.

During the November, and great part of December, previous to my birth, my father was traveling in Cornwall with Mr. Tom Wedgewood, as I learn by letters from him to my mother. The last of the set is dated December 16th, and in it my father speaks as if he expected to be at Ambleside Thursday evening, December 23d. He writes with great tenderness to my mother on the prospect of her confinement. I believe he reached home the day after my birth. Several of his letters, the last three, are from Crescelles, the house of Mr. Allan, father of Lady Mackintosh and of Mrs. Drew, the brother of Lady Alderson.

Mamma used to tell me that, as a young infant, I was not so fine and flourishing as Berkeley, who was of a taller make than any of her other children, or Derwent, though not quite so small as her eldest born. I was somewhat disfigured with red-gum. In a few months, however, I became very presentable, and had my share of adoration. "Little grand-lamas," my father used to call babes in arms, feeling doubtless all the while what a blessed contrivance of the Supreme Benignity it is that man, in the very weakest stage of his existence, has power in that very weakness. Then babyhood, even where attended with no special grace, has a certain loveliness of its own, and seems to be surrounded, as by a spell, in its attractions for the female heart, and for all hearts which partake of woman's tenderness, and whose tenderness is drawn out by circumstances in that particular direction.

My father wrote thus of Hartley and of me in a letter to Mr. Poole of 1803 : "Hartley is what he always was, a strange, strange boy, 'exquisitely wild;' an utter visionary—like the moon among thin clouds, he moves in a circle of light of his own making. He alone is a light of his own. Of all human beings, I never saw one so utterly naked of self. He has no vanity, no pride, no resentments; and, though very passionate, I never yet saw him angry with any body. He is, though seven years old, the merest child you can conceive ; and yet Southey says he keeps him in perpetual wonderment, his thoughts are so truly his own. His dispositions are very sweet; a great lover of truth, and of the finest moral nicety of feelings; and yet always dreaming. He said very prettily, about half a·year ago, on my reproving him for some inattention, and asking him if he did not see something : 'My father,' quoth he, with flute-like voice, 'I see it—I saw it, and to-morrow I shall see it again when I shut my eyes, and when my eyes are open, and I am looking at other things ; but, father, it is a sad pity, but it can not be helped, you know; but I am always being a bad boy when I am think-ing of my thoughts.' If God preserve his life for me, it will be interesting to know what he will become ; for it is not only my opinion, or the opinion of two or of three, but all who have been with him talk of him as a thing that can not be forgotten."

"My meek little Sara is a remarkably interesting baby, with the finest possible skin, and large blue eyes ; and she smiles as if she were basking in a sunshine, as mild as moonlight, of her own quiet happiness."

In the same letter, my father says: "Southey I like more and more. He is a good man, and his industry is stupendous ; take him all in all—his regularity and domestic virtues, genius, talent, acquirements, and knowledge—and he stands by himself."

Of this first stage of my life, of course I have no remembrance ; but something happened to me when I was two years old which was so striking as to leave an indelible trace on my memory. I fancy I can even now recall, though it may be but the echo or reflection of past remembrances, my coming dripping up the Forge Field, after having fallen into the river, between the rails of the high wooden bridge that crossed the Greta, which flowed behind the Greta Hall hill. The maid had my baby-cousin Edith, sixteen months younger than I, in her arms ; I was rushing away from Derwent, who was fond of playing the elder brother on the strength of his two years' seniority, when he was trying in some way to control me, and in my hurry slipped from the bridge into the current. Luckily for me, young Richardson was still at work in his father's forge. He doffed his coat and rescued me from the water. I had fallen from a considerable height, but the strong current of the Greta received me safely. I remember nothing of this adventure but the walk home through the field. I was put between blankets on my return to the house ; but my constitution had received a shock, and I became tender and delicate, having before been a thriving child. As an infant, I had been nervous and insomnolent. My mother has often told me how seldom I would sleep in the cradle ; how I required to be in her arms before I could settle into sound sleep. This weakness has accompanied me through life.

One other glimpse of early childhood my mind retains. I can just remember sitting by my Aunt Lovell in her little down-stairs wing-room, and exclaiming, in a piteous tone, " I'se miseral !" A poor, little, delicate, low-spirited child I doubtless was, with my original nervous tendencies, after that escape from the Greta. " Yes, and you will be miserable," Aunt Lovell compassionately broke out, as mamma has told me, " if your mother doesn't put you on a cap." The hint was taken, and I wore a cap till I was eight years old. I appear in a cap, playing with a doll, in a little miniature taken of me at that age by the sister of Sir William Benthorn, who also made portraits in the same style of my Uncle and Aunt Southey, my mother, Aunt Lovell, and cousins Edith and Herbert.

I can not leave this period of my existence without some little allusion to my brother Derwent's sweet childhood. I have often heard from mamma what a fine, fair, broad-chested little fellow he was at two years old, and how he got the name of Stumpy Canary when he wore a yellow frock, which made him look like one of those feathery bundles in color and form. I fancy I see him now, as my mother's description brought him before me, racing from kitchen to parlor, and from parlor to kitchen, just putting in his head at the door, with roguish smile, to catch notice, then off again, shaking his little sides with laughter. Mr. Lamb and his sister, who paid a visit of three weeks to my parents in the summer of 1802, were charmed with the little fellow, and much struck with the quickness of eye and of memory that he displayed in naming the subjects of prints in books which he was acquainted with. " Pi-pos, Pot-pos," were his names for the striped or spotted opossum, and these he would utter with a nonchalant air, as much as to say, " Of course, I know it all as pat as possible." " David Lesley, Deneral of the Cock Army," was another of his familiars. Mr. Lamb calls him " Pi-pos" in letters to Greta Hall, after his visit to the Lakes.

My parents came to Keswick in 1801. My father writes to my Uncle Southey, urging his joining him in the North, and describing Greta Hall, April 13th, 1800. See Southey's Life, vol. ii., p. 146.

I find in a letter of mamma to Aunt Lovell, written, but not sent, this record of early Greta Hall times:

"Well, after poor Mrs. Southey's* death, you all removed to Bristol, where the first child, Margaret, was born and died. Soon after this period, Southey, Edith, and you (Mrs. Lovell) came to Keswick. How well I recollect your chaise driving up the Forge Field ! The driver could not find the right road to the house, so he came down Stable Lane, and in at the Forge Gate. My Sara was seven months old, *very sweet*, and her uncle called her ' Fat Sal.'

" My husband, I think, was then in Malta, where he remained three years—there and in Sicily and Rome. Soon after his return in the autumn of 1806, Coleridge went away with Hartley to the Wordsworths at Coleorton ; thence he went to Lon-

---

* The mother of Robert Southey.—E. C.

don, and wrote to me to bring the other two children to Bristol, and wait there in College Street, at Martha's, with mother, till he should join us to go to Stowey and Ottery together. Accordingly I set off to Penrith, stayed a night at old Miss Monkhouse's, and next day proceeded toward Liverpool, where we were met by Dr. Crompton's carriage, and taken to Eton Hall, four miles out of Liverpool, where we stayed a fortnight, to the great happiness of Derwent and Sara. Thence we got to Birmingham, stayed a few days with the Misses Lawrence, saw Joseph Lovell and wife and children, and then proceeded to Bristol, to Martha's in College Street.

" After some time, Samuel Taylor Coleridge brought Hartley from London to join us, and we five all proceeded to Stowey, to Mr. Poole's most hospitable abode, remaining most pleasantly with him for more than two months, and did not go to Ottery at all. (I believe they had illness there.) We made visits to Ashhall (Mr. Brice's), to Bridgewater, at the Chubbs'. Then I, with my children, returned to Bristol, hoping to be rejoined by father. At length he came, but was not for returning with us to Keswick. We set forward with Mr. De Quincey to Liverpool, where we (*i. e.*, myself and children) remained a few days with the Koster family, and were again joined by Mr. De Quincey, and reached Grasmere, where we were joyfully received by the Wordsworths at their cottage, and the next day took a chaise to Keswick, on which occasion poor Hartley was so afraid that he should not again be a pet of dear friend Wilsy,* that he screamed out of a window of the chaise, 'Oh, Wilsy, Wilsy, let me sleep with you!'"

I was in my fifth year during this visit to the South, and my remembrances are partial and indistinct glimpses of memory, islanded amid the sea of non-remembrance. I recollect more of Derwent than of Hartley, and have an image of his stout build, and of his resolute, managing way, as we played together at Bristol. I remember Mrs. Perkins, with her gentle, Madonna countenance; and walking round the square with her daughter, who gave me currants when we came round to a certain point. I have faint recollections, too, of Stowey, and of staying at the Kosters' at Liverpool. At this time I was fond of reading the original poems of the Misses Taylor, and used to repeat some

* Mrs. Wilson, the landlord's housekeeper.—See Memoir of Hartley Coleridge, p. xxix.—E. C.

of them by heart to friends of mamma's. Aunt Martha I
thought a fine lady on our first arrival at College Street. She
wore a white veil—so it seems to my remembrance—when I
first saw her. I can but just remember Aunt Eliza, then at
Mrs. Watson's, and that there was an old lady, very invalidish,
at College Street, Mrs. Fricker, my mother's mother. At this
time I could not eat meat, except bacon.

My brothers were allowed to amuse themselves with the noble art of painting, which they practiced in the way of daubing
with one or two colors, I think chiefly scarlet, over any bit of a
print or engraving, in vol. or out of it, that was abandoned to
their clutches. It was said of Derwent, that upon one of these
pictorial occasions, after diligently plying his brush for some
time, he exclaimed, with a slow, solemn, half-pitying, half-self-
complacent air, "Thethe little minute thingth are *very* difficult;
but they *mutht be done!* ethpethially *thaithes!*"* This "*mutht
be done!*" conveyed an awful impression of resistless necessity,
the mighty force of a principled submission to duty, with a hint
of the exhausting struggles and trials of life.

Talking of struggles and trials of life, my mother's two un-
married sisters were maintaining themselves at this time by
their own labors. Aunt Martha, the elder, a plain, but lively,
pleasing woman, about five feet high, or little more, was earn-
ing her bread as a dress-maker. She had lived a good deal
with a farmer in the country, Uncle Hendry, who married
Edith Fricker, her father's sister; but not liking a female-farm-
er mode of life, came to Bristol, and fitted herself for the business. Uncle Hendry left her a small sum of money, some hundreds, and would have done more, doubtless, had she remained
with him. Burnet offered marriage to my Aunt Martha during
the agitation of the Pantisocracy scheme. She refused him
scornfully, seeing that he only wanted a *wife in a hurry*, not her
individually of all the world.

Aunt Eliza, a year or twenty months younger, about the same
height, or but a barleycorn above it, was thought pretty in
youth, from her innocent blue eyes, ingenuous florid countenance, fine light-brown hair, and easy, light motions. She was
not nearly so handsome in face, however, as my mother and
Aunt Lovell, and had not my Aunt Southey's fine figure and

---

* *i. e.*, chaises.—E. C.

quietly commanding air. Yet, on the whole, she was very feminine, pleasing, and attractive. Both sisters sang, but had never
learned music artistically.

Such were my Aunts Martha and Elizabeth Fricker in youth;
but they had sterling qualities, which gave their characters a
high respectability. Without talent, except of an ordinary kind,
without powerful connections, by life-long perseverance, fortitude, and determination, by prudence, patience, and punctual-
ity, they not only maintained themselves, but, with a little aid
from kind friends, whom their merits won, they laid by a comfortable competency for their old age. They asked few favors,
accepted few obligations, and were most scrupulous in returning such as they did accept, as soon as possible. They united
caution and discretion with perfect honesty and truth, strict fru-
gality and self-control, with the disposition to be kind and
charitable, and even liberal, as soon as ever it was in their
power. Their chief faults were pride and irritability of temper. Upon the whole, they were admirable women. I say
were; but one, Aunt Eliza Fricker, still survives, in the Isle of
Man. Aunt Martha died of paralysis, at the Isle of Man, September 26, 1850, at the age of seventy-three. Aunt Eliza is ailing; she must be seventy-three, I believe, now, or seventy-two.*

Our return to Greta Hall has left an image on my mind, and
a pleasant one. I can just remember entering the parlor, seeing the urn on the table, and tea things laid out, and a little
girl, very fair, with thick yellow hair, and round rosy cheeks,
seated, I think, on a stool near the fire. This was my cousin
Edith, and I thought her quite a beauty. She looked very shy
at first, but ere long we were sociably traveling round the
room together on one stool, our joint vessel, and our childish
noise soon required to be moderated. I was five years old the
Christmas after this return, which, I believe, was latish in autumn. I remember how Mr. De Quincey jested with me on
the journey, and declared I was to be his wife, which I partly
believed. I thought he behaved faithlessly in not claiming my
hand. I will now describe the home of my youth, dear Greta
Hall, where I was born, and where I resided till my marriage,
at twenty-six years of age, in September, 1829. It was built on
a hill, on one side of the town of Keswick, having a large nurs-

* Miss Fricker died at Ramsay, in the Isle of Man, in September, 1868.—
E. C.

ery garden in front. The gate at the end of this garden opened upon the end of the town. A few steps farther was the bridge over the Greta. At the back of Greta Hall was an orchard of not very productive apple-trees and plum-trees. Below this a wood stretched down to the river-side. A rough path ran along the bottom of the wood, and led, on the other hand (the Skiddaw side of the vale), to the Cardingmill Field, which the river near by surrounded ; on the other hand, the path led below the Forge Field, on to the Forge. Oh, that rough path beside the Greta! How much of my childhood, of my girlhood, of my youth, was spent there !

But to return to the house. Two houses inter-connected under one roof, the larger part of which my parents and my Uncle and Aunt Southey occupied, while the smaller was the abode of Mr. Jackson, the landlord. On the ground-floor was the kitchen, a cheerful, stone-flagged apartment, looking into the back place, which was skirted by poultry and other out-houses, and had trees on the side of the orchard, from whence it was separated by a gooseberry hedge. There was a drooping laburnum-tree outside our back kitchen, just in the way as you passed to the Forge Field portion of the kitchen-garden.

A passage ran from the kitchen to the front door, and to the left of this passage was the parlor, which was the dining-room and general sitting-room. This apartment had a large window, looking upon the green, which stretched out in front, in the form of a long horseshoe, with a flower-bed running round it, and fenced off from the great nursery garden by pales and high shrubs and hedges. There was another smaller window, which looked out upon another grass-plot. The room was comfortably but plainly furnished, and contained many pictures, two oil landscapes, by a friend, and several water-color landscapes. One recess was occupied by a frightful portrait of mamma, by a young lady.

The passage ran round the kitchen, and opened into two small rooms in one wing of the rambling tenement, one which Aunt Lovell sat in by day, and another which held the mangle, had cupboards as a pantry, but was called the mangling-room. Here we kept the lanterns and all the array of clogs and pattens for out-of-door roamings. The clog shoes were ranged in a row, from the biggest to the least, and curiously emblemed the various stages of life.

The staircase, to the right of the kitchen, which you ascended from the passage, led to a landing-place filled with book-cases; a few steps more led to a little bedroom which mamma and I occupied—that dear bedroom where I lay down, in joy or in sorrow, nightly for so many years of comparative health and happiness, whence I used to hear the river flowing, and sometimes the forge hammer in the distance, at the end of the field; but seldom other sounds in the night, save of stray animals. A few steps farther was a little wing bedroom, then the study, where my uncle sat all day occupied with literary labors and researches, but which was used as a drawing-room for company. Here all the tea-visiting guests were received. The room had three windows, a large one looking down upon the green with the wide flower-border, and over to Keswick Lake and mountains beyond. There were two smaller windows looking toward the lower part of the town seen beyond the nursery garden. The room was lined with books in fine bindings; there were books also in brackets, elegantly lettered vellum-covered volumes lying on their sides in a heap. The walls were hung with pictures, mostly portraits, miniatures of the family and some friends, by Miss Benthorn; of Uncle and Aunt Southey, by Downman, now engraved for the Life of Southey; of my cousin Edith and me, by Mr. Nash; and the three children, Bertha, Kate, and Isabel, by the same hand. At the back of the room was a comfortable sofa, and there were sundry tables, besides my uncle's library-table, his screen, desk, etc. Altogether, with its internal fittings up, its noble outlook, and something pleasing in its proportions, this was a charming room. I never have seen its like, I think, though it would look mean enough in my eyes, as a mere room, could I see it now, as to size, furnishing, etc. The curtains were of French gray merino, the furniture-covers, at one time, buff; I can not tell what they were latterly. My uncle had some fine volumes of engravings, which were sometimes shown to visitors; especially, I remember, Duppa's sketches from Raphael and Michael Angelo from the Vatican.

On the same floor with the study and wing bedrooms was a larger bedroom above the kitchen, looking into the back yard. This was my uncle and aunt's sleeping apartment. A passage, one side of which was filled with book-shelves, led to the Jackson part of the house, the whole of which after his decease (and some rooms before) belonged to our party. There was a room which used to be my father's study, called the organ-room, from an old organ which Mr. Jackson placed there ; a bedroom generally occupied by Aunt Lovell, looking into the back place—this was a comfortable but gloomyish room. At the end was a wing bedroom. Thence stairs led down to Wilsy's bedroom, Hartley's parlor, Wilsy's kitchen and back kitchen.

In the highest story of the house were six rooms, a nursery, nursery bedroom, maid's bedroom, another occupied by Kate and Isabel at one time, a sort of lumber-room, and a dark apple-room, which used to be supposed the abode of a bogle. Then there was a way out upon the roof, and a way out upon the leads, over one wing of the house, whence we could look far out to the Penrith Road, Brow Top, and the Saddleback side of the region.

I must now give one general sketch of the garden, of which scraps of description have already been attached to that of the house. It was very irregular. In front of the house and the two large windows of parlor and study, was the green, running out in the form of a long horseshoe, with a wide border of flower-garden all round, and sheltered by a hedge. The kitchen-garden was in two parts, on either side of this lawn. There was green sward also on the side of the house containing the front door, and there were green palings inclosing this part of the premises. A few steps from the front door of the larger side of Greta Hall was the front door of the landlord side, and that wing of the building was covered with ivy. The parlor of that part of the house, long called Hartley's parlor, looked out on a piece of green sward on the other side of our front door. From the back place a path led along to the gate of the nursery garden. To the right was another piece of green, with a large copper-beech at one end, and a sort of shrubbery; below that again, a set of beds, which were given up to us children as our garden.

That part of the kitchen-garden which lay below the hedge that bounded the lawn was divided into beds for the smaller vegetables, and there was at the lower end a little grove of raspberry bushes, white and red, and beyond this a plantation of under-ground artichokes, which my uncle was fond of, and a gooseberry hedge called Hartley's, I think, for what reason I forget. Peas and beans were in the lower part of the garden abutting on the Forge Field; in the upper compartment were the strawberry beds.

My young life is almost a blank in memory from that well-remembered evening of my return from our series of southern visits, till the time of my visit to Allan Bank, when I was six years old. That journey to Grasmere gleams before me as the shadow of a shade. Some goings on of my stay there I remember more clearly. Allan Bank is a large house on a hill, overlooking Easedale on one side, and Grasmere on the other. Dorothy, Mr. Wordsworth's only daughter, was at this time very picturesque in her appearance, with her long, thick, yellow locks, which were never cut, but curled with papers—a thing which seems much out of keeping with the poetic simplicity of the household. I remember being asked by my father and Miss Wordsworth, the poet's sister, if I did not think her very pretty. "No," said I, bluntly; for which I met a rebuff which made me feel as if I was a culprit.

My father's wish it was to have me for a month with him at Grasmere, where he was domesticated with the Wordsworths. He insisted upon it that I became rosier and hardier during my absence from mamma. She did not much like to part with me, and I think my father's motive, at bottom, must have been a wish to fasten my affections on him. I slept with him, and he would tell me fairy stories when he came to bed at twelve and one o'clock. I remember his telling me a wild tale, too, in his study, and my trying to repeat it to the maids afterward.

I have no doubt there was much enjoyment in my young life at that time, but some of my recollections are tinged with pain. I think my dear father was anxious that I should learn to love him and the Wordsworths and their children, and not cling so exclusively to my mother, and all around me at home. He was therefore much annoyed when, on my mother's coming to Allan Bank, I flew to her, and wished not to be separated from her any more. I remember his showing displeasure to me, and accusing me of want of affection. I could not understand why. The young Wordsworths came in and caressed him. I sat benumbed; for truly nothing does so freeze affection as the breath of jealousy. The sense that you have done very wrong, or at least given great offense, you know not how or why—that you are dunned for some payment of love or feeling which you know not how to produce or to demonstrate on a sudden—chills the heart, and fills it with perplexity and bitterness. My father reproached me, and contrasted my coldness with the childish caresses of the little Wordsworths. I slunk away, and hid myself in the wood behind the house, and there my friend John, whom at that time I called my future husband, came to seek me.

It was during this stay at Allan Bank that I used to see my father and Mr. De Quincey pace up and down the room in conversation. I understood not, nor listened to a word they said, but used to note the handkerchief hanging out of the pocket behind, and long to clutch it. Mr. Wordsworth, too, must have been one of the room walkers. How gravely and earnestly used Samuel Taylor Coleridge and William Wordsworth, and my Uncle Southey also, to discuss the affairs of the nation, as if it all came home to their business and bosoms—as if it were their private concern! Men do not canvass these matters nowadays, I think, quite in the same tone. Domestic concerns absorb their deeper feelings; national ones are treated more as things aloof, the speculative rather than the practical.

My father used to talk to me with much admiration and affection of Sarah Hutchinson, Mrs. Wordsworth's sister, who resided partly with the Wordsworths, partly with her own brothers. At this time she used to act as my father's amanuensis. She wrote out great part of the "Friend" to his dictation. She had fine, long, light-brown hair, I think her only beauty, except a fair skin, for her features were plain and contracted, her figure dumpy, and devoid of grace and dignity. She was a plump woman, of little more than five feet. I remember my father talking to me admiringly of her long light locks, and saying how mildly she bore it when the baby pulled them hard in play.

Miss Wordsworth, Mr. Wordsworth's sister, of most poetic eye and temper, took a great part with the children. She told us once a pretty story of a primrose, I think, which she spied by the way-side when she went to see me soon after my birth, though that was at Christmas, and how this same primrose was still blooming when she went back to Grasmere.

* * * My father had particular feelings and fancies about dress, as had my Uncle Southey and Mr. Wordsworth also. He could not abide the scarlet socks which Edith and I wore

at one time. I remember going to him when mamma had just dressed me in a new stuff frock. He took me up, and set me down again without a caress. I thought he disliked the dress; perhaps he was in an uneasy mood. He much liked every thing feminine and domestic, pretty and becoming, but not fine-ladyish. My Uncle Southey was all for gay, bright, cheerful colors, and even declared he had a taste for the *grand*, in half jest.

Mr. Wordsworth loved all that was rich and picturesque, light and free, in clothing. A deep Prussian blue or purple was one of his favorite colors for a silk dress. He wished that white dresses were banished, and that our peasantry wore blue and scarlet, and other warm colors, instead of sombre, dingy black, which converts a crowd that might be ornamental in the landscape into a swarm of magnified ants. I remember his saying how much better young girls looked of an evening in bare arms —even if the arms themselves were not very lovely; it gave such a lightness to their general air. I think he was looking at Dora when he said this. White dresses he thought cold, a blot and disharmony in any picture, in-door or out-of-door. My father admired white clothing, because he looked at it in reference to woman, as expressive of her delicacy and purity, not merely as a component part of a general picture.

My father liked my wearing a cap. He thought it looked girlish and domestic. Dora and I must have been a curious contrast—she with her wild eyes, impetuous movements, and fine, long, floating yellow hair—I with my timid, large blue eyes, slender form, and little, fair, delicate face, muffled up in lace border and muslin. But I thought little of looks then; only I fancied Edith S., on first seeing her, most beautiful.

I attained my sixth year on the Christmas after this my first Grasmere visit. It must have been the next summer that I made my first appearance at the dancing-school, of which more hereafter. All I can remember of this first entrance into public is that our good-humored, able, but rustical dancing-master, Mr. Yewdale, tried to make me dance a minuet with Charlie Denton, the youngest of our worthy pastor's home flock, a very pretty, rosy-cheeked, large-black-eyed, compact little laddikin. But I was not quite up to the business. I think my beau was a year older. At all events, it was I who broke down, and Mr. Yewdale, after a little impatience, gave the matter up. All teaching is wearisome; but to teach dancing, of all teaching the wearisomest.

The last event of my earlier childhood which abides with me is a visit to Allonby, when I was nine years old, with Mrs. Calvert. I remember the ugliness and meanness of Allonby (the town, a cluster of red-looking houses, as far as I recollect), and being laughed at at home for describing it as "a pretty place," which I did conventionally, according to the usual practice, as I conceived, of elegant letter-writers. The sands are really fine in their way, so unbroken and extensive, capital for galloping over on pony-back. I recollect the pleasures of these sands, and of the sea-side animation and vegetation; the little close, white Scotch roses; the shells; the crabs of every size, from Liliputian to Brobdingnagian, crawling in the pools; the sea-anemones, with their flower-like appendages, which we kept in jugs of salt-water, delighted to see them draw in their petals, or expand them by a sudden blossoming; the sea-weed, with its ugly berries, of which we made hideous necklaces. All these things I recollect, but not what I should most regard now—the fine forms of the Scotch hills on the opposite coast, sublime in the distance, and the splendid sunsets which give to this sort of landscape a gorgeous filling up.

Of the party, besides J. and R. Calvert and M., their sister, were Tom and William M——, two sons of Mrs. Calvert's sister, Mrs. M——. We used to gallop up and down the wide sands on two little ponies, a dark one called Sancho, and a light one called Airey, behind the boys. M. and I sometimes quarreled with the boys, and, of course, in a trial of strength, got the worst of it. I remember R. and the rest bursting angrily into our bedroom and flinging a pebble at M., enraged at our having dared to put crumbs into their porridge; not content with which inroad and onslaught, they put mustard into ours next morning, the sun having gone down upon their boyish wrath without quenching it. One of them said it was all that little vixen, Sara Coleridge; M. was quiet enough by herself.

I had a leaven of malice, I suppose, in me, for I remember being on hostile terms with some little old woman, who lived by herself in a hut, and who took offense at something I did, as it struck me, unnecessarily. She repaired to Mrs. Calvert to complain, and the head and front of her accusation was,

"That'un (meaning me) ran up and down the mound before her door." Mrs. C. thought this no heinous offense; but it was done by me, no doubt, with an air of derision. The crone was one of those morose, ugly, withered, ill-conditioned, ignorant creatures who in earlier times were persecuted as witches, and tried to be such. Still I ought to have been gently corrected for my behavior, and told the duty of bearing with the ill-temper of the poor and ignorant and afflicted.

At this time, on coming to Allonby, I was rather delicate. I remember that Mrs. Calvert gave me a glass of port wine daily, which she did not give to the other children. Oh, me, how rough these young Calverts and M——s were! and yet they had a certain respect for me, mingled with a contrary feeling. I was honored among them for my extreme agility—my power of running and leaping. They called me "Cheshire cat" because I "grinned," said they. "Almost as pretty as Miss Cheshire," said Tom M. to me one day, of some admired little girl.

Such are the chief *historical* events of my little life up to nine years of age. But can I in any degree retrace what being I was then?—what relation my then being held to my maturer self? Can I draw any useful reflection from my childish experience, or found any useful maxim upon it? What *was* I? In person, very slender and delicate, not habitually colorless, but often enough pallid and feeble looking. Strangers used to exclaim about my eyes, and I remember remarks made upon their large size, both by my Uncle Southey and Mr. Wordsworth. I suppose the thinness of my face, and the smallness of the other features, with the muffling close cap, increased the apparent size of the eye, for only artists, since I have grown up, speak of my eyes as large and full. They were bluer, too, in my early years than now. My health alternated, as it has done all my life, till the last ten or twelve years, when it has been unchangeably depressed, between delicacy and a very easy, comfortable condition. I remember well that nervous sensitiveness and morbid imaginativeness had set in with me very early. During my Grasmere visit I used to feel frightened at night on account of the darkness. I then was a stranger to the whole host of night-agitators—ghosts, goblins, demons, burglars, elves, and witches. Horrid ghastly tales and ballads, of which crowds afterward came in my way, had not yet cast their shadows over my mind. And yet I was terrified in the dark, and used to think of lions, the only form of terror which my dark-engendered agitation would take. My next bugbear was the Ghost in "Hamlet." Then the picture of Death at Hell-gate in an old edition of "Paradise Lost," the delight of my girlhood. Last and worst came my Uncle Southey's ballad horrors—above all, the Old Woman of Berkeley. Oh, the agonies I have endured between nine and twelve at night, before mamma joined me in bed, in presence of that hideous assemblage of horrors—the horse with eyes of flame! I dare not, even now, rehearse these particulars, for fear of calling up some of the old feeling, which, indeed, I have never in my life been quite free from. What made the matter worse was that, like all other nervous sufferings, it could not be understood by the inexperienced, and consequently subjected the sufferer to ridicule and censure. My Uncle Southey laughed heartily at my agonies. I mean, at the cause. He did not enter into the agonies. Even mamma scolded me for creeping out of bed after an hour's torture, and stealing down to her in the parlor, saying I could bear the loneliness and the night-fears no longer. But my father understood the case better. He insisted that a lighted candle should be left in my room, in the interval between my retiring to bed and mamma's joining me. From that time forth my sufferings ceased. I believe they would have destroyed my health had they continued.

Yet I was a most fearless child by daylight—ever ready to take the difficult mountain-path and outgo my companions' daring in tree-climbing. In those early days we used to spend much of our summer-time in trees, greatly to the horror of some of our London visitors.

On reviewing my earlier childhood, I find the predominant reflection

*   *   *   *   *   *   *   *   *   *   *

II.

Thus abruptly terminates, in the very middle of a sentence, the narrative of Sara Coleridge's childhood. The history of her wedded life and widowhood, which would have been of such deep interest as told by herself, had time and strength been granted, is, fortunately, to a great extent, contained in her cor-

respondence. In order, however, to combine the scattered notices of the letters, and put readers at once in possession of
the main facts; and still more, in order to provide some partial substitute for that chapter of her youth which would otherwise remain a blank, it has seemed desirable to preface the correspondence by a slight biographical sketch. In doing this, I
shall gratefully avail myself of the valuable reminiscences most
kindly imparted to me by friends, both of earlier and later date, as
well as of an interesting memoir of my mother which appeared
shortly after her death in an American journal,* composed by
one who, though personally unknown to her, was yet a highly
esteemed correspondent, the lamented Professor Henry Reed,
of Philadelphia.

In that dear home of her childhood, remembered with such
loving minuteness after more than twenty years of absence,
Sara Coleridge grew up as fair and sweet as one of the exquisite wild flowers of her native vale. The childish prettiness
which had excited the admiration of her young play-fellows at
Allonby, changed first into the maidenly bloom of fifteen; at
which age she is mentioned by the painter William Collins, as
"Coleridge's elegant daughter Sara, a most interesting creature," of whom he made a sketch, which was greatly admired by
her father for its simplicity and native refinement. It represents her in the character of the Highland Girl, seated in rustic
fashion under a tree. Five years later these girlish graces had
matured into a perfection of womanly beauty, which is thus described by Sir Henry Taylor:

"I first saw your mother," he writes in a letter which I have
lately had the pleasure of receiving from him, "when, in 1823,
I paid my first visit to Mr. Southey at Greta Hall, where she
and her mother were staying. I suppose she was then about
twenty years of age. I saw but little of her, for I think she was
occupied in translating some mediæval book from the Latin,
and she was seen only at meals, or for a very short time in the
evening; and, as she was almost invariably silent, I saw nothing and knew nothing of her mind till I renewed my acquaintance with her many years after. But I have always been glad
that I did see her in her girlhood, because I then saw her beauty untouched by time, and it was a beauty which could not but

---

* "The Daughter of Coleridge," written for the *Literary World*, July, 1852.

remain in one's memory for life, and which is now distinctly before me as I write. The features were perfectly shaped, and almost minutely delicate, and the complexion delicate also, but not wanting in color, and the general effect was that of gentleness, indeed I may say of composure, even to stillness. Her eyes were large, and they had the sort of serene lustre which I remember in her father's.

"After her marriage, I think, I did not see her till the days of her widowhood, in young middle life, when she was living in Chester Place, Regent's Park. Her beauty, though not lost, was impaired, and, with the same stillness and absolute simplicity which belonged to her nature, there was some sadness which I had not seen before in the expression of her face, and some shyness of manner. I think I was myself shy, and this perhaps made her so, and the effect was to shut me out from the knowledge, *by conversation*, of almost any part of her mind and nature, except her intellect. For whenever she was shy, if she could not be silent, which was impossible when we were alone together, she fled into the region where she was most at home and at ease, which was that of psychology and abstract thought; and this was the region where I was by no means at ease and at home. Had we met more frequently (and I never cease to wish that we had), no doubt these little difficulties would soon have been surmounted, and we should have got into the fields of thought and sentiment which had an interest common to us both. But I was a busy man in these years, and not equal in health and strength to what I had to do, and it was in vain for me to seek her society when I was too tired to enjoy it; and then came her illness and her early death, and she had passed away before I had attained to know her in her inner mind and life. I only know that the admirable strength and subtlety of her reasoning faculty, shown in her writings and conversation, were less to me than the beauty and simplicity and feminine tenderness of her face; and that one or two casual and transitory expressions of her nature in her countenance, delightful in their poetic power, have come back to me from time to time, and that they are present with me now, when much of what was most to be admired in her intellectual achievements or discourse have passed into somewhat of a dim distance."

Of all the personal influences which had to do with the formation of my mother's mind and character in early life, by far the most important were those exercised by the two eminent men with whom she was so intimately connected by ties of kindred or affection—her Uncle Southey, and her father's friend, Mr. Wordsworth.   In attempting to estimate the value of these various impressions, and trace them to their respective source, I am but repeating her own remark when I say that, in matters of the intellect and imagination, she owed most to Mr. Wordsworth.   In his noble poetry she took an ever-increasing delight, and his impressive discourse, often listened to on summer rambles over the mountains, or in the winter parlors of Greta Hall and Rydal Mount, served to guide her taste and cultivate her understanding.   But in matters of the heart and conscience, for right views of duty and practical lessons of industry, truthfulness, and benevolence, she was "more, and more importantly, indebted to the daily life and example of her admirable Uncle Southey," whom she long afterward emphatically declared to have been, "upon the whole, the best man she had ever known."

There is a third province of human nature besides those of the intellect and the moral sense—that of the spiritual—where the pure spirit of Sara Coleridge breathed freely, as in an "ampler ether, a diviner air."   In these serene and lofty regions she wandered hand in hand with her father, whose guidance she willingly followed, with a just confidence in his superior wisdom, yet with no blind or undiscriminating submission.   He, like herself, was but a traveler through the heavenly country, whose marvels they explored together ; and the sun of Reason was above them both to light them on their way.   In September, 1825, when not quite three-and-twenty, she was reading the "Aids to Reflection," "and delighted with all that she could clearly understand," as she says in a letter of that date to Sir John Taylor Coleridge.   "Do you not think," she adds, with modest deference to the opinion of a highly respected elder cousin, "that in speaking of free will, and the other mysteries of religion, my father, though he does not attempt to explain what I suppose is inexplicable, puts the subject in a new and comfortable point of view for sincere Christians?"   The "new and comfortable point of view," thus early perceived and adopted, was still more deeply appreciated when years of experience and reflection had increased her sense of its importance.   Led by circumstances, as well as by natural congeniality of mind, to a study of her father's philosophy, she then devoted herself, with all the fullness of matured conviction, to the task of illustrating those great principles of Christian truth which it was the main object of his life to defend. If, in following this path, she approached the dusty arena of controversy (though without actually entering it), and watched the combatants with approving or disapproving eye, it will yet, I believe, be acknowledged, even by those who differ most widely from her conclusions, that in her mode of reaching them she combined charity with candor. Possessing, as she did, a knowledge of theology, both as a history and a science, rare in any woman (perhaps in any layman), she had received from heaven a still more excellent gift—" even the ornament of a meek and quiet spirit."

These solemn investigations were, however, the appropriate employment of a more advanced stage of life than that of which I am now speaking. In youthful days my mother's favorite pursuits were chiefly literary and linguistic. Before she was five-and-twenty she had made herself acquainted with the leading Greek and Latin classics, and was well-skilled in French, Italian, German, and Spanish. These acquirements were mainly the result of her own efforts ; though it is needless to point out the advantages she derived in her studies from the advice and direction of a man like Mr. Southey, and from the use which she was kindly encouraged to make of his valuable library.

Natural History, too, in all its branches, especially those of botany and zoology, was a subject in which she found endless attractions. The beauty of nature manifested in bird or insect, flower or tree, delighted her poetical imagination ; while the signs of divine wisdom and goodness, revealed in all the works of creation, furnished a constant theme for the contemplations of a thoughtful piety. Other advantages accompanied these studies, so healthful both to mind and body. The out-door interests which they provided, the habits of careful observation which they rendered necessary, aided in the harmonious development of her faculties, and served to counterbalance the subjective tendencies of her intellect. She could turn at any time from the most abstruse metaphysical speculations to inspect the domestic architecture of a spider or describe the corolla of a rose.

The work referred to by Sir Henry Taylor in his interesting letter, as that upon which my mother was engaged at the time of his first visit to Greta Hall, was probably her translation of the " Memoirs of the Chevalier Bayard, by the Loyal Servant ;" which was published by Mr. Murray in 1825. The trouble of rendering the accounts of battles and sieges, from the French of the sixteenth century, into appropriate English, was considerable ; but was lightened by the interest inspired by the romantic character and adventures of Bayard, the Knight "sans peur et sans reproche."

This was not, however, her earliest appearance in print. Her first literary production was one concerning which Professor Reed gives the following particulars in the notice above referred to. After observing that it "manifestly had its origin in connection with some of Southey's labors,"* he proceeds thus : " In 1822 there issued from the London press a work in three octavo volumes, entitled, 'An Account of the Abipones, an Equestrian People of Paraguay. From the Latin of Martin Dobrizhoffer, eighteen years a Missionary in that Country.' No name of translator appears, and a brief and modest preface gives not the least clew to it ; even now in catalogues the work is frequently ascribed to Southey. At the time of the publication Miss Coleridge was just twenty years of age, and therefore this elaborate toil of translation must have been achieved before she had reached the years of womanhood. The stout-hearted perseverance needed for such a task is quite as remarkable as the scholarship in a young person. Coleridge himself spoke of it with fond and just admiration, when, in 1832, he said :

" ' My dear daughter's translation of this book is, in my judgment, unsurpassed for pure mother-English by any thing I have read for a long time.'

" Southey, in his 'Tale of Paraguay,' which was suggested by the missionary's narrative, paid to the translator a tribute so delicate, and so controlled, perhaps, by a sense of his young kinswoman's modesty, that one need be in the secret to know for whom it is meant. It is in the stanza which mentions Dobrizhoffer's forgetfulness of his native speech during his long missionary expatriation, and alludes to the favor shown him by the Empress Maria Theresa."

---

* The work was undertaken, in the first instance, for the purpose of assisting one of her brothers in his college expenses. The necessary means were, however, supplied by his own exertions ; and the proceeds of the translation (£125) were funded in Sara Coleridge's name for her own use.

"But of his native speech because well-nigh
   Disuse in him forgetfulness had wrought,
In Latin he composed his history;
   A garrulous but a lively tale, and fraught
With matter of delight and food for thought;
   And if he could in Merlin's glass have seen
By whom his tomes to speak our tongue were taught,
   The old man would have felt as pleased, I ween,
As when he won the ear of that great Empress Queen."

Canto III., stanza 16.

"Charles Lamb, in an epistolary strain, eminently characteristic, echoes the praise bestowed upon his friend's child, and
her rare achievement. Writing to Southey, in 1825, in acknowl-
edgment of a presentation copy of the 'Tale of Paraguay,' he
says:

"'The compliment to the translatress is daintily conceived.
Nothing is choicer in that sort of writing than to bring in some
remote impossible parallel—as between the great empress and
the unobtrusive quiet soul, who digged her noiseless way so perseveringly through that rugged Paraguay mine. How she Do-
brizhoffered it all out, puzzles my slender Latinity to conjecture.'"*

There is a graceful allusion to my mother's classical attainments in that lovely strain composed in her honor by the great
poet whose genius, especially in its *earlier* manifestations, she
so highly admired and reverenced:

"Last of the Three, though eldest born,
   Reveal thyself, like pensive morn,
   Touched by the skylark's earliest note,
   Ere humbler gladness be afloat;
But whether in the semblance drest
Of dawn or eve, fair vision of the west,
Come with each anxious hope subdued
   By woman's gentle fortitude,
Each grief, through meekness, settling into rest.
Or I would hail thee when some high-wrought page
Of a closed volume lingering in thy hand,
Has raised thy spirit to a peaceful stand
Among the glories of a happier age.
   Her brow hath opened on me, see it there
   Brightening the umbrage of her hair,
   So gleams the crescent moon, that loves
   To be descried through shady groves.

---

* "Talfourd's Letters of Charles Lamb," vol. ii., p. 189.

Tenderest bloom is on her cheek.
Wish not for a richer streak,
Nor dread the depth of meditative eye,
But let thy love upon that azure field
Of thoughtfulness and beauty, yield
Its homage, offered up in purity.
What wouldst thou more? In sunny glade,
Or under leaves of thickest shade,
Was such a stillness e're diffused
Since earth grew calm, while angels mused?
Softly she treads, as if her foot were loth
To crush the mountain dew-drops, soon to melt
On the flower's breast; as if she felt
That flowers themselves, whate'er their hue,
With all their fragrance, all their glistening,
Call to the heart for inward listening;
And though for bridal wreaths and tokens true
Welcomed wisely; though a growth
Which the careless shepherd sleeps on,
As fitly spring from turf the mourner weeps on,
And without wrong are cropped the marble tomb to strew."

My mother was once told by a poetical friend that, till he knew the original, he had always taken this passage in the "Triad" for a personification of the Christian grace of Faith. She used to smile at her involuntary exaltation, and maintain that there must be something exaggerated and unreal in a description which was liable to such misinterpretation. Yet the conjecture may have been a right one in the spirit, though not in the letter. Certainly no one who knew my mother intimately, and was privileged to see "the very pulse of the machine"—

"A being breathing thoughtful breath,
A traveler betwixt life and death;
The reason firm, the temperate will,
Endurance, foresight, strength, and skill"—

could doubt that such a life as hers could only be lived "by faith."

That light of faith, which shone so brightly in declining years, had been early sought and found between the troubled clouds of life's opening day. In 1828, when the "Triad" was written, Sara Coleridge was no stranger to the most powerful emotion which can agitate a woman's heart, either for joy or sorrow. The "anxious hope" alluded to by the poet, with almost parental tenderness, was for the joyful time when she might be enabled peacefully to enjoy the "dear and improving society" of him to whom she had given her affections; the "grief" that settled into the "rest" which is promised to the meek and lowly, arose not so much from the postponement of her own happiness as from sympathy with his disappointment, and sorrow for its cause, which was principally the uncertainty of health and means on both sides.

In 1822, while on a visit to her father at Highgate, she had first met her cousin, Henry Nelson Coleridge, a younger son of James Coleridge, Esq., of Heath's Court, Ottery St. Mary, who was educated at Eton College, and at King's College, Cambridge, where his course was not unmarked by academical honors. He was then practicing as a Chancery barrister in London, and made frequent pilgrimages to Highgate, one result of which was that series of notes to which the world is indebted for the "Table Talk of S. T. Coleridge."

The attachment thus formed between the two youthful cousins, under the roof of Mr. Gillman, was never for a single moment regretted by my mother, in spite of the solicitudes to which it exposed her, and the sorrows which in after years cast a shade of sadness over the stillness which characterized her gentle face.

"She was a maid," thus writes Hartley Coleridge of his only sister,

"Not easily beguiled by loving words,
Nor apt to love; but when she loved, the fate
Of her affections was a stern religion,
Admitting nought less holy than itself."

These "seven years of patience" did not pass without bringing forth precious fruits of piety and goodness in a heart already enriched with the dews of heavenly blessing. "Your virtues," writes my father to his betrothed in a letter of 1827, "never shone so brilliantly in my eyes as they do now; and it is a spring of deep and sacred joy in my heart to think that, however weak and wavering my steps may be in the ways of religion, you are already a firm traveler in them, and, indeed, a young saint upon earth. The trials to which our engagement has exposed you have been fatiguing and painful; but you have borne them all, not only without impatience or murmuring, but with a holy cheerfulness and energetic resignation, than which no two states of the heart are more difficult to man or more acceptable to God.

"I made a true remark to you once, which I feel every day justified by our own correspondence, that spiritual things differ from mere things of sense in this among other points, that sensual objects, capacities, and enjoyments are all naturally bounded, short, and fugitive, while pure love and pure intellectual communion are essentially without limits, and that to the pure-hearted a boundless ascent toward identity of moral being lies open, and that every day fresh depths of love and thought might open to the tender and assiduous sympathies of two mutually adoring persons. I have always loved you as much as my heart could feel at the time ; but my respect, my veneration for you has gone on increasing as I knew you more intimately. I hope I shall always have the sense to submit myself to your guiding influence in all cases of moral election. The more closely I imitate your habits, thoughts, and actions, the better and happier man shall I become."

The noble affection thus generously expressed was as fully returned by her on whom it was bestowed. In a letter written on the eve of her marriage, she thus addresses the expected bridegroom: "You will not, I know, grudge a few tears to my dearest mother, to dear Keswick, dear Greta Hall, and its dear and interesting inmates. These changes, these farewells, are types of the great change, the long farewell, that awaits us all hereafter. We can not but be thoughtful upon them. Yet I know and feel that *this* change is to be infinitely for the better ; and in your dear and improving society I trust I shall learn to look upon that other change as a blessed one too. The sadness of my present farewell will be tempered by the prospect of meeting all here frequently again upon earth, as, I hope, all dear friends will be reunited in heaven. But that speculation would lead me too far. Fear not, Henry, that such speculations, or, rather, such a tendency in my nature to speculation and dreaminess, will render me an unfit wife for you. Does not Wordsworth point out to us how the most excursive bird can brood as long and as fondly on the nest as any of the feathered race?* This taste for the spiritual I consider a great blessing, crowned by that other inexpressibly great one, the having found a partner who will tolerate, approve, sympathize in all I think and feel, and will allow me to sympathize with him."

---

* "True to the kindred points of heaven and home."—*The Skylark.*

On the 3d of September, 1829, Henry Nelson Coleridge and Sara Coleridge were married at Crosthwaite Church, Keswick. After a few months spent in a London lodging, they began their frugal housekeeping in a tiny cottage on Downshire Hill, Hampstead, where their four elder children were born, of whom the twins, Berkeley and Florence, died in infancy. In 1837, my parents removed to a more commodious dwelling in Chester Place, Regent's Park, where a third daughter, Bertha Fanny, was born in 1840, who survived her birth but a few days.

My mother's married life was, as Professor Reed has truly observed, "rich in the best elements of conjugal happiness; wedded to a gentleman of high moral worth, and of fine mind and scholarship, one who blended literature with his professional pursuits, she was not exposed to the perils of intellectual superiority."

The compositions (chiefly on classical subjects) which occupied his leisure, while his health lasted, and which displayed the varied powers of an acute and polished intellect, and the elegant taste of an accomplished scholar, formed a topic of common interest, and one which is frequently referred to in her letters of that period with visible pride and pleasure. With respect to moral and personal qualities, too, my father was, as she afterward said to a friend when describing her grief at his loss, "of all men whom she had ever known, best suited to her;" and this quite as much by force of contrast as of resemblance. Of sensitive temperament, reserved though deeply earnest feelings, and manners which illness and suffering rendered serious, though not usually sad, she was especially likely to feel the charm of the wit, gayety, and conversational brilliancy which, on social occasions, made her husband the "life and soul of the company," as well as of the joyous frankness and overflowing affectionateness which made him the delight of his home.

In that genial atmosphere of loving appreciation, free from the cares and depressing circumstances of her girlhood, she was encouraged and enabled to put forth all her best powers—

"A thousand happy things that seek the light,
Till now in darkest shadow forced to lie,"*

began to "show their forms and hues in the all-revealing sun." The imaginative genius which she inherited from her father (to-

---

* From a song in "Phantasmion."

gether with his turn for philosophical reflection, developed in her at a later date) found its most perfect expression in her romance of " Phantasmion," published in 1837. The wild and beautiful scenery of her birthplace, vividly remembered and fondly dwelt on in the enforced seclusion of sickness (for she was now unhappily an invalid), re-appears here, idealized by imagination, to form the main subject of the picture; while groups of graceful and dignified figures give animation to the landscape, and fairy forms flitting above or around them, Spirits of the Wind, the Woods, or the Waters, serve as a connecting link between humanity and nature.

" Nothing has appeared in this species of writing," says a friendly American critic, " to be for one moment compared with ' Phantasmion,' since Fouqué produced his inimitable ' Undine.' There is one characteristic feature in this book that will render it peculiarly acceptable to all lovers of nature. We do not allude to its accuracy in the delineating of the infinite phases of earth and air, sea and sky, though nothing can be more perfect in this respect; but what we mean is its remarkable freedom from the conventional forms and usages of life. It has the patriarchal simplicity, the beautiful truthfulness of primitive ages; while it is at the same time enriched and ennobled by the refinement of a more advanced period. * * * Do you ask what is its grand characteristic? It is beauty—beauty, truly feminine, beauty of conception, character, and expression. It is, indeed, a wilderness of sweets, illumined by the richest hues of earth and heaven, and through which a stream of magic melody is forever flowing. * * * The ' Songs of Phantasmion!' what sweetness of verse! what breathings of a tender spirit! whose voice—who but the writer's own spirit of the flowers— could do them justice?"

This beautiful fairy tale was at first intended (though it soon outgrew its original limits) as a mere child's story for the amusement of her little boy, whose beauty, vivacity, and early intelligence are described with maternal love and pride, in one of the letters of that period, in reply to the questions of her brother Hartley about his unseen nephew. The education of her children was now their mother's principal object—an object on which she deemed it no waste to lavish the charms of her genius and the resources of her cultivated understanding. Latin grammar, natural history, geography, and the " Kings of

England," were all made easy and attractive to the little learners by simple and appropriate verses, written on cards, in clear, print-like characters. Even a set of wooden bricks, which was a favorite source of amusement, was thus agreeably decorated, in the hope that those tough morsels, *hic, hæc, hoc,* and their congeners, might glide gently over the youthful palate, sweetened with play and pleasure. From these Sibylline leaves of the nursery a selection of juvenile poetry was published in 1834, by my father's desire, who wished that other children might have some share in the advantages enjoyed by his own. The little volume, entitled " Pretty Lessons for Good Children," proved a popular work, and passed through five editions.

> "Learning, Herbert, hath the features
> Almost of an Angel's face;
> Contemplate them steadfastly,
> Learn by heart each speaking grace.
> Truth and wisdom, high-wrought fancy,
> In those lineaments we trace;
> Never be your eyes averted
> Long from that resplendent face !"[*]

Happy the boy who is permitted to see those glorious lineaments reflected in the "angel-face" of a wise and tender mother! It may not be uninteresting to the sympathizing reader to learn that he who enjoyed the blessing of such rare guardianship lived to appreciate and reward it, and to attest its value by those public honors that are won by industry and talent.[†] And that, when disease came to blight the hopes of his manhood, and cut short a promising career, Learning was, to him as to her, a shield from the monotony of the sick-room and an exceeding great reward; and that as long as any thing earthly could claim his attention, it was seldom "averted from that resplendent face."

But it is time to return to an earlier stage of the narrative, when that domestic happiness, so patiently waited for and thankfully enjoyed, was smitten by the hand of death. All that

---

[*] Fifth stanza of a poem on the Latin declensions in "Pretty Lessons" —*Facies, a Face.*

[†] My brother was the Newcastle and Baliol scholar in 1847 and 1848, and took a double first class at Oxford in 1852, which latter honor his mother did not live to witness. He was a fine Icelandic scholar; and at the time of his death, which took place in 1861, he was engaged in preparations for the new English dictionary projected by the Philological Society, of which he was a member.

was earthly of it fell to the earth, and was no more; but there remained to the desolate widow the Christian's hope of a heavenly reunion, which proved an anchor of the soul, sure and steadfast, when the waves of affliction rose high. In 1841 my father's health began to give way; and in January, 1843, he died of spinal paralysis, after a trying illness of nine months.

In her deep distress, my mother again endeavored to act upon that principle of " energetic resignation" (so different from the aimless broodings of mere submission) which had been early noticed in her by the discriminating eye of affection. "I feel it such a duty, such a necessity," she writes to a friend three months after her bereavement, "to cling fast to every source of comfort, to be, for my children's sake, as happy, as willing to live on in this heart-breaking world, as possible, that I dwell on all the blessings which God continues to me, and has raised up to me out of the depths of affliction, with an earnestness of endeavor which is its own reward—for so long as the heart and mind are full of movement, employed continually in not unworthy objects, there may be sorrow, but there can not be despair. The stagnation of the spirit, the dull, motionless brooding over one miserable set of thoughts, is that against which, in such cases as mine, we must both strive and pray."

There is another, an equally interesting, though less personal, point of view, in which this great bereavement was an important turning-point in the life of Sara Coleridge. Her husband was Mr. Coleridge's literary executor, and the editorial task first undertaken by my father now devolved upon his widow. It has been beautifully remarked by Professor Reed, as a peculiarity of my mother's truly feminine authorship, that it was in no case prompted by mere literary ambition, but that there was ever some "moral motive"—usually some call of the affections, that set her to work, and overcame her natural preference for retirement. This helpful, loving, and unselfish spirit, which had actuated her hitherto, now took a more commanding form, and led her to dedicate the whole of her intellectual existence to the great object of carrying out a husband's wishes—of doing justice to a father's name. In the fulfillment of this sacred trust, she found occasion to illustrate and adorn the works which fell under her editorship with several compositions of no inconsiderable extent; and displaying powers of critical analysis, and of doctrinal, political, and historical research and discussion, of no common order. The most important of these are the "Essay on Rationalism, with a special Application to the Doctrine of Baptismal Regeneration," appended to Vol. II. of the "Aids to Reflection," the "Introduction" to the "Biographia Literaria;" and a Preface to the collection of her father's political writings, entitled, "Essays on his Own Times, by S. T. Coleridge," which contains, in Professor Reed's opinion, the most judicious and impartial comparison between British and American civilization, and the social and intellectual conditions of the two countries, that has yet been written. "And thus," continues her accomplished friend and biographer, "there have been expended in the desultory form of notes and appendices and prefaces, an amount of original thought and an affluence of learning, which, differently and more prominently presented, would have made her famous. There is not one woman in a thousand, not one man in ten thousand, who would have been thus prodigal of the means of celebrity."

> "Father! no amaranths e'er shall wreathe my brow;
> Enough that round thy grave they flourish now!
> But Love his roses 'mid my young locks braided,
> And what cared I for flowers of richer bloom?
> Those too seemed deathless—here they never faded,
> But, drenched and shattered, dropt into the tomb."*

This blended expression of the wife's and the daughter's affection was recorded when she was in the midst of her pious duties. Ere long she too was called upon to resign the work, still unfinished, into another, but a dear and well-skilled hand.† Seven years of waiting for the happiness so long expected—again seven years—not always of mourning, but of faithful memories and tender regrets for that which had passed away forever; and then came preparations for the "great change, the long farewell," to which she had learned to look forward when on the very eve of bridal joys and earthly blessedness. She who had once called marriage the type of death, now heard the summons to the heavenly Marriage Feast with no startled or reluctant ear. Solemn indeed is the darkness of the Death Valley, and awful are the forms that guard its entrance—

> "Fear, and trembling Hope,
> Silence, and Foresight;"

---

* From an unpublished poem by Sara Coleridge.
† Her brother, the Rev. Derwent Coleridge, the present editor.

but beyond all these, and revealed to the heart (though not to the eye) of the humble and believing Christian, are the blissful realities of Light and Love.

After a lingering and painful illness of about a year and a half, Sara Coleridge was released from much suffering, borne with unfailing patience, on the 3d of May, 1852, in the forty-ninth year of her age. In the old church-yard of Highgate (now inclosed in a crypt under the school chapel) her remains lie, beside those of her parents, her husband, and her son.

* * * * * * * *

The following letter will be read with pleasure, not only for its own sake, but as a tribute to my mother's memory, from one whose friendship, correspondence, and society helped to brighten her latter years, and to whom this work owes some of the most interesting portions of its contents.

"I rejoice to hear," Mr. De Vere writes to me, on the subject of the present publication, "that a portion of your mother's letters will be published so soon. To those who knew her she remains an image of grace and intellectual beauty that time can never tarnish. A larger circle will now know, in part at least, what she was. Her correspondence will, to thoughtful readers, convey a clearer impression than aught besides could convey of one who, of course, could only be fully understood by those who had known her personally and known her long.

"In their memories she will ever possess a place apart from all others. With all her high literary powers she was utterly unlike the mass of those who are called 'literary persons.' Few have possessed such learning; and when one calls to mind the arduous character of those studies, which seemed but a refreshment to her clear intellect, like a walk in mountain air, it seems a marvel how a woman's faculties could have grappled with those Greek philosophers and Greek fathers, just as no doubt it seemed a marvel when her father, at the age of fourteen, awoke the echoes of that famous old cloister with declamations from Plato and Plotinus. But in the daughter, as in the father, the real marvel was neither the accumulated knowledge nor the literary power. It was the spiritual mind.

'The rapt one of the God-like forehead,
The heaven-eyed creature,'

was Wordsworth's description of Coleridge, the most spiritual, perhaps, of England's poets, certainly of her modern poets. Of her some one said, 'Her father had looked down into her eyes, and left in them the light of his own.' Her great characteristic was the radiant spirituality of her intellectual and imaginative being. This it was that looked forth from her countenance.

"Great and various as were your mother's talents, it was not from them that she derived what was special to her. It was from the degree in which she had inherited the feminine portion of genius. She had a keener appreciation of what was highest and most original in thought than of subjects nearer the range of ordinary intellects. She moved with the lightest step when she moved over the loftiest ground. Her 'feet were beautiful on the mountain-tops' of ideal thought. They were her native land; for her they were not barren; honey came up from the stony rock. In this respect I should suppose she must have differed from almost all women whom we associate with literature. I remember hearing her say that she hardly considered herself to be a woman 'of letters.' She felt herself more at ease when musing on the mysteries of the soul, or discussing the most arduous speculations of philosophy and theology, than when dealing with the humbler topics of literature.

"As might have been expected, the department of literature which interested her most was that of poetry—that is, poetry of the loftiest and most spiritual order; for to much of what is now popular she would have refused the name. How well I remember our discussions about Wordsworth! She was jealous of my admiration for his poems, because it extended to *too many* of them. No one could be a true Wordsworthian, she maintained, who admired so much some of his later poems, his poems of accomplishment, such as the 'Triad.' It implied a disparagement of his earlier poems, such as 'Resolution and Independence,' in which the genuine Wordsworthian inspiration, and that alone, uttered itself! I suspect, however, that she must have taken a yet more vivid delight in some of her father's poems. Besides their music and their spirituality, they have another quality, in which they stand almost without a rival—their subtle sweetness. I remember Leigh Hunt once remarking to me on this characteristic of them, and observing that in this respect they were unapproached. It is like distant music, when the tone comes to you pure, without any coarser sound of wood or of wire; or like odor on the air, when you smell the flower, without detecting in it the stalk or the earth.

E

As regards this characteristic of her father's genius, as well as its spirituality, there was something in hers that resembled it. One is reminded of it by the fairy-like music of the songs in 'Phantasmion.'

"There is a certain gentleness and a modesty which belong to real genius, and which are in striking contrast with the self-confidence and self-assertion so often found in persons possessed of vigorous talents, but to whom literature is but a rough sport or a coarse profession. It was these qualities that gave to her manners their charm of feminine grace, self-possession, and sweetness. She was one of those whose thoughts are growing while they speak, and who never speak to surprise. Her intellectual fervor was not that which runs over in excitement; a quietude belonged to it, and it was ever modulated by a womanly instinct of reserve and dignity. She never 'thought for effect,' or cared to have the last word in discussion, or found it difficult to conceive how others should differ from her conclusions. She was more a woman than those who had not a tenth part of her intellectual energy. The seriousness and the softness of her nature raised her above vanity and its contortions. Her mind could move at once and be at rest.

" I fear that the type of character and intellect to which your mother belonged must be expected to grow rarer in these days of 'fast' intellect. Talents rush to the market, the theatre, or the arena, and genius itself becomes vulgarized for want of that 'hermit heart' which ought to belong to it, whether it be genius of the creative or the susceptive order. There will always, however, be those whose discernment can trace in your mother's correspondence and in her works the impress of what once was so fair. But, alas! how little will be known of her even by such! Something they will guess of her mind, but it is only a more fortunate few who can know her yet higher gifts—those that belong to the heart and moral being. If they have a loss which is theirs only, they too have remembrances which none can share with them. They remember the wide sympathies and the high aspirations, the courageous love of knowledge, and the devout submission to Revealed Truth; the domestic affections so tender, so dutiful, and so self-sacrificing, the friendships so faithful and so unexacting. For her great things and little lived on together through the fidelity of a heart that seemed never to forget. I never walk beside the Greta or the Derwent without hearing her describe the flowers she had gathered on their margin in her early girlhood. For her they seemed to preserve their fragrance amid the din and the smoke of the great metropolis."

To these high and discerning praises, any addition from me would be indeed superfluous. Yet one word of confirmation may here find a place: it is this, that such as Sara Coleridge appeared to sympathizing friends and admiring strangers, such she was known to be by those who, as her children, lived with her in habits of daily intimacy, and depended on her wholly for guidance, affection, and support. To such a one her memory is almost a religion ; or, to speak more soberly as well as more Christianly, it is prized not only out of love for herself, but as a practical evidence of the truth of that Religion which made her what she was.

CHAPTER I.

1833.

I.

Importance of Indirect Influences in Education.—Description of her Son
at Three Years of Age.—A Child's First Effort at Recollection.

To HARTLEY COLERIDGE, Esq., Nab Cottage, Grasmere :

Hampstead, 1833.—I think the present hard-working, over-busy, striving age somewhat overdoes the *positive* part of education, and forgets the efficacy of the negative. *Not* to make children irreligious by dosing them with religion unskillfully administered—*not* to make them self-important by charging them on no account to be conceited (which you used to complain of so bitterly)—*not* to make them busybodies and uncharitable by discussing the misdemeanors of all belonging to them, whom they ought to hold in reverence, in their hearing, giving them the fruit of the tree of ill knowledge (a fruit which both puffs up and imparts bitterness) before their stomachs have acquired firmness enough to receive it without injury (before the secretions of the mind are all settled, and such knowledge can subsist without disturbing the sweet juices of charity and humanity)—*not* to create disgust, or excite hypocrisy, by attempting to pour sensibility, generosity, and such other good qualities, which can not be supplied from without, but must well up from within, by bucketfuls into their hearts—*not* to cram them with knowledge which their minds are not mature enough to digest (such as Political Economy), the only result of which will be to make them little superficial coxcombs—in short, to give nature elbow-room, and not to put swaths on their minds, now we have left off lacing them upon their infant bodies ; to trust more to happy influences, and less to direct tuition ; not to defeat our own purpose by over-anxiety, and to recollect that the powers of education are even more limited than those of circumstances, that nature and God's blessing are above all things, and to arm ourselves against the disappointment that may attend our best directed and most earnest endeavors; all these considerations, I think, are treated too slightingly in the present day. Folks are all too busy to think; churches are built in a fortnight—but not quite such as our ancestors built. The only wonder is that there is so much childish innocence and nature left in the world. But, as an old nurse said, "Oh, Lord, ma'am, it's not very easy to *kill a baby*," so I think it not very easy to spoil a child. Nature has a wonderful power of rejecting what does not suit her; and the harangue which is unfitted for juvenile hearts and understandings, often makes no impression upon either. How often does a child that was certainly to be ruined by mismanagement disappoint all the wise Jeremiahs, and turn out an amiable member of society!

You say you can not bring before your mind's eye our little Herby. A mother is qualified to draw a child's portrait, if close study of the original be a qualification. High coloring may be allowed for. I will try to give you some notion of our child. He is too even a mixture of both father and mother to be strikingly like either; and this is the more natural, as Henry and I have features less definite than our expressions. This may, perhaps, account for that flowing softness and more than child-like indefiniteness of outline which our boy's face presents; it is all color and expression—such varying expression as consists with the sort of corporeal moulding which I have described; in which the vehicle is lost sight of, and the material of the veil is obscured by the brightness of what shines through it—not that pointed sort of fixed expression which seems more mechanically formed by strong lines and angular features. To be more particular, he has round eyes, and a round nose, and round lips and cheeks; and he has deep blue eyes, which vary from stone gray to skiey azure, according to influences of light and shade; and yellowish light-brown hair, and cheeks and lips rosy up to the very deepest, brightest tint of childish rosyhood. He will not be a handsome man, but he is a pretty representative of three years old, as D—— was a "representative baby;" and folks who put the glossy side of their opinions outermost for the gratified eyes of mothers and nurses, and all that large class with whom rosy cheeks are the beginning, middle, and

end of beauty, say enough to make me—as vain as I am.   I
don't pretend to any exemption from the general lot of parental
delusion—I mean that like most other parents I see my child
through an atmosphere which illuminates, magnifies, and at the
same time refines the object to a degree that amounts to a delusion, at least, unless we are aware that to other eyes it appears
by the light of common day only.   My father says that those
who love intensely see more clearly than indifferent persons ;
they see minutenesses which escape other eyes ; they see "the
very pulse of the machine."   Doubtless ; but, then, don't they
magnify by looking through the medium of their partiality ?
Don't they raise into undue relative importance by exclusive
gazing ; don't wishes and hopes, indulged and cherished long,
turn unto realities, as the rapt astronomer gazed upon the stars,
and mused on human knowledge, and longed for magic power,
till he believed that he directed the sun's course and the sweet
influences of the Pleiades ?

To return to our son and heir : he is an impetuous, vivacious
child, and the softer moments of such are particularly touching
(so thinks the mother of a vehement urchin).   I lately asked
him the meaning of a word ; he turned his rosy face to the window, and cast up the full blue eyes, which looked liquid in the
light, in the short hush of childish contemplation.   The innocent thoughtfulness, contrasted with his usual noisy mirth and
rapidity, struck my fancy.   I had never before seen him condescend to make an effort at recollection.   The word usually
passed from his lips like an arrow from a bow ; and if not forthcoming instantly, there was an absolute unconcern as to its fate
in the region of memory.   The necessity of brain-racking is not
among the number of his discoveries in the (to him) *new* world.
All wears the freshness and the glory of a dream ; and the stale,
flat, and unprofitable, and the *improbus labor*, and the sadness
and despondency, are all behind that visionary haze which hides
the dull reality, the mournful future of man's life.   You may
well suppose that I look on our darling boy with many fears ;
but "fortitude and patient cheer" must recall me from such
"industrious folly ;" and faith and piety must tell me that this
is not to be his home forever, and that the glories of this world
are lent but to spiritualize us, to incite us to look upward ; and
that the trials which I dread for my darling are but part of his
Maker's general scheme of goodness and wisdom.

II.

Mrs. Joanna Baillie.—"An Old Age Serene and Bright."—Miss Martineau's Characters of Children.—"A Little Knowledge" of Political Economy "a Dangerous Thing."—Comparison of Tasso, Dante, and Milton.

To Miss E. TREVENEN, Helstone, Cornwall:

Hampstead, 1833.—Our great poetess, or rather the sensible, amiable old lady that *was* a great poetess thirty years ago, is still in full preservation as to health. Never did the flame of genius more thoroughly expire than in her case; for though, as Lamb says, "Ancient Mariners," "Lyrical Ballads," and "Kehamas" are not written in the grand climacteric, the authors of such flights of imagination generally give out sparkles of their ancient fires in conversation; but Mrs. Joanna Baillie is, as Mr. Wordsworth observes, when quoting her non-feeling for Lycidas, "dry and Scotchy;" learning she *never* possessed, and some of her poetry, which I think was far above that of any other woman, is the worse for a few specks of bad English; then her criticisms are so surprisingly narrow and jejune, and show so slight an acquaintance with fine literature in general. Yet if the authoress of "Plays on the Passions" does not now write or talk like a poetess, she *looks* like one, and *is* a piece of poetry in herself. Never was old age more lovely and interesting; the face, the dress, the quiet, subdued motions, the silver hair, the calm *in-looking* eye, the pale, yet not unhealthy skin, all are in harmony; this is winter with its own peculiar loveliness of snows and paler sunshine; no forced flowers or fruits to form an unnatural contrast with the general air of the prospect.

I never could relish those wonderfully young-looking old ladies that are frequently pointed out to our admiration, and who look like girls at a little distance; so much the greater your disappointment when you come close. Why should an old person *look* young? ought such a one to *feel* and *think* young? if not, how can the mind and person be in harmony; how can there be the real grace and comeliness which old age, *as old age*, may possess, though not round cheeks and auburn ringlets?

Do you read Miss Martineau? How well she always succeeds in her portraits of children, their simplicity and partially developed feelings and actions; and what a pity it is that, with all her knowledge of child nature, she should try to persuade herself and others that political economy is a fit and useful study for growing minds and limited capabilities—a subject of all others requiring matured intellect and general information as its basis! This same political economy, which quickens the sale of her works now, will, I think, prove heavy ballast for a vessel that is to sail down the stream of time, as all agree that it is a dead weight upon the progress of her narratives, introducing the most absurd incongruities and improbabilities in regard to the dramatic propriety of character, and setting in arms against the interest of the story the political opinions of a great class of her readers. And she might have rivaled Miss Edgeworth! What a pity that she would stretch her genius on such a Procrustes bed! And then what practical benefit can such studies have for the mass of the people, for whom it seems that Miss M—— intends her expositions?—they are not like religion, which may and must mould the thoughts and acts of every-day life, the true spirit of which therefore can not be too much studied and explained; but how can poor people help the corn-laws, except by sedition? and what pauper will refuse to marry, because his descendants may, hundreds of years hence (if hundreds of things don't happen to prevent it), help among millions of others to choke up the world? Who, in short, will listen to dry and doubtful themes when passion calls? A smattering of Greek or Latin is, in my opinion, a harmless thing; nay, I think it useful and agreeable, just according to its extent; a little is good, more is better, if people are aware how short a way they have proceeded, and what a length of road is before them, which they have more opportunity of seeing than those who have never set out. But a little learning is, indeed, a dangerous thing, when no part can be seen clearly without a view of the whole, and when knowledge, or fancied knowledge, is sure to incite to practice. * * *

I admire the elegant and classical Tasso, but can not agree with those who call him the great poet of Italy. He borrowed from the ancients, not, as Milton did, to melt down the foreign with the original ore of his own mind, and to form out of the mass a new creation wholly his own in shape and substance, and in its effect on the minds of others. It appears to me that he only produced a vigorous and highly wrought imitation of former copies, into which he combined many new materials, but the frame and body of which was not original. Dante's was the master-mind that wrought, like Homer and Milton, for itself from the beginning, and which influenced the poetry of Italy for ages.

III.

Characteristics of English Scenery.—Somerset, Yorkshire, Devon, Derbyshire, and the Lakes.—Visit of H. N. Coleridge to Mr. Poole at Nether Stowey.

To Miss E. Trevenen, Helstone, Cornwall:

Hampstead, October, 1833. — Henry agrees with me in thinking the Somerset landscape the ideal of *rurality* where nature is attired in amenity rather than in grandeur. The North of England is more picturesque; you are there ever thinking of what might be represented on canvas; parts of Yorkshire are far more romantic, especially in the mellowing lights and hues of autumn, when its old ruins, and red and yellow trees, and foaming streams bring you into communion with the genius of Scott; Derbyshire is lovely and picturesque, but to me it is unsatisfactory, as mimicking, on too small a scale, a finer thing of the same sort. Dovedale may have a character of its own; I understand it is more pastoral than the English Lakeland, yet with a portion of its wilder beauty; but Matlock struck me as a fragment of Borodale, without the fine imaginative distance. Devon is a noble county, but less *distinctly* charactered, I think, than the sister one; it displays specimens of variously featured landscapes, here the river-scenery of Scotland, there a smiling meadow-land; in one place reminding you of the North of England, in another a wild, desolate moor, or fine sea-view peculiar to itself; still, in the general face of the country, I have felt that there was the want of individuality and a due proportion of the various features of the scene—in many parts the trees, though superb specimens in themselves, domineer, in their giant multitude, too exclusively over the land, and prevent the eye from taking in a prospect where the perfection of parts is subservient to the soul-entrancing effect of the whole. Devonshire has sometimes struck me as the work-shop of nature, where materials of the noblest kind and magnitude are heaped together. The only defect, Henry says, in Somersetshire, is the fewness and unclearness of the streams. With Nether Stowey he was especially delighted; it is, indeed, an epitome of the beauties of the county. He was much interested with the marked original character and gratified by the attentions of his host, our old friend Mr. Poole. He visited my father's tiny cottage, where my brother Hartley trotted and prattled, and where my unknown baby brother Berkeley, a beautiful infant, was born. The pleasant reminiscences of my father's abode in the village gave Henry much pleasure.

IV.

"Dodging."—Children best managed by Authority, not by Premature
Appeals made to their Feelings.

To her Husband :

Hampstead, October, 1833.— Herby begins his lessons now with "Oo shan't dodge me!" but I tell him (or tell myself rather) that without dodging no scholar was ever made. Short instructions at a time, and thorough cross-examination of those given, is the system I would go upon in teaching. Be sure that the first step is *really* taken before you attempt to proceed, and don't fancy that children will listen to lectures, either in learning or morality. Punish a child for hurting his sister, and he will draw the inference that it is wrong, without a sermon on brotherly affection. Children mark what you *do* much more, and what you say less, than those who know them not imagine. Another of my rules is, never to draw upon the sensibility of children, or try to *create* what must be a native impulse, if genuine ; neither would I *appeal* to what is so unsure a ground of action. I would not tell a child to refrain from what is wrong because it *gives me pain.* I know from experience how soon that falls flat on the feelings, and how can you expect sympathy where there can be no experience or conception of the evil suffered ? Do you remember how poor little ——— used to behave when told not to make his mother's head ache? Nothing is more sure to disgust than a demand for sympathy where there is a lack of all materials for its production. How can a child comprehend a grown person's bodily sensations, or parental griefs and anxieties? You must appeal to reason and conscience, not so much by argument as by such a medium as is most applicable to the mind of a child. If you have reason to think your motives misunderstood, in any way which may affect the child's feelings or conduct, a few leading hints may soon set the matter right.

V.

The Ancients' Close Observation and Accurate Delineation of Nature.—
Names of Colors in Classic Poetry.—"The Georgics."

To the Same :

Hampstead, December, 1833.—Martin says the ancients were vague in the description of colors. I doubt not, if we understood them thoroughly, we should find that what appears vague and shadowy proceeded from fineness and accuracy of discernment. · The ancients were precise in the delineation of nature. They did not see it with the spirit of Wordsworth—no more, I think, did Shakespeare. But they either drew and colored in the open air, and conveyed forms and tints closely and vividly, or they translated literally from the poets who did so, as Virgil appears to have done from Homer and Theocritus. This applies to their poetical diction. The spirit and form of Virgil's work were doubtless borrowed with modification; but the vague, dreamy imagery of Shelley, Keats, etc., I believe to be a thing of modern growth. The ancients did not modify and compose out of floating reminiscences of other books. *Purpureus*, as applied to a swan, of course is metaphorical, red being the most brilliant of colors, and a white swan gleaming in full daylight, one of the most resplendent of natural objects. The passages on the hyacinth, I think, are perfectly consistent, if closely examined, and express a peculiar shade of red belonging to one of the multitudinous tribe of lilies. *Glaucus*, too, has a precise meaning. *Pallens* is very expressive and true in the way it is applied, meaning yellowish-white. *Niger* must have meant *dark-colored*, not merely black. How exact the metaphors of the peasantry are. "The Georgics" is the Rubens portrait of nature. How exquisite is the expression, yet nothing is idealized. Herby must read that poem as soon as he has Latin enough to gather the meaning through the foreign garb. It will make him look at nature, and looking at nature will make him relish that sweet transcript. He has just come in from his walk, with a sprig of arbutus, with its red fruits, which, he says, are strawberries. He agrees with those who named the arbutus the strawberry-tree. Virgil affirms that folks once lived on these "mocking" strawberries and acorns, a thing which I make bold to disbelieve.

CHAPTER II.

1834.

LETTERS TO HER HUSBAND, AND TO MISS TREVENEN.

I.

Books for the Little Ones.—"Original Poems."—Mrs. Howitt's Poetry.—
Mrs. Hannah More.—Girlish View of her Literary Pretensions confirmed
by Maturer Judgment.—A Group of Authoresses.—Remarks on Jane
Austen's Novels by the Lake Poets.—Hannah More's Celebrity account-
ed for.—Letters of Walpole and Mrs. Barbauld.—Love of Gossip in the
Reading Public.

To Miss EMILY TREVENEN, Helstone, Cornwall:

Hampstead, August, 1834.—Mary Howitt's book* is a perfect
love, as to its external part; the prints are really exquisite. The
poems I have not read through, but what I have read confirm
me in my previous opinion that she has a genuine vein of poetry, though not, I think, a very affluent one. Some of the puffs
(one of them at least) said that she had even surpassed the au-
thoresses† of the "Original Poems" in hitting off something
truly poetical, yet *intelligible to children,* in verse. To this particular theme of praise I can not subscribe. I think Mary Howitt's verses do *not* contain what all children must enter into, in
the same degree that the "Original Poems" do; but in this respect I think them preferable even as regards fitness for youthful (I mean for childish) minds, that they represent scarcely
any thing but what is bright and joyous. Children should dwell
apart from the hard and ugly realities of life as long as possible.
The "Original Poems" give too many revolting pictures of mental depravity, bodily torture, and of adult sorrows; and I think
the sentiments (the tirades against hunting, fishing, shooting,
etc., for instance) are morbid, and partially false.

----

* "Sketches of Natural History."

† Ann and Jane Taylor, daughters of Isaac Taylor, of Ongar, and sisters
of the popular author of the "Natural History of Enthusiasm."—E. C.

When I say that Mary Howitt's vein is not affluent, I mean that she is given to *beat out* one fancy as a gold-beater does a bit of gold—that the self-same imagination is reproduced, with a little change of attire, in one poem after another.

You speak of Mrs. Hannah More. I have seen abundant extracts from her "Remains," and I think I could not read them through if I were to meet with them. I fear you will think I want a duly disciplined mind, when I confess that her writings are not to my taste. I remember once disputing on this subject with a young chaplain, who affirmed that Mrs. Hannah More was the greatest female writer of the age. "Whom," he asked, "did I think superior?" I mentioned a score of authoresses whose names my opponent had never even heard before. I should not now dispute doggedly with a divine in a stage-coach, but years of discretion have not made me alter the opinion I then not very discreetly expressed, of the disproportion between Mrs. More's celebrity and her literary genius, as compared with that of many other female writers whose fame has not extended to the Asiatic Islands. I can not see in her productions aught comparable to the imaginative vigor of Mrs. J. Baillie, the eloquence and (for a woman) the profundity of Madame de Staël, the brilliancy of Mrs. Hemans (though I think *her* overrated), the pleasant, broad comedy of Miss Burney and Miss Ferrier, the melancholy tenderness of Miss Bowles, the pathos of Inchbald and Opie, the masterly sketching of Miss Edgeworth (who, like Hogarth, paints manners as they grow out of morals, and not merely as they are modified and tinctured by fashion); the strong and touching, but sometimes coarse pictures of Miss Martineau, who has some highly interesting sketches of childhood in humble life; and last, not least, the delicate mirth, the gently hinted satire, the feminine, decorous humor of Jane Austen, who, if not the greatest, is surely the most faultless of female novelists. My Uncle Southey and my father had an equally high opinion of her merits, but Mr. Wordsworth used to say that though he admitted that her novels were an admirable copy of life, he could not be interested in productions of that kind; unless the truth of nature were presented to him clarified, as it were, by the pervading light of imagination, it had scarce any attractions in his eyes; and for this reason he took little pleasure in the writings of Crabbe. My Uncle Southey often spoke in high terms of "Castle Rackrent ;" he thought it a work of true genius. Miss Austen's works are essentially feminine, but the best part of Miss Edgeworth's seem as if they had been written by a man. "Castle Rackrent" contains genuine humor, a thing very rare in the writings of women, and not much relished by our sex in general. "Belinda" contains much that is powerful, interspersed, like the fine parts of Scotland, with tracts of dreary insipidity ; and what is good in this work I can not think of so high an order as the good things in "Castle Rackrent" and "Emma." I have been led to think that the exhibition of disease and bodily torture is but a coarse art to "freeze the blood." Indeed, you will acquit me of any affected pretense to originality of criticism, when you recollect how early my mind was biased by the strong talkers I was in the habit of listening to. The spirit of what I sport on critical matters, though not always the application, is generally derived from the sources that you wot of. Yet I know well that we should not go by authority without finding out a reason for our faith ; and unless we test the opinions learned from others with those of the world in general, we are apt to hold them in an incorrect, and, at the same time, a more strong and unqualified way than those do from whom we have derived them.

Though I think with the *Spectator*, etc., that Mrs. More's very great notoriety was more the work of circumstances, and the popular turn of her mind, than owing to a strong original genius, I am far from thinking her an *ordinary* woman. She must have had great energy of character, and a sprightly, versatile mind, which did not originate much, but which readily caught the spirit of the day, and reflected all the phases of opinion in the pious and well-disposed portion of society in a clear and lively manner. To read Mrs. More's new book was a sort of good work, which made the reader feel satisfied with him or her self when performed ; and it is agreeable to have one's very own opinions presented to one in handsome language, and placed in a highly respectable point of view. Then Mrs. More entered the field when there were few to make a figure there besides, and she was set agoing by Garrick and Johnson. Garrick, who pleased all the world, said that the world ought to be pleased with her ; and Johnson, the Great Mogul of literature, was gracious to a pretender whose highest ambition was to follow him at a humble distance. He would have sneered to death a writer of far subtler intellect, and more excursive imagination, who dared to deviate from the track to which he pronounced good sense to be confined. He even sneered a little at his dear pet, Fanny Burney; *she* had set up shop for herself, to use a vulgarism; she had ventured to be original. I must add that Mrs. More's steady devotion to the cause of piety and good morals added the stamp of respectability to her works, which was a deserved passport to their reception; though such a passport can not enable any production to keep its hold on the general mind if it is not characterized by power as well as good intention.

I admired some of Walpole's Letters in this publication, and I read a flattering one from Mrs. Barbauld, who was a very acute-minded woman herself. Some of her Essays are very clever indeed. I like Mrs. More's style—so neat and sprightly. The Letters seem to contain a great deal of anecdote, the rage of the reading public, but that is an article which I am not particularly fond of.

II.

Reasons why the Greek and Latin Poets ought to continue to form Part of the Course of School Instruction.—Lord Byron's Peculiar Experience no Argument against it.—Milton's Scheme of Education.—Conjecture as to the Effect of Circumstances on the Development of Poetic Genius.

To her Husband :

Hampstead, August 28, 1834.—I feel quite against the notion of substituting a lower set of books for the classic poets in the instruction of youth. Purity and force of language and of thought are not so much learned by rule as imbibed by early and long habit, so far as they are to be gained from without. They acquire an interest from association with the "visionary gleam" of our first years. The classic author is but dimly understood at first; but his various merits are developed with the developing mind of the student, and in the end he possesses the charm of an old affection and a new love combined. Such works present clear and pleasing images to the intellect in its very first stage: and the absence of all that is false in logic and corrupt in taste is a vast advantage.

Such, I think, is the effect of early classical reading in those who possess a sensibility and aptness for literature; and those who find no stimulus in the pursuit sufficient to make them recur to it in after years are surely better furnished with a little Homer, Virgil, and Horace, than with the words of an inferior writer.

I can not think Lord Byron, with his perverse, fastidious taste, is a fair instance in this question, great as his poetical taste may have been.   Horace, nine times out of ten, I should conjecture, is not the occasion of flogging; faults in construing are but a small part of school offenses.   As to Milton, he would have altered the system of Old England in many particulars; but I can not think that the Republic he advocated would ever produce a Miltonic mind, attired at least so gracefully as was that which presented to us the "Paradise Lost."

Query—what would Milton, Shakespeare, and Walter Scott have been, had they been born in the United States in the nineteenth century?   How would their genius have manifested itself?   Byron, Wordsworth, and Coleridge would, I think, have been less altered in the garb of their minds than the former three.   Shakespeare's plays are full of royal and courtly associations; Milton's style is based upon the ancient classics; chivalry and antiquity are the very spirit of Scott's creations. My father and Wordsworth philosophized upon man and nature; their writings are not strongly tinctured with any particular atmosphere; they wrote neither of nor for the fabrics of ancient power, and the French Revolution gave their minds a cosmopolitan impulse.   As to Byron, the tone of his mind in his most ambitious attempts was borrowed from them; and his Eastern tales have little to do with European antiquity.   A traveled American might easily have imbibed the spirit they display.

III.

Dryden and Chaucer.

To the Same:

Hampstead, September, 1834.—Dryden's fables are certainly an ideal of the rapid, compressed manner.   Each line packs as much meaning as possible.   But Dryden's imagination was fertile and energetic rather than grand or subtle; and he is more deficient in tenderness than any poet of his capacity that I am acquainted with. His English style is animated and decorous, full of picture-words, but too progressive for elaborate metaphors.

In "Palamon and Arcite" there is all Dryden's energy and richness; but you feel in such a subject his want of tenderness and romance. He seems ever playing with his subject, and almost ready to turn the lover's devotion, and the conquering Emily herself, into a jest. The sly satire of Chaucer suited his genius; but there is a simple pathos at times in the old writer which is alien to Dryden's mind. Chaucer jested upon women like a laughing philosopher; Dryden like a disappointed husband.

IV.

Concentration, not Versatility, the Secret of Success in Life.—Visionaries.
—The Passion of Envy and the Vice of Cruelty.—Is Sporting Wrong?
Practical Bearings of the Question.—Cruelty of Children seldom Deliberate.—Folly of Exaggerating Bird-nesting into a Crime.

To the Same:

Hampstead, September, 1834. — Persons who succeed in the world without moulding themselves on the world's model are those who command attention by doing some particular thing thoroughly well; a crowd of minor achievements pass for nothing, or convey only the notion of a studious idler. I would not give a farthing for you to be thought clever in architecture, or conversant with technicalities of the arts, a fine fencer, dancer, carver, or the best shot in England. Details which conduce to one great point are profitable, but not if they be entirely desultory. Would your moral and intellectual character, your whole man, be a grain the more respectable and admirable? I think it would be much less so if these pursuits diverted you in any degree from the main earthly objects of your life: your profession as the means of an honorable livelihood, and of benefit to others; literature as ennobling and blessing your own life, and enabling you to extend those advantages to the world which enhances the dignity of the pursuit; and those duties of home which love and religion impose. * * *

These writers on Natural History are quite as fanciful and vague in their theories, quite as often raise a structure on a

F

quaking bog, in their discussion upon facts, as those who are conversant with abstract matters. To be a visionary depends on the temper, not on the subject of contemplation, and none are more misled by imagination than the enthusiasts of mammon, or those who go about to establish the truth of facts in which they take an interest. I knew a man of the world who had a gold and silver dream about Peru, and who went thither upon such uncertain information, and drew such solid inferences from shadowy premises, as astonished many of his friends. Over-eagerness to find particular things true leads us away from the truth.

And what a visionary is the envious man! He walketh in a vain shadow, and disquieteth himself in vain; he is possessed and agitated and impelled by something which exists only in his own fancy. The dog in the manger is an old apologue; but I suppose a dog can no more be capable of envy than of veneration. May not envy be defined as a debility of the imagination, the condition or proximate causes of which are want of energy of mind and irritability of temperament? Envy no doubt tends to harden the heart, but it is not naturally connected with hard-heartedness. You will see very charitable and compassionate persons extremely envious. But people eminently envious are never good-tempered; and though persons of strong intellectual powers are not free from the feeling, it seldom tyrannizes over minds that reflect much, and are freshened and stimulated by a variety and choice of speculations. It is a modification of selfishness which can only exist through a false estimate of ourselves and others, and the things of this world. It is allied to pride and covetousness, but more closely to the former than the latter, because objects of pride are objects of imagination more than those of covetousness. Envious persons are always proud, but not always grossly covetous. Envy argues an obliquity of the reasoning powers, and never exists in any great degree in any very candid and sincere mind, but it does not imply willful injustice; candor is unconscious, or at least natural honesty, but justice is honesty of the will pursued upon principle. Envious persons are not necessarily unconscientious, though envy, like every irregular passion, tends to obscure the perception of right, and to weaken the moral power. I might add that envy is a weakness of human nature, not a peculiarity of individuals; and he who subdues it the most, or naturally has the least of it, is the person to be remarked, as he who is most under its influence is most noted for evil. It is not like shyness or openness, which is characteristic of one person, while the reverse is characteristic of another. * * * In the work on Natural History, I met with some good-natured, commonplace observations to this effect, that the coarse and ignorant are apt to be coarsely and ignorantly cruel. I added this note :

" Man is lord of the creation, yet his is not an absolute monarchy. There are limitations which the demands of his own heart rather than their rights insist upon ; but they are not very easily defined, and the line between use and abuse has never yet been strictly drawn. To take an abstract pleasure in sorrow of the meanest thing that feels, is the mark of a degraded nature—to indulge in such a pleasure is to degrade it willfully ; but how far may we justifiably consult our pleasure or our pride, regardless of such suffering? Falconry and hare-hunting have their apologists among the refined and reflective, as well as angling and shooting, which, indeed, occasion less protracted misery. Bird-nesting has not been defended, because peasant boys care not to defend themselves from imputations on their sensibility. All perceive that it is unworthy of a reasoning creature to inflict pain by way of venting irritated feelings ; but how far we may make it matter of amusement, or at least connect amusement with it, the conscience does not so readily determine. The contemplation of suffering for itself alone is, in very rare instances, I believe, the source of gratification. Cruelty is said to be natural, because children tease and kill living creatures, but in the same breath you are told that they do it out of ignorance, which no doubt is united with a pleasing sense of power. No, I believe that positive cruelty is a mark of the utmost corruption of our sin-prone nature, and, as in Nero and Domitian, the result of sophistication. Even boys that torture a mouse or a hedgehog are not delighted, I should think, with the pain of the animal—they do not image that very distinctly —but are amused with observing its conduct under those trying circumstances. In this case the sensibilities are dormant, or, put it at the worst, they are naturally torpid or obtuse, not excited and demonized, as in some extraordinary cases, where a hard and turbulent nature has been stimulated and trained by very peculiar circumstances. I think we may say that the more the excitement of any sport with animals proceeds from the exhibition of suffering, and the more inconsiderable are the benefit and pleasure arising collaterally in proportion to the suffering occasioned, the more it may be reprobated as cruel and degrading."

This note has swelled under my transcribing hand. I was going to add that, in treating of the conduct of man toward animals, we must not forget that they are *things*, as my father says, and not persons. They have no *rights* to regulate this matter, for an animal may be used in *any* way if the needs of man require it. But man violates his own dignity and hardens his heart if the suffering or evil is disproportioned to the necessity, and, as my father would say, every unhardened heart and unperverted mind is *"possessed"* by this idea. To strike an animal in passion is a cruel and degrading action more than an unjust one. It is cruel, because it is to inflict pain without necessity. To strike a man would be unjust as well as cruel; he has a right not to be struck, independent of all circumstances. He can only forfeit his right by his own acts and deeds. I can not think that slaves in the West Indies are *practically* treated as things. It would be impossible to manage any reasoning creature with advantage to the manager in this manner. There is a sort of compact between the master and slave. "If you will serve me well you shall have such and such advantages," is the strain of every prosperous slaveholder to his work people. But it was a vile state of things that the contrary was the theory which the laws of the country were regulated by, though, as you and many others think, this evil was not to be remedied on a sudden by Act of Parliament. However, to return from this excursion to the point of practice in my mind at present. It is very difficult to lay down rules for children or others on a matter which can not be brought to any standard more fixed than the varying requirements of different men, these requirements being defined by tastes, desires, and habits as various as the minds and situations of the agents. Nor is there any law by which you can condemn bear-baiting and uphold angling. Even if the fish are eaten, they are a mere luxury to the angling idler and his family. I think it ill-judged to lead children to look with contempt or dislike upon uneducated boys amusing themselves with bird-nesting. What precept of the Gospel, or the spirit of it even, do they infringe?

The sorrow of the bird is no part of the pleasure. The less we teach Christianity and humanity by way of censure upon others, the better. The animal suffering is very inconsiderable; the bird builds again immediately. But I would never put a child in the way of bird-nesting. I would say, "Don't take the eggs, it is a pity—the poor bird will miss them;" but I would not teach forbearance as a Christian duty, nor treat the matter with the same solemnity that I should do the unkindness to a sister or playmate, or insolence to a servant. If I saw a child tease or torture an animal, I should of course say, That is *cruel*, and I should let the child perceive that the animal feels bodily pain. The absence of all forethought or anticipation in the creature is not a reflection to which it would be useful to lead a child's mind. But all exaggerated pictures of animal suffering, the investing them with human sentiments (except in an apologue which the child soon understands), tirades against hunting, shooting, etc., I would let alone. And the author of "Hartleap Well" is as great an enemy of this false sentimentality as any in the kingdom.

V.

The Drama and the Epic.—Painting among the Ancients.—Sense of the Picturesque in Nature a Development of Modern Taste.

To the Same:

Hampstead, September, 1834.—In a drama the event is to display character; in an epic the characters are to carry on the event. Drama is biography, the Epic history. Lear, Othello, are the subjects of those dramas; the Loss of Eden, the destruction of Priam's power and domestic blessing by the anger of Achilles, those of Milton's and Homer's poems. In an Epic, only such a diversity of characters as the event would naturally assemble, and such qualities in the hero as would bring about the event, are essential to the conception of this sort of poem. In the Drama, characters are chosen for the subject, because their qualities are interesting and remarkable; and the proof of this is their bringing about particular events, or showing a certain line of conduct in peculiar circumstances. The Epic would be retarded by the exhibition of passion in all its stages, such as we have in Othello; it would be out of proportion, and would engross the whole attention from the general narrative. * * *

There can be no doubt that Cicero had a feeling of the interest to be derived from a copy of living objects on canvas, or even of those of still life, as the scene and circumstance of action. But the picturesqueness of the group may not have been the source of interest (at least not to the consciousness of the beholder, though no doubt it did enhance the gratification), but the life portrayed in the picture. The beholder was to be instructed, animated, or soothed by the story of some event or knowledge of some fact, rather than astonished, gratified, entertained by the exhibition of art, and spectacle of abstract beauty. I think this is the general distinction between the ancient and modern notions in regard to painting, though there may be exceptions, and the times of old may have had an infusion of our feelings, as we doubtless partake of that sort of interest which was the chief and most defined one to them. The pleasure to be derived from the power of art was by no means so decidedly modern, as a sense of the picturesqueness of inanimate combinations. The latter must belong to a people who have long been refined, a people who have leisure to luxuriate in things which have no being but in the imagination, and who have hit upon combinations and notions of the agreeable and beautiful, which were never suggested to the fancy even of sages and philosophers of simpler ages. Don't you think that much of the best modern poetry would be unintelligible to Cicero?—I mean as to the sentiment of it.

VI.

The Sublime and the Beautiful.—Comparative Popularity of Shakespeare, Milton, and Ben Jonson.—Education of Taste by an Exclusive Study of the Best Models.

To the Same:

1834.—It is perhaps more true to say that the sublime can not be so long dwelt upon as the beautiful, than that it is less *popular*. That style is, I think, as easily felt and estimated by the uncultivated taste as the other. But from its own nature it can not be long sustained, for awe and terror owe half of their being to novelty and surprise ; yet an appeal to those feelings,

or rather an attack upon them, is as surely effective as any in
the world. Indeed, I believe far more persons can appreciate
the merits of "Theodore and Honoria" (the supernatural scene
of which is sublime in the German style, though not in the more
elevated one of Milton and Dante) than of "Palamon and Arcite," which is beautiful ; or of "The Cock and the Fox," which
is witty and exquisite. Why and how far is Shakespeare more
popular than Milton ? Not (to *conjecture* merely) because there
is more of the sublime in Milton's poem, but simply because
persons unused to dwell upon what is abstract, who have acquired no knowledge of literary perfections, are unable to keep
up their attention during the course of an epic, especially one
which embodies a scheme of theology, and therefore demands
the cognizance of the understanding throughout the main part
of it, to be relished at all. The only parts of Shakespeare that
are popular, as you have stated,* are the selections for the
stage, the incidents of some of his plots, and the passions exhibited by some of his characters, though they are far from being understood. There is an upper surface which catches the
general eye, but what lies beneath, which is indicated to the refined taste, or to the fine perception of genius, is not generally
caught. The verdant lawn presents a pleasing aspect to the
eye of the rustic, yet it is not so interesting as to that of the
florist, the botanist, the physiologist, who perceives a thousand
peculiarities in that mass of vegetation which are unseen by
others, and who can pierce the bosom of the earth to discover
how and why and whence it has arisen. "Paradise Regained"
is less popular than "Paradise Lost," yet it contains comparatively little of the sublime ; but it is too abstract to be generally
relished ; it has no merits but those which a refined taste can
alone appreciate. "The White Doe," the "Flower and the
Leaf," and many other such plays of pure imagination, can
never be popular, in whole or in part. "The Pilgrim's Progress" has a complete upper surface of popularity. How little
is Shakespeare's delicate, sportive dialogue now appreciated,
such as that between Hotspur and his wife ! Coarser copies
have superseded it. Ben Jonson's plays were received with
rapture, when plot and incident were not to be had elsewhere,
or not in any more popular form ; and his reputation was up-

* In his "Introduction to Homer," a second edition of which was being
prepared by my father in 1834.—E. C.

held by the finer wits who frequented the theatre in those days. But now who except bookish persons knows any thing about them, or perceives that the "Fox" and the "Alchemist" are works of art a thousand times finer in design, and more exquisite in execution than those of modern vulgar dramatists? When good works alone were presented from the first to the populace, even their taste must have been simpler and finer than in times when it becomes sophisticated and yet degraded by inferior trash. If a peasant were shown daily a collection of Claudes and Correggios alone, he would be far more in the way of learning to admire them than if such pictures were thinly scattered among a set of glaring daubs.

VII.

Mrs. Joanna Baillie's Taste in Dress.—Opinion of the Poetess and of her Sister expressed by an Eminent Savant.

To the Same :

Hampstead, September 4, 1834.—I saw Mrs. Joanna Baillie before dinner. She wore a delicate lavender satin bonnet; and Mrs. J—— says she is fond of dress, and knows what every one has on. Her taste is certainly exquisite in dress, though (strange to say) not, in my opinion, in poetry. I more than ever admired the harmony of expression and tint, the silver hair and silvery gray eye, the pale skin, and the look which speaks of a mind that has had much communing with high imagination, though such intercourse is only perceptible now by the absence of every thing which that lofty spirit would not set his seal upon. Sir John Herschel says that Mrs. Agnes Baillie is "by far the cleverer woman of the two ;" but this is the speech of a *clever* man, a man whose acute mind can pierce some of the mysteries of the world of fact, but which does not sympathize with all the beings of the world of imagination. And then, in Mrs. Joanna Baillie, age has slackened the active part of genius, and yet is in some sort a substitute for it. There is a declining of mental exercitation. She has had enough of that ; and now for a calm decline, and thoughts of Heaven.

Miss Herschel.

Mrs. J—— says that Caroline Herschel, sister of the late Dr. Herschel, is a person of uncommon attainments and abilities, and is a Fellow of the Royal Society. She is now eighty-four; her letters from Berlin, where she resides, are full of vigor and spirit. She says: "My brother and I have sometimes stood out star-gazing till two o'clock, and have been told next day that, the night before, our neighbor's pigs had died of the frost."

Hard Words in the Latin Grammar Useful to Young Learners.

Those odd words, *Genitive, Vocative, Preterpluperfect,* etc., are helps to the memory. They have a quaint uniform of their own, and are something like one another, but unlike all other things.

Geography made Easy.

How much knowledge may be put into a child, by good economy of instruction, without employing his mind more than is perfectly wholesome! To Herby the map is a sort of game, and one that contains far more variety than any play that could be devised. To find out Sumatra or Owhyhee, to trace the Ganges, and follow the Equator in every different map, is a supreme amusement; and the notions of hot and cold, wet and dry, icy seas and towering palm-trees, with water dashing, and tigers roaming, and butterflies flitting, and his going and seeing them, and getting into tossing boats, and climbing by slow degrees up the steep mountain, are occupying his little mind, and give a zest to the whole affair. And then there is the pleasure of preaching it all over again to Nurse!

Right Opinions must be Held in the Right Spirit.

It is a fortunate thing to be induced by any circumstances to adopt the most edifying opinions, whichever they may be; but of still more consequence is the manner in which we hold and maintain them. Indeed, even in the most vital considerations, the *manner of holding it* is almost more than the speculative, abstract creed. I never can forget that the most (apparently) Christian-spirited creature I ever knew was a Unitarian.

CHAPTER III.

1834 (*continued*).

LETTERS TO HER HUSBAND AND HER ELDEST BROTHER, AND TO
MRS. PLUMMER.

I.

Composition of " Pretty Lessons for Good Children."

To HARTLEY COLERIDGE, Esq.:

Nab Cottage, Grasmere, ——, 1834.—What you say about
Natural History, dear Hartley, is quite accordant with my own
feelings ; but I am not *studying* it, or reading any thing system-
atically. A few pretty works with colored prints have been lent
to me, and I took an especial interest in the subject, not only for
the attractions you mention, but because I could talk to little
Herby about the birds and beasts, and show him the pictures.

I have also amused myself, and instructed him, with mamma's
assistance, by means of little rhymes, which I ink-printed upon
cards. Henry had a fancy for having some of them printed, as
a little record of some of my occupations during a season of
weakness and suffering, when I was shut out from almost all
pleasures and means of usefulness. In this view you will look
at the little book which I send you. It is worth nothing in any
other. It may amuse some other children, but it can not be to
any other child what these verses have been to Herby, struck
off as they were for the occasion, an occasion in which he was
specially interested.

II.

Chaucer's Poetry not that of a Primitive Age.

To her Husband:

It appears to me absurd to speak of Chaucer as living in the
"infancy of our poetry." Chaucer's metre is proved by Tyr-

whitt to be, as old Speght declared, quite perfect, if the words are pronounced as they were in his day. So says Sir W. Scott. Time only has "mis-metred" him, as he himself apprehended. Dryden says that numbers were in their nonage till Denham and Waller appeared. This is a strange misappreciation, as critics think now, of Spenser and Chaucer. And then as to the *matter* of Chaucer, it can not be called the offspring of a rude age, or even of a simple age. Much of it is satire, which is the growth of an age of social institutions. As to the refinements and complications of civilization, they may go on *ad infinitum*, and poetry will gain from that a greater variety of objects, and a different tone. Yet it may be perfect in kind at a very early period. Wordsworth, I think, would have been as fine a poet in Chaucer's age as now. The garb of his mind would doubtless have been different; perhaps some of his poetry would have been less exquisite; and certainly it may be supposed that certain circumstances are more congenial to certain minds than to others equally powerful. But a vivid imagination, with strong intellect and talent, must manifest itself, I imagine, under any circumstances.

III.

Note on Enthusiasm.—Mischievous Effect of Wrong Names given to Moral Qualities.

To the Same:

My mind misgives me about some notelets that I have penciled in J——'s "Journal of Art." Most of them are about facts in Natural History; but one is on the use of the word "Enthusiasm." Knapp says: "He must disclaim the epithet *Enthusiastic.* His is not an ecstasy that glows, fades, and expires; but a calm, deep-rooted conviction," etc. I have said— "Must enthusiasm expire? That of Linnæus survived through pain and weakness. Neither can I think that enthusiasm precludes calmness and rationality. That ardor which does so is fanaticism. But the enthusiasm of great minds is a steady heat, and though opposite, not contrary, to sobriety, as generosity is opposed to prudence, not exclusive of it. Enthusiasm with some persons is a synonym for extravagance. But how otherwise can we designate that habit of mind which impels to the most arduous and persistent efforts in pursuit of what must be its own reward, and the object of an abstract devotion? and was not this the primary meaning of enthusiasm?" I do think that words, from being used in a half wrong or wholly wrong sense, reflect upon the things originally signified a portion of that misapprehension. The word enthusiasm is taken for extravagance, and thus *genuine* enthusiasm is looked upon as in some sort extravagant. Over-strict religionists are called *serious*, till undistinguishing worldlings connect superstition or spiritual self-deception with staid reflective piety. Persons of warm fancy and weak judgment are called *romantic*, through which an elevated spiritual temper, and imaginative mode of viewing subjects and objects, is deemed inseparable from a certain degree of self-delusion and want of skill in the executive government of daily life; and people will not perceive that true poetry is truth, and that fiction conveys reality, because both have been falsified, and made false to their proper aim; the vehicle itself, and the thing to be conveyed, being both corrupted.

IV.

Cowper's "Iliad" and "Odyssey."—Requisites for a Successful Translation of Homer.

To the Same:

I hate Cowper's slow, dry, blank verse, so utterly alien to the spirit of the poem, and the minstrel mode of delivery. How could it have suited any kind of recitative or melody, or the accompaniment of any music? It is like a pursy, pompous, but unpolished man moving laboriously in a stiff dress of office. Those boar and lion hunting similes describing swift motion are dreadfully dragging in this sort of verse. In Milton there is little of this rapidity and flash to be conveyed. How meditative are the speeches of the fallen host? We feel conscious of the scope of the poem—that they have ages of time before them to work in, that they are not planning a scheme to be executed in days or weeks or months. In Homer, the time of action seems to be the life of individual men, and all is measured according to this scale. In Milton, we are reading of superhuman agencies, of times with which day, month, or year had nothing to do.

The only sort of translation of Homer, I think, which would be thoroughly gratifying, should be on Pope's plan, but better executed. There should be his brilliance and rapidity — or rather that of Dryden's in the Fables—with that thorough understanding of the spirit and proprieties of the whole poem, which would enable the translator (he being a person of some poetical genius) to give substitutes for the exact physical meaning of certain passages, yet to preserve the spirit and to maintain the rich flow of verse, and keep the genius of the language unviolated, at the same time that he transported us to ancient times and distant places. Cowper's poem is like a Camera Lucida portrait—far more unlike in expression and general result than one less closely copied as to lines and features. In a different material there must be a different form to give a similar effect.

V.

False Etymologies.—Dr. Johnson, his Mental Powers and Moral Character. —Quiet Conclusion of " Paradise Lost," and of the Part of Shylock in the " Merchant of Venice."—Silence of Revenge; Eloquence of Love and Grief and Indignation.

To the Same :

Hampstead, October, 1834.—I am often provoked by the silly derivations of words given in books. Two doctors (Johnson and Webster) have derived butterfly from *butter*—one because these flies come in butter season (they come from March to November, and what *is* butter season?), and the other because a very common butterfly is yellow! No, no; the *vox populi* that makes language is a much more accurate reporter of nature, and of all truth, than a guessing writer of books. Butterflies are *better* flies—larger flies, the largest sort of flies that you meet with. Poor Dr. Johnson was often dead tired when he made that dictionary, though it was on the whole a favorite work. But he had no fine perceptions about objects of sight—that is apparent in all that remains of his mind. He was, indeed, half blind; but I do not agree with those who attribute his coldness in regard to painting, natural landscape, etc., to that. He might have seen enough to admire, but his mind was anti-poetical; he was, as my father would have said, more keen than subtle. To call his mind gigantic, if the dimensions of the mind are meant,

I believe is erroneous; but he used his powers with giantly strength. If an ordinary scholar could bring readily into play all his latent power and knowledge, he would appear a giant in conversation. Johnson's written works leave no such impression; but he was a man of deep and strong feeling; his mind was vigorous, and saw all objects clearly within a certain range, and he had the power of arranging his thoughts and the various parts of a subject in an effective manner, and expressing his views with clearness and energy. Amid an apparent consciousness of frailty and sense of suffering, there is a strong cleaving to that which is good and holy. It is this mournful dignity, this religious humanity, which interest me in his writings, and he had just so much imagination as will enable a man to picture his views and feelings thus clearly to others. * * *

I think the concluding verses of "Paradise Lost" are truly sublime. There is an awful beauty about them.

> "The cherubim descended; on the ground,
> Gliding meteorous, as evening mist
> Risen from a river o'er the marish glides,
> And *gathers ground* fast at the laborer's heel,
> Homeward returning."

How skillfully are the points of likeness here just pointed at, and then the image is abandoned, just when it has done its work, and attention is drawn off to a new one: the flaming sword of God, the comet, and Libyan sands. Then the pathetic gentle-heartedness of the angel, hastening, yet leading them away; and they looking back once more saw their "once happy seat" waved over by that threatening hand; and then the few sad, subdued lines, so like human life and its submission, with a sort of sad effort after reparation, to an inevitable calamity. Just so quietly does Shylock go off the scene—"I am not very well, I would go home." It is remarkable how devoid all Shylock's language is of exaggeration. There is no amplifying, no playing with the subject, and waving it up and down like a streamer to catch different lights and display itself in various fantastic attitudes, as Shakespeare's lovers expatiate and add stroke after stroke to the picture of their possessed fancy. Shylock's passion of revenge is expressed, according to the view in my father's preface, by a bare, keen reiteration of certain matters of fact; he seems to shrink and double himself up like a crouching tiger, in order to shoot out all his energies when let loose upon their prey; when the moment patiently waited for arrives, he thrusts forth his cutting blade in the face of his enemy—you did thus and thus—see, you fool, what you imagined of me, and what I have made you. It is these sharp contrasts of neither more nor less than the actual facts which constitute all his oratory, and all his feelings of hatred are shown by hugging the reality with a fierce intensity, saying the very thing which was in every part of his heart over and over again. Indignation that breathes scorn, and believes deeply in the wrongfulness of the offender, but is not transfigured into malice; strong grief that has not collapsed into despair, are almost as expatiative as love; "Oh that I were a mockery-king of snow, to melt before the sun of Bolingbroke," is the language of a wandering fancy. And the Scriptures are full of such illustrations of sorrowfulness; for grief rushes out eager for a vent, and roams forth, seeking for employment, for a change from the intolerable misery of passiveness. Anger will talk much and strongly, but not so fancifully as love and grief; it stems the fancy by its violence, and those passions which, like revenge, impel to action, employ the energies in another way. As a watery mirror shaken by the wind presents only the confused fragments of a picture, the mind agitated by vehement anger reflects no continuous imagery, like sorrow which is still and meditative. Yet there is a sort of sullen resentment, which seems to stupefy the soul, and a scorn which is unutterable; it fears to be dissipated in words, and imparts an energy which facilitates restraint. Scorn argues self-possession; a man in a passion can not scorn.

VI.

Authority of Criticism.—The Judicial Faculty as much a Part of the Human Mind as the Inventive Faculty.—Great Art appeals to Sympathies which exist in all.

To the Same:

H——'s position is plainly absurd; for what but criticism is to establish the merits of any work? Does he mean that poets only can judge of poetry, and that they alone are to criticise each other? Even according to this view, how is he to prove that any particular critic is not a poet potentially, whether he have published or not? It seems to favor his notion that poets who write above the age, and whose productions are of an original mould, are often unjustly criticised in the beginning; but they are so as much by the critical poets of the day, as by the men of judgment who have no poetical power. Witness Dryden's first impressions of "Paradise Lost." By degrees it is perceived that the new type may be tried on the same principle as the old admired models, and that by *analogy* with them, though not by an unfair comparison, it will stand its ground. But the critical faculty must decide upon this question, be it in poet or prose-man, and the only question is, "Can the faculty of judging poetry be possessed apart from poetical power?" I should answer, Yes, undoubtedly. Waller had no perception of Milton's merits. But he was not a *great* poet. Neither was Dryden great in comparison with Milton; and according to that view none could judge of Milton but Milton himself. Certainly no critic could so mould and refine the taste and judgment of the age as he who afforded such models to exercise them upon: but the poet does not create in others the faculty of judging, though he may stimulate and direct it; that faculty must decide whether they are models or not, after all. My father and Wordsworth may have improved the poetical taste of the age, but that does not exempt them from being amenable to criticism, for unless they can touch the feelings, or win the verdict of the judgment of men, they are not great poets; I mean the judgment, not of the unlearned, but that faculty where it is really developed. Those poets were wronged by particular critics, who did not try their merits fairly, but that does not prove them above criticism. The same may be said of painting. The great painter is to be appreciated not by painters alone: he appeals to faculties latent in all, and possessed in various degrees by various men. They may be oftener developed in painters than in others; but I believe that he who can execute a fine Dutch piece may be a very indifferent judge of a poetical landscape, or sublime representation from Scripture, except as to the technical part. E—— thinks the Titian (Bacchus and Ariadne) is only excellent for color, and that Claude has no merit different from Turner. Then all that poetry, that sentiment, which others have perceived in those pictures, are either a mere accident or a matter of imagination in the beholder. "The critic is only to abstract rules from the poet's practice"—*that* I can not admit. If judgment be a faculty of the mind, it must be innate, consequently as old as the inventive faculty; and as soon as ever a poet wrote, a critic might judge whether he had written well or ill. "The critic has only to inquire whether the world has acknowledged the poet," then the world is the original critic that decided the matter; and the world decided that Byron was finer than Wordsworth, Campbell than Coleridge.

VII.

Botany.—The Linnæan System quite as *Natural* as the Modern Classification, though less Comprehensive.—Both Arrangements ought to be learned by Botanical Students.

To the Same:

Professor S—— makes an attack upon the Linnæan System of Botany, because a man on a savage island would find it of no use! Now, I think, that as the facts on which he founded it are true, it ought to be learned in addition to any more philosophical arrangement that may have been since devised. The knowledge of a science is truly useful, not for any one particular accidental purpose to which it may be applied, but generally for the enlargement of the mind, the confirmation of general principles, elucidation of the natural and metaphysical world, and consequently the practical good of mankind, on the broad scale, and in special instances. And then the very instance he adduces is so inconclusive. On a desert island a man that sees a herb without bracts may be sure it is fit to eat, because he may be sure it belongs to the cabbage tribe. Next year a new sort of cabbage, that is a deadly poison, may be discovered. Nightshade and potatoes are of the same natural family; but who that first saw the one after old acquaintance with the other could derive any practical benefit from the knowledge of that fact? Then, as if the new classification was more *natural* than the other! In one system plants are classified according to the number of pistils and stamens; in another according to some more general features of agreement; but in both nothing more than the agreement actually specified is implied. Both arrangements ought to be known. Certainly the one called Natural is better, because it embraces a combination

G

of agreements.   And it may be proved that plants, like the animal creation, may be arranged in classes, one within another,
till you come to the particular species.

VIII.

On the Death of Samuel Taylor Coleridge.*—Details of his Last Illness.
—His Will, Letters, and Literary Remains.—Respect and Affection felt
for Him by Those with whom he Lived.—Probable Influence of his
Writings on the Course of Religious Thought.—Remarks on his Genius
and Character by Different Critics.—His Last Readings and Notes.

To Mrs. PLUMMER :

Hampstead, October, 1834.—My dearest L——, your affectionate and interesting letter gave me great pleasure, and gratified
my feelings in regard to my dear father, whose memory still occupies the chief place in my thoughts.   Your appreciation of his
character and genius, my dear friend, would endear you to me
were there no other ties between us.   In his death we mourn
not only the removal of one closely united to us by nature and
intimacy, but the extinction of a light which made earth more
spiritual, and heaven in some sort more visible to our apprehension.   You know how long and severely he suffered in his
health; yet, to the last, he appeared to have such high intellectual gratifications that we felt little impulse to pray for his
immediate release ; and though his infirmities had been grievously increasing of late years, the life and vigor of his mind
were so great that they hardly led those around him to think
of his dissolution.   His frail house of clay was so illumined
that its decaying condition was the less perceptible.   His departure, after all, seemed to come suddenly upon us.   We were
first informed of his danger on Sunday, the 20th of July, and on
Friday, the 25th, he was taken from us.   For several days after
fatal symptoms appeared, his pains were very great; they were
chiefly in the region of the bowels, but were at last subdued by
means of laudanum, administered in different ways; and for the
last thirty-six hours of his existence he did not suffer severely.
When he knew that his time was come, he said that he hoped
by the manner of his death to testify the sincerity of his faith;

---

* At Mr. Gillman's house, the Grove, Highgate, on the 25th of July, 1834.
—E. C.

and hoped that all who had heard of his name would know that he died in that of the English Church.   Henry saw him for the last time on Sunday, and conveyed his blessing to my mother and myself; but we made no attempt to see him, and my brothers were not sent for, because the medical men apprehended that the agitation of such interviews would be more than he ought to encounter.   Not many hours before his death he was raised in his bed and wrote a precious faintly scrawled scrap, which we shall ever preserve, recommending his faithful nurse, Harriet, to the care of his family.   Mr. Green, who had so long been the partner of his literary labors, was with him at the last, and to him, on the last evening of his life, he repeated a certain part of his religious philosophy, which he was especially anxious to have accurately recorded.   He articulated with the utmost difficulty, but his mind was clear and powerful, and so continued till he fell into a state of coma, which lasted till he ceased to breathe, about six o'clock in the morning.   His body was opened, according to his own earnest request—the causes of his death were sufficiently manifest in the state of the vital parts; but that internal pain from which he suffered more or less during his whole life was not to be explained, or only by that which medical men call nervous sympathy.   A few out of his many deeply attached and revering friends attended his remains to the grave, together with my husband and Edward;* and that body which did him such "grievous wrong" was laid in its final resting-place in Highgate church-yard.   His executor, Mr. Green, after the ceremony, read aloud his will, and was greatly overcome in performing his task.   It is, indeed, a most affecting document.   What little he had to bequeath (a policy of assurance worth about £2560) is my mother's for life, of course, and will come to her children equally after her time.   Mr. Green has the sole power over my father's literary remains, and the philosophical part he will himself prepare for publication; some theological treatises he has placed in the hands of Mr. Julius Hare, of Cambridge, and his curate, Mr. Sterling (both men of great ability).   Henry will arrange literary and critical pieces—notes on the margins of books, or any miscellaneous productions of that kind that may be met with among his MSS., and probably some letters will appear if they can be collected.

---

* The Rev. Edward Coleridge, his nephew.—E. C.

I fear there will be some difficulty in this; but I have understood that many written by him at different times exhibit his peculiar power of thought and expression, and ought not to be lost to the world if they could be recovered. No man has been more deeply beloved than my dear father; the servants at the Grove wept for him as for a father, and Mr. and Mrs. Gillman speak of their loss as the heaviest trial that has ever befallen them, though they have had their full share of sorrow and suffering. Mrs. Gillman's notes, written since his death, are precious testimonies to me of his worth and attaching qualities. In one of them she speaks of "the influence of his beautiful nature on our domestics, so often set down by friends or neighbors to my good management, his forgiving nature, his heavenly-mindedness, his care not to give offense unless duty called on him to tell home truth; his sweet and cheerful temper, and so many moral qualities of more or less value, and all adorned by his Christian principles. His was indeed Christianity. To do good was his anxious desire, his constant prayer—and all with such *real* humility—never any kind of worldly accommodating the truth to any one—yet not harsh or severe—never pretending to faults or failings he had not, nor denying those he thought he had. But, as he himself said of a dear friend's death, 'it is recovery and *not death*. Blessed are they that sleep in the Lord—his life is hidden in Christ. In his Redeemer's life it is hidden, and in His glory will it be disclosed. Physiologists hold that it is during sleep chiefly that we grow; what may we not hope of such a sleep in such a Bosom?'" Much more have I had from her, and formerly heard from her lips, all in the same strain; and during my poor dear father's last sufferings she sent a note to his room, expressing with fervency the blessings that he had conferred upon her and hers, and what a happiness and a benefit his residence under her roof had been to all his fellow-inmates. The letters which I have seen of many of his friends respecting his lamented departure have been most ardent; but these testimonies from those who had him daily, hourly, in their sight, and the deep love and reverence expressed by Mr. Green, who knew him so intimately, are especially dear to my heart. My dear Henry, too, was deeply sensible of his good as well as his great qualities; it was not for his genius only that he reverenced him, and it has been one of many blessings attendant on my marriage, that by it we were both drawn into closer communion with that gifted spirit than could otherwise have been the case. There was every thing in the circumstances of his death to soothe our grief, and valuable testimonies (such as I have mentioned, with many, many others) from valued persons have mingled their sweetness in the cup.

We feel happy, too, in the conviction that his writings will be widely influential for good purposes. All his views may not be adopted, and the effect of his posthumous works must be impaired by their fragmentary condition ; but I think there is reason to believe that what he has left behind him will introduce a new and more improving mode of thinking, and teach men to consider some subjects on principles more accordant to reason, and to place them on a surer and wider basis than has been done hitherto. It is not to be expected that speculations which demand so much effort of mind and such continuous attention to be fully understood, can ever be *immediately* popular —the written works of master spirits are not perused by the bulk of society whose feelings they tincture, and whose belief they contribute to form and modify—it is through intervening channels that "sublime truths, and the maxims of a pure morality" are diffused among persons of various age, station, and capacity, so that they become "the hereditary property of poverty and childhood, of the workshop and the hovel." Heraud, in his brilliant oration on the death of my father, delivered at the Russell Institution, observes that religion and philosophy were first reconciled—first brought into permanent and indissoluble union—in the divine works of Coleridge ; and I believe the opinion expressed by this gentleman, that my father's metaphysical theology will prove a benefit to the world, is shared by many persons of refined and searching intellect both in this country and in America, where he has some enthusiastic admirers ; and it is confidently predicted by numbers that this will be more and more felt and acknowledged in course of time. My dear L——, I will not apologize to you for this filial strain ; I write unreservedly to you, knowing that you are alive to my father's merits as a philosopher and a poet, and believing that you will be pleased to find that he who was misunderstood and misrepresented by many, and grossly calumniated by some, was and is held in high honor as to moral as well as intellectual qualities by good and intelligent persons. "Hereafter," says a writer in Blackwood, "it will be made appear that he who was so admirable a poet was also one of the most amiable of men." The periodicals have been putting out a great many attempts at accounts of his life—meagre enough for the most part, and all more or less incorrect as to facts. We have been very much hurt with our former friend, Mr. De Quincey, the opium-eater, as he chooses to be styled, for publishing so many personal details respecting my parents in *Tait's Magazine.* As Henry says, "the little finger of retaliation would bruise his head;" but I would not have so good a Christian as my father defended by any measure so unchristianlike as retaliation, nor would I have those belonging to me condescend to bandy personalities. This, however, was never intended by my spouse ; but I believe he has some intention of reckoning with the scandal-monger for the honor of those near and dear to us. Some of our other friends will be as much offended with this paper of his as we are. He has characterized my father's genius and peculiar mode of discourse with great eloquence and discrimination. He speaks of him as possessing "the most spacious intellect, the subtlest and most comprehensive" (in his judgment) that ever existed among men. Whatever may be decided by the world in general upon this point, it is one which, from learning and ability, he is well qualified to discuss. I can not believe that he had any enmity to my father, indeed he often speaks of his kindness of heart ; but "the dismal degradation of pecuniary embarrassments," as he himself expresses it, has induced him to supply the depraved craving of the public for personality, which his talents would have enabled him in some measure to correct.

My next letter, my dear L——, shall be of a more lightsome and general nature, but this is dedicated to my dear father's memory ; and I could say much more on that subject if I had more strength and more paper, and were not afraid of wearying even you, who are a reader and lover of his works. When Mr. Poole, of Nether Stowey, received his copy of the will, in which his name was affectionately mentioned, he read it aloud to his niece, Mrs. Sandford, who expressed her admiration with tears in her eyes. One of the last books that my dear father ever perused is the "Memoir and Diary of Bishop Sandford," which he greatly approved; some notes penciled on the margin are among the last sentences he wrote.

IX.

Attachment of Mr. Wordsworth to the Church of England.—Arguments
for an Establishment in Mr. Coleridge's "Church and State."

To the Same :

Hampstead, 1834.—I am always hoping, my dear L——, that
the chances of life, happy ones I trust in your case, will bring
you to reside in the south. Of livings—of any thing connected with our dear, excellent, venerable Church Establishment, I
hardly dare to speak. I really shudder, as I turn over the
menacing pages of the *Spectator,* and that organ of destructive-
ness, *Tait's Magazine.* How well do I remember Mr. Wordsworth, with one leg upon the stair, delaying his ascent till he
had uttered, with an emphasis which seemed to proceed from
the very profoundest recesses of his soul—"I would lay down
my LIFE for the Church !" This was the conclusion of a long
and eloquent harangue upon that interesting subject.

My father, in his "Constitution of the Church and State, according to the Idea of each," has taken the *a priori* view of the
matter, and argued for an Establishment with reasonings which
none of the Destructives ever attempt to overthrow. Whatever
they may pretend, it is not by reasoning, but by very different
engines, that they are effecting their object.

CHAPTER IV.

1835.

LETTERS TO HER HUSBAND, TO MRS. PLUMMER, MISS TREVENEN,
MRS. HENRY M. JONES.

I.

Early Training.—How to Instill Right Principles of Conduct; and Teach a
　Child the Use of his Mind.—A Little Boy's Notion of Parental Disci-
　pline.

To Miss E. TREVENEN, Helstone, Cornwall:

Hampstead, January, 1835.—I was highly interested in dear
Derwent's last letter. I could subscribe to every word of his
remarks. I have always felt that such statements of "naughty"
and "good," as he objects to, have no effect in averting naughti-
ness or producing goodness; and I know well that you "can
not beguile a child to any useful purpose." But when you come
to practical management, a mother must say a thousand things
to her child which have no other use but this—they gradually
help to form his notions of right and wrong. "Oh, silly boy,"
we say, "to be afraid in the dark, which is as safe as the light!"
This will not take away the nervous fear which the very darkness produces; but will it not tend to avert mistaken notions,
if often repeated and consistently persisted in? "You ought to
give your sister your shells—you ought to like that she should
be pleased." I do not expect that he will act on this immediately; but is it not a little preparation for "Thou shalt love thy
neighbor as thyself?" As to reading for children, something
must be set before them which they will partly understand,
which they will like as much as they can like any thing of the
kind, and which will not pervert or mislead. It seems to me that,
with children four or five years old, more than this can not be
effected, and it would be waste of time to attempt it. D——'s
remarks are beautiful on the propriety of early habituating children to the yoke of duty—to labor and application. I would
never turn all lessons into play; but without losing sight of this

principle we may, perhaps, turn a child's play, to a certain degree, into lessons. For instance, when Herby looks over a book of colored prints, I never attempt to make a task of the thing; but I draw his attention to such points as are of a general interest—the knowledge of which may come usefully into play afterward. This flower is crimson, that is pink, that scarlet; I make him observe this difference, and his great amusement is to compare these different hues together. "These birds have small wings and large bodies—that sort of birds the contrary." In this way I think a child *may* be "beguiled usefully" into the habit of observation—into the *use of his mind;* the particular facts are of little consequence, or less consequence, but they are not totally useless: they form a nucleus of knowledge —they give an interest to other facts; and this little knowledge is gathered at a time when, if that were not done, nothing else would be. I am perhaps in some danger of attaching even too much importance to intellectual pursuits and to book-learning. I have been forced upon such considerations by circumstances, as well as led to them by natural taste, and what we dwell constantly upon we are too apt to magnify. A dancing-master thinks that the execution of a waltz, or the solo part of a quadrille, is the chief point of education. However, this is more for my own mind to beware of, than likely to lead to practical errors affecting the interests of my children. * * *

Herby and Dervy are unanimous in their views of ground-rice pudding. I was telling Herby what good order his cousin was in, and that he was made to do what he was bid by his papa. "Does he *force* him?" asked the urchin. "To be sure, unless he does what is right of his own accord." "It's naughty to *force* him," was the reply. "You know Ulysses said, 'We can't take Troy by *force!*'"

II.

Her Contributions to the "Table Talk."—Taking Notes a Useful Practice. —Education: a Quick Child may be Taught a Good Deal, without any Danger of Cramming.—Deaths of Charles Lamb and Edward Irving.

To Mrs. PLUMMER:

Hampstead, 1835.—As to my contributions to the "Table Talk," I am ashamed to say that they really amount to a mere

nothing. Two or three short memorables I remember recording; and I often wonder now how I could have been so negli-
gent a listener. But there were several causes for this. In the
first place, my father generally discoursed on such a very extensive scale, that it would have been an arduous task for *me* to
attempt recording what I had heard. Henry could sometimes
bring him down to narrower topics, but when alone with me he
was almost always on the star-paved road, taking in the whole
heavens in his circuit. Another impediment was this: When I
was at Highgate (I think of it with grief and shame, for I ought,
perhaps, to have had my mind in better order), my heart and
thoughts were very much oppressed and usurped by a variety
of agitating personal matters; I was anxious about my brothers, and their prospects—about Henry's health, and upon the
subject of my engagement generally. The individual of this
year often longs for the slighted opportunities of years ago; but
we can not be what experience makes us, and live over again
the years which have been gradually forming our tastes, desires,
and capabilities. This may seem a truism. What I wish to
convey to you is, that if I could have seen years ago how useless taking thought for all *those* things really was, and how permanently valuable every relic of my father's mind would be
(which I did not then perceive *to the extent* that I do now,
though well aware of his great powers), I should have tried to
be an industrious gleaner, instead of loitering about the harvest-
field as I did.

Writing down a discourse, or a part of it, is very useful also
to the mind, and a good test whether you have at all comprehended what you heard.

I must not finish my letter without telling you a little about
my secondary *selves*—my children—because they *are* self in a
second edition. I am on my guard how and how much I speak
of them, for fear of appearing or being selfish. Both are well
and brisk at present. Herby is reported to be a forward child,
and we have many admonitions against pushing, cramming, and
over-refining, which are all very just and sensible, and will, I
hope, keep us from straying into the wrong path. But I can
not think we have been betrayed into it yet; neither would our
admonishers think so, if they understood the whole state of the
case. The child in question has a show of Coleridgian quickness, and bookishness, and liveliness of mind. He retains what

he learns pretty well, and is mighty fond of sporting it afterward, which he does with great vehemence and animation. For instance, he informs every one he meets that Chimborazo, whatever Coley* may say on the subject, is not so high as Dhawalaghiri, the highest of the Himalayas; and that he is certain that the wedding of Mr. and Mrs. Day (domestics at his Uncle Patteson's, in Bedford Square), was not nearly so grand as that of Peleus and Thetis, on Mount Pelion. He is at this moment bent upon making bilberry preserve at Keswick, and rosefruit-jam from hips that must be gathered on Mount Caucasus. Hearing him talk in this way gives some people a notion that he is *crammed.* I can only say that I put no food into his mind which is not prepared as carefully for his childish digestion as the pap and panada which are recommended for infants; and he certainly never has any more of it at a time than he has the fullest appetite for. He hears certain stories about Troy and other antiquities over and over again, and looks at colored plates of flowers which are lent me, and gradually learns some of their names; and he is actually fond of poring over maps, and tracing the course of rivers. But what is there in all this (*done in the way he does it*) which can strain the intellect, or overload the mind of a young child? I assure you nobody can be more careful than I am not to err on these points, for I am fully aware of the mischief both to body and mind which may be caused thereby; but at the same time we all know that there is much in habit, in the gradual training both of hand and muscles. My boy will have to go through the mental labor required in a public school, and in after-life he will have to gain his bread by head-work. I can not, therefore, follow the advice of those who say, "Let him run about all day, and leave books entirely alone." I feel sure that such a plan would not be for his welfare, either for the present or in the long run.

I teach him writing too, because I think it a good thing to keep a child sitting still, and paying attention for a longer time than you are employing his intellect. The habit of regularity and submission should be taught early. As for the art of writing, it may be learned more quickly at a much later age; but it is a useful instrument in learning other things; and the time

---

* His cousin, John Coleridge Patteson; well-known to the Church and the Country as the "Martyr-Bishop" of the Pacific Islands.—E. C.

is not altogether thrown away that is spent in teaching an urchin of four years and three months to scribble. * * *

We have been much grieved lately by the death of our old friend Mr. Charles Lamb, of the India House. He was a man of amiable manners, and kind and liberal heart, and a rare genius. His writings exhibit a rare union of pathos and humor, which to me is truly delightful. Very interesting short memoirs of him have already appeared, and I see new editions of his works advertised. So soon after my father, whom, humanly speaking, he worshiped! Irving is also gone. He was one whose good and great parts my father saw in a strong light, and deeply did he lament the want of due balance in his mind, which ended in what may be almost called madness. Irving acknowledged that to my father, more than to any one, he owed his knowledge of " the truth as it is in Jesus."

III.

"The *Accomplishment* of Verse."—The Delightful Duty of Improving Natural Talents.

To Miss EMILY TREVENEN, Helstone, Cornwall:

Hampstead, July 12, 1835.—I rejoice, dear Miss Trevenen, to think of your versifying tastes (I am sure I have expressed that sentence as humbly as you yourself would dictate !).* As for poetry, in the strict sense of the word, I can not think that any woman of the present day, whose productions I have seen, has furnished the genuine article from her brain-warehouse, except Mrs. Joanna Baillie. I have read many of Mrs. Hemans's most mature productions with a due degree of attention. I think them interesting, full of poetical feeling, displaying much accomplishment, and a very general acquaintance with poetry,

---

* The lady who formed so modest an estimate of her own powers was the daughter of the Rev. Thomas Trevenen, rector of Cardinham, in Cornwall, and member of a good old Cornish family. She was a woman of accomplished mind and truly Christian character, and will long be remembered with affectionate respect by those who enjoyed the benefit of her influence and example. A small volume of juvenile poetry, entitled " Little Derwent's Breakfast," written by her for the amusement and instruction of her godson, Derwent Moultrie Coleridge, and published in 1839, was probably referred to by her correspondent in the present passage.—E. C.

and some proficiency in the art of versifying; but though poetry is an art, no truly excellent poem can be produced by art alone, and to practice the whole art there must be high natural endowments. Of poetical imagination, it appears to me that a very small portion is to be found in the works of Mrs. Hemans. Yet this lady has given delight to thousands by her verses; and they must have been the source of great delight and improvement to herself. Just as I would have any one learn music who has an opportunity, though few can be composers, or even performers of great merit, I would have any one, who really and truly has leisure and ability, make verses. I think it a more refining and happy-making occupation than any other pastime accomplishment.

IV.

Newspaper Criticisms on the "Table Talk."—Unreasonable Complaints Answered, and False Insinuations indignantly Rejected.—Mr. Coleridge not a Partisan either of Whigs or Tories, though he was a Friend of the People and Supporter of the National Church.—Mr. Southey's Opinion of the Book.

To Mrs. HENRY M. JONES, Heathlands, Hampstead:

Downshire Place, Hampstead, July, 1835.—My dear Mrs. Jones, we send you "Table Talk," thinking that you may like to see a little more of it than the fragments given in reviews. Henry desired me to tell you, with kind regards, that the *Morning Chronicle* is wrong in its conjecture respecting Lord Londonderry. The embassador alluded to was a "far less able man."*

The *Printing Machine* and other critical publications find fault with the editor of "Table Talk" for not having done what they themselves admit no reporter upon earth could do. They all allow that it was impossible to represent on paper the ample sweeping current of my father's discourse. They add, however, that the work has preserved much valuable matter, which would otherwise have perished; that it serves in some measure to confirm and elucidate my father's written works, and ought always to be printed as a companion to the "Friend," etc. This was all that Henry expected to do; he dreamed not of

---

* "Table Talk," p. 286.—Note of Aug. 28, 1833.

placing Coleridge *the talker* before his readers, but merely hoped to preserve some part of his talk.

One of my father's Whig friends insinuates that if he had told his own story, he would have told it more Whiggishly. The spirit of party is "father to this thought;" it is not true. Henry is a man of honor, though, as some may think, an illiberal Tory. I refer such objectors to my father's little work on "Church and State." Could he, who had such an "idea of the constitution of Church and State," think more favorably of the Reform Bill, and of the projected alienation of Church property, than he appears to have done in Henry's publication? I can truly re-assert what has often been asserted before, that my father was no party man. He cared for no public man or ministry, except so far as they furthered what he considered the best interests of the country. "He had a vision of his own," and he scrupled not to condemn and expose the acting Tories if they ran counter to it. He was no lover of great and fine people—the pomps and vanities of this world were distasteful to him rather than otherwise. He had lived in a cottage himself, and he loved cottages, and he took a friendly interest in the inhabitants of them. He thought himself a true friend to the people in upholding the Church, which he considered the most popular institution in the country.* If Henry had wished to please his own party, through thick and thin, he would not have printed many of the opinions recorded in "Table Talk." As to my father's having any interest in leaning to one side more than another, I really believe that figment is discarded by all but those who care not whether it be true or not, so that it serves an unworthy purpose.

Lord Brougham made a *kind offer* to my father, but it would not have been for his dignity and consistency to have accepted it.

I am glad that my Uncle Southey is pleased with "Table Talk." He says to Henry, "You have dealt well with De Quincey and the Benthamite Reviewer," *i. e.*, him of the *Westminster.*

Of course, when my father was in company with Whigs, he refrained from all strong expressions respecting Whig conduct, and rather sought those topics on which he could sincerely agree with them, than those on which they must have differed.

---

* See "Table Talk," pp. 159, 322.

V.

Union of Thought and Feeling in the Poetry of Wordsworth.—The " White Doe of Rylstone."

To Mrs. HENRY M. JONES, Heathlands, Hampstead :

Downshire Place, Hampstead, July, 1835.—We are expecting a new set of Wordsworth's poems, including the " Excursion ;" and I really think the murmuring River Warfe, the gray rocks, the dusky trees and verdant sod, the ancient abbey, and the solitary Doe, " white as lily of June," will be pleasant subjects of contemplation in this hot, languid weather. The poetry of Wordsworth will give you at least as much fervor and tenderness as you will find in Byron or Hemans ; and then, in addition, you will find in it a high philosophy, a strengthening and elevating spirit, which must have a salutary tendency for the mind.

Mr. Wordsworth opens to us a world of suffering, and no writer of the present day, in my opinion, has dealt more largely or more nobly with the deepest pathos and the most exquisite sentiment ; but for every sorrow he presents an antidote ; he shows us how man may endure, as well as what he is doomed to suffer. The poem of the " White Doe of Rylstone " is meant to exhibit the power of faith in upholding the most anguish-stricken soul through the severest trials, and the ultimate triumph of the spirit, even while the frail mortal body is giving way.

> " From fair to fairer, day by day,
> A more divine and loftier way ;
> Even such this blessed pilgrim trod,
> By sorrow lifted toward her God—
> Uplifted to the purest sky
> Of undisturbed mortality."
>
> *White Doe*, Canto VII.

The first and last cantos are much superior in point of imaginative power to the others, upon the whole ; but the speech of Francis to his sister in the second is beautiful. I remember that it was greatly admired by dear Hartley.

> " Hope nothing, if I thus may speak
> To thee, a woman, and thence weak ;
> Hope nothing, I repeat, for we
> Are doomed to perish utterly.

*   *   *   *

Forbear all wishes, all debate,
All prayers for this cause, or for that,
 * * * *
Espouse thy fate at once, and cleave
To fortitude without reprieve."
Canto II.

The address of the father to Francis in the fifth canto is a favorite of mine.

"Might this our enterprise* have sped,
Change wide and deep the land had seen,
A renovation from the dead,
A spring-tide of immortal green.
The darksome altars would have blazed
Like stars when clouds are rolled away;
Salvation to all eyes that gazed:
Once more the Rood had been upraised,
To spread its arms, and stand for aye!"
Canto V.

VI.

Charles Lamb, his Shyness and Tenderness.—A Life-long Friendship.

To Mrs. H. M. JONES, Heathlands, Hampstead:

Hampstead, 1835.—I agree to your criticism on Lamb, and sympathize most entirely in your preference of field and grove and rivulet to square, garden, street, and gutter. I always feel so particularly *in*secure in a street. Nevertheless I can quite understand Lamb's feeling. A man is more especially alone, very often, in a crowd. Nowhere can an individual be so isolated, so independent, as in London. Nowhere else can he see so much and be himself so little observed. This I think is the " sweet security of streets "† which the eccentric old bachelor delighted in. And then he had been educated at Christ's Hospital; all his boyish recreations, when life was new and *life-*

---

* The "enterprise" referred to was the " Rising of the North," in the 12th year of Elizabeth, 1569, under the Earls of Northumberland and Westmoreland, " to restore the ancient religion."—E. C.

† I care not to be carried with the tide that smoothly bears human life to eternity; and reluct at the inevitable course of destiny. I am in love with this green earth, the face of town and country, the unspeakable rural solitudes, and the sweet security of streets. I would set up my tabernacle here. —*Lamb's Essays. New-Year's Eve.*—E. C.

some, had passed in streets, and we all know that the circumstances of our childhood give the prevailing hue to our involuntary tastes and feelings for the rest of our lives. I can not picture to myself a Paradise without lakes and mountains. Our poor friend was much affected by my father's death,* and had a fanciful presentiment that he should not remain long behind. He must have remembered some interesting remarks† connected with this subject in an old preface of my father's, the preface to a volume containing united poems of Coleridge and Lamb.

VII.

Writings of Charles Wolfe in Prose and Verse.‡—His Defense of Poetry against the Attacks of the Utilitarians.—Wolfe with the Methodists.—Wesley's Interview with Two Crazy Enthusiasts.—Political Questions from a Conservative Point of View. — The Secularization of Church Property.—Projected Disestablishment of the Church in Ireland certain to Lead to the same Measure in England.—A Sisterly Wish on Behalf of the Sister Isle.

To Mrs. H. M. Jones, Heathlands, Hampstead:
Downshire Place, Hampstead, 1835. — My dear Mrs. Jones, the "Remains of C. Wolfe," kindly lent by Dr. Park, I return

---

* Mr. Lamb's visit to Highgate, shortly after my grandfather's death, is thus described by Judge Talfourd: "There he asked leave to see the nurse who had attended upon Coleridge; and being struck and affected by the feeling she manifested toward his friend, insisted on her receiving five guineas from him—a gratuity which seemed almost incomprehensible to the poor woman, but which Lamb could not help giving as an immediate expression of his own gratitude. From her he learned the effort by which Coleridge had suppressed the expression of his sufferings, and the discovery affected him even more than the news of his death. He would startle his friends sometimes by suddenly exclaiming 'Coleridge is dead,' and then pass on to common themes, having obtained the momentary relief of oppressed spirits."—*Letters of Charles Lamb*, vol. ii., p. 304.—E. C.

† The reference is probably to the Latin motto printed on the title-page of the second edition of "Poems by Coleridge, Lamb, and Lloyd," which appeared in May, 1797: *Duplex nobis vinculum, et amicitiæ, junctarumque Camœnarum ; quod utinam neque mors solvat ; neque temporis longinquitas.* Charles Lamb died on the 27th of December, 1834, five months and two days after the friend whom he loved so well.—E. C.

‡ Collected and published in 1825 by Archdeacon Russell. The Rev. Charles Wolfe (of the same family with General Wolfe) was born at Dublin in 1791, and died at Cork, in his thirty-second year, of consumption. He was for three years curate of Donoughmore, in the Diocese of Armagh,

with many thanks. As to the ode on Sir John Moore's Burial, and the Gra-ma-chree verses,* which suit the old melody to perfection, I have them almost by heart. The latter I have heard sung by Edith Southey in her tasteful way, and read aloud by Mr. Wordsworth with his deep, solemn voice, and exquisite intonation. The observations on poetry, though expressed with enthusiasm, are, in the opinion of a poet's daughter, absolutely true. When people say, Of what *use* is poetry? what need is there for works of imagination? "Oh, argue not the *need*," I am ready to exclaim. But I think if the cause *were* argued, it might be plainly proved that poetry and the sister arts are of use in more ways than one. It is the fashion now to cry up science at the expense of fine literature, on the ground that the former is more useful to mankind. The meaning of the term utility must be agreed on before the argument can proceed, but I think, unless a very narrow and *corporeal* definition is insisted on, both will be admitted highly useful in different, and also in some similar ways, and neither can operate so beneficially apart, as when they play into each other's hands. For poetry is truth as well as science, and truth of a most ennobling, and, therefore, improving kind. Your mark is also in another part of the memoir, which interested me no less—I mean Wolfe's explanations with the Methodists. I have lately been employed in transcribing my father's notes on Southey's " Life of Wesley." Many of them relate to sanctification and the new birth; to faith and works ; to free grace ; free-will and election ; subjects on which there have been long and bitter disputations—as my father thinks, because the disputants have not gone deep enough, and started from the very beginning. I could not help laughing, in the midst of all this grave reasoning, at my uncle's story of " two ignorant dreamers," who, thinking that Wesley's new birth had not taken place in the right way, informed him from the Lord that he must be " born'd again," and vowed that they would stay in his house till it was done. He showed them into the Society Room,

---

where he won the love and respect of his parishioners by his devotion to his professional duties, which he combined with literary pursuits. He is best known to posterity by his beautiful poem on the Burial of Sir John Moore, who fell at the Battle of Corunna, January 26th, 1809.—E. C.

* The lines beginning—
> " If I had thought thou couldst have died,
> I might not weep for thee."—E. C.

where they remained without meat, drink, and firing, till they were very glad to go away and mind their own business.*

Did I almost make thee a Tory? Truly thou hast almost made me ashamed to call myself one; but I believe, if you and I had converted each other, and changed sides as to politics, our respective wiser-halves would soon waltz us back again to our former creeds. I rest content, however, with having elicited from you a decided condemnation of O'Connell and such reformers as he; and you will rest content with my assuring you that the poverty of curates and incumbents of small livings, a grievance not unknown in the circle of my nearest and very dear friends, and the troubles of Ireland, are evils which I lament, and should be thankful to see *reformed.* How far some part of them are capable of a remedy at present, without bringing on greater calamities than themselves, and what are the best and safest measures which can be employed for their removal or mitigation, can be the only points of controversy, I should think, between disinterested *liberal* Conservatives and truly religious sane-minded Whig or Radical Reformers. The reason, I believe, why the former distrust the policy of Lord Brougham is because they *think* that, however unintentionally on his part, it would betray us finally into the hands of O'Connell and his band, as well as of English Church Destroyers and Revolutionists. I have been reading the *Edinburgh Review*, and am therefore not entirely unacquainted with the Liberal line of argument, and many are the long discussions which I have listened to on these questions. As to the English Church, surely it is apparent that there is a deficiency of funds for the spiritual wants of the people—to provide for them fully at least. If she enjoyed all the property originally intended for her use, this would not be the case. As to the grievances of those who have to help to support a Church to which they do not belong, I believe it is argued that the majority of the United Kingdom are Protestants, and that a Church Establishment can not subsist long if the nation at large does not contribute to its maintenance. This, of course, is only an argument to those who admit the beneficial effects of an Establishment, and have no wish to see Church and State disunited. The *Edinburgh* says, No, no; but it has yet failed to convince the Conservatives that de-

---

* Southey's "Life of Wesley," vol. ii., p. 273.—E. C.

priving the Irish Church of its property would not be the first step to the ruin of the Establishment both in England and Ireland. Put in, they say, the narrow end of the wedge, and there is a compact, indefatigable band of conspirators, who will drive it right onward till they have brought the fabric to the ground, and poor Mother Church to voluntary contributions, which many of her children consider a beggarly condition. "Look at America" is the cry of both parties. "We do look at her," the Conservatives make answer, "and we can not like her as to her religious condition;" and the *Quarterly* endeavors to prove that even were it the best in the world for her, it would not do equally well in England. But let me no longer betray my own cause by pleading it after my feminine fashion, nor misrepresent the arguments on either side by attempting to repeat them. When I read or hear of the mutual injuries of England and Ireland, I fancy it would have been a blessed thing had the sea never flowed between the two countries. Had they been all in one, surely there would have been more unity between them of interests and of feelings. But let us hope that days of peace and general enlightenment will arrive by ways past man's finding out. I am sure it is the duty of the Conservatives to *wish* that their opponents' cause may be the just one, for in all human probability it will be successful.—Believe me, my dear Mrs. Jones, most truly yours,   SARA COLERIDGE.

VIII.

Severity not the Right Mode of Treatment for an Obstinate Temper, in Spite of its Apparent Success.—Parental Discipline has a Higher Aim, and avails itself of Higher Influences.

To her Husband:

Hampstead, October, 1835.—Some people go on day after day and month after month pursuing a method, which day after day and month after month they find invariably to fail, without once saying to themselves, "Since this plan works so ill, is it, or is it not, the least bad that can be imagined?" They live from hand to mouth, as it were, impelled by feeling to a regular routine which they never correct by principle. Mr. ———, self-flattering man, says he has but one bout with all his children—*venit, videt, vincit*—and yet ——— was, up to the last time I had the opportunity of observing her, a most obstinate little animal. My aim is something far beyond extorting obedience in particular instances. Unless the wayward *will* is corrected, what care I for the *act;* unless the fount is purified, what care I for an artificial cleansing of the draught which falls to my portion this day or the next? If I thought that to force compliance by terror would induce a salutary habit, by which the heart might be bettered, it might be my duty to take this painful course. But I do not think so. I believe the experiment to be worse than dangerous; for the improvement of our children's moral nature I put my trust in no methods of discipline : these may answer well for a warring prince or general who has a particular external object to gain, and cares not for his instruments, except *as* instruments. I, too, have a particular object to gain— that our children should acquire a certain portion of book-learning ; but my *whole* aim is their general welfare—as it must be that of every truly parental heart—the growth of their souls in goodness and holiness ; to promote which I put my faith in no ways and means which I have power over, but the influence of good example, the constant inculcation of none but sound principles, and the opportunities which we can afford our children of gaining worldly experience and religious knowledge and impressions. For they must be *wise as serpents* and innocent as doves. Of course I do not mean to undervalue the advantage of sensible artificial management; I would but place it in a fair light, and show that it is no enchanter's wand, but more analogous to a doctor's drugs and diet, which may do good, but which are quite inefficacious in many cases, and can effect nothing unless other operatives combine to aid the work. Indeed, I do not strictly *put my faith* in any thing but the power of grace in the heart. What I mean is, that I hope more from favorable influences of this kind I have mentioned than from any mechanical routine ; and I really think that "you shall be beaten unless you do it, or you shall be mortified and annoyed till you look and speak humbly," *is* a sort of external force which does not touch the heart.

IX.

Spiders.—Their Webs and Ways.

To the Same:

This day, 5th of October, I saw a large primrose-colored butterfly, which looked the very emblem of April or May. Also, I examined three or four spiders, and saw quite plainly the spinnerets in their tails, and once I clearly perceived the thread issuing from the apertures. The thread of a spider's net is composed of such a multitude of threadlets that it gives one a good notion of the infinite divisibility of matter. A spider, when examined, feigns death, and lies back with all his arms and legs closely pinioned to his sides, so that he shrinks up into as small a space as possible. In this condition he is a good symbol of some wretched slave, stupefied and collapsed into stillness in the presence of a mighty one. I have often marveled at the strength of a spider's web, which offers far more resistance to my finger, as I push and bend it, than a net made of silken threads of the same apparent substance would do. This firmness is procured by the multiplicity of threadlets of which every thread is composed, which circumstance also hastens the drying of the fluid gum, so great a surface being exposed to the air. While we compare natural objects or operations with artificial ones, we are so taken up with the likeness that we forget the difference. There is no other thing in art or nature similar to the spinning of spiders. Evelyn would watch spiders for five hours together.

X.

Unpractical Suggestions of a Writer in the *Athenæum* on the Subject of Female Education.—Boarding-school Life not Unhealthy for Girls under Ordinary Circumstances.—Alleged Physical Superiority of Savage over Civilized Races not Founded on Fact, nor much Worth Regretting if it were.

To the Same:

Hampstead, October, 1835.—The *Athenæum* is fond of bringing out great mouthing articles against modern female education; but the huge mountain of denunciation brings forth but a mouse of instruction in the better way. The weakliness and imperfect forms of modern ladies are all laid to ignorance and want of sense in their governors, pastors, and masters. This seems to me by far too unqualified a charge. It may be true that the squaw and the copper-colored woman of the Western woods has a constitution that will bear wind and weather, and a pair of shoulder-blades that are as even as a pair of dice. It may be that the habits of civilized life—snug houses, warm, soft beds, abundant meals, and the habit of sitting on a chair while we make our complicated clothes, write numerous letters, read interesting books, converse with our friends, wait during compound meals, attend divine service, and *sit* under the clergyman—may be unfavorable to a certain sort of bodily vigor; but our women live as long as they used to do, they go through as uninterrupted a routine of duty, pleasure, and occupation (in one shape or another) as the female savages do; the *whole woman* is as much put into action among the former as the latter; and if it be true, which the *Athenæum* writer himself avers, that mechanical causes have little to do with spinal curvature, why are the employments of young girls at school so vehemently denounced? As to the harp or the tambour-frame, not one girl in thirty or forty in the middle-classes is confined by those exercises, or could be injured by them. When that old argument of savages is brought forward, it always seems to be forgotten that none but the strongest children ever pass the age of infancy in those communities. Many are put to death, and no weakly child survives the hardships of that mode of life. We, by medical and *nutrical* art, preserve hundreds of delicate infants, who grow up to be delicate men and women, and have still more delicate children. School-mistresses are abused for the mode in which they lead out their girls to take exercise; but let the writer take the poor women's place, and let us see how he would manage. There must be order, regularity, in a school as well as in an army. How are twenty girls to be kept out of mischief, and under the eye of the mistress, if they are to straggle about as they like? The shepherd has barking dogs to help him to keep *his* flock in order. Like Madame de Genlis, we may sit down and imagine a delightful scheme of education, all the circumstances being made on purpose by the writer's imagination; but in actual life we must do the best we can under such circumstances as we happen to light upon. It is only to a limited extent, indeed, that we can manufacture them to suit us. The *Athenæum* writer is like a clumsy fencer: he knows that something is to be hit, but he hits far too hard, and hits only half of the right place. He accuses imperfect civilization of all our evils and sufferings. Whether civilization *can* ever be so perfect as to preserve the good things we now enjoy, and divest them of their bad accompaniments, is a problem which I can not solve; but of this I feel quite sure—namely, that civilization and cultivation, such as we have, are well worth the price we pay for them.

* * *

XI.

Puns.—Affectation.

To the Same:

October, 1835.—I can't say I should care to know Mr. ———, from your account. Puns are often unacceptable to the feelings; they come like a spoonful of ice-cream in the midst of a comfortable smoking-hot steak, or as a peppery morsel when your palate was in expectation of a mild pudding. The *place for life* was a good thing; but the worst of a regular punster is that he picks up so many poor jokes, which any one equally on the look-out might have hit upon, merely because they lie in his way, while other people are content to say things worth hearing in themselves, but which there is no cleverness in saying. How much more agreeable is many a piece of news, a kind remark, a civil inquiry, than smart sentences which one is not in the humor of listening to. * * *

I believe G——— is what is commonly called affected; but the affectation in question is perfectly natural to the individual, though not natural to the occasion—*i. e.*, not what would be natural to most people on such an occasion. It is engendered by vanity; the desire to make an impression leads a vain man to think that all he has to bring forward is fitted to make an impression; consequently a disproportioned manner is produced, the manner is too big for the matter, too earnest, too *portentous*, or too exquisite for the occasion, according to the view which other people take of the occasion. Shrewd people seldom fall into these mistakes; shrewdness prunes vanity, but does not eradicate it.

CHAPTER V.

1836.

LETTERS TO HER HUSBAND, HER MOTHER, MRS. H. M. JONES, MISS
TREVENEN, MISS ARABELLA BROOKE.

I.

"Miscellaneous Plays," by Mrs. Joanna Baillie.

To Miss E. TREVENEN.

Hampstead, 1836.—Have you seen Mrs. J. Baillie's twelve
new dramas ?* One critique says they have the same vigor of
thought and felicity of language as her earlier productions, but
that they are not so sustained nor so well united, nor have the
same propriety of action and character. The passion of hatred
is powerfully exhibited in the comedy of "The Election." Successful and admirable as Mrs. Baillie's dramas are, I can not
think it a good plan to announce one particular passion in the
title-page of a play ; it leads you to expect to find the laboring
author, rather than a picture of life itself transmitted through
the author's mind and hand in the following pages.

II.

A *Perfect* Reticule.—Bridgewater Treatise by Dr. Roget.—Natural History
less Dependent on other Sciences than Astronomy—or Comparative
Anatomy.—Want of Reality in the Poetry of Mrs. Hemans.—Excess of
this Quality in Crabbe.

To Mrs. H. M. JONES,† Heathlands, Hampstead :

Downshire Place, Hampstead, 1836.—My dear Mrs. Jones,
a mock-heroical note-writer might commence a billet on the

---

* Published in three volumes, in 1836, nearly forty years after the appearance of the first volume of "Plays on the Passions." It was during our residence at Hampstead that my mother became acquainted with the aged poetess, whose genius she highly admired, and whose personal appearance and
manners are pleasingly described in several passages of her correspondence.
Mrs. Baillie died at Hampstead in February, 1851.—E. C.

† Our kind friend and neighbor, whose amiable attentions are here grate-

present occasion thus—"Oh, for the glowing language of a Hemans, or the lively fancy of an L. E. L., that I might return fitting acknowledgments for my kind neighbor's various and refined courtesies!" In sober earnest though, I do think you ought not to be thanked in a common, dry, cool manner for your friendliness, and I feel doubly obliged and flattered by your spending *time* upon me as well as other things. As to the reticule, it is a *gentlewoman's bag*—I could say nothing better of it were I to study for a fortnight; and when I consider how difficult it is to produce a perfectly lady-like reticule; how many would-be genteel people carry reticules, and infect every reticule fashion they adopt with an air of vulgarity or shabby gentility; how many laboriously wrought reticules I have seen in the course of my life, none of which came up to my beau-ideal of a bag; how many negative as well as positive qualities a perfect bag ought to have—I really think your success in this line is a triumph of art and tastefulness; you have completely embodied all my airy reticulous imaginations, and have combined satin and velvet into a shape fit to be patronized by an exclusive. This may perhaps truly be called *running on* about a reticule, but it will at least show you, dear Mrs. Jones, that your attentions give the pleasure you design: neither you nor I would be in raptures with a bag, or any other elegance, which was bought in a shop, and in no way connected with genial feeling.

If I may not saunter over "Roget" in my usual manner, will you be kind enough to bid me hasten my perusal. I am pleased and I hope instructed with what I have read. Dr. Roget, in this volume* more especially, treats of many matters which I am often wishing to know about. Comparative anatomy, though highly interesting, makes one often feel the want of the knowledge of mechanics; and one can not proceed far in astronomy without mathematics. But there are certain portions of physiology which I fancy may be understood sufficiently for a great degree of pleasure and profit without the aid of other sciences.

---

fully though playfully acknowledged, has been for some years a resident in her native country of Ireland; where I hope she will read these memorials of the happy past with feelings in which pleasure may predominate over regret.—E. C.

* On "Animal and Vegetable Physiology;" one of the Bridgewater Treatises, 1834.—E. C.

I return the "Forest Sanctuary," etc.　I think Lord Byron's remark on Mrs. Hemans was very just: he said she was a poet, but too "stiltified and apostrophical;" this you may remember in Moore's Life of Lord B.　But she was a very extraordinary woman, and had a wonderful command of language. Yet, various as her subjects are, I still feel, as I did after reading the other volume of her poems which you lent me, that there is a *sameness* in her productions upon the whole ; the spirit and tone of feeling are almost invariably the same ; she keeps one so long in a sublime region of thin ether that one craves to come down and breathe the common air, impregnated with odors that put one in mind of real life.　People say there is *too* much real life in Crabbe, and certainly he did not idealize enough ; but, in spite of this defect, he is a great and permanent favorite with me.　Mrs. Hemans's "Hebrew Mother" struck mamma from its great likeness to my Uncle Southey's style of poetry ; I thought it very beautiful.　"Evening Prayer at a Girls' School " is another of my favorites.

Believe me, my dear Mrs. Jones, your truly obliged friend,

SARA COLERIDGE.

III.

Etymology of *Plat* and *Plait*.—The *Plaits* (or *Plats*) of a Lady's Hair, and the *Plaits* of her Gown, originally the same Word, though Different in Meaning and Pronunciation.*—A Social Sunbeam.

To Mrs. H. M. JONES :

Hampstead, 1836.—My dear Mrs. Jones, my dictionaries are highly flattered by the appeal made to them from the Court in John Street ; and, after some consultations together, give it as their unanimous opinion that plat and plait have precisely the same pedigree—Gr., πλεκω ; Latin, *plecto* and *plico ;* French, *plisser* and *plier ;* Italian, *piegare ;* and *ployen*, Dutch.

---

* The former being called *plat*, and the latter *pleat*.　Might not the old English word *pleach* have been included among the derivatives of πλεκω ? The "pleached bower" in which Beatrice awaited her friends, in "Much Ado about Nothing," was one formed of the *plaited* or interwoven branches of the honeysuckle, which,

"Ripened by the sun,
Forbid the sun to enter."—E. C.

They have also come to the conclusion that to fold, weave, braid, twist, twine, plait, plat, and platt, are to a certain degree synonymous, though in making minor distinctions we use them in slightly different senses; plaiting is a sort of weaving, and weaving is a sort of infolding. The word platted is used in Scripture, as all must recollect : "They platted a crown of thorns"—they wove a garland. It was a remark of my dear father's,* that we can not ascertain the precise meaning of words by searching for their roots only; words that originally were the same become appropriated to separate uses, as there is a greater *demand* for language, and the knowledge and refinement of the speakers of the language increase. To *plait* now, with milliners and clear-starchers, means a particular way of folding muslin, and to plat with smart young ladies signifies nothing in the world but twisting their glossy tresses in a neat and elegant manner ; and yet plat and plait both come originally from plecto and from plico, and both plecto and plico, according to my aforesaid informants, are either derived from or cognate with the Greek word pleko, which must excuse my writing it in Roman character. * * *

You have a suggestive Byronic imagination, or you could never have fancied that your visit injured me ; this is turning a *beam* into a *cloud*, and a lively mind like yours ought to employ itself in doing the reverse.

IV.

"*Clever*" People not always *Thinking* People.—Serious Reflections Suggested by the Receipt of Taylor's "Holy Living and Dying," as a Present from a Friend.—Sympathy more to be Prized than Admiration.— "The Boy and the Birds," and the "Story without an End."—A Critic's Foible.

To Miss EMILY TREVENEN :

Hampstead, August, 1836.—Dear Miss B——! Henry and I quite agree on her character; she is one of the *thinking* class, which is so congenial to our tastes and feelings. A merely *clever* person, without depth of sensibility or reflection, I own is not congenial to me—I mean abstractedly considered. I

---

* See Coleridge's "Notes on English Divines," vol. ii., p. 259.—E. C.

might know a person in actual life to whom that description applied, whom yet I might love and like from early habit, or peculiar circumstances, or the predominance of other attractive qualities.

I must thank you, dearest friend, for the "Holy Living and Dying;" it would have pleased you to see how charmed and surprised I was on opening the bundle and finding what it contained. "Bibles laid open, millions of surprises,"* George Herbert says, are too often of little avail to sanctify the worldly spirit. There are two awful thoughts which often beset my mind, and must, I think, present themselves to all who dwell on religious considerations. The first is, the want of opportunity to become spiritually minded in such a large portion of the humbler classes, as well as of savage tribes and nations not Christianized; the other (its counterpart), what endless opportunities are either wasted or not turned to a sufficiently good account by persons in our line of life, their very commonness almost taking from their efficacy.

What you say of your sojourn near us is most gratifying, and expressed in your own refined, feminine, yet thoughtful way. It finds an echo in all our hearts, otherwise it would not be gratifying; for I hope we are passed those years of vanity when one desires to be considered exciting, even when the excitement is not mutual.

Both the children enjoy "The Boy and the Birds."† As to the "Story without an End,"‡ I admire it, but think it quite unfit for juvenile readers. None but mature minds, well versed in the artificialities of sentimental literature, can understand the inner meanings of it; and I do not think it has that *body* of visual imagery and adventure which renders many a tale and allegory delightful to those who can not follow the author's main drift. Bees and flies, and leaves and flowers are talked *about*, but not *described*, so as to give the child any clearer notion of them and their properties than he originally had, and all that is ascribed to them, all the sentiments put into their mouths, as one may say, are such as can breed naught but confusion in the juvenile brain. "*That child* is always asleep, or else dreaming,"

---

* From a Sonnet entitled "Sin," in Herbert's "Temple."—E. C.
† By Mary Howitt.—E. C.
‡ Translated by Mrs. Austin from the German of Carové.—E. C.

I overheard Herby say to himself, as he looked at the picture with an air of contempt. * * *

Oh, reviews! if you yourselves were reviewed, how you might be cut up and exposed. A common fault of reviewers, and one which makes them desert good sense, is that they are so desirous to take a spick-and-span new view of any debated point. They smell down two roads, and if both have been trodden before, they rush at once down the third, though it may lead to nothing, like a blind alley. So it is with the *Edinburgh* reviewer; he perks up his nose, and tries to say some third thing, which never has been said before, and which is the worst thing of the three.

V.

A Visit to Devonshire.—Advantages of Frequent Intercourse among Relations.—Forebodings of Illness, too soon Realized.—Maternal Cares and Interests.—Interruption of her Journey Homeward.

To Miss E. Trevenen, Helstone :

*Manor House,** Ottery St. Mary, Devon, October* 8, 1836.— Married relations should not live in the same house with each other, perhaps not next door; but it is a mutual disadvantage to be so far from each other that, unless health and purse are in the most flourishing state, they must pass years without the opportunity of intercourse. Even relations that often disagree, if there be any respect and affection at bottom, care more for one another, and love one another's society better, than those who seldom meet.

Our old acquaintance, Dr. Calvert, gave a cheerful account of Greta Hall, where all were well and in very fair spirits. Aunt Lovell seemed quite in good health, and tripped up to shake hands like a young girl. Such are the turns and changes of life. My turn of strength will perhaps come; but at present, the prospect of my health is like the prospect of lake and mountain at Keswick, when the whole being involved in mist, one might as well be in a flat unwatered country, for all the advantage one has of scenery. Could I be sure that health and strength were indeed behind the cloud! Little H—— tells me

---

* The residence of Francis George Coleridge, Esq., one of my father's elder brothers.—E. C.

that I " have come here for nothing," because I have only once been as far as the flower-garden, and that I am a "poor dull woman," who can have no enjoyment. But the pretty little maid is out there, I trust. It is true I have not enlarged my notions of the picturesque, nor much improved my acquaintance with Devonshire; but I have met several of my relations in a sociable way, gleaned a little out of Frank's library, and become better acquainted with the children than some would have been in three years. Herby and Edy have derived much benefit from this visit, I trust, and had their little minds ventilated by fresh scenes, people, and goings-on. Herbert's nervous temperament and general delicacy of frame have been placed in a clearer light to me by the change than ever, and I trust I shall use this knowledge aright. I listen to the advice and opinions of *all* experienced persons—let my notion of their discernment be great or small. Every kind and degree of experience on the management of young people obtains a fair hearing from me ; but I am now fully convinced how entirely it is the duty of a mother to act resolutely on her own judgment, when she has once formed it with all due deliberation, and with as much clear-sightedness as she has it in her power to exert. I would give a good deal if Herbert could have little A—— for his constant companion ; these two are so nearly matched in age that they run well together, and in temper are so well suited to each other, and so fitted to do one another good, that I regret the little opportunity they will have of playing and studying side by side. A—— is a sweet boy ; there is an innocent solemnity and a sprightly gravity about him which are charming, and contrast well with Herbert's quick, eager, mercurial temperament. Herby is excessively fond of him. It is pretty to see them play dominoes together, chattering all the time with a light-hearted earnestness and importance, the pomposity and intensity of their words contrasting prettily with the easiness of their looks and tones ; or to hear them read the Bible, verse about, with Henry ; A——, serious and steady, pronouncing his words dis-´tinctly, and proceeding smoothly to the end of the verse ; Herbert, poor fellow, more interrupted by his occasionally impeded utterance, and by the thoughts which the subject suggests. He does not skim the surface, but stops continually to look under the ice. * * *

Ilchester, October 21.—Dear Miss T——, you will be grieved to find that I am stopped on my journey home by nervous illness, and am here in bed under the doctor's care. All circumstances are favorable. I can not now write particulars. God bless you and your true   S. C.

VI.

"Blessed are they that mourn : for they shall be comforted."

NOTE.—This affecting letter, which breathes the very spirit of Christian resignation, was occasioned by an earnest desire to suggest topics of consolation to my poor Grandmother, who was alone at home when she received the news of her daughter's illness, and was thrown by it into a state of the greatest anxiety and trouble. During this period of suffering and weakness, my mother was, however, still able to read, and reflect on what she read, as appears from the following passages of her correspondence. The books which chiefly occupied her attention, while she was thus detained at Ilchester, seem to have been her father's " Literary Remains ;" the writings of Mrs. Hemans, a lady whose poetical talent gave her a good deal of pleasure, though she was apt to note its deficiencies; and several devotional works by Abbott, an author of the Evangelical School, much esteemed by serious persons of the last generation.—E. C.

To her Mother :

Castle-Inn, Ilchester, October 24, 1836.—Dear Mother, I entreat you to pray for cheerfulness and fortitude to the Giver of all good. Be sure that the effort to pray will be useful, however distracted your poor thoughts may be. Let us recollect that were we enjoying all that our worldly hearts desire, how rapidly does time move on ; how soon shall we arrive at the end of our earthly course—then what will worldly good things avail us? But these days of trial are more available for securing a happy seat in the eternal kingdom than those which our unsanctified hearts might deem more blessed. The merciful Saviour has given us a check in the midst of our heedless career, and bids us consider, ere it be too late, whither we are hastening, lest we think only of the roses on the way-side, and forget the glorious city in the clouds, which, would we raise our eyes, we might see right before us. Dearest mother, be not grieved for this visitation. When you go to heaven before me, if you leave your poor daughter with a more serious, chastened heart (though still a weak and sin-inclined one), you leave her in far better case than if her frame were as free from uneasy weakness as the best in the land. Look not on this as a poor consolation, only taken up because no better can be had. These which I have alluded to are substantial truths, which will abide to my weal or woe, when all this busy and bustling world for me exists no longer. I thought my business here was to teach my darling boy ; to be respected, admired, beloved ; my head said otherwise, but my heart felt thus. Now I feel, more feelingly, that my business here is to make my soul fit for eternity, and my earthly tasks are but the means by which that blessed work of my salvation is to be effected. Not according to what I do here, but according to the spirit in which I do it, shall I be judged hereafter. Is there any thing in this reflection that tends to weaken our zeal, prudence, industry, forecast, in the exercise of our earthly avocations? Our worldly things would be better done than they are could we but view them only in their due relations to heavenly things ; as children are best educated when they are accounted as children, and not treated with the state and ceremony and indulgence that rightfully belong to the mature.

God bless you, my beloved mother.—I remain, your warmly affectionate   SARA COLERIDGE.

VII.

"The *Shaping* Spirit of Imagination."

To her Husband:

Ilchester, Somerset, October 25, 1836.—Chemists say that the elementary principles of a diamond and of charcoal are the same ; it is the action of the sun or some other power upon each that makes it what it is. Analogous to this are the products of the poet's mind ; he does not *create* out of nothing, but his mind so acts on the things of the universe, material and immaterial, that each composition is in effect a new creation. Many of Mrs. Hemans's poems are not even in this sense creations ; she takes a theme, and this she illustrates in fifty different ways, the verses being like so many wafers, the same thing in blue, green, red, yellow. She takes descriptions from books of natural history or travel, puts them into verse, and appends a sentiment or a moral, like the large red bead of a rosary at the end of several white ones. But all these materials have under-

I

gone no fusion in the crucible of imagination. We may recognize the author's hand by a certain style of selection and arrangement, as we might know a room furnished by Gillow or Jackson, according to the same rule; but there is no stamp of an individual mind on each separate article.

———

VIII.

Speculations on Life and Organization.—Life considered as the Connecting Link between Mind and Matter.—Mr. Coleridge's Application of this View to the Scriptural Narratives of Demoniacal Possession;* and to the Christian Doctrine of the Resurrection.

To the Same :

Ilchester, October 27, 1836.—The sensorium is what we feel by; if I have a blow on the back, it is not the back that feels, but that organ; if I am *informed* that I shall have a blow on the back, it is the sensorium that gives the feeling of apprehension. In the one case the channel of communication is the body, in the other the mind; when the sensorium is affected through the body, it may affect the mind; when affected through the mind, it may affect the body; as this inn may convey news from Ilminster to Wincaunton, or news from Wincaunton to Ilminster. What *is* the sensorium?—what constitutes it the organ of feeling? surely something more than the material particles of which it is composed, and which alone our material senses recognize. *Life,* whatever that power may be; the same principle that animates the flower, the zoophyte, ant, elephant, man; a something which is neither the soul nor the visible, tangible frame, but keeps both united, or, rather, makes the human frame a fit receptacle and instrument of the reasonable soul—this life it is which feels by the sensorium. Now my father seems to imagine that the "evil spirits" spoken of in Scripture may be something akin to the fierce spirit or life of a tiger, the treacherous spirit or animating principle of a wolf, which might mysteriously have become connected with the human frame; and indeed we know, that when reason fails, the animating principle which remains in man, the mere life, appears endowed with evil, bestial qualities, malice, treachery, ferocity, unmitigable

---

* Coleridge's "Lectures on Shakespeare," etc., vol. ii., pp. 152-3, 155-6.

cruelty; in the presence of some madmen or idiots, we feel as in the presence of a wolf or a tiger, not in the presence of what is called a cruel, remorseless man. But to imagine that the soul of a demon, that is, a demon's identity, can inhabit the body of a man, co-tenant with his soul or identity, or that the two identities can be mingled together (two *alls*, made into a double *all*, as if fire or water could be made doubly fire or water by the addition of fresh fire and water), is surely an incredible creed, a proposition contrary to that very reason which is to decide on its acceptance or rejection. Equally monstrous is it to suppose that the man's soul is expelled, and that the demon's soul reigns in its stead; *then* the subject of discourse is *not a man at all*, but a demon in a man's body; we can not then say that a *man* is cured, but that a demon has been expelled from a mortal body, and the soul, which formerly dwelt in it, recalled, as the soul of Lazarus was recalled to his lifeless body. Is it not more reasonable to suppose that the almighty Saviour, by restoring the body to the conditions of health, freed the suspended soul, restored the instrument by which, in this world of matter, the soul can alone be conscious of its existence, and, so doing, expelled that evil nature which, in the absence of a higher power, reigned in the unruled realm? When we speak of being inspired by the Spirit, united to Christ, having our corrupt will purified by the influence of the Holy Ghost, do we ever mean that our personal identity is lost, that either Person of the Trinity is indisputably one with our person?

Life is the steam of the corporeal engine; the soul is the engineer who makes use of the steam-quickened engine. In life there is no more personal identity than in the body to which it belongs; indeed, the tangible frame and the life together constitute the body; it is *my* life, *my* body, not more myself than my clothes, and only seeming more so because in this world inseparably connected. The reason is the soul in its integrity, with all its faculties awake; the reason may be impaired, and yet some of its faculties may remain capable of action, as memory and imagination. While the reason, *as to its integrity*, is suspended, the evil life or nature may draw those faculties to the service of evil, and make them cry aloud, "What have I to do with thee, Jesus of Nazareth." Yes, the life and corporeal frame together constitute the body; therefore I have the same body that I had as a child, and God may raise me up with my identical body; for the same principle of life continues, and surrounds itself with new matter according to its need, as the fish forms its shell suitable to its own shape, and ever renewed according to its growing wants. Thus the *shell-fish* is ever the same, though the shell is yearly different. Thus the soul yearly expands, having yearly a tenement enlarged and accommodated for its expansion, till at length the conditions of the perfect soul are attained. The soul can never cease to exist, but it may cease to be conscious of existence, as in a trance; or as the soul of Lazarus was suspended during the four days that his body lay in the grave. In sleep, the soul, as to its integrity, seems to be suspended, and the life plays with the memory, the fancy, and the faculties of the soul; or rather with the soul itself, then capable only of exerting those partial faculties. It is plain that in the case of a madman afterward restored, his reasonable soul has been suspended, not destroyed or separated; and who knows but that the soul of an idiot *exists* in its integrity; that the soul of an infant who dies young *exists* in mature perfection, though destitute in this world of an instrument by which to exercise its faculties? And if life be not the result of organization, but the organizer, is it not conceivable that it may exist apart from the material frame, as the soul may exist apart from the body?

IX.

"The Remains."*—Metaphysics like Alum.

To the Same:

Ilchester, November, 1836. — How delightful are the "Remains!" I quite grieve to find the pages on my left hand such a thick handful. One wants to have such a book to dip into constantly, and to go on reading such discussions on such principles and in such a spirit on a thousand subjects.

It does not seem as if the writer was especially conversant with this or that, as Babbage with mechanics, and Mill with political economy; but as if there was a subtle imaginative spirit to

---

* Published now under the following titles: "Lectures on Shakespeare," etc.; "Notes on English Divines;" and "Notes, Theological, Political," etc. —E. C.

search and illustrate all subjects that interest humanity. Sir J. Mackintosh said that "S. T. C. trusted to his ingenuity to atone for his ignorance." But in such subjects as my father treats of, ingenuity is the best knowledge.

Like all my father's works, the "Remains" will be more sold at last than at first. Like alum, these metaphysical productions melt slowly into the medium of the public mind; but when time has been given for the operation, they impregnate more strongly than a less dense and solid substance, which dissolves sooner, has power to do. Why? Because the closely compacted particles are more numerous, and have more energy in themselves. By the public mind, I mean persons capable of entertaining metaphysical discussions.

X.

Abbott's "Corner-Stone," and other Religious Works.—Comparison of Archbishop Whately with Dr. Arnold, in their Mode of Setting Forth the Evidences of Christianity.—Verbosity of Dr. Chalmers.—Value of the Greek Language as an Instrument of Mental Cultivation.

To Miss ARABELLA BROOKE :

Ilchester, November 8, 1836.—My dear Miss Brooke, though I am under orders to write to no one except my husband and mother or sister, I must thank you with my own hand for thinking so affectionately of me in my trouble, as you evidently have done, and as I felt sure you would do.

    *   *   *   *   *   *   *   *

Since I saw you, I have read with great attention, and I humbly hope not without profit, Abbott's "Young Christian," "Corner-Stone," and "Way to do Good." In a literary point of view, these works are open to much criticism, though their merits in that way may be considerable; and certainly, in several points, the author is far from being what a sincere member of our Church can call orthodox. For instance, his view of the Atonement seems to me below the right standard; he dwells solely on the effect produced in man, entirely leaving out of sight the mysterious propitiation toward God; and his illustration of the "Lost Hat" strikes me as inadequate and presumptuous. But notwithstanding these exceptionable points, and several others—his very diffuse style, and a frequent want of harmony between his expressions and the deep reverential feelings which he aims to excite—I think very highly of Abbott, as an energetic, original, and fresh-minded writer ; and I think his works calculated to do great good, by leading those who peruse them to scrutinize their own spiritual state, and the momentous themes of which he treats with zeal and fervor, if not always with perfect judgment.

I wish I could put into your hand a book from which I have derived great pleasure—Whately's "Essays on some Difficulties in the Writings of St. Paul." The Archbishop does not seem to be a profound, subtle, metaphysical writer ; neither does he aim at any thing of the kind. What he does aim at, he seems to me to have well accomplished. He reasons clearly to particular points from a general view of Revelation, not from the nature of things in themselves ; and his style is vigorous, simple, and perspicuous. In this respect it resembles that of Dr. Arnold, but the latter does not so exclusively address the understanding ; he does more in the way of touching the heart, at the same time that (when party spirit is out of the question) he reasons forcibly and clearly—as far as I can judge, I mean.

The substance of what pleases you in Abercrombie* I have lately read in Chalmers's Bridgewater Treatise ;† and, oh ! when the wordy Doctor does get hold of an argument, what a splutter does he make with it for dozens of pages. He is like a child with a new wax doll; he hugs it, kisses it, holds it up to be admired, makes its eyes open and shut, puts it on a pink gown, puts it on a blue gown, ties it on a yellow sash ; then pretends to take it to task, chatters at it, shakes it, and whips it ; tells it not to be so proud of its fine false ringlets, which can all be cut off in a minute, then takes it into favor again ; and at last, to the relief of all the company, puts it to bed.

I wish very much that some day or other you may have time to learn Greek, because that language is an *idea*. Even a little of it is like manure to the soil of the mind, and makes it bear finer flowers.—My dear A——, your truly affectionate friend,

SARA COLERIDGE.

---

* "Inquiries concerning the Intellectual Powers and the Investigation of Truth." By Dr. Abercrombie.—E. C.

† "On the Adaptation of External Nature to the Moral and Intellectual Constitution of Man." By the Rev. Dr. Thomas Chalmers.—E. C.

CHAPTER VI.

1837.

LETTERS TO HER HUSBAND; TO MISS A. BROOKE; MRS. PLUMMER;
MRS. H. M. JONES.

I.

Difference between the Italian Satiric Poets and their English Imitators.

To Miss E. TREVENEN:

10 *Chester Place*, 1837.—I can not think that the English Beppoists have any authority among the Italians for their style. Ariosto conceived his subject to a certain degree lightly and sportively; and Pulci has a vein of satire; but these ingredients in them are interfused so as to form a *tertium aliquid*—not grape-juice and water, but *wine*. Their satire and their sentiment, their joke and their earnest, do not intersect each other in distinct streaks, like the stripes of red and white in the Union flag.

II.

Unsatisfactoriness of Desultory Correspondence.—"Phantasmion, a Romance of Fairy-land."—Defense of Fairy Tales by Five Poets.—Books *about* Children not often Books *for* Children.—Incongruous Effect of Scripture Lessons, intermixed with Nursery Talk and Doings.—Christianity best Taught by a Mother out of the Bible and Prayer-book.—"Newman's Sermons."—"Maurice's Letters to the Quakers."

To Miss ARABELLA BROOKE:

10 *Chester Place, Regent's Park, July 29,* 1837.—We always feel some difficulty in addressing those whom we are not in the habit of addressing frequently; we feel that the letter which is to make up for long silence, and epitomize the goings on of a good many months, ought to be three times as kind, satisfactory, and newsful as if two others had preceded it. And being at the same time quite sure that this very circumstance will

tend to freeze the genial current of our thoughts, and that occurrences which might have had some savor in them, if told when fresh, are now grown vapid, we are apt to look on the matter as a sort of task, something we would wish to perform better than we have any chance of doing; and this feeling is the stronger the more we desire to stand well with the letter-expectant. Letters that come seldom can not do without preambles; which are always stupid things, but sometimes seem necessary to prevent the appearance of abruptness.

Without extending *my* preamble quite over the whole first page, I will commence my true epistle by begging your acceptance of a little book which is to accompany it. This little book was chiefly written the winter before I last saw you, when I was more confined to my couch than I am now; and whether any friends agree with my husband (the most partial of them all) in thinking it worth publishing or not, they will attach some interest to the volume as a record of some of my recumbent amusements; and be glad to perceive that I often had out-of-door scenes before me in a lightsome, agreeable shape, at a time when I was almost wholly confined to the house, and could view the face of nature only by very short glimpses.* It requires no great *face* to publish nowadays; it is not stepping upon a stage where the eyes of an audience are upon you—but entering a crowd, where you must be very tall, strong, and striking, indeed, to obtain the slightest attention. In these days, too, to print a Fairy Tale is the very way to be *not read*, but shoved aside with contempt. I wish, however, I were only as sure that *my* fairy tale is worth printing, as I am that works of this class are wholesome food, by way of variety, for the child-

---

* L'ENVOY OF "PHANTASMION."

Go, little book, and sing of love and beauty,
To tempt the worldling into fairy-land;
Tell him that airy dreams are sacred duty,
Bring better wealth than aught his toils command,—
    Toils fraught with mickle harm.

But if thou meet some spirit high and tender,
On blessed works and noblest love intent,
Tell him that airy dreams of nature's splendor,
With graver thoughts and hallowed musings blent,
    Prove no too earthly charm.—S. C.

Written in a copy of "Phantasmion" about the year 1845.—E. C.

ish mind. It is curious that on this point Sir Walter Scott, and Charles Lamb, my father, my Uncle Southey, and Mr. Wordsworth, were all agreed. Those names are not so great an authority to all people as they are to me ; yet I think they might be set against that of Miss Edgeworth, powerfully as she was able to follow up her own view. Sir Walter Scott made an exception in her favor, when he protested against the whole generation of moral tales, stories of naughty and good boys and girls, and how their parents, pastors, and masters did or ought to have managed them. It is not to be denied that such stories are exciting to children, and, indeed, spoil their taste utterly for works which have less of every-day life, though not less of truth, in them. But the grand secret of their sale seems to be that they interest the *buyers* of the books, mammas and governesses, who see in such productions the history of their own experience, and the reflection of minds occupied with the same educational cares as their own. In this way, "Grave and Gay," by Miss Tytler, sister of the historian, was very interesting to me ; but I would not put it into the hands of my children, excellent manual of divinity as it is thought by some. It is not in such scraps, nor with such a context, however pretty in its way, that I should like to present the sublime truths of Christianity to the youthful mind : "Florence put the cherry in her mouth, and was going to eat it all up," etc.—just before or after extracts from the Sermon on the Mount, or allusions to the third chapter of St. John's Gospel. The Bible itself, that is, the five Books of Moses and the four Gospels, with a mother's living commentary, together with the Catechism and Liturgy, appear to me the best instruments for teaching the Christian religion to young children.

I have lately been reading, certainly with great interest, the sermons of John Henry Newman ; and I trust they are likely to do great good, by placing in so strong a light as they do the indispensableness of an orthodox belief, the importance of sacraments as the main channels of Christian privileges, and the powers, gifts, and offices of Christian ministers derived by apostolical succession—the insufficiency of personal piety without Catholic brotherhood—the sense that we are all members of one body, and subjects of one kingdom of Christ—the danger of a constant craving for religious excitement, and the fatal mistake of trusting in any devotional thoughts and feelings, which are not immediately put into act, and do not shine through the goings-on of our daily life.   But then these exalted views are often supported, as I think, by unfair reasonings; and are connected with other notions which appear to me superstitious, unwarranted by any fair interpretation of Scripture, and containing the germs of Popish errors.

The letters of Maurice to the Quakers should be taken in conjunction with these discourses, to qualify them and keep the mind balanced.   Maurice is a profound thinker, a vigorous though rough writer; and I trust you would not like him the worse for sharing my father's spirit.   His divinity seems based on the " Aids to Reflection;" and, though no servile imitator, he has certainly borrowed his mode of writing and turn of thought very much from S. T. C.

III.

"Mary and Florence; or, Grave and Gay," a Tale for Children.*—Right Interpretation of St. John iii., 8.—Heavenly Things should be set before Children, both " plainly " and " by a Parable."

To Mrs. H. M. JONES:

I have read " Mary and Florence," and have been charmed with it; the story has made me " grave " and "gay," according to the writer's intention.   As to the "utility" of this and other such works—that is, whether or no they answer their *professed purpose*—I could write a long sermon or essay, which my readers would suspect to be more than half borrowed from S. T. C. and H. N. C.   The illustration of the nature of the soul by the wind, I thought calculated, in some measure, to mislead.   The wind is as *material* a thing as the cheek it blows upon; we can not see it, but we can feel and hear it; it is cognizable by the senses, and therefore material.   The verse from St. John's Gospel does not, I think, bear upon this point at all, but has reference solely to the operations of divine grace.   " As the wind bloweth where it listeth," so grace comes by the will of God, not at man's pleasure; "thou hearest the sound thereof, but canst not tell how it cometh nor whither it goeth, so is every man that is born of the spirit."

---

* By Miss Fraser-Tytler.—E. C.

Thou knowest the existence of grace in the heart by its *effects*, but canst not understand the nature of it, nor of God's working : "how it cometh nor whither it goeth." This is the case with every man who has such grace given him that his heart and mind are *born again—i. e.,* totally renewed. Such, I believe, is the interpretation of this passage by good divines, and surely it has no reference to the nature of spirit as opposed to matter. Nicodemus did not fancy that he could *see* the soul of man, but he desired an explanation of our Lord's expression, "Thou must be born again." Miss T. gives a material description of heaven to her young catechumens. In this she goes contrary to the judgment of the celebrated Abbott, who, in his "Corner-Stone," declares this to be an injudicious method ; but John Abbott, author of the "Child at Home" (often confounded with the former), declares that young folks ought to have their feelings warmed by these visual pictures. To combine the two methods would be best, I should think. But let me say again that, in spite of all these critical thoughts, I was charmed with the book, and so much excited with the gypsy story at the end (which to be sure is as wild a romance, the conversion at least, as any thing in Mrs. Ratcliffe), that I almost feared being kept awake by it, and for a long time could think of nothing but Herby in a similar situation. He would not have *slept*, I fear, under such circumstances, as Florence did. The story of the "Mouse" is sweetly and humorously told.

IV.

Regent's Park.

To Mrs. PLUMMER :

10 *Chester Place, Regent's Park, August* 26, 1837.—In regard to our change of abode, we have great reason on the whole to be satisfied. From the up-stairs apartment we have really a nice look-out, which, however, I may not dignify with the name of *view.* The foreground consists of good houses, and to the right a garden with stone balustrade, and beyond, the trees of the park, behind which we can see a portion of many a glowing sunset. Where dark green foliage, backed with buff and crimson clouds, is clearly to be seen, one ought not to complain of being banished from the shows of nature.

The walks, too, are invaluable in this neighborhood. At Hampstead I always had to climb; here a few steps brings me into the park, with its acres of green turf, and flocks of country *looking* (and *sounding*) sheep. The grand want is the want of water ;* but even at Norwood (rural as that is) we should be no better off in this respect. You may imagine what a play-ground the park is for our children.

V.

Dryden's Censure of Ovid on the Score of the Rhetorical Expressions attributed to the Dying Narcissus.—His Observations not True to Nature, nor Applicable to the Case in Question.—Definition of "Force" and "Liveliness" in Poetry.—The Homeric Mythology not Allegorical.—Symbolical Character of the Imagery of Milton and Wordsworth.—Originality of Virgil.

To her Husband :

September 13, 1837.—Dryden's criticisms were fine for the times in which he wrote, which were corrupted from the purity of the Elizabethan age, and had not learned the metaphysical accuracy which some in these days have attained to. Comparing them with the best critics of this day, I should describe them as lively and distinctly expressed rather than profound. He finds great fault with Ovid's poems, but I think in one passage on wrong grounds. "Would a man dying for love express his passion by such conceits as 'Inopem me copia fecit,' and a dozen more of the like sort, poured on the neck of one another, and meaning all the same thing?" Shakespeare, in "Romeo and Juliet," showed forth the passion of love, which is so pre-eminently imaginative, venting itself in every variety of metaphor ; and I can assert from experience that it is the impulse of minds in strong emotion to eddy perpetually round the one magnetic theme, and to express the same feeling in twenty different forms of speech. I think "Inopem me copia fecit," which is not a mere verbal contrast, but a contrast of

---

* This was before the adjoining estate, with its artificial lake, wooded knolls, and islets, was added to Regent's Park. In after years, the walk right across the new park and up Primrose Hill to see the sunset (returning along the terraces) was a favorite one with my mother on fine summer evenings.—E. C.

things actually existing, is perfectly natural under the circumstances. "How strange is my fate! my very abundance causes me to be in want; possession makes me suffer the pangs of unsatisfied desire." Such reflections would be perfectly natural to a man who could pine away in love-sickness of his imagined self. Such a death is not to be described with the physical accuracy of a medical report. We are to be shown the passion of love incarnate, not flesh and blood dying in consequence of love. And surely Ovid's tone of description is to be modified by the nature of his subject; fears and sorrows that brought on such catastrophes as the being changed into a tree or a waterfall may be touched with a lighter hand than the agonies of Lear or Othello. * * *

In regard to *force* and *liveliness*, may we not call the latter one mode of the former, rather than a separate property? Scott's poems afford samples of lively force, but they contain little of that force which seizes the imagination, and obliges it to contemplate fixedly something spiritual, which has nothing in it of corporeal life. The "Leech Gatherer" is a poem which is forcible but solemn; it arrests and fixes the mind, instead of hurrying or leading it on. Yet the illustrations of this poem are as lively as the main design is far removed from bodily attributes. The stone is absolutely endued with motion by the comparison with a sea-monster that had crept out upon the shore to sun himself. Liveliness expresses the motion, the action of life, that by which life is manifested. When the lively is also sublime, as the "Battle of the Gods," we do not apply to the mixed effect the term of a quality which so generally describes the less exalted movements and acts of life; but Homer's force, as you have observed, always consists of liveliness. In him there is no force like that of Dante, Milton, Wordsworth, Schiller, Coleridge, where lively metaphors and life-like images are but to adorn or partly represent the various realities of abstract being. Their force results from the thing signified, together with the outward symbol, from the union and mutual fitness of the two. Philosophers may fancy that the Grecian mythology was allegorical, but the force of Homer is not derived at all from those inner significations. His divine and human battling is sublime, from being vast, fearful, and indistinct. It is *animated*, full of animal motion; it is a picture that strikes and pleases in and for itself alone; it is conceived and executed with all the power of mature genius, inspired by the circumstances, the wants, desires, hopes, lives of a peculiar state of human life—a state which precluded contemplation, and demanded action.   Compare Homer's poetry with Milton's first books of "Paradise Lost."   With what does the latter possess our minds?   "With greatness fallen, and the excess of glory obscured."   It is the *force* with which this subject is made to engross our contemplations, to tinge the whole of that dark, fiery region and those prostrate angel warriors with an awful sadness, the aptness of that region so described to shadow out eternal bale, of those vast and dimly lustrous images to represent the warring evils of our spiritual part—this it is which constitutes the peculiar perfection of that grand product of imagination. In this it is essentially different from Homer, life and progression are not its characterizing spirit.   They are represented by the older poet with the greatest conceivable truth and power, and Milton availed himself of that prototype in the embodying of his conceptions.   He imitated Homer in as far as he trod the same ground with him, but the main scope of his poem was an aboriginal of his own intellect.   In regard to Virgil, whom Dryden rather unfairly, as I think, contrasts with Homer, it appears to me that he has been rather misappreciated by being constantly looked at in his aspect of an imitator, and that his having cast his poem in a ready-made mould, has prevented most critics from observing the peculiarities of his own genius in the substance of thought, and in the external ornaments of diction.   A finer and more true criticism might be exerted by discovering and expressing that which was his own, rather than that which he borrowed.

VI.

" Parochial Sermons " by John Henry Newman.—Power and Beauty of his Style.—Tendency of his Teaching to Exalt the Passive rather than the Active Qualities of Humanity.—The Operation of Divine Grace on the Soul is a Mystery, the Visible Effects whereof is Holiness.—But Writers of the Oxford School appear to represent the Effect as no less Invisible than the Cause.—The Ordinance of Preaching.

To the Same :

Chester Place, September 23, 1837.—I think your expressions about Newman quite well chosen.   Decidedly I should say he is a writer, first, of *great talent*, secondly, of *beauty*. The *beauty* of his writing is shown, for the most part, in the tasteful simplicity, purity, and lucid propriety of his style; but now and then it is exhibited in well-chosen and brief metaphors, which are always according to the spirit of the subject. Speaking of children, in allusion to our Saviour's remark, that of such are the kingdom of heaven, he observes that this is only meant of little ones in their passive nature; that, like water, they reflect heaven best when they are still. However, it seems to be a point with the Oxford writers, either for good or evil, very much to represent, not children only, but men, as the *passive* unco-operating subject (or rather, in one sense, *object*) of divine operation. They are jealous of holding up, or dwelling much upon, grace as an *influence* on the conscious spirit, a stimulator and co-agent of the human will, or enlightener of the human intellect. That view, they think, is insufficient, leads to an inadequate notion of Christian ordinances, and of our Christian condition, and causes a confusion between God's general dealings with the human race, or His subordinate workings with Christians, and His special communications to the members of the New Covenant. "Salvation" is to be considered (exclusively) "as God's work in the soul." But whether it be not just as much God's work if carried on with the instrumentality of those faculties which He originally conferred, may be a question. Again, the Oxford writers dwell much on the necessity of a belief in mysteries not level to our understanding (of which my father says that they can not run counter to our reason, because they do not move on any line that can come in contact with it, being beyond the horizon of our earthly faculties). But the question is whether our Saviour ever spoke of any operations on men, the *effects* of which they were not enabled plainly and clearly (if their hearts be well disposed) to judge of. The *operations* themselves are not our concern, any more than the way in which God created the earth, and all that is therein. The operations themselves belong to that heaven which none can understand but He that is in heaven, and which consequently I can not believe that God ever meant us to understand, the symbols which the inspired writers employ on this subject being more probably intended to convey a notion of the desirability and accessibility of heaven than of heaven itself. Whately truly says, in relation to subjects of this kind, that a blind man may be made to understand

a great deal *about* objects of sight, though sight alone could reveal to him *what they are.*

To return to my theme.   It is an undoubted truth that the
manner in which God operates upon man is and must be as unintelligible to man as the way in which God created him at
first; but does it flow from this truth, or does it appear from
the tenor of Scripture, that Christ, who constantly appealed to
the reason and the will of His hearers (as Newman himself
urges against the Predestinarians), ever spoke of divine operations on man, the *effects* of which he might not judge of by intelligible signs.   The Syrian was commanded to bathe in a certain river, and how it was that bathing in that river could heal
his leprosy, it was not given him to know.   But was he commanded to believe that he had been healed of leprosy, while to
all outward appearance, and by all the signs which such a thing
can be judged of, the leprosy remained just as before?   Surely
it is not from the expressions of Scripture, but from the supposed necessary consequences of certain true doctrines, *according to a certain mode of reasoning*, that the non-intelligibility of
the *effects* of God's working is contended for.   Newman himself urges that baptism is scarcely ever named in Scripture without the mention of spiritual grace ; that baptism is constantly
connected with regeneration.   And then I would ask, is not
spiritual grace generally mentioned in Scripture, either with an
implication or a full and particular description of those good dispositions and actions which are to proceed from it, and which
men may judge of, as of a tree from its fruits?   And is regeneration ever mentioned in Scripture in such a way as to preclude
the notion that it is identical with *newness of life?* and is not
newness of life, according to our Saviour and St. Paul, identical
with doing justice and judgment for Christ's sake, doing righteously because of feeling righteously?   Are we ever led by the
language of Scripture to suppose that regeneration is a mystical
something, which, though it may, and in certain circumstances
must, produce goodness and holiness, yet of *its own nature* need
not absolutely do so ; which may exist in unconscious subjects,
as in infants, acknowledged incapable of faith and repentance,
which might, as to its own essence (though the contrary actually is the case), exist even in the worst of men?   In short, that
regeneration is the receiving of a new nature—a more divine,
and yet not better or more powerful nature.   Surely here are

words without thoughts. What notion have we of a *divine* nature which does not include or consist· of the notions of goodness and power? Newman illustrates the subject by the case of devils, who, he says, have a divine but not a good nature. To elucidate the obscure doctrine of regeneration by reference to evil spirits is like attempting to brighten twilight by the shades of night, and is a perfect contrast to the proceeding of our Saviour, who was accustomed to explain "the kingdom of heaven" by parables and stories about things which His listeners daily saw with their eyes and handled with their hands.

In the same spirit of being mysterious above what is written, Newman and his fellow-laborers in the Oxonian vineyard are wont to contend that preachers are bound to preach the Gospel, as a blind servant is bound to deliver a message about things which he can never see—as a carrier-pigeon, to convey a letter the contents of which it can not understand. They are not to preach for the sake of saving souls, nor to select and compose from the Gospel in order to produce a good effect, nor to grieve if the Gospel is the savor of death to those who will not hear. In short, it would be presumption and rationalism in them to suppose that their intellect or zeal was even to be the medium through which God's purposes were to be effected. What God's purposes *are* in commanding the Gospel to be preached, and sending His Only Son into the world, they maintain that we can not guess (as if God had not plainly revealed it Himself throughout the Bible). They are merely to execute a trust, to repeat all the truths of the Gospel, one as much and as often as the other. For what practical result of such a principle can there be, unless it be this, that a clergyman is to preach as many sermons on the Trinity and the Incarnation as on faith and hope and charity, and the necessity of a good life, along with its details. Yet Newman is the very man who would accuse such a proceeding of irreverence, and too great an exercise of intellect.

VII.

Graphic Style of the Old Testament Narratives.—Greek and Roman History less Objective.

To the Same :

September 30, 1837. — I think Herby is more struck with Exodus than with Genesis, for the former is even more strik-

K

ingly objective than the latter, and the account of the various plagues arrests the attention even of the youngest mind. The most objective passages in Roman and Grecian history unfortunately are *not* the really important ones and the hinges of great events; they are biographical episodes or anecdotes, for the most part; as the striking off the heads of the poppies, the death of Regulus, and much of what relates to Alexander, the Roman emperors and their private follies. But in the Old Testament a great battle is won by the Israelites because Moses sits upon a *stone* on a *hill*, and has his *arms held up* on either side by Aaron and Hur. The whole history is a series of pictures. If you make pictures of Roman history, you must imagine postures, the accessory parts, all the detail of surrounding objects; but in the Bible they are made out for you. Thus you can call to mind the main course of events in Jewish history by means of such pictures impressed upon the memory; but Roman history could not correctly be represented in any such manner. A series of its most picturable scenes would not recall the march of the principal events.

Married Happiness.

Marriage, indeed, is like the Christian course; it must either advance or go backward. If you love and esteem thoroughly, the more you see and do and feel and talk together, the more channels are opened out for affection to run in; and the more room it has to expand, the larger it grows. Then the little differences and uncongenialities that at first seemed relatively important, dwindle into nothing amid the mass of concord and tenderness; or if their flavor still survives, being thus subordinate, like mustard or other condiments which would be intolerable in large proportions, it adds a zest to the whole dish.

VIII.

"Phantasmion" a Descriptive Piece; not an Allegory, or Moral Tale.—
Want of Artistic Unity in Goethe's "Faust."

To the Same :

September 29, 1837.—In regard to "Phantasmion's" want of general purpose and meaning, I can only say that it does not belong to that class of fictions in which a single truth or moral is to be illustrated by a sequence of events, of which Miss Edgeworth's and Miss Martineau's tales are instances, or in which, as in the "Faëry Queen" and the "Pilgrim's Progress," the character and descriptions are all for the sake of an allegory, which not only shines through them, but determines the general form to be produced, as the osseous system of an animal under the flesh. It belongs to that class of fictions of which "Robinson Crusoe," "Peter Wilkins," "Faust," "Undine," "Peter Schlemil," and the "Magic Ring," or the "White Cat," and many other fairy tales are instances; where the ostensible moral, even if there be one, is not the author's chief end and aim, which rather consists in cultivating the imagination, and innocently gratifying the curiosity of the reader, by exhibiting the general and abstract beauty of things through the vehicle of a story, which, as it treats of human hopes and fears and passions and interests, and of those changeful events and varying circumstances to which human life is liable, may lend an animation to the accompanying descriptions, and in return receive a lustre from them. It may be a defect in "Phantasmion" that one thought is not as predominant throughout the narrative as in some of the above-mentioned tales; and I may venture to say (comparing little things with great) that this want of unity, exhibited in a somewhat different way, is also perceptible in "Faust." There the prevailing thought at the outset is quite merged in another, which arises adventitiously out of the progress of the story. We begin with the hopes and fears of a philosopher, with the Satanic principle of knowledge apart from goodness, working only potent evil; we end with a tale of seduction, of an innocent creature coming in contact with subtle and wicked beings, her beauty and goodness of heart being thrown into strong relief by the gloomy and awful circumstances in which she is placed; this black, with gleams of white, being Goethe's constant mode of producing effect, analogous to Martin's painting. The "Faust" is not a symmetrical whole, but a dual consisting of two halves; for, however the author might prove logically that the evils of the latter part of the story do arise out of the wrong-headedness and heartedness described in the first part, still, to the feelings of the readers (and they are the rightful judges in this case), the history of Margaret is an episode, an independent relation, which inspires its own peculiar thoughts, fancies, and emotions, in a superseding way, and does not act upon the whole as a mere vessel to carry forward the interests and concerns announced from the first. Compare "Faust" with any of Shakespeare's, Jonson's, or Massinger's fine plays, and we shall see its inferiority in regard to totality of impression.

IX.

Preparations for the Study of Divinity.—Tendency to Discursiveness inherited from her Father.

To the Same :

October 4, 1837. — I feel the strongest bent for theological topics; and it seems to myself that I should want neither ingenuity in illustration, nor clearness of conception, to a certain extent; but then I am utterly deficient in learning and knowledge. I feel the most complete sympathy with my father in his account of his literary difficulties. Whatever subject I commence, I feel discontent unless I could pursue it in every direction to the farthest bounds of thought, and then, when some scheme is to be executed, my energies are paralyzed with the very notion of the indefinite vastness which I long to fill. This was the reason that my father wrote by snatches. He could not bear to complete incompletely, which every body else does.

X.

A View of Grasmere.—"Prosy" Letters preferred to Practical Ones.—Inefficiency of Dames' Schools, and even of National Schools, as at that Time Conducted.—Effect of Church Principles and Practices in giving a Religious Tone to a School.*

To Mrs. PLUMMER :

10 *Chester Place, Regent's Park, October* 21, 1837.—You would have been pleased could you have witnessed the reception of your sweet picture in this house. It arrived the day before Henry's return home, and it was quite a pleasure to take him

---

* It was in order to remove this acknowledged inefficiency that the first Training College for National Schoolmasters was established at Chelsea by the National Society, under the direction of the Rev. Derwent Coleridge, in 1841.—E. C.

into the drawing-room, as soon as he had made himself neat after the journey, and show him the new "Grasmere." The view is a more characteristic one of the Lake and Vale than the other which we possess; and in it we can point to the very spot* where my brother Hartley lives, which, to mamma and me, is very interesting.

I can not now answer your nice full letter as it deserves, for I have a good deal of epistolary work on hand; but I must tell you one thing, which is, never to apologize to me for *prosing*. What some people call prosing, I like; and what I do dislike in letters is a long history of comings and goings, visitings and being visited, allusions to Mrs. A. B., and Lady C. B., and other folks whom I never saw, and do not care two-pence about.

Your remarks on National Schooling I fully accede to, as far as my knowledge extends; still, when the education of a people is to be considered, even allowing the truth of them all, it is hard to decide positively against institutions of the kind in some shape or other. Six Dames' Schools under your super-intendence, energetic body as you are, might be an excellent substitute; but I am sorry to say, in those which I have heard of lately, nothing, or next to nothing, is learned, and the parents merely pay for having their children kept out of harm's way. Have you ever thought much about Normal Schools? Till some better system is adopted than at present generally pre-vails, and the art of teaching is regularly taught, I fear the National Schools will continue very inefficient.

In regard to instilling religious *feeling*, that, I fear, no large school can ever do; but if a foundation of correct principles were laid, and the Church and her ordinances rendered more prominent objects for the minds of the children than they have hitherto been, this surely would be something. Feeling might come in other ways, by the nameless opportunities of life; and the two (what was taught at school and what accrued to the learner elsewhere) might work together for good.

---

* Nab Cottage, on the road between Grasmere and Rydal.—E. C.

XI.

Conservative Replies to some Arguments of the Radical Party.—The British Constitution not originally Popular but Paternal.—An Appeal to Universal Suffrage not an Appeal to the Collective Wisdom of the Age, but to its Collective Ignorance.—"The Majority *will* be always in the Right ;" but not till it has Adopted the Views of the Minority. —Despotism of the Mob in America Regretted by many Americans.— English Government not a mere Machine for Registering Votes.—How are the People to be Trained to a Right Exercise of their Liberties ?— "*Govern* them, and lift them up forever."

To Mrs. H. M. JONES, in Reply to a Political Essay by Dr. PARK :

" The British Constitution is *founded* on public opinion." The institutions and forms of government in which this idea is more or less adequately manifested have been wrought out by public opinion, yet surely the idea itself is not the result and product, but rather the secret guide and groundwork, of public opinion on the point in question, as embodied in definite words and conceptions. But what public opinion was that which moulded our admired policy, and fashioned the curious and complicated mechanism of our state machine? Did it reflect the minds and intellects of the majority? Or was it not rather the opinions of the best and wisest, to which our *aristocratic* forms of government gave both publicity and prevalence?

Surely we have little reason to say that public opinion, taken *at large*, is necessarily just and wise by virtue of its being public—necessarily that to which the interests of the nation may be safely intrusted. If we identify it with the opinions of the majority at all times and on all subjects, it can not be identified with the collective wisdom of the age. Like foam on the surface of the ocean, pure if the waters below are pure, soiled and brown if they are muddy and turbid, it can but represent the character of that from which it proceeds, the average understandings and morals of the community. How are the masses to be purified and tranquilized? How rendered capable of judging soundly on affairs of state, as far as that is possible to men of humble station? Surely not by the introduction of a vote-by-ballot system, which virtually silences the gifted few, and reduces to inaction the highest wisdom of the day. Truth, it is said, must ever prevail ; but unless utterance is given her —nay, more, unless her voice is heard, not drowned by the clamors of the crowd, what means has she of prevailing? Public opinion is consonant to reason and goodness only inasmuch as it is influenced by the wise and good. It is often grossly absurd, and the public opinion of one year or month is condemned by that of the next. There is some truth in the notion of Miss Martineau, to which, by stress of arguments, she has been driven, "that the majority *will be* in the right." The only rational interpretation of which seems to me to be this, that, *on given points*, the majority *ultimately* decide in favor of the truth, because, in course of time, the opinions of the wisest on those particular subjects are proved, by experience and successive accessions of suffrages from competent judges, to be just; they are stamped before the public eye, and in characters which those who run may read (or, as Habakkuk really has it, "He may run that readeth"), and in such points public opinion is in fact the adoption of *private* opinion by the public; the judgment approved by the majority is any thing rather than that which the majority would have formed by aid of their own amount of sense and talent, for "nel mondo non è se non volgo." In time the whole lump is leavened with that which emanated from a few; but what practical application should be made of this axiom, "The majority will be in the right?" Ought it to be such as would lead us to throw political power, without stop or stay, directly into their hands, and abide all the consequences of their blundering apprenticeship, while in particulars in which the public interests are concerned, in which immediate action is required, they are *learning* to be right? Will it console us under the calamities which their ignorance may inflict, that they will know better in the end? And when the Commonwealth is in ruins, will this after-wisdom restore the shattered fabric, or indemnify those who have suffered during its disorganization? This notion of a ruined Commonwealth appears no visionary bugbear to those who believe the continuance of a Christian and Catholic government essential to the well-being of the state.

Before we argue about public opinion, before we decide what this great power has already done, or what it ought to do, it would be as well to settle what we mean by the term. The public opinion of this country, on *particular points*, in *this* age of the world, is perfectly just and enlightened. On the Newtonian or Copernican system, for instance, public opinion now is identical with that of the philosopher in his closet. But what was public opinion on this same system in the age of Kepler and Galileo? (for Newton was anticipated in some measure by those great men). If, however, by public opinion be meant the opinions of the multitude taken collectively—the general body of their opinions concerning all matters of which man can take cognizance—this can no more be the best possible, than the mass of mankind are as able, moral, and enlightened as a certain number of individuals in every age. But ought not a state to be guided by the best possible opinions? Ought it to be swayed by the uncorrected thoughts of the multitude?

It is not high Tories and Churchmen alone who feel that in America public opinion is a tyrant—because it is a public opinion not sufficiently acted on by the wisest and best individuals; their voice has utterance, and in time is heard, but by the forms of society and of government established there—especially the want of a landed gentry and influential endowed Church—they do not enough prevail over the voices of the crowd; and the will of the majority is too much felt for the welfare of the majority themselves. Many Americans are now admitting this, and it appears either implicitly or explicitly in the pages of every American traveler. Miss Martineau would have helped us to find it out had we needed her information.

With us, government hitherto has not been degraded in its character to that of a machine, the functions of those who are engaged in it being simply this, to ascertain and obey a popular will, like the index of a clock worked by a pendulum. Our laws and institutions have been moulded by the suggestions of a wise minority, which the mechanism of our state machinery enabled to come gradually into play; so that the interests of the people have been consulted rather than their blind wishes. Thus our constitution, considered as an outward thing, has been formed according to an idea of perfection (never in this world to be more than partially realized)—an idea existing equally in the minds of all our countrymen, but most distinctly and effectively developed in those which are aided by an acute and powerful intellect, improved to the highest point by education, study, and reflective leisure.

Is it not obvious from Dr. Park's own abstract that our government has never been popular in the sense in which my father denies it to have been such? Has it not ever been "a monarchy at once buttressed and limited by the aristocracy?" Was it ever popular as the American government is so? If not, still less has it been popular after such a sort as our modern liberals —our separators of Church and State—will leave no stone un- turned to make it. On the other hand, is it not clear as noon- day—nay, gloried in by numbers—that, notwithstanding the prolonged duration of Parliament, the remnant of lordly influ- ence in the popular elections and House of Commons, the stand- ing army, and national debt, the British State is more demo- cratic in this nineteenth century than at any former period?* Ought it to be still more democratic? still more the mere rep- resentative of the multitude, and exponent of their will? Are we likely to fare better under the dominion of the people than this country did in former times, when government had not re- nounced its right to consult for the benefit of the community, even independently of its inclinations? On the answer to this question depends the answer to that of Dr. Park—were the acts above named constitutional?

The sage Whig, Hallam, is of opinion that the Reform Bill went too far in establishing democratic principles; and as to such politicians as Hume, Warburton, Roebuck, and their allies, I should imagine they sympathized but little in the anxiety of reasoners like Dr. Park and S. T. C. for the balance of powers, and so that they could but succeed in overthrowing the Church and the aristocracy, would care much less than a straw for the old and venerable idea of the British Constitution.

A noble national character belongs to the people of England, and grieved indeed should I be to suppose that they wanted a "foundation of moderation and good sense." But how are those good qualities to be most efficiently improved, confirmed, elicited? How does a wise mother act in regard to the children under her care—those children in whom she perceives with de- light the germs and first shoots of a thousand amiable affections and excellent dispositions? I need hardly say that she does not trust to them solely; that she remembers of what jarring elements man is a compound; and that she takes care to keep the passions and infirm tempers of her charge in due restraint,

* We can not surely imagine that more power and liberty were really enjoyed by the people under the sway of the strong-headed, strong-handed Cromwell, or that their interests were more attended to during the corrupt reign of Charles II.—S. C.

in order that their good feelings and reasoning habits may be strengthened and increased. Just so should a paternal government act toward the national family which it has to govern.

These are some of the thoughts which have been suggested to me by the perusal of Dr. Park's instructive abstract. I am aware that they are quite imperfect and inconclusive ; but they give a notion of the way in which I have been led to look on the subject of government.

XII.

Insanity.—Intermediate State of the Departed not distinctly Revealed in Scripture.

To Mrs. JOSHUA STANGER :

10 *Chester Place, November* 28, 1837.—In many cases of insanity, I believe there has been a lucid interval before death; but in such a case as that of ———— this was perhaps hardly to be expected. Where derangement has been brought out by some mental cause, the last illness may produce a change both in mind and body, which may for a short time restore reason. But derangement in ———— was merely a symptom of general bodily decay, and it was not likely that an increase of that very weakness which first disordered her faculties should be attended by any brightening of them.

It is very awful to think in how many ways the opportunity of a death-bed preparation may be denied us ; it may be prevented not only by sudden death, but also by loss of mental power, only to terminate in dissolution. We may trust, however, that for our friends "to die is gain," whatever may be the immediate or intermediate state of those who thus leave us. Mr. Dodsworth, Mr. J. H. Newman, and other influential writers, insist strongly on this point, that the Resurrection, and not the departure from this life, is the period on which the hope of a Christian ought to be fixed ; and they say it is too common to hear the bereaved enlarge on the *immediate* felicity of the released sufferer escaped from his tabernacle of clay. For my part, I can not think all the texts they bring to prove their points entirely conclusive ; and it does not seem clear to me that Scripture has left any thing positively revealed on this subject. For all practical purposes, the death of every Christian is to him the coming of the Lord.

CHAPTER VII.

1838.

LETTERS TO HER HUSBAND, TO MRS. JOSHUA STANGER, MRS. PLUMMER, MISS A. BROOKE, MISS TREVENEN.

I.

Letter of Condolence to a Friend on the Death of a Brother.*

To Mrs. JOSHUA STANGER, Wandsworth :

10 *Chester Place, Regent's Park, January* 16, 1838.—My dear friend, by this time I conclude you are returned from your distressful and agitating journey ; and I will no longer delay to express my grief at the melancholy termination of all your long anxieties for your dear brother. But in this case there really and truly is much to soothe and console your feelings, and there is no difficulty in finding a topic of comfort on the subject, when I have such a happy conviction that *he* was prepared to exchange this world for a more blessed state of existence, and that you have a heart sufficiently disciplined by thought and previous trial, and that heavenly aid of which thought and trial are but instruments, to take true pleasure in the contemplation of his "great gain ;" and look back on his past life, not so much to awaken earthly regret, as to find sources of satisfaction in regard to that which we trust he now enjoys. For, indeed, a more innocent and conscientious creature I really believe he has not left behind him, among all his survivors, as far as I know ; and purity, though no passport to heaven, is a great qualification for a blessed station there. The want of it for a course of many years, may be made up for by our Saviour's

---

* The youngest son of Dr. Calvert, of Greta Bank, Keswick, Cumberland, and nephew of the Raisley Calvert who was Mr. Wordsworth's friend. His only sister, Mrs. Joshua Stanger, was my mother's earliest friend and companion in their native vale ; to which she returned in 1843, after a few years spent in the South ; and now dwells there in the midst of her own people.— E. C.

perfect righteousness. Yet, "Blessed are the pure in heart, for they shall see God;" and surely those who have been pure and peaceful all their lives, as I imagine to have been the case with your dear brother, must have a special enjoyment of this heavenly privilege.

Your loss, and the tears of natural sorrow which I know you must shed, have made me vividly imagine what my own feelings would be on the loss of either of my brothers. The wrench would indeed be severe. I suffered much in parting with my beloved father, but, unfortunately, I had been so little in his society during my life, being separated from him by illness during two or three years of our residence at Hampstead, that his departure did not make so great a difference to my heart as it would have done otherwise. And so accustomed had I been to commune with him in his books, more than face to face, that even now I never feel, while I peruse his sayings, chiefly on religious subjects, as if he were no more of this world. I fear it will be difficult for me to learn resignation by your trials, but I trust they will not be altogether lost on me for salutary admonition; and I can represent them more strongly to myself than those of persons with whom and with whose connections I am less intimate. Dear Raisley's image, indeed, is associated with all my early recollections, and haunts the scenes of my childhood and girlhood, which memory presents with more warmth and distinctness than those of after-life.—Believe me, my dear Mary, your truly affectionate friend, SARA COLERIDGE.

II.

Mr. Gillman's Life of her Father.—Earlier Development of Mr. Coleridge's Mind in the Direction of Poetry than in that of Theological Research.

To Mrs. GILLMAN, The Grove, Highgate:

May 8, 1838.—I must tell you how gratified I have been by the perusal of the first volume of the Life.* I assure you we all feel deeply cheered and pleased to think that such a record of a good man's affection and respect for S. T. C. will exist for the world. The work contains many new and, as I think, valuable pieces of my father's writing and conversation; and I can

* "Life and Letters of S. T. Coleridge," by James Gillman, Esq.—E. C.

not but believe that it will be read with profit and pleasure by
many persons less nearly interested in the subject of the Memoir than myself. My father's life must necessarily seem deficient in outward events to those who care for nothing but
story. His letters would not tell his external history as those
of Sir Walter Scott did his ; and many circumstances must be
passed over cursorily or in silence by a biographer of strictly
delicate feeling. But there are many meditative, reflective readers in the world, many who appreciate my father's works and
admire his unworldly and deeply feeling character, and they
will be glad to peruse a memoir of S. T. C. such as the present,
undebased by the display of paltry vanity and selfish pride. I
am glad Mr. Gillman put a note and a comment on the letter
about the Trinity to Mr. Cottle. Not with such arguments did
my father defend the great Catholic doctrine in later years ; but
it is part of the history of his mind, and shows how far it was
from having attained to its full growth in philosophical theology,
when in poetry it had come into the most perfect blossom.

III.

Blessing of Fraternal Affection.—Danger to which it is Exposed from Human Infirmity.

To Mrs. PLUMMER, Gateshead :

10 *Chester Place, July* 20, 1838.—The longer I live the more
deeply I enter into the spirit of the Psalmist's animated expressions about fraternal unity and love. But minds must be in almost a heavenly state before this unity and love can reign un-
interruptedly among them. The contentions and passing anger
of childhood are succeeded by sources of disagreement and
alienation in too many cases of a much deeper kind. Brothers
and sisters marry, and the new interests and discordant feelings
of the fresh family connections are often found to weaken at-
tachments, and all but sever fraternal friendships, which would
otherwise produce a great deal of happiness. All this is expressed in the gross ; but a *something* of what I allude to alloys
the social comfort of most family circles which I happen to
know intimately. There would be little use in reflecting upon
these unpleasant topics, to mention which I was led away, I
scarce know how, if the contemplation of the evil did not lead

to such measures for its avoidance or mitigation as are within our power; and that there are many such, your cheerful temper will lead you very readily to believe and affirm.

IV.

Sea-side Occupations.—Bathing: Childish Timidity not to be Cured by Compulsion.—Letter-writing: Friendly Letters, like Visits, not mere Vehicles for News.

To Mrs. PLUMMER, Gateshead:

Herne Bay, August 30, 1838.—You ask for a letter from Herne Bay, and I take the opportunity to comply with your request now that papa and the children and Ann have just set off on the rumble of the coach for Canterbury. I have been strolling on the beach, rejoicing that the Canterbury visitors have so softly brilliant a day for their excursion, yet partly regretting that they have turned their backs on the bathing-place. This is quite a day to make Herby in love with the ocean waters. At first he suffered much from fear when he had to enter them, and he has not yet achieved the feat of going thoroughly overhead; but I think you will agree with us that no good would be done by forcing him. Troy town, as he long ago observed himself in reference to the treatment of children, after all was *not* taken by force. Bathing is not like a surgical operation, which does good however unwillingly submitted to; and we can not make children fearless by compelling them to undergo the subject of their fears. This process, indeed, has sometimes made cowards for life. There is much in habit doubtless, but persons who act upon this truth, without seeing its practical limitations, often commit great errors.*

I must not, however, proceed to state these limitations, and see whether or no they agree with your speculations on child management, seeing that my paper and my time have their limitations too. *Apropos* to this last point, however, I must digress again, to say how few people have what I consider just and clear

---

* It may be worth while to mention, in proof of the practical success of my mother's indulgent system, that the early nervousness here alluded to completely passed away. My brother learned to swim as easily as most boys as soon as he went to school at Eton, where bathing and boating became his favorite amusements.—E. C.

notions on the subject of letter-writing!* You are one of my few cordial, genial correspondents who do not fill the first page of their epistles with asseverations of how much they have to do, or how little news they have to tell, and how sure you are, as soon as it is at all necessary to your well-being, to hear it from some other quarter. Why do these people waste time in visiting their friends of an evening, or calling on them of a morning? Why do they not pickle and preserve, and stitch and house-keep all day long, since those and such-like are the only earthly things needful? The answer doubtless would be, "Friendships must be kept up; out of sight out of mind; and, as man is a social creature, he must attend to the calls of society." Now it is exactly on this ground, and not, in nine cases out of ten, for the sake of communicating news, that letter-writing is to be advocated. It is a method of visiting our friends in their absence, and one which has some advantages peculiar to itself; for persons who have any seriousness of character at all endeavor to put the better part of their mind upon paper; and letter-writing is one of the many calls which life affords to put our minds in order, the salutary effect of which is obvious.

V.

The History of Rome, by Dr. Arnold.—The Study of Divinity, Poetry, and Physiology preferred to that of History or Politics.—Christian Theology, as an Intellectual System, based on Metaphysics.—Importance of Right Views on these Subjects.—National Education the Proper Work of the Church.

To Miss ARABELLA BROOKE:

Herne Bay, September 8, 1838.—We are reading Dr. Arnold's "Rome," and feel that we now for the first time see the old Romans off the stage, with their buskins laid aside, and talking like other men and women. They do not lose by this: the force of the Roman character is as clearly brought out in Dr. Arnold's easy, matter-of-fact, modern narrative, as it could have been in the stilted though elegant language of their own historians. People say how Whiggish it is, in spite of the

---

* The lady whose letter-writing style is thus pleasantly described is the wife of the Rev. Matthew Plummer, Vicar of Heworth, and author of several useful works on Church matters.—E. C.

disclaimers in the preface. There is certainly a great deal of anti-aristocracy in it ; but then, I imagine, if ever aristocracy showed itself in odious colors, it must have been during the early times of Rome ; and no faithful historian could have concealed this, though he might have manifested less zeal and alacrity in the task of exposing it. However, I speak in ignorance : politics and history are subjects in which I have less of my desultory feminine sort of information than some others which seem rather more within my compass. Divinity may be as wide a field as politics ; but it is not so far out of a woman's way, and you derive more benefit from partial and short excursions into it. I should say the same in regard to poetry, natural history in all its branches, and even metaphysics—the study of which, when judiciously pursued, I can not but think highly interesting and useful, and in no respect injurious.

The truth is, those who undervalue this branch of philosophy, or rather this root and stem of it, seem scarce aware how impossible it is for any reflective Christian to be without metaphysics of one kind or other. Without being aware of it, we all receive a metaphysical scheme, either partially or wholly, from those who have gone before us ; and by its aid we interpret the Bible. It is but few perhaps who have time to acquire any clear or systematic knowledge of divinity. When the heart is right, individuals may be in some respects first-rate Christians without any speculative insight, because the little time for study is caused by active exertion ; and this active exertion, pursued in a religious spirit, and converted into the service of God by the way of performing it, is perhaps the most effective school of Christianity. But when there *is* time to read, then I do think that, both for the sake of others and of ourselves, the cultivation of the intellect, with a view to religious knowledge, is a positive duty ; and I believe it to be clearly established, though not cordially and generally admitted, that the study of metaphysics is the best preparatory exercise for a true understanding of the Bible. False metaphysics can be counteracted by true metaphysics alone ; and divines who have not the one, can hardly fail, I think, to have the other. * * *

My husband is warmly interested in a plan for improving National Schools, and bringing them into connection with the Church, on the basis of the National Society. Henry sent the explanatory papers drawn up by the Committee of the National

Society to Dr. Arnold; but he, "with regret," declined to sign, on account of the too great influence, which, in his view, the clergy would have over the education machine. Perhaps you will feel with him; but all must admit that it is a difficult problem how any education worthy of the name can be carried out without religion, and how religion worthy of the name can be taught without the frame-work of certain doctrines.

VI.

Literary Varieties.—Spirituality of Northern Nations, and Metaphysical Subtlety of the Greeks.

To her Husband:

Chester Place, September, 1838.—The introduction to this work* is an excellent piece of criticism, written in a good style, with a spice of your own living individual manner in it, a sort of refined downrightness; your manner compared with my father's is as short-crust to puff paste.

"A passion for descending into the depths of the spiritual being of men" is ascribed to the Scandinavians and Germans; true, they are more spiritual than the Southerns, and yet what could exceed the metaphysical subtlety of the ancient Greeks? The *feelings* of the former are more imbued with a seeking of the supernatural, and yet the intellect of the latter could sound any depths of the spirit which are fathomable by man, as S. T. C. seems to say in "The Friend," where he speaks of their great advances in metaphysical lore, compared with their backwardness in science.

VII.

Miracle of the Raising of Lazarus passed over by the Synoptical Gospels.

To the Same:

Chester Place, September, 1838.—The more one thinks of it, the more puzzling it seems that the raising of Lazarus is only re-

---

* The "Introduction to Homer," by H. N. Coleridge.—E. C.

corded in St. John's Gospel. The common way of accounting for the matter can not easily be set down, but yet it does not satisfy. We feel there may be something yet in the case which we do not fathom, and knowing as we do from constant experience how much there is in most things which transcend our knowledge—what unsuspected facts and truths have come to light, and explained phenomena of which we had given quite different explanations previously—we can not but feel that the true way of accounting for this discrepancy has never yet come to light.

VIII.

Connection between the Senses and the Mind.—Poetic Genius Implies a Sensitive Organization.—Early Greatness of Great Poets.—Poetic Imagination of Plato brought to bear upon Abstract Ideas.

To the Same :

Herne Bay, September 21, 1838.—Herbert is a most sensitive child, as alive to every kind of sensation as quick in faculties. Indeed, I believe that this sensitiveness does itself tend to quicken and stimulate the intellect. He will have especial *need* of self-control, and I trust in time that he will have it ; but at his age the sun of true reason has but sent up its rays above the horizon ; its orb is not yet visible. If we are fearfully and wonderfully made in body, how much more so in mind, and how much less can we fathom the constitution of the latter than of the former ! But considered in a *large sense*, they are *one ;* else how could the mind act on the body, the body on the mind ? Where the senses are active and rapid ministers to the mind, supplying it abundantly and promptly with thought materials, no wonder that the intellect makes speedy advances ; and such sensitiveness is doubtless one constituent of a poet. Still, whether or no true greatness and high genius shall be discovered must depend upon the constitution and properties of the intellect in itself ; and this is the reason that so many fine buds prove but indifferent flowers, rather than the popular account of the matter, that the sooner the plant blossoms, the sooner it will fade and fall. Now tell me that Milton and Shakespeare were not as wonderful children as the young Rosciuses, or any other modern prodigy, and hollow puff-ball ! How exquisitely does Plato illustrate his subject out of his own actual history, out of things moving, sensuous, and present, filling with life-blood the dry though clear and symmetrical vein-work of his metaphysic anatomy!

IX.

Treasures of English Literature.—Arnold's "Rome."

To the Same:

October 6, 1838.—I see you have Locke's works in folio, and a good Addison. How the possession of these works makes us feel the littleness of our reading—of what we can really mark, learn, and digest. "Amid a thousand tables we stand," and though we do not "want food," having access to those tables, yet how sparingly can we partake! Even as it is, what a strange, superficial thing is the ordinary way of reading a book, even when we fancy ourselves reading with attention. I more and more grudge to bestow time on the literature of the day, and the book club will not gain much of my devotion. Arnold's "Rome" is no mere ephemeral: that book seems destined to fill a permanent place, both as embodying Niebuhr, and from its own merits, as an able, animated history and historical commentary. I do not judge of it as to arrangement of parts, nor praise it as to the minute details of style; but the style, considered in a large view, is its great charm, and it is certainly a characteristic and vigorous work. The account of Dionysius the Tyrant, and remarks on his character, and that of the Greek tyrannies, are especially striking.

X.

The Homeric Ithaca.—Autobiographical Air of the "Odyssey."

To the Same:

October 2, 1838.—What an enigma the Homeric Ithaca is! It seems quite out of the question that it should be Thiaki. And why should it send only twelve suitors if it were the huge island Cephalonia? The vivid naturalness of the "Odyssey" seems to have inspired the notion of its being an autobiography into the minds of critics who differ in various particulars. No doubt it was so in the same way that the "History of the Plague" and other such fictions were true history. It brought together sundry incidents and places with which the writer or writers were perfectly familiar from some means or other. There is a very natural passage of this kind in "Don Juan," taken from some personal narrative, and merely versified. It seems as if some critics wrote by *feel*. Le Chevalier had a true *sense* of a certain characteristic of the "Odyssey," but how absurdly, as it appears to me, has he enunciated and reasoned upon it! Bryant's anti-Asiatic theory seems to run in the face of the poem. Surely he must have looked at some place in Egypt, and remembered detached passages in the "Iliad," without considering the general aspect of the whole.

XI.

Description of the Falls of Niagara in Miss Martineau's "Retrospect of Western Travel."

To Miss E. TREVENEN, Helstone :

October, 1838. — Miss Martineau's "Retrospect of Western Travel" I have read and enjoyed. It takes you through out-door scenes, and, though the politics are overpowering now and then, it freshens you up by wanderings amid woods and rivers, and over mountain brows, and among tumbling waterfalls. I think Miss Martineau made one more at home with Niagara than any other of the American travelers. She gives one a most lively *waterfallish* feeling, introduces one not only to the huge mass of rushing water, but to the details of the environs, the wood in which the stream runs away, etc. She takes you over it and under it, before it and behind it, and seems as if she were performing a duty she owed to the genius of the cataract, by making it thoroughly well known to those at a distance, rather than desirous to display her own talent by writing a well-rounded period or a terse paragraph about it.

XII.

Lukewarm Christians.

To the Same :

Chester Place, December, 1838.—I have no doubt that ———— disapproves of the Catholic party just as much as of the Evangelicals, and on very similar grounds. It is not the peculiar doctrines which offend thinkers of this description. About them they neither know nor care. It is the *high tone*, the insisting upon *principles*, to ascertain the truth or unsoundness of which requires more thought than they are disposed to bestow on such a subject. It is the zeal and warmth and eagerness by which tempers of this turn are offended. The blunders and weaknesses of warm religionists are not the *sources* of their distaste, but the *pretexts* by which they justify to themselves an aversion which has a very different origin. Be kind to the poor, nurse the sick, perform all duties of charity and generosity, be not religious overmuch—above all, keep in the background all the peculiar cardinal doctrines of Christianity—avoid all vices and gross sins—believe the Bible to be true, without troubling yourself about particulars—behave as resignedly as you can when misfortunes happen—feel grateful to God for his benefits —think at times of your latter end, and try "to dread your grave as little as your bed," if possible. Such will ever be— more or less pronounced and professed—the sum of religion in many very amiable and popular persons. Any thing more than this they will throw cold water upon by bucketfuls.

CHAPTER VIII.

1839.

LETTERS TO HER HUSBAND, MRS. PLUMMER, MISS A. BROOKE,
MISS TREVENEN.

I.

Characteristics of the Oxford School of Divines.--Combinations, even for
the Best Purposes, not Favorable to Truth.—Superior Confidence inspired by an Independent Thinker.—Are Presbyterians Excluded from
the Visible Church ?—Authority of Hooker cited against such a Decision. —Defense of the Title of Protestant. —Luther : Injustice commonly done to his Character and Work.

To Mrs. PLUMMER, Heworth Vicarage, Gateshead :

10 *Chester Place, Regent's Park, January* 17, 1839. — The
"Letter of a Reformed Catholic,"* and that on the "Origin of
Popery," I think remarkably well done—clear, able, and popular.   Such judgment as I have on such a matter I give unto
you, and this need not imply any presumption on my part.   But
though I can sincerely express my approbation of the way in
which these performances are *executed,* I must candidly confess
that I do not follow your husband on the Oxford road so far
as he seems to have proceeded.   On some subjects, specially
handled by Newman and his school, my judgment is suspended.   On some points I think the Apostolicals quite right, on
others clearly unscriptural and unreasonable, willfully and os-
tentatiously maintaining positions which, if carried out to their
full length, would overthrow the foundations of all religion.   I
consider the party as having done great service in the religious
world, and that in various ways; sometimes by bringing forward what is wholly and absolutely true; sometimes by promoting discussion on points in which I believe their own views
to be partly erroneous ; sometimes by exposing gross deficiencies in doctrine in the religion of the day; sometimes by keenly

---

* A Controversial Pamphlet, by the Rev. Matthew Plummer.—E. C.

detecting the self-flatteries and practical mistakes of religionists. But the worst of them, in my opinion, is that they are, one and all, *party men;* and just so far as we become absorbed in a party, just so far are we in danger of parting with honesty and good sense. This is why I honor Frederick Maurice, and feel *inclined* to put trust in his writings, antecedently to an express knowledge of their contents, because he stands alone, and looks only to God and his own conscience. Such is human nature, that as soon as ever men league together, even for the purest and most exalted objects, their carnal leaven begins to ferment. Insensibly their aims take a less spiritual character, and their means are proportionately vulgarized and debased. Now, when I speak of *leaguing together,* of course I do not mean that Mr. Newman and his brother divines exact pledges from one another like men on the hustings; but I do believe that there is a tacit but efficient general compact among them all. Like the Evangelicals, whom they so often condemn on this very point, they use a characteristic phraseology; they have their badges and party marks; they lay great stress on trifling external matters; they have a stock of arguments and topics in common. No sooner has Newman blown the Gospel blast, than it is repeated by Pusey, and Pusey is re-echoed from Leeds. Keble privately persuades Froude, Froude spouts the doctrines of Keble to Newman, and Newman publishes them as "Froude's Remains." Now it seems to me that under these circumstances truth has not quite a fair chance. A man has hardly time to *reflect on his own reflections,* and ask himself, in the stillness of his heart, whether the views he has put forth are strictly the truth, and nothing more or less than the truth ; if, the moment they have parted from him, they are eagerly embraced by a set of prepossessed partisans, who assure him and all the rest of the world that they are thoroughly excellent. (How many truly great men have modified their views after publication, and in subsequent works have written in a somewhat altered strain.)

These writers, too, hold the dangerous doctrine of the "economy of truth." Consistently with these views, if one of them wrote ever so extravagantly, the others would refrain from exposing him, for fear they should injure the cause, at least so long as he remained with them on principal points. God, of course, can bring good out of evil, and in this way I do believe that the errors of the party will serve His cause in the end as

well as their sound tenets.　Yet I can not think that what I
have described is the truest method of promoting pure religion;
and it seems to me that the most effective workmen in the
Lord's vineyard, those whose work tells most *in the end*, are they
who do not agree beforehand to co-operate, but who pursue
their own task without regard to the way in which others execute theirs.

*　　*　　*　　*　　*　　*　　*　　*

Well, I have looked at the "Reformed Catholic" again, and
think it is as well done as I did at first; but still there are
some points on which I am not quite of the writer's mind.

I can not yet bring myself to believe that the Kirk of Scotland in no sense belongs to the Body of Christ—in no sense
makes a part of the visible Christian Church.　Would Hooker
have said so?*　One Lord, one faith, one baptism : these are
the only essentials, I think, which he names.　A man may even
be a heretic, yet not altogether—nay, not at all—excluded from
this communion, though he can never belong to the mystical
invisible Church of the elect till he becomes a Christian in
heart and mind, as well as in outward profession.　The Kirk
may have deprived herself of a privilege by losing the episcopal
succession, may have thrown away a benefit by rejecting the
government of bishops (if we only put the matter in the outward
light), yet she may still make an erring part of that Church to
which Christ's Spirit is promised.

This, however, is a difficult subject.　I do not pretend to
have very decided convictions upon it.　Of one thing, however,
I feel pretty sure, that I shall call myself a *Protestant* to the end
of my days.　Yes! a Catholic Christian, as I humbly hope—
and, *moreover*, a Protestant of the Church of England.　I pro-
fess that "Reformed Protestant Religion" which our monarch
swears to defend on his coronation; the Protestantism of Cran-
mer and Hooker, of Taylor, of Jackson, and of Leighton.
These are great names, and dear and venerable are the associations with the title of Protestant in my mind.　To call myself such does not make me a whit the less Christian and

---

* But we speak now of the visible Church, whose children are signed
with this mark, "One Lord, one faith, one baptism."　In whomsoever these
things are, the Church doth acknowledge them for her children; them only
she holdeth for aliens and strangers in whom these things are not found.—
Hooker, "Eccl. Pol. Book," book iii., ch. i.—E. C.

Catholic, nor imply that I am so; it does not mix me up with sectarians any more than the latter term connects me with the gross errors and grievous practices of Romanists, who, whether they are entitled to the name or not, will always assume it. As for its being a *modern* designation—that which rendered a distinctive appellation necessary is an event of modern times; and that, I think, is a sufficient defense of it on this score. "Reformed Catholic" savors altogether of Newman and the nineteenth century.

In regard to Luther, I do not jumble him up with our reformers as to the whole of his theology—on some points he was less orthodox than they. But I can not think it altogether just to say that he "left, rather than reformed the Church." It is the Oxford fashion to dwell upon what he omitted, to throw into shade the mighty works which he did; to hold him forth as a corrupter, to forget that he was a great and wonderful reformer. If there were "giants in those days," the mightiest of them all was the invincible German. And how any man who thinks deeply on religious subjects can bring himself to speak scorn of this brave Christian warrior, or how he can divest his spirit of gratitude toward so great a benefactor, to whose magnanimity, more than to any other single instrument in God's hand, it is owing that we are not blind buyers of indulgences at this hour, I confess is past my comprehension.

> "In our halls is hung
> Armory of the invincible Knights of old."

Blighting breaths may tarnish the lustre of those trophies for a passing moment; but it is too late in the day to teach us that Milton is *not a poet*, and that Luther and Wycliffe and Ridley and Latimer were not worthy champions of the faith.

II.

A Little Lecturer.—Stammering a Nervous Affection, dependent on the Imagination.

To her Husband:

Chester Place, September 4, 1839.—Herby preached last night about chemical matters like a regular lecturer; I thought he looked quite a little Correggiesque Mercury—or something between Hermes and Cupid—as he stood on the little chair *lectur-*

ing volubly, and throwing out one leg and arm, with his round face glowing with childish animation, and a mixture of intelligence and puerility. The conclusion was, after a list of names a league long, "and the last is something like so and so; but the chemist's man had a pen in his mouth when he answered my question about it, and I could not hear distinctly how he pronounced the name." It is wonderful how clearly he speaks when there is an impulse from within which overbears and makes him forget the difficulty of articulation.* For it certainly is the pre-imagination of the difficulty of pronouncing a word that ties the tongue in those who stammer. F. M. could pronounce a studied oration without stuttering. I account for the fact in this way: it was the hurry of mind, excited by the anticipation of an *indefinite* field of words to be uttered, which paralyzed his articulating powers. With a paper before him, or a set speech on the tablet of his memory, he said to himself: thus much have I to pronounce and no more; whereas in extemporary speech there is an uncertainty, an unlimitedness, the sense of which leads most talkers to inject a *plus quam sufficit* of *you knows* into their discourse, and which causes others to hesitate. The imagination is certainly the seat of the affection, or rather the source of it. The disorder may be defined as a specific weakness of the nerves in connection with a particular imagination, or it may arise and be generated during the inexplicable reciprocal action, *wechsel-wirkung*, of one upon the other, in which, as S. T. C. says, the cause is at the same time the effect, and *vice versa*. The curious thing is that there is an idiosyncrasy in this, as perhaps to some degree in all other complaints, and every different stammerer stammers in his own way, and under different circumstances.

III.

Philosophy of the "Excursion."

To the Same:

Chester Place, September 17, 1839.—I am deep in the "Excursion," and am interested at finding how much of Kant and

----

* The slight impediment in his speech, to which my brother was subject as a child, was never entirely outgrown, though it diminished considerably in after years.—E. C.

Coleridge is embodied in its philosophy, especially in " Despondency Corrected." I should not say that the " Excursion " was as intensely poetical, as pure poetry, as ecstatic, as many of the minor pieces ; it holds more of a middle place between poetry, philosophy, and the thoughtful, sentimental story. But it is exquisite, be it what it may.

IV.

Lord Byron on the Lake Poets.

To the Same :

Chester Place, October 4, 1839.—" The Lake Poets are never vulgar." I often think of this remark of Lord Byron. Genius is an antiseptic against vulgarity ; but still no men that I ever met, except downright patricians, were so absolutely unvulgar as Coleridge, Southey, and Wordsworth.

V.

Writing to Order.—Sunday Stories and Spanish Romances.

To Miss E. TREVENEN, Helstone :

Chester Place, 1839.—Miss ———'s stories are, as you observe, " remarkably fit for their purpose." How she can contrive to write so exactly as a story composer for a Society ought to write ; how she can manage to be so wholly and solely under the dictation of the *proper sort* of spirit, I can not imagine. I, for my part, am neither *goody* enough nor good enough (and I humbly admit that to submit on proper occasions to *goodiness* of a certain kind is a part of goodness) for any thing of the sort. I should feel like a dog hunting in a clog, or a cat in gloves, or a gentleman's carriage forced to go upon a railroad ; or, to ascend a little higher, as Christian and his fellow-pilgrim did when they left the narrow path and got into the fields by the side of it. I should always be grudging at the Society's quickset hedge on the right hand and the left. As for Herbert, he is deep in " Amadis de Gaul ;" and the boy that is full of the Endriago and Andandana, and Don Galaor, and the Flower of Chivalry himself, and his peerless Oriana, is not quite in the right mood to relish good charity school-girls, and the conversion of cottagers that don't go to church, which Nurse, however, thinks worth all the Endriagos in the world.

VI.

Pain more Bearable when its Cause is Known.—Books and Letters *Composed* but never Written.—Musings on Eternity.—"We know not yet what we shall be."—Descriptions of Heaven: Symbolical, Material, and Spiritual.—Conjectures of Various Writers respecting the Condition of Departed Souls.

To Miss ARABELLA BROOKE, Gamstone Rectory, East Retford:

Chester Place, 1839.—It is painful to be unable to understand one's suffering, to translate it into an intelligible language, and bring it distinctly before the mind's eye. But it is already a sign that we are no longer wholly subdued by its power when we can analyze it, and make this very indefiniteness an object of contemplation. This evinces a degree of mastery over that which has of late been a tyrant. And if "to be weak is miserable" (oh, how often have I thanked Milton for that line !), to exercise any kind of power, or have any kind of strength, is so far an abatement of misery. To be sure, the explanation which my father gives of this mental fact, the uneasiness felt at the *unintelligibility* of an affection, when we can not tell whence it arises nor whither it tends, is not a little abstruse, and what is popularly called transcendental. "There is always a consolatory feeling that accompanies the sense of a proportion between antecedents and consequents. It is eternity revealing itself in the form of time."

Dear Miss Brooke, there are not many persons to whom I should quote a metaphysical passage of S. T. C. in a letter ; but I see you are one who like to be what the world calls idle— that is, outwardly still from the inward activity of thought—to pause and look down into the deep stream, instead of hastening on in view of the shallow, sparkling runnel. Dear me ! some people *think* more over the first page of an essay than others do while they write a volume. Thinking too much, and trying to dive deeper and deeper into every subject that presents itself, is rather an obstacle to much writing. It drags the wheels of composition ; for before a book can be written, there is a great deal to be *done:* contemplation is not the whole business. I am convinced that the Cherubim do not write books, much less publish them, or make bargains with booksellers, or submit to the ordeal of disgusting puffery and silly censure. I am convinced they do nothing but think; while the Seraphim are equally given up to the business of loving.

But I must consider the limits of this letter, and the observations which it ought to contain, and my letter-writing strength, which is at present but small. I am truly grieved that I can not give a proper answer to your last, or its interesting predecessor, which came with "Abercrombie's Essay." If I could but put on paper, without too much bodily fatigue, half the thoughts which your reflective epistles suggested to me, little as they might be worth your reading, you would see that your letters had done their work, and were not like winds passing across the Vale of Stones, but like those gales which put a whole forest in motion. That reminds me of another advantage enjoyed by the Cherubim and Seraphim. I am sure they do not write letters with pen, ink, or paper, nor put them into the post, nor stop to consider whether they are worth postage, nor look about for franks and private conveyances. They have a quintessence of our earthly enjoyments and privileges; the husk for them drops off, and all is pure spirit and intelligence.

All this nonsense is excusable in me, because I am poorly, out of humor with those activities in which I can not share, and quite cross and splenetic because I am not as free from fleshly ills and earthly fetters as the angels in heaven. *Apropos* to which, I have not read Mr. Taylor's book, and from your account of it am afraid I should not be such a reader as he would wish to have, unless, indeed, he confines himself to the statement of a few principles which may guide our views respecting the life to come, instead of attempting to describe it particularly, like Dr. Watts and others. It seems to me so obvious, both from the reason of the thing and the manner in which Scripture deals with it, that "if one came from the dead" to tell us all about it, he would leave us as wise as he found us. In what language could he express himself? In a language of symbols? But that we have already in the Bible; and we want to translate it literally, or at least into literal expressions. We know that they who have pleased God shall be eternally blessed; that they who have sinned against the light will suffer from a worm that never dies; and what more can we know while we are roofed over by our house of clay? A true account of the other world would surely be to the inhabitants of earth as a theory of music to the deaf, or the geometry of light to the blind.

Inquirers into the future state are all either Irvingites or Swedenborgians, horrified as most of them might be to be compared either with Irving or Swedenborg. They either give us earth newly done up and furnished by way of our final inheritance, observing that man is essentially finite, and must therefore have a material dwelling-place; or they talk of a *spiritual* heaven, while the description they give of it is only a refined edition of the things and goings-on of this world. What else *can* it be? All conjecturers may not talk of "wax-candles in heaven," but the spirit which dictated the thought is in every one of them.

I think I shall never read another sermon on the Intermediate State. Newman has no Catholic consent to show for his views on that subject, though doubtless they come in great measure from the Fathers. The supposition that blessedness and misery hereafter may both arise from increased powers, reminds me of an oft-quoted passage in a work of S. T. C., in which he conjectures that an infinite memory may be the Book of Judgment in which all our past life is written, and every idle word recorded in characters from which our eyes can never be averted. It was a fine thought in Swedenborg to represent the unblest spirits in the other world as *mad*. His visions are founded on many deep truths of religion. Had he given them as an allegorical fiction like the "Pilgrim's Progress," it would have been well.

CHAPTER IX.

1840.

LETTERS TO HER HUSBAND, HER ELDEST BROTHER, MRS. J. STAN-
GER, MRS. H. M. JONES.

I.

Love of Books a Source of Happiness, and likely to be Increased by Classical Studies.

To her Eldest Brother:

January, 1840.—I have a strong opinion that a *genuine* love
of books is one of the greatest blessings of life for man or woman, and I can not help thinking that by persons in our middle
station it may be enjoyed (more at one time, less at another,
but certainly during the course of life to a great extent enjoyed)
without neglect of any duty. A woman *may* house-keep, if she
chooses, from morning to night, or she may be constantly at
her needle, or she may be always either receiving or preparing
for company, but whatever those who practice these things may
say, it is not necessary in most cases for a woman to spend her
whole time in this manner. Now I can not but think that the
knowledge of the ancient languages very greatly enhances the
pleasure taken in literature—that it gives depth and variety to
reading, and makes almost every book, in whatever language,
more thoroughly understood. I observe that music and drawing are seldom pursued after marriage. In many cases of weak
health they can not be pursued, and they do not tell in the intercourse of society and in conversation as this sort of information does, even when not a word of Greek or Latin is either uttered or alluded to.

II.

Lord Byron's "Mazeppa" and "Manfred."—His Success in Satire and in
Sensational Writing.

To Mrs. H. M. JONES:

January 14, 1840.—I have had great pleasure in refreshing
my girlish recollections of the "Lament of Tasso" and "Ma-

zeppa." The latter is the only poem of Byron's which reminds me of Scott. I think it most spirited and impressive in its line. Byron is excellent in painting intense emotion and strong sensation of body or mind ; he is also good in satire and sarcasm, though not very amiable ; but I do not like him when he attempts the philosophic, invading the province of Goethe and Wordsworth, or when he tries his hand at the wild and supernatural, in which line I think him a mere imitator, and far outdone by Scott, Shelley, and many others. "Manfred," I think, has been greatly overrated, as, indeed, the public seems now beginning to see—the poetical public at least. Still there are fine things in it ; but the graphic descriptions in the journal are better, I think, than the corresponding passages in verse.

III.

Practical View of the Duties of God-parents.—Sponsorship Nowadays chiefly a Social Obligation.

To the Same :

1840.—Though writing even the shortest note exhausts and pains me in my present very weak and irritable state, yet I can not feel satisfied, dear friend, without expressing to you with my own hand how much I am pleased by your kind acceptance of the office which Henry and I both wish to put upon you, and the very kind words which you made use of on the occasion. In regard to *responsibility*, if I had thought that it involved any, I should have scrupled to attempt imposing such a burden on you, as, indeed, I should have scrupled, in regard to myself, to take upon me the name of godmother to six different children, as I unhesitatingly have done ; for whatever the theory of sponsorship may be (and I never yet met one who seemed to me to have a very intelligible and satisfactory theory on the subject, when one comes to examine the words which are usually uttered in this matter by rote), yet the fact is, and, as the world is regulated at present, must be, that the religious education of children rests almost wholly and solely with those who have the bringing of them up in other respects, together with the spiritual pastors and masters whom the Church appoints. "The duties of a sponsor," says a correspondent of mine, "are not very well defined ;" but those which I look for from you for my now expected little one, are clearly defined in my own mind, and are such as I am bold enough to reckon upon from your kindness. The truth is, you have ever shown such a special friendship toward me and mine, something so much more than mere lip-civility, or even slight though genuine good-will, such as the majority of our pleasant friends and acquaintances afford us, that I flatter myself you will view a child of mine with a certain degree of favor and partiality for my sake (indeed, I perhaps may add for its father's and grandmother's sakes), and the value of a *real* partiality from a person of worth, in this world of professions, of much speaking and less feeling, I am deeply sensible of. *This* kindness and interest of feeling is what I would fain secure from you, not merely a little nominal formal religious examination, which, as matters now stand in the world, is all in that way that sponsors ever do or can perform for their font-children. This interest I really believe you do feel for my H. and E. (it has ever been a pleasure to me to think so), and for their future brother or sister, if the dear hope is ever to be realized, I flatter myself you would feel, whether you were called the little Coleridge's godmamma, or simply its mother's friend. Only it is pleasant to link a *name* which implies kindliness and interest with the thing itself, though perhaps the latter would exist in almost equal degree independently of the former.

IV.

On the Death of an Infant Daughter.

To Mrs. JOSHUA STANGER, Wandsworth :

10 *Chester Place, Regent's Park, August* 10, 1840.—My dear friend, your last kind note was written in a strain which harmonized well with my feelings. Would that those feelings which a trial such as we have lately sustained must needs bring with it, to all who have learned, in any degree however insufficient, to trust in Heaven, whether for temporary consolation or for eternal happiness—would that those feelings could be more lasting than they are ; that they could leave strong and permanent traces ; that they could become " the *very habit* of our souls," not a mere mood or passing state without any settled foundation. My thoughts had turned the same way as yours, where all mourners and friends of those that mourn will natu-

rally go for sure and certain hope and ground of rejoicing, to that most divine chapter of the raising of Lazarus. "Thy brother shall rise again." This indeed is spoken plainly; this is "no parable," no metaphor or figure of speech. But in the next chapter we see the same blessed promise illustrated by a very plain metaphor. "Except a corn of wheat fall into the ground and *die*, it abideth alone; but if it die, it beareth much fruit."

Our loss, indeed, has been a great disappointment, and even a sorrow; for, strange as it may seem, these little speechless creatures, with their wandering, unspeaking eyes, do twine themselves around a parent's heart from the hour of their birth. Henry suffered more than I could have imagined, and I was sorry to see him watch the poor babe so closely, when it was plain that the little darling was not for this world, and that all our visions of a "dark-eyed Bertha," a third joy and comfort of the remainder of our own pilgrimage, must be exchanged for better hopes, and thoughts more entirely accordant with such a religious frame of mind as it is our best interest to attain. I had great pleasure in anticipating the added interest that you would take in her as your godchild. But this is among the dreams to be relinquished. Her remains rest at Hampstead, beside those of my little frail and delicate twins.—God bless you, my dear Mary, and your truly attached friend,

SARA COLERIDGE.

NOTE.—Bertha Fanny Coleridge was born on the 13th of July, 1840, and died eleven days afterward.—E. C.

V.

"They sin who tell us Love can die."

To her Husband:

The Green, Hampstead, September 13, 1840. — Will death at one blow crush into endless ruin all our mental growths as an autumnal tempest prostrates the frail summer-house, along with its whole complexity of interwoven boughs and tendrils, which had gradually grown up during a long season of quiet and serenity? Surely there will be a second spring when these firm and profuse growths shall flourish again, but with Elysian verdure, and all around them the celestial mead shall bloom with plants of various sizes, down to the tenderest and smallest shrublet that ever pushed up its infant leaves in this earthly soil. Surely every one who has a heart must feel how easily he could part with earth, water, and skies, and all the outward glories of nature; but how utterly impossible it is to reconcile the mind to the prospect of the extinction of our earthly affections, that such a heart-annihilation has all the gloom of an eternal ceasing to be.

VI.

A Sunset Landscape.

To the Same:

October 14, 1840.—I was thinking lately of my days spent in the prime of childhood at Greta Hall. How differently all things then looked from what they now do! This world more substantial, more bright, and clothed in seemingly *fast colors;* and yet, though these colors have waxed cold and watery, and have a flitting, evanescent hue upon them, to change my present mind-scene for that one, rich as it was, would be a sinking into a lower stage of existence; for now, while that which was so bright is dimmer, wholly new features have come forth in the landscape, features that connect this earth "with the quiet of the sky," and are invested in a solid splendor which more evidently joins in with the glories of the heavens. The softened and subdued appearance of earth, with its pensive evening sadness, harmonizes well with the richer part of the prospect, and, though in itself less joyous and radiant than it once was, now forms a fitting and lovely portion of the whole view, and throws the rest into relief as it steals more and more into shadow.

VII.

The True Art of Life.

To the Same:

10 *Chester Place, October* 20, 1840.—We ought, indeed, my beloved husband, to be conscious of our blessings, for we are better off than all below us, perhaps than almost all above us. The great art in life, especially for persons of our age, who are leaving the vale of youth behind us, just lingering still perhaps in

the latter stage of it, and seeing the bright golden fields at the entrance of it more distinctly than those nearer to our present station, is to cultivate the love of doing good and promoting the interests of others, avoiding at the same time the error of those who make a worldly business and a matter of pride of pursuits which originated in pure intentions, and bustle away in this secular religious path, with as little real thought of the high prize at which they should aim, and as little growth in heavenliness and change from glory to glory, as if they served mammon more directly. Any thing rather than undergo the mental labor of real self-examination, of the study, not of individual self, but of the characters of our higher being which we share with all men. For one man that *thinks*, with a view to practical excellence, we may find fifty who are ready to *act* on what they call their own thoughts, but which they have unconsciously received from others.

CHAPTER X.

1841, 1842.

LETTERS TO HER HUSBAND, MRS. PLUMMER, MRS. THOMAS FARRER,
MISS TREVENEN, MRS. H. M. JONES, THE REV. HENRY
MOORE, THE HON. MR. JUSTICE COLERIDGE.

I.

Necessity of Patience and Hope in Education.

To Mrs. PLUMMER:

April, 1841.—Patience is the most important of all qualifications for a teacher ; and the longer one has to do with managing young persons, or, indeed, persons of any sort or kind, the more one feels its value and indispensability. It is that resource which we constantly have to fall back upon when all else seems to fail, and our various devices and ways and means and ingenuities give way one after another, and seem almost good for nothing but to preach about. By patience I do not mean that worthless substitute for it which hirelings (in *temper*, for a paid governess is often a much better instructor than a mamma) sometimes make use of, a compound of oil and white-lead, as like putty as possible. With patience, hope too must keep company, and the most effective of teachers are those who possess most of the arts of encouraging and inspiriting—spurring onward and sustaining at the same time—both lightening the load as much as may be, and stimulating the youngsters to trot on with it gallantly.

II.

The Lake Poets on Sport.—The Life of Wesley a Wonderful Book.

To her Husband:

Chester Place, October 13, 1841.—Southey and Wordsworth loved scenery, and took an interest in animals of all sorts ; but not one could they have borne to kill; and S. T. C. was much of the same mind, though *he* would have made more allowance for the spirit of the chase than the other two. W——'s " Hart-leap Well" displays feelings of high refinement. Doubtless there is a sort of barbarism in this love of massacre which still keeps a corner even in cultivated minds, but which the progress of cultivation must *tend* to dissipate, and perhaps with it some habits that for some persons are more good than evil. Not-withstanding "Hartleap Well," Wordsworth always defended angling, and so did Dora; but the Southeys, from the great-est to the least, gave no quarter to any slaughterous amuse-ment. * * *

What a biography the life of Wesley is! What wonders of the human mind does it reveal, more especially in the mental histories of Wesley's friends and coadjutors!

III.

Coolness of Unimaginative People.—Imagination, like Religion, "requires looking after."

To the Same:

October 18, 1841.—There is a great coolness about the *minds* of the C——'s, though they have a *quantum suff.* of heart about them. The reason of this calmness of theirs is, that, though persons of good sense, they have no vividness or activity of imagination; things are not multiplied, heightened, and deep-ened to them by this mirror in the back part of the mind. "A great deal of religion," said old Fisher, of Borodale, "requires a great deal of looking after." There is so much acuteness and keen truth in this observation that I do not believe it original, but a popular saying. So we may say of imagination—the more a man has, the more sense and firmness he needs to keep it in order. An excitable imagination, united with a weak intellect and a want of force of character, is a plague both to the pos-sessor and his friends.

IV.

Inflexibility of the French Language.—The Second Part of "Faust:" its Beauties and Defects.—Visionary Hopes.

To the Same :

Chester Place, October 19, 1841.—I feel more than ever the inflexibility and fixedness of the French language, which will not *give* like English and German. It has few words for sounds— such as clattering, clanking, hanging, etc.—whereas the Germans are still richer than we in such. Derwent wanted, when here, to point out to me some of the beauties of the fifth act of the second part of " Faust," which, in point of vocabulary, and metrical variety and power, is, I do suppose, a most wonderful phenomenon. Goethe, with the German language, is like a first-rate musician with a musical instrument, which, under his hand, reveals a treasure of sound such as an ordinary person might play forever without discovering. D—— has a most keen sense of this sort of power and merit in a poet, and his remarks were interesting, and would have been more so if the book had been at hand. He gives up the general *intention* of the piece, which he considers a failure—the philosophy confused, unsound, and not truly profound. The execution of parts he thinks marvelous ; and as the pouring forth of an old man of eighty-four, a psychological curiosity. * * *

Your delightful letter and the after-written note both arrived at once. Your account of yourself is not worse, and that is the best that can be said of it. The lane is long, indeed ; we could little have thought of all its turnings and windings when we first entered it ; but I still trust that it will issue out into Beautiful Meadows at last.

V.

Reminiscences of a Tour in Belgium.—Hemling's "Marriage of St. Catharine" at Bruges, and Van Eyck's "Adoration of the Lamb" at Ghent. —Devotional Gravity of the Early Flemish Painters, and Human Pathos of Rubens.—Works of that Master at Antwerp and Mechlin.

To Miss E. TREVENEN, Helstone :

Chester Place, October 27, 1841.—Ostend is interesting merely from old recollections, especially military ones, and because it is foreign ; not so Bruges, which I think the most perfect jewel of a town I ever saw, and how completely is the spirit of the place transfused into my Uncle Southey's interesting poem—"The Pilgrimage to Waterloo." Here we visited the Hospital of St. John, saw the sisters tending the sick, and studied the beautiful and curious works of Hemling in the adjoining parlor. Do you remember the "Marriage of St. Catharine," with its beautiful background of vivid light green, and that exquisitely delicate and youthful neck of the bride Saint, shaded with such transparent gauze. Mr. Milnes (whom we met at Ghent on our return) specially admired Herodias's Daughter in the shutter of this picture. He said she looked at the bloody head in the charger so expressively, just as if she could not turn her fascinated eyes from it, and yet shuddered at it. The cathedral is large and impressive, and contains a noble statue of Moses—more like a Jupiter Tonans, however, than the Hebrew Legislator. At Ghent I visited St. Bavon's: what a superb cathedral it is, with its numerous chapels clustered round the nave! I do indeed remember that paradisiacal picture of the "Adoration of the Lamb," with its velvety green lawn and hillocks, and luxuriant rose-bushes. It is said that these old masters first opened the way to the Italian school of landscape-painting by the backgrounds of their pictures. There is a very peculiar air about them, an imaginativeness combined with life-like every-day reality, and a minuteness of detail which interferes with any thing like *intense* passion, but not with a sober, musing sort of emotion. A deeply religious character is impressed upon these pictures, and there is a mild and chastened wildness about them (if the seeming contradiction may be ventured on) which is very interesting, and specially suits some moods of the devotional mind. I think it is well, however, that the traveler for the most part sees these old paintings before he is introduced to those of Rubens; the fire, life, movement, and *abandon* of his pictures quite unfit one, for a time, for the sedater excellences of Hemling and Van Eyck. The "Descent from the Cross" is, perhaps, the finest and most *beautiful* of all that great master's performances; but no picture that I have ever seen (except in another line, the Sebastiano in our National Gallery) ever affected me so strongly as Rubens's "Christ Crucified betwixt the Thieves," in the Antwerp Museum. That is really a *tremendous* picture; in the expression of vehement emotion, in passion, life, and movement, I think it exceeds any other piece I ever beheld. How tame and over-fine Van Dyck shows beside Rubens! I can not greatly admire him as an historical painter, especially on sacred subjects. He should always have been employed on delicate fine gentlemen and ladies, and folks about court. Some of his Marys and Magdalens are most graceful and elegant creatures; but Rubens's youthful Magdalen at the foot of the Cross, imploring the soldier not to pierce the Saviour's side, moves one a thousand times more than all his lady-like beauties. However, I do not maintain, deep as is my admiration of Rubens, that his pictures thoroughly satisfy a religious mood of mind. They are somewhat over-bold; they almost unhallow the subject by bringing it so home, and exciting such strong earthly passion in connection with it. No sacred picture ever thoroughly satisfied me except the "Raising of Lazarus," by Sebastian del Piombo and Michael Angelo. The pictures at the Antwerp Museum, I believe, you did not see; but were you not charmed with those at Mechlin? What a delicately brilliant piece is the "Adoration of the Magi," at St. John's Church, with its beautiful shutters especially! and "St. John at Patmos," with that noblest of eagles over his head. Rubens ranked this among his finest productions. "The Miraculous Draught," too, in the Church of Notre Dame, painted for the Fisherman's Company, how splendid it is! And that *volet à droite*, "Tobias and the Angel," is the loveliest of all Rubens's shutter-pictures. What "colors of the showery arch" are there! What delicate aerial lilacs and yellows, softening off the scarlet and crimson glow of the centre-piece!

VI.

Prayer for the Dead.

To Mrs. J. STANGER:

Chester Place, January 12, 1842.—Some long to pray for their departed friends. How far better is it to feel that they need not our prayers; that we had best pray for ourselves and our surviving dear ones, that we may be where we humbly trust they are!

VII.

A Visit to Oxford.

To Mrs. THOMAS FARRER, 3 Gloucester Terrace, Regent's Park :

Chester Place, Easter, 1842.—Yesterday Mr. Coleridge and I returned from a very interesting excursion to Oxford. When I was in the midst of those venerable structures, I longed for strength to enter every chapel and explore the whole assemblage of antique buildings thoroughly. As it is, I have filled up the indistinct outline of imagined but unseen Oxford most richly. Magdalen Chapel, as a single object, is what pleased me the most; but the merit of Oxford, and its power over the feelings, lies in what it presents to the visitor collectively, the vast number of antique buildings which it presents to the eye, and of interesting associations which it brings into the mind.

VIII.

Illness of her Husband, and Death of his only Sister.

To Mrs. PLUMMER :

10 *Chester Place, December* 7, 1842.—My dearest Louisa, little did I think when I received your last but one letter that I should be thus long ere I communicated with the writer, and little did I think (and this was in mercy) what trials were to come upon me before I renewed my intercourse with you. I well remember beginning a letter to you soon after I received yours—explaining some of my theological views about Romish saints, or something of the sort—(you may remember our old theological discussions). Something prevented me from finishing it and sending it off; week after week went on, and the begun letter remained a beginning. Then commenced a new era with me of sorrow, and I humbly trust of purification. When these troubles began, I became reserved in writing to my friends, not from closeness of heart, but because I could not afford to expend my mental strength and spirits in giving accounts to them of my anxieties and troubles ; it was a prime necessity to keep all my stock within me. It is a bad plan, however, to put off writing to a friend from month to month, till we feel that only a very long and excellent letter can be fit to make up for such

a silence. You must excuse a very poor one from me now, dear friend, not proportioned, I assure you, to my interest in you, and wish that you should continue to feel an interest in me and mine. But to my present epistolary powers. I heard with great pleasure from dear E—— that you had been thinking much of my husband's prostration, and with friendly sympathy; on the whole, he has throughout this trying dispensation been wonderfully supported in mind. He has ever been as hopeful as any one under the circumstances could be, and he is quiet and resigned, and derives great comfort from devotional reading, from prayer, and religious ministrations. Our eldest brother has been a great soother and supporter to him during the most alarming and suffering part of his illness. J.'s company and conversation have been a constant blessing, and, indeed, all his family have shown him the tenderest affection during his illness. The bonds that unite us have been drawn closer by this trial of ours than ever before. Alas! one of our circle, who has for years been the centre of it, to which all our hearts were most strongly drawn, is removed. Oh, L——! hers was the death-bed of a Christian indeed. No one could die as she did who had not made long and ample preparation beforehand. She foresaw the present termination of her illness, when the rest of us were flattering ourselves with vain hopes that she would live down her wasting malady and see a green old age. Keenly sensible as she was of the blessing of her lot in this world, and no one could *enjoy* more than she did those temporal blessings—a good husband, honored among men, very promising, affectionate children, easy circumstances, and, if least, yet to her not little, a charming country residence in her beloved native county—she yet cast not one longing, lingering look behind when called to quit all and go to the Saviour. So strong was her wish to depart and *be with Christ*, that she even was not diverted from it by her tender love for her husband and children—which to me, who know her heart toward them, is really marvelous. Great must have been her faith to realize, as she did, the unseen world.* Her death-bed reminds me of the last days of one—a very dif-

---

* This lamented relative, both cousin and sister-in-law, between whom and my mother there always existed a most tender affection, was the daughter of James Coleridge, Esq., of Heath's Court, Ottery St. Mary, and wife of the Hon. Mr. Justice Patteson. She died in November, 1842, at Feniton Court, near Honiton.—E. C.

ferent person from her in many respects—my dear father. He had just the same strong, steadfast faith—the same longing to leave this world for a better, the same collectedness of mind during his last illness. *He* retained his intellectual powers to the last moment of his waking existence, but was in a coma for some hours before life was extinct. She was unconscious during the last two hours, and for some time previously it was only conjectured that she heard and joined in the prayers offered at her bedside.

IX.

On the same Topics.—Religious Bigotry.

To the Rev. HENRY MOORE,* Eccleshall Vicarage, Staffordshire:

10 *Chester Place, December,* 1842.—My dear Mr. Moore, I inclose to you my brother James's account of the last days and hours of our most beloved sister Fanny. Her call hence to what we can not doubt will be to her an unspeakably better world has left a blank in our circle which I can not describe. The event has long been anticipated. She herself has looked forward to it for some time; but there is a gulf between the real, actual things and these kinds of conjectural anticipations, the depth of which we find when all is over. She was a most impressive, influencive person. There was a strength of mind (not *intellect,* though she was clever) in her which would have approached to sternness but for her loving, tender disposition. She was the *deepest-hearted* creature! Henry has not been worsened in *body* by this affliction. Invalids often bear these shocks better than persons in health. * * *

We were amused by your account of the Puritanical Archdeacon. Religious bigotry is a dull fire—*hot* enough to roast an ox, but with no lambent, luminous flame shooting up from it. The bigots of one school condemn and, what is far worse, mutilate Shakespeare; those of another would, if they could, extinguish Milton. Thus the twin tops of our Parnassus would be hidden in clouds forever had these men their way.—Believe me, ever faithfully yours,   SARA COLERIDGE.

Henry desires his kindest regards to you, and wished this letter to be written.

---

* At present Archdeacon of Stafford.—E. C.

X.

"Hope Deferred."—Her Son at Eton.

To Mrs. HENRY M. JONES, Hampstead:

December, 1842.—I try to think of that better abode, in which we may meet each other free from those ills which flesh is heir to. *We* have a special need to look and long for the time when we may be clothed upon "with our house which is from heaven;" for in this tabernacle we do indeed groan, "being burdened." Bodily weakness and disorder have been the great (and only) drawbacks, ever since we met twenty years ago, to our happiness in each other. It will seem chimerical to you that I have not yet abandoned *all* hope. But this faint hope, which perhaps, however, is stronger than I imagine, does not render me unprepared for what all around me expect. The Lord has given; and when He takes away, I can resign him to his Father in heaven; and looking in that direction in which he will have gone, I shall be able to have that peace and comfort which in no shape then will the world be able to give me.

To-day I attended the Holy Communion. To be away so long from my beloved husband was a great trial to me (of course I did not attend the morning service); but I knew he greatly wished it, and I made an effort to satisfy him. It requires no great preparation for one who leaves the room of severe sickness, where all things point to a spiritual world—partly here around us, partly to come.

* * * * * * * *

You will be pleased, dear friend, to learn that Herbert has taken a good place in "trials" at Eton. Out of seventy boys, he had a 12th place assigned him in the 5th form—the highest but one, boys much older being down at 32, 39, and so forth.

XI.

Resignation.

To the Hon. Mr. Justice COLERIDGE,* 4 Montague Place, London:

January, 1843.—I now feel quite happy, or, at least, satisfied. Could I arrest his progress to a better sphere of existence by a

---

* My father's elder brother, now Right Honorable Sir John T. Coleridge, Member of the Privy Council.—E. C.

prayer, I would not utter it. When I once know that it *is* God's will, I can feel that it is right, even if there were no such definite assurances of rest and felicity beyond this world. I can not be too thankful to God, so far as my own best interests are concerned, that He is thus removing from earth to heaven my greatest treasure, while I have strength and probably time to benefit by the measure, and learn to look habitually above; which now will not be the spirit against the flesh, but both pulling one way, for the heart will follow the treasure. Thus graciously does the blessed Jesus condescend to our infirmities, by earthly things leading us to heavenly ones.

CHAPTER XI.

1843.

LETTERS TO HER SON, HER ELDEST BROTHER, MRS. GILLMAN, MRS. J. STANGER, HON. MR. JUSTICE COLERIDGE, REV. HENRY MOORE, EDWARD QUILLINAN, ESQ., MRS. THOMAS FARRER, MISS MORRIS, MRS. H. M. JONES.

I.•

To her Son :*

January 26, 1843. — My dear boy, my most beloved and honored husband, your excellent father, is no more in this world, but I humbly trust in a far better. May we all go where he is, prepared to meet him as he would have us! God bless you! Live as your beloved father would have you live! Put your trust in God, and think of heaven, as he would wish you.

May we all meet above! May we all join with him the Communion of Saints, and be forever with the blessed Jesus! Your good Uncle James was with me at the last.

I make an effort to write to you, my dear boy, from beside the remains of the dear, blessed, departed one. For you alone could I do this ; but it is due to his son, our child.—Your loving mother, SARA COLERIDGE.

II.

Her Husband's Death.—First Meeting with him at Highgate.

To Mrs. GILLMAN :

February, 1843. — My dearest Mrs. Gillman, you have ere now, I trust, received an announcement of my loss, of which I can not now speak. My sorrow is not greater than I can bear, for God has mercifully fitted it to my strength. While I was

---

* Written by my mother to my brother at Eton, on the day of my father's death.—E. C.

losing my great earthly happiness, I was gradually enabled to
see heaven more and more clearly, to be content to part with
earthly happiness, and to receive, as a more than substitute, a
stronger sense of that which is permanent.   I should have deferred writing thus to you, dear friend, till I was stronger ; but
I think it right to tell you that, at my strong desire, the remains
of my beloved husband are to be deposited in Highgate
church-yard, in the same precinct with those of my revered
father.

It was at Highgate, at your house, that I first saw my beloved
Henry.   Since then, now twenty years ago, no two beings could
be more intimately united in heart and thoughts than we have
been, or could have been more intermingled with each other in
daily and hourly life.   He concerned himself in all my feminine
domestic occupations, and admitted me into close intercourse
with him in all his higher spiritual and intellectual life.   It has
pleased God to dissolve this close tie, to cut it gradually and
painfully asunder, and yet, till the last fatal stroke, to draw it
even closer in some respects than before.—God bless you, my
dear friend.   I am ever your truly affectionate and respectful

SARA COLERIDGE.

III.

On the same Subject.—Trial of a Mourner's Faith, and How it was Met.

To the Rev. H. MOORE:

Chester Place, February 13, 1843. — My dear friend, letter-
writing is improper for me now, but I must pen two or three
lines to thank you for your last letter, and to tell you that I accept, from my heart, all your offers of friendship to me and
mine.   When I call your letter "most brotherly," with *such
brothers* as I have, it is the strongest epithet I can use.   You
loved, you still love and understand and value my departed
Henry ; this would forever make me a friend to you, even if
you had not expressed yourself so kindly, as you have ever
done, to me, and if we had not another thought or interest or
sympathy in common.

I must add but a line or two more, for I am suffering very
sadly from a nervous cough, which scarce leaves me a minute's
peace night or day, except for a few hours in the middle of the

twenty-four, when I am least weak. I caught a violent cold in attending on my husband on the Sunday and Wednesday nights of his final trial; but the weak and relaxed state into which I immediately sank as soon as the last call for exertion was over has more to do with my present suffering (the medical man thinks) than this exposure. Had I strength, I could tell you much that would interest you deeply of Henry's last days and months. His energy, while his poor, dear, outward man was half dead, was one of the most striking instances of the mind's independence of the body that can well be imagined. But oh! dear Mr. Moore, when I backward cast my eye, or rather when it reverts of itself, to the various scenes of his last illness, I feel that I have an ocean of natural tears yet to shed. At the time (except during the last fortnight) I but half felt the deep sadness, because I looked upon all his bitter sufferings as painful steps in the way to comparatively easy health, and felt as if every one of them was so much misery out of the way. Now that delirium, stupor, death are at the end of them, they have a different aspect. There is a comfort (I am speaking now of *mere* human feelings) in thinking that the anguish I have gone through, which will be merged, I humbly trust, before I go hence, in that peace which the world can not give, is probably the heaviest part of my earthly portion, or that it must have seasoned me to bear well what remains behind.

But in this mingled cup there are other sorrows of a still deeper kind; for physical evil is not *evil* in the most real sense. The separation is a fearful wrench from one for whom, and in expectation of whose smile, I might almost say, I have done all things, even to the choice of the least articles of my outward apparel, for twenty years. But even that is not the heaviest side of the dispensation. It is to feel, not merely that he is taken away from *me*, but that, as *appears*, though it is but appearance, he is not—that the sun rises in the morning, and he does not see it. The higher and better and enduring mind within us has no concern with these *sensations*, but they *will* arise, and have a certain force. While we remain in the tabernacle of the flesh, they are the miserable, cloggy vapors that from time to time keep steaming up from the floor and the walls, and obscure the prospect of the clear empyrean which may be seen from the windows. The most effective relief from them which I have found is the reminding myself that he who is passed

N

from my sight is gone whither I myself look to go in a few years (not to mention all those of whom the world was not worthy, before the publication of the Gospel and since), and that if I can contemplate my own removal, not with mere calmness, but with a cheerfulness which no other thought bestows, why should I feel sad that he is there before me? But these of which I have spoken are only the sensations of the natural man and woman. I well know in my heart of hearts and better mind that if he is not now in the bosom of God, who is not the God of the dead, but of the living, or if all these hopes are but dreams, I can have but little wish to bring him back to earth again, or to care about any thing either in earth or heaven. In my weakest moments, indeed, I have *never* wished that it were possible to recall him, or to prevent his departure hence. I thank God and the power of His grace, there has been no agony in my grief, there has been no struggle of my soul with Him. I have always had such a strong sense and conviction that if this sorrow *was to be*, and was appointed by God, it was entirely right, and that it was mere senselessness to wish any thing otherwise than as Infinite Goodness and Infinite Wisdom had ordained it. Forgive so much about my own feelings. Give my very kind regards to Mrs. M., and respects to Miss H., and believe me ever your affectionate friend, SARA COLERIDGE.

IV.

Affectionate Kindness of Relatives and Friends.—Special Gifts of a Christian Minister in his Attendance upon the Sick and Dying.

To HARTLEY COLERIDGE, Esq., Grasmere :

10 *Chester Place, March* 9, 1843.—My dear brother, I have long been wishing to renew my suspended intercourse with you. To do this requires some resolution, after all that has passed since I last wrote to you. When I have thought of taking up my pen to address you, a crowd of strong emotions and deeply concerning thoughts and remembrances have rushed upon me, pressing for utterance, and my spirits have sunk under the eagerness and intenseness of their requisitions. It is not because I anticipated an inadequate sympathy from you that I have felt thus, but from the very contrary. I have been answering kind and tender letters from persons less near and dear to me,

who could not and *ought* not to feel for me as I am sure you
have done, with comparative—I will not say calmness (for
since all uncertainty was removed, and my loss presented itself
to me as fixed and inevitable, I have been more deeply calm
in spirit than ever I was before in my life)—but with comparative lightness of feeling. Now, however, I take the first step
of renewing a correspondence with you, which I hope will be
cheerfully continued with pleasure and benefit to us both (if I
may so far assume and presume) to the end of our lives. It
is better to write little and often than much at a time, and in
this way, without formally asking your *advice*, which in a woman of my years is for the most part a mere form, I shall learn
your views and feelings on many interesting subjects, and be, I
humbly trust, improved and strengthened thereby. The great
moulder of my mind, who was, perhaps, more especially fitted
to strengthen my weak points and supply my deficiencies, and
altogether to keep my mind straight and even, than any other
man or woman living, is gone where I can not come—removed
out of the sphere of my human understanding—though not, I
trust, out of spiritual communion both with me and all who
are, or seek to be, in any vital sense Christians. On this account I have the more need to make much of the friendship of
my brothers ; and no widow, I think, when withdrawn from the
arms of a husband, can ever have been more affectionately sustained by those of brothers than I have been. The sadder my
prospect grew, the more closely they circled round me ; but a
thousand times dearer to my heart than their kindness to me
were the proofs they gave of affection, respect, and admiration
for him who was soon to be taken away from our mortal sight.
The expressions of dear John and of Frank were especially affecting. Of James* you have doubtless heard what he was to
me through all the last scenes of my trial. Upon this so important occasion, I found a brother—I may say an individual
man—in him whom before I knew not. I now saw for the
first time what was the secret of his influence and popularity
in his own pastoral sphere. He appears by the bed of sickness
and coming death (and he could not *so* appear unless his heart
were interested) entirely forgetful of self, absorbed in what is
before him. His own opinions, habits of mind, private inter-

---

* Dr. Coleridge, Vicar of Thorverton, near Exeter, was my father's eldest
brother.—E. C.

ests, seem gone, to a degree which strikes a by-stander like my-self as unusual. Then, in performing his professional part, he is the more effective from the absence of the intellectual in his mode of thought. There is nothing theological about James. From him you have the pure spirit of Gospel consolation and assurance—conditionally expressed—as it is in the Bible itself, with as little mixture of foreign matter as possible. This is not art in him, or knowledge. It is the result of the simple though not weak character of his intellect. He does not reason on one side or the other, but lets the moral and spiritual content of the inspired Book produce its own effect upon his mind, and find its own suitable utterance. His countenance and tone of voice are highly affecting and impressive, when he is thus seen in his best attitude of mind. Frank seemed gratified by my evident appreciation of his brother. But I can not thus speak of them without mentioning dear Edward* and Derwent too. Both in their several ways have been most soothing and help-ful to me. * * * My children are both going on well. Herbert is very well reported of from school, where his character for general cleverness continues ; though he fails in verse com-position, and in other more essential points, I feel hopeful and happy about him. His letters to his sister are an amusing mixt-ure of pure childishness, childish pedantry, and affectionate ruffianism. * * *—Believe me, my dear Hartley, your much at-tached sister,   SARA COLERIDGE.

V.

Memoir of Nicholas Ferrer.

To the Hon. Mr. Justice COLERIDGE :

March 11, 1843.—I am reading a very interesting Memoir of Nicholas Ferrer,† who lived in the times of James I. and Charles I. Were it not for certain expressions on the subject of grace, which clearly show that the writer is no disciple of

---

* The Rev. Edward Coleridge, Rector of Mapledurham, my father's young-er brother.—E. C.

† The friend of George Herbert, and editor of his Poems. Izaak Walton, in his Life of Herbert, gives a striking account of this remarkable man, who founded a Christian Society at Giddon Hall, Huntingdon, for purposes of de-votion and charity, in accordance with the principles of the Church.—E. C.

Pusey, one might suppose it a publication of the Oxford School —the sentiments, and some of the principles which it illustrates, being just such as Paget seeks to recommend by his amusing Tales. Without intended disparagement to Paget, how great is the superiority of the narrative to the fiction as a vehicle of truth !—the one bears something the same relation to the other, when carefully criticised, as the piece of linen or lace, viewed through a microscope, to the natural leaf or slip of wood examined in the same way.

VI.

A Quiet Heart.

To the Hon. Mr. Justice COLERIDGE :

March 22, 1843.—* * * I chat away thus to you, my dear brother, as if I had a light, gay heart, but I have only a quiet one. When I go out of doors from the incessant occupation of mind and hands, the full sense of my widowhood comes upon me, and the sunshine only seems to draw it out into vividness. Hampstead is a sadder place to me than Highgate. Yet sadness is not quite the word for my feelings—that seems too near to unhappiness. When I hear of happy marriages now, I do not feel that wretched sense of contrast with my own solitary state which I should once have felt. I rather feel a sort of compassionate tenderness for those who are entering on a career of earthly enjoyment, the transitoriness of which they must sooner or later be brought to a sense of. But for them, as for myself, there is a better communion beyond this present world, which, if begun here, will in the end supersede all other blessedness arising from union with objects of love.

VII.

Monument of Robert Southey.—Recumbent Statues.

To the Hon. Mr. Justice COLERIDGE :

March 28, 1843.—I scarce know what is finally settled about my uncle's monument. A modification of Lough's design seems most approved. The recumbent figure is all right in theory, but awkward in practice. Do what you will, it looks deathy, with too real and actual a deathiness. This is one of the instances, I think, of the difficulty of reviving old fashions; if you alter them at all, or even take them from amid the circumstances and states of feeling among which they were originated, you have a spectre of the past rather than the living past itself —a kind of resurrection. The recumbent figures on the old tombs are rather death idealized than death itself. The armor veiled from view the lifelessness of the limbs, and brought the body, as by a medium, into harmony with the sepulchral stone. The full robe of the dame by the warrior's side did the same thing in another way, and contrasted well with the male attire; and that one attitude of the hands crossed upon the breast, or pressed together in prayer, alone perfectly agrees with the whole design. The brasses are not open to these remarks, because they are much farther removed from life, and therefore can not offend by the semblance of death.

VIII.

On her Loss.—Injury Done to the Mind by Brooding over Grief.

To Mrs. PLUMMER, Gateshead:

10 *Chester Place, April* 27, 1843.—Your letter was very welcome to me, and I will thank you for it at once, though I can not now write at all as I wish, either as to matter or manner, so much am I occupied, and so unequal am I to getting much done in a short time, from bodily weakness and sensitiveness of nerves.

What you say, dearest, of your own particular grief in the loss that bears so heavily upon me, that but for very special mercy it must have crushed me to the earth, is extremely gratifying to me. Nothing soothes me so much as to hear *his* deserved praises, and to have assurances from his friends of the esteem and affection he excited. Few men have been ever more generally liked, or more dearly *loved* in a narrower sphere. Never before his illness did I fully know what a holy, what a blessed thing is the love of brothers and sisters to each other. By my bereavement all my relations seem to be brought closer to me than before, for pity excites affection, and gratitude for kindness and sympathy has the same effect. But my beloved Henry's brothers are twice as much to me as in his precious lifetime. John is such a friend and supporter as few widows I think are blessed with. You will not, I am sure, dear friend, think me boastful, but grateful for saying all this. I feel it now such a duty, such a necessity, to cling fast to every source of comfort—to be for my children's sake as happy, as willing to live on in this heart-breaking world as possible—that I dwell on all the blessings which God continues to me, and has raised up to me out of the depths of affliction, with an earnestness of endeavor which is its own reward ; for so long as the heart and mind are full of movement, employed continually on not unworthy objects, there may be sorrow, but there can not be despair. The stagnation of the spirit, the dull, motionless brooding on one miserable set of thoughts, is that against which in such cases as mine we must both strive and pray. After all, it would be impossible for one bereaved like me to care for the goings-on of this world but for the blessed prospect of another; and it is a most thankworthy circumstance that the more agitating our trials become, the brighter that prospect, after a little while, beams forth, through the reaction of the mind when strongly excited. The heaviest hours come on after the subsidence of that excitement, when we come out again from the chamber of death and mourning into all the common ways of life. All the social intellectual enjoyments—new books, the sight of sculpture, painting, the conversation of pleasant friends—are full of trial to me. I turn away from what excites any lively emotion of admiration or pleasure, now that I can no longer share it with him who for twenty years shared all my happiest thoughts.

IX.

God's Will the Best Consolation.

To Mrs. FARRER :

May 8, 1843.—My dear Mrs. Farrer, this morning I received your letter, of the kindness of which I have not time to speak adequately. I feel very glad to be able to avail myself of your offer. Broadstairs I have often wished to visit. I was to have visited it with my beloved invalid, but God ordered things otherwise, doubtless better for us both. As my friend, Mr. Frederick Maurice, truly says, in answer to some remarks of mine, there is more calmness in the thought, "It is God's will," than in all other consolations. I had been saying to him how impossible it is for any religious, reflective person to look back upon the bitterest dispensations of the Almighty Hand with a serious wish that they had never been awarded, that the web which Providence has woven could be unraveled, and all the good though trying gifts which our Father in heaven has bestowed taken back again. Sorrow makes us very egotistic, and, to those that understand not the house of mourning, very tedious and commonplace. But to those who are feeling deeply, or sympathizing with those who feel, the sense of *reality* in the oft-expressed sentiment lends it freshness and force.

X.

New Friends.—A Happy Pair.

To her Eldest Brother:

Broadstairs, May 30, 1843.—My dear brother, this is my last day at Broadstairs. To-morrow I depart for Chester Place, after a fortnight spent here with my little Edith and our maid Elizabeth, at the temporary abode of Mrs. Thomas Farrer, a lady whom I must rank among my friends, though not among my old acquaintances. My first introduction to her, not two years ago, was through her sons, favorite pupils of Edward C——, whom I met at Eton, and who thereupon felt desirous that their family and mine should be on visiting terms, as we were already neighbors in Regent's Park. To this wish I acceded, though a little dismayed at that time at the way in which the circle of our acquaintances was beginning to widen. I have since, however, rejoiced that I did not withstand the proposal, having been greatly pleased with the clan of the F——s, a large and very united one, so far as I have seen and come to know them. Mrs. F——'s eldest daughter, a very sweet and pretty girl of nineteen, is to be married next August to the heir of the N——'s, a most amiable and promising young man; and I have taken pleasure in resting my eyes on the smooth true-love course of this young couple, which appears to my fancy at present like the quietest of rivulets gliding along in the sun, with pretty wild flowers upon its banks. How will it run in that part of the region which is not yet in sight? May it not break over rough stones, or become suddenly lost under-ground, as mine has been? These are questions which the sight naturally suggests, and which cast an air of melancholy over it, in spite of all its sunshiny brightness, to the mind of the widow in her weeds. But the young pair, and even their friends at large, appear to see only the present sunshine. C——'s lids are unsullied by a tear; and long may the brown orbs under them (I have seen few so beautiful) beam darkly forth as now, full of calm happiness undimmed and unclouded.

XI.

Dryness of Controversial Sermons.

To the Hon. Mr. Justice COLERIDGE, Heath's Court, Ottery St. Mary:

June 27, 1843.—Dr. Arnold's sermon is all you described it. Would that of this sort, so practical, and appealing to the heart and religious mind, were at least the *majority* of *preached* sermons! Some doctrinizing from the pulpit may be necessary. But surely it ought to be subservient and subordinate to the practical; whereas, nine times out of ten, the practical point merely serves as an introduction or a pretext for a setting up the opinions of one school of thinkers, and a pulling down the opinions of another, with charges against the latter almost always one-sided and unfair. This sermon of Dr. A——'s, and one which I heard from Dr. Hodgson at Broadstairs on Death and Judgment, are quite oases in the hot, sandy wilderness of sermons which my mind's reverted eye beholds. I do not mean that many of them were not good; but, when they are viewed altogether, a character of heat and barrenness seems to pervade them.

XII.

Preliminary Essay to the "Aids to Reflection," by the Rev. James Marsh.—Her "Essay on Rationalism."*—Consolation and Instruction derived from Theological Studies.

To the Hon. Mr. Justice COLERIDGE:

Chester Place, July, 1843—I am glad that you think Marsh's essay *very good*. My dear husband read it during his illness,

---

* Appendix C to the Second Volume of the "Aids to Reflection," Sixth Edition.—E. C.

and was confirmed in his high opinion of it. As to my own production (*much as I admire it myself!*), I do not expect that it will be admired by any one else. It makes larger demands on the attention of readers than I, with my powers, have perhaps any right to make or can repay. Even if the thinking were sound or important, the arrangement is bad. If bad arrangement in S. T. C. is injurious to readability, in S. C. it will be destructive. Moreover, I have made to myself *no friends.* A follower out of the principles of S. T. C. myself, whithersoever they lead me, because they seem to me the *very truth,* I can not join hands with any of his half or quarter disciples. I praise and admire and applaud all the combatants on the theological arena, even the hearty opponents of my father, but I can not entirely agree with any one of them; and some of his friends have done him more harm, if such ephemeral harm were worth talking of, than his foes. Yet I should never regret the time spent on this little composition, though I should be rather out of pocket and not into reputation by it, as will certainly be the case; for it has sometimes brought one part of my mind into activity, when the other part, if active, could only have been alive to anguish; and it has given me a more animated intercourse with some great minds now passed from our nether sphere than I could have had from merely reading their thoughts, without thinking them over again myself.

XIII.

A Visit to Margate.—Domestic Economy in its Right Place.—An Eton School-boy.—Reading under Difficulties.—High Moral Aim of Carlyle's "Hero-worship."—Joy of a True Christian.—The Logic of the Heart and the Logic of the Head.

To Mrs. FARRER:

12 *Cliff Terrace, Margate, September* 5, 1843.—My dear friend, here we are—my children and nurse and self—on the East Cliff at Margate, a few miles from the spot where I sojourned with you in June. That fortnight is marked among the fortnights of this my first year of widowhood with a comparative whiteness, in the midst of such deep (though never, I must thankfully acknowledge—never, even at the earliest period of my loss—quite unrelieved) blackness. I fixed upon this

place, instead of Broadstairs or Ramsgate, on account of its greater cheapness, and because it could be reached with rather less exertion. Lodgings certainly *are* cheaper than I could have got them in an equally good situation at more genteel sea-bathing places; but provisions are dear enough — lamb 8½*d.*, and beef 9*d.* ! I am so often twitted with my devotion to intellectual things, that I am always glad of an opportunity of sporting a little beef and mutton erudition, though I can not help thinking that, as society is now constituted in the professional middle rank of life—still more in a higher one—women may get on and make their families comfortable, and manage with tolerable economy—by which I mean economy that does not cost more than it is worth of time and devotion of spirit— with less knowledge of details respecting what we are to eat, and what to put on, than used to be thought essential to the wise and worthy matron. I dare say your dear C. will make her loved and honored S. as comfortable as if she had been studying butchers' and bakers' bills, and mantua-making, and upholstery in a little way, for the last seven years, instead of reading Dante and Goethe and Richter and Wordsworth and Tennyson. But to return to this place: it is a contrast to Broadstairs as looked out upon from the White Hart, where we took up our abode the first night; but the East Cliff, where, by medical recommendation, we have settled ourselves for a fortnight or three weeks, is neither more nor less than the Broadstairs Cliffery continued; and as we return from the gully leading down to the sands (the very brother to that which I so often went down and up with you), Edy and I might almost fancy that we were returning to the Albion Street lodgings, if it were not for the tower of the handsome new church, where we attended morning service last Sunday, which reminds us that we are at Margate.

We were delayed in coming hither for some days by Herbert's prolonged stay at Rickmansworth, where he spent nearly three weeks in a sort of boys' paradise, bathing two or three times a day. Both Baron and Lady A—— wrote about him to me in very gratifying terms. It is perhaps not right to repeat things honorable to our children without being equally communicative about their faults and ill-successes. But you have been so specially friendly with me, and shown such kind interest about all that concerns me, that I think I should withhold a pleasure from you in not telling you what has very much pleased me. H. thinks this place very *seedy*, and despises the bathing. The tide seems never in a state to please him; but the truth is, he wants companions, and does not like to be a solitary Triton among the minnows, or rather, as those are fresh-water fish, among the crabs and sea-weed. However, he has got "Japhet in Search of a Father," from the circulating library, reads a portion daily of Euripides, and has begun learning French; and it is quite right that a little *seediness* should come in its turn after "jollity," and quietness and plain fare after "splendid lark," with "sock" of all sorts, that he may learn to cut out interests and amusements for himself out of home materials.

I must tell tales of the vessel that brought us hither, in order to deter you, dear friend, from ever trusting yourself to it in future. The "Prince of Wales" does certainly make its way fast over the water, but the vibration of its disproportionately small frame under the energy of its strong steam-engine is such that it fatigued me much more than a slower voyage would have done, and gave both nurse and me a headache. The motion almost prevented me too from reading. Carlyle's "Hero-worship" trembled in my hand like a culprit before a judge; and as the book *is* very full of paradoxes, and has some questionable matter in it, this shaking seemed rather symbolical. But, oh! it is a book fit rather to shake (take it all in all) than to be shaken. It is very full of noble sentiments and wise reflections, and throws out many a suggestion which will not waste itself like a blast blown in a wilderness, but will surely rouse many a heart and mind to a right, Christian-like way of acting and of dealing with the gifted and godlike in man and of men. Miss Farrer lent me the work, and many others. Very pleasant to me was her stay at Gloucester Terrace, if *pleasant* is a fit word for an intercourse which awakened thoughts and feelings of "higher gladness" than are commonly so described. She is one who loves to reveal her mind, with all its "open secrets," to those who care at all for the one thing which is, and which she happily has found to be, needful; and few indeed are the minds which will so well bear such inspection as she invites; few can display such a pure depth of sunny blue without a cloud, such love for all men, and Christ above all—ascending from them whom she has seen to God whom she has not seen, and again honoring them and doing good to them, on principle, for His sake. My doctrinal differences from her (and *some* doctrine we all must have in this world) are considerable; but I could almost say that, were all men like her, no Christian *doctrine* would be needed. She has much knowledge, too, of men and things—has read and seen much; and pray tell your T. H. that I learned to thread the at first bewildering labyrinth of her discourse after a while much better than at first. Even to the last her rapid transitions confounded me very often, and some of her replies to objections are rather appeals to the imagination and affections than properly answers. But she has a logic of her own; and though I do maintain that Christendom would fall abroad if it were not knit together by a logic of another sort, the want of which would be felt sorely, if it were possible that it could ever be wholly wanting, which the nature of man prevents, yet this logic of the heart and spiritual nature is more than sufficient to guide every individual aright that possesses it in such high measure as she does.

XIV.

Beauty of Sussex Scenery.—Congenial Society.

To Mrs. JOSHUA STANGER, Fieldside, Keswick, Cumberland:

Tunbridge Wells, September 26, 1843.—I am having every advantage here which a most agreeable family circle and daily drives in an easy carriage, in the most inspiriting air, through a lovely country, can give me; and I do fully believe that I shall be better in the end for having made the effort to come hither, and to mix myself up with my neighbors' concerns. I seek to take an interest in all their little belongings, and cultivate cheerfulness as much as possible. Enough of melancholy remembrance and deep irremovable regret is sure to remain, let me do what I may to enter thankfully and genially into the present.

The landscape here, which I believe you are well acquainted with, continually puts me in mind of Milton's description of Paradise—the slopes are so emerald-velvety, and the clumps and clusters of trees so varied and beautiful. But there is an imperfection in the prospect from the want of water. I long to introduce dancing rills and fairy waterfalls and lucid pools into the midst of these basin-like valleys, and to people the glades with deer and the villages with a freer, finer peasantry.

There is a great want of water generally in the South of England. Devonshire has plenty of it; but the climate of Devon is to me a drawback for which nothing can compensate.

The family party here consists of Judge E——, his wife, two daughters, and eldest son: the youngest is at Eton. The visitors are Miss M——, a charming young woman, most animated and intelligent, a niece of Judge E——, and myself. Judge E—— is one of the most agreeable men in the family circle that I have ever known. He has the indescribable air and way of a man of high birth about him; and there is in his conversation that happy mixture of seriousness, with light sportiveness and arch remark, which every body likes, and which is never jarring or oppressive, whatever mood one may be in.

XV.

Friendly Recollections and Anticipations.

To Miss MORRIS:

October, 1843.—You can not think what pleasure I have in looking back upon my late visit. The verdurous, soft, quiet beauty of the country at Tunbridge Wells seems to form a very harmonious *ground* for the more prominent remembrances with which it has furnished me. Your relatives of the honorable and honored name of E——, like glow-worms, shine in the shade; they come out *most* brightly in family life, as indeed do all characters who have much in them. How can that *much* be shown in company? That part of my recollections in which you figure, dear Miss Morris, of the character of *that* I do not now speak to you, but I trust it will appear more and more in our future lives, as a suitable beginning of a happy and fruitful friendship. —Believe me, affectionately yours,   SARA COLERIDGE.

XVI.

On her Loss.—Cheerfulness instead of Happiness.—Visits to Eton and Tunbridge Wells.

To Mrs. HENRY M. JONES, Hampstead:

Eton, October 13, 1843.—Of course I am not up to the mark of easy, quiet enjoyment; yet I feel that, for a time, it is good for me to be here. I can not withdraw myself from the world; I must live on in this outward scene (though it continually seems most strange to my feelings that I should yet be mixed up in it, and Henry *gone from* it forever). But since I have been doomed to outlive my husband, I must, for my children's sake as well as my own, endeavor to enter, with as much spirit as I can, into the interests and movements of the sphere to which it is God's will that I should yet belong. Ever since my widowhood I have *cultivated cheerfulness* as I never did before. During my time of union I possessed *happiness;* mere *cheerfulness* I looked upon as a weed, the natural wild produce of the soil, which *must* spring up of itself. Now I crave to see fine works of art, or the still more mind-occupying displays of nature. I try to take an interest in the concerns of my friends, to enter into the controversies of the day, to become intimate with the mood of mind and character of various persons, who are nothing to me (*I* being nothing to them) except as *studies;* just as a lichen or a curious moss may be, only in a higher manner and degree. All this with an earnestness unfelt in former times. To a certain extent I find my account in this; my mind is restless, and rather full of desultory activity than, what is far better, concentrated energy; but it does not stagnate. I do not brood miserably over my loss, or sink into an aimless, inert despondency; I have even an upper stratum of cheerfulness in my mind, more fixed than in my happy married days, but then it is only an upper stratum; beneath it, unmoved and unmodified, is the sense of my loss.

I have been interrupted, to see Dr. Hawtrey. He was such an intimate friend of my beloved Henry. I shall always, on this account, feel a special interest in him. And he is in himself much to be liked and approved, most amiable in his domestic character, as son and brother, and full of intellectual refinement; a good scholar, and an accomplished modern linguist.

I came hither for a holiday, but I assure you I have no complete one. Herbert *makes* me read Euripides with him, and hear his Latin theme, I being as good a judge of Latin composition as a Great Cham of Tartary is of English.

My visit at Tunbridge Wells was a very agreeable one. I was quite astonished at the picturesque beauty and great variety of the country there, and found the family of Judge E—— quite charming in every-day, familiar life. Miss M——, who was my fellow-visitant, I found more than an agreeable companion, though she is that in a high degree; her brilliancy and amusing humor is the mere sparkling, polished surface of a genuine jewel, in which the ground is invaluable. I can not but add her to my list of *friends* made since marriage, in which list you, dear friend, are so prominent. Mamma is looking anxiously for a sight of you. Your affectionate conduct towards her, dear Mrs. Jones, gives me more comfort than I can well express. I do not think she fails at all in mind, and in body her declension is very gentle and gradual.

I must get ready to drive out and see the oak forests of Windsor, in all the charming drapery of autumnal gleam and shadow. —I remain your truly attached friend,   SARA COLERIDGE.

Excuse the egotism of this letter. Sorrow makes one egotistical.

XVII.

Sympathy Inspired by the Sorrows of Childhood and Youth.

To EDWARD QUILLINAN, Esq. :*

Eton, October 24, 1843.—I scarce know why it is that I feel far more moved by the griefs of childhood and of youth than those of middle-age. One has a sense, I suppose, that the young have a sort of *right* to happiness, or rather to gladsomeness and enjoyment; that if they ever are to be gay and pretty, then is the time. Sorrow and sallow cheeks come to me at my time of life not unnaturally. Reflection has preceded them, and ought at least to have enabled the fading mourner to look beyond them, to see a new world wherein dwelleth righteousness, and to drown in its lustre, superinduced over the worsening remnant of our earthly life, all its own melancholy hues. The comparative health and beauty of those who have fairly parted with youth is but a poor thing at the best. But you will laugh at my moralizing on the subject of beauty, at least if you do not bear in mind that I am not thinking of that which we ascribe to *a beauty*, the admired of the ball-room, the celebrated

---

* The son-in-law of Mr. Wordsworth. Mr. Quillinan was well acquainted with the Portuguese language and literature, and has left a translation of the first five cantos of the "Lusiad of Camoens."—E. C.

toast, but rather of that general attribute which the Psalmist must have referred to when he complained so heavily that his "beauty was wasted for very trouble." We all have, or have had *beauty*, though we are not all "beauties."

XVIII.

Restoration of the Jews.—Literal Fulfillment of the Promise apparently Indicated by Old Testament Prophecy, and by the Words of St. Paul in his Epistle to the Romans.

To Mrs. JOSHUA STANGER, Keswick:

10 *Chester Place, December* 18, 1843.—The passage which has always seemed to me very strong for the restoration of the Jews, or at least very remarkable, and seemingly hitherto unfulfilled, is Jeremiah xxiii., 5–8.* Ben Ezra and Mr. Dodsworth, take great pains to show that this can not be understood of any restoration of the Jews to their own land that has *already* taken place. I never read any argument against the opinion of the restoration of the Jews; and should like to know how Mr. Myers and others, who have a positive belief that Scripture is not to be so understood, interpret that passage. My own mind has hitherto been quite suspended on the subject, which I have but very cursorily examined; I have no positive formed belief against this view, as I own I have against the doctrine of the Millennarians.

Zechariah xiv., 4, 5, "And his feet shall stand upon the Mount of Olives," has more apparent reference to the restoration of the Jews than to the Millennium.

There seems, too, to my mind to be a sort of internal probability—or rather, I mean, a sort of fitness and propriety in the thing; it looks like a completion of a design of which two parts were already accomplished—I mean the setting apart of the chosen nation, then the dispersion among the Gentiles. Does it not seem as if their restoration were the proper last act of the

---

* "Behold, the days come, saith the Lord, that I will raise unto David a righteous branch," etc. "Therefore, behold, the days come, saith the Lord, that they shall no more say, The Lord liveth which brought up the children of Israel out of the land of Egypt; but the Lord liveth which brought up and which led the seed of the house of Israel out of the north country," etc. (Jer. xxiii., 5–8).

O

great drama? Of course, I speak of this only as an auxiliary argument; and then the latter part of Romans, chapter xi.,* seems to favor this view not a little.

XIX.

Readings in Aristophanes.—Cheerfulness and Simplicity of Early Poetry.

To the Hon. Mr. Justice COLERIDGE:

Chester Place, December 26, 1843.—As to Aristophanes, I quite accede to the justice of your representations of his not altogether fitness for the joint perusal of Herby and me. I had clean forgotten the uncleanness, till my boy discreetly observed that there was a word in the next line which would not do to be voiced aloud. We shall only read the "Frogs;" but Herby is so delighted with this play that it would be a pity for him not to finish it, as I believe, from what Frere says, that there is but little, after the first scene, to object to in it. The *spirit* of the humor of Aristophanes a boy like Herbert may well enter into, when the *material* is once cleared out of its concealing husk and set before him. The temptation to read Aristophanes is that his plays are mirthful, and "as there's naught but care on every hand," I am glad of every scrap of cheerfulness which I can lay before my children, now in their spring season, when they can enjoy it. I feel sadly for them that this is a widowed home. But they appear as glad as others of their age, and the great change to me bears lightly upon them in comparison.

* * * * * * * *

We have been laughing heartily at the "Frogs" again. It would be a lounge to read Homer with Herby; but I feel a wish to get him through some of the harder, more troublesome parts of the classical task that lies before him. It is wonderful —*not* wonderful so much as noticeable—how fitted the ancient classics are in general for the youthful mind. They contain, indeed, the youthful mind of our human race, are less abstract and subjective than modern compositions.

---

* "For I would not, brethren, that ye should be ignorant of this mystery, lest ye should be blind in your own conceits: that blindness in part is happened to Israel, until the fullness of the Gentiles be come in.

"And so all Israel shall be saved: as it is written, There shall come out of Sion the Deliverer, and shall turn away ungodliness from Jacob" (Romans xi., 25, 26).

CHAPTER XII.

1844.

LETTERS TO MISS MORRIS, JOHN KENYON, ESQ., MRS. EDWARD
COLERIDGE, MRS. FARRER, MRS. J. STANGER.

I.

"Traveling Onward."—Differences of Mental Perspective in the Contemplation of Truth.—Doctrine of the Millennium.—Symbolism in the Bible.—"Messiah's Kingdom" and the "Reign of the Saints" both signify the Establishment of Christianity.—Literal Explanation of the latter Prophecy by some of the Fathers not Founded on Tradition.

To Miss MORRIS, Mecklenburg Square :

Chester Place, January, 1844.—"Geneva !" and " Rome !" My hope and trust is that we are *traveling onward,* and shall in time leave these names, these badges of division, behind us. So far I understand and sympathize with Mr. Maurice, that I think there has been much of "notionalism" among all parties ; by which I take him to mean, in general, a losing sight, or at least a steady view, of spiritual *substance,* through the perplexing and deluding atmospheric medium of the mere understanding, its refractions and distorting reflections ; so that differences have arisen, not from pure perversity of heart, as believers are so apt to say of those who disagree with them, nor from an absolute blindness to truth, but from difference of position and a variableness and uncertainty in the medium itself. I sympathize with him, too, in this, that from being very strongly possessed with the thought which I have just mentioned, I am a good deal isolated from all the conflicting parties now on the arena, and can not agree wholly either with Tractarians or Anti-Tractarians. For Maurice is at bottom quite as unlike any *party* in his views as I have been led to be, though his language would put him into the class of High Churchmen, somewhere between the old section and the new, with those who read him but cursorily, without asking him and themselves very strictly what that language in *his* mouth means.

If you will soon be addressing Mr. Bickersteth, pray convey my best thanks to him for his last gift. I think I have read all that he says on the Promised Glory, and know the texts which he brings to the service of his view. Certainly, looked at in one way, they serve it effectively. I can not, however, help seeing them in another. The more we look back to the development and expression of thought in past ages, the more, I think, we find that great spiritual and moral truths were in the earlier times continually presented in the form of the fable or myth. Instead of sermons and scientific treatises, they had allegories and symbolical representations: all doctrines—moral, religious, or metaphysical—were embodied and clad in sensuous forms. To speak of this, and draw inferences from it in the interpretation of that old book, the Bible, is considered a modern refinement, a piece of rationalism. But rationalism did not invent the mythical mode of writing; it does but point it out, and compare what it presumes to be instances of it in Scripture with countless others out of Scripture. I seem to myself to see plainly that the descriptions of the Messiah's kingdom in the Prophets are descriptions of Christianity itself, in all the glory and gladness and purity of the idea, under the guise of actual history, and with all the pomp of sensuous imagery to render the symbol significant. In the same way I read the Revelations; and it seems to me that on this plan an interpretation may be given, which, though at first it seems bold, yet is in truth more consistent with itself, and more accordant with the language of Scripture, when that is tried by the proper rules, than any other. I can not but think that the whole theory of the earthly millennial kingdom stands on an insecure foundation, because I always find from writers on the subject that at bottom it rests with every one of them on Rev. xx., 4, as it did from the first; and I do verily believe that the language of that text will not admit of the interpretation which their theory gives to it. The early Fathers, some of them, understood it so; but such symbolical texts they made sad work with, I believe, for the most part. We should not, any of us, like to accept their Biblical criticism all through; and criticism it was plainly enough, not traditional knowledge of any clear description.

II.

Critique on the Early Poems of Elizabeth Barrett (Mrs. Browning).—Favor-
ite Pieces.—Exuberance of her Style Inappropriate to Solemn Themes.
—Hasty Objections made by Miss B—— to the Ideal Philosophy of
Berkeley, and to the Wolfian Theory of Homer.

To JOHN KENYON, Esq.:*

Regent's Park, 1844.—My dear Mr. Kenyon, at last I return
with thanks the Poems of Miss Barrett, which I now always
mention in high terms to any of my acquaintances, when the
conversation affords an opportunity. I think my favorites are
the "Poet's Vow," "A Romance of the Ganges," "Isobel's
Child" (so like "Christabel" in manner, as mamma and I both
thought), "The Island," "The Deserted Garden," and "Cowper's Grave." But my conception of Miss B——'s poetical
merit is formed from lines and stanzas occurring here and there
in most of the poems—from the general impression produced
by the whole collection, rather than from any number of entire
pieces. "The Seraphim" contains *very* fine passages; and perhaps no other single poem in the volume has impressed me so
strongly with the writer's power; and yet, taken as a whole,
with reference not to what others could produce, but with what
it ought to be, I confess it does not altogether please me. If
there be a subject throughout the range of human thought
which demands to be treated (if treated at all as the prominent
theme of any metrical composition) with a sober Miltonic majesty of style, rather than with a wild modernism and fantastic
rapture, surely that subject is the Crucifixion of a Saviour and
the Redemption of a fallen world. Even in that clever translation of the "Prometheus Bound" (for very clever it is), there
occur some phrases which want the Hebraic simplicity of the
original. "The faded white flower of the Titanic brow"—do

---

* A friend of Mr. Southey's, and relative of the gifted lady whose earlier
works form the subject of this letter. It is proper to add that the two concluding paragraphs are only inserted here for the sake of the interesting remarks which they contain on Berkeley's system and the Homeric question,
since the notes which originally called them forth were withdrawn in subsequent editions. In Mrs. Browning's later publication, my mother particularly admired the "Drama of Exile" (the subject of which she thought "more
within the sphere of poetic art" than that of the "Seraphim"), "Lady Ger-
aldine's Courtship," "The Cry of the Children," the "Rhyme of the Duchess May," and the "lovely sonnet" called "Irreparableness."—E. C.

you think that quite comes up to the manly broadness and
boldness of the Greek Dramatist, or suits the awful circumstances of the Titan fixed upon his rock? There is a *flower* in
both cases, to be sure ; but Æschylus meant that *the whole outward man* of Prometheus would be parched and discolored by
the sun's heat ; and this he expressed by a plain but untrans-
latable Græcism.   I think that your cousin should study a noble simplicity, especially as her poetical aims are so high, lest
she should be obliged to finish the lofty temples of imagination
with brass instead of gold.   You see how easy it is to *preach*
even for those who can not practice ; but Miss Barrett *can* practice, and will benefit, I trust, by preaching of more authority than
mine, the presumption of which will never reach her ears.

I can not make an end of my preaching, however, without
venturing a remark or two on her summary manner of dealing
with the Homeric question, and with the opinions of Berkeley.
Surely no one who understands what Berkeley's scheme of
Idealism really was would suppose that the poor bishop was
bound, in consistency with his metaphysical principles, to let a
cart run over him ! He tells us plainly that if by material *substance* he meant only that which is *seen* and *felt*, then is he
"more sensible of matter's existence than any other philosopher." I question whether Miss B—— did not confound Idealism with unreality, as persons new to the subject invariably do.
Few metaphysicians would ratify her sentence that Berkeley
was "out of his senses ;" though none now perhaps believe his
system true in fact, or look upon it as other than a platform on
which a certain number of pregnant truths were exhibited in a
strong point of view.   Channing observes how it has influenced
the modes of thinking among metaphysicians.

Then, again, Miss B——'s censure of all who believe in the
"Homeric speculation" is sweeping indeed.   It sweeps away,
like chaff before the wind, not only almost all the great scholars and fine critics of learned Germany—not only "the eloquent
Villemain," and numbers of French savans—not only men of
genius and learning, such as Wolf and Heyne, and the Italian
Vico—but those of the highest *poetic* feeling, who, both in this
and other countries, are converts to the system.

Before I conclude, however, let me add that I do not quarrel
with any one for sticking resolutely to the "blind old man of
Scio's rocky isle," nor pretend to have formed a decided opin-

ion on this puzzling point upon which great doctors have agreed to differ; though I *incline* to the belief that, if Homer ever existed, he no more wrote *all* the books of the "Iliad," than one Hercules performed the twelve labors ascribed to him. The books, to be sure, are extant, the labors fabulous; but I mean that the one, as the other, *may* have been a nucleus around whose works those of others were collected, but whose name remained to the whole.

P. S.—Since writing the above, I have again read the "Seraphim," and am more impressed with its merit than at first. It is *full* of beauty.

III.

Gladsomeness a Natural Gift of Childhood.—Severe Discipline not Suited to the Period of Early Youth.

To her Eldest Brother:

Chester Place, 1844.—There is a gladsomeness generally found in children happily circumstanced and managed by those who understand and will to act upon the simple rules, by observance of which these little ones are made and kept as happy as they can be—keeping black care quite out of their sight, addressing them with cheerful looks and tones, never keeping them long at any one task, yet enforcing a certain amount of work, with occasional half and some whole holidays regularly—never letting any trouble remain as a weight and grinding pressure upon their minds—but inflicting at once whatever is absolutely necessary, and then diverting their minds to what is easy and pleasant. A child must also have a certain amount of health and of intellectual activity, imaginativeness, and so forth, to be perpetually *gladsome;* but with the positives and negatives that I have named, we shall find any child in a country or town cottage not only cheerful, but joyous.

Of course, I am not implying that to produce and maintain this gladness is the great work of education; but I feel assured that it is a true part of education, and that amid this ease from without, and consequent happiness from within, the affections, temper, and understanding expand and grow more favorably, and take a better and more generous form, than under other circumstances. What I am now saying, however, applies to children as such; this I think the best *preparatory* state, because it best enables the native powers to develop themselves; but trial and hardship are proper to exercise and consolidate them from time to time as soon as they have gained a certain measure of strength; and, to put the matter practically, I think that parents should make their children as easy and happy as ever they can without indulging them in what is wrong, leaving *discipline* to be supplied by the ordinary and inevitable course of events, the sorrow, difficulty, and suffering which life in this world brings to every individual. The young people that are spoiled by an indulgent home are spoiled, I think, not by over-happiness, but from having been encouraged in selfishness, never made to understand and led to practice Christian duty.

IV.

The Temple Church.—Color in Architecture.

To Mrs. EDWARD COLERIDGE, Eton:

June, 1844.—Yesterday I saw with delight for the first time the restored Temple Church. The restoration seems to me to be in excellent taste, with the exception of the altar. No doubt the great beauty of this interior consists in what it always had, its general form, with the clustered pillars, and exquisite interlacing of arches. But the decorative part brings out and illuminates this original and essential beauty, as I have so often seen the rich colors of sunset illuminate the fine forms of my native hills.

V.

Use of Metrical Rules in Poetry.—Versification of "Christabel" and "The Ancient Mariner."—Artificial Character of some of the Greek Metres.

To Miss MORRIS:

June 10, 1844.—Have you been poetizing of late? Mind, I do not tie you down to those longs and shorts; but, depend upon it, there is much use in them. The more our ear can direct us, the better; but rules help and educate the ear. Poetry is more of an *art* than people in general think. They know that Music and Painting are arts; but they imagine that Poetry must flow forth spontaneously, like the breath which we breathe, without volition or consciousness. All our finest metrists knew these rules: how far they went by them, I can not say; but I know that my father, whose versification has been greatly admired by critics, was fond of talking about anapæsts and iambuses; and if people admired "Christabel," as it were, by nature, he was never easy till he had put them in the way of admiring it more scientifically. Dr. Carlyle says he never succeeded in making him admire "The Ancient Mariner" properly. He was obliged, after all, to go back to his own first rude impressions, and rely upon them.

The manner in which the ancient verse was constructed is a curious problem. It seems as if those very artificial metres, dependent on syllabic quantity, could never in any degree have been written by ear, or otherwise than as such verse is written now. All critics, however, agree that the best and seemingly most *easy* and *natural* styles, both in prose and verse, are those that have been most artfully written and carefully elaborated. Art alone will do nothing, but it improves and educes the natural gift. Cobbett taught wrong doctrine on this head; and so, I believe, did my Uncle Southey.

VI.

The "Life of Arnold" a Book to be "Gloried in."—The Visible Church not to be Identified with any Single System.—Dr. Arnold's Opinion that there ought to be no Distinction between the Clergy and the Laity.

To the Hon. Mr. Justice COLERIDGE:

July, 1844.—I can not tell you in one short day, or the longest summer day that ever shone, what I feel and think about the "Life of Arnold"—how I rejoice over it, how I glory in it, what good I augur from it. Not that I can see my way through the *whole* of Arnold's view, or perceive the justice of all his practical conclusions. I can not but think with him that the *visible* Church is a human institution, sanctioned and blessed by God, and rendered the vehicle of His grace, just so far as it is really an efficient instrument of the preservation and propagation of true Christianity. I can see no sufficient reason to believe that it was supernaturally ordained by Him in detail—

that it is not in this respect essentially different from its Jewish predecessor.   I can not doubt that it was full of error from the first, the Apostles during their life repressing, but not radically removing, wrong notions of the faith.   I imagine that the Church, as a spiritual power co-ordinate with the Word and the Spirit, is certainly realized through *a* visible machinery and system of outward ordinances, but by no means confined to one alone, and that one prescribed by Christ himself; so far as any one answers its great end better than another, so far it is a more divine and a fuller organ of the Spirit.   But putting the question on the grounds upon which Arnold himself would have placed it—moral evidence, reason, and the plain speaking of Scripture—I can not but infer that religion and affairs of policy ought to have distinct functionaries; and certainly the general judgment of mankind, and not a mere sect and party of Christians, has inclined to this view rather than the other.

VII.

"Nothing to Do."—Isaac Taylor's Suggestion that there will be Work as well as Rest in Heaven.—Sea-side Views and Walks.—Fellow-Lodgers. —Idleness and Extravagance of London Shop-keepers.—Two Sorts of Diffuseness. — Lord Eldon. — Reflections on his Character and Portrait.

To Mrs. FARRER:

5 *Nelson Place, Broadstairs, August* 27, 1844.—Dearest Mrs. Farrer, I will not defer writing to you till I have "nothing else to do;" for I hope that time will never come.   Mr. Taylor, of Ongar, in his "History of Enthusiasm," takes pains to show that we shall have a great deal *to do* in heaven, and even have to work hard there.   My remark, however, is quite limited to the time of this mortal life; for I think we are scarcely qualified as yet to cut out our work in the world to come, or determine upon the manner in which we shall spend eternity.   Probably our present ideas of labor and rest will not be among the things which we shall carry along with us into the other state; and I can not think Mr. Taylor is justified in accusing other Christians of having *indolent notions* of heaven, because they have not exactly his view of the *exertions* that are to be made there.   Be that as it may, however, the main part of my

business here at Broadstairs is to scribble on scraps of paper,
sometimes on sheets; and I am sure that after all your great
kindness to me, and concern shown for my comfort, I ought to
fill one of these little sheets as well as I can to you, little indeed as I have to put into it.

I know you will be pleased to hear how very satisfactory I
find these lodgings. I never before had a *bedroom* with an interesting prospect, and I undervalued to you what I had scarce
learned to prize. But nothing can be more charming than the
view which I have before me now. The cornfield betwixt me
and the sea takes off the sense of dreariness, and occasional
bleak chilliness, which a full view of the "unfruitful ocean,"
and *that alone*, relieved only by the not more fruitful or lifesome
shore, has always inspired me with. The sea thus viewed has
something of a lake-like aspect; but that soft green hue was
never seen upon any of my native lakes, although their calm
bosoms used to exhibit a great variety of hues. I take short
walks sometimes two or three times a day; yesterday I walked
out between seven and eight in the evening in hopes to see
the moonlight shining on the sea. But the moon, which had
bathed the landscape in tender light the night before, was hidden in clouds; still I had a pleasant walk toward Dampton
Stairs, and saw the *earth*-stars—the lights on Goodwin sands,
and others—to advantage. For a day and a half after your departure, I felt low and unequal to walking; but since then my
mercury has risen a little, and I feel as if the sea was (or
"*were?*" no, *was*, in this case, I think) doing me that kind and
degree of good which it generally has done, whenever I have
tried it under tolerably favorable circumstances. The only
drawback has been the noisiness of the children. Yesterday
afternoon I began to think it went quite beyond bounds, and
all my self-remindings that I had loud-voiced chatterers of my
own did not bring me to feel complacently on the subject of so
much rattling up and down stairs, incessant slamming of doors,
and squeaking and squabbling. They say there is no lane so
long but it comes to an end at last. I find, however, that *my*
lane is a very short one, for the noise-makers depart in a day
or two; indeed, they have been very bearable ever since yesterday. Their "pa" and "ma" keep a shop in Oxford Street;
and now that I am able to make some calm, disinterested philosophic reflections on all that I have observed in this family,

I am confirmed in my old opinion that the inferior London shop-keepers are an ill-managing class. I *suspect*, at least (I will not venture to say more), that they have more luxury with less in proportion of real respectability, that they partake more of the *civilization* of their times with less of the *cultivation*, than almost any other portion of the community. These children live on the stairs or in the kitchen, and never take a book or needle in their hands, and yet their parents are overburdening Mrs. Smith with cooking attendance, dressing well, and living for many weeks by the sea in commodious lodgings. The extravagance and recklessness that go on in the families of tradesmen in London is beyond what the rank above them even dream of. No wonder they hate the Church, and band against her. The farmers may be still worse in grudging their money; but shop-keepers turn against the Church, I think, because they are better fed than taught, and because they hate regularity, and all that is stern and strict. Methodism and Quakerism have their own strictness; but *they*, many of them, stick to no sect, but go after this or that preacher. They represent the *bad* spirit of this age more completely than almost any other large class among us; but I believe they are to be pitied more than blamed, having great temptations to all they do amiss.

I heard Dr. H—— again last Sunday, and continued to like his manner of preaching, for its earnestness and practicability, and aiming at the one thing needful. The fault of his style is a verbosity and diffuseness: he gives you five branches of illustration where one good solid bough would be quite enough. It is well to be reminded that we are better than the beasts that perish, and can give greater glory to God; but the various particulars of our superiority, beginning with our erect posture, etc., etc., might be left to our own minds to suggest. This is very different from such diffuseness as that of Lord Eldon, who had not, I conjecture, *more words than matter*, but more matter of various kinds than he could arrange to perfection; the minor matters overlaid the major, as the muffling ivy prevents the fine figure of a noble oak, with its well-proportioned trunk and branches, from being clearly discerned. He was perspicuous in thought, but not equally perspicuous in expression. I read to the end of this last volume of his life with very great interest of various kinds. The concluding portion, containing the vin-

dication of his professional character, appeared to me very ably
written, and, upon the whole, more than triumphant, and the remarks on Chancery business, and the legal anecdotes interspersed, are very good also.   The perusal brought home to me,
what I have long felt, how impossible it is that any eminently
good and great and useful man should go through life without
being perseveringly and violently misrepresented and ill-used.
That review by Justice W—— is such a specimen of able but
untruthful and unfair writing !   The portrait of Lord Eldon, the
more I look at it, the more it seems to be the very man—mild
sensibility and weight of intellect and moral firmness and sound
judgment are all marked in that countenance.

VIII.

Religious Discussion Necessary to the Church; and Useful, under Certain
Conditions, to the Individual Christian.

To Mrs. JOSHUA STANGER, Keswick :

10 *Chester Place, November* 7, 1844.—You spoke in your last
to me of controversy and its spiritual inutility.   I quite agree
with you that it is of no *direct* benefit to the soul, and that it
may be pursued injuriously to ourselves and others.   But still
I think it has its use even in a religious point of view, and that
it may be used without being abused.   I would exchange the
term controversy (which gives a notion of *quarreling* to many)
for the milder one of discussion.   This surely is necessary for
the Church at large, if it is to be preserved from error, while
the human understanding is so prone as it is to self-deception.
But I own I should be disposed to go further ; and 'to say that,
in reason and in season, it is useful for the individual.   We can
not have clear, definite views, or know well what our professed
tenets really are, or why we ought to hold them, unless we reflect upon them, and compare them with the opposite ones
which we reject.   Persons who never do this (such persons, I
believe, are very few, even among those who disclaim controversy) are apt, I think, to become narrow, superstitious, and
bigoted ; to think their own belief the only one that any wise
and good person can hold, yet all the time not to know what
that belief really is, or how far it substantially (not in words
only) differs from that of other Christians, with whom they dis-

agree.   Such, I mean, is the *tendency*, in my opinion, of an un-discussing, taking-for-granted frame of mind, though I fully believe that practical Christianity is found both among those who discuss and those who leave alone discussion ; and where that is, nothing else can be deeply amiss.

CHAPTER XIII.

1845.

LETTERS TO THE HON. MR. JUSTICE COLERIDGE, HARTLEY COLE-
RIDGE, ESQ., AUBREY DE VERE, ESQ., MISS MORRIS,
MISS ERSKINE, MRS. FARRER, THE HON.
MRS. HENRY TAYLOR.

I.

Memories of her Native Vale.—The *Quarterly Review* a greater Authority on Practical than on Poetical Matters.—Dr. Arnold as a Man
and a Writer.—His Peculiar Theory of Church and State.—Definition
of Humility and Modesty, suggested by a Note in the "Northern
Worthies."

To HARTLEY COLERIDGE, Esq., Nab Cottage, Grasmere:

Chester Place, January 20, 1845.—Your communications and
comments are ever most interesting to me, partly because they
are upon persons and things in my native land, to which I
have turned since my loss with renewed love and longing—to
thoughts of the hills and the lakes, and still more of the rivers and
streamlets; my dearly beloved Greta, rushing over the stones
by the Cardingmill Field, or sweeping past, swollen with rains;
and all the lovely flowers, especially the yellow globe flower,
which fringe the banks, or lurk in the woods, or crowd and
cluster in the open glades. But then my remembrance of all
these things is inseparably associated with the feelings of early
youth, which lends a glow to them. *Now,* if I were at the Blue-
bell Bog, or on the slope of Goosey Green, I should be sinking
with fatigue, not knowing how I should get back again. Even
an easy saunter by Greta's side would be a very different thing,
now that life, or the best part of it, is all behind me, from what
it was when this same life was *before* me—a vision often broken
and obscured indeed by fear and anxiety, but yet with the Sun
of Hope burning in its centre. This thought prevents me from
lamenting, as I otherwise might, that I can not look to spend

my latter years in the lovely country of my youth.   Yet I never
take a solitary walk in the Park without longing that I could
turn my steps toward dear old Friar's Crag.   I think, in spite
of middle-age and sickness and sorrow, I should still have
much enjoyment in looking on the Lake, every day differently
complexioned from the last, in gazing on the hills lit up by sunset, and all the manifold shows of nature among my native hills.
Herbert H—— seems to miss the richness and variety of the
lake-land exceedingly.   In his last letter he observed how flat
countries lose all their attractions in winter, which does but
interestingly vary those of a mountainous district.   Do not
think, however, from my speaking of having left the best part
of life behind me, that I am unhappy.   I do not in the least
wish to be happier, in the sense of having more satisfaction and
animated enjoyment in the things of this world.   It is best for
me as it is. * * *

It is remarkable how strong the *Quarterly Review* is in
dealing with *matters of fact:* various as the writers in it must be,
they always shine in that department.   In abstract reasonings
this *Review* is not great, and in æsthetics it is generally poor
enough.   Its poetical criticism is arbitrarily vague, without the
slightest attempt at principle, and in a sneering, contemptuous
spirit.   Its treatment of Keats and Tennyson was ultrazoilian.
I admire Keats excessively.   Mr. Wordsworth used to say of
Shelley and Keats that they would ever be great favorites with
the young, but would not satisfy men of all ages.   There is a
truth in this saying, though I should say that it is not *literally*
true, for I myself and many other *mediævals* can read their productions with unabated pleasure.   But yet I feel that there is
in those writers a want of solidity : they do not embody in their
poems much of that with which the deeper and the universal
heart and mind of man can sympathize.   To be always reading
Shelley and Keats would be like living on quince-marmalade.
Milton and Wordsworth are substantial diet for all times and
seasons.

Your admiration of Arnold I fully share.   I admire, and,
what is more, deeply honor him as a man, and as a writer so
far as the man appears in his writings.   As a reasoner and
speculator I surmise that he was not *great*, though what he
does see clearly he expresses with great energy and lifesomeness.   It seems to me that he arrived at much truth which sub-

tler men miss through sheer honesty and singleness of heart and mind, through sheer impatience and imprudence, not through philosophy. His views of Church and State I can not well understand (I have not seen his fragment on the Church): so far as I *can* understand them, I imagine (it seems presumptuous for such as I to *opine* positively on such a subject) that they are incorrect and inadequate. He was a great historian; yet I would fain see how he reconciled them with history, let alone philosophy. By unifying the State with the Church, does he not nullify and destroy the latter as a spiritual power, the antagonist of the world, and confer privileges and functions on the former incompatible with its proper and peculiar ones? I should say, in my ignorance, that this is after all but Romanism in disguise, at least practically. But perhaps I do not apprehend his scheme. He was and is a burning and a shining light in this country. His "Life and Letters" seem to have made a greater impression on the public mind than any book that has been published for many a day. * * *

Reading your "Life of Mason" lately (during the height of my illness I read the "Doctor" and your "Worthies:" I did not want *new* books, but soothing ones in which I took a special interest), I noticed that you said in a note, "Modesty and vanity are only different phenomena of one and the same disposition, viz., an extreme consciousness and apprehensiveness of being observed."[*] But this degrades modesty, methinks, into mere bashfulness, which belongs to the physical temperament, and is but modesty's shadow. Many a youth has both modesty and vanity; for modesty is directly opposed, not to vanity, but to impudence. Still, modesty is surely something more than the *fear of being observed*, which is, indeed, but a phase or mood of vanity, when it is not mere nervous bashfulness.

How shall we define Modesty? Surely it is an important virtue, and a grace to boot. Is it not *moderation*, viewed in its moral rather than its prudential aspect—ingenuous shame, and keen sensibility to all that is unseemly, unfitting, disproportionate in reference to self? It is closely allied to Justice, for he who does not overrate himself is the less likely to arrogate to himself more than is his due: it borders upon Humility and

[*] "Lives of Northern Worthies," by Hartley Coleridge, vol. ii., p. 256. —E. C.

P

Piety, for he who is not disposed to exalt his own merits in his own eyes or in those of others, though not necessarily humble on that account, is yet far more in the way of being so than if he had a high notion of his relative excellence, and a desire to parade and proclaim it.   Humility is not the mere consciousness of our low estate, but the disposition to act and suffer as if we had no high claims; and this is different from modesty, yet, I think, akin to it.   Humility, perhaps, is the being *content* with the low place and scant portion; Modesty, a sense of the impropriety of claiming a higher and a better.

II.

The Royal Academy of 1845.—Turner's Painting.

To Miss ERSKINE:

May 18, 1845.—It is commonly said that this is not a striking Exhibition, simply, I think, because there is in it no great glaring Maclise, nor the usual number of fine animal pieces, with fur which one longs to stroke, by Landseer.   I should say, as some others say too, that it is upon the whole a very interesting collection of specimens of our modern English school of painting: it contains so many sweet landscapes by Stanfield (no Callcotts, alas!), by Collins, Creswick, Lee (one of whose pictures is almost a Gainsborough), Leitch, Harding, and Roberts, though about the productions of this last there is rather a tiring sameness.

In this list I have not included Turner, because I can find but few persons who agree with me that he *is* to be admired; but I had the comfort of an accordant voice with mine in dear Lady P——'s.   I do not like Turner's Venetian views, of which he has four in the present Exhibition, so much as two pictures called "Whalers," in which sea and sky are mixed up together in most (by me) *admired* confusion.   No other man gives me any notion of that infinity of hues and tints and gradations of light and shade which Nature displays to those who have eyes for such sights, except Turner: no one else gives me such a sense of the power of the elements, no one else lifts up the veil and discloses the *penetralia* of Nature, as this painter does.   The liquid look of his ocean and its lifesomeness, and that wonderful steam that is rising up and hovering over the agitated vessel, are what one might look for in vain in any but the Turnerian quarter.

On the other hand, I can not admire Landseer's "Shepherd in Prayer" so much as it is the fashion to do. In this picture he aims at something in a higher line than he has attempted before; and, to my mind, in this higher line he wants power. There is doubtless a sweet feeling about the picture: the shepherd is good, and he kneels before a most picturesquely rural crucifix; but the sheep are *de trop*—such a quantity of dead fleece scattered around, and continued on to the very horizon, I can not away with, or, rather, I wish it away. Neither can I satisfy D—— in the amount of admiration which he demands for Eastlake's "Comus." It is very pure and harmonious, and finely colored, but it wants intensity and meaning and spirit. The "Heiress," by Leslie, is a most lovely girl; and Clater's "Bride" as fair and vernal as the hawthorn wreath with which she is encircling her head, in contempt of Fashion with her orange-flowers. Etty has seven or eight pictures, all of which have his usual merits, more or less, and some of them are beautiful. His *flesh* is first-rate; but one may look in vain in him for the spirit—that is, the spiritual and refined.

III.

Visitors before Luncheon.

To Miss MORRIS:

Chester-Place, 1845.—First, I must reply to your proposal of coming to see me between twelve and one o'clock. My *rule* is, not to let my friends visit me at that early hour when they can with no great difficulty come at a later one; because the two hours before my mid-day meal are with me the most uneasy in the whole twenty-four. Still I do not wish to be more subjected to my bodily weakness than is unavoidable, and every now and then I am called down to some old friend whom I do not like to send away unseen. Old gentlemen especially *will* take their own way in such matters, and look in when it suits them rather than when it suits me. At first I feel faint and cross; but when they begin laying down the law about this and that—the Church and the Tract doctrines, and other such subjects—as if there was but one opinion in the world that was

really worth a straw, and that their own—all other reasoners
and thinkers dancing about after vain shadows and will-o'-the-
wisps—I am provoked into a sort of enraged strength—my
controversial muscles begin to plump up—I lose sight of lunch-
eon (a vision of which had been floating before my dull eyes
before), and as soon as a pause occurs, I fill it up with my voice,
and, whether listened to or not, improve by exercise my small
powers of expressing opinion.

IV.

Interpretations of Scripture Prophecies by Writers of the Evangelical
School.—Antichristian Character of the Papacy supposed to be Predicted by the "Little Horn" in the Book of Daniel, the "Man of Sin"
in the Second Epistle to the Thessalonians, and "Babylon the Great"
in the Revelations.—Contents of the Sixth Vial.—Shelley's Atheism.—
Not Papal, but Pagan Rome the Real Object of the Apocalyptic Denunciations.

To Miss MORRIS :

10 *Chester Place, June* 21, 1845.—I have felt that I ought to
have been conversing with you of late on a subject upon which
I have been venturing to write (I mean a *letter* only)—the subject of prophecy.

I told Mr. B—— the impression which the different passages
in Scripture, most important in the Antichrist controversy, and
most dwelt upon by each party, as proving their own particular
views, make upon me, when I read them without the medium of
note or comment, and with no theory intervening betwixt my
mind's eye and the text. The "little horn" of Daniel presents
to me a staring likeness of the Pope. That it was intended for
him, and for none other than he, I will not venture to say. I
do not feel sure of *that*, all things considered, so far as I can
consider them. But I. say it is *awfully like* him—that he *is* a
little horn that speaks great things, and has eyes, *such eyes* as no
other power in this world possesses, that he changes times and
laws presumptuously and iniquitously, and has worn out a great
many saints of God with persecutions. But when I read the
language of the New Testament on the Man of Sin and Antichrist, instead of seeing this picture enlarged and rendered
more distinct, on the contrary, I see only a generalization. The
mystery of iniquity is in the Papacy; but that Popery, and Popery

alone, is the mystery of iniquity, I can not persuade myself. Here, I think, Horsley, Palmer, and a hundred others, who oppose the theory which identifies Antichrist with the Pope or Popery, are strong. That "wicked that is to be consumed by the spirit of the Lord's mouth, and destroyed by the brightness of His coming," is certainly no popery that has existed yet. But it is said there is to be another manifestation of popery and its corruption, and this it is which is to be destroyed. Now it is just this way of interpreting Scripture, this putting into the sacred text *ad libitum*, and filling up ever so great a gulf and gap with supposition, which seems to me so unwarrantable, and a method, too, which never leads to any conclusion, because every different theorist can resort to the same expedient to justify his opinions. See the tracts on Antichrist, and the use *they* make of this argument. If all the abominations, persecutions, presumptions, and impious pretensions of the Papacy, which history records, are the characters of the Man of Sin, then surely he has been already revealed, as he was not revealed in St. Paul's own day. To say that we have already witnessed these things, and that they constitute the wickedness of the wicked one, and yet that he is *still to be revealed* close before the advent of the Lord, and His reign upon earth, is not, in my opinion, to submit our minds to the text of Scripture, but to make it say what we like. The "powers and signs and lying wonders" of Romanism have been manifested at full. It is highly improbable that they can ever deceive the world again as they have done. What a crafty priesthood can contrive in one part of the civilized world, an active press and an irrepressible spirit of inquiry and opposition to superstitious falsity exposes and counteracts in another part. The passage in Timothy, on forbidding to marry, does not, to my mind, describe Romanistic errors, but religious notions of a somewhat different kind.

If such are my impressions from the Epistles, still more strongly do I feel on going on to the Apocalypse that Popery was not the object of the apostolic predictions and denunciations, except so far as *all* falsehood and corruption is so. I can not pretend to assign the meaning of all the various symbols—I *never* have seen them to my mind satisfactorily explained. The "vials" are filled, to every man's fancy, with just those exhibitions of evil which most strongly have excited his aversion and alarmed his fears. Mr. B—— notices Shelley's

"Revolt of Islam," under the sixth vial.   Alas! poor Shelley!
"I'se wae to think of him," as Burns was to think of old Nick
and his gloomy fate.   He had a religious element in his nature,
but it was sadly overborne by an impetuous temper, and a certain presumption, which made him cast aside all the teaching
of other men that did not approve itself at once to his judgment.   But to mention him under the sixth vial is to give him
an infamous sort of fame which he scarcely, I think, deserved.
As an unbeliever, he was utterly insignificant—made no prose-
lytes, had no school, nor belonged to any school.   He had
ceased to be an atheist before he died, and never had any
power, or excited any great attention, I think, except as a poet.
In that line he has a station from which he can not be moved,
while any genuine taste for poetry, as such, exists.

To conclude my impressions of prophecy, not from commen-
taries, but from the text: I own I can see nothing but Imperial
and Pagan Rome in the Revelations, as the great object of the
prophet's denunciations, from beginning to end.   It should be
borne in mind, I think, that the persecutions under the Roman
Empire were the only warfare that ever has been carried on
against Christianity as such—against the *religion* itself under
any form.   The martyrs during that warfare were the only sufferers who could *properly* be said to have died "for the testimony of Jesus."   There have been anti-Papal martyrs enough
for the purity of the faith; but is it not putting the less before
the greater to imagine that these, and not the thousands that
were put to death and tortured for professing Christianity at
all, are those of whom the apocalypt wrote with such a pen of
fire?   But the whole description of this Babylon the Great, and
her downfall, this city on seven hills, to my mind, is expressive
of the great Roman *Empire*, of which Rome itself was the representative, and not Papal Rome, which never sat upon seven
hills; and to convert those seven hills into seven Electors of
Germany, seems to me a more incredible transformation than
any in Ovid's "Metamorphoses."   Nothing can exceed the boldness of Scriptural metaphor; but this boldness has its own laws,
and the same figure which fits one sentence fits not another.

V.

Occasional Recurrence of Millennial Preachings.—Unpractical Nature of the Doctrine.—Bearing of the Parable of the Ten Virgins on this Subject.—Various Styles of Contemporary Divines.

To Miss MORRIS:

1845.—I find that there has been a very general preaching of the Millennium in various parts of the country of late years. So it will continue to be, I think, ever and anon, till some victorious arm shall arise, or some victorious pen shall write some book in which a real advance shall be made in the elucidation of the subject. Hitherto there has been nothing more than a repeated eddying round a certain number of arguments, which contain a certain quantity of force, and are especially striking when first presented to the unprepared mind, but which, as I have been led to think, are not strong enough to bring the matter to a conclusion with the majority of the reflective and judicious. Hence the subject is often brought forward, eagerly enforced, makes a number of converts—some few permanent ones, others only for a season; but then it dies away again, without taking any deep hold of the Church at large. I know how your brother disposes of this fact in that judicious sermon of his on the "Actual Neglect," etc., which shows a clearer insight into the difficulties of the question, I think, than most Millennial discourses do. He observes that the *wise* virgins slumbered as well as the foolish while the Bridegroom tarried. But if the *wise* as well as the foolish neglect this doctrine, what are they that attend to it? Our Lord leaves no room for them in His parable at all. Looking at the structure of it, I can hardly persuade myself that He meant by this slumber to indicate a blamable inattention to His coming again ; for what more could the wise virgins have done, had they kept awake the whole night, than provide oil for their lamps? what would they have gained more than admission to the marriage-feast? * * *

I agree with you quite about Mr. B——'s sermon and its "dry brilliancy." It reminds me of those bright, burnished insects whose juiceless bodies clink and rattle as they whisk glittering along. His style wants oiling.

Newman's sermon, "Faith against Sight," one of those addressed to the University, is an admirable specimen of his mind and manner. I think he is the finest writer, upon the whole, that we have at present; but, with all his power, he will never be able, as I believe, to establish more than one half of his body of opinion in this land.

VI.

Dr. Pusey's Preaching.

To Miss MORRIS, Mecklenburg Square:

Chester Place, July 7, 1845.—We have had Pusey and Manning preaching here lately, the former three times. Pusey's middle sermon, preached in the evening, was the perfection of his style. But it is wrong to talk of *style* in respect of a preacher whose very merit consists in his aiming at no *style* at all. He is certainly, to my feelings, more impressive than any one else in the pulpit, though he has not one of the graces of oratory. His discourse is generally a rhapsody, describing, with infinite repetition and accumulativeness, the wickedness of sin, the worthlessness of earth, and the blessedness of heaven. He is as still as a statue all the time he is uttering it, looks as white as a sheet, and is as monotonous in delivery as possible. While listening to him, you do not seem to see and hear a *preacher*, but to have visible before you a most earnest and devout spirit, striving to carry out in this world a high religious theory.

VII.

Sunset over the Sea.

To Mrs. FARRER:

Herne Bay, August 9, 1845.—Yesterday evening the soft blue of sea and sky, illumined with windows of bright rose-color, which seemed like windows of heaven indeed, with the Apocalyptical City stretched out in gemmy splendor on the other side, as fancy suggested, was most lovely and tranquilizing.

VIII.

Canterbury Cathedral and St. Augustine's College.

To the Hon. Mr. Justice COLERIDGE, Heath's Court, Ottery St. Mary:

Herne Bay, August 10, 1845.—Last Wednesday we went to Canterbury to see the Cathedral and St. Augustine's. The former I admired more than ever; and D——'s architectural lore made our excursion all round the outside, and through the inside of this more beautiful than sublime structure, all the more rememberable and interesting. Some of the old painted glass is the very ideal of that sort of thing, rich and gemmy with minute designs, and far removed from the modern *picture* style of painted window. We visited the precincts of St. Augustine's with very great interest, and were pleased to see with our own eyes how considerable a part of the ancient structure will be woven into the view, and what a *physical continuity*, as D—— says, there will be of the one with the other. The new dining-hall takes in the wood-work, to a great extent, of the old refectory for strangers; and the antique architectural forms (in the middle-pointed style) will be carefully reproduced. The old gateway will form a very imposing entrance to the modern college.

IX.

Reunion of Christendom.—The Romish Clergy and the Roman Church.

To the Hon. Mr. Justice COLERIDGE:

Chester Place, August 26, 1845.—As for desire for reunion with the Church of Rome—I verily think that no one can exceed me in desire for the union of all Christendom, that all who call upon the name of the Lord, and acknowledge the moral law of the New Testament, and the necessity of obeying it, should be in communion with each other—the millions of Methodists, Baptists, Congregationalists in America, as well as the Romanists of Italy and Spain. But such a union can not be without concessions on one side or the other, if not on both, unless the parties were to change their minds to a great extent, in which case the debate and the difficulty would be at an end; and I for one could never give up or adopt what would satisfy either body. I suppose, however, that you have a desire for a reunion with *Rome* of a very different kind from any you may entertain for union with all Christians; you look upon Rome as a branch of the true Church, and the others above named as out of the pale of the true Church. With this feeling I can not pretend to have much sympathy, though it may be my error and misfortune not to have it. I think that the Congregationalists belong to the Church of Christ as well as the others. The Church of Rome I am accustomed to regard, not as the aggregate of Christians professing Romish doctrine, but as the body of the Romish clergy, together with the system of religious administration upon which they proceed. For the former, the multitude of Romish individuals, I have no feelings of dislike or disrespect whatever—I believe that numbers of them are full of true religion and virtue, and worship God in spirit and in truth. The Romish clergy, considered in their corporate capacity, I can not but look upon as full of worldly wisdom and worldly iniquity, and I think, as you do of the Reformation, that Old Nick contemplates it—*i. e.*, this body—with great satisfaction, the cockles of his heart leaping up with delight at the view. My Uncle Southey was abused for calling the system of the Romish Church "a monstrous structure of imposture and wickedness;" yet I think he did a good deal to substantiate the charge; he certainly had far more *information* on the subject than our young inamoratos of the modern Romish Church can any of them boast, and he had no sort of sympathy with Dissenters and Low Churchmen to inspire him with enmity against the opposite quarter of Christendom. Still I am endeavoring to get rid of Protestant prejudice—of all feelings and views merely founded on habit, apart from reflection and genuine spiritual perception — and to consider quietly whether or no there be not some good even in the Romish ecclesiastical system; and some good I do believe there is, *especially for the lower orders*, as I also think there is some good in the Methodist system, with which, as well as with the religious practices of the strict Evangelicals, Blanco White is always comparing the system in which he, to his misery, was brought up. But I own it seems to me that the good, whatever it may be, is inextricable from the evil, both from the nature of the thing, and also because the Romish body has never been known to make any *real* concession of any kind or sort—none that was not meant as a mere temporary expedient, to be withdrawn on the earliest opportunity; and looking upon it as I do, as *a power of this world*, aiming at political domination, and not inspired, as a body, with any pure zeal for the furtherance of the *truth*, be it what it may, I can not believe it ever will.

X.

"New Heavens and a New Earth."

The following lines may fitly be inserted here, as a poetical expression of the writer's sentiments on these high subjects.—E. C.

TO A FAIR FRIEND ARGUING IN SUPPORT OF THE RENOVATION, IN A LITERAL SENSE, OF THE MATERIAL SYSTEM.

PHILONOUS TO HYLASIA.

I.

Keep, oh! keep those eyes on me,
  If thou wouldst my soul persuade,
Soul of reasoner, bold and free,
  Who with pinions undismayed
Soars to realms of higher worth
Than aught like these poor heavens and earth.

II.

Talk no more of Scripture text,
  Tract and note of deep divine:
These but leave the mind perplexed—
  More effectual means are thine:
Through that face, so fair and dear,
The doctrine shines as noonday clear.

III.

Who that sees the radiant smile
  Dawn upon thy features bright,
And thy soft, full eyes the while
  Spreading beams of tender light,
But must long those looks to greet,
When perfect souls in joyance meet?

IV

Who that round some verdant home
  Day by day with thee hath strayed,
Through its pathways loved to roam,
  Sat beneath its pleasant shade,
But must hope that heavenly bowers
May wear such hues as these of ours?

v.

O ye fair and pleasant places,
  Where the eye delighted ranges;
O ye dear and friendly faces,
  Loved through all your mortal changes;
Are ye but stars, to shine through this life's night,
Destined, in Heaven's great Day, to vanish from our sight?

S. C., 1845.

To Miss MORRIS:

Eton, September 8, 1845.—I have often spoken of you to Mr.
De Vere; and yesterday I told him that the views which he
was setting forth in regard to the future world, the glorified
body, and the new heavens and earth, were in spirit, and to a
great degree in form, extremely similar to those I had heard you
express and warmly enlarge upon. *I* am much more *dry*, alas!
on these subjects; at least, I am aware that my belief must appear very dry and cold to all but those who entertain it. *We*
somehow fancy that we are to have a quintessence of all that
is exalted and glowing and beautiful in your new-world creed
hereafter, only not in the same way. Mr. De Vere can not bear
to part with our human body altogether, nor with this beautiful
earth with its glorious canopy. He wants to keep these things,
but to have them unimaginably raised and purified and glorified! *I* think that *they* must go, but that all the loveliness
and majesty and exquisiteness are to be unimaginably extracted and enshrined in a new, unimaginable form, in another, and
to us now, inconceivable state of existence. He said (so like
you), "But I want *this earth* to have a fair trial, to have it show
what it can be at the best, in the highest perfection of which
it is capable, which never has been yet manifested."

XI.

Poetry of Keats: its Beauties and Defects.—"The Grecian Urn" and
"Endymion."

To AUBREY DE VERE, Esq., Curragh Chase, Ireland:

Eton, September, 1845.—I admire Keats extremely, but I
think that he wants solidity. His path is all flowers, and leads
to nothing but flowers. The end of the "Endymion" is no point:
when we arrive there, it is looking down a land of flowers,
stretching on *ad infinitum*, the separate parts indistinguishable.

I admire all the minor poems which you have marked, three of them especially. In the "Grecian Urn" I dislike the third stanza: it drags out the substance of the preceding stanzas, which, after all, is stuff of *fancy*, not of the higher *imagination*, to weariness; and it ends with an unpleasant image, expressed in no very good English. "High sorrowful" is Keats' English, if English at all.

I must say that, spite of the beautiful poetry, as far as words and images go, I've no patience with that Adonis lying asleep on a couch, with his "white arm" and "faint damask mouth," like a "dew-lipped rose," with lilies above him, and Cupids all round him. If Venus was in love with such a girl-man as that, she was a greater fool than the world has ever known yet, and didn't know what a handsome man is, or what sort of a gentleman is "worthy a lady's eye," even as far as the mere outward man is concerned. I do think it rather effeminate in a young man to have even dreamed such a dream, or presented his own sex to himself in such a *pretty-girl* form. And where is the sense or the beauty of setting one woman opposite another, for a pair of lovers, instead of an Apollo and a Venus? This effeminacy is the weak part of Keats. Shelley has none of it. There is no greater stickler than I am for the rights of woman —not the right of speaking in Parliament and voting at elections, but of having her own sex to herself, and all the homage due to its attractions. There is one merit in Byron: he is always manly. The weaknesses he has are weaknesses of an imperfect man, not a want of manliness.

You will perhaps tell me that the Greek poets have sometimes ascribed a delicate beauty to Adonis. But I say those poets must have been thinking of their own lady-loves all the while, and that *Venus herself* would have admired a very different swain. It is not the possession of any beauty of form or hue that will make a man effeminate; but it is the presence of such beauty apart from something else to which it is subordinated. It is the absence of this *something else*, and the presentation without it, of that which in woman is characteristic and prominent, which makes this picture of Keats' so disagreeably feminine, at least to my taste. I think I have a right to preach on *this* theme, just because I am a woman myself. Men in general are frights, especially before and after five-and-twenty. Nothing provokes ladies more than to hear men admiring one another's beauty. It is less affronting for each man to admire his own ; they fancy *that* is for their sakes !

I must take another half-sheet to quarrel with you about the "Endymion." How could you possibly, after making so many marks, pass over that powerful description of Circe torturing the metamorphosed wretches in the forest, one of the most striking passages in the whole poem. I am afraid you like nothing that is *horrid*, that you are too fond of the "roses and the thistle-down," and find such things "too flinty hard for your nice touch." To me it is *refreshing*, after the sugar upon honey and butter upon cream of much that precedes. It is fine, too, as an allegory. And is not that an energetic expression ?—

> "Disgust and hate,
> And terrors manifold, *divided me*
> *A spoil among them.*"

Especially powerful is that part beginning—

> "Avenging, slow,
> Anon she took a branch of mistletoe."

The deliberate way in which she does the thing is so fine, and their anticipation of agony, and the poor elephant's pathetic prayer ! One feels the cumbrous weight of flesh weighing one down in reading it.

Again, you take no notice of Cynthia's speech to her lover, so Beaumont and Fletchery—

> "O that the dreadful smiles
> Had wanéd from Olympus' solemn height,
> And from all serious gods !"

Brimful of love-sick silliness, no doubt, but so is the whole poem ; and, instead of flattering the fellow in that way, she ought to have given him a sharp dig with her keenest arrow for having the abominable bad taste to call her lunar lips "slippery blisses." By the bye, what think you of "nectarous camel-draughts?" Is it not enough to horrify the very genius of osculation into a fit? Surely, after a *camel-draught* of nectar, Glaucus might have found the contents of the "black, dull, gurgling phial" an agreeable change, and after such a drench of roses and ambrosia, who would not cry aloud for camomile and wormwood ?

These are your omissions. Then, in the way of commission, you put a stroke of approval at these lines—

> "Old Œolus thy foe
> Skulks to his cavern, 'mid the *gruff* complaint
> Of all his rebel tempests.
> * * * "Dark clouds faint
> When, from thy diadem, a silver gleam
> Slants over *blue dominion.*"

Gruff is a ludicrous word; and if we may talk about *blue dominion*, I know not what classes of words there are that may not intermarry with every other class.

You approve also this—

> "While ocean's tide
> Hung swollen at their backs, and *jewel'd* sands
> Took *silently* their foot-prints."

Ocean's tide hangs swollen from a dike, which keeps it back; but does it ever thus hang from a sandy beach, and how should sands be *jeweled*, and why should it be noticed that they took foot-prints *silently*?

It seems to me that Keats not only falsifies language very frequently, besides making words, such as *orby*, *serpenting*, etc., *ad libitum*, but that he also falsifies nature sometimes in his imagery. He turns the outer world into a sort of raree-show, and combines shapes and colors as fantastically and lawlessly as the kaleidoscope. The kaleidoscope certainly has a law of its own, and so has the young poet, but it is not nature's law, nor in harmony with it. The old masters, in all their vagrancy of fancy and invention, never did thus. They always placed their wild inventions in the real world, and while we wander in their realms of faëry, we have the same solid earth and blue sky over our heads as when we take a walk in the fields to see Cicely milking the cow. This I think is occasionally the fault of Keats, and another is that sameness of sweetness and over-lusciousness of which I have already spoken. Reading the "Endymion" is like roaming in a forest of giant jonquils. Nevertheless, I take great delight in his volume, and thank you much for putting it into my hands.

XII.

Sudden Death of her Mother.*—Reflections on the Event.

To the Hon. Mr. Justice COLERIDGE :

Chester Place, September 26, 1845.—My dearest John, thank you for your most kind letter.   My soul is indeed very sorrowful.   The death-silence is awful.   I had to think of her every minute of the day, to be always on my guard against noise ; and she was one that made herself *felt*, dear creature, every hour in the day.   *I* shall never be *so* missed by any one, my life is so much stiller, and more to myself.

I feel more than ever the longing to go and join them that are gone—but for my children.   But the greatest tie to earth is gone from me, for even the children could do better without me than she could have done.

All that Nurse tells me of her last days is soothing.   She wrote contentedly, thankful for Nurse's devotion to her, and speaking even of Caroline's desire to please her.   She had said to me, as I was going away, "This is the last time you must leave me."   I said, "If you are in the least ill, let me know, and I will return directly."   I knew it would only vex her to give up the visit *then*.

I always looked forward to nursing her through a long last illness.   I know not how it was, I could never help looking forward to it with a sort of satisfaction.   I day-dreamed about it —according to the usual way of my mind—and cut it out in fancy all in my own way.   She was to waste away gradually, without much suffering, and to become more and more placid in spirit, and filled with the anticipation of heavenly things.   I thought, too, that this would help to prepare me for my change. Now I seem as if a long-cherished prospect had been snatched away from me.   I thank God I was not thus suddenly separated from Henry.—Ever your very affectionate sister,

SARA COLERIDGE.

---

* At Chester Place, on the 24th of September, during my mother's absence on a visit to the Rev. Edward Coleridge at Eton.—E. C.

XIII.

Peculiar Sense of Solitude arising from the Loss of a Parent.—Editorial Labors on the "Biographia Literaria."—Mr. Coleridge's Immense Reading, and Striking Quotations made from Obscure Authors.

To the Hon. Mrs. HENRY TAYLOR:

10 *Chester Place, December* 8, 1845.—Your kind invitation I feel quite grieved to decline, but I must decline it, as I have done many others that have lately been made me. I do not feel sufficiently equable in spirits to leave home *now*, and can not agree with my friends in general that I should regain this quietude better elsewhere than at home. But I hope to see more of you, dear Mrs. Taylor, some time hence. The death of my mother permanently affects my happiness, more even than I should have anticipated, though I always knew that I must feel the separation at first as a severe wrench. But I did not apprehend, during her life, to what a degree she prevented me from feeling heart-solitude, and the full forlornness of a widow's state. Her age and infirmities, though they caused me great uneasiness, had not made any sensible alteration in her mind or heart. I lost in her as apprehensive a companion, and one who entered as fully into life, as if she had died at fifty. She had a host of common remembrances with me, and interests, which my children are strangers to. They can not connect me, as conversation with her so constantly did, with all my early life. But the worst is the loss of cares and duties, due to her, which gave additional interest to my existence, and made me feel of *use* and important.

I am not, however, brooding over grief from want of employment. I am just now, indeed, *absurdly* busy. I have to edit my father's fragmentary work, the "Biographia Literaria," or at least to continue the preparations already made for a new edition. To carry on these upon the plan on which they were commenced, and to do for the "Biographia" what has been done for "The Friend," and other works of my father, I have found, as I advanced into the first volume, *for me*, exceedingly troublesome. A clever literary man, who reads and writes on a large scale, would make nothing of the business, but it makes me feel as if I had no rest for the soles of my feet, and must be continually starting up to look into this or that volume, or find it out in some part of Europe.   As little boys at school do *so* wish that Virgil and Livy would but have written *easily*, so I am sometimes tempted to wish that my father would just have read more *commonplace-ishly*, and not quoted from such a number of out-of-the-way books, which not five persons in England but himself would ever look into.   The trouble I take is so ridiculously disproportioned to any effect that can be produced, and we are so apt to measure our importance by the efforts we make, rather than the good we do, that I am obliged to keep reminding myself of this very truth, in order not to become a mighty person in my own eyes, while I remain as small as ever in the eyes of every one else.

Then my father had such a way of seizing upon the *one* bright thing, out of long tracts of (to most persons) dull and tedious matter.   I remember a great campanula which grew in a wood at Keswick—two or three such I found in my native vale, during the course of my flower-seeking days.   As well might we present one of these as a sample of the blue-bells of bonny Cumberland, or the one or two oxlips which may generally be found among a multitude of cowslips in a Somersetshire meadow, as specimens of the flowerhood of the field, as give these extracts for proof of what the writer was generally wont to produce.

XIV.

"S. T. C. on the Body."—The Essential Principle of Life not Dependent on the Material Organism.—Teaching of St. Paul on this Point.—The Glorified Humanity of Christ.—Disembodied Souls.—Natural Regrets arising from the Thought of our Great Change.

To Aubrey de Vere, Esq.:

"What did Luther mean by a body?   For to me the word seemeth capable of two senses, universal and special ; first, a form indicating to A, B, C, etc., the existence and finiteness of some one other being, *demonstrative* as *hic*, and *disjunctive* as *hic et non ille*, and in this sense God alone can be without body ; secondly, that which is not merely *hic distinctive*, but *divisive ;* yea, a product divisible from the producent as a snake from its skin, a precipitate and death of living power, and in this sense the body is proper to mortality, and to be denied of spirits made perfect, as well as of the spirits that never fell from perfection, and perhaps of those who fell below mortality, namely, the devils."*

What did S. T. C. mean by a *form* not material? A material form is here *divisive* as well as *disjunctive,* and this he denies of the essential body or bodily principle. Did he conceive the body in essence to be supersensuous, not an object of sense, not colored or extended in space? Of the bodily principle we know only this, that it is the power in us which constructs our outward material organism, builds up our earthly tenement of flesh and blood. Can this power, independently of the organism in and by which it is manifested, be conceived of as a *form* indicating the existence and finiteness of some one being to another? I believe that with our present faculties we are incapable of conceiving how a soul can be embodied otherwise than in a sensuous frame ; but knowing, as we do, that our fleshly case is not a part of ourselves, but that there is a something in ourselves which thus clothes us in matter, I think we may infer that the human body, in the deepest sense, is independent of matter, and that it may, in another sphere of existence, be our *form,* that which indicates to other beings our finite distinct individual being, in a way which now we are not able to know or imagine.

But what did St. Paul mean when he declared so emphatically, "Now this I say, brethren, that flesh and blood can not inherit the kingdom of God." Is he not to be understood literally? Must we suppose him to have meant only this : the carnal mind, or the man in whom the lower animal nature has the upper hand, can not inherit the kingdom? But how will such an interpretation suit the context? St. Paul has been speaking not of holiness and unholiness, but of soul and body, and the state after death, when this mortal tabernacle shall have been dissolved. In reference to this subject, he affirms that as we have borne the *image of the earthy,* that is, a material body, we shall also bear the image of the heavenly, and then straightway adds that flesh and blood shall not inherit the divine kingdom. To this, indeed, he adds again, "Neither doth *corruption inherit incorruption,"* evidently identifying flesh and blood with the corruptible, not introducing the alien topic of spiritual corruption. Jeremy Taylor affirms, in reference to this passage in Corinthi-

---

* Coleridge's "Notes, Theological, Political," etc., p. 49.—E. C.

ans, that "in the resurrection our bodies are said to be spiritual, not in substance, but in effect and operation;" upon which my father observes, " This is, in the first place, a willful interpretation; and, secondly, it is absurd, for what sort of flesh and blood would incorruptible flesh and blood be? As well might we speak of marble flesh and blood. In the sense of St. Paul, as of Plato and all other dynamic philosophers, flesh and blood is *ipso facto* corruption, that is, the spirit of life in the mid or balancing state between fixation and reviviscence. 'Who shall deliver me from the body of this death' is a Hebraism for 'this death which the body is.' For matter itself is but *spiritus in coagulo*, and organized matter the *coagulum* in the act of being restored: it is then repotentiating. Stop its self-destruction as matter, and you stop its self-reproduction as a vital organ."*

St. Paul declares that in the resurrection we are to be clothed with a spiritual body, and to leave behind the natural body which we had from Adam. Now what is a spiritual as opposed to a *natural* body? Surely the latter is a material and fleshly body, and no body of flesh and blood can be otherwise than natural, or can be properly spiritual. Make the flesh and blood ever so thin, fine, and aerial, still the difference betwixt that and any other flesh and blood will be one of degree, not of kind. But the Apostle does not promise us a body of refined flesh and blood, such as, according to some theologians, Adam had before the fall, but sets aside our Adamite body altogether; and seems, indeed, to imply that the first man had no spirituality at any time, for he is opposed to the second man as being of the earth, earthy, as if in his character of the *first man*, and not as fallen man, he was the source of earthiness, the Lord from Heaven alone being the foundation of the spiritual.

There are some who believe that the Lord from Heaven is now sitting at the right hand of the Father in a material and fleshly body, such as He wore upon earth, and appeared in after the Resurrection—a *metaphorical* right hand, as Pearson explains it, but the body of Him who sits thereat of flesh and blood. It is quite natural for such believers to expect that the bodies of the saints in the resurrection will be fleshly too. As the first fruits, so they must think will be all that follow. This argument, however, seems to prove too much for those who con-

---

* "Notes on English Divines," vol. ii., p. 284.—E. C.

tend that our bodies in the future world are to be of flesh and blood, but refined and glorified, and no longer natural; for the body in which our Lord ascended was the same as that which He had before He rose from the dead. It was certainly a natural body, that could be felt as well as seen, and which ate and drank.

But my father believed that there will be a resurrection of the *body*, which will have nothing to do with flesh and blood; he speaks of a *noumenal* body, as opposed to our present phenomenal one, which appears to the senses, "no visible, tangible, accidental body—that is, a cycle of images and sensations in the imagination of the beholders—but a supersensual body, the *noumenon* of the human nature."* In truth, he considered *this* body inseparable from the being of man, indispensable to the actual existence of finite spirits; the notion of disembodied souls floating about in some unknown region in the intermediate state, after the dissolution of the material organism, and before the union of the soul with a celestial, incorruptible flesh-and-blood body, he looked upon as a mere dream, a chimera suited only to the times when men were wont to convert abstractions into persons, and to ascribe objective reality to creatures which the intellectual and imaginative faculty engendered within itself. He laughed at the notion of the separability of the *real* body from the soul—the arbitrary notion of man as a mixture of heterogeneous components. "On this doctrine," he says, "the man is a mere phenomenal result, a sort of brandy-sop, a toddy-punch, a doctrine unsanctioned by, indeed inconsistent with, the Scriptures. It is not true that body plus soul makes man. Man is not the syntheton or composition of body and soul, as the two component units. No—man is the unit, the prothesis, and body and soul are the two poles, the positive and negative, the thesis and antithesis of the man, even as attraction and repulsion are the two poles in and by which one and the same magnet manifests itself."†

I continually feel sorrowful at the thought of never again beholding the faces of my friends, or, rather, about to be sorrowful. I come up to the verge of the thought ever and anon, but before I can enter into it am met by the reflection, "O vain and causeless melancholy!"—whatever satisfaction or happiness I

* "Notes on English Divines," vol. ii., p. 52.—E. C.
† Ibid., vol. ii., p. 96.—E. C.

can conceive as accruing to me in this way, can not the Omnipotent bestow it upon me in some other way, if this is not in harmony with His divine plan? The loss, the want, is in this life only, for whatever that other sphere of existence may be, I shall be adjusted to it. Still in this life it is a loss and a trial to feel that we can not image or represent to ourselves veritably the state and happiness. We long to see again the very faces of our friends, and can not raise ourselves to the thought that in the other world there may be no seeing with the visual eye, but something better than such seeing, something by which it is absorbed and superseded. The belief that the future world for man is this world reformed, exalted, and purified, is one which I can not reconcile with reason.

CHAPTER XIV.

1846.—January-July.

LETTERS TO AUBREY DE VERE, ESQ., REV. FREDERICK D. MAU-
RICE, HENRY TAYLOR, ESQ., MISS MORRIS, MRS. H. M.
JONES, MRS. RICHARD TOWNSEND.

I.

The Conviction of Sin.—Exaggerated Self-Accusations of the Religious.—
Substantial Agreement among Christians of all Denominations.

To Miss MORRIS, Mecklenburg Square :

10 *Chester Place, January* 14, 1846.—I will at once tell you
the thought or two that occupied my mind as I read your letter
on the subject of the comparative sense of sin. I quite agree
with you that the *sentiment*, the feeling, is natural, and perhaps
necessary, in an awakened or awakening state of mind, respecting sin, its odiousness and its danger. But, then, I think it is
capable of being modified or balanced by the representations
of the reasoning mind. This latter must tell most sinners,
whose overt acts are not of the most flagrant description, that,
in all probability, if they saw the hearts of others as they see
their own, they would behold a very similar train of goings-on
to that which they discern by inward inspection. And when
they hear so many of those who appear to be trying to please
God express this opinion of their own *superior* wickedness in
terms equally strong—as strong as human language will admit
—how can they, without suspending the use of reason, avoid
drawing the inference that it is no more to be relied on as *absolute truth* than the unawakened Pharisee's notion that he is
holier than other men ?

The feeling in itself I believe to be a good one ; but I do
think it is plainly the intention of our Maker that man should
not be guided by feeling alone, or by his intellect alone, but
that he should be kept in the right path by the alternate or mingled action of the two. The sense of being worse than any

one else, if thus kept in its sphere by reason, will be nothing more than a keen spiritual sensibility; if it went further, and clouded that inward eye which makes us acquainted with *truth*, we know not what perversions might follow, what evil reactions and corruptions, even of the spiritual mind by means of the understanding. How often has it appeared as if excessive spiritual humility passed over into spiritual pride, and the very man who was calling himself a worm, and really fancying himself such, has shown by his acts and words that he considered every soul alive that did not embrace his notions of election, justification, and such parts of theology, as far beneath himself, in the eye of God, as a soul that is and is to be cast out forever, is beneath a soul that is to be saved. Yet this same self-deceiver, as he referred to feeling alone, felt sure that he was really humble. Had he tried himself by all the different criteria whereby we may arrive at a knowledge of ourselves — by the state of his heart and by his outward course of action, by the conclusions of his judging and comparing faculty, as well as by his emotions—he could hardly have been thus ignorant what spirit he was of.

My clergyman friend, who is to spend this evening with me, speaks strongly and sadly of the mutual misunderstandings that prevail among Christians, and I own I daily more and more lament these *dogmatic* differences. I know the parties on both sides insist that they are substantial and not merely logical (*ens logicum*) differences; but I do believe that most persons who have gone between various parties as I have done, not merely *read* on both sides—that is by no means enough—but eat and drunk and slept, and talked confidentially, and interchanged, not only courtesies, but heart kindnesses on both or all sides, would have very much the same impression with myself, that though logical truth is one, and can not belong equally to those who logically differ, yet that the life and soul and substance of Christianity may be pretty equally partaken by those who logically differ. And, to confess the truth, my own belief is that the whole logical truth is not the possession of any one party; that it exists in fragments among the several parties, and that much of it is yet to be developed.

II.

Grace in Baptism.

To AUBREY DE VERE, Esq., Curragh Chase, Adare:

1846.—People talk about a *seed* of grace sown in the heart remaining latent, then springing up, bearing fruit, etc., in all which, I think, they deceive themselves by material analogies, and forget the true nature of that which they speak of. The use of those metaphors in Scripture is quite different. I think that error and confusion have arisen on the subject from confused notions of the nature and predicates of *spirit*. Men think of the "heart" as if it really were a fleshy receptacle. They do not consider that the *heart* means the mind considered as feeling, and that the mind is essentially *action*. The very passivity of the mind is an *act* of suffering. Again, men sophisticate the doctrine of regeneration by departing from the idea involved in the word, and presented in Scripture. It is nearly the same with recreation, and must therefore be a general and inalienable change. The gift in baptism is regeneration (as I believe) in a *secondary* sense. It is a power unto regeneration, surrounding the soul as with an atmosphere, and influencing it perpetually with the subordinate co-operation of the will.

III.

Defense of Mr. Coleridge's View of Baptism.—Regeneration, in its Primary Sense, means the Work of God upon the Soul, which leads to Sanctification.—Baptism effects a Change of State (not of Nature) by giving the Promise of the Holy Spirit.—"The Gospel of the Poor."—Use of Rationalism in rectifying Popular Theology.—Negative Character of German Philosophy.

To AUBREY DE VERE, Esq., Curragh Chase, Adare:

Chester Place, January 23, 1846.—By *actual regeneration*, I mean that change of the soul from evil to good by the Spirit of the Redeemer, which fits it for eternal bliss. This is the idea of regeneration contained in Scripture, where to be a son of God and to be freed from sin are identified. Regeneration *in this sense* is very fully described by South and Taylor, and many other (not merely evangelical) divines. Dr. Pusey calls it the secondary regeneration, and has sometimes described it quite scripturally.   St. Paul speaks of the same thing when he talks of the "new creature," which is the soul of man renewed by the Spirit, its dispositions raised and purified, grace and goodness predominating within it, and sin being put down.   Now no divine ever has said, or can say, that regeneration in this (which I must own I consider its proper and primary) sense is produced in the moment of baptism.   The spirit of man and spiritual action, *as it is in itself*, considered apart from our representations, has no real relation to time, at least according to the philosophy adopted by my father, whose views of baptism in my essay I attempted to set forth and defend (a lady to-day told me that Mr. Newman wondered that the said essay was not more read).   But regeneration, which I suppose to be the under-side or co-extensive ground of justification and of sanctification (unless we take it as including them), *phenomenally* viewed, is a gradual process.   What, then, is *baptismal* regeneration?   Surely it must be neither more nor less than *a power given to the soul of the baptized for the production of the actual regeneration.* So far divines are agreed.   All worth speaking of admit that the regeneration I have described is required in Scripture, and that it can not take place in a moment in the soul of an infant. They differ when they come to define the power unto regeneration granted in baptism, or rather *how this power belongs to the soul.*   Newman, in his desire to adhere to the primitive doctrine, or at least that which the early Christian writers *most* inclined to (for I believe their conceptions to have been vague and unsettled), and which the Council of Trent adopted, described it to be *within* the soul, to constitute an entire change and spiritualization of its nature.   Now this my father considered to be utterly irrational, and I must add that I consider it, though not so meant, in itself most irreverential and profane. According to this view, the very same soul which is given to all evil is an abiding-place of the Spirit of God.   Indeed, Keble affirmed this in express terms: "almost in all evil," were his words.   I can not believe that any human being, whose soul had been spiritualized and recreated in the image of God, ever grew up a "scandal to the Church."   I hope it may be sufficient to say, with Waterland, Bethel, and, as I understand him, Thorndyke, that baptism *consigns* the regenerative Spirit to the soul, or, to adopt your expression, *introduces it into spiritual circumstances,* which is a very different thing from merely giving it outward means and opportunities. In virtue of baptism we have the Spirit, as it were, at *our right hand*, ever ready to lead us into all goodness and truth, and make means and opportunities available to our welfare. It is not within us from the first, but ever *coming within* us as fast as we admit it, and operating upon us from without, so that we can not help admitting it, except by an act of resistance, an exertion of the rebellious will. Does not this doctrine secure all the same spiritual results as the other, without, as the other does, bringing us into conflict with Scripture and experience and the spiritual sense? One who has received the baptismal gift may indeed grow up a scandal to the Church, because he may continually resist the Spirit. But holding fast by the *idea* of regeneration given by reason and Revelation, I hold it right to say that no *really* regenerate person ever became reprobate and ungodly, or ever ceased to be a true follower of Christ. If a man falls away from grace, as the Epistle to the Hebrews affirms that men may, it is because he never received grace more than partially; he did not *so* receive it as to prevent the sinful principle, though latent, from being the master-principle of his spirit. So far, I own, my doctrine coincides with that of Calvin, and I think that our Saviour's words plainly affirm what I have just expressed. If there is no such thing as a state of the soul as preclusive of a final fall and general corruption, as the state of a butterfly is preclusive of a relapse into the caterpillar, how should Christ so positively have predicted that His sheep should never perish, and that no one should pluck them out of His hand? St. Augustine, that sophisticator of theology (of whom the late Bishop Butler said that, if he and Pelagius had been hung upon two cross-sticks, it would have been all the better for the Church), was the first, I believe, who brought in the notion of the possible fall of the regenerate.

With a very deep sigh, my dear friend, I partly admit what you said about Rationalism, that it can not be the religion of the poor and simple. But, then, I believe that every *refined* view of Christianity is more or less a rationalistic system. What, think you, do the poor make of correct Anglicanism, or of Newmanic Romanism? A philosophic Christianity maintains all the spiritual ideas of the Catholic faith; neither does it preclude the belief in an outward and visible system, but continually tends to rectify, purify, and explain it. The spirit and the principle have been at work in the Church from the beginning. But then I am not prepared to say that a perfect scheme of philosophic Christianity has ever yet been developed, or that it is the possession of one party or any individual. The Rationalists of Germany have shown their philosophy for the most part destructively and negatively, more than in any other way. But this is not true of Neander, or, as far as I know, of Schleiermacher. *They* have a body of substantive belief in their minds, not a world of unbelief on one hand, and a chaos of uncertainty and something-undetermined-ness on the other.

IV.

"Moral Effects the Test of Spiritual Operations."*—Dream-Verses.—Milton's Beauty.

To AUBREY DE VERE, Esq., Curragh Chase, Adare :

10 *Chester Place, January* 17, 1846.—I find that two clergyman-friends of mine, who attacked my little essay on Rationalism, hold, after all, precisely the same opinion of baptismal efficacy which I have endeavored to set forth in that essay, namely, that it is not, as Newman teaches, an internal, total, instantaneous, spiritual, non-moral change, giving a *power* unto righteousness, but a consignment of the regenerative spirit, made instantaneously, for the purpose of producing a total spiritual *and* moral change gradually realized, an introduction of the soul, as it were, into a new spiritual atmosphere, or, as my father somewhere expresses it, " the periphery of graces belonging to the Church of Christ." This is Waterland's doctrine, and, I believe, that of Arthur Thorndyke. I found that they disliked, as much as I do, the severance in Newman's theory of the spiritual and the moral (which he continually tries to cloak over, but is obliged to reveal, when he comes to display the root part of his doctrine), " the notion that a soul, in spite of being actually spiritually regenerate, may grow up a scandal to the Church !" This is a notion which common-sense and common feeling protest against at the outset, and which the subtlest metaphysical sense, as I imagine, condemns, as an empty phantom, at the end of reflection's career. * * *

---

* " Aids to Reflection," vol. ii., p. 66.—Essay on Rationalism, by Sara Coleridge.

Your sister's verses are very sweet and lovely. Thank you for sending them. Sir W. H.'s are mighty good ones to be written in a dream. My Uncle Southey had some good stories of dream verse-making. He was a skeptic on the subject. He thought that, on these occasions, men either dreamed that they composed in a dream (if the poem was good for any thing, like "Kubla Khan"), or dreamed that their dream verses were good poetry. He used to repeat some most inane verses which a certain poet composed in his sleep, and kept repeating in the hearing of his wife. He assured her, when he awoke, that he had produced, while under the dominion of Morpheus, the finest poem in the world—if he could but recollect it. He was rather crestfallen when she repeated to him the nonsensical couplet which he had voiced aloud over and over again, while he supposed himself to be rivaling Milton.

Speaking of Milton, do you think that the human face divine ever fell into a finer form than his? It has all the beauty which Italian painters give to St. John, and is infinitely more manly, meaning, and intellectual.

V.

Originality of Milton's Genius.—Love of Nature Displayed in his Poetry.

To AUBREY DE VERE, Esq. :

1846. — Milton "not *characteristically* one of *nature's great men?*" *Every* great man is characteristically *nature's* great man. When did art or learning ever make the most distant approximation to a Milton? Learning may be the *form* of Milton's poetry, but nature is its matter—or, at most, learning is the body, while nature inspires the soul. Book-knowledge was more to Milton, world-knowledge to Shakespeare; but I believe that the latter owed as much to what he *acquired*, what he took into his mind from without, as the former. But book-knowledge, after all, was less to Milton than observation of external nature. It is this lore surely which forms the master-charm of "Comus," "Lycidas," the "Allegro," and "Penseroso," the descriptions of Eden, which are the most perfect part of the "Paradise Lost." Wordsworth has *humanized* nature; but Milton glorified it, *out of itself,* in showing how divine a thing it is, in its own, and none but its own loveliness, how evidently the

work of God.   Here he is, as you, and Wordsworth before you,
say, essentially Hebraic, so far as the Hebraic mind appears in
the Old Testament.   Hence his sublimity—his simplicity and
grandeur, as to the nature of his theme, which the classical or-
nature by no means injures or misfits.   He never is *so* ornamental as not to be "sensuous and impassioned," for his ornaments are all, in themselves, the fresh products of nature, and
the use that has been made of them, since they were first gathered, has deadened, in no least imaginable degree, their ever-
lasting verdure.   Milton is more profusely, more thickly and
richly poetic than Wordsworth; his felicities of diction and brill-
iancies of imagination are more uniformly spread over the mass
of his productions.   As for the Homeric poetry, it is perfection
in its way; but in regard to *thought*, the work of the intellect-
evolving reason and the spirit, it displays the childhood of the
human race, and that under an imperfect, obscured, and broken
Revelation.

VI.

Blanco White.—Comparison between his State of Mind and that of Cowper
and Shelley.

To the Rev. FREDERICK D. MAURICE, Chaplain's Lodge, Guy's
    Hospital :

Chester Place, February 4, 1846.—I was disappointed with the
review of Blanco White's* life in the *Quarterly*, which I had
heard highly praised for liberality and beautiful feeling.   To
my mind it by no means does justice to Blanco White's head
or heart.   It does not set in a strong point of view that in B. W.'s
character in which he was superior, as it strikes me, to the mass
of even good men—a determined, far-going, all-sacrificing truthfulness.   Neither does it render justice to the powers of thought
in Blanco White.   It is easy to point out vacillations, inconsistencies.   The more a man thinks for himself and looks *into*
things, the more will be his apparent inconsistencies.   There is
an external superficial consistency with which the masses of

* The Rev. Joseph Blanco White, author of " Letters on Spain, by Don
Leucadio Doblado," was born at Seville, of a Roman Catholic family, in
1775.   He came to England, and joined the English Church about 1817.
After passing through various phases of belief and skepticism, he died a
Deist, in 1841.—E. C.

men are contented. And the review does no justice to the faith Blanco White evidenced in his last illness; nor does it fairly compare Cowper's state of mind with his, though the comparison is in one point instituted. Cowper was quite as unhappy as B. White—far more so than Shelley. A great deal of Shelley's misery was merely poetry; and he, too, had wretched health, and suffered habitual pain. It is also to be taken into account that men who have separated from the Christian world do not conceal their heart-wretchedness, nor affect to receive comfort as others are apt to do.

I hope and believe that the Christian has the more consolation for being such. But the dearer this hope is, the less can one bear to hear half-truths and make-believes pressed into the service of it.

VII.

Character of her Mother.

To Mrs. H. M. JONES, Hampstead :

February 21, 1846.—I really feel more and more that your appreciation of my mother was just and clear-sighted. Her character rises upon me now as I look back upon it, and compare her *perfect* simplicity and honesty, her union of steady, deep affection for those she was connected with by blood or friendship, her earnest gratitude, with an artless way of dealing respecting them, and dispassionate views. Hasty she was at the moment of provocation, but never was any one more just to all mankind, as far as her knowledge and insight extended, less swayed by peevish resentment in her deliberate judgments. There are some more devout in temper, more exalted in the world's eye, who are far inferior to her in those Christian tempers, who are perpetually on the watch *to set up* those they love by studied representations, while negatively or positively they are depreciating and unjust to those whom they love less, and whose praise seems to them so much taken from their own dear ones. *She* never disparaged others that those she loved might shine the more, though she sometimes too bluntly and straightforwardly commended her loved ones.

VIII.

Unfair Criticism of Mr. Coleridge's Religious Opinions.—His MS. Notes.
—Care taken of them by Mr. Southey.

To HENRY TAYLOR, Esq., Mortlake :*

February 26, 1846.—I would always invite and welcome for
my father, as he did for himself, the closest examination of the
character and merit of his writings. The sooner they are clearly understood, both for praise and for usefulness, or for detec-
tion of delusive appearances of truth and excellence, the better.
His complaint always was that nobody would question his views
in *particulars*—that nobody would fight with him hand to hand,
but that random missiles were discharged at him from a distance, by men who fled away while they fought.

I do not know how any of the Notes came to be effaced,
never having seen the copy of the "Life of Wesley" in which
they were written by my father himself. He did sometimes
forget to finish a note, in some instances most tantalizingly.
Perhaps he broke off to think, and then either did not satisfy
himself, or forgot to record his conclusions. Some of his *marginalia* have been cruelly docked by binders, some rubbed out.
My Uncle Southey used to ink over his penciled notes, "that
nothing be lost," as he said, with his usual diligence. When
shall we see such diligence again, such regularity, with such
genius and versatility? I think if he had not been a poet, he
would have been called a plodder, and have become a respectable and useful writer by sheer industry.

IX.

Beauties of Crabbe.

To Mrs. RICHARD TOWNSEND, Springfield, Norwood :

Chester Place, June 17, 1846. — I am glad that you enjoy
Crabbe. Sir Francis Palgrave praised him most warmly, and
was pleased and rather surprised to have a warm response from
me the other day at Mr. Murray's. The "Tales of the Hall"
are what I now like the best of all his sets of poems. In my

----

* Author of "Philip van Artevelde," now Sir Henry Taylor.—E. C.

earlier days I did not perceive half their merits, the fine observation of life, the tender sympathy with human sorrow, the gentle smile at human weakness, the humor, the pathos, the firm, almost stern morality, the excellent, clear, pure diction, and the touches of beauty (as I think) interspersed here and there. The Songs I much admire: the descriptions of Nature are decidedly poetical, in my opinion, though they bear the same relation to Milton's and Wordsworth's descriptions as the expression of Murillo's pictures does to that of Raphael's and Leonardo's.

X.

Reflections of an Invalid.—Defense of Luther.—Charges of Irreverence often Unjustly Made.—Ludicrous Illustration found in a Sermon of Bishop Andrews'.—Education : how far it may be Secular without being Irreligious.—Mr. Keble's "Lyra Innocentium."—Religious Poetry.

To Miss ERSKINE :

July 23, 1846.—My dear A——, I thought to have answered your letter very soon; but I have been ever falling from one poorliness into another, each slight in itself, but producing a general weakness in me which is no slight evil, or rather it is the general weakliness which rendered me liable to those little attacks, and the attacks make it worse. But I am making the vestibule of my letter a doleful sick-room, in which the most interesting and refreshing objects that present themselves are bottles from the apothecary's shop full of tonics, sedatives, liniments, gargles, and so forth. Your letter, on the contrary, was full of fresh air, and made me think of you, both when I read it and from time to time ever since, riding away on a spirited pony, with most *countrified* cheeks and eyes and a very light heart, and mind *less* light than ever. I could wish your heart and mind to be like two buckets, the latter to be ever filling, fuller and fuller, with the streams of sacred and all other lore, pure as water and rich as wine—while the former grows constantly more and more empty of earthly cares and troubles. I hope that your dear mother continues well and does not walk too much. She is rather apt, I believe, not to think of herself when others are concerned. There are so many dépôts, of the largest possible extent, where selfishness and self-preservativeness may

be borrowed to any amount, that if she can but be persuaded
of the necessity, she might readily furnish herself with a little
of the needful article. But this I have said, as it were, with
one eye open and the other shut, for, though there are in every
street and lane and country village such vast stocks of selfishness to be found, yet those who are in want of the article never
know how to get at any of it. Every particle clings to its native place like petrifactions in marble. But all this moral reflection is enough to *petrify* you by its stupidity, and, in order to
put a little life into both of us, I must e'en turn for a while to
controversy.

How say you, my A——, that you are not *growing in love for
Luther*, but rather becoming hardened in a *Tracts for the Times*-y
view of that great and good man, the noblest divine instrument,
in my opinion, which the world has seen after the Prophets and
Apostles? *Coarse?* What is coarseness in such a man, of
such dimensions, of such mental and spiritual thews and sinews,
with such a heart and soul and spirit, and such a mighty life-
long work as he had to perform, and performed most heroical-
ly? If Luther had been a " nice man for a small tea-party,"
if to write a few tracts for the times, or publish a few volumes
of sermons, or to put a church in proper ecclesiastical order,
after a modernized-primitive fashion, had been all his vocation
upon earth, then truly a little coarseness would have quite
spoiled him. But he was, as Julius Hare says, "a Titan;" and
"when a Titan walks abroad among the pigmies, the earth
seems to rock beneath his tread." It is vain to tell me that
Luther could not have been spiritual-minded, because he used
rough, coarse, homely expressions. His whole life, public and
private, the general character of his writings, so far as I know
them, prove *to me* that he *was* a spiritual-minded man, and the
most deeply convinced of sin that ever lived. That Luther
was profane I can not admit. I have always thought that the
language of the Oxford theologians respecting profaneness in
religion had much in it that was both narrow and uncharitable.
They confound want of good taste with want of piety, homely
breeding with that irreverence which springs from the heart;
in the mean time *they* are teaching doctrines and expressing
opinions which appear to many earnest and thoughtfully religious minds in the highest degree derogatory to God and
Christ and Christianity. Every one is profane who does not

adopt their peculiar ceremoniousness in religion, who can not specially revere all that they have made up their minds to think worthy of reverence.

Think of this comparison from the pen of Bishop Andrewes, one of their highest favorites among our Anglican divines: "Are they like to *buckets?* one can not go down unless the other go up." The "*buckets*" are the Saviour and the Comforter! Now would not this be pronounced highly profane by the Luther-haters, had it been found in a book of Luther's? Yet Andrewes is considered the *beau ideal* of a reverential spirit by the Oxford writers, and I have no doubt that he never for a moment lost the feeling of reverence out of his heart. Yet with all Luther's occasional scurrility and violence, I doubt whether an example so unworthy of the highest of all subjects could be found in his works. That instance from Andrewes is brought forward in a long note in the new work of Archdeacon Hare, "The Mission of the Comforter, and other Sermons." The second volume is twice as long as the other, and full of notes. Note W contains a most warm, thorough, searching, resolute defense of Luther against all his modern censors. It is not to be expected, indeed, that they who dislike the work which Luther did, can ever like the workman ; still they should not bring up again the refuted slanders of Romanists, and quote his writings out of the books of his Romish adversaries instead of out of his own.

Yesterday I discussed with Mr. M——, or, rather, he with me, Dr. Hook's remarkable pamphlet on National Education. M—— contends that no part of education should be dissociated from *religious* education, that we ought not to divide our life or our teaching into secular and religious, and that such a plan as the one proposed would clamp and rivet a wrong principle of education, and prevent the arising of a higher and more deeply religious system.

I think certainly that no man could teach History in an effective, living manner, without infusing into it the tone and principle either of Socinianism or Trinitarianism. But I believe that in the routine of the National School, except where religion is formally introduced, the spirit of Christianity is not felt at all. And certainly a man may teach reading, writing, spelling, and arithmetic without letting it appear whether he is a Mohammedan or a Christian—nay, more, I do not see how he could keep steadily to his business in teaching these branches without keeping his peculiar form of religion in the background. Still I believe that M—— is right, and that we who embrace with our hearts the Divinity of Christ, should not allow a disbeliever even to teach our children to cipher; though I would by no means admit that we ought to keep *out of all intercourse* with such disbelievers, and that is another point on which I think the Oxford teaching injurious.

I meant to talk with you a little about the "Lyra Innocentium," but have hardly left myself room. I am doing it all possible justice, for I read it slowly, two or three poems a day, and some two or three times over. I like best "Sleeping on the Waters" and the "Lich-gate." Still it would be quite insincere to say that I either like or approve of it, *upon the whole*, either as religion or poetry, though there are beautiful passages. I hope you do not *wholly* approve of it as religion. Surely the Marianism is far more than our best and greatest divines would approve. The article in the *Quarterly* is the article of a friend, and in the main a partisan; the reviewer mentions some important faults in the volume as poetry, but to my mind there is a deeper fault than any he mentions, namely, want of truth and substance, and not only of doctrine, but of human child-nature. The incidents recorded are quite insignificant in themselves: they add nothing to our knowledge, no richness to our store of reflections. They are used as mere symbols, suggestive of analogies. They are just so many pegs and hooks on which Mr. Keble can hang his web of religious sentiment. The reviewer says that to *excel as a poet* is not Mr. Keble's aim. This seems to me something like goodyism. He who writes poetry surely should aim to excel as a poet, and the more if his theme is religion, and his object to spiritualize and exalt. Every great poet has a higher aim, of course, than that of merely obtaining admiration for his poetic power and skill. Wordsworth's aim was to elevate the thoughts of his readers, to enrich and purify their hearts, but he sought to excel as a poet in order that he might do this the more effectually. I believe that Isaiah and Ezekiel sought to excel as poets, all the more that their poetry was the vehicle of divine truth—of truth awakened in their souls by inspiration.

XI.

Composition of "Phantasmion."—Love in Fairy-land.

To AUBREY DE VERE, Esq. :

Before writing "Phantasmion," I thought that for the account of Fairy-land Nature I need invoke no other muse than Memory; my native vale, seen through a sunny mist of dreamery, would supply all the materials I should want, and all the inspiration; but for the love part, and the descriptions of personal beauty, I invoked Venus to aid me. On my application, she told me that Fairy-land love was such weak, sirupy stuff, and so little in demand, that it was hardly worth her while to keep any in store. She would send out Cupid as soon as she could catch him, to gather cowslips and primroses enough to make a few small bottles, that to ferment it she would use a little sea-foam which he might whisk off the surface of the waves after bathing, and that I should have it, fresh and fresh, as I wanted it in the progress of the story.   In the mean time, though she could by no means lend me any of her swans or golden-breasted pigeons, she had a sick dove, which had broken its leg, and lost its health for want of exercise, which was at my service for any use I could put it to.   These handsome offers I was glad to accept, seeing that they were the best I could obtain, and so, if the love-poetry of the volume is rather mawkish and soporific, or if some of it tastes a little brackish, as if tears had trickled into the liquor, you must bear in mind what poor wild flowers and froth I had to brew it of; and if the story is but a lame affair, and the whole piece a faint and sickly piece of painting, you must lay it all to the account of the broken-legged dove, and the shabbiness of Venus in lending me no better help.   Coarse-minded thing! she can't endure Fairy-land, where the lovers are as fine as mists, and the ladies evanescent as rainbows.   She admires heavy hulks, downright, visible, tangible wretches, and would have the very ladies perceptible to the mere unpurged visual orb!   There was Venus Cœlestis, but I dared not apply to her, *she* was too exalted for me.   There ought to be a Venus Fairy-landensis, abiding between earth and heaven, to assist writers of fairy tales.

Since you desired to know particularly what I did and where I was when I wrote the book, and all the circumstances attending its composition, I must further inform you that Cupid behaved abominably about the cowslips. He wove them into tisty-tosty-balls, and tossed them up in the sun, so that they were absolute hay before he brought them to make the love-small-beer. I begged Venus (who, by the bye, is just like her picture by Correggio in the National Gallery) to take him by the wing and give him a good shake, but she merely snatched up one of the cowslip balls and flung it in his face, which he took as a signal for a game of romps, threw a whole handful at her, then let fall his basket and ran away, screaming and laughing. Foreseeing how vapid the beer would be when the flowers were thus banged about, I grew very cross, and reproached Venus for taking the matter so lightly. But she only laughed, and told me that I should have done just the same with my urchin ; just at that moment Herby came in, and began to be as naughty as Cupid, looking all the time equally pretty, so that I thought it as well not to push the dispute any further just then.

Another misfortune to me was this, that Mercury, at my request, put off Cupid's reading-lesson, in order that he might have full time to gather the cowslips in the morning ; consequently he came cross and tired to his master in the afternoon, and at last fell asleep over his book. This put Mercury out of humor, and he was heard to say that, since I had made a dunce of his pupil, I might appear like a dunce myself, for all the help he would give me toward the invention of my tale. However, I have since heard that he has taken the book into favor, so far as to teach Cupid to read out of it, and that the little fellow is well pleased with the descriptions of the butterflies and bees, and other creatures with wings, insect and human, and both his mother and his uncle think that Hermillian was intended as a portrait of him.

A Character.

To the Same :

* * * His manner is not shy or taciturn, yet is essentially reserved ; all that is said seems meted out beforehand : so far it is to go, and no farther ; and the smile is sweet, yet seems too intentional. I like more overflow and self-abandonment to the subject of discourse ; but then I was bred up among poets, who are enthusiastic, overflowing people for the most part, and

let their thoughts run away with them now and then, as the dish ran away with the spoon. F. N—— talks in a very finished way, but his talk is *all* finished when it is presented to you : it is stereotyped, as it were—not to be modified or enlarged by alien suggestions. Thus it is as perfect as he can make it— that is, very perfect on its own scale : you are to take it, and be thankful. He has a *Latin* sort of intellect.

December 30, 1846.

XII.

Comparative Merits of the Earlier and Later Poems of Wordsworth.— Burns.

To AUBREY DE VERE, Esq. :

1846.—Your scheme of a critique on Wordsworth would be very noble and comprehensive, if adequately executed. The difficulty would be to avoid obscurity and vagueness. I agree to all your characteristics, so far as I understand them, except those of the later poetry, of which I take a wholly different view from that expressed in your prospectus. You have brought me to see more beauty in them than I once did ; but when you say they have more *latent imagination*, are more *mellow*, exhibit "faculties more perfectly equipoised," you seem to me to have framed a theory apart from the facts. They have more *fancy*, but surely not more imagination, latent or patent. They can hardly be mellower, for they have not the same body ; their substance is thinner ; and some of the author's poetic faculties are, to my mind, not *there* to be equipoised. What! are any of the later poems, in the blending and equipoise of faculties, beyond " Tintern Abbey," " The Leech-gatherer," " The Broth- ers," " Ruth ?" Did the instrument become mellower than in " Three Years She Grew," " The Highland Girl," " The White Doe?" Surely there is far more real strength in the " Sonnets to Liberty," " Song at the Feast of Brougham Castle," " Platon- ic Ode," " Rob Roy's Grave," than in any thing the author has produced during the last twenty years.

That is a good distinction of meditative and contemplative.

Your characteristics of Burns are excellent. I agree to them all heartily. I am glad you are not too *genteel* to like Burns.

XIII.

Classification of Mr. Wordsworth's Poems, with a View to Proving the Superiority of the Earlier Ones over the Later.—Earlier Poems : Meditative ; Lyrical.—Poems of Incidents : Reflective and Pathetic.—Poems
of Sentiment : Reflective and Imaginative ; Descriptive.—Ballad Poems.
—Homely Strains.—Sonnets.—Later Poems.

To AUBREY DE VERE, Esq. :

SCALE OF MR. WORDSWORTH'S POETRY.

The poems are arranged in classes according to the character of the composition, but in a loose, inexact manner, as such
classes are apt to run into one another, some poems having the
characteristics of more than one.

The degrees of excellence are marked by the letters of the
alphabet—*a* being the highest, and so on.

Meditative strains, sedate in character, and in which solem-
nity and tenderness mutually succeed or flow into each other :
The Old Cumberland Beggar.   *a, a, a.*
Tintern Abbey.   *a, a, a.*
Address to my Infant Daughter.   *a.*
The Happy Warrior.   *a.*
Lines on the French Revolution.   *a.*
When to the Attractions.
Nutting.
To M. M.
There was a Boy.
The Yew-tree Seat.
A Little Onward.
Certain passages of " The Excursion." See further on. (The
    excellences of " The Excursion " are of a diffusive kind :
    you must gather them from a large surface. The most
    condensed passage is in the 4th book, " Within the soul
    a faculty abides.")

Lyrical compositions, more rapt and fervid than the former,
and equally exalted in spirit :
Intimations of Immortality.   Ode sublimely imaginative.
    Thorough Wordsworthians think this poem transcendent,
    and that its merits baffle description.
Song at the Feast of Brougham Castle.   *a, a, a.*

Ode to Duty. *a, a.*
Rob Roy's Grave. *a, a.*

Elegaic, but with a solemn fervor which connects them with
the two former classes :
Peel Castle. *a, a.*
Laodamia. *a, a.* "Laodamia" partly belongs to the next.

Poems containing some history or incident, dignified and
solemn in tone, or, when less elevated, full of a deep, reflective
pathos :
The Leech-gatherer. *a, a, a.* (A title I prefer to the new one,
    "Resolution and Independence." Derwent says, "The
    Old Cumberland Beggar" might, in the same spirit, have
    been changed into "Advantages of Mendicancy.")
The Female Vagrant. *a, a.*
The Brothers. *a, a.*
Ruth. *a, a.*
Michael. *a.*
The Matron of Jedburgh. *a.* There is a lyrical air about
    this poem.
The Thorn. *b.* Fine in parts, but unequal.
The White Doe. First and last cantos, especially the for-
    mer ; interview of Francis and Emily, in the second ; and
    speech of the Father, in the fifth. *a, a.*
Peter Bell. Unequal, but striking and impressive in general
    conception, with passages of deep passion and potent im-
    agination.
The Wagoner. Humbler in its aim and general conception,
    but more equal in execution, more tender and harmonious
    in tone, more truly in keeping, if lower in tint, and with less
    depth and brilliancy of coloring. The Epilogue I prefer
    to the Prologue of Peter Bell.

Poems, reflective and pathetic, in which the *habit* of grief is
more impressively described than any particular acts or accesses
of the passion :
The Affliction of Margaret. *a.*
The Emigrant Mother. *a.* Pleasing, but not powerful.
The Two April Mornings. *a, a.*
The Fountain. *a, a.*

'Tis said that Some have Died for Love.   *a.*

Vaudracour and Julia.

History of Margaret, in "The Excursion;" of the Solitary's
Wife, and of Ellen.

Song for the Wandering Jew.   Not improved by the new stanzas.

The Mad Mother.

The Complaint.

The Complaint of the Forsaken Indian Woman.   This poem
describes grief, not as the attendant on a permanent state,
but arising from sudden misfortune.   Schiller has a poem
of the same sort, "Nadowessische Todtenklage," but less
intense in feeling.

Poems of sentiment, imaginatively presented, distinguished by
exquisiteness of expression, in which the language seems more
especially one with the thought, or inseparably incorporated
with it.—*b*, not so great as the two first classes.

Three Years She Lived in Sun and Shower.   *a, a, a.*

The Highland Girl.

She was a Phantom of Delight.

To H. C., Six Years Old.

Farewell, thou Little Nook.

Yarrow Unvisited.

Castle of Indolence.

A Poet's Epitaph.

All these first six are almost equally excellent; the two last
very good, but less sweet perhaps.

Less perfect in execution, or lighter and humbler in the tone
of feeling:

The Cuckoo.

To a Skylark.

I Traveled among Unknown Ways.   (Last stanza exquisite.)

She Dwelt among the Untrodden Ways.

If Nature for a Favorite Child.

A Slumber did my Spirit Seal.

The Green Linnet.

The Sparrow's Nest.

I Wandered Lonely as a Cloud.   (Unequal; second stanza
beautiful.)

I met Louisa in the Shade.
The Solitary Reaper.
To the Daisy.
To the Same Flower.
O Nightingale, thou surely art.

Inferior, but of the same class:
To a Butterfly.
Stepping Westward.
Glen Almain.

Of this set, some are as perfect in their way, having as much unity of execution, as those of the first set; and some, as the verses on Matthew, "If Nature," etc., are as deep in feeling. But none of them so finely unite harmony of expression with a high poetic spirit.

"Beggars" belongs to this class, and has some power about it. But, though thoroughly Wordsworthian, it is to my mind unsuccessful.

Poems of reflection imaginatively conceived:
Gypsies.

I can not yet feel quite satisfied with this poem. I wish that such fine language had a more clearly justifying subject. Mr. De Vere alleges that though, if the reality of the case be considered, the "tawny wanderers" were quite in the right to take their rest, yet the poet, looking at the matter poetically, did very well to be indignant at them, and to express his indignation in the most magnificent manner. Now I know that the poetical aspect of things, and the common-sense, unadorned aspect of them, are different; but can it be right to make them clean *contrary*, the one to the other, on any occasion? The poet may *add* to truth of fact "the light that never was on sea or land"—but this light ought surely to exalt and glorify, not to reverse or misrepresent it. The actual ought to underlie the whole fabric, and even regulate its form, though it be not itself immediately visible. Otherwise we convert poetry, which ought to be truth of a peculiar kind, into falsehood. The great merit of Mr. Wordsworth's best poems is that they present realities of the heart and mind of man and of external nature in the grandest forms, and under the most glowing and glorifying lights wherein they can possibly appear.   Some deny that these lights are glowing.   They have seldom, indeed, any such glow as is opposed to purity and solemnity.   But in his finest poems they are intense, and transfigure the objects, not changing the form and lineaments so as to render them unrecognizable, but exalting, refining, illuminating them.

The small Celandine—There is a Flower, the lesser Celan-
dine.   Last stanza is in the pithy manner of some of the
old poets.
Fidelity.   Last four lines fine.
My Heart Leaps up.
The Kitten and the Falling Leaves.
Yes, full surely 'twas the Echo.
It is no Spirit.
Preface to the White Doe.
Animal Tranquillity and Decay.   A prosy didactic title.

Descriptive pieces highly imaginative, and pervaded with a sentiment inspired by the objects of the description, the outward forms of nature, not arising from other sources, and arbitrarily arrayed therein :
Yew Trees.   Sublime.
To Joanna.   Containing the fine passage finely imitated by
Lord Byron in "Childe Harold," about the echo among the
mountains.
The Danish Boy.   A fragment.

Here I might have placed—
There was a Boy.
To M. H.
When to the Attractions.
Nutting.

The "Evening Walk" and "Descriptive Sketches" are energetic, but seem to want a point to seize the heart and fancy.
They want unity of aim.

Passages in the Blind Highland Boy.
Idle Shepherd Boys.
Description of Skating at Sunset.

Night Piece.
Emma's Dell.   "There is an Eminence."
The Haunted Tree.
Influence of Natural Objects.

There are fine descriptive passages in "The Excursion," especially that beginning, "Such was the boy; but for the growing youth, What soul was his," p. 10, 1st book; and the description of the cloud city, at the end of the 2d book, p. 71.

"Characteristics of a Child Three Years Old" is pretty and graceful, like a woman's writing.

Poems of the ballad character—serious and pathetic:
The Horn of Egremont Castle.
The Last of the Flock.
The Force of Prayer.
The Childless Father.   "Up, Timothy."   Very affecting and
    pleasing.
Poor Susan.   Still better in the same line.
Ellen Irwin.   My old friend Mr. Calvert wore me out with
    this poem.   I have pleasing juvenile associations with it,
    but not poetical ones.   He was always half-admiring, half-
    quizzing his friend's muse.
The Seven Sisters.
Lucy Gray.
Repentance.

More homely, and with an occasional sportiveness not sufficiently distinguished from the ludicrous.   Mr. Wordsworth's utter want of all sense of the humorous seems to me connected with his mistakes on this head.
The Idiot Boy.   Admired by Charles James Fox.   I think
    that none but a poet and a man of power could have
    written, or dared have written, " The Idiot Boy;" but, like
    "Peter Bell" and "The Thorn," and, in less degree, some
    of his other poems, it has in it a radical defect in the
    original cast and conception.
The Two Thieves.
The Farmer of Tilbury Vale.
The Pet Lamb.
The morality of the first two of these poems is dubious.   It

is not well to be so figurative and poetic in a matter of morals, that the wrong sense is the more obvious. But I do not see that there is any humility of thought and diction in these poems which is not within the rules of taste, rightly and liberally understood.

Lower again, but still not without power and marks of an individual mind, which to me are pleasing :

Goody Blake. That is surely a stanza which has some efficacy toward freezing the blood—"She prayed, her withered hand uprearing."

We are Seven.

Written in Germany. "A fig for your languages."

Homely strains, not ballads :

To a Sexton. "Let thy wheelbarrow alone." Quaint, but with a sort of vivid realizing of the country church-yard which used to please me, as Tennyson's vivid realizations of cottage gardens, old country mansions, reedy swamps where swans expire, and spots about the country village, please me.

A Character.

Sonnets. The finer sonnets belong to the first class of sedate, meditative strains, 1; or the less elevated sentimental class, 2; some are imaginatively descriptive, 3.

With how sad steps.   3.

Surprised by joy.   2.

Among the Mountains.

I watch, and long have watched.

I am not one. The series of four Sonnets beginning thus.   1.

Three Sonnets on Sleep.   2.

Earth has not any thing.   1.

Lady, the songs of Spring.   1.

The world is too much with us.   1.

Once did she hold.

Toussaint.

Inland, within a hollow vale.

Two voices are there.

Milton, thou shouldst be living.

It is not to be thought of.

When I have borne in memory.
These times touch monied worldlings.
Shout, for a mighty victory.
Another year, another deadly blow.
Clarkson, it was an obstinate hill.
Hail! Zaragoza.
Brave Schill.
Ah! where is Palafox?
The power of armies.
What need of clamorous bells.
From the dark chambers.
Calvert, it must not be unheard.
Pure element of waters.
Calm is all nature.
With ships the sea.
It is a beauteous evening.
Praised be the art.
The fairest, brightest hues.
Methought I saw.
The Imperial Consort.
Fallen and diffused.
Grief, thou hast lost.
As the cold aspect.
While not a leaf.
Ye sacred nurseries.
Shame on the faithless heart.
Ward of the Law.
  Etc., etc., etc.

———

"THE EXCURSION."

Such was the boy, p. 10 of 6th vol. of last edition.
Story of Margaret, p. 36.
Cloud City, p. 71.
Voiceless the stream, p. 96.
Description of the Solitary's married life and mental history
  after his bereavement.
His wife's death, p. 101–113.
How beautiful this dome of sky, p. 116. Miltonic.
Religion of the Ancients, p. 138, 139, 140.
A Curious Child—passage that Landor quarreled about, p. 155.

Of the later poems, those that have pleased me best are—
Lines on a Portrait.*
Dion.
On the Longest Day.*
The Triad.*
Evening Ode.
Ode to Licoris.
The Minstrels Played.†
Ethereal Minstrel.
Yarrow Visited.
Yarrow Revisited. Inferior, but elegant.
Remembrance of Collins.
Lines in a Boat.
The Pass of Kirkstone.
Some of the Duddon Sonnets. My father said the best of
   them were written early..

Of these poems, I like best those that I have marked
with a *.

I have purposely exhibited the earlier poems by themselves,
in order to make it appear whether or no the author's fame
rests principally on them—whether any thing approaching to
the like amount of poetic *stuff* can be produced from the later
productions, which almost equal them in bulk. How comparatively few of the former could lovers of his poetry afford to part
with! Perhaps my great preference of the earlier set may not
be defensible by æsthetic rules : I might not be able to prove
that there is a difference of *kind*, more than of mere degree,
between the first and the last; that the former are poetry and
works of genius in a higher sense than the latter ; that the latter are produced willfully by the author's poetic skill and talent, while the former were effluxes of the poetic spirit, and results of inspiration ; that the latter are imitations and elaborate
reproductions of what was produced *in substance* before, rather
than fresh products of thought and feeling. But so it is, that I
feel they never can have any great hold on my mind. I have
heard some of them to the greatest advantage ; for if any thing
can *teach* one to love poetry, it is to see that it is loved, and

---

† "Laodamia" and the "White Doe" are intermediate in style between
the early and later poems, and mark the transitional state of the Wordsworthian genius.—S. C.

hear it repeated in tones of love and admiration by those who are themselves poetical. And I shall read it through again, and see much more in it than I have ever yet done, though nothing, I fear, comparable to two thirds at least of the old set.

My notion of the superiority of such poems as "Tintern Abbey," "The Song at the Feast of Brougham Castle," "The Female Vagrant," etc., over such as "Dion," "The Triad," "The Ode to Lycoris," I might *partly* illustrate by referring to the difference betwixt such a face and countenance as that of J——H——, or of B—— N——, at the same age, with the face and countenance of Schiller, or any of the handsomer of the ancient Greeks. The former are graceful, refined, and elegant; but they want breadth, mass, and expansion. There may be all, and more than all, their elegance, with greater breadth; for where the features are more solid and on a bolder scale, the face may be altogether wider, with no loss of beauty, but the contrary, and with an infinite gain in grandeur and force. So, too, the expression may be as refined, yet far more impressive and energetic.

XIV.

Critique on "Laodamia."—Want of Truth and Delicacy in the Sentiments attributed to the Wife in that Poem.—No Moral Lesson of any Value to be Drawn from such a Misrepresentation.—Superior Beauty and Fidelity of a Portrait taken from the Life.—Leading Idea of Shelley's "Sensitive Plant."

REASON FOR NOT PLACING "LAODAMIA" IN THE FIRST RANK OF WORDSWORTHIAN POETRY.

"Laodamia" is, in my opinion, as a whole, neither powerfully conceived nor perfectly executed. I venture to say that there is both a coarseness and a puerility in the design and the sentiments. I see a want of feeling, of delicacy, and of truthfulness in the representation of Laodamia herself. The speech put into her mouth is as low in tone as it is pompous and inflated in manner. Would even a Pagan poet—would Homer have ascribed such an address to Andromache or Penelope? Would he have made any virtuous matron and deeply loving wife address her lord returned from the dead so in the style of a Medea or a Phædra? Surely in Ovid's "Epistle of Laodamia to Protesilaus" there is nothing so unmatronly and un-

wifely, bold and unfeminine. Not only does the poet make
Laodamia speak thus—he clenches the imputation by a commentary. He ascribes to her *passions* unworthy of a pure
abode, *raptures* such as Erebus disdains—implies that her feelings belong to mere sense, the lowest part of our nature. By
what right does he impute to the spouse of Protesilaus such
grossness of character, and how can he do so without representing her as quite unworthy of that deep sympathy and compassion which yet he seems to claim for her? "Oh, judge her
gently who so deeply loved." *Deep* love is utterly incompatible with such passions and raptures as Erebus can have any
pretense to disdain. Even where they existed, they would be
consumed, burned up as a scroll, in the strong, steady fire of
conjugal affection. After all, what is the moral of this much-
pretending, lofty-sounding poem? What is it that the poet
means to condemn and to warn against? To judge by his
words, we must suppose him to be declaiming against subjuga-
tion to the senses, because these things earth is ever destroy-
ing and Erebus disdaining. Now if Laodamia really longed to
be reunited with her husband only for the sake of his "roseate
lips" and blooming cheeks, she would deserve censure and contempt too ; but the true reason of her sorrow and reluctance to
part with him is this, that *she* is chained to the sphere of outward and visible things, while he is gone, Heaven knows whither, and that, except through a sensuous *medium*, she can have
no communion with him—none of which she can be conscious,
not the highest and most spiritual. Love can have no other
fruition than that of union. The fervent apostle longs to be
dissolved and to be *with* Christ. The poet's machinery, too, is
extremely ill-adapted for bringing out any deep or fine thoughts
on such a subject. His heaven itself is a heaven of *sense*, Elysian fields, with purling brooks and lilied banks, "purpureal
gleams," and all that we have here on a brighter and larger
scale, where the pride of the eye, by far the strongest and most
seductive of all the senses, is to be oceanically gratified. But
is submission to the will of God, and a patient waiting to be
made happy in his way, true faith and *trust* in the Author of our
being, that He who gave us our hearts and the objects of them,
can and will give us the feelings and the fruitions best adapted
to our eternal well-being, if we rely upon Him with an energy
of self-abandonment and patience, what the poet meant to in-

culcate? I can only say that, if this be the case, nothing can be more circuitous and misleading than the way which he takes to arrive at his point; all along, if he aims that way, he shoots another.

In this poem Mr. Wordsworth willfully divested himself of every tender and delicate feeling, in the contemplation of the wife and the woman, for the sake of a few grand declamatory stanzas, which he knew not else how to make occasion for. Of course a poor woman is glad to see the external form of her husband after a long and perilous absence; right glad, too, to see him with a ruddy cheek, thankful under such circumstances to receive ever so dislocating a squeeze—a thing to the mere sense unluxurious, nay painful, but comfortable to the heart within, as making assurance doubly sure that there he is, the good man himself; no vision or spectre like to vanish away, but a being, confined like herself within the bounds of space, and likely for many a day to be perceptible within that portion of space which is their common home; proof also, or, at least, a strong sign, that whether or no he be as glad to rejoin her as she is to have him back, at all events he is more glad than words can express.

Why did Mr. Wordsworth write in this hard, forced, falsetto style of "Laodamia?" Was this a sketch taken from *very* nature? Was it drawn by the light of the sun in heaven, or by real moonlight in all its purity and freshness? No—but by the beams of a purple-tinted lamp in his study, a lamp gaudily colored, but dimmed with particles of smoke and fumes of the candle. Compare with this the thoughts and feelings embodied in that exquisite sketch, "She was a Phantom of Delight," the fine and delicate interweaving of the outward and sensuous with the things of the heart and higher mind in that poem. Can we not see in a moment that the poet had been gazing on the deep and manifold countenance of Nature herself, of Truth and Reality, when he threw forth those verses—that he had been *seeing*, not inventing? Yet is it not far more finely imaginative than the other? Would any but a great poet have so seen the face of Nature, or so portrayed it? Mrs. Wordsworth lies, in essence, at the bottom of that poem. How angry would the bard be to have her connected in any way with the other, and its broad, coarse abstractions! So long as sense *is* divorced from our higher being, it is, indeed, a low thing, but may it not be redeemed, and by becoming the minister and exponent of the other, be purified and exalted? I have ever thought those doctrines that seek to sever the sensuous from our humanity, instead of retaining and merging it in the sentimental, the intellectual, and the spiritual, "a vaulting ambition that o'erleaps itself and falls on the other side."

I have received more consolation from Mr. Wordsworth's poetry than from any sermons or works of devotion at different times of my life, but I must have more truth and freshness than there is in "Laodamia" to be either highly gratified or consoled. I would not have poetry always dwell in the *common* world, but still it must always have truth at the bottom. I admire, for instance, and see great truth in Shelley's "Sensitive Plant." It is wild, but there is nothing unreal or forced about it. I look upon it as a sort of apologue, intended, or at least fitted, to exhibit the relations of the perceptive and imaginative mind, as modified by the heart, with external nature.

CHAPTER XV.

1846.—*July–December.*

LETTERS TO AUBREY DE VERE, ESQ., REV. HENRY MOORE, MISS
FENWICK, MRS. FARRER, MISS MORRIS.

I.

Mr. Ruskin's "Modern Painters."

To Miss MORRIS:

1846.—A book which has interested me much of late is a
thick volume by a graduate of Oxford, whose name is Ruskin,
on the superiority of the modern landscape-painters to the old
masters in that line. The author has not converted, and yet he
has delighted me. I think him a heretic as regards Claude,
Cuyp, G. Poussin, and Salvator Rosa; but his admiration of
Turner, whom he exalts above all other landscape-painters that
ever lived, I can go a great way with; and his descriptions of
nature, in reference to art, are delightful—clouds, rocks, earth,
water, foliage, he examines and describes in a manner which
shows him to be quite a man of genius, full of knowledge, and
that fineness of observation which genius produces.

II.

A Talk with Mr. Carlyle.—Money as the Reward of Virtue.—Different Effects of Sorrow on Different Minds.—Miss Fenwick.—Milton, Good as
well as Great.

To AUBREY DE VERE, Esq.:

Carlyle, I think, too much depreciates money as an instrument. I battled with him a little on this point when I saw him
last. He is always smiling and good-natured when I contradict him, perhaps because he sees that I admire him all the
while. I fought in defense of the Mammonites, and brought
him at least to own that the laborer is worthy of his hire. Now
this contains the pith of the whole matter. The man who de-

votes himself to gain riches deserves to have riches, and, like Hudson, to have a monument set up to him by those whom he has enriched; and if he strives for riches to spend them nobly or kindly, then he deserves to have the luxury of *that sort* of doing good. A Burns or a Berkeley aims at, and works for, and ought to find his reward in, other harvests. But Carlyle seems angry because the Burns or the Johnson or the Milton has not the same honors, or from the same men, as millionaires and fashionists; because the whole world—unphilosophical and un-poetical as the main part of it is—does not fall down and wor-ship them, and cast forthwith into the sea or some Curtius gulf all the gauds and playthings which *they* do not care about. This is overbearing and unfair. Let him teach the world to be philosophical and poetical as fast as he can; but till it is so, let him not grudge it the rattles and sugar-plums and hobby-horses of its infancy. * * *

Your last letter, received at Herne Bay, gave a delightful ac-count of your mother and her consolations. Soon after reading it, I saw a fine appearance in the sky—for then I was always watching sky and sea and atmosphere spectacles—the sun and moon in a mist, the latter pallid and sickly, while the former burned through the veil, and converted all the vapor around it into a vehicle of golden radiance. This seemed to me an apt image of the diverse effect of sorrow on different minds. To a warm and deeply benevolent spirit it becomes the means of a more diffusive charity and kindliness; the sorrow itself is pierced through and overpowered, yet serves to spread abroad and augment the benevolence which it can not damp or ex-tinguish; while to those who have but a comparatively scanty stock of love belonging to them it is the extinguisher of all so-cial amiability, it renders them dull and cold, the mere ghosts of their former selves. * * *

I take great delight in Miss Fenwick and in her conversa-tion. Well should I like to have her constantly in this drawing-room to come down to from my little study up stairs—her mind is such a noble compound of heart and intelligence, of spiritual feeling and moral strength, and the most perfect feminineness. She is intellectual, but—what is a great excellence—never talks for effect, never *keeps possession of the floor*, as·clever women are so apt to do. She converses for the interchange of thought and feeling, no matter *how*, so she gets at your mind, and lets you into hers. A more generous and a tenderer heart I never knew. I differ from her on many points of religious faith, but on the whole prefer her views to those of most others who differ from her. Once she said something against Milton, which made me feel for the moment as Oliver Newman did when Randolph denounced the "blind old traitor"—

> " With that his eyes
> Flashed, and a warmer feeling flushed his cheek."

"Time will bring down the Pyramids," he said, and so forth. Randolph's respondent did but defend Milton on the score of his poetry. But I think he was great as a *man* and a *patriot*, very noble in the whole cast of his character, and very far from being what she thinks him—for his writings against that weak, wily (or at least *un*-straightforward, not ingrainedly honest) despot King Charles I.—"malicious." It is seldom that so brave, so public-spirited a man as Milton harbors malice in his heart; he, too, who had "never spoken against a man, that his skin should be grazed." So, like Oliver, though I kept "self-possession as a mind subdued," yet was I " a little moved."

III.

A Picture.

To the Same :

Her features are not Grecian, but a most graceful contour of figure, head, neck, and arms, having that χαρις ευμορφων κολοσσων —that *grace of well-formed statues*—of which Æschylus speaks ; a camellia-japonica complexion and gazelle-like eyes go far toward making a pretty girl. You must stand off a little to see her beauty, and look at her as you would at a tree, a weeping birch or delicate ash, the lady of the woods or the princess, as Mr. Wordsworth used to call it.

IV.

Danger of Exclusiveness in Parental Affection.

To the Hon. Mr. Justice COLERIDGE :

Chester Place, August 5, 1846.—It is certainly right that parents should form, as much as possible, a friendship with their children, and seek mental association with them ; but it seems to me that their desire for this, and endeavor after it, should not be without limits. Parents and children can not be to each other as husbands with wives, and wives with husbands. Nature has separated them by an almost impassable barrier of time ; the mind and the heart are in quite a different state at fifteen and at forty.

Then, too, we must consider that, though so many difficulties attend the comfortable marriage of young people in our rank of life, yet marriage, somewhere between seventeen and thirty, is what we should look to for them, as a possible and, upon the whole, desirable event for them in ordinary cases. This probability alone must interfere with our forming such habits of *continual* intercourse with them, and dependence upon them for hourly comfort and amusement, as it would be very painful to break off in case of their doing what it is certainly most for their life-long happiness that they should do—forming a marriage connection which may endure when we are gone to our rest. Whatever is most *natural,* so that it be not of the nature of sin, is in all ordinary cases the best and safest. I have seen and heard of a great deal of distress and misery arising from parents setting their hearts too much on the society and exclusive or paramount love of their children ; and have always felt, especially since I have been a widow, that this was a rock which I had to avoid.

V.

St. Augustine's College. — Holiday Tasks. — The Evening Gray and the Morning Red.

To Miss FENWICK :

St. George's Terrace, Herne Bay, August 20, 1846.—One day last week we drove to Canterbury to visit the rising Missionary College of St. Augustine, which will be completed and set agoing—made alive, as it were—before the end of next spring, as is now expected. I was much struck with the true collegiate air of the pile of buildings, and the solid handsomeness and appropriate beauty of the separate parts. I was particularly pleased with a long gallery running between the two ranges of fifty students' rooms : it will be such an excellent walk for the meditative student in bad weather, and at all times when he wishes to relieve his sitting posture. There he may untie many a knot occurring in his studies, which has *stuck him up*, as the boys say, while he was sitting on his chair. There he may cast his eye over his future prospects—though, perhaps, as to some part of them, it may be as well not to "proticipate," to use Mrs. Gamp's expression, for hardships seem still harder at a distance, I think, than close at hand.

D. and M., and their sweet chattering C——, who looks, when in a madcap willful mood, even prettier than when she is good —like a little wild cat of the woods, or kitten ocelot in a playful fury—returned to St. M—— some days ago. They left their son for some time longer to be Herbert's companion. I can not say that I have an absolute holiday even here, as I am bound to read Homer and Æschylus with these youths (of whom my son is to be sixteen, my nephew eighteen, in October) every day; and though their lessons at present are not long—yet to rein them in when they are galloping on, leaving sense and connection of thought in the far distance, and to have my own way about the disputed passage when I *am* in the right, and let them have theirs and their little triumph when *Ma* has proved to be a "verdant creature," as my boy has the coolness to call me when I have betrayed an ignorance of something that he knows—is to me some little exertion; but not too much, for I see very little good in entire holidays, especially when there are so many sad remembrances in the background of the mind as there are in mine, ever ready to come forward when the foreground is not well filled up. Sad, indeed, they are not, by this time—at least, not always and wholly. They begin to lose their blacker hue, and to be tinged with the soft though sober gray of thought and meditation on things to come, with which they blend, and in which they seem to sink, and at times almost to be absorbed. Still I am glad to have my eyes turned for a while toward brighter objects, and the rosy dawn of youth and health and gladness. These young ones are as hoity-toity and fantastical and *crest-perky* as boys who have never known care or want, and are full of health and strength (if not naturally of very sedate dispositions), usually are. They are fond of chattering about the pretty girls they meet and fascinate. M. and I make a point of thinking the young ladies they admire particularly plain and vulgar, and assuring them, on our own early life experience, that young ladies seldom have any eyes for the

charms of gentlemen, but are solely intent on the degree of admiration which their own charms excite. Well, this is a very
motherly and auntly tale; you will think that these young beaux
have one admirer at least, their own mamma and aunt.

VI.

"Saintism."—Untrustworthiness of Religious Autobiographers.

To Miss MORRIS:

Herne Bay, August 22, 1846.—Dear friend, I have read a part
of the memoir of the "Sisters," and have been much interested
by it; but I think I do not feel about it *quite* as you do. It
seems to me to present a mixture of real, pure Christianity and
of *Saintism,* that spurious or semi-spurious piety which is to be
found, not among Methodists alone, but among Christians of
all names, and sometimes *leavens* the religion even of the truly
religious. But why do I feel thus? What is there in the book
that is otherwise than pure and holy? Dear Miss M——, you
will perhaps think me very wrong and over-captious, but it is
just this absence of every thing that is not presentable in the
record that makes me distrust it, as not being the whole truth,
and nothing but the truth. So far as my reflection and experience, and knowledge of life, and knowledge of biography go
(I do not say they go far, but by such as I have I must judge),
souls seen *as they are,* without a glorifying mist, do not look quite
as those souls do in that book—scarcely ever, if ever. Yet if
Papistical and Methodistical and other religious biography be
absolutely trustworthy, and to be taken literally, there must be
thousands upon thousands of such white lambs in every country.
The very same sort of things which I read there are to be read
in so many other volumes. There is too little individuality about
them; they do not read (like poor Blanco White's Memoirs) like
actual life, with all its peculiarities; for if every leaf is unlike
every other leaf, how much more is every soul unlike every other
soul! True it is that religion, like love, levels many distinctions;
but yet in every portrait of a living face we recognize a thousand lines and expressions peculiar to itself. These girls call
themselves worms, poor sinners, *as in reference* to their God, to
Infinite Perfection. There is not much humility in making this
avowal. But see, after all, what a fine character, what a noble,

elevated character, with none but *noble* faults, is traced of each of them in those pages! And by whose hands is that character traced? By any other than *their own*, and that of their memorialist, partial and proud, as their biographer, and as their own sister? I can not, and I never could, feel deeply impressed by such representations as these. I always feel that there may be, that there probably is, much of unconscious self-deception about them. A man's own journal, his own book of private confession, so far as it reports well of him, is not to be entirely trusted; for we can not help drawing flattering pictures of ourselves even *for* ourselves; we do not give an exact copy of our own hearts— we involuntarily soften it off. We say we are evil, but we do not *show* it and prove it. I admire, and am often deeply affected by the goodness of many of my fellow-Christians, but then it is such as I have had the means of witnessing myself in their daily acts and course of life, or such as is attested by persons not interested on their behalf, or from some record that has that life-like air about it, that natural light and shade, those *vera*, and not *ficta peccata*, of one kind or another, which I believe that every *real* life, faithfully and fully drawn, would exhibit. Still I think that Anne and Emma must have been girls of a very high stamp; the whole family of the M——s appear to me to be very superior.

VII.

Human Sorrow and Heavenly Rest.—"The Golden Manual."—Blue and White in Sky, Sea, and Land.—Landor's "Pentameron."—Comparative Rank of Homer, Shakespeare, Milton, and Dante.

To AUBREY DE VERE, Esq., Curragh Chase:

Herne Bay, August 31, 1846.—Of all the thoughts that press upon us on the loss of nearest friends, that which presses hardest and strongest is the self-question, "How have I done my part toward him that is gone? Is he now or has he been the worse through any fault of mine?" Then how earnestly we pray, when he is in the hands of his Heavenly Father alone, in the bosom of Infinite Mercy, that he may have that perfect kindness and boundless compassion shown him which we failed to show him here, even humanly and as far as we might. For then the double-faced glass is reversed: it magnifies all our trespasses against him, and exaggerates our shortcomings, while it reduces our efforts to serve and please, our bearings and forbearings, to narrow room, or at least takes the color out of them, and makes them look as wan as the dear face that used to smile and glow in our sight. But I meant to have said something different from this, more calm and soothing. I was going to speak of the religious peace and firmness of your father's dying hours, the *sure and certain hope* he seemed to feel of mercy through the " Merits and Death of his Redeemer." These are remembrances on which the mind may repose as on a bed of balm—more lasting in their fragrance than any balm that ever grew in Arabia, for they will yield fresh odors from time to time as long as they are pressed upon. As those dying hours of our dearest ones can never be far out of mind, it is a blessing, indeed, when they have more of the rest of heaven in them than of the sting of the grave. Those you spoke of to me remind me of my own father's. He, too, was calm and clear to the last, till he fell into the coma that so often precedes death, and neither afraid nor grieved to depart; and he was thoughtful for others still struggling with the world when he was leaving it. Perhaps it is easier to die at sixty (he was near sixty-three) than at forty. It ought to be so, if we make use of our time. A man who reaches that age may feel that he has done a day's work; and then life, as it runs on, changes its color and aspect, just as the natural day changes from meridian light to afternoon mellowness, and then to evening gray. It seems right and fit to go hence in that evening gray, when the shadows are falling on all things here to our altered eyes—not to leave the sun full behind us when we enter the darkness of the tomb. It is true that this darkness exists but in our imagination; we transfer to the state of the departed the obscurity of our minds respecting it, or, at least, our incapability of beholding it visually as we behold this present world ; still it has a real influence upon our feelings, although by efforts of thought we can dispel those shades of Hades, and bring before us that place where there is neither sun nor moon—no need of them, 'or the glory of God will lighten it, and the Lamb be the light thereof. May we more and more dwell upon that place and state, remembering that, whatever be the form and outwardness of it, whatever be its relation to the beauty of this world in which we now dwell, it is to be a spiritual state more fully than that which we abide in here, and yet that here we must be prepared for it, and, in part, conformed to it. I am at this time reading a little book of mystic divinity, the "Theologica Germanica," or little "Golden Manual," a great favorite with the Platonist divine, Dr. Henry More. It contains very high spiritual doctrine, and dwells on the necessity of setting aside all "selfness and egoity," and serving God purely for love's sake alone, without respect to even a *heavenly* reward.

We are just come in from a sea-side walk, driven home by the glaring sun. Scarce a breath is stirring, sea and sky are all one hue, and the air is heavy. The sunniest day in last week was fresher than this; then there was one light wreath of white but shaded clouds rolled along the horizon, and to match it there was a fringe of still whiter foam along the edge of the retiring sea—all else of sea and sky was brightly blue. Herbert reminded me of Homer's expressive phrase about spirting off the divine sea, which sounds low in English, but is not so felt in the Greek ἀποπτύει ἄλα δῖαν. The sea-side plants and insects, too, all do their part of brightness on these sunny days, none more than that shiny blue flower, which grows upon a shrubby stem and emulates the sky so boldly.* Veronicas make a fine show of azure in the mass, as they creep over a bank, and beds of harebells are earth-skies in the clear spaces of the wood, but the single blossoms of this plant are each a little sky in itself. Quite as lovely and as lustrous in its way is the foam-white convolvulus, which looks so exquisitely soft and innocent, as it gleams amid the brambles and nettles which its lithe stem embraces. Critics have made a "mighty stir" to find out what Virgil meant by his *ligustrum :*

"Alba ligustra cadunt, vaccinia nigra leguntur."

Surely he must have meant this snowy-blossomed bind-weed. Privet is out of the question. It is neither very white nor very caducous. The flowers of the bind-weed are especially so; they soon sink into a twisted roll, and fall to the ground, though not wafted away so early as the petals of the anemone and gum-cistus. Then near the sea there are always blue and white butterflies hovering over these blue and white flowers.

I have just finished reading Landor's "Pentameron." It is full of interest for the critical and poetical mind, but is sullied by some *Landorisms*, which are less like weeds in a fine flower-

---

* Centaurea Cyanus (Corn blue-bottle).—E. C.

bed than some evil ingredient in the soil, revealing itself here
and there by rankish odors, or stains and blotches on leaf and
petal. The remarks on Dante, severe as they are, I can not
but agree with in the main. I believe you expressed some dissent from them. I think that Dante holds the next rank in poetic power and substance after Homer, Shakespeare, and Milton, perhaps above Virgil, Ariosto, and Spenser; but there is
much in his mind and frame of thought which I exceedingly
dislike—and I have ever *felt* much of what Landor expresses
on the subject, though without speaking it all out even to myself. It happened that just after I had been declaring to Derwent my opinion of Milton's superiority to Homer, and he had
been upholding the paramountcy of the latter, I came upon
Landor's sentence on the subject. *He* pronounces Homer and
Dante both together only equivalent to Milton "shorn of his
'Sonnets' and 'Allegro' and 'Penseroso.'" I suppose he thinks
that the objectivity of the one and subjectivity of the other
(which, however, is not equal to that of still later poets), blended into one, might come up to the epic poetry of Milton; and
truly, in poetic matter and stuff of the imagination, they might
even surpass it; but there is to my mind, in the latter, a tender
modern grace, a fusion of sentiment and reflection into the sensuous and outward, which is more exquisite in kind than any
thing you would obtain from Homer and Dante melted together. I must tell you, however, that Mr. Wordsworth considers
Homer second only to Shakespeare, deeply as he venerates
Milton.

VIII.

Age and Ugliness.—"Expensive Blessings."—Æschylus.—Principle of Pindaric Metre, and Spirit of Pindaric Poetry.—Physical and Intellectual
Arts of Greece.

To the Rev. HENRY MOORE, Eccleshall Vicarage, Staffordshire:
Herne Bay, September 5, 1846.—You kindly renew your invitation, and put it in a new shape. I can only thank you for it,
alas! and try to keep alive a hope that I may enjoy your hospitality some future autumn. We read much in books, among
other things about women which to many of our sex are altogether new and surprising, that the softer sex are apt to tough-
en as they lose the graces of youth. Really, if this were the

case, it would be such a set-off against gray hairs, and withering
roses and lilies, and all those ugly, unflourishing dells which
time gradually introduces into our face-territory, that we might
behold those changes with at least half-satisfaction; but I should
say from experience that, on the contrary, we grow weaker and
more sensitive in advancing life, quite as fast as we grow ug-
lier. Then women who are so *unfortunate* as to have a boy
and girl growing up under their eyes, are reminded of their age
and weakness continually. It is a miserable thing to be sure!
and then how much money it costs! Why, if it wasn't for these
plagues, I should be quite rich, and should not have to cast an
anxious eye toward railways, or be tossed up and down in soul
and spirit with the fluctuations of the money-market. I need
never care whether I got 5 per cent. or only $3\frac{1}{2}$. I *was* rather
pleased, certainly, when my fellow-lodgers expressed their as-
tonishment that I should be the mamma of "that fine boy."
They expected to see a buxom dame, after seeing him first.
But matters are not always ordered so; and, even in this
way, the race is not always to the swift, nor the battle to the
strong.

During Herbert's stay here, before he left us to return to
Eton, he read with me the " Eumenides " of Æschylus, and great
part of the " Chœphoræ," and the " Olympics " of Pindar. The
drawback to pleasure in reading the former is the corruptness
of so many of the choruses. You may read Latin, German,
French, English translations of those compositions, all different
and all unsatisfactory. Pindar is much easier: one can make
him all out at last—bring him back from his long excursions to
the spot whence he started—though not without some trouble.
But the drawback to pleasure in reading *him*, for me, is the im-
possibility of realizing to my ear his strange metre, so strictly
regular, yet of a regularity so varied and complex, that it seems
like lawlessness and wild extravagance to those who can not
feel, though they may *understand* the law of it. To judge from
the eye, I should say that its flow somewhat resembled the sea
with its waves, growing ampler and ampler for a while, then
sinking back again; and that this suits well with his style of
thought and imagery, that combination of impetuosity with a
majestic gravity—a tempered enthusiasm, controlled and regulated by the law of reason, and a deep spirit of reverence for
the Supreme and the Invisible—the things that are above us,

and at the same time are lying at the very depths and foundations of our nature.

What a high rank bodily exercises held in those ancient days! A man's feet or fists, or skill in horsemanship or driving, lifted him to renown and wreathed his brow with laurel—and yet, in those same days, the intellectual arts had reached a point in some respects (in execution, certainly) unsurpassed. The celebrated race-hero now lives in memory of man only in virtue of the poetry devoted to his celebration. Pindar seems but half to have foreseen this when he intimates that the mighty man of feet or of fists would have had but a brief guerdon but for his glowing strains. It is some exertion for me to keep pace with Herbert's Greek now; his eye is rapid, more so than mine ever was—I wish he would unite with this a little more of my pondering propensities and love of digging down as far as ever one can go into the meaning of an author—though this is sometimes unfavorable to getting a given thing done for immediate use—it takes one off into such wide and many-branched excursions. As long, however, as I can *keep pace* with the youth, I shall be able, in virtue of my years and experience, at least for some time, to *shoot ahead* of him when we come to any really hard passage, in which it is not so much the knowledge of one particular language, but of thought in general, that is required for the elucidation. John often exhorts me to let my mind *go to grass;* but who can do this while their mind can do any sort of good in harness? After all, it is a gain, even for our own mental enjoyment, to be led back to these evergreen haunts of the Muses, which, but for the sake of accompanying our children, we might never revisit; and I am thankful that the limbs of my mind are still agile enough for these excursions, and that I am not aged for rambling in those literary fields, or for enjoying myself there, which in some respects I am able to do far more than when I first entered them.

IX.

Miss Farrer.

To Mrs. FARRER:

10 *Chester Place, September* 21, 1846.—My dearest Mrs. Farrer, since I read the last pages of your kind and interesting

letter, I have been thinking almost continually of dear Miss Farrer.* I feel as yet as if I could scarcely understand or reconcile myself to her death. The event is so unexpected, as well as unwelcome. When I first saw her, she struck me as one full of firmness and vigor, in rich and undeclining autumn. To say I shall never forget her is nothing. I might *remember* a far less impressive person; but she will remain in my mind as one of the most marked and interesting persons whom I have met with in my walk through life—one of those who most made me feel that religion is an actual reality—not merely a system, but a vital influencive truth, which, even in this world, can give such happiness as the world can not give. I am unable to remember many of her sayings, but I well retain the spirit of her discoursings, and her deep, glad, earnest voice will often sound in my ears. How graceful and persuasive, too, she was in her gestures! These are the outward things, and it seems wronging her who had such riches within, such a depth of heart and spirit, to speak of them; but they were a part of her here, and they bring her vividly to mind, such as she was altogether, outwardly and inwardly; and never was any one's outward part—countenance, carriage, and even bodily form— more expressive of the soul within than hers was.

How many must there be, and in what distant quarters of the world, that will truly mourn her death! I am sure she must have a large interest in the heavenly habitations. How many years she was doing good, and how steadily she trod the path of Christian charity and bounty! I think she was not clear-sighted on some points, and that she fixed her eyes too exclusively on one side of truth, though she sought so earnestly to look upon all who call on the name of Christ as belonging to one fold under one Shepherd, let them shut themselves up within walls and hedges of partition as much as they might. She would have embraced all *believers* with the arms of her charity, but did not always do full justice, I think, to the *belief.* She was, however, a sincere and bountiful Christian. Her example has been a burning and shining light, and will, I trust, be remembered for good long after the tears are dried that will be shed for her. What attracted me so to her was to see her,

* This lady, whose acquaintance my mother made in the autumn of 1843, is mentioned in one of the letters of that date, in which her interesting and remarkable character is dwelt upon with cordial admiration.—E. C.

T

wide as her charities were, so warm and liberal and loving in her own family.   I mean by *liberal*, so full of sympathy, so ready to see all things in the best light, and to promote all that is gay and gladsome and beautiful.   There have been philanthropists, and sincere and noble ones too, who have been oppressive and inconsiderate and morose in their own families.   Some who do good abroad, from ambitious motives, are selfish and even cruel at home. . But she was so faithful and tender and affectionate !

   X.

On the Establishment.—The Church Supported by the State, not in its Catholic, but in its National Character.—Bishops in Parliament.

To AUBREY DE VERE, Esq.:

What Dr. Hook says on the Establishment in his pamphlet on the Education of the People, I rather admire.   A correspondent of mine exclaims with indignation, " Conceive his asserting that the State is no more bound to the Church than to Methodists, etc., and asking, if it is, by what Act of Parliament?   As if the Church were not an estate of the realm, as much as the monarch is, or either House of Parliament."   I can not quite understand what my friend means by this.   Our Church, with the sovereign at its head, and with its present formularies, dates only from the sixteenth century.   Dissolve its present connection with the State, and merge it in the Church of Rome, still the State remains essentially the same ; but take away the monarch, or either House of Parliament, and you, at least organically, derange the State.   It will remain, but as a different thing, with its character quite altered.   Dr. Hook seems to mean only this, which seems to me undeniable, that the British *nation* is not of one form of Christianity, but of several, and that the State, which surely must conform itself to the nation, acting through Parliament, does not, and must not, protect, support, and, so far, help to *establish* one form alone, but as many as the nation embraces.   It is true that the Church of England has some special relations to the State, which other bodies of Christians have not.   But how has she obtained these ?   Is it simply from her being spiritually the Church of Christ, apostolically descended, while those other bodies are not the Church of Christ, or any part of it ?   It seems to me chimerical to say

so. The special relations of the Church of England to the
State, as I understand the matter, are of a temporal character,
derived from her having once been the Church of the whole
nation, still being the Church of the majority, and consequently
having a greater amount of property than other religious communities, and that in a more imposing and dignified form.
The Council of the nation *may* be filled with Dissenters and
Papists. It never, therefore, can be the duty of that Council, *as
such*, to support the Church of England more than other religious
bodies, except in proportion to numbers. The bishops do not
represent that Church in Parliament, for they sit there as temporal peers. I believe that Christianity, religion in its deepest
form, is interwoven with the State, and every State, in a vital
and intricate manner. We know of no civilized State that was
not in alliance with religion ; but I can not think that one particular form of Christianity, though it be the truest form, is a
component and essential part of the State, while the large body
of Methodists, with Quakers, Independents, and others, are in a
totally different predicament. I can not think Dr. Hook so far
wrong for asking in what real, substantial sense is the Church
of England *established* here, or how has it a right to *peculiar*
State support and protection, to be supported as the *Church
of England*, not merely as a part of the Christianity of the land.
Of course it is still formally the Established Church, and long
may it be.

XI.

The "Divina Commedia."—Barbarous Conception of the World of Fallen
Spirits exhibited in the "Inferno." — Dante compared with Milton,
Lucretius, and Goethe.—Dante as Poet, Philosopher, and Politician.

To AUBREY DE VERE, Esq., Curragh Chase :

October, 1846.—I can not quite agree with you (*yet*, at least)
on the superlative merits of Dante, whom you seem to me to
view through a glorifying glass bigger than that with which
Herschel inspected the sun ; but your reflections on the state
of your country are full of that heart-poetry and spiritual wisdom which, methinks, you "half-create," and do but half, or
scarcely half, "find," in the great Epic Poem of the Middle
Ages. What you say of hungry people, that they should not
be convened in multitudes, is a part of this wisdom. The

clamors of the *Times*, and the mingled yells and hisses of the *Dublin Review*, are—a disgrace to a Christian country. This is quite a bathos. I had something in my mind much more energetic, which I forbore to utter, lest you should think that I had had a little bite of Cerberus myself, and that my preference of the "Inferno" to the other parts of Dante's poem arises from a fellow-feeling with those amiable gentlemen in the City of Dis, who shut the gates in the face of Virgil.

How graphic all that is! How one can enter into the *spite-fulness* (if Dante had not been spiteful, he couldn't have written it) with which they proposed that Virgil should stay with them, and Dante find his way home by himself; how one can see them tearing off as hard as they could go to bar the entrance! Milton could not have conceived this intensity of narrow malice; he could not have brought his rich and genial mind, his noble imagination, down to it. It may truly be said that Dante brings the violence and turbulence of the infernal world into heaven—witness his 27th canto of the "Paradiso," which is all denunciation after the splendid introduction, yet comprises, to my mind, with slight exceptions, almost the whole power of the "Paradiso," on the merits of which, as at present advised, I quite agree with Landor; while Milton invests even the realms below and their fallen inhabitants with a touch of heavenly beauty and splendor. And is this in an irreligious spirit? Oh! far from it. This is consonant with religious truth and with the Bible, which leads us to look upon the world of moral evil as a wreck, a ruin, rather than a mere mass and congeries of hideous abominations. It is this which renders Milton's descriptions so *pathetic:* sympathy with human nature, with fallen, finite nature, pervades the whole. If this be "cotton-wool," then cotton-wool forever, say I. But this cotton-wool I believe to be a part of the substance of Christianity. For pure, unmixed wickedness, we can have no feeling; we can but shudder and turn away. Dante utterly wants this genial, expansive tenderness of soul; wherever he is touching, it is in the remembrance of something personal—his own exile, or his love for little Beatrice Portinari, or the sorrows of his patron's daughter, Francesca. Let him loose from these personal bandages, and he is perpetually raging and scorning, or else lecturing, as in the "Paradiso." How ferociously does he insult the sufferers in the "Inferno"—actual, individual men! You say this is but imagination. Truly, if it were not, the author would have been worthy of the maniac's cell, chains, and darkness; but surely the heart tinctures the imagination. I know my father's remark upon this very point, and admit its truth as a general remark; but I think it is not strictly applicable to Dante. His pictures *are* like the visions of heart-anger and scorn, not mere extravagant flights of merry petulance, or pure, high-flown abstractions, but have something in them deep, earnest, real, and individualizing. It is a hard turn of mind, to say the best of it. Carlyle does Dante more than justice—rather say generous *in*justice—on this point, when he tells us of his softness, tenderness, and pitifulness, at the same time extolling his rigor. Rigor is all very well in the right place; but such rigor as Dante's could scarce be approved by Him who said, "Judge not, lest ye be judged." It is well enough to be rigid against the *passion of anger*, but not to stick a certain Filippo Argenti up to the neck in a lake of such foulness as few men could have conceived or described, and then to express a "fearful joy"—or what is fearful to the reader, rather than himself—in seeing the other condemned ones fall furiously upon him, and duck him in it all but to suffocation! And he makes Virgil (who would have been above such school-boy savagery) hug and kiss him for it, and apply to him the words spoken of our Blessed Saviour—Luke ii., 27! Dante ought to have looked upon the tortures of the lower kingdom with awe and a sorrowful shuddering, not with triumphant delight and horrid mirth. But the whole conception was barbarous, though powerfully executed.

You must not think that I am wholly an armadillo or rhinocerean, insensible to the merits of Dante, from what I have said. I think that his "Divina Commedia" is one of the great poems of the world; but of all the great poems of the world, I think it the least abounding in grace and loveliness and splendor. There is no strain in it so fine as the address to Venus at the beginning of Lucretius's great poem; scarce any thing so brightly beautiful as passages in Goethe's great drama. I think, certainly, that the religious spirit displayed in it, especially in the "Purgatorio," is earnest and deep, but far from pure or thoroughly elevated. If you set up a claim for Dante, that his is the great Catholic Christian mind, then αφισταμαι—I am off, and to a great distance. The following description of Carlyle seems to me to point at what is Dante's characteristic power:

"The very movements in Dante have something brief, swift, decisive—almost military. The fiery, swift Italian nature of the man—so silent, passionate—with its quick, abrupt movements, its silent, pale rages—speaks itself in these things." Yes; it is in this fiery energy, these "pale rages," that Dante's chief power shows itself, as it seems to me, not in genial beauty and lovingness, not in a wide, rich spirit of philosophy. You compare a passage in the "Aids to Reflection" to the conclusion of Canto I. of the "Paradiso." They are, indeed, in a neighboring region of thought; but as neighbors often quarrel violently when they come into close contact, so I think would these if strictly compared. S. T. C. in this passage speaks of the *scale* of the creation—how each rank of creatures exhibits in a lower form what is more fully and nobly manifested in the rank above. Of this Dante says not a word. How should he? The thought is founded on facts of natural history unknown in his day, and a knowledge of zoology in particular, to which his age had paid no attention. The chief beauty of my father's aphorism consists, I think, in the striking manner in which instances of his remark are particularized, and the poetic elegance with which they are described. Then he proceeds to a concluding reflection, which is spiritual indeed—no mere fancy, but a solid truth. But Dante's passage ends with that confusion of the material and the spiritual which my father made it his business to drive out of the realms of thought as far as his eloquence could drive it. The next canto—the Beatrician lecture on the spots in the moon—I think now, as I thought when I first read it, the very stiffest oatmeal porridge that ever a great poet put before his readers, instead of the water of Helicon. If it were ever such sound physics, it would be out of place in a poem; and its being all vain reasoning and false philosophy makes it hardly more objectionable than it is on another score.

October 29.—For saying that Dante's spots-of-the-moon doctrine is, as the commentators say, a mere *fandonia* and *garbuglio*, we have no less authority than Newton. Canto III. you put your own opinions into. But I must not enter the field of Spirit *versus* Matter. I only beseech your attention to this point. God is a Spirit, and yet He is Substance, and the Head and Fountain of all Substance, and the Son is of one Substance with the Father. If the tendency of the whole creation, when not dragged down by sin, is upward to the Creator, then surely there is a progress away from matter into spirit. This I believe to be Platonism, and this Platonism Schelling, Coleridge, and others, have tried to revive. You oppose to them Mediævalism, or the semi-Pagan doctrine of the primitive Christians, *converts from Paganism*, and both parties appeal to Scripture. We think the Bible plainly teaches that flesh and blood, however *smartened up*, can not enter into the kingdom of Heaven, but that things, such as *eye* of man hath *not seen*, nor *ear heard*, are prepared by God for them that love Him. It is true we can not here, in this life, *image* to ourselves that kingdom. God himself tells us that we can not, both in Gospel and Epistle. However, few new books would give me so great delight as a full, wide, particular criticism from your pen of Dante, Milton (yes, I would trust you with him; you could not but do him glory and honor, in spite of yourself, when you took him up, though you might have thought you were going to depreciate him), and Wordsworth.

Herbert keeps me busy. He writes continually about his studies, asking for explanations, advice, and so forth. He is learning Icelandic, of which he brags greatly, and is reading Dante, Tasso, and Ariosto. I sent him a sheet of Dantian interpretations lately. I take the political view of the beasts in the first canto, instead of the merely moral. Dante's politics are very remarkable. Born a Guelph, he became the most intense and vehement Ghibelline. It was Ghibellinism that perverted his mind into that strange judgment of Brutus and Cassius.

XII.

Dante's Lucifer and Milton's Satan.—The Anthropomorphism of Milton an Inheritance of the Past.—Personality of the Evil Spirit.—Confusion between the Spiritual and the Material in the "Divina Commedia."— Poetic Merits of Dante.

To AUBREY DE VERE, Esq.:

December 24, 1846.—I am sorry that you differ so *toto cœlo* from S. T. C. in your estimate of Milton's Satan. He, the poor old "silly bard," thought the character deeply philosophical, as well as poetically sublime in the very highest degree, "the height of poetic sublimity," and the passage* in which he expatiates

---

* Coleridge's "Lay Sermons," p. 69.—E. C.

on its excellences, Mr. Hallam, in his "History of Literature," has cited as a proof of the great advance of the present age over Addison's in deep and thoughtful criticism. My father was looking at this creation of genius poetically and dramatically. *You* seem to be looking at it religiously, and in reference to a high, pure, philosophical Christianity; the objections to it in that point of view no one saw more strongly than my father, no one was less disposed to "bind up his Milton with his Bible." *He* had a right to condemn Milton's anthropomorphism, if obtruded upon us for religious truth; but I can not think that the Antiquarian High Churchman has the least right to look down upon it, and I hail the sentiments you utter on the subject as a sign that your hold on that antiquarian system is beginning a little to relax. The Christian of antiquarian views can not reject the legend of the Fall of the Angels, because a sacred writer refers to it *as if he believed in it.* The passage in Jude plainly refers to the Book of Enoch; now that book contains an account of the Fall and Apostasy in Heaven substantially the same as Milton's, and certainly involving all the absurdity which you and others find in "Paradise Lost." The passage in Isaiah about Lucifer is supposed by *orthodox* divines of this school to refer to the same subject. And look, I pray you, at the preamble of the Book of Job. Do you think it right to take that as literal verity? If you saw that account expanded in a modern poem, and did not know it to be in the Bible, would you not apply very much the same language to it that you now apply to Milton's "War in Heaven?" And just consider the common High-Church view of the Atonement. Is not that as derogatory to the Supreme Being, does it not bring Him to a level with weak, erring mortals, and their blind, selfish acts, fully as much as Milton's representation? Yet for pointing this out, and for other such anti-anthropomorphisms, my father has been set a mark against, as *an unsafe and unsound writer*, by the Antiquarian High-Church School, even by men who admitted him to be rather above his fellows in genius and intellect, than below them; strange, as Carlyle said, if he be a man of genius, with rather more wit than the common herd, instead of less, that on these deeply concerning points he should know *less* than the multitude, and this without one motive on the face of the earth to bias his mind; whereas to hold fast by the old system, *every* man has *some* inducement, clergymen the greatest inducement that it is possible to conceive. You think that Dante would have been above such a conception as Milton's. *I* think he would have been right thankful for such a conception, but that nothing so refined and sublime ever entered his pate. What is Dante's Lucifer? Has he not all that contrariety to reason which you find in Milton's Satan, without one particle of the sublimity? He is a fallen angel, too, but every bit of the angel is well done out of him, and how he ever could have been aught of the kind is inconceivable. After all, is not the irrationality of which you speak contained in the very idea of a personal evil Being, the adversary of God? What better account of such a Being can you give, what better conception of him can you frame, than Milton's, or rather, I should say, how can you avoid some such conceptions as his, if you admit the idea at all? If he be a personal agent, he must be powerful, he must be proud and rebellious, he must be capable of assuming splendid and alluring aspects ; and if he be a personal being and have a personal history, how can the symbol be realized more finely than as Milton has done it? The fault is not in the poet, but in the gross idolistic system to which he adhered, which system writers of the Tractarian School have endeavored to bring back whole in all its self-consistent absurdity, but, as I believe, in vain, for as soon as men forget their theology, they fly out against such notions as you do against "Paradise Lost." Of course I do not mean that "God the Father talks like a school divine" in the Book of Enoch, but I believe that the author of that book would have made Him talk so, had divinity been the fashion of his day. What I mean is that the ancient writers were all anthropomorphic in their conceptions of God, and some things are found fault with in Milton that are actually in the Bible, or just like things that are in the Bible, as God's laughing at the vain thoughts of men. M——'s sermon last Sunday was all against Rationalists who oppose anthropomorphism, and consider *"I shall behold his face"* as symbolical. I do not think that any mere Pantheist, who does not believe in a moral, intelligent Creator, cares for the Bible at all. No Rationalist that does hold to the Bible would say that these words did not express something deep and spiritual. The literal meaning is *not* deep and spiritual.

The offenses in the "Divina Commedia" against a pure, philosophical Christianity seem to me as great as possible. I pass by his "Regina Cœli," and the prayer addressed to her, versified from St. Bernard, though *I* hold it a fearful giving of God's glory to another ; but think of the ridiculous jumble of Pagan mythology with the Christian religion which runs through the "Inferno," and think of this absurdity which stares you in the face from beginning to end—the poem treats of disembodied spirits, not angelic beings that may have a *kind* of bodies merely, but *souls divested of their bodies ;* yet to these Dante assigns corporeal pains, and every attribute of matter.   I admit that in the "Paradiso" his representations of the Supreme, and of heavenly things in general, are not so derogatory as Milton's— they are not so broad and bold—but to my mind they are most insipid and fatiguing.

You do not exceed me in admiration of Dante, any more than in admiration of Wordsworth, though you admire some things in both more than I do.   I admire in both their passages of plain, broad vigor and humble pathos—humble, I mean, not in thought or feeling, but in circumstance.   When they put on jewelry and fine linen, I do not like them so well as in their plainer garb. Dante can describe an old *Graffiacane* with a grappling-hook in his hand to the very life.   I like that better, I own, than most of his sweetnesses in the "Paradiso," though some of them are very sweet.   His bird comparisons I like better than his baby ones.   He makes a baby of himself too much beside Beatrice—it puts one in mind of Gulliver and Glumdalclitch. However, the devylles, good as they are, are not the best parts of the "Inferno ;" the best parts are his meetings with old associates in that dolorous realm, his sorrow for their fate, their punishments, some of which are not simply horrible, graphically hideous, but most*

---

* The conclusion of this sentence is missing.—E. C.

CHAPTER XVI.

1847.—*January-July.*

LETTERS TO AUBREY DE VERE, ESQ., HON. MR. JUSTICE COLE-
RIDGE, MISS FENWICK, MISS ERSKINE, MISS
MORRIS, MISS TREVENEN.

I.

Characters of Milton, Charles the First, and Oliver Cromwell.

To AUBREY DE VERE, Esq., Curragh Chase:

Chester Place, January, 1847. — To rebel against a tyrant,
himself a rebel against the laws and liberties of his country, and
a traitor to its constitution, is no disgrace to Milton's memory.
Both parties were wrong and both were right, in my opinion
—the struggle was to be, and on either side there was much error and much wrong-doing, from a blindness, under the circumstances, scarce avoidable. Charles I pity, admire, but do
not deeply respect. Cromwell I respect more, but do not ven-
erate. He was a man of great firmness, courage, and ability.
Charles had personal, not moral courage—*he* had both. I think
he was sincere and patriotic at first, but became in some measure corrupted, just as Artevelde became corrupted in the
course of his career.

II.

Reserve in Friendship. — A Labor of Love. — Dedication of the Second
Edition of the "Biographia Literaria" to Mr. Wordsworth.—"The Silence of Old Age."

To Miss FENWICK, Queen Square, Bath:

Chester Place, 1847. — Your affectionate assurances I value
more than I can well express, not for lack of words, but because
there is a natural shyness, a little of that reserve which Mr.

Keble talks so much about, both in reference to poetry and prose, in most minds, when they have to speak of what they feel very seriously about. There is always a sense that bringing the feelings up to the light tends to fade them a little, and that some may see them with a cold or careless eye, or that the very friend to whom you utter them, and to whom they refer, may not be thoroughly pleased with them. But there may be too much of this reserve in the intercourse of friends with each other, and it is a little to be fought against.

I am seriously thinking of availing myself of your kind invitation, but if I do, it must be during the latter part of your stay at Bath. The printers are now sending the sheets of the " Biographia Literaria," and I can not correct the proofs any where but at home. Dear Miss F——, the trouble I have taken with this book is ridiculous to think of—it is a filial phenomenon; nobody will thank me for it, and no one will know or see a twentieth part of it. But I have done the thing *con amore*, for my father's book ; and after this I shall not scribble or search in books (except for reading with H. and E.) perhaps any more.

I lately had thoughts of writing to ask you a question, but recollecting that Mr. Robinson* was at Rydal, and that quick dispatch of the matter was desirable, I wrote to him instead. It was about dedicating this new edition of the " Biographia" to Mr. Wordsworth. Soon I had from himself an affectionate and gracious accedence to my wish. He said, what I wished him to say and feel, that no one now had so good a claim.

Mr. Robinson thought dear Mr. Wordsworth aged in mind— not that there was any confusedness, but an inertness, an absence of activity. He said himself, "it is the silence of old age," when Mr. Robinson remarked how little he had said the evening before.

---

* This was Mr. Henry Crabb Robinson, "the friend of Goethe and Wordsworth," whose interesting diary, extending over three large volumes, has been lately given to the public. The name of another honored guest at Rydal Mount, Isabella Fenwick, will also be familiar to readers of the " Memoir of Wordsworth."—E. C.

III.

A Visit to Bath.—Her Son's Eton Successes.—School-boy Taste.—The
Athanasian Creed.—Doctrine of the Filial Subordination not contained in it.—The Damnatory Clauses.—Candor in Argument.

To the Hon. Mr. Justice COLERIDGE :

8 *Queen Square, Bath, March* 20, 1847.—My dear John,
here we are at Bath, in the commodious temporary abode of
Miss Fenwick, with my dear old friends, Mr. and Mrs. Wordsworth. Our journey on Thursday was a bright and pleasant
one. Mr. and Mrs. W. were waiting to welcome us at the station, and most affectionate was their greeting. Mr. Wordsworth
has always called me his child, and he seems to feel as if I
were such indeed. * * *

Since I wrote the first page of this letter, I have had to answer two notes from Edward on a very pleasant occasion ; the
first told me that Herbert was in the number of the select, and
also that he had gained the essay prize in a very distinguished
manner ; the second announced, with very hearty congratulations, that he had been declared the medalist, Whymper being
the Newcastle scholar. I could not help thinking with special
keenness of feelings on those who are gone, who would have
shared with me and E. in the pleasure of this success; but it
is best, for my final welfare at least, that all is as it is, and that
the advantages of this world and its drawbacks have ever been
mingled in my portion. It is a great addition to the pleasure
to feel that Herbert's success gives real delight to others besides myself. Any thing of the kind is received at St. M——'s
quite as a little triumph. Edward says that to Latin composition and the general improvement of his *taste* he must chiefly
address himself during the next year. His taste will certainly
bear a great deal of improvement during many a year to come,
for the formation of a sound literary taste is a matter of time.
His taste, taking the word in a positively good sense, as the appreciation of what is excellent, is now in fragments, not a general embryo, apparently, but much more developed in parts
than on the whole. He has a much better notion of the true
merits of ancient writers than of modern ones—modern *subjectivity* he does not understand in the least, hence his preference
of Southey's poetry to that of Wordsworth.

* * * Mr. Dodsworth asked me in his last call what I thought
of the article on Development in the *Christian Remembrancer.*
I mentioned to him, among some other part objections, a statement toward the end which seems to me rather awkward for
those who hold by the Athanasian Creed—I mean those who
not only believe the doctrine of the Trinity and Incarnation
which it sets forth, but defend the imposition of it upon the
Church, and the propriety of its expressions from beginning to
end. The statement is that the Subordinateness of the Son,
as the Son, to the Father, "an awful and sacred doctrine," taught
by the early Fathers, had been suffered "to fall into the shade,"
"to become strange to modern ears," and thus (according to
the writer's own argument, that mere explicit knowledge is
practical ignorance) to remain unknown to the mass of Christians—Christians who are anxiously instructed by their pastors
in all the most subtle mysteries of the faith, except this (as, for
instance, that our Lord had *two wills,* against the Monothelite
heresy); that, on account of its tenderness as a matter of theological handling, the Church had discouraged any handling of
it at all. It is natural to ask, can that be *the Church,* led and enlightened by the Spirit of Christ, which shrinks from the statement of any true and sacred doctrine, which is unequal to
guard it from running into heresy, and actually sets forth a
creed which virtually denies it; for the expressions of the Athanasian Creed, "none is afore or after other," "none is greater
or less than another" (although Christ said "my Father is
greater than I," and Bull applies this to the Filial Subordination—indeed, as applied to the human nature, it would be a truism inconceivable for our Lord to have uttered), unaccompa-
nied by the admission of *any* sense in which the Father is before the Son, are, to all intents and purposes, a denial of the
doctrine. Nor does the Nicene Creed remedy the defect, as
the article seems to insinuate. It expresses the *Origination,* as
the Athanasian does also, but not the *Subordination;* and if the
latter be a direct and necessary inference from the former, is it
not the extreme of faithless cowardice to be afraid of a direct
and necessary inference? After all, what I most object to in
the "pseudo-Athanasian" Creed is the damnatory clauses, which
I take according to the common-sense of mankind, and consider to be a positive assertion of what no man *now* believes,
though when that Creed was written the belief was common

enough. To go back to Mr. D——, he agreed with me, as I understood him, in this and some other objections to the article, interesting and suggestive as it is, and in some parts satisfactory. Mr. D—— is remarkably candid in discussions of this sort. Most persons, if an objection to their view is stated, which they know not how to meet, will oppose it by a general non-admission, waiting in hope that something will turn up to justify that which they hold as part and parcel of their creed; but he always says frankly at once "that is very true," to any point which he may have at first denied, if reasons are alleged in favor of it which seem to him sufficient.

IV.

Reasons why Popular Fallacies on Religious Subjects ought to be Exposed. —Gradual Advance of the Human Mind in the Knowledge of Divine Truth.—Admission of Objections to the Athanasian Creed by Churchmen.—The Nicene Creed.

To AUBREY DE VERE, Esq.:

Bath, April, 1847.—The opinions of A, B, or C may not be weighty in themselves, but if they are signs of the times, samples of the kind of stuff which is accepted by the would-be orthodox as wisdom and truth, and which numbers of persons not deficient in sense or discernment in practical matters, or in any matters which they have really examined with study and earnestness, adopt (even if they adopt them implicitly merely because they like the sound and look of them), they are worth controverting and exposing, so far as they are unsound and spurious, though specious. As soon as ever their hollowness is plainly shown, men say, why take the trouble to break bubbles which will burst of themselves? The truth is, that bubbles of false opinion will last whole ages and deceive whole generations, till they are broken by some powerful breath, and even then how often they reunite, and again shine in the eyes of men, who hold them solid as cannon-balls! What you say about the agile feats of theologians playing with texts, is true enough; but, on the other hand, there is, I think, a change and a progress made in course of ages in divinity as in other applications of the human mind, and this change is brought about by individual labors, as huge rocks are built by the labors of coral insects, each insect laboring individually. It is also true enough that theological subtleties are of no direct practical value; but so long as a practical system, of no little weight in its effects and consequences, and a whole attitude of thought and feeling are supported mainly on the adherence, explicit or implicit, to certain theological tenets, the establishment or overthrow of which involves a development and explication which must appear subtle to all that have not become familiar with it, I can not think it a mere cat's-cradle pastime, or rather waste-time, to endeavor to show what the nature and internal consistency of these tenets really are. The more I look into these subjects, the more persuaded I am that the *practical* value of the various forms under which Christianity is embraced by various sects of Christians varies far less than is commonly supposed by the various parties themselves. The means and instrumentalities by which morality and religion are sustained and promoted differ in efficacy among different bodies of Christians; but I believe that the real spiritual substance of the belief of well-informed and well-disposed men, who have the Bible constantly in their hands, differs far less. I verily believe that *Tritheism* is the intellectual form in which numberless Trinitarians hold the faith of the Godhead, and that their view of the subject is as wide of the truth, and as inconsistent with the voice of Scripture, as that of many whose creed they speak of with horror as a "God-denying heresy." The Unitarian who worships Jesus as the Way, the Truth, and the Life, the Source of salvation, and believes in one God, to whom all fealty and submission from man is due, ought not, in my opinion, to be described as holding a "God-denying heresy." But this opinion is so very unpopular, that if I were prudent I should keep it to myself. I am like the poor pigeon who painted herself black in order to escape ill-usage from the crows, and thus, looking neither like crow nor pigeon, was driven away with scorn by both parties.

I certainly agree with you that the Church was neither dove nor eagle when she uttered the so-called Athanasian Creed; or, rather, I do not believe that it was the true Church at all who uttered it, the Church led by the Spirit of Truth. Athanasius himself would have been right sorry, I doubt not, to hear it called by his name. I will not trouble you with my reasons for this opinion, but will just say that the article on Develop-

ment in the last *Christian Remembrancer* contained a statement on this subject which those who object to that creed may
lay hold of to their own advantage. There is nothing new in
the statement ; S. T. C. said it long ago. But the *admission* is
a triumph. You must not suppose me to doubt or deny that
the doctrine of the Godhead taught in the Nicene Creed, which
I firmly and reverently hold, is quite irreconcilable with Uni-
tarianism ; but I would suggest that the errors of the Unitarian
ought to be looked on indulgently, when it is considered how
difficult it is to preserve the mind from intellectual error upon
this subject, when it is opened out as it is in the Athanasian
Creed. Well! how much I have said on the Athanasian Creed,
and yet not said half that I should say if I spoke of it at all !

V.

Mr. and Mrs. Wordsworth.—Walks and Talks with the Aged Poet.—His
Consent obtained to a Removal of the Alterations made by him in his
Early Poems.

To AUBREY DE VERE, Esq. :

Bath, April, 1847.—I have made an effort to come hither,
availing myself of Miss Fenwick's most kind invitation, although
it separates me from Herbert during his holiday time, because
I felt that the opportunity of being once more under the same
roof with my dear old friends was not to be neglected. I find
them aged since I saw them last in many respects ; they both
look older in face, and are slower and feebler in their movements of body and mind. Mrs. Wordsworth is wonderfully active ; she went three times to church on the Fast Day,* and
would have fasted almost wholly had not Mr. W., in a deep, determined voice, said, " Oh, *don't* be so *foolish,* Mary !" She wisely felt that obedience was better than this sort of sacrifice, and
gave up what she had "set her heart upon," poor dear thing!
She is very frail in look and voice, and I think it very possible
that a real fast might have precipitated her downward progress
in the journey of life—I will not say how many steps. Mr.
Wordsworth can walk seven or eight miles very well, and he
talks a good deal in the course of the day ; but his talk is, at

---

* The Day of Fasting and Humiliation appointed on account of the Irish
Famine. This occasion gave rise to the general remarks on fasting, as a
religious exercise, in the ensuing letter to Miss Trevenen.—E. C.

the best, but the faintest possible image of his pristine mind as shown in conversation ; he is dozy and dull during a great part of the day; now and then the dim waning lamp feebly flares up, and displays a temporary *comparative* brightness—but *eheu! quantum mutatus ab illo!* He seems rather to recontinue his former self, and repeat by habit what he used to think and feel, than to think any thing new. To me he is deeply interesting, even in his present state, for the sake of the past ; the manner in which he enters into domestic matters, the concerns and characters of maids, wives, and widows, whether they be fresh and gay, or " withering in the stalk," is really touching in one of so robust and manly a frame of mind as his originally was, and, in a certain way, still is. We sit round the fire in the evening, his aged wife, our excellent hostess, your friend S. C., Louisa F., a very handsome and very sweet and good girl, and my E., and talk of our own family matters, or the state of the nation, or the people of history, Tudors and Stuarts, as subjects happen to arise, Mr. W. taking his part, but never talking long at a stretch, as he used to do in former years. Sometimes we walk together in a morning, and one day I had the satisfaction of hearing him assent entirely to some remarks which I ventured to make upon the alterations in his poetry, and even declare that they should be restored as they were at first. I say "they," but it remains to be seen to what extent he will do this. He promised, in particular, that the original conclusion of " Gypsies " should be restored in the next edition ; he also seemed to assent to my view of the new stanzas in the " Blind Highland Boy," that, though good in themselves, they rather interfere with the effect of the poem. I would have them preserved, but detached from the poem, and the story of the tub retained with a little alteration of expression, if possible. One day I contrived to draw Mr. W. out a little upon Milton, and to hear him speak on that subject in a *to me* satisfactory manner.

VI.

Fasting and Self-Denial.

To Miss E. TREVENEN, Helstone, Cornwall :

Bath, April 9, 1847.—As for the sham fasts or semi-fasts, with a great heavy supper afterward, which some people prac-

tice by way of obeying the Church and following the example
of the ancient Christians, I can not believe that they are of any
great service to Christendom ; and real fasts are so injurious
to the health of a large proportion of Christians, that I can
never believe them to be an acceptable sacrifice to God. However, on this point I differ from many whom I deeply respect,
while I agree with some whom I deeply respect also, and I will
enter into the subject no further than to say that I believe in
fasting in a high and spiritual sense, that of abstaining from
self-indulgence for the sake of doing good to others. Contract-
ing our wants into as narrow a compass as possible, without
injury to our body or mind, is a most important part of Christian duty, and no one can be a true Christian who does not
practice it. They who give largely to the poor *must fast* in this
sense, because they diminish their means of indulging in the
pride of the eye, and all kinds of unnecessary luxuries and el-
egancies.

VII.

The Irish Famine.—Defects and Excellences of the Irish Character.—
Bath Churches.—The " Old Man's Home ;" an Allegory.

To Miss ERSKINE :

8 *Queen Square, Bath, April,* 1847.—My dear A——, I thank
you for your kind congratulations, and for your wish that this
visit may encourage me to avail myself of an invitation to Little Green at some future time from dear Mrs. E——.   I strained
a point to come hither in order to be with my dear old friends
Mr. and Mrs. Wordsworth.   They are aged since I saw them
last, but still wonderful people of their age, very active in body,
and in mind to me most interesting.   We have many, many
mutual recollections and interests and acquaintanceships, and
should have enough to converse about even if *news* reached us
not here.   It is impossible, however, not to dwell a good deal
on the state of Ireland.   I have just received a long letter from
Adare.   No one has died of starvation in his neighborhood, my
friend tells me, though there is want and trial enough.   He is
indignant at the abuse of Irish landlords in our papers, which
he treats as absolute slander.   " People who can not get rent
enough to keep them in snuff," says he, " are spoken of as having £10,000 per annum ; and men who are feeding their poor

on the venison of their parks are accused of living in palaces
among beggars, just as if they could grind down the statues in
their halls into powder, and make the poor people live on lime-
stone broth." He calls the English subscriptions "magnificent,"
but says that all the good-hearted people he converses with are
dreadfully incensed at not being allowed to feel as grateful as
they would wish to feel. I believe that there are good, bad,
and indifferent among Irish landlords, as among other sets of
people, and that *some* are as bad as they have been represented.
We have reports of some from persons resident among them,
which describe them as most selfish and unfeeling. Surely,
too, there are some besetting faults in the poor of that land;
they seem to be indolent, improvident, not truthful. How much
of this arises from misgovernment is hard to say, but I am inclined to think that the *circumstances* of the Irish would never
have been so bad as they have ever been had their original
disposition and character not been wanting in certain elements
conducive to prosperity and well-being. They have passive
courage, but they want persistent energy and activity, and
steady, effective principle, though there are many excellent, amiable points of character in them, and they have produced some
admirable men. Bishop Berkeley I have long thought one of
the best and most-to-be-admired of mortals, and have warmly
assented to that line of Pope's, in which he assigns

"To Berkeley every virtue under Heaven." * * *

Since we have been here we have tried more churches than
the Little Old Woman tried chairs of Bears to sit down in, and
at last have fixed on one about the middle of the hill, as more
comfortable in its arrangements and inoffensive in doctrine than
any other.

I have no time, or scarce any, for reading here, but have read
by snatches Adams's "Old Man's Home," which is sweet and
pleasing in style, but in aim and import, as it seems to me,
very vague and unsatisfactory. It is difficult to see exactly
what moral or maxim or sentiment the author means to en-
force; if you take it one way, it seems scarce worth making a
tale about; if another, then it is an untenable falsity, such as it
is scarce worth any one's while to take the pains to refute.
Equivoques and paradoxes I never could entertain any respect
for myself, though they are often very popular: 'a sentiment
looks well in a mist, and has a sublime air, like our terraces in

the park, which look like common houses of £200 or £300 a year, instead of romantic palaces, when the vapors clear off.

VIII.

Last Visit of Mr. Wordsworth to London.

To Miss FENWICK, Queen Square, Bath :

Chester Place, April 26, 1847.— * * * Last Saturday I saw dear Mr. and Mrs. Wordsworth probably for the last time during this visit of theirs to the south. He has looked remarkably well since he came to town ; when I have seen him there has been a rosy hue over his face, and he struck my nephew, J. D. C., who saw him on his arrival at Paddington, as wondrously full of vigor, quite a grand old man, and as one might expect the poet Wordsworth to be. * * * I was not able to obtain a dinner or breakfast visit from the great man, though several times promised it. But I believe he dined out nowhere, and even declined breakfasting at Mr. Robinson's. You have heard, no doubt, that he has written part of the Installation Ode ; Miss F. says that there is a great deal of thought in it ; but he says himself that it is but superficial thought, and that it is not worth much. However, I am glad that his mind is still lithe enough to perform such tasks, even in an ordinary manner, if ordinary it be. There will probably be a manner in it that reports of himself, even if the substance be not very new or powerful.

IX.

Illness of Mrs. Quillinan.—Answer to the Question " Whether Dying Persons ought to be Warned of their State at the Risk of Hastening their Departure ?"—Holy *Living* the only Real Preparation for Holy *Dying*.

To Miss FENWICK :

Chester Place, May 3, 1847.—My dearest Miss Fenwick, I return to you, with many thanks, poor Mr. Quillinan's very affecting letter, which conveys the impression that our sweet, dear Dora* has but a few weeks, perhaps not many days, of life in this world before her.

---

* Mr. Wordsworth's only daughter, whose early life was spent in sisterly intimacy with the family at Greta Hall. She died of consumption in the first week of July, 1847.—E. C.

In my reply to Mr. Quillinan, I expressed briefly my own strong opinion against communicating to the patient medical opinions that destroy all hope of prolonged life. The truth to me seems this, dear Miss Fenwick. That we ought not to deprive our friends of a certain or even highly probable spiritual advantage for the sake of saving them any *trial* or *suffering here*, I most entirely agree with you; but I can not help greatly doubting, as I believe James Coleridge doubts too, that the spiritual advantage is such as many suppose it. Have we a right to hasten death, to destroy (as in *some* cases we may) a remaining *chance* of recovery, to cut short what may be days of *real*, if not formal preparation, to produce a state of, perhaps, unspeakable distress and terror, preclusive of that calmness and self-possession which are so indispensable to the best and most efficacious spiritual reflection? Every medical man will say that such communications have generally a bad effect upon the body; can spiritual guides *assure* us that they have a good effect upon the soul, or give us great reason to think so? What Mr. Wordsworth expresses seems to me to be the simple truth; my Uncle Southey held the same opinion. It is very true that numbers of persons view the approach of death with composure, even welcome it; this was the case with my sister Fanny Patteson; she had long thought that she was death-stricken, and not regretted it; when her time came, she *knew* the truth, without being told it, and, great as her blessings in this life had been, was "glad to go." But there are other persons equally good, equally religious, to whom the near prospect of dissolution is intolerable; to persons in general, I think we may say, the shock is awful. I fear you may not agree with me, but I must express my doubt whether the agitated prayers which persons offer up in this terrified state—prayers produced more by a vague horror and dread of punishment, than a calm, clear sense of the odiousness and unhappiness of sin as *sin*, let it bring further consequences beyond itself or not—are of such service in a religious point of view as persons generally suppose. It seems a trite thing to say that it is the use we make of life and all our active powers, what we make ourselves to *be* inwardly by the life we lead, that our well-being hereafter depends upon, and not the thoughts of our final change specially occupying the mind during our last few days, and producing a special preparation. Yet this special preparation, if it can be brought about, well or *usefully*, is by no means to be disregarded. I am inclined to think, however, that even where there is still hope of life, and not an absolute coming face to face with approaching death, there is often a most salutary discipline and real preparation : a sense of the precariousness of life, and the weakness and liability to suffering of this our earthly state, must be strongly impressed on any *impressible* mind under such circumstances ; and to this preparation, with its subdued yet quiet and cheerful frame of spirits, I should trust more than to any which the prospect of speedy dissolution brings about. I would not go so far as to say that *true* penitence may not be produced by this prospect, but I think it is best for Christians through life to feel that if they do not repent of sin effectively while they yet may practice it, the mere sorrow that they *have* practiced it when they are on the verge of a state where only the misery of it can survive will stand them in little stead, or at least is nothing to rely upon.

If you ask me how would I myself be dealt with under such circumstances, I scarce know what to say; only I feel *now* that if I do not now prepare to go, it will signify little then. I should be resolved to have every thing temporally, as much as I can, in readiness, and as I should wish it to be were a disabling illness to come upon me ; and I always pray to be prepared for my final change, and enabled *now* to realize the short interval between my present existence and that other state. I earnestly hope that I may be, as Fanny was, aware when the time is approaching, by my own inward feelings, so that friends about me will not have the pain of breaking it to me. Alas! I have neither husband nor parents to be grieved ; and children, however loving and beloved, can not feel as they feel. But, dear friend, this is not altogether to be deplored. I doubt not you feel with me that there is a calmness, even if a sadness, in this thought. We must, as Keble says, take that last journey alone ; we must learn to be alone *in heart* here first. I always felt that my deep losses would make it easier to die.

X

To Miss MORRIS, Mecklenburg Square:

Margate, May 31, 1847.—This place is very refreshing. The larks twittering in the fields of dwarf beans, now in fragrant bloom, and the lush green oat crops, and the clover-beds, not yet in blossom, but soon to be, and the sight of the blue field of ocean beneath the blue sky, are all very pleasant. I think of the time when I came hither first, four years ago—a sad, sad widow. My children were with me, and their gambols and ex- treme vivacity were not like what any other gayety would have been to my feelings, as "the pouring of vinegar upon nitre, and the taking away a garment in cold weather." They "sang songs to my heavy heart," without seeming to increase its burden. Then the dying bed of my beloved husband, who had ever been such a lover to me, his last illness and dying hours, were all fresh in my mind; but a little space interposed between the present and that sorrow. *Now* I have to dwell on the dying bed of one of my very earliest companion-friends, dear Dora Quillinan, once Wordsworth, who is sinking in the last stage of consumption. You know I was with her parents at Bath in March. In April they were for a week in London, were hast- ened home by a report that the medical man had discovered fatal symptoms in her. Now for the last fortnight she has known her prospect, that she is death-stricken, and that it is only with her a question of time, and nothing can exceed the heavenly composure, sweetness, and piety of her frame of mind. She bore the communication, which she solicited herself, with perfect firmness, seemed quite happy to go, though full of love to all around her, and no dying bed can be more full of amia- ble dispositions, or more perfect in its resignation than hers. I must write to Mrs. Wordsworth in reply to a detail of her be- loved child's sayings and doings in this her season of death- expectancy and final weakness, which she thought due to me as her earliest companion-friend. Scarcely a day passes that I do not receive, either from Rydal Mount or from our mutual friend, Miss Fenwick, accounts of the dear sufferer. It is quite a privilege to be admitted to dwell on such a dying bed as hers. In the day my children and other interests share my thoughts with her, but at night, in my sleepless hours, I am ever with her, or dwelling on my own future death-bed, or going back to that of my dear husband, or the last days and hours of my beloved mother. The parents are wonderfully supported, but deep, deep is their sorrow. Mr. Wordsworth can not speak of it without tears. Poor Mr. Quillinan! But I must say no more of this, to me, engrossing sorrow.

The "Biographia" has various misprints, omissions, etc., in it, which I have been correcting in my friends' copies. Some of my "Catholic" friends have been objecting to my remarks, and I have been replying and explaining. I find no difficulty in this. People never do. Replying and rejoining may go on *ad infinitum*, because, somehow or other, different thinkers assign such a different value to the same considerations. There is always a something left which can not be churned up, like the buttermilk which can not be turned into butter; there is always a something which can not be absolutely settled by logic and reasoning, and this something determines whether you are to be on this side or that.

Mr. D——, still judging by circumstances, instead of looking straight at the opinions themselves, will have it that my father's views would have been much modified had he read the ancient Fathers. I think he would have read them more at large had he not felt assured, from what he had read of them, that this would not bring an adequate return in the way of sound Christian knowledge. We have the grain without the chaff, I should imagine, in our great divines.

However, time fails, and if I go on defending my statements as I have done of late, I shall have no time left ever to think of any thing else. It is impossible to please one's opponents, so it does not signify trying. If we argue weakly, they triumph, and if strongly, they don't know that they are beaten; but, having a sort of half-suspicion of it, they are far worse satisfied than if the argument against them had been more unsatisfactory! However, I admit that I can be no great judge of the satisfactoriness or the reverse of my own arguments. But sometimes one is attacked for not considering a position which one thought so very untenable that, if one took it in hand, folks would say one was fighting with a shadow.

I dined at the Chevalier Bunsen's not long before I left town. It was a most pleasant party. I was also at pleasant ones at Lord Monteagle's, where I met Whewell, and was delighted with his talk, at Sir Robert Inglis's, and Sergeant Stewart's, and met Carlyle at Mrs. W——'s one evening. I should have had party fever had I not run away.

I saw the Exhibition, admired the landscapes, a lovely Danby, Rippingille, Cooper, Stanfield. I liked the Mulready, and the first of the Joan of Arcs. I also liked the great Landseer, and the lion picture, too, in its way. The good-natured look of the lioness is true to nature, though perhaps exaggerated. The amiability and good-humor of lionesses are very remarkable.

Talking of lionesses, Mrs. Southey's volume of poems contains many of merit, though I do not like her continuation of "Robin Hood." Her "Young Gray Head" is exquisitely pathetic, and beautiful, too, in the style, of all others, that suits her best.

XI.

The Earnest of Eternal Life.

To Miss FENWICK, Bath :

Chester Place, July 1, 1847.—Poor Mr. Quillinan's letter increases the sad feeling with which I approach in thought that sick-room at Rydal Mount. But while the mind is so far from sick, these are, indeed, as you say, but temporary emotions: the natural horror of continuous pain and suffering will go ; the remembrance of the sufferer's strength and sweetness will remain. We can not need arguments and sermons on immortality ; or, at least, after being instructed in Christianity, we can not need them to strengthen and refresh our faith when we have such living documents and earnests of Eternal Life before us as these. If the mind seemed to weaken and die with the body, we might doubt ; though even then I trust the written Word might sustain us ; but up to the last breath, how brightly the light shines in some ! It would be impossible to think, even without the Word, that such a power of thought and feeling was in a few moments to cease to be forever !

XII.

The Sister of Charles Lamb.

To Miss FENWICK :

Margate, July 6, 1847.—I see that Mary Lamb is dead. She departed, eighty-two years old, on the 20th of May. She had survived her mind in great measure, but much of the *heart* remained. Miss Lamb had a very fine feeling for literature, and was refined in mind, though homely, almost coarse, in personal habits. Her departure is an escape out of prison, to her sweet, good soul more especially. To put off the clog of the flesh must be to the sanest an escape from a body of death.

XIII.

Religious Tendency of Mr. Coleridge's Writings.—Her Father, her Uncle, and Mr. Wordsworth.

To Miss FENWICK, Queen Square, Bath :

Chester Place, July 7, 1847.—Dear friend, I have been extremely gladdened by what you said in your last but one on the use that my father's writings had been to you. No better compliment could be paid them than to say that they *sent you to the Bible;* and this exactly describes my own feelings and experience. I, too, feel now, that though I read books of divinity—especially of Jeremy Taylor and our old divines—with delight, and a certain sort of advantage, I do not *want* any book spiritually except the Bible, now that by my father and Mr. Wordsworth I have been put in the way of reading it to advantage. They, indeed, have given me eyes and ears. What should I have been without them ! To my Uncle Southey I owe much —even to his books; to his example, his life and conversation, far more. But to Mr. W. and my father I owe my *thoughts* more than to all other men put together.

XIV.

Margate in a Storm.

To the Hon. Mr. Justice COLERIDGE:

Margate, July 16, 1847.—Yesterday I longed for E——, or any of our dear young people, in my pleasant, long walk with nurse. A storm came on, and I stood, backed and screened by a hedge, and saw Margate looking really fine under the dark, tumultuous sky, with her two churches of opposite characters— the young, tall, upright Trinity Church, crowning the town; and at the farther end of it the little, old, dumpy, yet venerable St. John the Baptist's. I prefer this place, upon the whole, to Herne Bay or Broadstairs: there is more to see—more of human life in this long-established, half-new, half-old town, than in those later-settled spots; and the country and the views are pleasanter.

CHAPTER XVII.

1847.—July–December.

LETTERS TO AUBREY DE VERE, ESQ., HON. MR. JUSTICE COLE-
RIDGE, MISS FENWICK, REV. HENRY MOORE, MISS ERS-
KINE, MISS MORRIS, MISS TREVENEN, MRS. H.
M. JONES, MRS. RICHARD TOWNSEND.

I.

Grasmere Church-yard.

To Miss FENWICK :

August 2, 1847.—Your account of dear Mr. and Mrs. Wordsworth is very consolatory. I am sure they must be soothed and
sustained by the remembrance of their blessed child's sweet,
loving, beneficent life, and of her calm, happy, patient death-
bed, so full of faith and Christian graces. I should think that
a visit to the church-yard where she lies must, under these circumstances, be soothing. Well do I remember Dora shedding
tears when we, her thoughtless companions, read aloud the
names of her little departed sister and brother in that church-
yard. How little did I think, full of life and strength as she
then was, that she would be laid there herself while I survived,
and her own parents still lived to lament her loss !

II.

The Installation Ode.—"The Triad."

To the Rev. HENRY MOORE, Eccleshall Vicarage, Staffordshire :

Chester Place, August 4, 1847.—The visit to Bath was very interesting, though I saw in Mr. Wordsworth rather a venerable
relic, so far as his intellectual mind is concerned, than the great
poet I once knew; and I do not agree with H. T. in thinking
highly of his Installation Ode.* It is only so far Wordsworthian

---

* Written on occasion of the Installation of the Prince Consort as Chan-
cellor of the University of Cambridge.—E. C.

that it is not vulgar, not decked out with a second-hand splendor that may be bought at any poetry-mart for the occasion. But the intercourse with my dear old friends was saddened by the bad news they were receiving of their beloved daughter. A week after they came to town they received a report of her which hastened them home, and now she is in her grave—has been in her grave for some weeks. She was one of my earliest friends, and her death has saddened this summer to me. Never was there a more blessed death-bed than hers—one fuller of faith and love and fortitude, and every Christian grace. Still it is sad for those who knew her from childhood to see her light go out in this world. Look at "The Triad," written by Mr. Wordsworth four or five and twenty years ago. That poem contains a poetical glorification of Edith Southey (now W.), of Dora, and of myself. There is *truth* in the sketch of Dora, poetic truth, though such as none but a poet-father would have seen. She was unique in her sweetness and goodness. I mean that her character was most peculiar—a compound of vehemence of feeling and gentleness, sharpness and lovingness—which is not often seen.

III.

High-Church Principles practically carried out.

To the Rev. HENRY MOORE:

Chester Place, August, 1847.—*To be sure* I should vote for Gladstone! Why, don't I always *support* the High-Church party with all my *mighty power and influence?* What can you be thinking of? Didn't I give money to St. Augustine's—more than I could afford—and always stand up for Mr. D—— to his back, though I oppose him to his face? And am I not as constant to his church* as a dove; and wouldn't I rather join the Tractarians than any other *party*, if I was forced to join any? I am only provoked with High-Church divines for some of their dry dogmas, which, as distinctive opinions, have no practical value whatever, so far as I can see, but which they set up as saving truths, and denounce all other Christians for doubting. Their theology, on the whole, I think better than that of any other

---

* This was Christ Church, Albany Street, where my mother was a regular attendant for many years, till her health failed.—E. C.

party. But the theology of all parties wants ventilating and sifting. The abuse of Rome in the Anglican party is vulgar and ignorant, and their representations of Calvinism are the finest specimens of misrepresentation that I am acquainted with.

IV.

Intellectual Ladies, Modern and Ancient.

To AUBREY DE VERE, Esq. :

Chester Place, August 20, 1847.—I had a very interesting talk last night with Mr. H. T., who is looking remarkably well. He put in a strong light the unattractiveness of intellectual ladies to gentlemen, even those who are themselves on the intellectual side of the world—men of genius, men of learning and letters. I could have said, in reply, that while women are young, where there is a pretty face, it covers a multitude of sins, even intellectuality; where there is not that grand desideratum to young marrying men, a love of books does not make the matter much worse in one way, and does make it decidedly better in the other: that when youth is past, a certain number of persons are bound to us, in the midst of all our plainness and pedantry; these old friends and lovers cleave to us for something underneath *all that*, not only below the region of good looks, skin, lip, and eye, but even far deeper down than the intellect, for our individual, moral, personal being, which shall endure when we shall be where all will see as angels ken, and intellectual differences are done away: that as for the *world of gentlemen at large* —that world which a *young* lady desires, in an indefinite, infinite way, to charm and smite—we that are no longer young pass into a new, old-womanish, tough state of mind; to *please* them is not so much the aim as to set them to rights, lay down the law to them, convict them of their errors, pretenses, superficialities, etc., etc.; in short, tell them a *bit of our mind.* This, of course, is as foolish an ambition as the other, even more preposterous; but it is so far better that even where the end fails, the means themselves are a sort of end, and a considerable amusement and excitement. So that intellectualism, if it be not wrong in itself, will not be abandoned by us to please the gentlemen.

God bless you, and prosper you in all your labors, for your country's sake and your own. But do not forget the Muses al-

together. Those are intellectual ladies who *have* attractions
for gentlemen worth pleasing, and who retain "the bland composure of perpetual youth" beside their refreshing Hippocrene.

V.

Sacred Poetry: Keble, Quarles, and Crashaw.

To Mrs. RICHARD TOWNSEND, Springfield, Norwood :

Chester Place, September, 1847.—I am much pleased to hear
of your undertaking,* and feel provoked that I can not aid you
in it—poet's daughter and niece and friend, as I am—I mean
in the way of pointing out some green haunts of the sacred
Muses which you have not yet found out. But though sacred
poetry abounds, good sacred poetry is more scarce than poetry
of any other sort. I do but half like the " Christian Year," I
confess ; but this you will think bad taste in me, though I could
quote some poetical authorities on my side. I admire some
stanzas and some whole poems in the collection exceedingly,
but they seem to me quite teasingly beset with faults both of
diction and composition. Of these, the former annoy me most,
and most interfere with my pleasure in reading them. I know
no other mass of poetry so good, that is not at the same time
better, showing more poetic art and judgment.

I can only mention to you Quarles, a great favorite with my
Uncle Southey, and Crashaw,† whose sacred poetry I think

---

* A collection of sacred pieces, chiefly from the elder English poets, entitled "Christmas Tyde," and published by Mr. Pickering in 1849. It was
followed by " Passion Week," a companion volume.—E. C.

† Richard Crashaw, a contemporary of Herbert, Quarles, and Vaughan,
became a Roman Catholic during the troubles of the Civil War, and died a
canon of Loretto, A. D. 1650. His poetry is marked by a dreamy, fanciful
sweetness and devotional fervor, which give it a peculiar charm. The following elegant little poem, "On Mr. George Herbert's book, entitled the
Temple of Sacred Poems, sent to a Gentlewoman," must surely have been
prized by the receiver, as adding to the value of the gift :

"Know you, Fair, on what you look?
Divinest Love lies in this book,
Expecting fire from your eyes
To kindle this his sacrifice.
When your hands untie these strings,
Think you've an angel by the wings—

more truly poetical than any other, except Milton and Dante. I asked Mr. Wordsworth what he thought of it, and whether he did not admire it; to which he responded very warmly. My father, I recollect, admired Crashaw; but then neither Quarles nor Crashaw would be much liked by the modern general reader. They would be thought queer and extravagant.

VI.

The Art of Poetry.—A Lesson on Metre.

To Miss MORRIS:

1847.—My dear friend, I may not on Wednesday, or before —for I hope we shall meet again before—be able to squeeze in a word about the Art of Poetry; and so I will write a few lines on the subject now, only as a prelude to much talk on such subjects which I hope to have with you from time to time.

I must begin with telling you that I never wrote blank verse in my life, and smile at myself when I think that I am about to attempt giving instructions, or even hints, on metre. I always, in attacking Wordsworth's later poetry with Mr. De Vere, admit that, from his far greater practice in verse-making and executive skill in poetry, he is more alive to delicacies of metre and elegances of diction than I am. However, though I never wrote Latin verses myself, I could often inform Herbert of the faults of his; and so in regard to your lines. I can perceive that some of the lines have not quite the right metre, without too much humoring.

You know blank verse consists of ten feet called iambuses, each foot containing a short and a long syllable, represented in the symbols of ancient prosody thus : ⌣ ‒, as forbear.

One that gladly will be nigh
To wait upon each morning sigh,
To flutter in the balmy air
Of your well-perfumed prayer.
These white plumes of his he'll lend you,
Which every day to heaven will send you,
To take acquaintance of the sphere,
And all the smooth-faced kindred there !"—E. C.

X

This heroic measure is called pure when the accent rests upon the second syllable through the whole line, as—

But who | can bear | th' approach | of cer | tain fate.

Still it would be very wearying and tame if the accent was never transposed in the course of a composition. Very often spondees are introduced in the place of the iambus—the spondee is a foot formed of two long syllables, as *wax-light*—or a trochee, a long and a short, as *daily.*

Here Love | his gold | en shafts | employs, | here lights |
His con | stant lamp | and waves | his pur | ple wings—
Reigns here | * * * * * *

In the second line you see the iambic measure is pure, in the others mixed. (I should have said above that the ancients have *syllabic* quantity, their short and long syllables depending upon the number and position of the consonants, and the time taken up in pronunciation; we have only *accentual* quantity, at least as an absolute rule, though some attention to the length of syllables is also paid by every fine versifier.) Milton often crumples two short syllables into one for the last half of his iambus at the end of a line, as—

Your bod | ies may | at last | turn all | to spirit.

Equivalent in time to a short and a long, for two shorts are equal to one long.

So again—

Eter | nal King, | the au | thor of | all being.

In this line there is a pyrrhic in the fifth place, and a dactyl (– ◡ ◡) in the last, which forms a very agreeable variety. Here you see the time is equal to that of the pure iambic, if you take the two last feet together, because the long syllable "all" is in the place of a short syllable. The time in the two last feet is the same as six shorts or three longs, or two shorts and two longs, which is the usual distribution. Only the change of arrangement, introduced but very seldom, and in an appropriate place, is a beauty. Do just mark the exquisite metrical variety in the passage—book iii., lines 344–371—especially from "With these that never fade" to the end of the paragraph.

By way of practice you ought to scan Milton's "Paradise Lost." That is, read passages, attending principally to the metre, and putting them on paper with the prosodiacal marks, as—

Pāvemĕnt | thăt līke | ă sēa | ŏf pūr | plĕ shōne ;

and mark in a paragraph the varieties of accent and their relation to the sense and the feeling of the verse. Does it not seem brutal thus to anatomize and skeletonize poetry? but so painters learn to paint, and so poets must learn to poetize, I believe.

It is the sense of the great difficulty of writing blank verse that has always kept me from attempting it. In rhymes and stanzas there is a mechanical support, a sort of *frame-work* of poetry which my weakness rests upon. But some persons' thoughts (probably yours are such) naturally flow into that form more than any other.

I have criticised you as freely as I do many of my other friends. I think that writing verse is useful in a secondary way, as learning music is also; it teaches us to feel doubly the excellences of the great poetic artists, as musical practice to understand fine playing.

VII.

Lodging-house Discomforts.—A Programme Unfulfilled.

To AUBREY DE VERE, Esq., Curragh Chase :

Margate, September 20, 1847.—We came hither on Friday in pouring rain. I had not been able to secure our former nice lodgings, and was not disposed to spend money at the inn as on previous occasions, so on we went to find a shelter amid the cats and dogs, and rushed into apartments as a hare rushes into her form when pursued by her enemies. The little sitting-room has a pleasant view, but the moss-rosebuds that adorn the paper of the walls are emblematic in their very conspicuous thorns of the discomforts of the abode. I put my foot on a tea-caddy, by way of a foot-stool, and E—— eats her plum-tart with a salt-spoon. But all this is naught to the brawling of the people who keep the house; never did I hear the like, except in fancy, when I have been reading that passage of the "Inferno" about the

> "Diverse lingue, orribili favelle
> Parole di dolore, accenti d'ira,
> Voci alte e fioche."

Talking of the "Inferno," you accuse me of want of love and reverence for Dante! Oh, that you would come as near me in respect and affection for Luther as I near you in admiration of the stern Florentine! I see more faults in the "Paradiso" than you do, and I can not place it relatively so high; but I think you no more outgo me, dear friend, in reverence for the genius of Dante than in general estimation of Wordsworth. I marvel that you do not think Luther a great man, and that you do not love, as my father did, as Carlyle and Hare do, one side of his character. It is the union of force, gigantic energy, constancy, indomitable resolution, dauntless courage (Mr. Wordsworth calls him "dauntless Luther"), with tenderness of spirit, and in his writings a deep insight into the meaning of St. Paul, and a most animated and expressive style, perfectly adapted to the work it was to do, which I so admire. Different men have different gifts and missions to perform, and are great in different ways; but I do not think the world has ever seen a greater man, *upon the whole*, than Luther, or one who was the instrument of greater works, except the worthies of the Bible, Lawgiver and Leader, Prophets and Apostles. Are you thankful for the Reformation? Do you prize a reformed and Scriptural Church? Do you think we have a purer faith than that which Rome taught in the sixteenth century, and even now teaches? If you do, how can you not honor God's instrument in effecting the noble work—heroic Luther? Do you admire and love our good old divines "the Anglican Fathers?" * * *

I was going to inflict on you a lecture in the shape of a parallel between English divinity and that of the Continental divines, a recapitulation of all the testimonies to the merits of Luther in our Church, and a history of the rise and progress of Anti-Lutherism in the Church of England; but my heart relents toward you. I think that you are working hard to be useful to your fellow-creatures in a tedious way. I have eaten my early dinner since I began the Lutheran lecture, and though the hash was hard, scarcely less so than the "rhinoceros veal" of which Herby and Dervy complained at Herne Bay, and the

French beans were fit fare for Nebuchadnezzar in his state of humiliation, yet, having a philosophic mind, I am not exasperated, but softened, by this lodging-house repast, and will leave you to repent about Luther at leisure.

VIII.

Modern Novels: "Grantley Manor," "Granby," "The Admiral's Daughter."

To Miss FENWICK:

Fort Crescent, Margate, October 2, 1847.—We have both read "Grantley Manor," with which we have been rather disappointed after the ecstatic reports of it which we received. The story proceeds languidly, though never devoid of interest, till the middle of the third volume, and whether or no it was Anglican prejudice, but so it was, that the heroism and oft-repeated agonies and anguishful trials of the Romish heroine were to me more wearying than affecting. It was so easy to give the fine, elegant, heavenly-minded, firm-souled, poetical sister to the Church of Rome, and the little, short, half-worldly, half-coquettish, pretty, but cross-mouthed sister to the Church of England! The trap for admiration is too palpable. We see it afar off, and will not walk into it. Still there is much to admire in this book, and some scenes are extremely good. There is every wish on the part of the authoress to be candid, and in Ann Neville she has portrayed a character quite as excellent and admirable as Ginevra, and given her to our Church.

But I confess, fond of the poetical as I am, and of reflection and sentiment, I do not like so much of this sort of thing *in a novel* as Lady Georgiana Fullerton gives us. At least, I think the best sort of *novel* is that which deals chiefly in delineation of character, dialogue, and incident. I have been much pleased, more than I expected to be, with a novel by Mr. Lister—"Granby." The *ease* with which it is written throughout is admirable. This ease is quite inimitable. It results from birth, breeding, and daily association with that sphere of thorough gentility where the inhabitants have little else to do than to be refined, and are cut off from all particular occupations that give a particular cast and impress to the manners. Dickens could as little give this air to his dialogue by letters or narrative as the author of "Granby" could have produced Sam Weller and his father, or Ralph Nickleby, or Sairey Gamp.   Do you like Mrs. Marsh's books?   "The Admiral's Daughter" seems to me one of the best tales of the day.   It is deeply pathetic, and the scenes are admirably well wrought up.

IX.

"Marriage," by Miss Ferrier.—Novel Writing.

To Miss FENWICK:

Margate, October, 1847.—I am now engaged with " Marriage," by Miss Ferrier, which I had read years ago.   It is even better than I remembered.   The humor reminds me of that of our good old plays.   Lady Maclaghlan and Sir Sampson are excellent, and there is an easy air of high life in Lady Juliana which makes it bearable to dwell so long on a heartless, childish creature.   To read novels is all very well; but to write them —except the first-rate ones—how distasteful a task it seems to me to dwell so long as writing requires on what is essentially base and worthless!

X.

Mrs. Gillman, of Highgate.

To Miss FENWICK :

Chester Place, October 30, 1847.—I was much pleased to see my dear old friend, Mrs. Gillman, at Ramsgate, looking far better, and evidently in better health, than several years ago.   She is wondrously handsome for a woman of seventy, far more interesting than I remember her in middle age — for she has more color, and becomes the fine cap close to her face, all hair put away, more than her more commonplace head costume of former days.   Her profile is quite Siddonian, and her black eye is bright; the only drawback is rather too keen an expression, inclining almost to hard and sharp, when she is looking earnestly and not smiling.   She is still lame from the effects of a fall which, I think, she had in running once hastily to my father when he was ill.   It was interesting to me to see her surrounded with portraits of old familiar faces, now passed away from earth, and pictures that I used to know at Highgate.

XI.

The Salutary Discipline of Affliction. — Earthly Enjoyments and Heavenly Hopes.

To Miss MORRIS:

24 *Fort Crescent, Margate, October* 6, 1847.—My dear friend, most sincerely do I thank you for your letter,* which affected me deeply—affects me, I may say, for I can not look at it or think of it without feeling my eyes fill with tears. It contains a record which will ever be precious to me—a testimony to the power of faith, one of those testimonies which make us feel with special force that Christianity is no mere speculation or subject of abstract thought, but a blessed and glorious reality—the *only* reality, to speak by comparison. But I believe it impossible for us in this earthly sphere to realize religion without an attendant process of destruction. While this destruction of the natural within us goes on gradually, we do not note it ; but in great affliction, when much work is done at once, the disruption is strongly felt, and the body for a time gives way.

After a while, even the body seems to gain new strength ; it has adjusted itself to a new condition of the soul ; it remains attenuated, but firm. We seem to have passed into a partly new state of existence, a stage of the new birth. One coat of worldliness has been cast off ; the natural is weaker and slenderer within us, and the spiritual larger and stronger. I seem to myself scarce worthy to talk of such things. I have not profited by affliction as I ought to have done. Better than I once was, possessed of a far deeper sense of the beauty and excellence of Christianity, I do humbly hope that I am. But I have had, perhaps, too much worldly support — *earthly* support, I should rather say. Things of the mind and intellect give me intense pleasure ; they delight and amuse me, as they are in themselves, independently of aught they can introduce me to instrumentally ; and they have gladdened me in another way, by bringing me into close communion with fine and deep minds. It has seemed a duty, for my children's sake and my own, to cultivate this source of cheerfulness, and sometimes I think the result has been too *large*, the harvest too abundant, of inward

---

* Containing the account of a sudden and severe affliction in the writer's family, and of the Christian resignation with which it was borne.—E. C.

satisfaction. This is dangerous. How hardly shall the rich man enter into the kingdom of heaven! and these are the richest of earthly riches. They who *use* intellect as the means of gaining money or reputation are drudges, poor slaves—though even they have often a high pleasure in the means, while they are pursuing an unsatisfactory end. But they who live in a busy yet calm world of thought and, poetry, though their *powers* may be far less than those of the others, may forget heaven, if sorrow and sickness, and symptoms of final decay, do not force them to look up, and strive away from their little transitory heaven upon earth to that which is above. Bright, indeed, that little heaven continually is with light from the supernal one. But we may rest too content with those *reflections*, which must fade as our mortal frame loses power. Hope of a higher existence can alone support us when this half-mental, half-bodily happiness declines.

XII.

Controlling Grief for the Sake of Others.

To Miss ERSKINE:

Chester Place, October, 1847. — I have always gone upon a plan of avoiding all excitement and agitation on the subject of my own deep, irretrievable losses. This for me was an absolute necessity: had I not kept sorrow at arm's-length, as it were, with my very irritable state of nerves, I should have been perpetually incapacitated for doing my duty to my children. In early youth one thinks it impossible to keep grief at bay. To banish it is indeed impossible; keep it off as far as we may, there it stands dark and moveless, casting its shadow over our whole life, tingeing every thought and action, and every would-be sunny prospect with at best a twilight evening hue. But this is far better than to be forever at close quarters with sorrow, continually plunged in tears, and stung with keen regrets. I take no credit to myself for what I have done in this way, because it was not I that did it, but my circumstances. I had children to consider and to act for; and the sense of how cruel and selfish it would be to shadow their young lives by the sight of a mother's tears was a motive for exertion in cultivating all cheerful thoughts, which I could never have supplied to myself.

Hence, as soon as possible, I put away all the special reminiscences of my past happy wedded life which lay in my daily path ; this was not to diminish the remembrance of the departed—that remains vivid as ever, without a hue faded or a line erased—but it prevented me from continually beholding the image of the departed in the midst of my daily work, when I could not afford to stand still and gaze upon it, and forget the present in the past.

XIII.

"Anti-Lutherism."—Charges made against Luther of Irreverence, Immorality, and Uncharitableness.—Luther's Doctrine of Justification adopted by the English Church.—"Heroes," and the "Worship" due to them.—Luther's Mission as a Witness for Gospel Truth.

To AUBREY DE VERE, Esq., Curragh Chase :

Margate, October 12, 1847.—I regret our difference of feeling and opinion concerning Luther more than on any other subject, but differences on persons are not such discrepancies as differences on things. Did I conceive the old Reformer as you conceive him, I should admire him no more than you do. But a totally different person is before my eyes, when I think of him, from what you present. I marvel how you can admit him to be a *hero*, if you believe his strength to have been "of a very physical kind"—look upon him as a religious demagogue, a "self-intoxicated man." It seems to me that you do by Luther what has so often been done by my father—that is, that you present an exaggerated image of the mere surface of the man— the outside of his character—for the man himself. I believe that Luther was not that *mere* tempestuous struggler for liberty, that coarse, bold, irreverent, self-deceiving fanatic, whom you present to me.

The truth is, your view of the objects of Luther's warfare, the things for which and against which he strove, determines your view of his personal character. You call him irreverent. Why? Because he did not revere much that you look upon with veneration. But has it yet been shown that Luther wanted reverence for the objects of faith and religious awe to which there is a clear testimony of reason and the spiritual sense—which are *Christian*, not mediæval? He had no reverence for the priesthood, considered as the possessors of *mystic* gifts and ecclesiastical privileges—*pseudo*-ecclesiastical, I should say. I confess I have just as little as he. I think no one can exceed me, according to the powers and energies of my mind, in love and respect for the Christian pastorate. I honor the minister of Christ both in his office and, still more, when he is what he ought to be, for his personal gifts and graces. I look with deep interest and gratitude to God on the *succession* of Christ's shepherds from the Apostles to the present day, but the Succession *dogma*, taught in the "Tracts for the Times," I can not behold with any respect whatever; just because it seems to me absolutely devoid of evidence, and, secondly, a mere spiritual mockery, which adds nothing to religion but a name and a notion.

It is true that Luther, in the beginning of his career, spoke rashly of St. James's Epistle; but I can not permit this fact to nullify for me all the evidence of deep religious feeling which I see in his writings and in his life. As for his want of charity, I do not defend his language; but vehement language alone can never convict him or any man of an uncharitable heart. Luther began with *great moderation;* but the murderous malice and violence of his enemies, who would have martyred him ten times over, and would be content with nothing but absolute renunciation of what he held to be the truth of God, goaded him to a degree which a writer of "Tracts for the Times," sitting quietly in his study, does not fairly allow for.

What are those moral enormities, those *thicks and thins*, that Mr. Hare defends? There is but one moral offense of any magnitude that has ever been brought home to Luther—the affair with the Landgrave of Hesse—and surely Hare does not defend his part in that matter. He only shows, very ably, as I thought, all the extenuating circumstances, and exposes the ridiculous unfairness of the representation of it by his adversaries. Those Romanists, and admirers of Romanism, treat it as an unprecedented crime in Luther to have done, with deep repentance afterward, what their infallible Vicegerents of Christ had done before, without repenting of it at all. That Luther ever meant to defend or recommend polygamy, he shows, I think, very clearly to have been one of the ten thousand calumnies uttered against him by his untruth-telling foes. He said, I think justly, that we ought not to look upon polygamy as *essentially* a crime. What God has once sanctioned (surely the words of Nathan to David show that it was sanctioned) can not be compared with sins against which there is a fiat of the Eternal.

Do you think that I admire Luther's doctrine for its energy and spiritual boldness? No, I admire the energy and boldness for the sake of the doctrine. What are those most vehement assertions of his which you consider heterodox? The great assertion of Luther's life as a theologian was justification by faith alone. Is this heterodox? Then is the Church of England heterodox in her Articles and her Homilies. It is vain to say that they teach Melancthon's doctrine. There is no real difference, I believe, and I have studied the subject a good deal, between Luther's view of the subject and that of his bosom friend Melancthon. But Philip was a mild, calm man. He explained the doctrine, and put it into language less liable to be taken by a wrong handle, though far less calculated to make way for it in the first instance. The "Commentary on Galatians" was spiritual thunder and lightning. That it reads as well as it does now, when we consider the sort of work it did, and compare it with other such instruments by which great changes are made suddenly in masses, we may see, and ought, I think, to acknowledge, that if Luther was a spiritual demagogue, he was of the first order of such after-inspired men. Indeed, my father, as appears in the "Remains," put him in the next rank after St. Paul and the Apostles. That article of our religion which the "Commentary on Galatians" is specially devoted to set forth —the manner of our justification—he thought more clearly seen, with greater depth of insight, by Luther than by any other man after the Apostle to the Gentiles. Such are his and my heresies.

As for hero-worship, if by *Hero* you mean only a strong man, able to produce great changes and make a sensation, and by *worship* such homage as Romanists pay to the Virgin and the Saints—which I believe to be too near that which belongs to God alone—I am as little a hero-worshiper as you are. I mean by a Hero a great, good man, endued with extraordinary gifts by the Father of Lights, which he employs for the benefit of mankind. Ought we not to *worship*, that is, honor and praise and listen to such men? It seems to me that Luther's ends were great and noble, and that his motives were always disinterested, high, and pure. In some instances, his means were blameworthy. He was embarked in a mighty, and most perilous, laborious, and difficult enterprise ; and if, in the conduct of it, he sometimes, through fear of losing what had been gained, departed from the strict rule of right, surely a liberal and charitable judgment will not deny him the praise due to a benefactor of men. That he was a true religious enthusiast, not one who makes religion either a source of self-glorification or worldly advancement, seems clear from his dedication of himself at first, before the struggle with Rome began. He was raised up, as I fully believe, by Providence, to resist the practical corruptions of the Church, and to bear witness to the truth that it is the state of the heart, and not any number of outward acts or course of observances, on which our spiritual prospect depends.

XIV.

Performance of " Philip van Artevelde," by Mr. Macready, at the Princess's Theatre.

To Miss FENWICK :

Chester Place, November 27, 1847.—Rather imprudently, I went to the Princess's Theatre last night, and have not improved the state of my cold thereby. However, I can not feel sorry to have gone, for I really seem to have gained something of knowledge of "Philip van Artevelde." We live and learn in regard to any really good and important work of the mind. It is wonderful how it keeps opening out to one fan-wise. The fan is soon unfurled to its full length, but a good play or poem is a sort of hundred-fold fan, that *bides* a good deal of unfolding.

During the first act I felt as if the piece was being murdered. The dresses had an unfavorable effect on my irritable imagination. Myk accused Van den Bosch of *hounding his pack upon him;* Bosch, as far as I could hear, having uttered no word of the menace whereto that is a natural reply. Macready did not take possession of me, *on his first essay,* as Kean did. He did not flash out the fine and uncommonplace actor all at once. He began to be effective in the scene where he wins over Ryk and Much, and threatens Occo. Thence onward the piece continued rising in power or sustaining itself on to the end.

The closing scenes were very spirited in the way of mere stage effect. The interviews between Van Artevelde and Van den Bosch were most powerful ; the most moving scene of all was Philip's address to the people, when he makes the three propositions. All the interest centred in the hero, even more than in the play as read. Macready was the only good actor ; he evidently had entered into the character with enthusiasm, and the nobleness of the conception rose more strongly before me as the play proceeded, or at least was more keenly felt than ever before, though this might not have been had I not been imbued beforehand with a knowledge of it from perusal of the play. Many parts, well omitted in the representation, aided the effect by being remembered.

I think it was in some respects advantageous to the effectiveness of the drama that Van Artevelde was thrown into even stronger relief than in the reading play ; scenes good in themselves being cut away, his part became more prominent, and proceeded more rapidly.

XV.

Dr. Arnold on the Wickedness of Boys.—Social Oysters.—A Liberal High Churchman.

To the Rev. HENRY MOORE, Eccleshall Vicarage, Staffordshire :

Chester Place, December 3, 1847.—Dr. Arnold took a strong view of the wickedness of boys. I wish I could think that men were so very much better. Men conceal a good deal which boys show ; and this is pleasanter to me in boys than in men, that they so seldom assume the virtuous, or talk as if they were far more charitable and disinterested and religious than they are practically. But perhaps Dr. Arnold meant only a lamentation over the weakness and pravity of human nature, not to put *boy* nature at so much lower a level than that of adults.

I was much struck, in conversation with Mr. G——, at the appearance of amiability in his countenance and manner—a sort of simple frankness amid his intellectual refinement, which I much admire. There is in some men a kind of pride, in the guise of modesty, a reserve and self-shelterment, as of a cold fish in its self-made shell still colder than itself, which is to me most disagreeable. These men, if they have talent, are always highly esteemed and extolled by the few who enter with zeal into their peculiar views, and can accept their narrow terms (for they always are narrow in such tempers) of soul-communion.

Now I must say good-by; so farewell, *High-Church* friend! though, after all, your High Churchmanship, when you come to explain it, looks wonderfully like the *lowness* and *liberality* of some whom you set down on the wrong side of the hedge—the contrary to your own side! I am sure you gave a fearfully liberal and philosophical account of Apostolical Succession, which would make a stanch Anglo-Catholic's hair stand on end, while his tongue clave to the roof of his mouth, and on getting free would be employed in showing you, if he condescended to hold any communication with such a Rationalist, how utterly un-Catholic, how unmystical, and how abominably intelligible and rational, such a conception of the matter is! Why, such a view as yours need not be taken implicitly, like a pig in a poke! the pig can be *seen*, and commends *itself!* The truth is, you may talk as you will about your *highness*, but you are not very high according to the Tract standard, which places height in this, exaltation of the *outward* in reference to religion, with a proportionate depression of the acts of the intelligent will in the individual mind. Not but that they would like reason well enough, if she declared in their favor, but they hate her as the angry king did the prophet, because she always prophesieth against and not for them—that is, against their priest-exalting system. Now *you* are too Coleridgianized in mind to adopt their philosophy. There are some who affect to think my father's a great mind, who play with his doctrine as a hungry cat does with meat that has mustard on it. What to them is mustard you take as the natural gravy of the meat; and then, though I must say you are remarkably honest and bold, more so than most men, especially of the clergy, you try to stir up your High-Church reputation and keep it brisk, by declaring how desperately *high* you are—knocking at the stars with your head, so that one is in fear for the planetary system, and calling poor unpretending things like me *low* and *liberal*, who are not a bit more liberal than yourself, if you come to that.

"Take that now, Father M'Grath!" and believe me your faithful and ever obliged friend,   Sara Coleridge.

XVI.

Pamphlet by a Seceder to the Roman Church.—The Hampden Controversy.—Church Ornamentation.

To AUBREY DE VERE, Esq. :

December, 1847.— * * * I have lately been reading "Reasons
of my Conversion to the Church of Rome," by Mr. Gordon, one
of our late curates. The pamphlet is very able, and the first
six or seven letters contain, I think, a good deal of *ad hominem*
truth. The writer's aim is to show, what we who never have
wholly submitted to the Tract Doctors have been saying all
along, that Anglicans of the Oxford School are in a false position in the Church of England, that for them to remain here is
to be in constant collision with their own principles—a very
uneasy rock to knock against. He urges that such thinkers
have no living Church at all, which is to them a guide and a
mother, the pillar and ground of the truth. The Church in
which they abide they treat as a child and a pupil, whom they
are to instruct and improve ; so long as this pupil-Church keeps
within certain bounds, they will remain, trying to un-Protestant-
ize and improve her ; if she transgresses these bounds, they
must leave her — and for what? form a body of their own?
But they can not create a Church — they can not reproduce
Apostolical Succession. In that case, therefore, they will be
out of the Church of Christ, absolutely churchless.

Then he takes them up on *private judgment*, and shows what
a system of private judgment they are themselves involved in,
while they are condemning private judgment ; that their appeal to the Fathers is after all, at bottom, but an appeal to
themselves, and their own determination what is the true import of patristic teaching, and what its value. He insists that
when the Church of England accuses Rome of corrupt doctrine
and of schism, this is but the protest of the culprit against the
judge. Like many other assailants, he is strong while he
points out the defects of the Anglican system, and the inconsistency of Anglo-Catholics. But when he comes to the positive defense of his own position, to speak of that system which
he has preferred, then the strong man is palsy-stricken ; his
firm, rapid march is turned into staggering weakness ; assumption and one-sided representation take the place of careful exam-

ination; and audacity that of candid reasoning. By the line of argument that he adopts, the worship of Baal and Moloch, and the restitution of the calves and groves, and other heathen abominations, might be quite as well defended as Purgatory and the cultus of the Virgin Mary.

What think you of Hampden's elevation? Are you of those who think the war made upon him at Oxford was right? A High-Church clergyman friend of mine was here last night, and I had the rare felicity of hearing him say on this subject what seems to me the golden mean; with Hare, he regrets the appointment, but thinks the measures taken against Hampden unjust (hundreds voting who had not read his books, condemning on the authority of another), and that his doctrines are misrepresented. He *has* read that heavy book, the "Bampton Lectures," which few of the many that condemn Hampden have done.

Mr. ———— is raising a subscription for a painted window; and I scarce know what to do about it. I must confess—though here again I am out of sympathy with most of my friends, for, like Mr. ————, I am ever protesting against my own party (that is to say, the party which to my mind embraces *most* of the truth, and with whom I can in general concur in all that is practical)—but I must confess that I have scruples about giving spare money for painted windows when there is spiritual destitution still to provide for. "Oh! the more is given in one way, the more will be given in the other," is the cry. This seems to me an equivoque. The same spirit which excites one kind of giving will excite both; but that any man who gave *all* he properly could and ought for the higher object would have any thing left for the lower, I can not believe; and thus, while some churches are smartened up (and there is no limit to the expensive smartness that may be lavished upon a single edifice), others are erected of the meanest description. I do not feel quite satisfied that church grandeur was ever based on pure Gospel *faith*, as Keble and others maintain. Pure faith does so much *else* for God, so much for her neighbor during lifetime, that she leaves not great sums behind to build a temple, to make up for the temple to God's honor and glory that she did *not* build, while she might, with her own hands. Then our modern church splendor is so poor and petty and equivocal; so vulgarized by patterns displayed in shops, and all kinds of trade associations. It does not flow from any great universal spirit which will last, but is supported by an effort of a busy section, running counter to the age instead of concurring with it.

XVII.

Origin of the Dislike felt to Dr. Hampden's Views.

To Mrs. H. M. JONES, Hampstead :

1847.—Hampden has offended the bigots and zealots of all parties, Romanistic and Puritanical, by his charitable and conciliative sentiments, by daring to say that good and well-disposed men, with sound heads and sound hearts, who hold in their hands the one Gospel of Christ, believing it all to be the Word of God, can not and do not differ substantially, in their vital operative faith, as much as they appear to do in dogmatical statements and intellectual schemes of belief. This has given far more deep and bitter offense than if Hampden had been really a disbeliever in any of the truths generally acknowledged in Christendom; the self-styled orthodox love to think themselves up in heaven, those who differ from them in the gulf below—themselves to be the soft, snowy, lovely, innocent sheep, others the great coarse, rough, ill-scented goats. Hampden's doctrine partly fills up the gulf, the wide chasm which they would establish betwixt themselves and all who are not ready to swear to all their articles, and embrace what the Middle Ages determined on matters of faith by the mouths of uninspired Ecclesiastics, with implicit faith.

XVIII.

Dr. Hampden's "Observations on Dissent."

To Miss ERSKINE :

1847.—As to the Hampden controversy, you guess rightly, indeed, dear A——, if you think I am not with the opposition. I wish to know what has ever been *proved* against Dr. Hampden, showing him to be unfit to be a Bishop in our Church? All the allegations against him appear to me to be either false or insufficient. Quite false, I think, is the charge that he represents the Divinity of Christ as being no essential part of the Christian

Y

faith.   His arguments all along suppose the contrary—that it is essential for all men.   I do not like or agree to all he says in the "Observations on Dissent," but I believe that the leading principles of Hampden's teaching, and *those positions which have brought upon him the enmity under the effects of which he is at present laboring,* are true and valuable.

What is considered such a crime in Hampden is his having dared to proclaim what are simple facts, of which proof has been given, and which have never been disproved; as, for instance, that the phraseology commonly used by divines in theological statements has been established by dialectical science; that the *forms* of doctrine have been determined by the psychological philosophy of the period when they arose; and that the doctrine of the Sacraments (that is, the Scholastic theories concerning them) is "based upon the mystical philosophy of secret agents in nature Christianized."

CHAPTER XVIII.

1848.

LETTERS TO AUBREY DE VERE, ESQ., REV. HENRY MOORE, MISS
MORRIS, MISS FENWICK, MRS. H. M. JONES, MRS. RICHARD
TOWNSEND, MRS. GILLMAN, C. B. STUTFIELD, ESQ.

———

I.

Mr. Coleridge's Religious System addressed to the Heart and Conscience,
not to the Intellect alone.

To Miss MORRIS:

1848.—This can not be an answer to yours, dear friend; but
in reply to some of your concluding sentences, I would reiterate
my former assertions that my father's religious views have in
reality no more connection with the reasoning faculty—neither
more nor less—than yours or any one's else; although he has
written so much about reason and the understanding. His theory of faith pre-eminently appeals to the *heart*, to the moral and
spiritual being. He never supposed that the inspiration of
Scripture, a spiritual subject, could be known or apprehended
by mere intelligence. But he did maintain that the human mind
is one, though it has many different powers, and that the moral
and spiritual only subsist by the co-inherence of the intelligential—that Reason and Will are necessary each to the other, so
that the one is what it is as existing in union with the other.
Have you not a *doctrine* of inspiration as well as *feelings* on the
subject? If yes, by what faculty of your mind is that doctrine
apprehended? Has reason, has thought, nothing to do with it?
And have the heart and spirit naught to do with the views you
seem to reject? My father does not judge of Inspiration by
the intellect an iota more than others. Nay, I am sure his objection to the views he rejects is because they are so heartless,
so empty, and unmeaning. Why should you assume that he
judges Inspiration more than you judge it, by the view you take?
On the subject of Reason and its province in religion, my father

says nothing that has not been said by Christian philosophers and great divines in all ages. To say otherwise than as my father says, on this point, if carried out, is sheer Romanism. Denial of it is a denial of the Reformation, and makes every act of the Reformers flat rebellion and falsehood.

What think you is my last appeal which is not your last appeal? Whither can either of us go as the last resort, the ultimatum of our religious search, but to the depths of the human spirit, the heart and conscience of which Reason is the pervading light, and in which God and His Truth are mirrored? Have *you*, then, any place or object of appeal beyond this? Can *you* contemplate God and His Christ except in your own soul?

II.

Her Son's Preparation for the Newcastle Examination.—School Rivalries.

To Mrs. GILLMAN, Ramsgate :

Chester Place, March, 1848.—Herbert is now preparing for the Newcastle contest. On the 3d of April it will commence, the Scholarship will be declared on the 8th, and on the 10th he returns home. He bids me have no expectation of his gaining the Scholarship. His most formidable competitor, the eldest son of Sir Thomas F——, is nearly a year older than he, very clever, and very desirous to conquer, and has had much instruction during the holidays—more than H. has.

It is a comfort to see what an excellent state of feeling exists between him and F——, not a shade of jealousy, I am sure. Indeed, I think that rivalry at public schools and at college is not the source of evil generally. Boys are generally inclined to like and respect those whose pursuits are similar to their own, and who exhibit talent in the line in which they are trying to distinguish themselves. They are oftener unjust to those of different habits, pursuits, likings, and dislikings—are apt to set them down as "brutes" and "asses," and to be perfectly blind to their abilities and good parts.

III.

The Newcastle Scholar.—The Chartist Demonstration.—Lowering of the Franchise. — Moral and Material Improvement the Real Wants of the Poor, not Political Power.

To Aubrey de Vere, Esq., Curragh Chase, Ireland :

Chester Place, April 14, 1848.—The news of Herbert's success, on which you congratulate me in a manner which adds greatly to the pleasure of it, was indeed very pleasant. He darted in upon us like a beam of light on Saturday afternoon, and received from us an awful account of the Chartist preparations for insurrection and violence. You at a distance, except by comparing our troubles with your own, not by reports, can hardly have a notion of the alarm and excitement that was produced all in a day or two. I had been thinking of the matter a week or two before, and consulted our intelligent neighbor, Mr. Scott, whose opinion with regard to the state of the poor I thought more important than any other. He told me that he had been trying by private letters to rouse people in authority to a sense of the necessity of making a determined show of the power and will to put down violence. The middle or shop-keeping class, he said, think all these points of political arrangements and government very much the gentry's affair. Still they will side with the gentry, feeling them to be their natural protectors, and the class with whose interests, in the present state of things, theirs are interlinked, if they feel that the gentry can stand up for themselves, and present a bold front to the insurgents ; otherwise, having no *principle* to guide them one way or the other, and not being given to theories or abstractions, or to go beyond the present hour, they might throw themselves into the arms of the mob, as did the shop-keepers and National Guard, who are so much composed of that class, in Paris. But then the army? Well, he did not think we could be certain of the army. There was no knowing how they might act if the Chartists proved very formidable. He thought the danger lay at present in the apathy and inactivity of the upper classes, who carried a good principle of not interfering with the liberty of the people much too far. At this time no one was alarmed. Nothing was said about the Chartists in the large print part of the *Times*. On Saturday people began to be frightened. I was resolved, though the maids were terrified and we had no man-servant, not to go away. The gentlemen of the neighborhood — several of them — called on me on Sunday morning to tell me all the arrangements for the defense of the Park, to offer protection, etc. On Sunday morning I went to St. Mark's College. The young men brought alarming reports from the city. The Bank and other offices were bristling with artillery; it was reported that the Government had received bad news. Now, for the first time, I did feel a little alarmed. The report was (quite false, as it turned out) that two regiments were disaffected. I did not wholly believe this. I hoped it was not so; but Miss T—— had heard the report about the Coldstream Guards at Plymouth—and it seemed to me that if the Duke of Wellington *was* unpopular, as was said, and the troops *were* discontented, and should refuse to act against the people, there might be a revolution. Still I should have stayed in the Park (for how was one to run away from a revolution that would reach one in Cumberland?), had I not received a letter from Eton pressing me to go thither with plate, etc. I accepted this offer, because I feared that otherwise Herbert would hardly be prevented from coming home on the dangerous Tuesday. So we flew to Eton on Sunday evening, and there heard the happy event of the dreaded Chartist demonstration. Now all feel that the attempt has been a blessed thing for the country, since it has plainly discovered the weakness of the physical-force party, and the power of that body in the State who are interested in the preservation of our present constitution. I really feel, with the *Times*, that our country has afforded a "sublime spectacle" to Europe on the late occasion. The arrangements of the Duke for the preservation of the metropolis were worthy of the hero of Waterloo; and how merciful thus to preclude, by the formidable and complete nature of the preparations, any attempt on the part of the misguided Chartists. Even if their demands were in themselves reasonable, or such changes as they propose could benefit the people at large, the *manner* of making them is contrary to all government whatsoever, and if yielded to must lead to pure anarchy alternating with despotism. Some think that these events will lead to an extension of the franchise. It does not seem at all clear to me that there would be the slightest use in giving votes to more and poorer men, without bettering their condition or improving their education beforehand. They say not more than a fourteenth part of the population is represented. I do not see the grievance of not being represented *per se.* What the poor really want is to be better off; they care not for more representation except as that may favor their pockets. An extended representation can not produce more bread and cheese. As it is, taxation does not affect the very poorest people. The income-tax is hard upon professional and trading persons who make only just enough for their wants. Hardly any of these persons are Chartists. I believe the Chartist body to be composed principally of men who have nothing to lose, are not doing well in any trade or calling, for the humblest char-woman who has work is furious against them, and looks to the upper classes for support. A great proportion of them are sufferers by their own fault; though there may be some bodies of men, thrown suddenly out of employment, who are in great distress through pure misfortune, and who became Chartists in pure ignorance, with a blind hope of bettering their state by changing the present order of things.

IV.

Youth and Age.

To Miss FENWICK:

1848.—I am glad, dear friend, that you have had some enjoyment at Teignmouth. I felt a good deal as you do, that there is not so much greater a proportion of happiness in youth (and, I would add, still less in childhood) than in more advanced periods of life, when thought and experience have brought more knowledge of all that it concerns us most to know, and more tranquillity. Youth and childhood are indeed beautiful and interesting to look back upon; but I feel as old Matthew did about the lovely child, *I do not wish them mine—* mine to go over again.

V.

Early Marriage.

To C. B. STUTFIELD, Esq., Hackney:

Chester Place, 1848.—I have been much interested by your note; it really gives the *pith* and *marrow* of the case in *pithy* language. I agree to it all without reserve, except a partial one on a single point. You say that a "young man much occupied will not generally think of marriage till past thirty." I know a good many exceptions to that rule, I think. It seems to me, I own, that the time to form a marriage engagement, in an ordinary case, for a man, is between twenty and thirty. It is not so naturally, easily, or well done afterward. D——, who has had some experience of youth, laments exceedingly the difficulties in the way of early marriage for men, and my Uncle Southey was of the same mind. But the difficulties are often insuperable. What I like is to see a young man ready to work hard, and ready to be married. Energy, energy, that is the thing— if it be kept in order by a religious mind.

VI.

Charms of our Native Place.—Country Life and Town Life.—Portrait-painters.—Portraits of Middle-aged People.

To Mrs. RICHARD TOWNSEND, Norwood :

Chester Place, July 7, 1848.—It strikes me, dear Mrs. Townsend, that you would be better off, as regards your health and spirits, if you resided in Regent's Park, or some airy part of London, than at Norwood, sweet and (for a summer-spell) enviable as Norwood is. Your husband seems to be much engaged, and the society of any country place is necessarily limited. Our native place is quite a different affair. *There* every stick and stone, or, at all events, every nook and woody clump, and turn of the well-known river, whose sounds were the first that struck upon our infant ears—*there* all the old familiar faces, however humdrum, or even unpleasing to strangers, are full of interest from old association. We see in these objects not simply their present selves, but a host of past impressions, which, as it were, illuminate them—impart to them both a general luminous glow and a rich mosaic embroidery, which render them far more interesting in our eyes than new ones—though infinitely more striking, as seen for the first time.

Here I have almost too much excitement from intercourse with interesting people. I feel the charm of London society deeply, but my nervous system is so weak and irritable that I seem always on the verge of being outdone, even though I keep quite on the outskirts of the gay, busy world, and go out little in comparison with most of my friends—very seldom (never if I can help it) two nights consecutively.

I broke through that rule this week. I had on Thursday a little party to meet an old friend, C. H. Townshend, known most to the public as author of a book on Mesmerism, but to me and my brother Derwent as a poet and a lover of poetry, amateur painter, and collector of paintings. To meet him, I had my brother's party from St. Mark's, Mr. R——, the artist, and his wife, Mr. L——, the artist, and a few more. Both R—— and L—— are highly interesting men in very different ways. The former is more genial, mild, and popular; and, oh, how he is improved in his art! His picture of my Herbert is the very youth himself. Every one says so. He told me that he enjoyed taking his portrait, and gratified my mother's heart by describing him as a capital subject.

L—— has a severe cast of mind. He is very intelligent, and a beautiful speaker, and when he is successful, his success is of a high order. He paints the mind. So, indeed, does R——, but L—— sees the mind, I think, in a sterner way. Both contemn the old, fashionable Sir Thomas Lawrence style of painting.

I am now sitting to Mr. L—— for my dear old friend Mrs. Stanger. E. thinks that the picture promises well. Some of my friends decline sitting because they are middle-aged, and middle-age is neither lovely nor picturesque. *My* objection is not the plainness of the stage of life, but the variability of my nervous state, and consequently of my looks. Sometimes the artist is forced to work away at the gown (at least Mr. R—— was sometimes) because the *face* is actually gone away *pro tempore.*

VII.

Teaching Work.—Dickens as a Moralist for the Young.

To Mrs. H. M. JONES:

Herne Bay, August 17, 1848.—My sister and C—— left us last Monday; young D—— remains with us till Friday. He reads Homer to me, and this, with H.'s readings, and E.'s, is as much in that way as my nerves will stand; for I can do every thing that I ever could, *a little*, but nothing much or long. The hundred lines with each youth, and sometimes Pindar or Horace besides, which seems nothing to my brother, is a good deal to me. They like to talk with me and each other about "Harry Lorrequer" and other military and naval novels, and above all about the productions of Dickens, the never-to-be-exhausted fun of "Pickwick," and the capital new strokes of "Martin Chuzzlewit." This last work contains, besides all the fun, some very marked and available morals. I scarce know any book in which the evil and odiousness of selfishness is more forcibly brought out, or in a greater variety of exhibitions. In the midst of the merry quotations, or at least on any fair opportunity, I draw the boys' attention to these points, bid them remark how *unmanly* is the selfishness of young Martin, and I insist upon it that Tom Pinch's character, if it could really exist, would be a very beautiful one. But I doubt, as I do in regard to Pickwick, that so much sense, and deep, solid goodness, could co-exist with such want of discernment and liability to be gulled. Tigg is very clever, and the boys roar with laughter at the "what's-his-name place whence no thingumbob ever came back;" but this is only a new edition of Jingle and Smangles; Mark Tapley, also, is a second Sam Weller. The new characters are Pecksniff, and the thrice-notable Sairey Gamp, with Betsy Prig to show her off.

VIII.

Mr. Coleridge's Philosophy Inseparable from his Religious Teaching.—
His View of the Inspiration of Scripture.

To Miss MORRIS:

1848.—I doubt not that though your American semi-Coleridgian, or rather Coleridgian only in fancy, imagines my father a "Heretic" in his *formal-divinity mind*, yet that his heart and spiritual being, if he really have benefited in any way or degree worth speaking of by his writings, is making a far different report. Why should a fine intellect (and most men allow my father *that*), united with a disposition to believe, and strong desire to be in sympathy with the religious, become suddenly effete and worse than useless when applied to the discernment of religious truth? I know how vain it is to argue. But I say this to show you my own state of mind on these matters, not in any expectation of altering yours, or that of any of those who see the subject of religious belief, or rather *the theory of faith*, as you do. My father's religious teaching is so interwoven with his intellectual views, as with all deep and earnest thinkers must ever be the case, that both must stand or fall together; and in my opinion those persons dream who think they are improved by him intellectually, yet consider his views of Christianity in the main unsound. There are some portions of his theology on which I feel unresolved, some which I reject; but in the mass they are such as both embrace me and are embraced by me. His view of Inspiration, as far as it goes, I do entirely assent to; and it is my strong anticipation, as far as I have any power to anticipate, that, after a time, all earnest, thoughtful Christians will perceive that such a footing, *in the main*, as that on which he places the Inspiration of Scripture, is the only safe one—the only one that can hold its ground against advancing thought and investigation. I refer not so much in this to examination of outward proof, but to reflection on the nature of the thing in itself, the discovery of the internal incoherency of the ordinary schemes of belief on this subject. I think it will be found how satisfyingly spiritual it is.

IX.

Mr. Spedding's Critique on Lord Macaulay's Essay on Bacon.—The Ordinance of Confirmation.—Primitive Explanations of its Meaning and Efficacy.

To AUBREY DE VERE, Esq.:

1848.—I am delighted and interested in a most high degree by the vindication of Bacon. It seems to me no less admirable for the principles of moral discrimination and truth and accuracy of statement, especially where character is concerned, which it brings out and elucidates by particular instances, which, as it were, substantiate and vitalize the abstract propositions, than for the glorious sunny light which it casts on the character of Bacon. Then how ably does it show up, not Macaulay's character individually and personally, so much as the class of thinkers of which he is the mouth-piece and representative.

There are numbers who dislike and suspect that anti-Bacon article, and would take in with avidity the refutation.

But can it be true that Bacon doubted whether Confirmation were a *subsequent* to Baptism? How can it be doubted by any one who knows what Confirmation is, what are the purposes of it?

There can be no doubt that Confirmation was in the beginning considered, if not a component part of the whole sacrament of Baptism, yet certainly a sacrament in which the regenerative Spirit was received. The two were united in time, and formed one double rite. Confirmation or Imposition of Hands was performed directly after Baptism; and Tertullian affirms that men are prepared for the Spirit, or purified by the Baptismal rite—that they receive the Spirit by Imposition of Hands.

I think we may argue from this, and many like dogmas of the early Fathers, that it is not possible to follow out the primitive *rationale* of Sacraments on all points. The Church afterward separated Imposition of Hands from Baptism, and taught that the gift of the Regenerative Spirit appertained to the latter. Still Confirmation is surely a complement of Baptism, has a special reference to it, though it be not necessary to salvation, or an essential part of Baptism. The term "subsequent to Baptism" is ambiguous. Confirmation is not to *confirm the Baptism*, but to confirm or corroborate *the baptized* in the graces and spiritual edification originally received in baptism.

X.

Pindar.—Dante's " Paradiso."—" Faustina," by Ida Countess Hahn-Hahn.—Haziness of Continental Morality.—A Coquette on Principle.—Lord Bacon's Insincerity.

To AUBREY DE VERE, Esq., Curragh Chase, Ireland:

Chester Place, 1848.—One feels proud of reading Pindar. It is like being at a fountain-head, at the fresh top of a lofty aerial mount, a wide prospect of the land of beauty spread out before one. The second Pythian Ode contains one of those Scripture-like passages which one seems to have read somewhere in the Old Testament, but knows not exactly where—perhaps in the Psalms, in Job, or Isaiah. * * *

Canto V. of the " Paradiso" is in the main rather dry, sententious, and unsensuous, but it reads impressively; and I feel this time, more than before, how finely the light *keeps growing* as one goes on in the " Paradiso," how the splendors accumulate, the glory deepens, the colors glow out more and more in ever richer variety.

I was very glad, however, to conclude the evening with Countess Ida ; and now I have read her story carefully to the end, and what do I think of it ?   Why, that it is in the style of execution very exquisite, full of grace, beauty, light rich fancy ; but that it is as strong an instance as I ever met with of that pseudo-morality, that vague, slippery, luminous-misty view of right and wrong, which it would be unfair to call German, as if it belonged to the Germans more than to the French, Italians, Danes, or Swedes, but which we may certainly call *un-English*.   If the plant appears among us, it is recognized as a foreigner at once. Goethe's morality has been much questioned among us, but there is nothing in his tales surely of worse tendency than this " Faustina," more false and insidious.   The conduct of the heroine is that of an unprincipled coquette—a frail, fickle, faithless, self-indulgent, passionate creature ; nay, more than that, heartless and cruel in the extreme.   Yet, forsooth, we are assured that these acts in *her* proceed from superlative *purity of heart!* the simplicity of genius—an innocent desire to *mould her being*, to take to herself whatsoever is beautiful, noble, and excellent ; to keep it as long as it suited her, and then fling it away like a sucked orange, or let it fall, as she does the wild flowers when she is tired of them !   It is a libel, a shocking libel, on purity of heart and genius, to lay such sins as these at their door, or even to suppose them compatible in any way with the former.   No woman that united a fine intellect with a generous, noble, and tender heart, or even a heart of tolerable goodness, could have acted the part of Faustina, even suppose her to have been ever so badly educated : so at least it strikes me.   I complain of the whole representation as radically *false*, and can not be reconciled by the delicacy and beauty of the execution to what is so deeply wrong in the main conception. " Faustina" is entirely a woman's book, a Continental woman's book, as " Jane Eyre" is that of an English *man*.*   And, oh !

---

* My mother's critical discrimination was at fault here. She felt sure that the mysterious " Currer Bell" was a *man ;* and used to declare that she could as soon believe the paintings of Rubens to have been by a woman as " Jane Eyre."—E. C.

how vastly superior in truth and power is the latter, coarse and hard in parts as it certainly is. Faustina is false in another way, too, I think. She does nothing but what any exquisitely beautiful and graceful woman might do. Hers are not, as seems to be pretended, the triumphs of genius. Jane Eyre, without personal advantages, gains upon the mind of the reader by what she does, and we can well understand how she fascinates Rochester. We *see* that she is heroic, we are not merely *told* so. "Faustina" reminds me of two novels by women—"The History of a Coquette," by a daughter of the well-known Bishop Watson, and "Zoe," by Miss Jewsbury. The latter is less refined than "Faustina," but contains greater variety—I should say, exhibits more power upon the whole. It has the same moral falsity that strikes me in "Faustina"—that of uniting noble qualities of head and heart with conduct the most unworthy and unvirtuous. T. F. warmly defends "Zoe," declaring it to be but a true picture of life. If I could think it a true picture, I too would defend the representation. But I believe that such compounds as "Zoe" and "Faustina" are to be classed with the griffins and sphinxes of ancient fable. Nay, those have at least subjective truth; in these I can see none at all.

* * * * * * * *

I dissent from Spedding's defense of Bacon's slight dissimulation about the calling of Parliament. Silence is one thing, but untruth, ever so slight, will never do.

XI.

Romanist Secessions.

To Miss FENWICK, Bath:

1848.—I have just been writing to dear ———, to express my concern and sympathy in her sorrow at the secession of her son, who has joined the Church of Rome. I told his mother, what I could say with sincerity, that though such a step on the part of a child could not but be a great trouble, yet that, so far as the interests of the soul are concerned, it would not deeply afflict me, because I never can think that any youth bred up in the bosom of our Church will, or almost can, enter into the "cult" of the Virgin idolatrously; though I fear with many *born* Romanists it does absorb some part of the feelings due to

God and His Christ alone. Nor can I think such a person will ever really ascribe a redemptive merit to works, or any thing in man whatsoever. And in regard to the denial of the cup in the Eucharist—I should hope (to the faithful receiver) the bread alone conveyed the spiritual benefit, whatever sin may rest with those who first altered and impaired the institution of Christ. So I should feel with respect to the *individual* who has been nurtured in our Church. I do believe the religion of enlightened Romanists, who have conversed much with our clergy of the better sort, does not differ materially from Anglicanism. Still it would be a grief to me to think that a son's descendants (if he married) should all be brought up in a system which *may* be, for some, such a wide departure from the religion of Christ, and substitution of a new Gospel. And it is painful, too, to be regarded by a seceder, if he be near and dear to us, as not in the true Church or the regular way of salvation.

CHAPTER XIX.

1848 (*continued*).

LETTERS TO THE REV. HENRY MOORE, AUBREY DE VERE, ESQ.,
MISS FENWICK, THE REV. EDWARD COLERIDGE.

I.

Dr. Arnold's School Sermons.—His Comment on the Story of the Young
Men who Mocked Elisha.—Individuals under the Mosaic Dispensation
dealt with as Public, not as Private Characters.—Dr. Hammond's proposed Rendering of 2 Peter i., 20.

To the Rev. HENRY MOORE, Eccleshall Vicarage:

1848.—I must write a line to thank you for giving to my boy
those excellent Sermons of Dr. Arnold's, more comfortable to
my spirit than most of the sermons addressed to men. I think,
in his application of the judgment on the young people who
mocked Elisha, he seems not sufficiently to bear in mind that
they were punished for contemning the character and authority
of an Envoy of the God of Israel, not for teasing an old man.
The judgment would be frightfully disproportionate if we did
not look upon it thus nationally, in analogy with the whole sacred history. In the Old Testament, individuals appear to be
dealt with not primarily in reference to their own merit or de-
merit in the sight of God, or their own private destiny, but as
they are parts and instruments of one comprehensive scheme
for the advancement of the human race by their Creator. Now
I say that Carlyle, in his "History of the French Revolution,"
whether consciously or otherwise, has in some sort written upon
the Scriptural plan. He looks at the French Revolution, in all
its horrors and miseries, as an awful retribution for the accumulated crimes of selfishness, cruelty, and profligacy of the
wealthy and powerful classes—a long-delayed vengeance—to
be a grand beacon and instruction for the ages to come, and at
the same time the preparation for a new and better state of
things. The actors in the Revolution he considers *principally*

as instruments of this divine work, and he therefore views them chiefly in reference to their *powers*. What he says of Mirabeau's powers, his wisdom and insight, I believe to be quite true. There is a sketch of the life and character of Mirabeau by my husband in a periodical work, written before Carlyle's book appeared, which contains in substance all that Carlyle maintains on that point. Mirabeau had, however, not only *powers*, but virtues, though mingled with great vices, and it is not true that Carlyle disguises or disregards the vices : he speaks of them as to be lamented and wept over with bitter tears.

* * * * * * * *

I am looking at Horsley's Sermons on 2 Peter i., 20, 21.* But he appears to me to have, to a certain degree, a wrong notion of the drift of the text from neglecting Hammond's explanation. Hammond says that ἐπίλυσις is an agonistical word, and signifies the starting or watch word upon which the racers set out in their course. According to him the passage has nothing to do with interpretation whatever, no bearing of any kind upon private judgment, as it has been a million times quoted for or, rather, against. I think, if you consult Scapula or Passow, you will find that the good doctor is right, and that ἐπιλυσεσθαι means to let loose, as dogs or hunting-leopards from a leash (though it also means to solve or explain), and this is more accordant with the context. "No prophecy is ἰδίας ἐπιλύσεως—*for* the prophecy came not in old time by the *will* of man, but holy men of old spake *as they were moved* by the Holy Ghost." Now is it not better sense if we render the Greek, "of his own starting," "without particular mission from God," than if we understand it of private interpretation, which has nothing to do with what goes before or what comes after? St. Peter was not warning men against self-willed uncatholic views of prophecy, but simply exhorting them to trust to prophecy, because it was from God.

---

* "Knowing this first, that no prophecy of the Scripture is of any private interpretation. For the prophecy came not in old time by the will of man : but holy men of God spake as they were moved by the Holy Ghost."—2 Peter i., 20, 21.

II.

To AUBREY DE VERE, Esq., Curragh Chase, Ireland:

Chester Place, September, 1848.—Thank you much for "Evangeline," which is full of the beautiful, and is most deeply pathetic, as much so as the story of Margaret in the "Excursion." Perhaps you will think me paradoxical (no, *you* would not, I believe, though many would) when I say that this deep pathos is not the right thing in a poem. I could not take the story and the poetry together, but was obliged to skim through it, and see how the misery went on, and how it ended, before I could *read the poem.* I think a poem ought not to have a more touching interest than Spenser's "Faëry Queen," Ariosto, and Tasso. The agitations of the Drama may be quoted against me. I can but say that I feel the same objection to "Romeo and Juliet;" but then the edge of the strong interest is rubbed off after a first perusal, and we recur to it as to a poem—and so we may in any other case. But those fine old dramas contain so much *more* than the mere story, even in the material; so much wit, and display of character and humor and manners, that they are hardly to be compared with our modern affecting metrical tale.

It does not clearly appear why Gabriel should lose sight of Evangeline on leaving Acadia. Perhaps we shall be told, as we are of the story of Margaret, that it is matter of *fact.* This would not excuse it, if it *looks* improbable; and, depend upon it, *in the fact* there was something different, something that prevented the difficulty which suggests itself in the written tale. "Evangeline" seems to be, in some sort, an imitation of Voss's "Luise." The opening, especially, would remind any one who had read the "Luise," of that remarkable Idyll. It is far inferior to that, I think, both in the general conception and in the execution. Voss's hexameters are perfect. The German language admits of that metre, the English hardly does so. Some of Longfellow's lines are but quasi-metre, so utterly inharmonious and so prosaic in regard to the diction. I do not think there will ever be a continuous strain of good hexameters in our language, though there may be a good line here and there.

Goethe's hexameters are excellent; those of Schiller in "Der Tanz," a poem in longs and shorts, exquisite.

You should read Longfellow's "Hyperion," which is an imitation of Jean Paul Richter, in the same degree, perhaps, that "Evangeline" is an imitation of Voss. It is extremely refined and pleasing. It is, however, a collection of *miscellanea* strung together on the thread of a Rhine tour, with very little of a story, only an event to begin with, and an event to end with.

The "Letters and Remains of Keats" are highly interesting. The "Eve of St. Mark" is an exquisite fragment; "Otho the Great" an utter failure, in my opinion. I do not agree with Milnes about the "splendor and glory of the diction." There is a speech or two that might have suited Lamia or Endymion, but nothing of proper *dramatic* force or beauty, from beginning to end; and the blank verse is poor.

Severn's journal of poor Keats' last days is deeply affecting. But how sadly he wanted fortitude. He was manly in some respects; but in others he was but "five feet high" after all.

Compare the death-bed of the Deist, Blanco White, with that of poor Keats, and I think it must be admitted that both in faith and fortitude the former has immeasurably the advantage. It ought, however, to be recollected that Blanco White was older, and had had more time to gain strength of mind. But he was also of a more religious turn from the first.*

*   *   *   *   *   *   *   *

* The following lines, written in 1845, with a marginal note added later, will find an appropriate place here.—E. C.

BLANCO WHITE.

Couldst thou in calmness yield thy mortal breath,
Without the Christian's sure and certain hope?
Didst thou to earth confine our being's scope,
Yet, fixed on One Supreme with fervent faith,
Prompt to obey what conscience witnesseth,
As one intent to fly the eternal wrath,
Decline the ways of sin that downward slope!
O thou light-searching spirit, that didst grope
In such bleak shadows here, 'twixt life and death,
To thee dare I bear witness, though in ruth—
Brave witness like thine own—dare hope and pray
That thou, set free from this imprisoning clay,
Now clad in raiment of perpetual youth,
Mayst find that bliss untold 'mid endless day
Awaits each earnest soul that lives for Truth.—S. C.

I have never defended Blanco White, but I do insist on looking at his

III.

Justice and Generosity.—"Vanity Fair."—The World, and the Wheels on
which it Moves.—Thackeray, Dickens, and Currer Bell.—Devotion of
Dobbin to Amelia.

To Miss FENWICK :

November, 1848.—It is commonly thought that justice and
generosity belong to different characters, but it seems to me
that a want of both often goes together, and that people are
seldom thoroughly *just* who are ungenerous. But perhaps the
truth is that the ungenerosity to which I allude is a sort of injustice—the temper that grudges not only the outward things
of this life, but can not bear to bestow praise, honor, and credit
where they are due, and where perfect justice would award
them.

I believe "Vanity Fair" presents a true view of human life—
a true view of one aspect and side of it. We can not live long
in the world, I think, with an observant eye, without perceiving
that pride, vanity, selfishness, in one or other of its forms, together with a good deal of conscious or unconscious pretense—
pretense to virtue and piety especially, but also to intellect, elegance, and fashion—to disregard of praise and admiration, and
various other supposed advantages—are among the great main
wheels which move the social machine. Still these are uneasy
reflections, and perhaps we are not in the best frame of mind
when such things present themselves to us very strongly. I
hope that "Vanity Fair" presents but one side of the author's
own mind, else it must be a most unhappy one. Still, I must
say I think very highly of the book. None of the kind ever ex-
ceeded my anticipations so much. In knowledge of life and
delineation of character, it seems to me quite equal to "Jane
Eyre," though it has never been so popular, and I can not but
think that it afforded some hints to that celebrated novel.

---

virtues and struggles and powers of mind with the naked eyes, and not
through the glass of an opinion concerning his religious opinions. In thus
dealing, I put forth no new view of Christian justice and toleration. I do but
carry out the received view consistently, and without vacillation. Men *will*
not believe that B. W. died a firm believer in a Moral and Intelligent Creator and Governor to whom our homage and submission is due, because he
rejected outward Revelation, and was unconvinced of the resurrection of
man's soul to conscious existence.—S. C.

Thackeray is not good where he imitates Dickens—where he describes houses, for instance. The *still* part of his descriptions is often tedious; whereas in "Jane Eyre" the landscape-painting is admirable, and Dickens shines in Dutch pieces, descriptions of interiors, and so forth. But Thackeray has a vein of his own, in which he is quite distinct from his predecessor and successor in the novel-writing career, and it is a keen and subtle one. I believe the description of Sir Pitt Crawley is hardly an overdrawn picture of what may have existed fifty years ago.

Dobbin's devotion to a weak woman like Emmy is perfectly natural. That sort of devotedness is seldom bestowed on very worthy objects, I think, for they do not excite tenderness in the shape of pity, are more independent, and turn the admirer's thoughts into a better and higher direction.

IV.

Essay on "Money."—Prodigality and Avarice.

To Miss FENWICK, Bath:

1848.—That part of the essay on "Money"* which will be thought severe (perhaps), I believe indeed to be most true—I mean the part about creditors. It is merciful to be harsh on such subjects, in public declaration, and nip the *tadpole* in the *bud*, to use an incongruous metaphor.

I think that prodigality and avarice taken early may be checked. I believe, however, that the former is more curable than the latter, as belonging to less tough natures, and depending more on the outward and less on the mind. For avarice is especially, I suppose, a disease of the imagination.

---

* "Notes from Life," in Six Essays, by Henry Taylor, Esq.—E. C.

V.

To the Rev. EDWARD COLERIDGE :

REPLY TO STRICTURES OF THREE GENTLEMEN UPON CARLYLE, SUPPORTED BY A REFERENCE TO CERTAIN PASSAGES IN HIS WORKS.

In order to do justice to the views of an author, especially such an author as Carlyle, who less than most men can be understood in fragments, a want of finish in the parts being the characteristic defect of his style, we must take care to place ourselves in his point of view, to possess ourselves of his aim. Now Carlyle's great theme in the work before us is worship—the instinct of Veneration in man (but see his limitation of the term, p. 381—or intimation that he has been using it in a limited sense). The religion of nations, as to its superficial and outward part, he considers to be, in great measure, a system of empty forms, dead conventionalisms, and lifeless ceremonies—the worthless remains of a something which once had life. On the other hand, he believes that, in all religions which have ever held sway over masses of men for a considerable time, there has been at bottom a living and life-exciting principle. This principle, which he sets up as the *work of God*, against the artefacts of men—vain substitutes for genuine gifts from on high—he maintains to be *Veneration*—the principle or feeling which leads men to bow down before the image of God in the soul of man. Power is an attribute of God—Carlyle maintains that the instinct whereby we are impelled practically to adore and obey mental power, wherever we behold it, is a salutary and high instinct, which instrumentally redeems mankind from the dominion of sense and the despotism of moral evil. (But power in God is joined with benevolence, and so it is in all whom Carlyle sets up as objects of " worship.")

In the first passage referred to (*Hero - Worship*, p. 22, 23),

Voltaire is spoken of as a *kind* of hero, a man gifted by God with remarkable *powers* of thought and expression, and who, whatever evil he may have done, exceeding any good that can be ascribed to his authorship, was nevertheless believed by those who "worshiped" him to have devoted his life and abilities to the "unmasking of hypocrisy," and "exposing of error and injustice." Carlyle's proposition seems to me to be simply this: The French nation being such as they were, that is to say, in a comparatively low, dark, unspiritual state, their enthusiasm about Voltaire was a favorable symptom of their mental condition—the spirit evinced therein, a redeeming spirit (in its degree)—their feeling of admiration and veneration for one whom they thought *above* them, in its own nature a noble and blessed feeling. Poor and needy, indeed, must that people be who have no better object of such a feeling than Voltaire. Our author means only to affirm that Frenchmen were better employed in "worshiping" him even for supposititious merits than in groveling along in utter worldliness, pursuing each his own narrow, selfish path, without a thought or a care beyond the gratification of the senses. Here is no intention to set the intellectual above the moral, or to substitute the one for the other, but to insist on the superiority of *natural gifts*, as means of bettering the souls of men, to the vain shows and semblances which commonly pass for religion in the world, according to the author's opinion.

The second passage (p. 166, 167) I remember noting when I first read the work in which it is contained, as announcing a doctrine either wrong in itself or wrongly expressed. But I can not see that it is erroneous by the exaltation of intellectual power above goodness, but rather by too bold and broad an affirmation that the former is the measure of the latter. So far I agree with Carlyle, that I believe the highest moral excellence attainable by man is ever attended by a certain largeness of understanding; not that intellectual power is a part of goodness, but that moral goodness can not be evolved, to the greatest extent, without it. Men of high virtue and piety are ever men of insight, the moral and intelligential in their mixed nature reciprocally strengthening and expanding each other. To transfer these remarks to a lower subject, every *great* poet must be possessed not merely of a fine imagination, a lively fancy, or any other particular intellectual faculty, but of a great understanding; he must be one whose mental vision is deeper and more acute than that of other men, who sees into the truth of things, and has a special power of rendering what he sees visible to others. He must be practical, as well as percipient, else he is not a poet, a maker or creator; he must see keenly and (if the expression may be allowed) *feelingly*, else his poetic faculty has no adequate materials to work upon. Shakespeare was inclusively a great philosopher. "Lear," "Hamlet," and "Othello" could never have been produced by one who did not see into the human mind deeply and survey it widely. But to be a Shakespeare, a man must have certain peculiar gifts of intellect added to this great general powerfulness; or, to express myself more distinctly, his mind must be specifically modified, and that from the first—*à priori*. I can not at all agree with Carlyle in thinking that the sole original qualification of every great man of every description is a strong understanding, and that, where there is this common base, circumstances *alone* determine whether the possessor is to be a Cæsar or a Shakespeare, a Cowley or a Kant, a Wellington or a Wordsworth. To return to the moral side of the subject, I think that Carlyle expresses himself too broadly when he says "that the degree of vision that dwells in a man is the correct measure of the man," and illustrates his meaning by a reference to Shakespeare. Was Shakespeare as much better than other men as he was deeper and clearer sighted? The truth is that *vision* considered in the concrete, as found in this or that individual, is always specific. The saints and servants of God have a vision of their own—but here let me pause, for I am at the mouth of a labyrinth. Lord Byron, to whom Mr. A—— refers, was a very *clever* man; but I think that Carlyle would not allow him any very remarkable "degree of vision;" his "superiority of intellect," *sensu eminente*, he would plainly deny, and, in my opinion, with justice. But still Byron had a stronger understanding than many a better man, though his fame during life may have been no "correct measure" of his intellectual size (in literary and poetical circles his fame is now fast shrinking into more just proportion therewith). Carlyle's statement is, at best, confused and inadequate, probably because he had not properly thought out the subject when he undertook to speak upon it.

Much waste of words, and of thought too, would be avoided if disputants would always begin with a clear statement of the question, and not proceed to argue till they had agreed upon what it was that they were arguing about. The proposition which I understand Mr. A—— to maintain (when he censures Carlyle as a worshiper of intellect, implying that he worships it in a bad sense), and which I venture to deny, is this: That Thomas Carlyle, viewed in his character of author, as appears upon the face of his writings, exalts intellect taken apart from the other powers of the mind—that he sets up mere intellect as the ultimate object of esteem and admiration, and represents a man as truly great and worthy of all honor purely on the score of intellectual gifts, without reference to the use he makes of them. In disproof of this position (or by way of attempting to disprove it), I appeal to the fact that all his heroes, whom he describes as being the deserving objects of what, "not to be too grave about it," he chooses to call "*worship*," are represented by him as benefactors of the human race, just in proportion as they were *deserving* objects of worship. He describes them as men whose powers have been employed by God's will and their own, for good and noble purposes on a large scale, chiefly for the purpose of leading men, directly or indirectly, from earth to heaven, from the human to the divine. This, indeed, is the key-note of Carlyle's writings—it is the beginning and the end of his whole teaching; it is this which gives a character of elevation to all the productions of his mind, and renders him so widely influential, as, with all his bad taste and frequent crudity and incompleteness of thinking, he certainly is, that in all he puts forth there is an immediate reference to man's higher destiny, under the power of which thought all his other thoughts are moulded and modified. His vocation is that of an *apostle*, in the sense in which the title may truly and reverently be bestowed upon uninspired men. If it be objected to this view of his drift and purpose that Voltaire and Rousseau are mentioned among his heroes, I reply that he has done this, not from blindness to their faults and deficiencies, but from the supposed perception of a certain degree of merit in them not commonly recognized by admirers of goodness. This supposition may be well or ill founded—he may be wrong in supposing those writers to have exerted any beneficial influence; but the character of his aim is to be determined by the supposition and not by the fact. He places them very low in the scale of benefactors, and brings them forward rather as illustrations of his meaning in the lowest instances, than as considering them worthy to be placed by the side of the best and greatest men in the scale of moral greatness. His account of Cromwell I think very fine as a sketch, and very well framed as an exponent of his doctrine: with regard to its truth in fact, my judgment is suspended. Be that as it may, Carlyle's heroes are all men who have striven for truth and justice, and for the emancipation of their fellow-mortals. He represents them as having been misunderstood by the masses of mankind, in the midst of all their effectivity and *ultimate* influence, simply because the masses of mankind are not themselves sufficiently wise and good and perspicacious to understand and sympathize with those who are so in an eminent degree. There is *some* originality in Carlyle's opinions; but he seems to me to be more original in manner than in matter: the force and feeling with which he brings out his views are more *remarkable* than the views themselves.

Carlyle has somewhere spoken as if he thought that bodily strength gave a just claim to the possession of rule and authority, and this passage has been quoted against him with considerable plausibility. But is it not true that superior strength of body and mind have ever enabled the possessors, sooner or later, to command the herd of their inferiors? This is a fact which Carlyle does not invent, but only reasons upon, and his reasoning is that native strength and other personal endowments, conferred directly by God, without man's intervention, convey a better claim to the obedience and service of men, and are a safer ground whereon to erect sovereignty, than arbitrary human distinctions and titles established conventionally, which by a certain theory of theologians are made out to have been instituted by God Himself. The only divine right of kings which he will acknowledge is *native might*, enabling a man to rule well and wisely, as well as strongly. Hereditary sway, pretending to be divine, he looks upon as a mere human contrivance, one that has never adequately answered its purpose, that arose originally from false views and bad feelings, and, as it had in it from the beginning a corrupt root, is ever tending to decay and dissolution. For myself, if it is worth while to say what I think, I can not clearly understand the *divine right* of kings as taught by High Churchmen, but neither do I believe that Carlyle has seen through the whole of this matter, or that there is not much more to be said for conventional sovereignty than appears in his notices of the question. If all men were at all times wise enough to choose the best governors, there need be no such contrivance as hereditary sway—but, till they are, elective sway is no better ; and in the mean time, according to Carlyle's own admission, native strength has a sphere of its own, in which it governs with more or less effect, according to its intensity.

Carlyle's *manner* of describing the character of Mirabeau is, perhaps, the most questionable part of his writings; yet even here, I think, his main drift is quite consistent with morality. He is not judging the eminent Frenchman as a divine, nor examining him as a moralist. His theme is the French Revolution, which he regards as a tremendous crisis, the result of a long series and extensive system of selfishness, cruelties, and injustices, and he views all the persons of his narrative principally in reference to the part they acted, and the effects they wrought, in this great national convulsion. Whatever Mirabeau's private character may have been before God, yet as far as he was a powerful and conspicuous agent in carrying forward the work of the French Revolution, Carlyle was justified, as it seems to me, in setting him forth as an object of interest, and even of admiration, proportioned to the amount and rareness of the gifts which rendered him a potent instrument in the hands of Providence for a particular purpose ; and this he might have done without calling evil good, or good evil. But it is abundantly evident that Carlyle did *not* consider Mirabeau's mind and dispositions as *upon the whole* morally bad ; he ascribes to him high purposes and public virtues—that is, virtues specially calculated to benefit the public. Whether his account of him be true in fact, or whether it is a fiction, our argument does not require us to consider. The question only is, does Carlyle's language respecting Mirabeau confound the distinction betwixt virtue and vice—does it tend to dim the lustre of the first, and to surround the last with a false and falsifying splendor? Now I am inclined to answer this question in the negative, both from consideration of Carlyle's general turn of mind, as displayed in his books, and from a survey of all that he says of Mirabeau, taken in connection with the spirit and principles of the work in which it appears, though I admit that he has not taken sufficient pains to prevent his sentiments from being taken for that which they are not. The writings of Lord Byron are really open, in some measure, to such a charge, because they array in attractive colors imaginary personages to whom no real good or noble qualities are ascribed; they are not reprehensible for that they represent men as worthy to be admired in spite of great vices, but because they tend to produce admiration of the very vices themselves — to detach it from virtue altogether, and place it on inferior objects. Lord Byron's heroes have no higher merits than gallantry and courage; they are invested with a kind of dignity from romantic situation, and the possession of outward elegance, not dignified by their instrumentality in great and important events. Such representations are essentially mean and worthless, but such is not Carlyle's representation in the present instance. He describes Mirabeau, not only as a man of vast energy and amazing political sagacity, but, amid much personal profligacy and unruliness of passion, as being possessed, like his father before him, of a philanthropic spirit, high disinterested aims, and a zeal to serve his country. He affirms, and in this, whatever Macaulay's opinion may be, he is borne out by other authorities, that Mirabeau took a right view of the political needs of the French people; that he sought to bring in a limited monarchy on the English model, knowing it to be the only form of public liberty for which the French nation was fit; and that, had God spared his life, and permitted him to go on in the career which he had commenced, he would have been the saviour of his country, so far as this, that, without the horrors of the Revolution, he would have established all that the Revolution ultimately brought about in so violent and calamitous a manner. Such, according to Carlyle, was Mirabeau's aim; such his insight. That he was in many respects a bad man can not make such an aim not to have been good; the sagacity with which he directed it, and the resoluteness with which he pursued it, not to have been admirable—and to *deny* this character of excellence appears to me to be a confounding of good and evil, not to *affirm* it. Would it not be an approach to the ill practice of lying for God, if we were to refuse all honor to the name of Mirabeau on account of that bad side of his mind and actions, supposing Carlyle's account of him to be correct? Carlyle represents this remarkable man as a voluptuary and a libertine. Libertinism is of the nature of wickedness, but mere libertinism, though it may be accompanied by, and though it tends to produce, hardness of heart, and is a contempt of God's Word and commandments, does not alone constitute the man who is guilty of it "an atrocious villain." It may be villainously pursued, but it is not in itself the same thing as villainy; for a villain, according to the common acceptation of the word, is a man basely malignant as to his general character, incapable of generous thoughts and actions; but libertinism is not absolutely incompatible with generosity and benevolence, however it may *tend* to weaken and fret away all that is better than itself in the mind of the libertine. Again, a *mere* voluptuary is a contemptible being. But Mirabeau, according to Carlyle, was much else besides being a voluptuary. He seems rather to have acted the rake, as a form of activity, than through a slavish subjection to mere sensual appetite; and Carlyle brings forward his exploits in this line, rather to show his multifarious energy—how many different kinds of things he was able to do at once, and with the force of a giant—than with any intention of admitting that he was a selfish sensualist in the main; that this was his distinguishing character. I am afraid his way herein was made all too smooth before him, and that the women sank before his genius with fatal facility. They are too apt to yield their whole heart and mind to men of power and distinction, let their other qualities be what they may, and there was little Christianity in Paris during Mirabeau's career to keep such a disposition in check. However, I am far from defending the *tone* in which Carlyle deals with this part of his subject; there is something of exultation in it highly reprehensible. As a defender of truth, he should not have referred to such things without a mark of reprobation, nor, as a pretender to refinement and elevation of feeling, should he have touched upon them without expressions of disgust and contempt.

On one other point, however, I do think Carlyle may be defended without sophistry or straining. It was said, as I understood, that whereas this writer treats his own favorites with undue indulgence, he displays a bitter and vehement spirit against their adversaries, and generally all who are not of his school and party. I should say, on the contrary, that Carlyle treats all historical characters that come under his cognizance with leniency; he speaks admiringly and indulgently, for instance, of Marie Antoinette; and I can perceive no *scorn* in his exposure of the weakness and dullness of her husband—which who can deny. In speaking of Laud, he less decries the *man* than the circumstances of which he was the creature. One of Carlyle's opinions, whatever his candor, could not look upon Laud as a large and free-minded man, a martyr in a wholly good cause.

Carlyle is a satirist, but he is not given to satirize individuals, or even parties of men. The object of his satire, as it appears to me, is the weakness and wickedness of *mankind*—systems of opinion, not bodies of believers. He speaks occasionally with contempt, though not always with unqualified contempt (see his last work, "Past and Present"), of Puseyism, as a resurrection-system of defunct things ; but he says nothing of any of the resurrection-men, nor has he ever joined any person or party, that I am aware of, in impeaching the conduct of the Puseyites, considered as a party.

Macaulay's opinion of Mirabeau is cited by Mr. A——. Macaulay may be more correct than Carlyle as to the facts of the case (though I do not see that this has been proved), but I can not think him fit to be trusted with the character of any great man. He is a thorough Utilitarian and anti-Spiritualist, and though he makes judicious remarks upon this person and upon that, yet scarcely sees at all that element of greatness, that spark of the divine in these marked agents of Providence, which Carlyle sees too exclusively. Macaulay finishes fully, but his conceptions are on a confined scale. Carlyle aims at something higher and deeper, his views are more novel and striking, but they are hastily and often inaccurately set forth. Carlyle writes paradoxically about great men. Macaulay, on similar subjects, is liable, in my opinion, to write untruly, from defective perception of a certain side of greatness. I would refer to Carlyle's character of Johnson, in his "Essays," as a most interesting sample of his style and mode of thinking.

In the comparison of Byron and Carlyle, with regard to the moral tendency of their writings, I would add, that if the latter had *invented* the character of Mirabeau, or if the character thus invented was untrue to nature, in representing high and noble qualities in combination with evil ones, so as they never appear in actual life, he might justly be accused of depreciating the former, and varnishing over or softening off the latter. But Carlyle has not been found, I believe, to have misrepresented the life and actions of Mirabeau; nor has it yet been shown that he has misrepresented human nature in his account of them. Neither this nor that, indeed, is the charge against him; but rather that he has described him as a wicked man, and yet has held him up to honor and admiration, on the score of marked talents and striking qualities, apart from virtue. This charge is unsupported, I think, by sufficient evidence; Carlyle has not exalted him as a *man*, still less as a subject of the *Prince of Life*, but as an actor in a great historical drama; nor has he held up his worst actions to positive admiration; he has but given them a place beside his worthier ones, without drawing the line betwixt them with sufficient sharpness. But he was not called upon by the nature of his undertaking to sum up all the points of Mirabeau's character, and decide whether it was good or bad in the eye of God. He had undertaken to describe, and to moralize and philosophize, implicitly rather than expressly, upon the French Revolution; and this I think he does in a deeply religious spirit, ever bearing in mind and bringing before the minds of his readers that there is a God that both ruleth and judgeth the world, and exposing the *moral* bearings of his subject, whether justly or not, yet with a constant regard to the law of conscience and the inward revelations of the Spirit. It was not his province to censure the private vices of Mirabeau (I mean that this was not within the scope of his principal design, though I admit that he ought not to have spoken of them without noting his disapprobation of them more clearly). It was his province to show how the selfishness and godlessness of *numbers*, how spiritual wickedness in high places, gradually reared up a pile of misery and mischief; and how this mass of evil, when at last it exploded with ruinous violence, was at once a remedy from God and a retribution.

CHAPTER XX.

1849.—January-July.

LETTERS TO MISS FENWICK, MISS MORRIS, MRS. J. STANGER,
MRS. R. TOWNSEND, MRS. PLUMMER, AUBREY DE VERE,
ESQ., HON. MR. JUSTICE COLERIDGE, EDWARD
QUILLINAN, ESQ., HENRY TAYLOR, ESQ.,
REV. EDWARD COLERIDGE.

I.

A Sad New-Year.—Alarming Illness of her Brother Hartley.

To Miss FENWICK:

Chester Place, January 7, 1849.—My dear friend, you may perhaps have heard from the North of my present sorrow and anxiety; but, whether you have or not, I must write to tell you of it. On Christmas-day came from dear Mrs. Wordsworth an alarming report of my dear brother Hartley. Several other reports were still worse, and after one of them I almost mourned him as dead. Then a report that he had happily passed the crisis, as was hoped, assured me for a while of his restoration. When the news worsened again, Derwent went to him. The news he sent was cheering at first, but ever since the first has been worsening. On Wednesday night he grew faint, his countenance changed, and D—— thought his last hour was approaching. D—— gave him brandy and water; * * * he revived upon this, and conversed a good deal; talked on Pindar, Cary, Dante—on Ireland, and such topics. * * * Yesterday's report was that he was no better—weaker, if any thing. * * * He has every advantage of medical skill, the most excellent and affectionate nursing, and testimonies of love and regard from numerous friends, more than I can express. No man, I do think, can ever have been more beloved who had no means of attaching men to him but his mere personal qualities.

His state of mind in regard to religious feeling is all that can be desired. Nothing, D—— says, can be more devout, more pious, resigned, simple, and loving. But he appears at times greatly depressed, both in his mind, from itself, and by his bodily sufferings. Dear Mrs. W——'s letters were all you could expect from her—wonderfully clear and strongly written, and most kind and affectionate. On Friday D—— wrote: "Mr. W—— has seen him, and was much affected. His own appearance was very striking, and his countenance beautiful, as he sat by the bedside." * * * He took the Sacrament some days ago. I suffer greatly in being unable to be at his bedside. The journey, taken at once, would render me useless; and, after our long separation, for me to arrive at Rydal shattered and prostrate, would do nothing but harm. * * * His illness has brought up strongly before my mind all my past early life in connection with my dear brother. I feel now more than I had done before how strong the tie is that binds me to him. Scarce any death would make me anticipate my own with such vividness as would his. Children and parents belong each to a different generation; but a brother, a few years older, who has never suffered from any malady—in him I should seem in some sort to die myself. I trust, if he is spared, we shall all be more serious for the future—not more sad—more cheerful, but more earnestly thoughtful of the true end of life, and desirous to make ready for departure.

II.

His Long Absence and Unexpected Death.—Disappointment of Long-cherished Hopes. — His Attaching Qualities. — His Grave in Grasmere Church-yard.—His Last Hours.

To Miss MORRIS:

10 *Chester Place, January* 17, 1849. — Many, many thanks, dearest Miss Morris, for your note. I am so thankful that you can anticipate my deep grief! We had long been separated from each other, as to outward sight, but oh! how much he occupied my thoughts, and how dear he was to my heart!—never till now did I know how dear.

There were three who loved me best in this wide world, to whom I was most dear, most important. Now all three are gone; and I feel, even from earthly feeling, as if that other world were more my home than this.

I never thought of surviving him. I always thought he would live to old age, and that, perhaps, in our latest years we might cherish each other; meantime, that I might see much of him in some long visit to the North, when I might make my children known to him.

It seems as if he were snatched away from me all on the sudden, and all the thoughts and visions of so many, many years are swept away all at once. This has brought my mind into a strangely agitated state. I have felt worse since yesterday evening than I did before. Dear friend, I can not as yet reconcile myself to this loss. For a time I feel resigned—then comes back a tide of recollections which deluge me with tears. It is so grievous to me that I could not attend on him in his last illness. That was impossible. The sight of me, after so long a separation, would have agitated him, I know, and been too injurious. I thought to go with Nurse had the illness continued. He was the most attaching of men; and if tributes of love and admiration from those who knew him well, and tears shed for his unlooked-for death, could remove or neutralize sorrow, my cup would have lost its bitterness. Never was a man more loved in life or mourned in death; indeed, within the circle of my acquaintance, I might even say, *so* loved and mourned.

It soothes me to think of all the love and sorrow of the Wordsworths, and that by their wish—it would have been his too—his remains are laid as near as possible to the spot where they are to lie, in the southeast corner of Grasmere churchyard, near the river, amid the cluster of graves which belong to the Wordsworths—dear bright-minded, warm-hearted Dora, who never spoke of him but with praise and affection, and others of the family still earlier removed. But, oh, how little did I think that I was never to see him more!

I should like you some day to see the letters which give account of his state in illness, his dying hours, and then of the funeral. Nothing could be more gentle, loving, pious, and humble—more deeply penitent for sin. Long and severe was his parting struggle—severe both to body and mind; but at the very last he went off gradually.

III.

Affectionate Behavior of the Old Friends at Rydal Mount on this Occasion.
—Mr. Wordsworth's Opinion of Hartley's Character and Genius.

To the Rev. EDWARD COLERIDGE, Eton College :

10 *Chester Place, Regent's Park, January*, 1849.—My dear Edward, I think you will be glad to see the letters I inclose. They will tell you more of my dear Hartley's last days than you could otherwise hear. Our old friends, Mr. and Mrs. Wordsworth, are more endeared to me and Derwent than ever, by the love and tender interest they have shown ; not more, indeed, than I should have looked for from them, but all I could have thought of or hoped. "You should have heard the old man say, 'Well, God bless him !' and then turn away in tears. 'It is a sad thing for me, who have known him so long ! He will be a sad loss to us ; and let him lie as near to us as possible, leaving room for Mrs. Wordsworth and myself. It would have been his wish.' "

In another letter, when all was over, D—— says : "Mr. and Mrs. W—— had been at the cottage during my absence. Mrs. W—— kissed the cold face thrice, said it was beautiful, and decked the body with flowers. This has also been done by others. Mr. W—— was dreadfully affected, and could not go in. Miss S—— had told her father that the face was still the same—the same countenance. 'Is it strange,' he replied, 'that death should not be able to force a mask on him who in his lifetime never wore one ?' "

. It soothes me to think that my dear brother, the greater part of whose life has been spent in our dear old friend's daily sight, should in death not be parted from them—the same neighborhood in their last homes as in the abodes where they have lived—that his remains should rest beside those of dear, bright-minded, kind-hearted Dora, who never mentioned his name but to say something of praise or affection. Her father's expressions about Hartley, when I met him at Bath nearly two years ago, have been a treasure of memory to me ever since, and ever will be. Tributes of admiration to his intellectual endowments, his winning, though eccentric manners, were plentiful as flowers in summer. This was *more*. It showed me that he was esteemed in heart by one who knew him well, if ever one man could know another—one not too lenient in his moral judgments. I valued this testimony as confirming my own belief, which, because it related to one so dear, I held tremblingly, not as making me feel what I had not felt before. "It falls to the lot of few," another old friend says, "to have been so beloved and so worthy of love as poor Hartley Coleridge." No one could be loved as he was without a great share of those qualities to which our Saviour referred when he said, "Of such is the kingdom of heaven."

IV.

Christian Use of Sorrow.

To the Hon. Mr. Justice COLERIDGE, Heath's Court :

January, 1849.—I am sure, dear John, this most unexpected death of my dear brother is a spiritual benefit to me. Nothing has ever so shaken my hold upon earth. Our long separation made me dwell the more earnestly on thoughts of a reunion with him, and the whole of my early life is so connected with him, he was in my girlhood so deep a source of pride and pleasure, and at the same time the cause of such keen anguish and searching anxiety, that his departure brings my own before me more vividly and with more of reality than any other death ever has done. If thinking of death and the grave could make me spiritual and detached from the weaknesses of this earthly sphere, I should be so ; for I am perpetually dwelling on death and that other unimaginable state. But, alas! more is required than the sense of our precarious state here, to fit us for a better and a higher.

V.

Sensitiveness about Public Opinion.

To the Hon. Mr. Justice COLERIDGE :

Chester Place, February, 1840. — The accompanying letter shows a sensitiveness about any exposure of private matters to the public in which I can not *now* quite sympathize. A good deal of thought upon the subject, through a good deal of experience, has brought me to think that a serious, anxious concern on such points is hardly worth while. If we could but overhear all that people say of us, when we are supposed out of hearing, all their careless comments and detailed reports of our affairs, I believe it would cure a good deal of this anxiety, by showing us how vain it is to aim at keeping ourselves out of the reach of observation ; that it is but an ostrich-like business of hiding one's head in the sand. More especially with respect to money matters and *age*, it is politic to tell our own story, for if we do not, it will surely be told for us, and always a degree more disadvantageously than truth warrants. The *desire* to be the object of public attention is weak, but the excessive dread of it is but a form of vanity and over-self-contemplativeness. The trouble we take in trying not to *seem* would be better spent in trying not to *be* what we would rather not appear to be. If a strain of thought is beautiful and interesting in itself, I would not generally withdraw it from a collection of poems about to be published because it touches on private affairs. I remember the time when I felt otherwise ; but now I can not help thinking that we should so order our lives, and also our feelings and expectations, that we may be as far as possible independent of the opinions and judgments of our fellow-men ; and that whatever is the truth on a subject of any sort of interest can very seldom in the long run be effectively or beneficially concealed.

VI.

Lecture at the Royal Institution.—Visit to the Dudley Gallery.—Early Italian Masters, Fra Angelico and Fra Bartolomeo.—Comparison between the "Last Judgment" of Fra Angelico and the "Divina Commedia" of Dante.—Her Brother Hartley : his Countenance and Portrait.

To Mrs. PLUMMER, Gateshead :

Chester Place, February 20, 1849.—Of Herbert's *progress in life* you have perhaps heard all the heads from E. G., who is such a kind friend of his, and so interested about him. He is a great admirer of her, and a great admirer of her husband. I wish that both he and you could have heard Mr. G——'s last lecture at the Royal Institution on Voltaic Ignition. It was most masterly—quite perfect, I should say, in its line—so far as I could judge, for I pretend not to have been able to follow the whole train of thought, though I believe it was as clearly expressed, and it certainly was as clearly and fluently delivered, as can be imagined. The experiments were all successful, and very brilliant and striking.

My nieces have just sent a messenger to arrange with me about a visit to the Dudley Gallery—Lord Ward's pictures—in Brook Street. This collection I saw a little while since with the D——s; now I wish to show it to E. and the P——s. It contains many beautiful pictures by the older Italian masters, as well as some, *to my mind*, still greater beauties by Correggio, Guido, and Salvator Rosa. I confess I can not feel that enthusiasm for the pictures of Fra Angelico which some mediævalists in taste as well as in doctrine tell us we ought to feel. I have seen pictures of Fra Bartolomeo which I admired exceedingly; they struck me as uniting some of the grace and fine finish of Raphael with that simple, severe, or serious air of devotion which characterizes many of the older painters. But the productions of the earlier school are often grotesque, feeble, wanting in richness, grace, and beauty to my eyes; and though I respect them as devotional pieces, where they really do express a religious sentiment, I can not much admire them as works of art. The admired Fra Angelico in Lord Ward's gallery is a representation of the Last Judgment, and is to my mind more curious and interesting than beautiful. On one side is a most debased copy of a portion of Dante's "Inferno," quite devoid of the pathos and sublimity of the Florentine's poetic place of retribution. Dante, amid all his mediæval grotesqueness and monstrosity, is almost always elevated or affecting. What a study his great poem is!—what a compendium of the religion, philosophy, ethics, politics, taste of the Middle Ages!

I can not tell you how deeply my dear brother's death has affected me. Hartley's image is so connected with all my early life, which is life pre-eminently, that it seems strange to be left here without him. Separated as we had so long been by a set of very peculiar circumstances, I was always looking forward to the time when I should see much of him, and make my children known to him. If testimonies of warm and strong attachment, the liveliest admiration and deep regard—in spite of his sad infirmity, which did himself such wrong—to my dear brother's memory could console for his loss, I should be abundantly consoled, for I think I never knew any man so wept for out of his own immediate circle. Some of the letters of his friends and

admirers are most affecting and beautiful. But I meant to refrain from this theme, which must either be tedious or sadden-
ing. D—— has undertaken to collect his writings in prose
and verse, and will, I hope, find time for this, as well as to preface the poems with a memoir. The outward events of our
dear Hartley's life are few and slight—all except one. There
is little to tell, but much to describe, could description convey
a living image of what he was, what he appeared in heart and
mind to his many friends, as child, boy, man. L——, the artist, told me not long ago that he hoped to induce him to sit to
him for his portrait when he was next in the North; that such
a face as his ought to be preserved, and that the picture I have
of him does him injustice. I grieve that this was not done before. L—— admired his mind so warmly that he would have
been the better enabled to do justice to his countenance, and
he possesses the art and knowledge which were wanting to the
limner whose work I had bought, and which, in spite of its
faults as a painting, is to me very interesting.

VII.

Strong-minded Women.

To Mrs. JOSHUA STANGER, Fieldside, Keswick:

Chester Place, March 6, 1849.—Young ladies who take upon
them to oppose the usages of society, which, as I fully believe,
are the safeguards of female honor and happiness, and sup-
porters of their influence over the stronger and wiser sex, and
have arisen gradually out of the growing wisdom of mankind,
as they increase in civilization and cultivation, are generally
found to possess, I think, more self-confidence than thorough
good sense, intellect, and genius. Certainly all the women of
first-rate genius that I know have been, and are, diffident, feminine, and submissive in habits and temper. For none can
govern so well as those who know how to obey, or can teach
so effectively as those who have been docile learners.

VIII.

Dean Stanley's Sermons.—Study of German Theology.

To Mrs. R. Townsend, Springfield, Norwood :

Chester Place, March 27, 1849.—I am reading with great delight Stanley's Sermons, which, strange to say, I never read through till now. He brings out the distinct characters of St. Peter and St. Paul, and their different missions, quite grandly.

He speaks of the study of German theology, in his preface, in what seems to me the right spirit and the right way. Some of the chief aids in his task had been found in " the labors of that great nation from which we should be loth to believe that theology alone had derived no light, or that, while we eagerly turn to it in every other branch of study, we should close our eyes against it here. Until we have equaled the writers of Germany in their indefatigable industry, their profound thought, their conscientious love of knowledge, we must still look to them for help. I know not how we should be justified in rejecting with contempt the immense apparatus of learning and criticism which they have brought to bear on Sacred Writings."

In truth, this *can not* be. If there is light in Germany more than here, it will shine in upon us. In these days light travels fast. It is not as it was centuries ago, when light might shine in corners here and there, yet ages pass away before it had become diffused, on account of the thick masses of palpable cloud and smoke which occupied the main part of the region. What a significant fact it is that Strauss' book was translated into French and English as soon as ever it appeared —that four translations of it were offered as soon as it came to England ! The worst books—those which contain some portion of truth so presented that it has all the effect of deadliest error, half-truths, and truths without their proper accompaniments—are sure to penetrate and spread fast among us. Hare and Stanley and Arnold would have the German mind brought *whole* in among us, convinced that, as a whole, it will promote the cause of spiritual religion ultimately, and that its philosophy will counteract its pseudo-philosophy—that German error is more easily to be fought by arms from Germany than from elsewhere. Those men who declaim against German theology in the mass are sometimes absolutely ignorant of a single German author, and uniformly unable to appreciate the true meaning and value of German philosophic speculations. They never really combat German opinions, nor disprove them: they do but raise a hue and cry against them. I would be a conservative, too; but is there not a kind of conservatism that is most self-destructive? Such, I think, is the conservatism of T—— and P——, which leads them to attempt to stifle the products of German thought, instead of boldly accepting it, examining the mass, and winnowing the good from the evil. It is a want of faith to doubt for a moment that religious truth can maintain its ground against all that the heart of man can conceive or the human mind imagine.

IX.

Essay on the "Idea of Life," by S. T. Coleridge.

To Miss FENWICK:

Chester Place, March 29, 1849.—My dear friend, is it to you that I am indebted for the *Guardian* of March 21, containing a review of my father's "Idea of Life?" If it be, my thanks.

The best review of the "Idea of Life," or what I liked the best, as showing most insight into and agreement with my father's views, was in the *Athenæum.* Another critique has been sent me from America, where, at Philadelphia, the Essay has been republished. This little work, of which we have been deprived, has made a more immediate impression than almost any philosophical production of my father's.

I marvel at the objections of the *Guardian* and Dr. W—— to my father's personification of Nature. This seems to me rather old-womanish. Do they suppose my father meant that Nature was an independent, self-subsisting power, like a pagan deity, walking about the visible universe in a green robe, a sky-blue bonnet, and earth-colored petticoat?

X.

To EDWARD QUILLINAN, Esq., Loughrigg Holme, Ambleside :

Chester Place, March 31, 1849.—You would have been amused
to hear the critical dispute at tea yesterday, just after Mrs.
W—— had left us with a parting word about Matthew Arnold's
poetic volume, which Herbert greatly admires.   E—— began
to extol "The Kitten" and "The Falling Leaves," and then
went off into a rapture about the "Platonic Ode," when H——
interrupted her recitation of one of the sublimest passages with
"What's *that* compared with those exquisite lines of Byron :

> "'Away with your fictions of flimsy romance,
>   Those tissues which Folly has wove !
> Give *me* the mild beam of the soul-breathing glance,
>   Or the rapture which dwells in the first kiss of love !'"

He knows better than this, however.   But he was rather successful yesterday in quizzing Keats, by hitting upon that line
in the "Endymion"—

> "When shoals
> . Of dolphins *bob their noses* through the brine."

And that stanza about the

> "Unimaginable lodge
> For solitary thinkings, such as dodge
> Conception to the farthest bourne of heaven."

These things do not well bear to be taken out of their poetic
places, and exhibited through a frame-work of broad grins.

I am awaiting with some curiosity the arrival of the *Quarterly,* in which Mr. Lockhart has dealt with Macaulay.   I wonder whether he will prove him wrong in any of his points with
respect to the career of James II.   Since finishing Macaulay's
highly attractive volumes, the second of which has an enchaining interest, I have perused Miss Strickland's Memoir of James
II.'s wife, Maria d'Este of Modena.   The book seems to me
childishly perverted and partial in much that relates to James
II., but the account of his wife grows upon one.   Proud and
impetuous she must have been, but certainly she must have had
a heart.   The history of her feelings in the first days of widow-

hood, and in her husband's last illness, was to me, on reading, a mere repetition of that which is written in my own memory of my own experience. Macaulay's cool way of speaking of her person, which must have been one of the finest in Europe, is one of the greatest signs of party-spirit in his book, unless it is not party warmth, but mere temperamental coldness and apathy on the subject of female charms. Yet that it can not be, since he can use strong words enough about some of Charles II.'s good-for-nothing beauties.

Miss Rigby's[*] article on "Vanity Fair" was brilliant, as all her productions are. But I could not agree to the concluding remark about governesses. How could it benefit that uneasy class to reduce the number of their employers, which, if high salaries were considered in all cases indispensable, must necessarily be the result of such a state of opinion? Many governesses, as it is, receive £80 and £100 a year. When the butler has £40, and lady's-maid £20, or housekeeper £30, this is surely the average. Besides, hard and unsentimental as it may seem, I must think that the services of the ordinary tradesman's governess are not worth more than £30 a year. After all, let the governess' discomforts be what they may, is not the situation in all respects far more tolerable for a lady, or semi-lady, than that of lady's-maid or upper house-maid, or the health-destroying slavery of the milliner's or dressmaker's business, or the undignifying, if not positively degrading place behind the counter, which really in London partakes of some of the disadvantages of the stage, so obviously are the young women dressed · up, and *selected*, perhaps, to attract the eyes of customers and their lounging companions? But to some one of these situations must many a destitute young woman descend, if that of governess in some family of limited means was not to be procured.

XI.

"Une Femme Accomplie."

To Edward Quillinan, Esq.:

1849.—Did you ever meet Miss R——— in London? She is perhaps the most brilliant woman of the day—the most accom-

---

[*] The present Lady Eastlake.—E. C.

plished and Crichtonian. She draws, takes portraits like an
artist, and writes cleverly on painting; she plays with power,
and writes most strikingly on music; she speaks different languages. Her essays and tales have both had great success, the
former as great as possible. To put the *comble* to all this, she
is a very fine woman, large yet girlish, like a Doric pillar metamorphosed into a damsel, dark and striking. No, this is *not* the
comble: the top of her perfections is that she has well-bred, court-
eous, unassuming manners, does not take upon herself and hold
forth to the company—a fault of which many lionesses of the
day are guilty. At this moment no less than *four* rise up before
me, who show a desire to talk to the room at large, rather than
quietly to their neighbor on the sofa. Miss R—— is honorably
distinguished in this respect. She is thoroughly feminine, like
that princess of novelists, Jane Austen.

XII.

Failure and Success.—Her Son's Choice of a Profession.—Metaphysical
Training a Desideratum in University Education.—Confusions arising
from the Misuse of Philosophical Terms.—A General Council of the
Church to be desired for the Settlement of Controversies.

To the Hon. Mr. Justice COLERIDGE:

10 *Chester Place, April* 10, 1849.—I am glad you think it some
credit that Herby obtained a second place in the "Ireland"
contest. Disappointments, interposed between successes, are
decidedly useful to a mind of any native strength, as are all the
trials of this life; and it is a good point in H—— that he is
never so discouraged by failure as to lose a just confidence in
himself, and become listless and inactive. As for my boy's
prospects at the bar hereafter, it is all dimness and darkness to
me. Herbert will take the law as a profession, because no other
bread-making career is open to him, not because there is any
particular eligibility in it for him. He is fitted for the profession
by his power of application and of continuous study; but I know
not whether it will suit him in all respects. I hope he will prove
to have some logical ability, but I can not judge at present
whether his interest in the reasonings of Plato is a true indica-
tion of this or not. I have long thought it a desideratum in the
education of our young men that they should undergo some

systematic metaphysical training, and acquire some of that learning and power of analyzing thought of which the schoolmen display so much. Many debates would be cut short, and long webs of theory would be swept away, before they had wasted the time of authors and readers, if men were regularly taught at college the import of such terms as *nature, person, matter, soul, spirit, will, reason, understanding,* and so forth. I mean, if they were but taught those principles which *all regular* metaphysicians of all schools admit, but which many writers of the present day lose sight of in their arguments, simply from being quite out of the habit of abstracting and reflecting on the processes of the mind within itself. Men who show great ability and good sense while they keep to the *practical,* often commit, as I believe, the greatest blunders, which the merest tyro in mental science could detect, when for some practical end they set up explanatory theories involving metaphysical distinctions. I think I could give some instances of this; but I must not ask your attention to matters of this sort, exercised as you are with head-work of various kinds. In support of my remark, I will merely say that educated, well-principled men could hardly come to such opposite conclusions, one among another, as we see them do, on points which are not mere matters of taste and feeling, but seem to be altogether within the domain of logic, if they were better instructed in the meaning of the terms they make use of. I often, on this account, feel a great yearning for a General Council of the Church. Surely, if there could be even such general discussion as took place before the Council of Trent, when Cardinal Contarini—that admirable Cardinal and other good men—sought so hard to bring about a reconciliation between the Protestants and the rest of the Western Church, *some* questions must at least be set at rest forever, and the range of debate somewhat narrowed. Now every man writes what seems good in his eyes; and if the book is eloquent, and shows some reading, it is extolled to the skies by the party whom it serves, even though its main arguments are such as the reflective among them would not subscribe to were they fairly put before them, and which, in fact, *they never notice,* even though they form the *pith,* or at least contain the chief point in the whole work, and that for the sake of proposing which it was composed and published.

XIII.

Modern " Miracles."

To Miss FENWICK, Bath :

Chester Place, April 13, 1849.—The cases of L'Addolorata and L'Ecstatica in the Tyrol, are very interesting.* But Mr. Allie's conclusion respecting the object and use of the supposed miracles is, to my mind, very inconclusive. He thinks they are intended to awe and impress a skeptical, unspiritual age. But the worst of it is that no one not already brimful of what A—— calls *faith,* but what some would designate superstition, would ever consider them for a moment in the light in which he regards them, or indeed as having any connection with religion; and no one not already a believer in the Gospel would take the least interest in them, except as strange *physical* phenomena.

XIV.

Claims of Society.—A Practical Philosophy.

To HENRY TAYLOR, Esq., Ladon House, Mortlake :

Chester Place, May, 1849.—I find it difficult to break away from London. Friends come pouring into London in the spring in an uninterrupted stream. Go when you will, you are going away from somebody, doing an unfriendly action, and showing coldness of heart. I wish to feel for about a fortnight that I am at liberty to be a poor, faint, spiritless creature, that is not called upon for a single smile, or the slightest outward sign of sympathy. Oh ! that, like you, I had a play, an original dramatic composition, dependent on my obtaining a spell of leisure ! But it is ungrateful to speak thus, so much pleasure as I have in the works of others. We may easily be content " to enjoy what others understand ;" but to enjoy understanding what others have the enjoyment of producing is a practical philosophy which some in these times lose sight of (I mean to be *content* with this),

----

* This passage refers to an account, which attracted some attention at the time, of two peasant women in the Italian Tyrol, whose prolonged trances, and other strange symptoms, excited the wonder of their neighbors, and were looked upon by some persons as direct communications from heaven. —E. C.

but which I should feel it right to cultivate, if it did not grow of its own accord in my mind.

XV.

Lights and Shadows.—" Latter-day Pamphlets."—" Chartism."—" Shirley."
—Walking Powers not Lost.

To Mrs. H. M. JONES, Heathlands, Hampstead :

3 *Zion Place, Margate, May* 19, 1849.—I enjoy the quietness of this place. Very few visitors are here. We have the cliff all to ourselves for the most part, or share it only with the caroling larks. This place is better than Herne Bay : it has a fuller sea, and the water comes up to the bottom of the cliff, along which we walk ; and although the inland country is much prettier between the Kentish coast and Canterbury, yet as I come for refreshment and bracing sea-breezes, I do not miss the shady lanes and lawns and copses about Herne, but take my two walks a day, with E—— beside me, in perfect tranquillity and contentment, if not in hilarious glee. Who can be very *gleeful* for more than a few minutes at a time in such a world as this, dear friend, so full of sorrow and misery and crushing want, spiritual and physical, and so surrounded by impervious shadow, the awful mystery of the world to come ?

Have you read Carlyle's " Pamphlets?" The last, called " The Stump Orator," contains some good things, and the *Guardian* can not sneer it down, with all its talent at sneering. People affect to despise its *truisms*, when I believe, in fact, at heart they are galled by some of its bold, broad *truths*, expressed with a graphic force and felicitous humor which it is easier to rail at than to hide under a bushel. Put what bushel over it they may, it will shine through, and indeed burn up the designed extinguisher, as the fire eats up a scroll of paper. " Chartism," by the same author, however, is better than any of these new pamphlets, which repeat in substance a good deal of its contents. That book seems to me prophetic, as I read it now. The accounts of the poor, of the savage Irish, etc., are wonderfully powerful.

Have you read " Shirley?" We are delighted with it. The review in the *Edinburgh* made far too much fuss about its little faults of style and breeding. When you read the sen-

tences in question, *where they occur*, they do not appear very
shocking. The worst fault by far is the development of the
story. Mrs. Pryor's reason for putting away her daughter is
absurdly far-fetched and unnatural. No wonder the "Old Cos-
sack" disliked her, and thought her a queer sort of maniac.

I think my sleeping is a wee bit improved, and I am very
active on my legs. The country folks at Keswick, when I was
a little one, sometimes called me a "lile Jenny spinner," and I
can spin along yet, though my face is so pale and small, and
tells such a tale of sleepless nights, a weakly wifehood, and
nervous widowhood.

XVI.

Afternoon Calls.—Hurried Composition.—"Metaphysico - phobia."—Middle-aged Looks.—Simplicity of her Mother's Character.

To AUBREY DE VERE, Esq.:

1849.—I find it difficult to carry on literary business, all I
have to do in editing my father's books (and a long task in
that way yet lies before me) and worldly business, to see about
the various investments of our little property, besides domestic-
ities and social business, the last by far the hardest to me of
the three. Oh! how I do abominate the afternoon calling, to
pay or to receive it! To go out *prepared* to meet our friends
is pleasant enough, but in the afternoon, when one is engaged,
their coming is felt as an interruption. Nothing is so fatiguing
as to go through a round of afternoon visits, to initiate half a
dozen different conversations in different styles, take up half a
dozen different tunes, pitch one's self at half a dozen different
keys, and then feel obliged to rush away just as the strain begins to have a little heart in it. However, it is not the feminine visitations (if I were to begin the list of exceptions of ladies
I am always glad to see, *even in an afternoon*, I should fill up
too much of my paper), it is the evening visiting that knocks
me up.

I am truly sorry that you feel it necessary or desirable to
compose hurriedly and within *a limited time*. It is that which
makes intellectual exertion so injurious, so ruinous. It has
killed its thousands, and invalided its tens of thousands. I hope
you will have strength of mind to give it up, come what may.

I read your Landor article with great admiration. It may not show Landor's poetry in a captivating light, but it showed Mr. Aubrey de Vere in a handsome, engaging one. I quarreled with naught in it but a certain sentence about modern metaphysics, by which I suppose you mean Kant, Jacobi, Schelling, and Co., "like a dog questing after old philosophies." *Pray what do you mean by that, sir?* As if dogs ever quested after philosophy. Now don't attempt to set me right about the sentence—I remember it distinctly. I consider your view of modern metaphysics quite canine, almost inclining to mad-dog-ish. You have a German metaphysico-phobia! You ought to smother, not yourself, but *it*, that same *phobia* of modern metaphysics.

You ask me how I am. R——- asked me to sit for a chalk drawing, on my return from the sea, but my phiz, to judge by the glass here, which, however, is always in the shade, because the toilet-table is covered with my books and papers, and half the only chest of drawers is filled with the same, is not improved since my stay here. It is even more hollow and hatchety than it was. Middle-aged faces are very bad and difficult subjects. The lines and sinkings appear in them as worsenings, impairments, impoverishments, deficiencies; a few years afterward they look like seasonable marks of time, having a grace and a meaning of their own. I remember mamma, at my age, put on quite the old woman, and the Keswick people called her "auld Mrs. Cauldridge," though her complexion was a hundred times clearer and rosier than mine is now, and her cheeks rounder. As for her hair, she cut it all off, and wore a wig when she was quite a young woman, and her every-day front (a sort of semi-wig, or wig to wear with a cap), for she was too economical to wear the glossy one in common, was as dry and rough and dull as a piece of stubble, and as short and stumpy. Dear mother! what an honest, simple, lively-minded, affectionate woman she was! how free from disguise and artifice! how much less she played tricks with herself, and tried to be and seem more and better than she was, than the generality of the world!

B b

XVII.

Early Associations with the Seasons.—Vaughan, Herbert, and Crashaw.

To AUBREY DE VERE, Esq. :

10 *Chester Place*, 1849.—My dear friend, I had great pleasure in transcribing the inclosed poem ; it brought spring so vividly before me, beloved spring, which is as closely unified to my mind with my childhood, as autumn with my girlhood. I can scarce recall what I did as a *child* in *autumn*. Winter was a glorious season ; summer heat I well remember, and the throng of flowers in June, with the June Pole, and all our garden and river doings in May and June. But autumn brings no visions of childhood, except of seeking for plums in an old worn-out orchard, where the plum-trees were in the last stage of imbecility and dotage, and of standing in a sweet apple-tree, eating half the apples off the boughs, carrying on a lively dispute with my cousin Edith, who was swinging away, in the warmth of the debate, on an opposite apple-tree.

And now even my children's childhood is passed away !

Do you know Vaughan's " Silex Scintillans," a collection of sacred poems, a few years younger than those of George Herbert? They are very sweet, some lovely, but have less power and thought than Herbert's, less perfect execution than Crashaw's.

XVIII.

Miss Sellon at Plymouth.—Lord Macaulay's History.—Cruelty of James II.

Miss FENWICK, Bath : ˙

Chester Place, June, 1849.—I have heard nothing of the Sellon case at Plymouth, except at second hand. Substantially the reformeresses must be in the right. But it struck me, as I heard the case stated by one quite on her side, that it was a pity she could not have done her good things after a more Protestant fashion as to externals, avoiding party badges, however silly it may be in her opponents to consider such externals as necessarily connected with Popery and unsoundness toward our Anglican Church in the main. The bishop seems to have taken the lady's part with great warmth. However, when I speak of *party badges*, I may speak on misinformation, and she may have used no fashions but such as have been approved or allowed by our authorities here.

Macaulay's History has had, and is still having, an immense run. It is certainly a fascinating book; but in some respects, perhaps, too fascinating and attractive to be thoroughly good as a history. Dry matters are skipped, and many important events are rather commented on than narrated. And yet every true history that is to be a useful and faithful record must contain much that is dry and heavy to the common reader. His account of James II. makes the profligate, unpatriotic despot Charles II. appear like an angel of light; for what can be more hideous in the human character than implacable malice and revenge, deliberate barbarity, and love of human suffering and misery for its own sake?

XIX.

Revolutions of 1848.—Chester Place and Hyde Park Gardens.—A Little Beauty.

To AUBREY DE VERE, Esq.:

Chester Place, June 18, 1849.—Your remarks about Rome are most *apropos* to my thoughts. I have been wanting exceedingly to understand a little what is going on in that most famous of cities—what papers I ought to get for the report of late events there. When you next enter our small drawing-room, be prepared to give E—— and me a regular lecture on Roman and French political affairs, and to receive nothing in return but our best attention.

"*Small* drawing-room," I say emphatically; for a lady from Hyde Park Gardens was so "frightened" at the smallness and shabbiness of my room here, that poor Martha, my late housemaid, loses the place she hoped to obtain in her household thereby. This lady of spacious apartments seemed to contemplate her own rooms in Hyde Park Gardens (which she need not have so minutely described, since I had lately been actually admitted as a guest into the house adjoining) with the same sort of awe and admiration which Carlyle archly ascribes to Lockhart with respect to Sir Walter Scott—"an object spreading out before him like a sea without a shore."

I wish that when you come next I could show you a splendid little two-year-old who resides at No. 4 Chester Place. Such eyes, hair, and complexion, and form! Her hair is really what Mr. Wordsworth used to call his Dora's—"*angelic*"—the curls are so thick, so perfect, so large and bossy and Raphael-esque, and such a lovely golden flaxen.

XX.

A Fatiguing Task.—Comparison of Mr. Coleridge with Mr. Fonblanque as a Newspaper Writer.—Vindication of his Character for Industry and Political Integrity.—Plato on the Immortality of the Soul.—Mr. Newman's Sermon on the Intermediate State. — Opinion concerning Paradise held in the Primitive Church.

To the Hon. Mr. Justice COLERIDGE:

Chester Place, July, 1849. — My dearest John, * * * many thanks for your kind wish to see Herbert in the West. He departs on Thursday, and would that I could go on the same day; but I am beleaguered with piles of the *Morning Post* of near fifty years since, and with *Couriers* above thirty years old. I hope to get away next week, but it will be difficult. This is the last editing work, I trust, in which I shall engage that will be very laborious and confining. The mere bodily exertion which it involves is not small; and if I were as *weak* in muscle as I am disordered and uneasy in nerves, I could not get on with my task at all, far less in the exact, complete sort of way in which it is my nature to execute whatever I undertake, as far as my abilities extend (for I am now speaking only of pains-taking and jog-trot drudgery). Mr. Kenyon tells me that such collections do not sell; that Fonblanque's did not, though his articles were very elaborate and brilliant. I do not quite despair on this account. Fonblanque had a great name as a writer *for the day*, but perhaps a less one than S. T. C. as a producer of the permanent. There is a small but very affectionate and respectful audience who take an interest in knowing all that my father thought, and the words in which he uttered his sentiments on every subject, knowing that, however transient the immediate topic, he always referred it to the permanent, and shed the steady light of the past, and the bright gleams of the future, on every present of which he treated. Still no one would undertake such a business with any view to money profit. My only anxiety is that it may not be a dead loss, and Picker-

ing's willingness in the matter encourages me to hope that it
may not be that. The deepest reason why I have been anxious to do it relates to my father's moral, not his intellectual
reputation. I think it will show, first, that he *did labor* before
he fell into paralyzing ill-health, and contributed far more to
the *Morning Post* than any one would dream from Stuart's representation ; and, secondly, I believe it will show his political
course to have been characterized by honesty, strong feeling
for his country, especially the poor, and a sagacity almost prophetic. In the midst of all this, the accounts of the cholera are
very disturbing ; and sometimes, when an afternoon caller has
been dwelling on its ravages, I feel ready to run away to Herne
Bay, and leave the newspapers on the floor undispatched.

I am reading the "Phædo" with Herbert, which long ago I
read with my dear husband. I can derive as little comfort as
ever from all that seemingly profound trifling (though perhaps
there is more in it than I see) about the idea of bigness and littleness, unity and duety, and so forth. But it is decidedly a
comfort to perceive, in the midst of all this, that a thoughtful
and fine-minded man, like Plato, looked upon the soul as something too good to have been made by a wise and good Creator to last only during a short, uneasy life, in a state of existence
which seems utterly disproportionate to the desires and aspirations which inhere in its constitution, and become stronger
and fuller the better and more knowing it grows.

Lady P—— says, in answer to a remark of mine on Newman's sermon on the Intermediate State, of which her husband
expressed to me great admiration, "Do not you think, if we
were allowed to hear, like Job, the only unerring Voice, we should
truly find that counsel had but been darkened ? that we had
better try to throw our minds out of discussions into prayer for
being enabled in faith to leave such points ?" I do indeed
think that great darkness rests on what is called the Intermediate State. But the primitive Church did not seem to think
so ; at least, it made no doubt that disembodied souls met in
some *place* called Paradise, and that friends and relations knew
each other. And if we cast these views aside, then we depart
from that early theology which it was the endeavor of Newman
and his school to re-establish. Then the old doctors and bishops were not wiser than we without their light can be, because
nearer in time to the apostles.

CHAPTER XXI.

1849.—*July–December.*

LETTERS TO MRS. JOSHUA STANGER, AUBREY DE VERE, ESQ.,
HENRY TAYLOR, ESQ., MISS FENWICK, MRS. FARRER,
HON. MR. JUSTICE COLERIDGE.

I.

"Sacred and Legendary Art," by Mrs. Jameson.—Parallel between the
Classic Mythology and the Hagiology of the Roman Catholic Church.
—Hartley Coleridge's Poems.

To AUBREY DE VERE, Esq., Curragh Chase:

1849.—I am delighted with Mrs. Jameson's two volumes on
"Sacred and Legendary Art." It interests me doubly from its
descriptions of curious and beautiful works of art, and even
still more from the picture it presents of what may be called
the *Christian Mythology.* It is very curious to see how the saints
and saintesses of the Middle Ages, after the secular establishment and worldly enrichment of Christianity, succeeded to the
places of the Pagan Deities, and inherited their honors, in some
cases were invested with their attributes. There are the four
great Catholic Saintesses—St. Catharine, St. Barbara, St. Ursula, and St. Margaret. One can plainly see that the first corre-
sponded to Minerva, as Mrs. Jameson suggests, and the second
to Pallas or Bellona. The Virgin Mary, as Regina Cœli, is a
purified, elevated, glorified Saturnian Juno, the spouse of Jove,
and Queen of Heaven. St. Ursula rather resembles one of the
protective matron goddesses. "Mild Maid Margaret," that
loveliest conception of them all, in her purity and courage, may
be compared with Diana; in her lovely gentleness and humility,
has no prototype out of Christianity. Mrs. Jameson's way of
treating these subjects will not please religionists of any kind
or class, except the very Latitudinarian, whom some will call
the *Ir*-religionists. Antiquarians and Mediævalists and Romanizers will feel indignant at her treating the legends as cun-

ningly devised fables, highly as she praises their devout religious spirit and effective embodiment of moral and spiritual truth; while zealous Reformists will frown at the favor with which she regards them, and her indifference to the large amount of superstition and idolatry which they have suggested and fostered. The legends are, many of them, full of beautiful, picturesque incident, and expressive allegories and emblems. Many of them I knew before, but, like ribbons in a shop, or the different stripes in the rainbow, they set one another off, and the whole is a most interesting panorama of Devotional Art and of Christian semi-evangelical Polytheism.

The collection of dear Hartley's poems is going on. They spring up here and there and almost every where, like flowers in April. Some are but showy weeds, perhaps, and many are rich and lovely flowers, while others are of an intermediate character. The last I had to transcribe were some fine lines on Lucretius.

II.

Principle of a Poor Law.—Mortality in Ireland.—Poetry and Farming.

To AUBREY DE VERE, Esq.:

10 *Chester Place*, 1849.—Your note comes too late to save me from the "*worry*" of your "Nine Letters,"* seeing that I am looking through them again, after a regular attentive perusal of the whole nine. I hope some good will come of them.

I wish they could be reprinted in better type, and prefaced by an Essay on the principle of a Poor Law in general. You say well that here it is a sort of insurance for property.

But this is looking at it merely as matter of expediency. You *could* only so consider it in these letters. But I should like to know your view, whether it is not also matter of *justice;* whether accumulation of property should be allowed and protected by positive laws and artificial arrangements, without being accompanied by a provision that none who desire to work are to starve, while there is provision in the land enough to sustain all, if distributed. One of the great mischiefs of Ireland seems to be the way in which property is held, the occupants and managers of the land being one set of men, and the proprietors another.

* On Irish Affairs, published in the *Morning Chronicle.*—E. C.

Is it not strange that the mortality has not at least done some good, as a bloody battle generally does, by diminishing numbers?

Your style and your preaching away about agriculture, while poetry seems your vocation, is so like my father at your age, who would turn away from "Christabel" or the "Ode to Dejection" to give Mr. Poole his ideas about fattening pigs with acorns! At least, I know that the economical letters and the ethereal poems are of about the same date.

III.

Durability of Early Impressions.—Morbid Depravity.—Swedenborg.

To the Hon. Mr. Justice COLERIDGE, Heath's Court, Ottery St. Mary:

St. George's Terrace, Herne Bay, August 21, 1849.—It seems clear to me that impressions once made upon the mind are not really effaced, as they *seem* to be, but only, as it were, covered over and hidden for a time. Otherwise they could not come forth again so fresh and strong, when there has been no new impression, only some stimulus to the memory from a renewal of similar circumstances or sight of similar objects to those which were present when the impression was first made. * * *

You seem to have had a horrid circuit, though not a heavy one. The more I read and hear and see, the more forcibly it strikes me that crimes are perpetrated less from the apparent motive than from some strange, mysterious, horrible fascination in the thing itself. If we examine the history of man, we shall find that in not solitary instances only, but whole classes of instances, the ordinary feelings of human nature seem to be inverted. I believe there are thousands to whom bodily torture becomes a species of excitement, sought for its own sake, while the fancy is engaged and kept quiet by visions of indefinite grandeur and felicity to be gained by endurance of pain. There are many who become swindlers, forgers, etc., evidently from the love of playing tricks with other people, exerting their power of dupery, and acting forever a sort of practical drama, of which themselves are the heroes. This state of mind seems to be near akin to insanity, and yet not to be it, though all insanity seems to have these dispositions inclusively, with something besides. It was a fine thought of Swedenborg to represent all the spirits in hell as madmen. He should have written a "Divina Commedia," like Dante, instead of putting forth a system purporting to be literal truth and reality.

IV.

Hearing and Reading.—Facts and Opinions.

To HENRY TAYLOR, Esq.:

10 *Chester Place*, 1849.—If it is not too greedy, what I should like is to *read* the play first, and then to *hear it read* by you. I do not catch very quickly by the ear, and I have got into such a slow, musing way of reading that I can not easily follow a reader aloud of any thing interesting. I am staying behind, picking flowers and finding nests, and exploring some particular nook, as I used to be when a child walking out with my Uncle Southey, whom I found it hard to overtake when thus tempted to loiter.

How the *Quarterly* and *Edinburgh* contradict each other about the Dolly's Brae affair! I believe there is nothing so uncertain and slippery as *fact*. Theories and opinions, much as they differ, are scarce so different as the reports of what purport to be the same facts by the different parties.

V.

Judgment of the Privy Council in the Gorham Case. — Functions of the Council Declaratory, not Legislative.—Depreciatory Tone of the "Latter-day Pamphlets." — Pictures belonging to Mr. Munro, of Hamilton Place.

To HENRY TAYLOR, Esq., Mortlake:

1849.—My dear Mr. Taylor, I was horrified when late yesterday evening my eyes fell on the inclosed preface as I was searching in a drawer for the Key to Cattermole's great picture of the "Protest at the Diet of Spires," my print of which I have had framed and hung up, partly in honor of the late triumph of toleration and moderation, grand characteristics of the Reformed Religion, in the decision of the Privy Council in the Gorham case. I believe two thirds of the clergy, had the decision been in the Bishop of Exeter's favor, must either have given up their livings or cures, or have retained them with *peine forte et dure* of conscience. *Now* where is the *practical* difference in the affairs of the Church and interests of Churchmen? The judgment has but declared that to be an open question which has always in fact been so. As for Lord John Russell being the "Pope of our Church," in one sense he is so, and, as I believe, very properly and profitably for the country; in another sense, the only one that concerns truly spiritual matters, he is not aught of the kind. Infallible guide we have none, and do not think it possible to have upon earth, but the doctrine of the Church of England has always been settled by the Church interpreting Scripture. This judgment does but declare what the law of the Church is, what our formularies mean, and to make such a declaration is quite within the province of the learned body of which the Privy Council is composed. There were three bishops for the supply of theological information, and that all the body were not divines was in favor of truth and impartial justice.

* * * I wonder what you think of the "Latter-day Pamphlets?" They are much to be admired, especially for felicity of particular expressions, and they please some persons whom the author never pleased before. But I, for my part, like all his former works better than these. The drift of "Hero-Worship," and most of his other writings, was to defend and exalt, to set in a clear light, neglected merit. In the present publications I feel as if the drift were depreciatory. I do not see why we should try to take any thing from the good name of Howard. Nobody ever said that he was a brilliant man, but it was to his credit that he found his Bedfordshire estates insufficient to fill up the measure of his mind, and to satisfy his aspirations.

E—— and I have lately seen such a fine collection of Italian pictures at the house of Mr. Munro, Hamilton Place. The "Candelabra Virgin," by Raphael, most exquisite. One most lovely Claude, with a mountain which Ruskin would criticise, but which (*i. e.*, the picture) you ought to have engraved as an embellishment for your new play. A space in a wood, with a lovely pool, a clump of tufty, waterish-looking trees, goats roaming in the afternoon sunlight under the trees, and figures in front. There was also a splendid "Venice" by Turner; and Watteau's darling little town-girls, a famous picture.

VI.

Scotland and Switzerland.—Historical Interest attaching to the Former.—
Bathing in the River Greta.

To Mrs. FARRER, Greenway, Dartmouth, Devon :

12 *St. George's Terrace, Herne Bay, August*, 1849.—How I long to visit Scotland! I think there is more *romantic* interest attached to it than even to poetic Switzerland. The latter puts me in mind of my father's Ode or Hymn in the Vale of Chamouni, and of the poem* of the beautiful Duchess of Devonshire on crossing Mont St. Gothard, verses that might almost have been admired for their own sakes, and not merely as coming from the pen of a popular Duchess and Beauty. But Switzerland has no historical associations in my mind higher than Aloys Reding, or at most William Tell, celebrated by the modern Schiller. While Scotland is connected with history from Macbeth as he appears in Shakespeare's play to James I., and from him down to the romantic, foolish, wrong-headed times of the Jacobites. That wild heath on which the witches met Macbeth almost symbolizes Scotland for me, or at least that with the "Lady of the Lake" to fill up the picture, or to present the picturesque of the land in another aspect.

That wooded bank of the Dart which you speak of, overlooking Torbay, takes especial hold of my fancy. I am pleased to hear of the primitive river-bathing. It reminds me of my Greta Hall days.

VII.

Tunbridge Wells.

To Miss FENWICK :

August 28, 1849.—I do not wonder that you are not fascinated with Tunbridge Wells. It is a fine place to drive out from in

---

* This poem, entitled the "Passage over Mount Gothard," forms the subject of the "Ode to Georgiana, Duchess of Devonshire," by S. T. Coleridge, beginning—

"Splendor's fondly fostered child!
And did you 'hail the platform wild,'
　　Where once the Austrian fell
　　Beneath the shaft of Tell?
O Lady, nursed in pomp and pleasure,
Whence learned you that heroic measure?" E. C.

various directions.   But there is far more refreshment and change in a sight of the changeful ocean while we are stationary.   The lie of the country is beautiful at T. W.; the terrace roads, and rich, green glades, and basin-like valleys want only running streams, and herds of deer and kine and sheep and goats, to be delightful.   But they *do* want life and movement. There is something to me quite depressing in their stillness. The beautiful trees seem made in vain, with no living things to frolic around them or lie under their shade, and the eye quite thirsts for water.   How oddly, too, the stones and rocks are seated on the turf, as if they had been taken from their native bed, and placed there by some giant who had been playing at bowl with them.

VIII.

Cholera and Infection.—Need of Sanitary Improvements.—Evening Walks at Herne Bay.—Sisterhoods : what they Are, and what they Might Be. —Remarks of Sir Francis Palgrave on the Resurrection of the Body, and on the Gospel Narratives of the Healing of Demoniacs.—Proposed View of the Miracles in Question does not " Explain them Away."—A Last View of Herne Bay. — Home and Social Duties. — Archbishop Trench on the Miracles.—Associations with Places.—Love and Praise.

To AUBREY DE VERE, Esq. :

Herne Bay, September 18, 1849.—Here I am still, kept here for a week longer than I intended by the encroachments of that fiend cholera, and the advice of our careful medical friend Mr. N——, who expressed his regret to my servants that I should return to town when the disorder was on the increase. I, for my part, believe that the cholera atmosphere is all over England, and that the complaint kills off most people where there are most people to kill, and in the most unfavorable circumstances in regard to diet, clothing, and the air of their dwellings.   I strongly suspect that the disorder is in some degree infectious, since one hears so often of many dying in one house, and sometimes when there seems to be no special cause of malaria.   I have been saying to John that it is an ill wind that blows no sort of good, and that it is to be hoped the present pestilence will improve the drainage of England.   Yet how little is done and doing in this way compared to what ought to be !   If men would but expend as much energy and ingenuity upon this subject, or half as much, as they do upon making money fast, or adding to the sum of amusements and luxuries, what a blessed, odoriferous nation we should be! I speak feelingly, dear friend, and beg you will feel for me, and for my E—— and our good Nurse, for Herne Bay, in a high wind blowing inland, as at present, resembles a certain compartment in a certain circle of Dante's "Inferno" in point of olfactory horribleness. E—— and I have to fly like chaff before the wind when we pass certain parts of the town, which we must pass daily to post our letters, and to strike into the two best walks of the neighborhood. I wonder whether the drainage of this good land, and the sewerage, and all that sort of thing, will ever be so perfected as to prevent all escape of noisome vapors. I often day-dream what England will be five hundred years hence—whether it will be free from coal-smoke, from butcher's meat exhibited openly in the street, from the abominations of Smithfield market, from rookeries like St. Giles, from nuisances affecting the atmosphere of every sort and kind; and I am sure, if there are seventy different species in Cologne, there must be seven thousand in London. But stop! let me turn the current of my thoughts into a better channel, or, rather, let me open a different spring and display a clearer, fresher stream, which will make its own banks green and flowery, and fit for your eye to rest on.

Imagine us on our evening walk out upon the East Cliff, a mile and a half from our present abode. We have passed a rough pathway, and, weary of a long, low hedge, the very symbol of sameness and almost of nothingness, have struck in by a breach which the sailors, who sit there with their observatory telescopes, have made upon the grassy cliff, and are looking upon the sea and sky and straggling town of Herne Bay. The ruddy ball is sinking; over it is a large, feathery mass of cloudage that *was* swan's-down, but now, thrilled through with rosy light, resembles pinky crimson flames, and the dark waters below are tinged with rose-color. In the distance appears the straggling town, with its tall watch, or, rather, clock tower, and its long pier, like a leviathan centipede, walking out into the waves. This time we are home before dark; another evening we set out later, and by the time we descend the cliff it is dark, and as we are pacing down the velvet path, as we call the smooth, grassy descent which leads to the town, there is Nurse in her black cloak waving in the wind, moving toward us through the dusk like a magnified bat. As we pass the town, what a chrysolite sky is before us, passing off above into ultramarine, spangled with one or two stars, and below into a belt of straw-color and orange above the horizon, over the οἴνοπα πόντον. Then we enter our lodging, and begin to feel—

> "Com 'è duro calle.
> So scendere e il salir per le altrui scale."

Thirty-six steps, steep ones too, have we to ascend to our sleeping apartments.

Then see us on the West Cliff. Just below us is a collection of huts, where live a set of people who gain a poor maintenance by picking copperas from the beach and cliff. When I first looked upon this hovelage, thinks I, this is like an Irish hamlet, and the people have an Irish look about them. Afterward I heard that they were Irish, and that the old Nelly, who so glad-ly received the scraps and fragments from our not very extrav-agant repasts, is from the good town of Cork. It seems that she went not long ago to her mother-land, and there received such unnatural treatment that she was very fain to turn her back upon it. And now she applies a transitive verb that be-gins with *d*, the harsher form of the verb condemn, both to Ire-land in general, and to Cork in particular.

Wednesday evening.—Right glad were we this evening on the East Cliff to welcome back the moon from her "interlunar cave." Lovely gleamed her crescent in the chrysolite depth above the crimson, yellow border of the vault serene. The sea was darkly steel colored, and all the vessels upon it looked black. How much do they lose who walk out only in the full daylight!

I am writing to dear Miss Fenwick, and wish to interest her for poor M. S——, who has lately lost her mother, and is left quite desolate and destitute. She tried a religious establish-ment, but found the life too hard, and fell ill there. Now she is trying another. But she complains of want of fresh air, and it is evident she only remains there for a home. She has sent me a plan of hours, showing how the time of the inmates is to be spent, and indeed it must require a burning zeal to render such a life tolerable. It is not so much the hardness and la-boriousness that must be trying, though it *is* hard and labori-ous, but the dryness, the monotony—nothing but private devo-tions and public, parish-visiting, and teaching. The only relaxation, almost, is reading aloud, with the needle. It is a pity that the bow is bent so tight ; or at least it is a pity that there can not be an honorable retreat of this kind, where persons who have no home of their own, no domestic duties to fulfill, might take refuge and be useful, without being worn out by requirements more than can be well complied with by any but the very strong, or those who gain an unnatural, feverish strength from zeal, and what some will consider fanaticism. I believe that worldly people much misjudge the zealous members of these institutions, but still I think that such systems can not answer in the long run, except by aid of superstition, if to succeed by superstition is to succeed at all. Whenever they withdraw active, earnest-minded women from home duties, or service to those with whom they are connected by blood or early intimacy or claim of gratitude, they are doing, I think, most serious mischief, for which they never can compensate.

September 21.—A note from Sir Francis Palgrave this morning. He says, " The Antiquarian theologian will tell you what he means by a celestial body, when the scientific philosopher of the nineteenth century shall have explained the nature of the ultimate atoms of which the matter constituting a terrestrial body is composed." Now I had not been complaining of the Antiquarian that he does not attempt to explain the celestial body. I remarked that he does attempt, not to *explain*, but to *describe* the celestial body, or, rather, takes it for granted that it is describable and conceivable by our present senses and faculties—that it is a sort of improved, brightened, subtilized, glorified earthly body, having the same form and lineaments, visible and tangible, as our present body. The question is, whether this notion is not disclaimed by St. Paul, and negatived by reason and by philosophy.

Sir Francis says, too, " The theologian of the nineteenth century, who explains away the narratives of demoniacal possession in the Gospels, is on the verge of explaining away the Gospels altogether." The subject often causes me anxiety, because I feel that it is going very far to believe that our Lord spoke as if He entertained the popular belief, while the popular belief was a delusion—*going far*, though only on the same road that all must enter who would reconcile the language of Scripture on many other subjects with truth of science. Still the case is not so bad, not at all such as Sir Francis says it is, if by " explaining away " he means understanding the demoniacs to have been madmen possessed with a belief that they were possessed by evil spirits, or, what is common with the insane, that they were evil spirits themselves. All that is related by the Evangelists may have taken place—a miracle been performed of which the moral purport, the use and aim, is the same as it would be on the popular supposition. Our Lord healed a madman, and sent the spirit of madness into the swine, probably in order to render the display of his power the more striking and impressive. It is unfair to call such a view an *explaining away* of the miracle : it is but another interpretation of the nature of the miracle—all the moral effect and the exertion of superhuman power remaining the same. This is a subject that has given me anxiety ; I can only say that the popular view is obviously a part of the old false philosophy which confounds the material and the spiritual—a philosophy now obsolete, except where it is retained for the sake of retaining certain ancient interpretations of Scripture, involving not mystery, but plain contradictions, which no human mind can really receive, however the owner of the mind may blink, and fancy that he is believing. As for the view substituted by Trench and others, namely, that the afflicted persons were influenced by evil spirits, as the sons of God are influenced by the Holy Spirit, I own it does not satisfy me, because it is, in fact, as irreconcilable with the language of the Evangelist, and the reported words of our Lord, and the manner in which His words were understood at the time, as the other modern interpretation, or, at least, it is quite irreconcilable by fair methods with them. I confess I have other objections to it, relating to the general view which it involves of the existence of personal evil spirits ; but it is sufficient to say that, to my mind, it does not accomplish what it undertakes, that is, to reconcile the Scripture narrative (understood as we may suppose the narrator understood it) with that view of the state of the demoniacs which Trench deems preferable to the ordinary ancient mode of possession. But no belief that is irreconcilable with reason will stand its ground among *reasoners,* upon whom ultimately the form of the popular religion depends. In all ages the learned and thoughtful have given to religion a frame-work accordant with the philosopy of their times, and with the highest reason which, in their times, had manifested itself. The Antiquarian must show the reasonableness of his creed, if he seeks to defend it. If he fails in this, he loses the game. But you perhaps think that he will not fail.

Friday night.—We have looked from the East Cliff down upon the sea, on one side, and the quiet inland view, with the village of Herne, upon the other, perhaps for the last time. The bright crescent of the moon was shining in the white depth, above a bank of soft blue clouds, broken into vultures' heads and many bold promontories, and the waters looked bluish gray, while swan's-down clouds, shaded as with India ink, were overhead.

The rapidity of agricultural operations, and continual changes going on upon the surface of the earth, give a spirit to the country. The canary, which, I believe, is raised chiefly in Kent, is a very pretty crop, looking at a distance like wheat. The ear is of the form of the hop blossom, but yellow. The grain is used for birds, and is very dear—as dear as wheat—nine pounds a quarter, I think I heard. There is more canary in this neighborhood than any other grain.

Monday.—As soon as one returns home, even in this season of London desertedness, one is dropped in upon in such a way that leisure goes away as fast as a plum-cake under the maw of a hearty, munching child. One young gentleman drowned half yester afternoon, and another took a large slice out of the evening. In the night I read "Trench on the Miracles," a book with which E—— and I are delighted. The author is High Church, but in point of doctrine follows very closely the early Reformers, as, for instance, on justification by faith, and is in decided opposition to the Romish views on the Virgin Mary, on the superior sanctity of a retired and celibate life, etc. He does justice to Spinoza, even in arguing against his views, refuting the charge of atheism and impiety brought against him, but deals with Woolston, Paulus, Strauss, and the other misnamed Rationalists, with all due severity. In his interesting section on the water made wine, he sets forth a metaphysical view which you and I anticipated in one of our searching, lengthy discussions. "He who does every year prepare the wine in the grape, causing it to drink up and expand with the moisture of earth and heaven, did now gather all those His slower processes into the act of a single moment, and accomplish in an instant what ordinarily He does not accomplish but

C c

in many months." This comes from St. Augustine, as so many fine-spun speculations do.

Yes, Curragh Chase must indeed be full of pensive recollections. So was Herne Bay to me. It brought back my children's early childhood, and my own anxious, yet on the whole happy wifehood. You can scarce imagine the change from wife to widow, from being lovingly flattered from morn to night, to a sudden stillness of the voice of praise and approbation and admiration—a comparative dead silence it seems. Vanity and the affections have such a mixed interest in this that it is hard to disentangle them, and the former during a happy state of marriage grows up unperceived under the shadow of the latter, and absorbs some of its juices.

IX.

Kentish Landscapes.—Scenery of the Lakes.

To Miss FENWICK :

September 19, 1849. — Strode Park, near Herne Church, is very interesting in its quiet Kentish beauty. There is a stillness in the landscapes of this county, owing to the want of water and moving objects, which is to my feelings almost melancholy. I can *admire* other counties besides my own native lakeland, other sorts of nature-beauty, abundantly; but I can not thoroughly *like and enjoy* any but that in which I was born. When in the country, I am full of thoughts and longings for my native vale. Friar's Crag, and Cockshot, and Goosey Green, and Latrigg side—all my old haunts, I long for. Yet, if I were there, I should find that my youth was wanting, and the friends of my youth, and that I had been longing for them along with the old scenes, the old familiar faces, and the old familiar places together.

X.

To AUBREY DE VERE, Esq.:

10 *Chester Place, October* 2, 1849.—My dear friend, after reading your letter this morning, perhaps from some stimulus to memory which it supplied, I recollected a repository within reach where your poem might be ; I searched, and lo! there it was. I have a copy of it in that less accessible store-house. But it is best to send at once the lost—not *sheep*, though there is no objection to calling it a pretty lamb, or a *serpentagnus*. My childish name for Herby was the *Onalopex*, which he generally uses now as the signature to his filial epistles. After coining this expressive and euphonious title, I was amused to find that I had been partly anticipated by Aristophanes with his *Chenalopex*. Between *Goose-fox* and *Ass-fox* the difference would not be enough to acquit me of plagiarism in a court of the Muses, unless I could bring evidence to show that I was ignorant of the Greek comedian when I invented the name. This was true. I never read Aristophanes till I was far from the period of chickenhood, and then only a few of his plays. So similar is *fun* in all ages of the world. Indeed, the fun of Aristophanes, which is but the light, sweet, creamy froth that floats over the rich substance of his serious satire, is especially child-like and playful — almost infantine. I have now in my ears Herby's childish, hearty giggle at the grotesque burlesque in the "Frogs," about Hercules and his greediness in the eating-shops of Hades.

Mr. Myers' book I have never found time to read yet ; but read it I will. I hardly ever read books of writers of Mr. Myers' opinions. I have a sort of dread of writers professedly on the same side as my father: they so often do an injury to his cause, either by their tone of mind or by their reasonings. Almost all the theology I read is what you would call Catholic, in its various shades and grades. Trench, for instance, is chiefly on your side, at least as to the points last discussed between us. He follows the reformed doctrines upon faith and the subject of *grace* generally; but he is of the old school on the matter of superhuman beings and existences. He is quite Coleridgian on the question of evidence, and often quotes S. T. C. with high respect. His doctrine of demoniacal possession is, I believe, the only one which is regularly sustained in argument at the present day; and, from *one* of your expressions, I should suppose it to be the same as your own, though you do call it an evasion. Another of your expressions seems to say the contrary. I should like much to know what your view, metaphysically set forth, really is, and how you distinguish it from that of Trench and St. Augustine.

Your reply to the theological avowals of my last letter would surprise me exceedingly, if I had not had considerable experience of such like discussions, if I did not well know how difficult it is for disputants to see clearly and fairly the opinions they do not themselves hold. You, dear friend, certainly do not see *my opinions;* but, looking toward the quarter where they lie, you behold a strange set of objects, with their feet where their heads ought to be, clad in hues worthy of some of the murky passages leading from certain colleges of skeptical philosophers down into Tartarus, or the twilight region which forms its outermost circle. *We* turn the miracle of healing the demoniac into "scenic illusion!" S. T. C.'s reasonings respecting a personal Satan founded on the "faculty *according to sense!* and swine are not subject to hypochondriacal delusions!" I do not wonder, in the least, at your shrinking from opinions which you behold in this odious and ridiculous light. Do come a little to particulars. What are those reasonings of my father on the subject of personal evil spirits which seem to you founded on premises and deductions of the mere isolated understanding? The objections which I principally referred to were *moral*—founded on the moral idea of God, and suggested by the spiritual sense. What these have to do with the faculty according to *sense,* I can not imagine. So far is it from being true, according to my view of the subject, that the objections against believing personal evil spirits are merely logical and deceptive—they rest upon an *intuition,* as we think, which is not the subject of logic. The logic has been all on the other side, and there has been plenty of it. But to all arguments, from the belief of the ancient Church, difficulty of disproving the doctrine, and so forth, we reply that to our religious sense it seems a discord and an anomaly. However, I know well that no one can in consistency reject this belief, who does not adopt principles with respect to the interpretation of the Bible which you have never adopted. I never dreamed of you *approving* the view; but am surprised at the particular form of your charge against it. But the truth is, that since my father introduced the distinction between reason and the understanding, we are very apt to ascribe every reasoning in favor of what we dislike to the inferior faculty, reserving the heavenlier one for the imputed parent of our own lucubrations. Perhaps I have done the same myself ere now.

It seems to me that you misrepresent our view of the miracle in Gadara, when you say we represent all that passed on the part of our Lord as a *scenic illusion.* To defend our opinion at full, and in all particulars, would take more room and time than you and I can spare just now; and I will admit to you that this is a question respecting which I have felt more anxiety than any other in which I have been led to adopt an interpretation which would commonly be considered unorthodox. It seems to be *going far* to suppose that our Lord took up the thoughts of His day concerning demoniac possession, if those thoughts were wrong. Still, as I said before, and you do not notice, it is but going on the *same road* as all must enter, who believe that there are errors or contradictions to truth of science involved in the language of the inspired writers of the Bible, in any case or to any extent. You take a distinction, as does Trench and all on your side, in this question. You say that belief in demoniac possession is not a mere matter of science. But here we come to an issue with you. We think that belief in demoniac possession belongs to psychology. Now psychology *is* a science— and, as a science, distinguished from truths respecting the soul which are purely spiritual and moral in their nature and consequences. According to our notions of the subject, at least, whether the beholders believed that our Lord expelled a fiend which was causing the effects of madness, or whether he expelled the spirit of insanity, is not strictly a *religious* question, but rather one of metaphysical divinity. I can not think, for instance, that the difference between your view of the miracle and mine is an *essential* one, in respect of the moral and spiritual purport, and of vital influences. This distinction serves as an answer to your argument for a personal Satan, founded on the language of Holy Writ. It seems to me that if we thoughtfully survey all the teaching of our Lord, we can not reasonably avoid the conclusion that He did speak more than is commonly supposed in *parables*, adopting the notions and psychologies of that day, as the vehicle for permanent, unalterable spiritual and religious truth. I could say a great deal to show how impossible it was for our Lord, compatibly with the aim and objects of His mission, the actual *scheme* of Divine Providence in His ministry upon earth, to have done otherwise than adopt the views of His age and country in these matters. I could derive many arguments, or what seem to me such, from a detailed examination of His language. But all this I must leave. I will only add on this subject, that pigs are not subject to hypochondriacal delusions after the manner of men—that a hog would not rush out of his sty, distressed by the imagination that he was one of Lucifer's fallen angels, and was to be reserved in chains and darkness to the last day. But that, nevertheless, madness is an affection to which brutal natures are subject—nay, that it belongs more properly to the bestial than to the human or higher part of our nature, when it afflicts men or women. You might fairly triumph on the score of this suggestion, or more fairly, if the swine, or a voice from the swine, had cried out "We are legion," and entreated our Lord not to torment them before the time. If swine are not subject to hypochondriacal delusion—*à fortiori*, how can they be fit subjects for the influence of evil *spirits?* After all, what is your view of demoniac possession? What is it you mean exactly when you say that evil spirits were first *in* the men and afterward *in* the swine? Was not rushing down the steep an act of madness?

As to our not being a whit nearer the true philosophy of the relations of the material and spiritual than the ancient Fathers, I must repeat, in substance, what I said before. In one sense we are not, perhaps—in another, I think, we are. I think men see more clearly the idea of the spiritual—perceive its essential difference from the material more clearly—than the ancient Fathers did, near two thousand years ago. (I do not decide about Plato.) *You* do not believe on these points what Irenæus and Tertullian believed. You *assume* in all your reasoning, consciously or unconsciously, something different. At least, if you do not, I think most reasoners on your side do, and that there are no *systematic metaphysicians* now living who would maintain with the old Fathers that the soul consists of very subtle matter. Kant, and the German metaphysicians who followed in his steps, and tried to go a little beyond him, pretended to no positive discoveries in the region of the spiritual. Kant's undertaking was to complete what Aristotle had begun—to describe more accurately than had been attempted before his day the nature of the human intellect, or power of cognition, and to demonstrate the limitedness of our knowing faculties.

I am sure you can not recollect my father's "Letters on Inspiration," if you think they deprive men of the guidance of the Bible; I believe that they make the Bible a surer and clearer guide than it can be on the other theory. Neither would we deprive men of the help of Catholic tradition—of any universal tradition which really and truly exists, and is not a mere image, a mere reflection of preformed theory in the mind of the believer.

Well, I must not send this off without telling you that I am wishing to see your article on Tennyson. Upon politics and poetry you and I think more alike than on metaphysical divinity, if I may venture to speak of my having an opinion on politics at all.

Do you know " Master Humphrey's Clock?" I admire Nell in the " Old Curiosity Shop " exceedingly. No doubt the whole thing is a good deal borrowed from Wilhelm Meister. But little Nell is a far purer, lovelier, more *English* conception than Mignon, treasonable as the saying would seem to some. No doubt it was suggested by Mignon.

XI.

Remarks on an Article on "Tennyson, Shelley, and Keats," in the *Edinburgh Review.*—Inferiority of Keats to Shelley in Point of Personal Character.—Connection between Intellectual Earnestness and Moral Elevation.—Perfection of his Poetry within its own Sphere.—Versatility ascribed by the Reviewer to Keats in Contrast to Coleridge.—Classification of her Father's Poems, showing their Variety.

To AUBREY DE VERE, Esq., Curragh Chase, Adare :

10 *Chester Place, November* 4, 1849.—My dear friend, I have just read your article on Tennyson, Shelley, and Keats, and

can no longer delay expressing to you my delighted admiration. I think it quite your finest and most brilliant piece of prose composition. It is full of beautiful sayings and pithy remarks, and it does a justice to Keats, not only which was never done to him before, but I should almost say a higher justice than any poet of this age has ever yet received from the pen of another. Nothing can be more admirable than your characterization of Keats; I was quite excited by it. What you say of Shelley is excellent, too; but this is more *entirely* new, and the whole article is worthy of you, which I think a good deal to say, for you have been rather tardy in bringing out your mind in prose writing. However, it is all best as it is, and I am sure the richest products are those which are delayed, so that they unite the peculiar qualities of the youthful mind carried forward with the greater force of a maturer age. I must some day soon talk with you about the article at large in detail. I wish you could see the copy I have marked.

One general criticism I must make, which you will not admit, because the *effect* I shall notice flows from your general temper and mental complexion as its cause. You have a propensity to aggrandize and glorify; you over-praise, both negatively and positively, by omission of faults and drawbacks, unless they are of a kind (such as Shelley's want of reverence, and Cromwell's antagonism to bishops and kings) especially to excite your disapprobation and dislike, and by the conversion of certain deficiencies into large and glorious positives. You are more displeased with Shelley's *wrong* religion than with Keats' *no* religion. That very deficiency in the mind of Keats which prevented him from being a *very* good man, and must, I think, forever prevent him from taking the highest rank as a poet—want of power or inclination to dwell on the intellectual side of things, or the spiritual organized in the intellect as soul in body, or, indeed, to embrace things belonging to the understanding at all—do you contrive to represent in the light of a very sublime, angelical, seraphical characteristic. It is all very well to distinguish meditation from contemplation, and to intimate that the mind may feed on deep thoughts and soul-expanding spiritualities, when it is quite apart from the region of logic and intellectual activity. But is it not the fact, and a painful truth which must forcibly strike every reader of Keats' letters and life, together with the mass of his poetry, that Keats never dwelt upon the great exalting themes which concern our higher peace, in any shape or form? "Oh, he was dark, very dark," said Miss Fenwick to me one day about Keats, and I heard her say it with pain. "He knew nothing about Christianity." You say he had no interest in the intermediate part of our nature, "the region of the merely probable." You give him "*intuitions*" (of the highest things which humanity can behold implicitly), and call his nature "Epicurean on one side, Platonist on the other." I wish I could see the matter as you do, or rather I wish the matter really were as you describe. But the truth seems to me to be rather this, that by means of a fine imagination and poetic *intellect*, Keats lifted up the matter of mere sensation into a semblance of the heavenly and divine, while the heavenly and divine itself was less known to him than to the simplest Bible-reading cottager who puts her faith in Christ, and bears the privations and weaknesses, or even agonies of a lingering death, with pious fortitude. The spectacle of Keats' last days is a truly miserable one; and I must say I think that, beautifully gentle as is your treatment of Shelley, if viewed in itself, yet *taken together with your judgment of Keats*, it is hardly fair. Surely Shelley was as superior to Keats as a moral being as he was above him in birth and breeding. Compare the letters of the two, compare the countenances of the two, as they are imperfectly presented to us by the work of the graver, see how much more spiritual is Shelley's expression, how much more of goodness, of Christian kindness, does his intercourse with his friends evince! Shelley, in his wild way, was a philanthropist; Keats was social, but the same spirit which led him to turn away from earnest questions which agitate the religious world—which agitated Augustine and Pelagius, Luther and Calvin, Hooker and Taylor, some of the greatest and best men that have ever lived—rendered him careless of promoting the good of mankind, or any but those individual felicities of the passing hour which added to his own earthly sensational enjoyment. He showed a pettish jealousy respecting the estimation of his works in his intercourse with contemporaries, and in his love affair he betrayed all the weakness, all the passive non-resistancy of a passionate girl of eighteen, together with the impetuosity of a young man and the sensitiveness of a poet. Again I must say that it is a *miserable* spectacle. I have read of late numberless lives of poets, philosophers, and literary men, not one that upon the whole inspired me with so much contempt as that of Keats. His effeminacy was mournful, and his deliberate epicureanism, with the light of the Gospel shining all around, even worse than mournful. I quite agree with you as to the excellence of his poetry, and that he was even, upon the whole, more highly gifted in that way than Shelley. There is even a greater intensity in his productions, a perfection in the medium of repose. Upon all that part of the subject you are as just and discriminating as you are eloquent and inwardly poetic. But when you go on to endow Keats with all the nobler qualities of a man and a writer, and, not content with showing him to be an exquisite, sensational poet, must exalt him into a poetical seraph, why, either I am too narrow and ill-natured, or I am too simple and straightforward and truth-requiring, to accompany you to the far end of your eulogium.

Shakespeare as little preached and *syllogised* as Keats does. But Shakespeare was a great philosopher, implicitly. Shakespeare furnished *material* for the contemplative, inquiring, discriminating intellect, and consequently intellectualists like Goethe, Schlegel, and S. T. C. find a perpetual feast in his writings, and are forever converting into the abstract what he presented in a concrete form. Not so will any great thinker ever be able to do with the writings of Keats. His flight was low, his range narrow; he kept on a lower level; and in that poor rejected critique of mine which Lockhart cut out of my article on "The Princess," I endeavored to show what advantage he derived from his unity of purpose, from his confining himself so entirely, and with such a faith and complacency in his own genius, within his native range of power and beauty. I did not attempt to do *justice* to Keats, I knew *that* would not be allowed in the *Quarterly*, even if I had been equal to the subject, which I am not, for no woman can give the portrait of a man of genius in all its masculine energy and full proportions. I did not present him with a grand chaplet of bays, as you have done in your noble criticism, but culled a nosegay of sweet flowers out of his own poems, and bound it about with a silken band of subdued praise and temperate characterization.

But this is a digression. I must make an end about Keats. I was astonished at your calling the last act of that, to my mind, wretched tragedy of his "very fine." I thought, as I read it carefully more than once, that any thing so poor and bad from a man of real, great poetic genius, never proceeded. I do not quarrel with it for not having the slightest merit as a drama. It has scarce any merit, as it seemeth to me, in any other way. It is as vapid as the little fragment "The Eve of St. Mark" is exquisite. Lastly, to conclude my objections on this part of the article, I do not understand why you ascribe *versatility* to Keats, and deny it to my father. What you say of my father on this head I think a deserved compliment, by which I mean, of course, not a flattery, but a just recognition of excellence. But it seems to me that you should have commenced with a *definition* of versatility, if not explicit to the reader, yet at least in your own mind. I should say that my father had shown a greater range of poetic power, that he had exhibited more *modes* of the poetic faculty, than Keats has done, or Tennyson either. Let us enumerate them :

1. The love poems, as "Lewti" and "Genevieve," which Fox thought the finest love poem that ever was written.

2. The wild, imaginative poem, treating of the supernatural, as "The Ancient Mariner" and "Christabel."

3. The grave strain of thoughtful blank verse, as "Fears in Solitude."

4. The narrative ballad, homely, as "The Three Graves ;" or romantic, as "Alice du Clos."

5. The moral and satirical poem of a didactic character, as the lines on "Berengarius," and those lines in which he speaks of seeing "old friends burn dim like lamps in noisome air," and "Sancti Dominici Pallium."

6. The high, impassioned lyric, as "The Odes to France," and on "Dejection."

7. The sportive, satirical extravaganza, as the "War Eclogue," "The Devil Believes," etc.

8. The epigram and brief epitaph.

9. The drama.

I must say good-by to you, though I shall chat with you again soon about your splendid article, which contains matter enough for four such as the *Edinburgh* has usually favored the world with. Think of the *Edinburgh* beginning in her old age to criticise poetry poetically ! "Age, twine thy brow with fresh spring flowers !"

XII.

Personal Likeness between Mr. Coleridge and Lord Macaulay.

To Miss MORRIS:

Chester Place, November 16, 1849.—I met Mr. Macaulay on Tuesday at a very pleasant party at Sir Robert Inglis's. He was in great force, and I saw the likeness (amid great unlikeness) to my father, as I never had seen it before. It is not in the features, which in my father were, as Lawrence says, more vague, but resides very much in the look and expression of the material of the face, the mobility, softness, and sensitiveness of all the flesh—that sort of look which is so well expressed in Sir Thomas Lawrence's beautiful unfinished portrait of Wilberforce. I mean that the *kind* was common to Wilberforce, but the species alike in Macaulay and S. T. C. The eyes are quite unlike —even opposite in expression—my father's in-looking and visionary, Macaulay's out-looking and objective. His talk, too, though different as to sentiment and matter, was like a little, in manner, in its labyrinthine multiplicity and multitudinousness; and the tones, so flexile and *sinuous*, as it were, reminded me of the departed eloquence.

CHAPTER XXII.

1850. —*January – July.*

LETTERS TO EDWARD QUILLINAN, ESQ., REV. HENRY MOORE,
AUBREY DE VERE, ESQ., MISS FENWICK, MRS. H. M.
JONES, MISS MORRIS, MRS. R. TOWNSEND,
PROFESSOR HENRY REED.

I.

Chinese Selfishness.—The Irish Famine.—Objects of Charity.—Church
Decoration, and the Relief of the Poor.—Butchers' Prices.—Sudden
Death of Bishop Coleridge.—The Anglican Formularies a Compromise.—Non-natural Sense put on the Baptismal Service by One Party,
and on the Articles and Homilies by Another.—Mystic Theory of Regeneration, Unsupported by Antiquity, Opposed to the Moral Sense,
and Contradicted by the Epistle of St. John.

To AUBREY DE VERE, Esq., Curragh Chase, Adare :

10 *Chester Place, Regent's Park, January* 4, 1850.—Some philosopher observes that not a man in Britain would make a
worse dinner if he heard that the whole Empire of China was
swallowed up quick. Of all people on the face of the globe,
the Chinese are those I should feel the least inclined to cry
about, whatever befel them ; and I think the reason is because
I have a strong impression that, less than any other people, do
they care what becomes of the rest of the world, that their
sentiments and sympathies are of the dullest possible description. But this starving state of the Irish does occupy my mind
a good deal. Here we are much better off, and yet it is dreadful to walk the streets of London, and to think that the poor
wretches who moan for alms are by no means the worst-off
class of the community. If I happen to have left my purse at
home, I am almost sure to come home unhappy about some
object whom I would fain have relieved. One day I was quite
upset by the piteous cry and pale, sickly face of a little old
woman. I had no money, and felt ashamed to ask Herbert
for a shilling, knowing that there were hundreds whom he would

think as deserving of charity. You must know that ever since I lost my dear mother, the sight of any feeble old woman agitates me. I felt quite glad that Lady Inglis was out, and that I had not to present my nervous visage to her. Soon afterward I walked the same way, and luckily found the old woman. I gave her 6*d.*, and had to give 3*d.* away before I got home. I will never go out again without a pence purse.

My niece Mary was talking the other day of the beautiful Ottery Church, with its groining and arches and painted windows. The siren drew me on; and on hearing that some of the small windows cost only £5, I cried, in a fit of enthusiasm, "I *will* give a window myself," though I had signified to her father that a sovereign for the eagle lectern in our church was the last money I meant to give for church decorations. I think I shall tell her that the £5 she shall have, but that I would rather she gave it among those poor, distressed, underfed slaves, whose condition she had been describing to me when we last went out together to dine at Baron Rolfe's, than spend it on the colored window.

Then what a shameful conspiracy there is among the butchers against the poor!—for such it may be called—when they are selling the inferior parts of animals to poor creatures by gas-light for 6*d.* per lb. My cook overheard a butcher extorting that price from a poor creature for *shin* of beef (mere *shin*) a few days ago. The farmers complain that they can not obtain a decent price for their stock—nay, sometimes can not sell it at all—and these butchers are putting into their abominable pockets all the profit, instead of lowering the price proportionably to the consumer. I have been writing notes about this to many of my friends, and all agree to make a stand. But I wish, when we make a stand for ourselves, we could do something in this matter for the poor.

Our Christmas has been saddened, as you may suppose, by the sudden and most unexpected death of William Coleridge, the only son of my never-seen Uncle Luke Coleridge.* He

---

* Luke Herman, seventh son of the Reverend John Coleridge, of Ottery St. Mary, was a surgeon at Thorverton, where he died at the early age of four-and-twenty. His wife, daughter of Mr. Hart, of Exeter, was a woman of much feeling, united with firmness of character. It is related that when her only son, William, asked the consent of his widowed mother before accepting the appointment of first Missionary Bishop of Barbadoes and the

was conscientious in public and in private, doing scrupulously whatever he thought right, and in his own family he was most loving, even-tempered, and amiable. William, in person, was just fitted for a Missionary Bishop. He was *six feet* in all his proportions, not merely in height, with a stentorian voice, fit to preach on a mountain, which he has been known to do in the Leeward Isles, and with a stout, robust, but not corpulent frame. We thought he had twenty years of vigorous life in him yet. He shone in the practical more than in the exercise of the speculative intellect; he managed the clergy under him admirably, and was much beloved in Barbadoes, spite of the war he had to carry on against selfishness and prejudice.

You are capital upon the Gorham controversy. Your witty saying about our good-natured Church, that, in trying to be *comprehensive*, she is sometimes *incomprehensible*, I have already repeated to a correspondent. I feel such disagreement and dispathy with both parties, that I know not which to oppose first. It seems to me that Gorham betrays an ignorance of the history of thought and the nature of language on this particular subject of Baptism and the New Birth, when he affirms, in common with Goode and many of the Evangelicals, that the framers of the Baptismal Service and of the Catechism, intended what they said of infant regeneration to be understood *hypothetically.* That they were not very clear in their minds what they meant I fully believe. But still they had some vague sort of notion that some sort of internal influx of the Spirit, or infantine *commencement* of regeneration, took place in the moment of baptism; and, although Waterland interprets the baptismal service in conformity with his own view, as if it pointed to no more than a *consignation* of the Spirit unto a future regeneration, I

Leeward Islands, she replied to him in the following letter : "MY SON,— Abraham's faith can be imitated. Go.—I am your mother, SARAH COLERIDGE."

Bishop Coleridge left England in 1825 for his tropical diocese, where his evangelical labors among the negroes, and untiring advocacy of the cause of justice and humanity, are well described by my father in his "Six Months in the West Indies," which contains an account of the Bishop's first visitation-tour among the Islands. Some time after his return to this country, he undertook the office of Warden of St. Augustine's College, Canterbury, a post for which his missionary experience rendered him peculiarly fitted. He had not been there more than a year and a half when the tidings of his sudden removal, with no warning of previous illness, caused a shock of grief and surprise through a wide circle of friends and relations.—E. C.

do not myself think (and in *this* point I differ from my father) that the baptismal service requires no such hypothesis as that of an instant internal change, or that any man would have written, "This child is regenerate by the Holy Spirit," who did not think the child had been internally affected. He would have chosen other words in which to express himself had he held Waterland's notion.

But no doubt it is very easy to interpret the expression into the doctrine of Waterland and of Burnet, and to say that "*is regenerate*" means "*is taken into a new relation with* the Church, and brought into a *new state*, which is the way of the Spirit."

Granting that the deniers of momentary internal regeneration are unable to use that one sentence in the sense of the framer, would it not be grossly inequitable to press that sense upon all the clergy, to exact it as a condition of ordination, when it is so well known that all those clergymen, or at least the major part, who construe the baptismal service strictly, do *not* construe the articles on justification strictly, but put a non-natural sense upon them, besides turning up their noses at the Homilies, which certainly the Reformers set forth as formally explanatory of their doctrine, and declared such in more than one article? Secondly, does it not seem hard and unfair, when there is an article expressly on Baptism, meant to be the rule of doctrine upon that point, to exact belief in a dogma not contained therein? The article obliges to no more than the general belief that the Sacrament conveys grace; how or when is not stated. Surely Turner argued fairly that the articles are the sole rule of doctrine upon all the points of which they treat. The Liturgy has a different use—not to keep opinion in bounds, but to give a tongue to religious faith and spiritual belief.

But what think you of Mr. B——'s *rationale* of baptismal regeneration? An adult coming to the font faithless and impenitent obtain spiritual regeneration! Surely, my dear friend, this is an awful perversion of the Scriptural doctrine. I will venture to say that not an authority could be cited for any such view from Polycarp to Pusey inclusively. Actual sin has ever been held to preclude the entrance of the Spirit; and yet, doubtless, it is more consistent with the ritual, momentary theory of passive regeneration, to suppose that a sinful adult may be a fit subject for it, than the contrary. This B——, with his lawyer's logic, may have seen. If the spiritual change, or indwelling, or both—for both are affirmed—are irrespective of the will and moral being—if they do not keep off sin from the soul to which they belong, why may they not be imparted to a soul in which sin is?

But the logical coherency, the reason of the thing in itself, is no sufficient argument for a High Churchman, who pins his faith on authority and tradition and the belief of past times. This mystic, non-moral regeneration was unknown to St. Augustine, unknown to any divine before the present age; and that great Father, "who is a host in himself," and who identifies regeneration with baptism, in more passages than could be recited in a summer's day, is, after all, substantially and in the spirit, far less distant from the Evangelical view of this question than from the Tractarian. For St. Augustine believed regeneration to be no mere potentiality, but a moral change begun in some inconceivable infantine way in infant baptism. I can cite a passage of his quite explicit upon the subject. In this way of expounding the matter he was followed by our great divines generally before Waterland. Tell me of one who explains regeneration in the same way as Newman and his school, and I will beg B——'s pardon.

That mystic doctrine is a pure modern development, and, like many developments after the fashion of Rome, it is even contrary to the views anciently held. B—— misrepresented the Romish doctrine of Baptism also.

What grieves my soul most in all the teaching and preaching of the Tractarian new-old divines is their treatment of St. John's Epistle. I would fain know how you reconcile the teaching of that Apostle of divine intuitions with the momentary theory. Does he not expressly declare that he who is born of God sinneth not, and that his seed (*i. e.*, divine, new-born nature) *remaineth* in him? How, then, can we affirm that they who sin habitually and grievously, and who do *not* retain a holy spiritual nature, preclusive of sin, are truly and essentially, and internally, regenerate.

The new-old theologian argues that, since every man commits *some* sin, therefore the Apostle's description is but a *beau ideal* of regeneration, attained by no man upon earth; and, therefore, spite of his definition, men who are full of sin, predominantly sinful, may be regenerate. This seems to me a monstrous inference and conclusion.

D D

Sinneth not, Hammond and other great divines interpret to
mean, *is not a sinner*, is led by the Spirit, and leading a holy
life. Would you scruple to say of a true saint, a justified person, fit for heaven, he *sinneth not*, in opposition to men who affirm, as the Jews affirmed in the days of the Apostles, that men
may be sons of God, by virtue of an outward revelation imparted to them, even while they are leading sinful lives? The
Tractarian shrinks from this interpretation, as a fearfully lax
mode of construing the Apostle's words, a doing away of the
high idea presented by the sacred writer — he, who explains
away the Apostle's words as we have seen! But there is no
laxity in the case. The Apostle is describing the character of
the regenerate estate, as one opposed to sin; if this or any other Scriptural description of the internal state of a true Christian is to be applied to actual persons, it must be *cum grano salis*.

Does it not make the Apostle's teaching nugatory and ob-
jectless to suppose him to have meant no more than that a
regenerate person *would* become incapable of sinning if he improved his advantages, although a true essential regeneracy is
compatible with a sinful life? What correction would this be
of the profligate pretensions of the Jews? Even they would
not have denied that a son of God would put down sin if he
acted as beseemed a son of the Most High. But they affirmed
that sonship was a matter of privilege, not conditional upon
inward dispositions, or necessarily accompanied by holiness;
and does not that Churchman say the same, who will have it
that, in spite of the regenerate nature, a man may continue in
sin?

If this is not Antinomianism, I know not what it is. Can
you really think that St. John would express himself, as he does
express himself in this epistle, were he conscious all the time
that genuine regeneracy, and that very blessed estate of which
our Lord spake to Nicodemus, may belong to those who can
and do sin habitually? Surely this is still more inconceivable
than that the framer of the baptismal service meant no more
by "is regenerate by the Holy Spirit" than Goode and Gorham
will have him mean.

It seems to me, after circumnavigating this doctrine of the
Tracts as often as Cook sailed round the world, that, from whatever point of view you consider it—whether from the nature of
our spiritual being, or from the language of Scripture, or from

the universal usage of the term regeneration—when it is not applied technically to baptism, but used according to the idea of a spiritual new birth—whether we try it by the nature of will, or by the *facts* of the moral *phenomena* visible in the baptized—it is equally untenable. I seem to see the lines of truth converging to one centre from off the different points of circumference. Change of the will, from carnal to spiritual, from enslaved to emancipate, from contrariety to reason, to coincidence, and confluence with it, is the central truth. Substitute for this a mystic, non-moral spiritualization, and you may labor forever before you can make all the different facts that relate to the subject of spiritual new birth converge and meet together in this notion for a centre.

The Spiritual in man is the Will; the Will, because it is will, can only be changed by its own act, under a higher impulsion.

St. John declares that the regenerate can not live in sin. We find that none abstain from sin but by acts of will, and an energy of submission to God. Thus the idea of a spiritual being born into a divine and sinless nature, and St. John's description, taken in the plain, undistorted sense, perfectly coincide.

II.

Various Occupations of S. C.—Fatigues of Chaperonage.—Barry Cornwall at a Ball.—Waltzing.—Invitation to the Lakes.—Effect of Railway Traveling on her Health.

To E. QUILLINAN, Esq., Loughrigg Holme :

February 9, 1850.—My dear friend, I must give you an installment of my letter debt to you at once, because your last contains a very kind and agreeable proposal, which should be noticed at once. A proper response I must defer. I have all my life been rather a busy person ; but I now have more work of various kinds to perform than ever before. There is first the domestic business. I can not spin this out, as some ladies do—ladies in the country more than in town. Still the inevitable part consumes a good bit of time of every year. Changing servants is specially troublesome : I have had to give Martha's character three times, and Caroline's twice, and to see nine or ten more servants, and write about others, in order to fill their places.

Then, 2dly, there is the care of my father's books—new editions and new publications; and of this work the unseen part, which does not appear, is more than that which does appear. I might have written many volumes in the time, of a certain sort, with far less trouble.

3. Reading with my children. This, I am sorry to say, has come to very little of late. But I shall resume my studies with E—— in a few days.

4. Money managements, letters of business, and all that relates to the care of my income. A *wife* knows nothing of this; but a widow, even with fellow-executors, has something to do in this way every year.

5. Business of society. This is the hardest, in one sense, of all the work I have to attend to. It is always beginning, never ending. For the sake of the children, I keep up the game more than I once thought I should ever have attempted. I go sometimes to evening parties, and twice, nay thrice, of late, have chaperonified at balls! I do think, of all the maternal self-sacrifices and devotednesses that can be named, that is the greatest. If it was not for the supper!—actually I have gone down to supper *twice*, in the course of the evening, out of sheer exhaustion. On the last occasion I fell in with Barry Cornwall. It was like getting into an oasis, with a clear stream bubbling along under beeches and spreading planes and rose-bushes and geranium tufts, and an enameled flooring of crocus, auricula, and violet, to be taken care of by a literary man, and have a bit of poetical and literary talk, after the weariness of witnessing for hours that eternal scuffle and whirl — H—— whirling around the room forever and ever, with first a black-haired, and then a brown-haired, and then a flaxen-haired damsel in his arms. (What queer indecorums these waltzes are! If twenty years ago one could have seen a set of waltzers of to-day through a time-telescope or *future*-scope, how we should have turned up the corners of our eyne!)

I have been interrupted, and forced to write notes of sociality and domesticity, till all the edge of my epistolary zest is rubbed off. I have seen friends, and hired a satisfactory damsel, as well as transacted lunch, since I began the letter. I dine out *homishly* with E—— at six, and so, instead of translating from my brain to the paper the letter, or an abridgment of the letter, which I have been writing to you in thought ("How swift is a thought of the mind," and what pen can more than toil after it at a measureless distance), I must speak of your kind invitation, and then say farewell for the present, though with an intent of renewing intercourse by pen and with you ere long.

I can hardly describe to you my longings to revisit my native vale and dear Rydal. But there are difficulties in the way. Twelve hours by the railroad at a stretch I could quite as little accomplish as I could walk twenty miles. Indeed I think the latter would not disorder me more than the former. I can by the sea-side walk ten miles, five in the morning and five in the evening, on a strong day, without disorder or any injury or exhaustion. But three hours of passive motion, or, if that is an incorrect expression, of suffering motion, the muscles unexerted, is enough to set up nervous irritation in me ; and this goes on at an increased ratio from that time till the journey's end. I should arrive a shattered creature, unable to enjoy any thing for six weeks or more. The journey might be managed by stoppages on the road, and I am always visionizing on the subject. But there is much to be thought of before it can be effected. I can hardly bear to think of the changes I shall witness. Keswick will be a place of graves to me ; but there would be a melancholy pleasure and interest in thinking of the departed. The changes in things and persons that remain are far more unwelcome.—I am yours, very affectionately,

SARA COLERIDGE.

III.

"Telling" Speeches not always the Best.

To Miss FENWICK, Bath :

February 15, 1850.—Derwent was full of the great Educational Anti-Government Meeting at Willis's Rooms. S——'s was the grand speech of the evening. His oration must have been very lively and ingenious and impressive, from D——'s report. But I have little respect for speeches that *tell* in assemblies of this kind. The probability always is, I think, that a speech accurately true and just, entering into the depths and intricacies which really exist in great questions, and doing justice to the views of all parties, would not *tell* half so well as a superficial harangue, full of half-truths and bold assumptions and affecting irrelevances, which call down a thunder of claps and "hear, hears!" yet, if read in the closet, would not convince a single soul who was sincerely seeking the truth, and was not decidedly of the speaker's mind beforehand.

IV.

Death of Mrs. Joanna Baillie.

To Mrs. H. M. JONES, Hampstead :

Chester Place, February 24, 1850.—Your note has affected me very much. Dear Mrs. Joanna Baillie, that unique Female Dramatist, thorough gentlewoman, and (last and best) good Christian, gone at last, leaving not her like, in some remarkable respects, behind her ! You were privileged, dear friend, to have that sight of the dear face after death, and to see that "friendly look," so consolatory to survivors, and so precious a treasure for memory. Her aged sister must feel desolate indeed. Blessed are they, says a famous old poet, whom an unbroken link keeps ever together. But this is not the lot of humanity, for death comes at last to break every chain, whether a hated or a loved one.

V.

Mr. Carlyle's "Latter-day Pamphlets" compared with his "Chartism."— Ideal Aristocracy.—English Government.

To the Rev. HENRY MOORE, Eccleshall Vicarage :

Chester Place, March 15, 1850.—Carlyle's "Latter-day Pamphlets," I own, I like less than any of his former works. It has all his animation and felicity of language in particular expressions, and there is much truth contained in it. But the general aim and purpose is, to my mind, less satisfactory than in any of his former writings. It has all his usual faults in an exaggerated form. His faults I take to be repetition, and the saying in a roundabout, queer way, as if it were a novel announcement, what every body knows, without any suggestion of a remedy for the evils he so vividly describes. "Chartism" had finer passages than any in these papers. Yet *that* was decried, and these are almost universally received with favor. The address to the horses in " Chartism," besides being new, was far better turned, more seriously pathetic in its humor, than the repetition of the thought in "The Present Times." Then I can not bear the depreciation of Howard, and the sneers at the Americans. His former works have all been devoted to exalting and elevating, defending and raising from the dust. The great drift of these is of a depreciatory, pulling-down character. As for the Irish, I would be right glad to see them coerced for their good, only they should be treated as children, not slaves ; and the great mass of the barbarous English, too, especially the class of little, prejudiced, pig-headed, hard-handed, leather-hearted farmers, who are grinding the poor laborers, and grinding their own nobles to nine-pence by mismanagement and asinine methods of tilling the ground. But who is to do these things? Who is to bell the cat? Then Carlyle tells us, as he told me in conversation long ago, that the few wise ought to govern the many foolish. But who doubts that? This is a kind of aristocratic sentiment which is common to all mankind who think at all. But we shall be none a bit the nearer to this millennial state of wise-man government by sneering, as Carlyle does, at the attempts of mankind to do things carefully and justly and methodically—sneering at all that by introducing the words "bombazine, horse-hair, red tape, periwigs, pasteboard, and so forth."

I, for my part, believe that the English government does *approximate* to this nearer than any other ; that Pitt and Percival, Peel and Russell, *upon the whole*, have governed—so far as they individually governed—as well as any man in the country would have done. Among men of letters have been many wiser, speculatively, and cleverer for some things. But it does not follow that they would have done better as Premiers, or could have filled such a place.

VI.

Home Amusements.—Reasonings of an Anti-Gorham Controversialist.—
Holiness the Evidence of Election, not its Ground.

To the Rev. HENRY MOORE, Eccleshall Vicarage :

March 21, 1850.—Herby tunes and grunts away at his cornet-a-piston ; and it is wonderful how little I care about his practicing, nervous as I am about sounds. Nurse said yesterday, "Now, if it was not Master Herbert, how mad we should be at all this trumpeting!" I feel that a young man must have some amusement, and that this is as harmless as he can possibly choose. I prefer it to the eternal chess-playing of last vacation ; for that brought him into company of which I could not judge, as they were out of my circle.

Talk of woman's reasoning! Tell me if any woman's reasoning could possibly be weaker than that of Archdeacon W——in his Anti-Gorham-and-Goode book on Holy Baptism? wherein he divides a man in two, putting his will, reason, understanding, appetites, affections—all that belongs to his common or general humanity—on one hand, and his personality or individuality on the other ; and represents the former as regenerate in baptism, the latter not. As if there were literally and truly two moving powers, two wills in one man—the one regenerate, the other unregenerate ; as if what is merely mentally distinguishable were practically separable! As if a man's personality were a distinct thing from all the rest of his being, and could remain unaffected, while "the common humanity" partook of the Redemption in Christ! Just as if you were to suppose the *roundness* of an orange (a mere abstraction) to be a distinct thing from the orange itself. And just as if the idea of personality itself did not belong to the common nature of man, or our general humanity!

And, then, how does this solve the difficulty, that the so-called regenerate prove unholy? Are not persons who lead unholy lives after baptism corrupt in their *will, appetites*, and *affections*, darkened in their *understandings*, unregenerate and unrenewed in all which he ascribes to the *common humanity*, which he supposes to be regenerated in baptism!

Then about Election. All the way through he misrepresents his adversary's opinions, and puts his opponent's objections on a wrong ground. For instance, he says (p. 101) that "to suppose that a gift is offered to all infants, bestowed only on those who are seen to be about to use it, is to rest the discriminating condition on the recipient's excellence, a notion opposed to the whole teaching of the Church," etc.

What an utter misconception of the views in question! The future faith and repentance of the infant are not supposed to be the *ground* on which the grace of election and regeneration is given ; but these moral attributes, when they appear as being effects of the grace unconditionally bestowed, as far as they go, are criteria and tests of election. They show *who* the elect are, but are never supposed to be the cause or *ground* of election, or that which determines God to elect some and not others.

VII.

Illness of Mr. Wordsworth.

To E. Quillinan, Esq. :

March 25, 1850.—My dear friend, I have just heard from dear Miss Fenwick of our beloved Mr. Wordsworth's illness. It is most painful to hear of this trouble, and not be able to be of use in any way. I am full of anxiety and sorrow. I have been dwelling much of late on dear Mr. Wordsworth and his state of health and spirits. My thoughts hover around him. He is the last, with dear Mrs. Wordsworth, of that loved and honored circle of elder friends who surrounded my childhood and youth ; and I can imagine no happiness in any state of existence without the restoration of that circle.

But I must not write more to you now. My earnest prayers for dearest Mr. Wordsworth's restoration will be preferred, both in selfish feeling and in sympathy.

Believe me, with most affectionate regards to dear Mrs. Wordsworth, and dearest love, whether it can be given or no, to the beloved sufferer.—Yours, in much friendship and sympathy,

SARA COLERIDGE.

VIII.

Lives of the Lake Poets.—Presumption of Incompetent Biographers.

To E. Quillinan, Esq. :

Chester Place, March 27, 1850.—Thank you, dear friend, for sending me the C—— notices, and do not think me stiff and stuck-up for saying that I should opine we had best keep aloof from them "*awthegither*," and let them "maffle and talk" as they like. There is not a grain of ill-nature in the composer or patcher. Persons have served my father far worse who had ten times as much reason to serve him well, from ability, knowledge, nearness to him, obligations of a certain sort to his mind, etc. It is not on account of any disparagement, too low estimate, liberty of criticism, or so forth, that I wish to have naught to do with the publication. I do not wish to correct its blunders, because this would seem to be a sort of sanction to the undertaking in itself—a tacit approval of the rest; and it is *this*, and not merely the way in which it is executed, that seems to me so unapprovable. Mr. C—— can not be expected to know clearly and fully his incompetence as a critic and biographer; but he must, if he has common-sense, be aware that he has not the means of correct information upon subjects on which he has undertaken to instruct the public; he must know, or ought to know, that he could not *honestly* engage in such a task. What should we think of any grocer or draper who set up in trade without some surer and more special means and opportunities of supplying the commodities he professes to deal in to his customers genuine, than this Mr. C—— has to supply readers with true accounts of Coleridge, Southey, and Wordsworth?

A man ought to have some special claim, some very particular qualifications for writing the life of another, who takes upon him this most difficult and delicate task. He ought to have been appointed to it by the subject himself, or to have some close connection with him—of blood or friendship—or intimate knowledge, from long and deep study, and special sympathy. It is true, these lives are but the stringing together of a few outstanding, external facts. But it is a fallacy to imagine that any sketch of a man's life, however meagre, can be given correctly without intimate knowledge. It is like what Sir Charles Bell so condemns, the attempt to draw outlines of the human figure without knowledge of anatomy and of inward structure. Besides, ought such meagre, coarse lives to be executed at all? To talk of my father's disagreeing with the Governor of Malta, a man whom he worshiped! Surely Mr. C—— knows little of Esteesian* anatomy. He can never have read the "Friend," to talk thus; yet he pronounces judgment upon it with a grand air of superior understanding—not love, but toleration, like Adam smiling on Eve!

---

* S.T.C.ian.—E. C.

IX.

Hopes of Mr. Wordsworth's Recovery. — His Natural Cheerfulness. — Use of Metaphysical Studies.

To E. QUILLINAN, Esq.:

Good Friday, 1850.—My dear friend, I must write a few lines, though in haste, to thank you for your welcome letter, and tell you of my joy in dearest Mr. Wordsworth's safety and his beloved wife's happiness. May he be restored to his former measure of strength, and may this crisis work a change for the better in his spirits! I have often mourned to think that he was no longer glad as of yore. He used to be so cheerful and happy-minded a man. No mind could be more sufficient to itself, more teeming with matter of delight, fresh, gushing founts rising up perpetually in the region of the imagination, streams of purity and joy from the realm of the higher reason—joy and strength and consolation, both in his own contemplations for his own peculiar satisfaction, and in the sense of the joy and strength and solace which he imparted to thousands of other minds. No mind was ever richer within itself, and more abundant in material of happiness, independent of chance and change, save such as affected the mind in *itself*. I felt with grief that his powers of life and animal spirits must have been impaired from what I heard of his fits of unjoyousness.

A visitor has taken away all my letter-writing time, so that all I meant to say must be screwed up into narrow room.

But one thing I must disown. Where upon earth, or under the earth (in the apartment of some gnome, I suppose, that lives under Loughrigg, in a darksome grot), did you learn that I supposed that you, "who do not study metaphysics all day long," can not understand S. T. C.? All the most valuable part of my father's writings, can, of course, be understood, as the writings of Jeremy Taylor or Milton or Gibbon or Pascal or Dante or Shakespeare, without specific study of mental metaphysics or any other *science*. Still I do think that some careful study of psychology, some systematic metaphysical training, ought to form a part of every gentleman's education, and more especially of every man who is destined for one of the learned professions, and still more especially for men who undertake to write on controversial divinity. A writer on doctrine and the *ration-*

ale of religious belief ought at least to know those principles of psychology and other branches of metaphysics in which all schools agree, and to have had some exercise of thought in this particular direction, and of course such a study must improve the faculty of insight into all works of reasoning which treat of the higher subjects of human thought.

X.

A Relapse.—Regeneration in the Scriptural Sense implies a Moral Change.
—Importance of Correct Statements in Theology. — Reason the only Standard of Spiritual Truth. — Distinction between Original Sin and Hereditary Guilt.— Views of Baptismal Grace: Anglican and Romanistic.—Hooker, Jackson, Taylor, and Waterland, on Baptism.

To AUBREY DE VERE, Esq.:

10 *Chester Place, April,* 1850.—My dear friend, I am much pleased at your wishing me to send invitations to Mr. and Mrs. T. and Mrs. J. M., and at your intention of attending at St. Mark's on the 18th yourself, and of what you say of the Institution, that it is one of the signs of life in the times. All this is saddened to me by thoughts of dear Mr. Wordsworth, and of his dear afflicted wife, his partner for nearly fifty years. How she will seem to live in waiting for death and to rejoin him and her beloved Dora !—if he goes now. For myself, I feel as I did in my own great bereavement and affliction—the thoughts and feelings which the event and all its accompaniments induce are, in the poet's own words, *too deep for tears;* they are deeper than the region of mere sorrow for an earthly loss or temporary parting. Sorrow for the death of those nearest to us, in whom our life has been most bound up, is absorbed in the gulf of all our deepest and most earnest reflections—thoughts about life and existence here and hereafter, which are more earnest, more *real,* and permanent and solid and enduring, than any particular thoughts and sorrows and troubles which our course here brings with it, or which contains them all virtually. The particular becomes merged in the general, happily ; and when we seem most bereft, most afflicted by the inevitable law of death and corporeal decay, we are only led to feel that this is but a part of the universal doom, that the loss and calamity which has come upon us at *this* time is but what, in a very short time, and in some form or other, we must bear. My grief respecting my

dear old friend has been to see him *grow old*. To my mind he has been dying this long time—not the man he was. I see in this, his final struggle, if such it prove, but the termination of that career of mortality. My tearful feelings are more for Mrs. Wordsworth than for his departure. The stupor and dejection which have long been upon him, when he was not roused by the presence of strangers, have been the precursor of dissolution and beginning of the stage of final decay. * * *

I have read your reflections on Baptism with deep attention and interest, and shall read them again and often. They come home to me more than other remarks ever did. Still they can not, and I think never will, move me from my standing-place, because, indeed, that has been chosen with all the powers of my heart and mind after the deepest and fullest consideration which I can give to the subject. It seems to me that the tendency of your reasoning is rather to withdraw the mind from what, after all, must be the foundation of all reasoning in religion, from the *real sense* of Scripture, interpreted according to the generally admitted rules of human language, and from the spiritual ideas, of which all true religion consists, combined and arranged according to the laws of thought. I hold the very highest doctrine of Baptism which is consistent, as I think, with a right scriptural, spiritual, substantial view of *regeneration*—with that view of regeneration which Scripture presents. The mystical view involves the belief that a soul in which the heart and understanding, the will and moral being, are wholly unaltered from the state in Adam, a soul which passes from the neutral state of unconscious infancy into positive immorality and ungodliness, pervading the whole character, has in baptism undergone that *regeneration, that new birth* in the Spirit, of which our Lord spoke to Nicodemus, that such a soul is really and inwardly incorporated into Christ, and a branch of the true Vine. Now it needs not long discussions. If you can look at this belief, and not feel shocked by it; if it does not seem to you contrary to the moral sense, contrary to the tenor of Holy Writ, and a profanation of sacred language—the direct and obvious sense of which denotes something *essentially* different, namely, a cordial, earnest, and unalterable acceptance of the Gospel of Christ, or of what the Gospel contains virtually and substantially, with such a spiritualization of the heart and life as constitutes the good Christian in character and conduct—I think we never can see alike on this point. There is a world-wide difference between a converted and an unconverted spirit ; it is the greatest soul-difference conceivable. Now I think the former *alone*, and not the latter at all, is internally, and in the primary sense, regenerate. No other view of regeneration than this appears to me reconcilable, fairly, with the declaration concerning being "born of God" in the Epistle of St. John, and indeed with whatever is said on the subject in the Bible.

The texts concerning Baptism in the Bible appear to me to be constantly misinterpreted and misrepresented by the maintainers of mystic regeneration.

Then what is that for which you contend? The belief that an unconverted soul has a high spiritual gift, an indwelling of Christ? This seems to me a shadow and a contradiction.

It is true that any words of human speech—*in, with, at,* or *by* —fall far short of the proper expression of any spiritual subject. Still they are the best, the only guides to the truth that we have. To us they are inexpressibly important. If once we let go that clew of our own inward ideas, the presentations of our minds, and the conceptions of which human language is the exponent, we plunge at once into the region of the dim and indefinite, where any monster with visionary pinions and uncertain lineaments may be presented to us as an angel of light and messenger from heaven.

Have you sufficiently examined the *ground* of your own belief with respect to baptismal regeneration? Are you sure that you stand on a sufficient spiritual evidence? Is your belief a coherent thing, or is it a mongrel, a heterogeneous compound of spiritual *ideas* with the *forms* and intellectualisms of a vague materializing philosophy, which had never yet separated in its conceptions the spiritual from the material?

Should we not recollect that there is but one standard to which all mankind can be referred on such subjects as these— but one last court of appeal? Is not that reason, or the power within the human mind of beholding religious truth, in substance, with the understanding or faculty by which the intellectual form of faith is determined? Whatever comes to us from without, by this inward medium we must receive it. If you accept a doctrine merely on authority which you can not prove to others to be reasonable and coherent, how can you look for unity of doctrine among mankind?

Have you asked yourself sufficiently, or examined carefully what are your real inducements to accept the mystical doctrine of Baptism? Is it from aught you perceive in the doctrine, *or what is proved by Scripture?* or is it not rather from a vague impression that this, because the strangest and hardest to believe, is therefore the highest form of faith, from early association, and the having heard from childhood that this is the true spiritual, orthodox creed, and from hearing a very forward, much-professing, much-assuming, and high-vaunting minority of the clergy evermore proclaim and declare that this is the *high*, and all others the low doctrine?

Some of the wisest men in our Church are, for good reasons, silent on this subject, and the wise men out of the Church are not attended to by those in it.

Then in my studies I perceive that the theory of Baptism has changed and varied from age to age, and that the primitive doctrine, though not that which I think the best, was certainly *not* that which is now set forth as the *ancient* orthodox doctrine of Baptism.

You thought some parts of my essay unsound. I should like to see what they are; I wish you would point them out particularly. But the truth is, do we admit the same principle by which the sound or unsound is determined? My view of Original Sin would be held unsound by ecclesiastics in general. But it is impossible for you to adduce any considerations by which my view of that subject could be altered, because it is matter of immediate intuition. To hold a creature guilty in the sight of God before it has acted, willed what it knows to be wrong and contrary to the divine law, is a decided anti-moralism. It is, as I apprehend, subversive of the very foundations of religion, or at least it strikes against, and, as far as it goes, it loosens and unsettles the foundation-stones of the faith. And, indeed, this is why I fear that there can be no further agreement between us—that you can have this thought presented to you, and yet do not positively and on the instant reject it. You say whatever is in the soul potentially exists truly. But how does sin in the sense of guilt exist in the soul of an infant? There is in every child born into the world a *capability* of *becoming* guilty. Will you treat a mere capability as if it had been actualized? As well might you say that the potentiality of fire in a flinty rock is to be treated as an actual conflagration, which men are to shun lest they be enveloped with flames and burned alive.

Now this notion that an infant has sin, in the form of absolute *guilt*, incurring the wrath of God, is the corner-stone of the whole " High " baptismal system.   How can I ever accept a system the very corner-stone of which I believe to be a gross error, a relic of Paganism?   There is no such thing in the Bible ; no intimation that a soul shall bear the consequences of any sin but that which itself has committed.   From one man we all inherit sin, because from him we all inherit a temptable body, and we all fall *as* he fell.   He is the representative of the whole race.

Then I feel quite assured that the view of Baptism which I hold is the only one which has been consistently held by the wisest men of our Church.   Bishop Taylor, when he is not on the subject of Baptism, always identifies a regenerate person with a holy person under the habitual influence of the Spirit. He teaches that regeneration is *begun* in Baptism, because Baptism is the first ordinary current in which the Spirit descends upon the soul.   This is a very different doctrine, though, in my opinion, not quite free from errors of statement, from the modern view, which declares that regeneration is *essentially* and at full a mystical change, having no *necessary* connection with change of heart and life whatever !

Hooker held baptismal regeneration to be the first reception of grace by the elect, the first inclination of their powers to future goodness.   This exposition also appears to me somewhat distorted from the truth.   Still both of these views avoid that monstrous anti-moralism which severs regeneration wholly from the restoration of the fallen will.

Jackson's view seems to have been the same as Taylor's. Waterland's doctrine is the same as mine as to *things*, differing only in words.   But Taylor, in saying that baptism and its effects may be disjoined, and that it grants effluxes to all periods of life, recognized that notion of the sacrament upon which Waterland proceeds.

It seems to me that the modern doctrine leads the maintainers into a great deal of quibbling and uncandid statement. People will not allow the inevitable deductions from their own tenets.   If we say that it separates the spiritual from the moral, they deny this.   But how can this truly be denied, if they give regeneration to a soul in which there is not, and never is to be, a moral new birth, or even the commencement of renewal?

Your mode of reasoning seems to be this. You do not attempt to remove the contrariety to the moral sense and to Scripture which I see in the modern development of the doctrine of baptismal regeneration. But you assume that this doctrine is a great precious truth; and then you say, if this be so, all your little fallible human reasonings about regeneration, considered as that change of the moral being which is commonly called conversion, must give way. You must suppose that all is right with moral regeneration and every other verity of religion, whatever you may fancy you perceive to the contrary. The Church doctrine must be served first. You must give *that* ample room and verge enough. You must see with your own eyes that this doctrine is not curtailed and defrauded, and then you must take it for granted that moral regeneration fares well enough, though to you it may seem to be screwed into a corner. This seems to me, I own, to be the upshot of your reasoning, and I can not think it safe or sound; it is essentially Romanistic. "Believe on the word of the Church (by the 'Church' being meant the dominant body of ecclesiastics for the time being), and shut your eyes to all seeming anomalies and contradictions. No belief enjoined by the Church *is* contrary to reason, but you, the individual, have no reason by which you can judge what is or is not reasonable or moral."

You would have me not regard Final Perseverance if it stand in the way of the Church doctrine. But we can not, if we would, set aside an inevitable deduction from undeniable premises. It will come to us even if we go not to it. Without putting fetters on the power of thought and reflection, we can not help arriving at it. That doctrine of baptism, which is incompatible with it, can not be true.

Have you any deeper, stronger proof of baptismal regeneration, according to a certain school, than Hooker, Davenant, Jackson, Hooper, and our greatest metaphysical divines had of the indefectibility of the regenerate estate? Regeneracy is a new nature, a *habit* of holiness wherein the soul is changed into an incapacity of sinning. What is the justified estate if it is not this? "Can a *son* cease to be a son?" Is there no such thing as a fixed habit of goodness which can not be lost? But I meant not to defend the doctrine itself. I only ask, have you

E E

any surer ground for your doctrine than I for believing this? But the modern tenet does not so much disprove, or seek to disprove, indefectible grace, as maintain that regeneration has nothing to do with it.

I would thankfully learn of you to heighten my view of baptismal grace, could this be done without lowering and degrading regeneration. But what you call a *high* view of Baptism seems to me a low one. You do not yourself hold that Baptism, without faith and repentance, renews the soul in all the higher provinces of our being. What is there high or exalted in the idea of a change which leaves the heart and mind unchanged, which does not even produce the necessary *ground* of a moral change?

The true sublime idea of regeneration is given by St. Paul— *"But we all with open face, beholding as in a glass the glory of the Lord, are changed into the same image, from glory to glory, even as by the Spirit of the Lord."*

This is regeneration, as I firmly believe—this gradual change into the Divine Image, in the light of truth, by knowledge. Nothing short of this, nothing but this, can be that change of which our Lord spoke to Nicodemus. Do you not lower the idea of the new birth when you cast out of it knowledge and goodness? You say that regeneration is a change passively undergone in the darkness of the spirit, without faith, without love.

What relation has the change described by the apostles to this mystical affection? We are told that *if* afterward the will consents to the "suasion of the new nature," to the power of the spirit in the soul, *then* a renewal of the moral being ensues. Does not this remind one of the *stone broth*, and is not the primary essential regeneration of the Pusey and Manning school mere stone and water? I must say for Dr. Pusey, however, that he is less unevangelical than most of his followers, and is content with defining baptismal regeneration after Jeremy Taylor's fashion, and yet, inconsistently enough, he calls it a *new nature*. But a mere *incipient* regeneration can not be a new nature.

My father was most desirous to hold the highest doctrine of Baptism compatible with reason and Scripture; but, like me, he never could accept the instant change of soul, in the *moment* of baptism, and agree that this was the new birth of which our Lord spoke to Nicodemus.

XI.

Death of Mr. Wordsworth.—Sense of Intimacy with her Father, produced
by her Continual Study of his Writings.

To E. QUILLINAN, Esq. :

1850.—My dear friend, your letter of this morning has made
me but a little more sad and serious than I felt before, and have
been feeling since the later reports. Thank God, that our dear
and honored friend was spared severe suffering! For days I
have been haunted and depressed with the fear that he had to
go through a stage of protracted anguish. He could afford the
torpor of the dying bed. His work was done, and gloriously
done, before, and will survive, I think, as long as those hills
amid which he lived and thought, at least, if this continues to
be a land of cultivated intellects, of poets and students of poetry.

Still, though relieved and calmed, I feel stunned to think that
my dear old friend is no more in this world. It seems as if the
present life were passing away, and leaving me for a while behind. The event renews to me all my great irremediable losses.
Henry, my mother, Fanny, Hartley, my Uncle and Aunt Southey,
my father—in some respects so great a loss, yet in another way
less felt than the rest, and more with me still. Indeed, he seems
ever at my ear, in his books, more especially his marginalia—
speaking not personally to me, and yet in a way so natural to
my feelings, that *finds* me so fully, and awakens such a strong
echo in my mind and heart, that I seem more intimate with him
now than I ever was in my life. This sort of intercourse is the
more to me because of the withdrawal of my nearest friends of
youth, whom I had known in youth. Still, the heart often sinks,
and craves for more immediate stuff of the heart. My children
are much. I trust that dear Mrs. Wordsworth will find hers, those
still left to her, sufficient to make life dear and interesting to her.

He is "gone to Dora!"* Yes; may we all meet where she

---

* Mrs. Wordsworth, with a view of letting him know what the opinion of
his medical advisers was concerning his case, said gently to him, "William,
you are going to Dora!" More than twenty-four hours afterward one of
his nieces came into the room, and was drawing aside the curtain of his
chamber, and then, as if awakening from a quiet sleep, he said, "Is that
Dora?"—*Memoirs of Wordsworth*, vol. ii., p. 506. Mr. Wordsworth died on
the 23d of April, 1850.—E. C.

is! She has been spared this parting. Would it have come so soon, had she not been severed from his side?

Will you convey to dear Mrs. Wordsworth, when it is desirable, my deep sympathy and assurance of my earnest prayer for her support and consolation, and in respect of the revered departed all the blessedness that our Father in heaven has to bestow on His faithful servants that are returned to His house of many mansions.—Believe me, dear friend, yours in deep sympathy and most faithfully,   SARA COLERIDGE.

Archdeacon Hare says to me, in a letter of late date: "I have a letter saying that his remaining days are few. If it is indeed so, a glory is passing away from the earth. Oh, what sweet odors of thankful love will mount with his departing spirit from thousands of hearts whose affections he has enlightened and enlarged and purified! This world will seem so much poorer without him; and yet his mind will still live in it as long as our language lives; and the treasures which he has been hoarding up for so many years will be found out among us!"

XII.

"Now we see through a glass darkly; but then face to face."

To Miss FENWICK, Bath:

10 *Chester Place, May* 6, 1850.—Dearest Miss Fenwick, I shall be thankful to see any letters from Rydal that you can forward. How dear Mrs. Wordsworth is to bear the trial of separation, and parting sorrow, and fatigue undergone in the last illness, is perhaps yet to appear. I trust we may augur well from the long-prepared state of her mind, and her living faith in the resurrection, and our reunion with departed friends.

Still, in some respects, the more we dwell upon that prospect, the more we strive to realize it, the deeper is the trial to our weak bodily frame. We know that another state of existence must be far other than this—that a spiritual world can not be like an earthly world. We can not penetrate the shades that hang over the state of souls on their departure. The subject that is spoken of under the name of the "intermediate state," of this what brief notices we have, and how ambiguous! How the best and wisest men differ about the interpretation of them! The more we think of the state after death, the deeper is the awe with which we must contemplate it; and sometimes, in weakness, we long for the happy, bright imaginations of childhood, when we saw the other world vividly pictured, a bright and perfect copy of the world in which we now live, with sunshine and flowers, and all that constituted our earthly enjoyment! In after years we strive to translate these images into something higher. We say, All this we shall have, but in some higher form: "Flesh and blood can not inherit the kingdom of heaven, neither shall corruption inherit incorruption." All this beauty around us is perishable: its outward form and substance is corruption; but there is a soul in it, and *this* shall rise again; and so our beloved friends that are removed, we shall see them again, but changed—altered into what we now can not conceive or image, with celestial bodies fit for a celestial sphere.

XIII.

Breaking of Old Ties.—The *Times* on Mr. Wordsworth's Poetry.—True Cause of its Different Reception on the Continent and in America.

To Mrs. H. M. JONES, Hampstead:

April, 1850.—I have been feeling and thinking much, as you will have anticipated, about the last days and hours of my dear and honored old friend Mr. Wordsworth. I feel as if life were passing away from me in some sort; so many friends of my childhood and youth removed, so few of that generation left. It seems as if a barrier betwixt me and the grave were cast down. Happily for me, friends of my married life and children have risen up to prevent me from feeling solitary in the world. Still there is something in the breaking of these old ties that specially brings the shortness and precariousness of our tenure here before us. Hartley and Mr. Wordsworth were great figures in my circle of early friends, and leave a large blank to my mind's eye.

Many thanks, dear friend, for sending me the *Times*. The article on the departed dear and revered poet, the *great poet*, I think, of his age, is respectful, though not up to the measure of what his warmest admirers think and feel. The remarks on his non-popularity on the Continent I consider mistaken; they ascribe, in my opinion, the ignorance of French and Germans of Mr. Wordsworth's poetry not to the true cause. If he were so peculiarly " English" that he could not be relished out of England, why is he so great a name in British America? There he holds even a higher place, or at least his claims are more fully and universally admitted among our transatlantic brethren than in England ; and his poetry has moulded that of the Americans far more than that of any poet of this age or of any other age. I was assured by Mr. Bancroft, the American minister, what I had often and often heard before (and he spoke it before a whole company at the Chevalier Bunsen's table), that my father's and Mr. Wordsworth's reputation in America was —I can not recall the expression, but I know he used the strongest and most energetic language on the subject. The Chevalier had just been saying that Wordsworth was not understood or cared for in Prussia. Moore and Byron were the great English poets there.

The reason to me is plain. Moore and Byron and Campbell are poets of a popular cast, and are admired by thousands who can not appreciate very refined and elevated poetry. This popular sort of writing sooner makes its way among foreigners than that which students would consider to be possessed of higher merits. Shakespeare is *now* read in Germany ; but he did not make his way there till during the course of this last century. He was never admired in France or Germany before the time of Lessing, nor generally appreciated before the lectures of Schlegel asserted and explained his immeasurable superiority to all other dramatists. While Shakespeare was neglected and called a " barbarous writer," the novels of Richardson and of Goldsmith were read and admired all over the Continent, not long after their appearance here. Why was this difference, but because they were far more easily understood than the great dramatist, and were, both in stuff and manner, such as would be relished by less cultivated minds ?

XIV.

"The Prelude."

To E. QUILLINAN, Esq. :

Margate, June 13, 1850.—All you tell me about the poem*
is delightful.   How wonderful it seems that the great man, our
dear, departed great one, should have deferred the publication
till after he had departed from this world !   How satiated he
must have been with praise and fame !   And what a glorious
existence must his have been to be the composer of such strains,
of such noble poetry—if, indeed, this poem is all that my father
ever thought of it, and you now say !

It is great pride and pleasure indeed to me that it is addressed to my father.   They will be ever specially associated in
the minds of men in time to come.   I think there was never
so close a union between two such eminent minds in any age.
They were together, and in intimate communion, at the most
vigorous, the most inspired period of the lives of both.

XV.

"The Prelude" a Greater Poem than "The Excursion."—Collection of
Turners at Tottenham.—"Lycidas," by Fuseli.

To Mrs. R. TOWNSEND, Springfield :

*   *   *   *   *   *   *   *

1850. — I have found your critique on "The Prelude."   I
tell you, as I do another friend—who is blind, as I think, to its
merits—that she must read again, and not run away from it on
account of the unusual, seeming-prosaic sound of many parts.
It is the production of a great poet in his vigorous period, and
I think it will be felt, on full consideration, to be a pregnant
and most energetic efflux.   The residence at Cambridge, which
my friend cries down, will live and command attention when
we are passed away.   I agree with those who say that it is a
greater poem than "The Excursion."   But there will always be
readers, and even lovers of poetry, who will never enjoy Wordsworth or Milton.   How many there are who can not under-

---

* "The Prelude."—E. C.

stand or relish Pindar, Petrarch, Dante, Spenser, not to speak of their scorn of Keats and indifference to Shelley.

I wish you could have had the treat we had to-day, in seeing a splendid collection of Turner pictures,* at the nice country-house of Mr. Windus, at Tottenham. I much admired a Fuseli —Lycidas lying asleep in the moonlight at earliest dawn, his dog baying the moon beside him ; Lycidas, in throat, cheek, and figure, wonderfully like my Uncle Southey. A most striking and poetically sublime production. * * *

XVI.

A Staffordshire Country-House.—Visitors at T—— Wood.

To Miss MORRIS, Mecklenburg Square, London :

T—— Wood, Wolverhampton, Staffordshire, July 1, 1850.— This beautiful domain—the house, which is built and furnished in the antique style with consummate elegance, and the grounds, which are in some respects the most to be admired of any that I have seen, especially in the velvet smoothness of the turf, and the fine effect of the endless-seeming vistas and clusters of tufted flower-beds seen from the windows—is the creation of Mr. M——. Twenty years ago an ordinary old mansion, amid ordinary pleasure-grounds, the abode of Miss H——'s father, stood where now stands a show residence, which is as fine a specimen of modern taste and ingenious arrangement as any I know. Perhaps I am the more struck because I have not ventured from my own home for several summers, and have never left Chester Place except for sea-side lodgings. When I compare, however, with this place, any of the seats I have formerly visited, they seem to my remembrance almost rough and unkempt in comparison. The only want is of water. We have no lake, no river, no streamlet here to give an eye and a smile to the "sylvan scene," only a sparkling fountain. The cedars scattered here and there among trees that sweep the green floor with their ample robes, in this leafy month of June, and others that tower upward in finest majesty, form a beautiful variety, the horizontal growth of their boughs contrasting with that of all the rest.

---

* Now dispersed, since the death of Mr. Windus.—E. C.

We have had a succession of gay parties, not only dinner company, but sets of guests coming to spend a few days, and soon after their departure succeeded by fresh sets, since we arrived here on June 22d.

Among the most interesting of the visitors have been Mr. and Mrs. B——, and Mr. and Miss H——, of B—— Park.

Mr. B——, the Prussian embassador's eldest son, is one of the smallest and most boyish-looking of men; his mind is all intelligence; his manners distinguished by a cordial frankness and sweet simplicity. His whistling to his own piano accompaniment is one of the sweetest musical performances I ever heard. Mrs. B—— is a picturesque, elegant young woman, and sings delightfully.

XVII.

Critique on Mr. Ruskin's "Modern Painters."—Figures and Landscapes Painted on the same Principles by the Old Masters. — Instances of Generalization in Poetry and Painting.—Turner "the English Claude." —Distinct Kinds of Interest inspired by Nature and by Art.—Subjective Character of the Latter.—Truth in Painting Ideal, not Scientific.—Imitation defined by Ancient and Modern Writers.—Etymology of the Word. — Death of Sir Robert Peel. — Vindication of his Policy.

To Professor HENRY REED, Philadelphia :*

T—— Wood, Staffordshire, July 3, 1850.—We have had several discussions of Ruskin's theory of the superiority of the modern landscape painters over the Cuyps, Poussins, and Claudes of old time. Wrong as I believe that theory to be, on the whole, and as to its conclusions, both from my own observations and from the remarks of artists and pictorial critics unprofessional with whom I have talked on the subject, I do not wonder at all to find you and other correspondents of mine in America warmly admiring and believing in his book, at a distance, as you are, from the works of genius which he disparages. It is a book of great eloquence, though the style has the modern fault of diffuseness, and the descriptions of nature with

---

* Mr. Reed was a Professor at the University, Philadelphia, and author of "Lectures on English Poetry and Literature," and other works. This lamented gentleman, as will doubtless be remembered, perished in the loss of the *Arctic*, on the return voyage, in 1854.—E. C.

reference to art which it contains are full of beauty and vivacity, evincing great powers of observation, and a mind of great animation; and no doubt there is some portion of truth in what he throws out concerning the defects of the old landscape paintings. But I think he is far from having perceived clearly and fully either the nature of the art of painting, or the true relations between the state of that art, as exhibited in the old landscape paintings, and as it appears in our modern English school. As that accomplished artist, R——, a great friend of Ruskin, observes, he ought, by the same principles upon which he condemns the old landscape pieces, to condemn the historical and sacred paintings of the same and an earlier age, and to these he attributes the same merits that the world has agreed to think they possess. I have heard that grand solemn picture, the "Raising of Lazarus," by Sebastian del Piombo, designed by Michael Angelo, declared unnatural, and an inferior production to what modern art could produce, by an accomplished artist, who applied to it the same tests of pictorial excellence as those with which Ruskin detects the vast inferiority of Claude to Turner. Now that picture (it is in our National Gallery in London) is pronounced the most sublime composition of the kind in the world by the first connoisseurs in Europe; and yet its merits are appreciated by persons of taste and sensibility in general, even those who have no particular, or what may be called *technical* knowledge of painting. Then Ruskin laughs at the notion of *generalizing*—but he says nothing that shakes my faith in the slightest degree in the common creed of critics on this point. Milton generalizes in word-painting in the fourth book of "Paradise Lost;" his description of the Garden of Eden brings together all the lovely appearances of nature which are to be found in all beautiful countries of the warm or temperate zones, not a single object which is peculiar to any one place in particular. His Eden is an abstract, a quintessence of the beautiful features of our mother Earth's fair face; and who shall say, or what man of sense and sensibility has ever yet said, that this generalized picture was painted on a wrong principle! Now what Milton has done in words, Claude, to my thinking, has done with the pencil; and all Turner's finest and most famous pictures are offsprings of Claude's genius. Turner was called "the English Claude" when he was at the height of his fame, and his beautiful "Dido and Eneas," or "Rise of Carthage," never would have been painted as it is painted but for the splendid prototypes, as I think they may be called, from the hand of Claude, in which sea, sky, and city are combined after a manner of his own, which, I scruple not to say, reports of the combiner's mind as much as of the material furnished by the world without. What Ruskin *meant*, I undertake not to say; but he *says* what I believe to be as great a mistake as can be entertained on this particular point — that a painter has nothing to do but to produce as close a copy as possible of particular objects, and combinations of objects, in nature. The fact is, that the works of every great painter are recognized as the product of an individual mind. If it was not for this individual subjective character, I believe they would be utterly uninteresting. May we not arrive at the truth of the matter by ascertaining what is, and ought to be, the painter's aim when he employs himself in imitating the natural landscape on canvas. Surely it is not to make the spectator acquainted with some particular spot or set of objects: it is to produce a *work of art;* not to present a camera-lucida copy of nature. It is not merely to call up the identical feelings which the very contemplation of the natural landscape itself is apt to excite ; but to remind us of those feelings in conjunction with the sense of the presence of an individual mind and character pervading and presiding over the whole. We may not, in looking at a Cuyp or Hobbima, a Claude or a Salvator Rosa, explain to ourselves the source of our interest in the picture, and its peculiar character, and yet it may be the impress of an individual genius— of this man's or that man's frame of intellect and imagination, that delights us when we contemplate a fine landscape painting far more than any thing else. The old painters were superior to the moderns, in my opinion, because an individual mind was stamped upon their works more powerfully and impressively. Their paintings have more character; it is *that* which I look for in these works of *art*. I do not go to them to improve my knowledge of *nature*. This is a difficult subject, and I am aware that I have been expressing myself broadly and laxly, and perhaps have gone as far from the exact truth on one side as Ruskin on the other. But this I do deliberately think, or at least strongly suspect, that as the power of representing nature on canvas must necessarily be very limited, and is rather suggestion than representation, the attempt to imitate the outward object beyond a certain point may injure the general effect of the work as a whole, and that the departure from truth which Ruskin points out in the old masters as faults and deficiencies may be part of the power and merit of their works as suggestive compositions. I believe that they did quite right to address themselves to the common eye of mankind, not to the eye of the painter. They present clouds and woods as we see them, when we rather feel their loveliness than think about it or examine into it. Turner has aimed at cramming into a piece of canvas or paper a foot square, or less, as much as possible of all that he sees in an actual sky on a certain day of the year, and has succeeded so well that critics complain of his skies as top-heavy. I have heard a clever engraver say that some of them might be turned upside down ; that they are solid enough to stand upon. It is impossible, in the too eager devotion to truth, to *all* the truth of the sky and her appurtenances, to do justice to earth, and exhibit the due relation of solidity between her and the firmament above her.

I have ever been a very warm admirer and ardent defender of Turner against his ordinary assailants. He is a poetical painter, and gives me more delight than any other modern artist. But Ruskin is extravagant, and defends him, in part, I think, on wrong grounds. If Ruskin is right, none can appreciate Turner but Turner himself. No doubt, every great creator must teach the world how and what to admire ; but if he does not succeed in being admired in the end, he has not done the work he pretended to do. No doubt Ruskin says rightly that a painter must aim at truth in his representations ; but the question is how much truth he can obtain without sacrificing the general effect—the emotions which the whole is to produce ; and I think he goes upon wrong, because one-sided principles, when he argues as if the only merit of a painting were its truthful representation of the outward object. A certain mode of doing this, derived from the painter's individual mind, is that which interests beholders more than aught besides, and I think I am referring to fact when I say it is this principally which assigns value to the picture. The pictures of Claude are not so true as those of many a painter whose works are not worth any thing in the market—Glover's, for instance, which people bought eagerly on their first appearance, because they were like the places of which they were portraits. Ruskin is quite mistaken, too, I think, in his remarks on the distinction made by my father and others between the terms "imitation" and "copying." Aristotle, in the "Art of Poetry," a standard authority, has used the former in the broad general sense, which Ruskin seems to suppose was the proper one, to produce a likeness of some object of observation by art, the intention of which is not that it should pass for the original by way of delusion, but to delight the spectator by the very sense of the art exercised. "Othello" is an imitation of a domestic story, in which the passion of jealousy was the principal feature, and the chief mover of the event. Mr. Burke says, quite in accordance with this usual meaning of the terms : "Whenever we are delighted by the representation of things which we should not delight to see in reality, the pleasure arises from imitation." I have not Ruskin's book at hand; but I remember he says upon this—"the very contrary is the case;" because he determines that imitation properly means no more than copying—the mere production of a duplicate or *fac-simile* of the original. Usage determines the meaning of terms, and I think it is against him. Even etymology, as far as it goes, is against him; for imitation comes from the Greek word which we render by "mimicry;" and he who mimics another man never means to pass for the man he mimics by disguise; the pleasure he gives rests upon the spectator's sense that the likeness is presented in a medium of diversity.

It is time to conclude this rambling epistle. Before you receive it you will have heard of the sad event which puts our papers in mourning—the death of Sir R. Peel, by a fall from his horse. I am one of those who honor Peel as a practical statesman. I am no politician, and always speak on such subjects with a reserve on account of my inadequate insight. But we can not help seeing, or seeming to see, some broad facts and acts in connection with them. It seems to me that Peel had the sagacity to see, when the time had arrived, what his country required, and *would* have, either from him or some one else, with more or less of struggle and commotion; and that he had come to the resolution to do what he had come to think, under the circumstances, necessary, let them say what they might, let him lose office or retain it. If he acted upon self-interest, it is not of the vulgar kind, but of that which was one with the good of the country; he could preserve the character of a statesman who would not sacrifice the public advantage to his own reputation for consistency. To say he should let others do what he would not do himself, with all the chances of their omitting to do it, or deferring to do it, seems to me a superficial, unpractical way of putting the matter.

XVIII.

The Black Country.—T—— Wood; the Dingle; Boscobel; Chillington.
—Liberality and Exclusiveness.—The Wolverhampton Iron-works.—
Trentham.—B—— Park.—Leicestershire Hospitality.

To AUBREY DE VERE, Esq.:

T—— Wood, Wolverhampton, July 9, 1850.—When we had passed Birmingham and entered the region of cinders and groves of chimneys, I thought it almost equaled the hideousness of a certain manufacturing portion of Lancashire. On the side of Tettenhall and Penn, Staffordshire has its share of sylvan beauty. The Worcestershire hills rise in several ranges faintly blue on the horizon. This house is all built (by Rickman) and furnished in the olden style, with great elegance and harmony of effect; the painted glass and old carved oak furniture are fine in their way; and the prospect from the windows reminds one of pictures of the garden of Boccaccio—the vistas are well managed, so as to *seem* ended only by the Wrekin in the distance; the turf is in high perfection—such an expanse of emerald velvet I scarce ever saw before; and the cedars scattered among the other trees delight me especially. I have been so long shut out from scenes of this kind that the place appears to me a finer one perhaps than it does to those who go from one smooth, ornate country-seat to another year by year. I do feel, however, the want of water. In the Dingle, a picturesque glen in the grounds of Mr. C——, of Badger, water has its due part in the scene, now in the foamy water-fall, now in the wide, quiet, gleamy pool, that reflects the sky and the branching of the tall, picturesque trees around. Yesterday we visited Boscobel, and E—— crept down into the hole where Charles II. is *said* to have hidden himself. I tried to go too, but felt too much stifled to proceed. I was pleased to see, in returning by the artificial lake at Chillington, which made me think of Curragh Chase and a certain poem of yours, that Mr. G——, the owner, allows the people of the neighborhood to disport themselves there on a certain day every week. How much more lively enjoyment he must have in seeing a crowd of people, whom his bounty has refreshed, than in keeping the whole spacious domain to himself all the week round, closed up in silent, melancholy state, no one going near that fine sheet of water embosomed in woods from hour to hour. Surely men will, in the course of time, become wiser about such matters than they have been, and frame for themselves deeper and keener pleasures, more stirring and expansive enjoyments, than wealth and large possessions have brought to our grandees for the most part. There is something to my feelings always deeply sad and sombre in the sight of a large domain belonging to some stately reserved proprietor, living alone there with but few inmates except domestic servants. It puts me in mind of the poor, bounded nature of our existence here, when it is regarded in a worldly point of view. There is great amusement in constructing a fine house and superintending the laying-out of a large pleasure-ground, such as my friend Mr. M—— has had here; but when all is done, and the place perfect in its way, I fancy the lawns and groves breathing sadness to the spirit of a proprietor, which is never felt when we gaze upon the wild woods and fields with a sense that we are not bound to enjoy them because they are ours.

From these reflections I was called away yesterday to go and see the Iron-works, a stirring spectacle strongly contrasted with the scenes which were in my mind's eye on my return from Boscobel and Chillington. First we saw the rolling-mills, and all the glowing processes of hammering down the masses and shaping the metal; then we proceeded to the huge furnaces, were hoisted up to the top of those enormous chimneys on a movable floor, inspected the craters of the artificial volcanoes on the platform at the top of the edifice, looked out over the land of iron and coal, and paid a visit to the engine, which cost £2500.

Regent's Park, Monday, July 23.—Dear friend, from my account of the furnaces, just as I was about to describe the red-hot river of melted metal, like Phlegethon bursting upward from Pluto's realm and rushing on under the light of the day, while a blast was let forth from an orifice above, and forth went the two impetuous elements, fire and air, flaming and roaring together—I was called away, and from that hour to this have never had time to write aught but necessary letters, accounts, etc. Before my return home on Saturday last I saw a great deal more of Staffordshire, and gained a strong impression of its richly sylvan beauty, enhancing a regret that those green lawns and fields, and full-foliaged banks of wood, are not enlivened with clear waters, living sparkling streams, and have no opportunity of mirroring their own charms in any but the sluggish, unclear, seemingly reluctant floods of made lakes and rivers. We visited Trentham, saw Broughton, Sir Henry Broughton's Staffordshire abode, and, lastly, went to stay at B—— Park, Mr. H——'s seat near Loughborough, which is as good a specimen of modern magnificent comfort, which is the proper phrase rather than *comfortable magnificence*, which, however, may be fitly applied to the grand and imposing hall. At Trentham the ministrative part of the establishment—the offices and kitchen and fruit gardens—are on a princely scale and in a princely style. The useful is nowhere abroad, I apprehend, so extensively and elegantly maintained, and this is truly characteristic of the English nobleman. The show-part of the house and grounds may be found fault with. Ten acres of flower-garden defeats its own object by disproportionateness. Some compare it to fairy-land; but fairy-land, so far as my travels have gone, includes more of the inimitable charms of nature—lucid streams, glittering lakes, basins of water, in which, by optical alchemy, liquid crystal is transmuted into beryl and emerald, forming rainbowy water-falls, and splendid masses of blossom, all of one hue, opposed to others, such as you describe in the Delphic region—instead of that endless succession of flower fantasticalities, and lawn and shrubbery artificialities. The park with its deer is good; but I like not the Arabian desert of gravel extended far as eye can go before the house, with the dull series of clipped laurel clumps to imitate the Versailles orange-trees, which seem intended to illustrate the stupidity of identity. The house is full of elegant apartments, but has no grand room; and abounds in pretty paintings without any fine pictures. It seems a show-place for pretty chintzes and Derbyshire ware. Some of the statues are to be admired, especially a bronze cast, in the garden, of the Perseus of B. Cellini, a sort of mediæval Apollo; a marble sitting statue of Paris listening to the prophecy of Nereus, which is most graceful, and listens all over. The Perseus has this defect: it wants the repose and decorum which characterize ancient art, not in the figure of the hero, which is but a variation of the Apollo, but in the victim. Under his feet is the death-stiffened figure of what, to the eye, appears no noxious monster, but only a beautiful woman distorted in the last agony; and the blood bursting from the neck looks like large ringlets of hair. Thus the Perseus seems a horrid murderer rather than a dauntless conqueror.

But I must run on to B—— Park, and tell you of that noble hall, which certainly is the most imposing house-interior, from the size and proportions of the whole, the rich, carved oak balustrades, etc., that I ever beheld, not even excepting the hall at the Duke of Sutherland's town mansion. There is a gorgeous window emblazoned with all the H—— heraldry. Mr. M—— criticises this, and maintains that it is too much covered with deep color, that a hall-window ought to admit a silver light; and again he criticises the formal garden, and objects to the abrupt transition from that artificialism into the park. But this criticism seems to me founded on too narrow a principle. The soul of B—— Park is heartsome ease, luxury, and comfort. T—— Wood is more poetical and picturesque, with its silver light and rainbow reflections on the white stone staircase. But for a dwelling-house, give me the comfortable brown light, which looks warm when you come in from a cold, wintry sky, and wraps you in cosy shadow when you enter weary with the heat, and eye-oppressed with the glare of our sudden summer sultriness and sunshine. Give me, too, the richly carpeted staircase, instead of cold stone. As for the garden, when you are *in it*, and look back upon the house (late Elizabethan, early James I.), you feel that it is the necessary adjunct to such a mansion, and that a picturesque Boccaccio garden, a sort of imitation of Armida's pleasure-ground, would be quite incongruous in such a place. But I must not go on describing at this rate. And, after all, the magnificent oaks of the park are the great boast of B——, for the oak is the weed of that district, as the elm in England generally, and Mr. H—— had only to clear judiciously. The owner of all this accumulation of showy luxury is, or will be, one of the richest commoners in England, and is as rich in amiable qualities as in worldly possessions. From the testimonies of those who know him well, and from his conversation, I judge that he is as faithful, generous, and affectionate

in heart, as he is frank, simple, and cordial in manner.   His
sister is a feminine copy of him ; and I do trust they will live
long together, like Baucis and Philemon.   They were all kindness to me, and Mr. H—— said I must come again to make a
longer stay ; and I am sure he paid me twice as much attention as he otherwise would, with so many guests to entertain,
because I seemed weak and delicate, and suffered dreadfully
from an accident, a minute grain of metal getting lodged in my
eye, between Derby and Loughborough, and causing me great
misery, till after I don't know how many searchings of the afflicted orb and its coverings, and assurances that whatever I
might feel or fancy, nothing *was* in it, the tormentor walked out
of its own accord.   There was an archery-meeting near the
rocks, a mile from the house, in Mr. H——'s grounds, on Friday, and our party was met by a select set from the neighborhood.   Mr. H——'s little speeches at the dinner had an air
of grave playfulness and business-of-society straightforwardness
about them which pleased every one.   Indeed, his whole manner is calculated to put all persons at their ease, and to excite
nobody's vanity.   Such blandness is like oil on the waves of
society.

CHAPTER XXIII.

1850. — *July – December.*

LETTERS TO MRS. MOORE, MISS FENWICK, AUBREY DE VERE,
ESQ., PROFESSOR HENRY REED, REV. EDWARD COLE-
RIDGE, MISS MORRIS, EDWARD QUILLINAN, ESQ.,
HON. MR. JUSTICE COLERIDGE.

I.

Rain, Roses, and Hay.—Experiences of Wesley as a Preacher among the
Agriculturists and Manufacturers.—Influences of Society, Education,
and Scenery on the Development of Poetic Genius.

To Mrs. MOORE :

Chester Place, July 26, 1850.—I have had a most agreeable
letter from dear Miss H—— this morning. She tantalizes me
with an account of the flood of sunlight which has been pouring into B—— Park, to illuminate all its beauties and glories
within and without, since our departure, and she almost brings
tears into my eyes by reminding me of the roses "laughing and
singing in the pouring rain," a touch worthy of Shelley, the
poet of the "Sensitive Plant;" and in the thought of these darlings rejoicing in the dews of heaven, which they think, I dare
say, made on purpose for them, she magnanimously adds—
"Never mind my hay." Now where is the farmer, or any *masculine* professor of hay, from the Land's End to Johnny Groat's
House, who would have said or felt, "Never mind my hay?"
All that set of men think their hay and stubble far more important than other men's gold and silver and precious stones.
So Wesley found, and Whitefield too. All their diamonds and
pearls did the farmers set at naught, and they were harder to
be taught to prize the great pearl of the Gospel itself than even
the poor benighted sinners and gin-soddened manufacturers.

All this is very uncharitable and narrow, perhaps you will
think, with a more fortunate race of husbandmen around you
than those I am thinking of. In truth, these field-preacher ex-

periences impeach particular circumstances rather than men. I
suppose if the farmers are more prejudiced and less ready to
give than manufacturers, and agricultural laborers more like
clods than operatives of the loom and the mill are like lumps
of greasy wool, it is because they have a less brisk intercourse
with their fellow-men, and the Promethean sparks of their
minds are not elicited so constantly by mutual attrition. "A
parcel of auld fells" will leave the men who live around them
as hard and savage as their own rocks and wild woods, if a
book-softened mind is not brought to bear upon them; and this
thought comes strongly upon me in reading Mr. Wordsworth's
great posthumous poem. He ascribes his poetry to his poetical
mode of life, first as a child, and then as a school-boy. But
whatever he might or might not have been without that training, certain it is that of the many companions of his early years
who shared it, none proved a poet, much less a great poet, but
himself. And there was my father, as the author remarks at
the end, city-bred, yet ready with an "Ancient Mariner" and
"Christabel," as he with his volumes dedicated to Nature. And
Milton was city born and bred too. I suppose, however, that the
detailed observation of the forms of nature exhibited, as Ruskin
remarks, in the works of Mr. Wordsworth, could not have been
but for his mountaineer education. How I should like to ru-
minate over this new feast with Mr. Moore !

II.

Domestic Architecture, Mediæval and Modern.

To Mrs. MOORE, Eccleshall Vicarage, Staffordshire :

Chester Place, July 27, 1850.—Mr. S—— is coming to see me
this evening. He appears charmed with my descriptions of
T—— Wood, Eccleshall, and B—— P——. He concludes
with, "An old manor-house is to me only less sacred and venerable than a church, and many degrees more so than a Dissent-
ing chapel !" I love and admire genuine remains of antiquity
in every way; and there certainly was a practical poetry in old
times, both ancient and mediæval, which showed itself not only
in books, but in pictures and statues and buildings. All we
can now do, for the most part, is to reproduce this old poetry,
to make likenesses of it in new material.

I must say, however, in regard to dwelling-houses, that the imitation is vastly better than the original, and that no houses of our ancestors could have approached in enjoyableness to T—— Wood and B—— Park. The *lowness* of the rooms is, to our modern feelings, the greatest possible preclusion of comfort. The loftiness of the sleeping-rooms at B—— Park is one of their greatest advantages, even more than all the sumptuous and elegant upholstery and pottery. At the house of Sir Thomas Boleyn (father of the unfortunate consort of Henry VIII.), though it is called Castle—something—with much state, or pretension to it, and much that indicates stately living for those times, there is a rudeness in the whole fabric, and a stifling want of height in the rooms, which made me feel that our ancestors' way of daily life must have been what we should now pronounce worthy of Gryll, who had such a "hoggish mind," in the days of Spenser.

III.

Biographical Value of "The Prelude."

To E. Quillinan, Esq., Loughrigg Holme, Ambleside :

August, 1850.—To all genuine admirers of Mr. Wordsworth's poetry, this strain of verse, so long kept back, will seem a treasure of high value as poetry, and most important as biography. The self-revelation of such a mind, the value of this—the *full* value—can not be perceived at once, it will be recognized more and more.

I must not go on pointing out fine passages, but begin the other business of the day. I will but name that on books at p. 108–9, and the fine touches at p. 157. All the addresses to my father, and notices of him, are, as you may suppose, a deep joy to me.

IV.

Mr. Tennyson's "In Memoriam."—Favorite Passages.—Moral Tone of "The Prelude."—Review of "The Prelude."—Neuralgia, and Dante's Demons.—English Reserve.—Interchange of Thought between Mr. Coleridge and Mr. Wordsworth.

To Aubrey de Vere, Esq. :

10 *Chester Place, August* 6, 1850.—I have just received your kind present of "In Memoriam ;" many thanks. What a treas-

ure it will be, if I can but think of it and feel about it as you do, and as Mr. T—— does! You said, "The finest strain since Shakespeare;" and afterward that you and Mr. T—— agreed that it set the author above all modern poets, save only W. W. and S. T. C.

My impression of the pieces you recited was that they expressed great *intensity* of feeling—but *all* that is in *such* poetry can not be perceived at first, especially from recitation. The poetry of feeling gains by impassioned recitation, but where there is deep *thought*, as well as emotion in the strain, to do justice to it, we must adopt the usual attitude of study, and dwell with our eyes upon the page; for the mind is a creature of habit, and moves but in the accustomed track.

Evening.—I have read "In Memoriam" as far as p. 48. I mark with three crosses—

"One writes that other friends remain,"
which you recited; with one cross the next—

"Dear house," etc.

Ditto the next—

"A happy hour," etc.

Most beautiful and Petrarchan is—

"Fair ship, that from the Italian shore."

Very striking is XIV., p. 22—

"If one should bring me this report."

XIX. and XX. I specially admire; and XXI., and still! more XXII.—

"The path by which we twain did go."

There is a very Italian air in this set of mourning poems throughout, as far as I have read. It is Petrarch come again, and become an Englishman.

Morning.—I read "In Memoriam" in the night, and was much affected by XXX.—

"With trembling fingers," p. 48.

The last stanza but one is to me obscure, and obscurity mars pathos. At present many passages are to me not clear, and some, which I *do* understand, strike me as too quaint. For instance, p. 43, last stanza. My father used to complain of Petrarch's eternal *hooks* and *baits* and *keys*, which "turned the lock on many a passage of true passion." "A shadow waiting with *keys*, to *cloak* him from his proper scorn," is to me all shadowy and misty, like some of Turner's allegorical pictures, the wantonness and willfulness of a mist-loving genius, who yet could clear off the mist, and display underneath a bold and beauteous plan, to delight the engraver and the lover of engravings.

This poem, and p. 14, and the betrothed tying a ribbon or a rose, are in his old vein of bright, fanciful imagery, vivid with detail. But the poems, as a whole, are distinguished by a greater proportion of thought to sensuous imagery than his old ones; they recede from Keatsland into Petrarchdom, and now and then approach the confines of the Dantescan new hemisphere.

I must tell you that "The Prelude" gains to my mind by reperusal. That is a fine passage at p. 306. Did you note the explicit recognition of eternal life, eternity, and God, at p. 361?

Perhaps one of the most striking passages of those that had not been printed before is that in "The Retrospect," describing the shepherd beheld in connection with nature, and thus ennobled and glorified. And, oh, how affectionate is all the concluding portion! I do feel deeply thankful for the revelation of Wordsworth's *heart* in this poem. Whatever sterner feelings may have succeeded at times to this tenderness and these outpourings of love, it raises him greatly in my mind to find that he was able to give himself thus out to another, during one period of his life—not to absorb all my father's affectionate homage, and to respond no otherwise than by a gracious reception of it. There are many touches, too, of something like softness and modesty and humbleness, which, taken in conjunction with those virtues of his character which are allied to confidence and dignified self-assertion, add much to his character of amiability. To be humble, in *him* was a merit indeed; and this merit did not appear so evidently in his later life as in these earlier manifestations of his mind.

Some friend has sent me the *Examiner*, which contains a review of "The Prelude," very exalting upon the whole, and in the main, I think, very just. I should not say, however, that the poem "will take a place as one of the most perfect of the author's compositions," although I agree with the critic in preferring it greatly to his later performances. The review is vigorously written, and worth your glancing your eyes over.

How wonderfully the wheel has turned! This poem, which you and I, strong Wordsworthians, do not think equal to his poetic works in general of the same date, is now received with such warm welcome, such high honor and hearty praise; while those greatest works of his, when they first appeared, met with only ridicule from the critical oracles of the day, scorn or neglect from the public, and admiration and love only from the few.

The diffuseness, want of condensation, is just noticed ; but I am pleased, I own, at the warmth and high style of the praise. I think you and I had not *quite* done justice to the poem, from comparing it with the author's most finished and finest compositions, rather than viewing it by itself, or as compared with other men's productions. * * * Passages are quoted from the "Residence at Cambridge," not as best and noblest in themselves, but, I suppose, as most suited to the *Examiner* newspaper, and certainly they are energetic, and contain strong thoughts in strong language. The passage on Newton I had stroked for admiration myself. The reviewers emphasize several passages, among the rest those on Milton—

> "With his rosy cheeks,
> Angelical keen eye, courageous look,
> And conscious step of purity and pride."

That noble line—

> "Uttering odious truth,
> Darkness before, and Danger's voice behind,
> Soul awful—,"

I never knew the birthplace of before.

But I must say good-night. This fierce pain clings to me. Oh! how well can I imagine that all the frightful shapes with which the infernal realms have been peopled, the demons with their prongs and pitchforks, may have been mere brain images —the shaping forth, by way of diversion and relief, in order to send it off from self, of these sharp pangs, and shattering, piercing nerve tortures! The vulture of Prometheus is more mental, but Dante's demons are personifications of Neuralgia and Tic-douloureux, or, at least the latter, if they sat for their pictures, would come out just like them. I don't wonder that Dante begged Virgil to dispense with their company, and would rather wander through the horrid circles without guide, than with those fierce ones—

> "Deh; senza scorta andiamci soli,
> Se tu sa 'ir, ch'i per me non la cheggio."

I always fancy I see Dante's piteous, frightened face, and hear his tremulous, eager tones, when he makes this petition.

Don't you observe how much less of sturdy independent pride and reserve there is in Italians, and all foreigners, than in us Englishmen? An English poet would not have written this of himself—he would have thought it babyish; and still more much of Dante's behavior with Beatrice, which I always have thought has a touch of Jerry Sneak in it. Indeed, he actually compares himself to a baby, fixing its eyes on its ma.

The *Examiner* says, "Coleridge was perhaps the only contemporary from whom Wordsworth ever took an opinion; and that he did so from him is mainly attributable to the fact that Coleridge did little more than reproduce to him his own notions, sometimes rectified by a subtler logic, but always rendered more attractive by new and dazzling illustrations."

I don't think this quite correct. I can see in this poem and in "The Excursion" also, some of the substance of my father's mind. I believe W—— took quite as much as he gave in this interchange.

V.

"In Memoriam;" its Merits and Defects.—Shelley's "Adonais."

To Edward Quillinan, Esq., Loughrigg Holme, Ambleside:

Chester Place, August 15, 1850.—I agree with Mr. Kenyon and Lady Palgrave, who are not mere *friend*-critics, that "In Memoriam" is a highly interesting volume, and worthy to be compared with the poems of Petrarch. I think it like his poems, both in the general scheme and the execution of particular pieces. The pervading though not universal fault, as you, I think, say too, is quaintness and violence, instead of force; in short, want of truth, which is at the bottom of all affectation, an endeavor to be something more and higher and better than the aspirant really and properly is. The heaven of poetry is not to be taken by these means. It is like the Elysium described to Laodamia, whatever is valuable in that way flows forth spontaneously like the products of nature, silently and without struggle or noise. How smoothly do all the finest strains of poetry flow on! the noblest passages in the "Paradise Lost," and in Mr. Wordsworth's and my father's finest poems! The mind stumbles not over a single word or image.

Shelley's great fault is occasional obscurity, I think. I find this even in "Adonais."

VI.

Public Singers.—Lovers at the Opera.

To Mrs. MOORE:

Chester Place, August, 1850.—I made a great effort last night to take advantage of Mrs. W. B——'s offer of a seat in her opera box, or one lent her, for myself and Herbert. We heard Sontag, and for the first time I was thoroughly entranced by a woman's singing. There is a softness and tenderness in the very highest warble of this lady-like singer, a combination of delicacy and brilliancy, which distinguishes her singing from that of all other women whom I have ever heard.

I delight in a man's tenor and contralto voice, but the fine, powerful, high-toned singing of women in general gives me little pleasure, wearies me in less than ten minutes. It wants body to my feelings; with a masculine background, I like it well. Catharine Hayes, in "Lucia," moved me not in the least, and tired me very soon. Coletti, in the "Barber of Seville," the huge Lablache, the pretty-handsome Gardoni—all pleased me greatly. But, oh! how comical it is to see those opera lovers without a particle of love, grief, or any other emotion in their faces, evidently full of their song, and not a bit of their middle-aged or unpretty sweetheart, feign to stab themselves in desperation, plump down most inelegantly, warble away to the last, and two minutes afterward pick themselves up, and appear before the curtain to bow, and receive the claps and compliments of the audience.

VII.

Simplicity and Sublimity of "The Prelude."

To Mrs. MOORE:

Chester Place, August, 1850.—I can not help thinking that a second perusal, when you have got over the shock of the style of certain passages, will bring you over to my opinion of the poetic energy of Book III. of "The Prelude." To my mind it is an earnest strain poured forth from the deep heart and soul of a great thinker and feeler. Those lines about Milton, p. 67, are such as none but a kindred spirit, who is to walk hand in hand with the blind bard, blind no longer, in Elysium, could ever have conceived or composed—

> "Yea our blind poet, who, in his latter day,
> Stood almost single, uttering odious truth,
> *Darkness before, and Danger's voice behind.*"

That underlined verse is a volume, a folio volume. It is sublime, worthy of the author of "Paradise Lost" in its pregnant sublimity. That plainness which reminds you of the "Rejected Addresses" is a noble simplicity, worthy of the depth and earnestness of the meaning. Then I admire greatly all that passage, p. 72, 73, and the passage at p. 76, "Like a lone shepherd on a promontory," and that subtle one at p. 78, "The surfaces of artificial life," and *very* fine indeed I think is the paragraph at p. 80—

> "And here is Labor, his own bond slave, Hope,
> *That never set the pains against the prize,*
> And Decency and Custom starving Truth,
> And blind Authority beating with his staff
> The child that might have led him;"

as he does at this hour—witness the Gorham Controversy, and the lists of subscribers to a great old proposition, least *understood* of all propositions perhaps that ever made a stir in Christendom, as Arthur Stanley so well shows in the *Edinburgh Review.*

VIII.

"One Baptism for the Remission of *Sins.*"

To EDWARD QUILLINAN, Esq., Loughrigg Holme, Ambleside:

August 19, 1850.—The article on the Gorham Controversy in the last *Edinburgh* is by Arthur Stanley. It seems to me very able. The argument about the article of the creed, "One Baptism for the Remission of *Sins*"—not *sin*, not *original* sin, in the sense in which any infant can have it—I had lately put on paper myself, and it seems to me, I own, very cogent. "Remission of sins" is a Scripture phrase spoken of adults, and can not surely be twisted into remission of an hereditary taint, without extreme violence.

IX.

Mr. Coleridge's Influence as an Adviser.

To the Rev. HENRY MOORE :

August 25, 1850.—In order to a good practical judgment, two things are required, a clear, strong understanding, and still more, perhaps, a generous, loving, sympathizing nature, which makes the state of another person's affairs, thoughts, feelings, present to the imagination. It was from the possession of these properties that my father's advice in matters of life and action was valuable, that his counsel to men in religious difficulties was felt to be of real service, as many have declared to me since his death. Men who are confined in their thoughts and affections to the narrow circle of self, and self at second hand, can not give valuable advice to those who are out of that circle; and the world is very apt to confound moderation in discourse, and prudence, with deep and comprehensive judgment, which rests on a very different basis, and results from far deeper qualities.

X.

Spiritual Truths beheld by the Eye of Faith in the Light of Reason.—The Gospel its own best Evidence.

To EDWARD QUILLINAN, Esq. :

Chester Place, September 10, 1850.—What I said to you the other day about the inseparability of faith from reason was only an attempt to express a characteristic doctrine of my father's, which has planted itself firmly in my mind. I spoke of reason, not as the faculty of *reasoning*, of reflecting, weighing, judging, comparing, but as the organ of spiritual truth, the eye of the mind, which perceives the substantial ideas and verities of religion as the bodily eye sees colors and shapes. It seems to me that a tenet which does not embody some idea which our mental eye can behold, is no proper object of faith. St. Paul says that we are to *know* the things that are given us of God, that they are to be spiritually *discerned*, that God *reveals* them to the faithful, yea, the deep things of God. Our saving faith consists, I think, in a spiritual beholding, a perception of truth of the highest order which purifies the heart, and changes the soul from glory to glory, while it gazes on the image of the divine perfections. The holy apostle prays that "the eyes of our understanding being enlightened," we may *know* Jesus Christ, and what is the hope of His calling. The doctrine of implicit faith, that men are saved by believing *something* to be true of which they have no idea or knowledge, I can not find in the Bible. My not finding would be nothing, if others could find and show it to me. But who can show it there? It seems to me to be a doctrine of fallible men, not of Christ himself, who always speaks of His teaching as being in accordance with the constitution and faculties which God has given us, as having its *witness* in our own hearts and minds, if they are not darkened by clouds of prejudice and passion. Reason is alike in all mankind; I therefore arrogate nothing to myself in particular when I express my agreement with the maxim of my father and many other thoughtful men, that faith consists in a spiritual beholding, "the evidence of things not seen" with the bodily eye. "By faith we *understand*," says the writer to the Hebrews, "that the worlds were framed by the word of God."

The Divinity of our Saviour, His Atonement, Justification by Faith, all the great doctrines of our religion, have been shown by the great fathers and doctors of the Church to be doctrines of reason, which may be spiritually discerned. If it were not for the witness of our hearts and minds to these great truths, I can hardly imagine that they would be generally received. The outward evidences are not appreciated by the masses, and by themselves would never suffice, I think, to a hearty reception of the Gospel. We are early *told* that the Bible is the Word of God, and believe it implicitly. But if we did not find and feel it to be divine, as our minds unfold and we begin to inquire and seek a reason for our beliefs, surely this early faith would fall from us as the seed-leaves from the growing plant, the husk from the blossom and fruit.

I can not think that there is any *outward* proof of the divinity of the Bible at all adequate to its general reception. People do not always theorize rightly on their faith; but many think they have had proof of their religion *ab extra*, when in reality it clings to them from its direct appeals to their heart and spiritual sense.

XI.

To E. QUILLINAN, Esq.:

1850.—My dear friend, last night in my sleeplessness I recollected rather uneasily my letter to you, and felt that I had spoken my mind too boldly and freely on the High-Church systems, one of which belongs to your creed.

This is in reality a compliment to you, or what I esteem very highly such; I should never have been betrayed into such plainness with any ordinary High Churchman. But I have ever felt in conversing with you on matters of religious belief, as if your mind was free, and your moral sense at liberty to judge of what came before it. I have always thought that your way of maintaining the credit of the " Catholic " religion was rather to ignore what we Protestants consider its errors of doctrine and injurious practices than to uphold and defend them, to represent them as at least no necessary part of the Romanistic system, and in your thoughts and reasonings to reduce the whole to that common ground of spiritual ideas which, as I firmly believe, alone is vital influencive Christianity. Possessed by this notion of your frame of mind, and recollecting how often I had heard you speak as if you were a disengaged spectator, *ab extra*, of formal Christianity—Christianity as it has been modified in its outward expression by national diversities, though Heaven forbid I should suppose you to be thus disengaged and on the outside of the Gospel faith, as it is a thing of the heart and spirit—I told you simply what impression I received from history, and the reports I read of the present procedure of the Papacy in different parts of the world; and what I had in my mind was, not to speak disrespectfully of your Church in a religious point of view, but rather to convey to you how far I was from sharing the popular notion of Romanism or Tridentinism, as if it embodied a kind of corruptness from which reformed Christianity is wholly free. You will hold me pseudo-philosophical, rationalistic, and so forth, I fear, when I avow my belief that popular dogmatic Christianity, whether of your Church or of ours, is not pure truth, and that a greater approximation to just views of the Bible and of the grounds of religious belief belongs to individuals than is found in any *party.* I think our state is better than yours, because, however inconsistently, it does allow more freedom of thought, and does in some sort, though imperfectly, bear witness to the great truth that saving faith is insight—perception by feeling, or knowing with the heart, and what Scripture calls the understanding, and philosophy calls the higher reason or spiritual sense of religious truth—not mere acceptance of doctrines, no matter whether felt or understood, which is to confound faith with obedience. I think, also, that there exists in our communion the same spirit of exalting the clerical body and representing them as *the Church,* which to us Protestants seems so objectionable and injurious to the true interests of Christianity. By this spirit, as it appeareth to me, the Synod of Thurles is actuated. What pretense is there for calling institutions "godless" which permit every pupil to be instructed in the religion of his parents, and merely require him to receive knowledge distinct from religion, without reference to his particular form of faith? History and metaphysics are perhaps the only branches of learning in which the particular form of faith of the professor would be even perceived, and surely a youth brought up in Romish principles would not have his faith undermined by listening to a Protestant's account of the Reformation. Is it genuine fear for pure religion that prompts these scruples, and leads the Catholic clergy " to deprive the Irish youth of their communion of a liberal education," rather than let them receive it, even in its secular branches, from any but the servants of Rome? Did they ever object to Trinity College, Dublin, on this score, at least for the laity? There is just the same jealousy in our Anglican High Churchmen—they would rather keep the people in ignorance than let them receive light not tinted by themselves. If the light they have to dispense is pure and strong, it will subdue every other to itself, and can only be increased by independent influxes from other quarters.

Pure metaphysics are in reality as distinct from religion as mathematics. No man could tell from the philosophical essays of Leibnitz or of Berkeley whether the author was a Roman or Anglican, or whether he was or was not a believer in Revelation, or even whether he was Theist or Pantheist or Polytheist, or at least even this would not be necessary to the enunciation of the philosophy. Leibnitz applies metaphysical principles to the elucidation of doctrine, and tries to defend transubstantiation on his own particular theory, the result of which seems to me to be that he arrives at the Anglican idea of the Real Presence as a spiritual power in the soul of the receiver. But in his pure metaphysical treatises his creed is not to be discovered.

XII.

Character of Christian in "The Pilgrim's Progress."

To the Hon. Mr. Justice COLERIDGE:

October 9, 1850.—I have been reading right through "The Pilgrim's Progress," with as much pleasure as if it was the first time. The only fault I *feel*, or care about, is that Christian, in his discourse with Talkative and with Ignorance, appears somewhat captious, peremptory, and overbearing. And, indeed, I must ever think that poor Ignorance had rather hard measure from first to last. The conclusion is sadly kill-joyed by the lugging of him off and poking him into that horrid hillside. Many a good Christian would be willing enough to adopt Ignorance's declaration of faith just as it stands.

XIII.

Comparative Merits of Sir Walter Scott's Novels.—Severity of Satirists on the Faults of their own Country or Class.

To AUBREY DE VERE, Esq. :

Chester Place, October, 1850.— * * * I am reperusing some of the earlier Walter Scott novels with great delight. "The Antiquary " is one of the very best, the fullest of genuine original matter. Oldbuck himself is a Sternean character. Elspeth is Macbethish, but Edie Ochiltree is the charm of the work. He is true poetry, a conception between Scott and Wordsworth, or at least with a third part of Wordsworth. The marrow of Scott's genius was put into this old Gaberlunzie and Bluegown. "Rob Roy" is *very* good, but not *so* good—more manufactured and will-wrought, in part. How admirable, though, is all that description of the Sabbath and the Laigh Kirk congregation at Glasgow. The Bailie, too, is very amusing. Andrew Fairservice is a satire on the Scotch of the keenest description. Do not we always find that the sharpest, most home strokes of satire come from those who are *near* to the subject of it, or even identified with it? Hook showed up the lords and lordlings of his day. Mrs. Gore exposes the follies of her fellow-fashionists. Berkeley and Swift have published all the characteristic faults of their countrymen to the world; and Scott and Galt and Miss Hamilton betray all the meanest and most odious peculiarities of theirs. Miss Edgeworth, too, in her "Absence" and "Castle Rackrent," has drawn as dark a picture of Ireland as the most decided enemy could have exhibited; and the author of "The Collegians" has written about Irish middlemen what, from an English pen, would have been considered a libel.

XIV.

Sympathy of Friends.—Collection of her Brother Hartley's Works.—Article in the *Quarterly* on the Homeric Controversy.—Infidelity.—Repeated Attacks on Revelation must be repeatedly met.

To the Rev. EDWARD COLERIDGE:

1850.—Your letter is, what I expected from you, kind and comfortable. Since my trial* began (and it is not light, all circumstances considered), I have received so many marks of warm sympathy and active kindness from friends, and from dear D—— and M—— such affectionate treatment, that some good has grown out of the evil. My estimate of the kindliness of my fellow-creatures, and the goodness of my own set of friends in particular, has been raised some degrees higher. The collection of our dear Hartley's Remains, with D——'s Memoir, is in the press, and I confess I have warm expectations from both, that they will at least deeply interest and delight a certain circle, if not a wide, yet a refined and genial one.

If we could but obtain the Worthies, and had encouragement to publish a collection of the printed essays, with the beautiful critique on "Hamlet" in *Blackwood*, there would be a compact little set of works, doubly gratifying to us as evidence that poor Hartley did not wholly waste the gifts with which he was intrusted, or dream away his genius without an attempt to bene-

---

* It was during the summer of 1850 that serious anxiety first began to be felt about my mother's state of health.—E. C.

G G

fit his fellow-creatures by it, by affording them refined amuse-ment, and in some sense enlightenment.

The article in the *Quarterly* on Mure's book and the Homer-ic Controversy is able, and contains much truth; but it is also full of unfairness, misrepresentation of argument, and plausible, but not deeply considered positions. This I can not but think, though I never pretended to a positive general opinion on the authorship of the Homeric poems; and while I entertained Wolf's idea of the possibility that the poems were national and the work of a school, as did also Mr. Wordsworth, Southey, and I believe Scott (and *they* may be supposed to have a poetic in-tuition), I have always seen unity in the plan of the "Iliad," what seems to me a true Achilleid. The unfairness of the ar-ticle to the Germans is gross, and to lay on their shoulders those opinions about "Titus Andronicus" and "The Two Noble Kinsmen," which were English before they were German, is ri-diculous. The proof from internal evidence—the delineation of character, knowledge of the human heart, etc.—seems to me very doubtful. You may see the tenderest touches of pathos, of very similar character, in our old ballads, which none deny to be by different hands.

Did you mark what is said in the beginning of that article (p. 438) on the subject of the *common foe* to Christianity? No attempt at answering *Strauss* amid all the thousand pamphlets upon theories of doctrine, the practical result of which is insig-nificant. *That* is indeed a fearful subject; that way the danger lies; and as there are sorrows too deep for tears, so are there perils and ills too real and serious for noise and agitation.

Infidelity creeps on in silence. Men whisper it to each oth-er; no man boasts of it or parades it; few even argue for it. Dr. Newman said the other day to some controversialist, "Let us talk about the prospects of Christianity itself, instead of the differences between Anglican and Catholic." Why does not he answer the adversary? Silent contempt is not politic in such a case. It is too ambiguous. Let our Churchmen con-quer first and contemn afterward. So our doughty old divines proceeded; and every age needs its own evidences and argu-ments against infidelity, as in every age the attack upon reveal-ed religion takes a form suited to the time.

P. S.—What I have said about infidelity is from the informations and lamentations of truly religious men. I talk with none but such. It is not the mere boasting of the foe.

XV.

Her Native Vale of Keswick, and the Valley of Life. — The Papal Aggression.—Reception of it by John Bull.—"Alton Locke."

To E. QUILLINAN, Esq. :

10 *Chester Place, November* 14, 1850. — The sight of your handwriting this morning gave me great pleasure, first, as coming from you ; secondly, as coming from a place and neighborhood in which, to the end of my mortal pilgrimage, my heart and imagination will ever be most deeply interested. Keswick and Rydal and Grasmere—then Netherhall and its neighborhood, but the two first far before the last—will ever be the scene of the millennial reign for me. They are my Eden—watered with my tears as they were. But how truly says the Poet—

> "Dewdrops are the gems of morning,
> But the tears of mournful eve."

Now there is a knock at the door ! Oh ! how I hate these peremptory knocks, now I have no goodman to expect, either morning, noon, or night. Well, well ! it is one comfort in sorrow that he and my dear mother had not to share my present trouble. Poor Nurse* has accompanied me all through this thorny valley, step by step; indeed she has her own thorns and stones on her side of the way, and we mutually pity and seek to console each other.

As for his Holiness and his false move, and Cardinal Wiseman and his unwisdom, I can not help thinking that while the Pope continues to be an Italian ecclesiastic, clear insight into the character and circumstances of John Bull will never be among his gifts, either human or divine. He might have

---

* This humble but faithful companion, whose sympathy is here affectionately recorded, is now gone to her rest, "full of years and labors." Ann Parrott entered our family in 1831, as nurse to my brother Herbert, and soon won the confidence of her master and mistress by her valuable qualities, displayed in many a trying crisis of sickness and sorrow, under which weaker minds and more selfish characters would have given way. After attending on my father, my mother, and my brother in their last illnesses, she enjoyed a period of well-earned repose and comfort, only troubled by the infirmities of her advanced years, and ended her days at Hanwell Rectory, Middlesex, in the summer of 1869.—E. C.

launched forth all sorts of spiritual fulminations—John would
have taken it as coolly as a cow would mesmerism, I was going
to say; but, really, after Miss Martineau's experiences, that is
no longer an available comparison, but would prove too much
on the wrong side. I was going to observe that this kind of
territorial pretension is just the sort of thing to rouse old John's
ire. It *sounds* at least practical and tangible; and unless the
Italian Potentate was prepared to take the Bull by the horns
in a material and tangible way, he had best not have ventured
the experiment. It was, as you justly observe (sensible man as
you are in reality, and Roman Catholic by courtesy and ances-
try), "an unwise move." His Holiness should have stuck to
spiritual primacy and supremacy — successorship to St. Peter,
the head of the Apostles. John would listen to all that with a
stolid air, as if it went in at one ear—as dear mother used to
say—and out at the other. But any attempt to parcel out his
acres, and dispose of his sees, which are closely connected in
his mind with revenues in solid coin of the realm—any attempt
of this kind enrages him; and without staying to inquire whether, after all, it is not as shadowy as the reflection in the stream,
for the sake of which the dog let go the solid meat in his
mouth, he ups with his hoofs and his horns, and plunges about
in as mischievous a style as that veritable bull whom some enthusiast of mesmerism lately endeavored to magnetize into the
rigid or the soporific state, and if he doesn't throw the Pope
himself over the hedge, not being able to get at him, he may
perhaps toss and maltreat no small number of his Holiness's
servants in this country. The sight of a Cardinal's hat will, for
some time to come, perhaps, make him as dangerous as a scarlet rag makes the four-footed sovereign of the meadow.

Have you read "Alton Locke?" Sir F. Palgrave thinks it
"poetry, and of a high order of conception."

XVI.

Objections to the Use of Mesmerism as a Medical Agent. — The Papal
Aggression.—Romanism in Ireland, in England, and in Spain.—"Anglo-Catholicism" a Transient Phase of Opinion.

To Miss FENWICK:

Bath, November 19, 1850.—Mr. T—— has shown most active
kindness on my behalf with respect to the mesmeric scheme,

and has supplied me with useful information at a sacrifice of
his own time, for which I feel truly grateful. His high intelligence and calm philosophic temper make me feel much favored
to have an adviser in him. Perhaps he will wonder why I am
still pausing, after having told him that I meant to apply to
Mr. P——, one of the mesmerists whose address he procured
for me from Dr. A——. The reason is that I do feel a repug-
nance, more than I can well express, to put myself in the hands
of one of these professional practitioners of an art, the grounds
of which are at present so little understood. I believe, from
what I have heard, that these men are capable of pretending
what is utterly incredible. One of them said he had cured ty-
phus fever in Mauritius, before there was time to know the result of any operations of his here, or that his friend was ill in
time for his mesmerizing. And even if it could be shown that
the fever ceased or had a favorable turn at the moment he was
mesmerizing, what proof would that be that his passes had cured
it? * * * As for the prospect of obtaining sleep regularly by it,
you see Lady Charlotte P—— is mesmerized almost daily by
her husband. Now I would never permit E—— to mesmerize
me. I have quite as much belief, quite as much data for believing, that it is exhaustive, and may be in many ways injurious, as I have for thinking it may have a beneficial effect. It
is an agent for good and for evil, and I have always thought
we ought to know the nature of it better before we meddled
with it. And yet, if none will try the experiment, science can
not be benefited. I should not like any young woman to mesmerize me, lest I should communicate to her any of my ailments. With professional persons it is different; they are paid
for what they do, and, if they do it not for me, will do it for
others.

Mrs. J—— has just been telling me of a benevolent friend
of hers who fell a sacrifice to mesmerism. She used to go about
administering mesmeric sleeps to sick people who were greatly
in want of rest, and among other patients she had one who was
subject to epileptic fits. After mesmerizing him, she had not
gone far from his house when she fell down in a fit. She was
subject to epilepsy ever after, and died of it. Up to the time of
her thus catching the brain-affection she was a healthy person.

Mesmerism has a special effect on the brain, and this was
one of my old objections to it. I thought, from the accounts I

had read, it had a strong tendency to produce epilepsy. It made Mrs. J. L—— delirious, and the visions called clairvoyance are all signs how strongly it acts on the brain.

* * * As for the concessions to the Romish bishops in Ireland, however unwise the measure, it does seem to come under a different head from tolerance of any territorial jurisdiction attempted to be usurped by the Papacy here. Romanism is the religion of the nation in Ireland, and a stout argument may be held for the opinion that it ought to be the inclosed and established Church. I own I have long been inclined to think so myself.

But this aggression is a political worldly movement, and ought, as it seems to me, to be treated and resisted accordingly. It makes one's blood first run cold, then boil, to read of the state and doings of the Papal religion in Spain, where it is rampant, and not kept down by surrounding Protestantism. It is a great pity that Blanco White's "Poor Man's Preservative from Popery," which in itself is very effective and well written, is known to come from a renegade priest, who broke his vow, and in the end renounced the belief in Revelation. I know no other book of the kind which is so powerful a warning against the insidious fiendish wickedness of uncontrolled Romanism. "Lencadio Doblado," too, is very powerful. The setting of parents against children, and children against parents, brothers and sisters against each other, both by the horrible Inquisition, and by the monastic system, which acts on a far larger scale— as we too often see the facility of lunatic asylums do here— seems to me so dreadful a fruit of the Romish system, that nothing in any other religious system of Christianity, at least, is at all to be compared with it in evil.

As for the Chelsea churches, it does indeed seem putting the cart before the horse to give them such prominence among the causes of the Pope's move. They are a part of the tide which has been rolling Romeward for some time, but had nothing to do with the first impulse. My own belief certainly is, and always has been, though I have been seeing it, in course of time, more and more distinctly, that what is called Anglo-Catholicism —vulgarly Tractarianism or Puseyism—is out of place in the Church of England, and if it has not a place here, it is hard to say where its place can be, for in the Church of Rome it can not exist, except as enlarged into Romanism. The principles of the Anglo-Catholic writers are contrary to the principles of the Reformation, those on which the formularies of our Church were framed. It is very true that our first Reformers held many of the opinions of the Anglo-Catholics, but they did not carry them out as Anglo-Catholics do now; their new doctrines did not harmonize with the old ones which they still retained. They reformed *doctrines* only to a certain extent, and this is the less to be wondered at because reform of doctrine, as such, was not the original chief object of the Reformation, but the putting down of corrupt immoral practices, which had grown out of doctrine, and were more and more overshadowing the truths of the Gospel, and darkening its pure light.

XVII.

Troubles and Anxieties.—The Shortness of Life not to be Regretted.

To Miss MORRIS:

10 *Chester Place, November* 24, 1850.—In a new Memoir of Gray, sent to me by a kind American correspondent, Professor Reed, of Philadelphia, I read just now the words of the poet— "Alas! I am a summer bird, and can only sit drooping till the sun returns." This brought in an instant to my mind Mrs. A—— with a special vividness. Day after day have I been thinking of her and of you, dear friend, longing to renew intercourse with you, and to know how you are. Little did I think when I perused with delight (though greatly affected by the opening) your letter to me at T—— Wood, that troubles and anxieties would intervene to prevent my answering it till the latter end of November. Oppressed as I have been with penwork, it was not of course the fatigue of writing a note that kept me silent, but the reluctance to enter upon the anxious matters which have been occupying my mind. Some of these related to my health, about which I have been more alarmed than ever before. Now I am better and in better spirits; but there are so many troubles pressing upon my mind relating to dear friends, that I have felt of late more strongly than ever how little cause we have to regret that the probationary period of our existence is such a brief one, unless a longer one would really bring more minds to repentance, which is much to be doubted.

XVIII.

Early and Late Periods of the Wordsworthian Poetry compared with Ancient and Modern Art.—Mr. Ruskin's "Modern Painters."—Scott's Novels. —Character-drawing in the "Black Dwarf."—The Anti-Papal Demonstration.—Aversion to Popery in the English Mind.—The Pope's Move Political, not Religious.—Intolerance of Romanism.

To Professor HENRY REED, Philadelphia:

10 *Chester Place, Regent's Park, November* 29, 1850.—My dear friend, many thanks to you for two most interesting volumes. The "Descriptive Sketches," with your inscriptions, is a very gratifying present to me. I have always wished to possess early. editions of Mr. Wordsworth's works, but have not been able to lay hold of many. I can not bear the arrangement of his poems in the later editions by subject, without regard to date. The *tone* of the productions of the poet's second and third eras is as unlike that of his great vigorous day as a picture of Stanfield to one by Claude or Poussin; and who would mix modern painting in a gallery with those of the old hands? I remember seeing an exhibition of Calcott's landscape painting in the third room of the British Gallery, ancient masters occupying the first and second. You can hardly imagine the deadening effect upon them. They were reduced to chalk and water. Any believer in Ruskin, I think, must have been staggered by that most odious, or at least injurious, comparison and contrast. Not that I do not admire Ruskin's *first* book: it has great merits; but it never converted or perverted me from Claude and Cuyp and S. Rosa, though it made me more than ever, if possible, a worshiper of the great mistress of all painters—Nature. The edition of Gray and your Memoir are a valuable addition to my library. I possess the Eton edition, and had lately been reading Mitford's Memoir, which rendered yours all the more interesting. Yours ought to supersede every other. I think your conclusion about Gray's poetic power is the truth of the matter. The author of the "Elegy," admirable as his poetry is, in its line, would never, I think, under any circumstances have helped to found a new school of poetry. His mind did not present a broad enough surface for the spirit of the age to operate on, even if the new age, which moulded and was moulded by the last generation of poets and romancers, had set in while he was in his vigor. No new aspect of human-

ity or nature is exhibited in his writings. Even Cowper was, in my opinion, far more original as to thought and way of viewing things; and the personal character of Cowper was more broad, bold, and interesting than that of Gray. I am reperusing with great delight the *Scotch* novels of Walter Scott. I do not think "Ivanhoe" and the later works, not on Scottish ground at all, to be reckoned among the great influencive literary productions of the age—productions of genius—along with "Waverley," "Guy Mannering," "The Antiquary" (perhaps the best of all), "Rob Roy," "The Black Dwarf" (which has been underrated), "Old Mortality," "The Heart of Mid-Lothian," and "The Bride of Lammermoor." "The Black Dwarf" has an especial merit in exhibiting the odd mixture of feelings and opinions on particular subjects which may exist in uneducated, unreflective minds. Hobbie is persuaded that Father Elshie has dealings with the Evil One, and would try to prejudice his salvation if he had an opportunity, yet is willing to receive a benefit at his hands, and is grateful for it, and is affectionately disposed toward the donor, as if he believed him as "canny" as other folks. The tale, however, was overshadowed by the superior merit of "Old Mortality;" and no doubt it has more than the ordinary amount of absurdity in the foundation.

I own I rejoice in the anti-papal demonstration. The fear and anger of this crisis will, of course, subside; but what has taken place proves, and will show the Romanists and Romanizers that there is a deep-seated and wide-spread aversion to Popery in this fair realm of England, which will come into effective action whenever any attempt is made to reintroduce a form of religion which is the natural and necessary enemy to liberty in all times and in every place. I can not agree with C—— S——, who thinks we are straining at a gnat after swallowing the camel of Emancipation. There was nothing that directly endangered our Church in a Romanist's sitting in Parliament; and the principles of toleration and equal dealing with all religions, *as such*, seemed to demand the concession. But this act is, in reality, a political movement, and ought to be politically resisted. My Uncle Southey would have refused Emancipation in the foresight of this and similar aggressions; but it was better to give them *rope* enough to strangle their own cause in the hearts of the whole nation. Now no man can say that the intolerance and ambition of Romanism are obsolete;

all must see that it is a born Ishmael: its hand is against every other form of religion, and every other form must keep a controlling hand upon it.

————

NOTES ON PROFESSOR REED'S MEMOIR OF GRAY.

To Professor HENRY REED, Philadelphia:

1. "Now, gentlemen, I would rather be the author of that poem than take Quebec."* This is indeed a most interesting anecdote. Query, is it characteristic of military men to be thus liberal and unappropriative? I certainly think that no class of men are so antipathetic to poetry as men of science, mathematicians, and students of the particular sciences to which mathematics are applied. The wider study which we call philosophy, the science of mind and of being, metaphysics at large, is not thus antagonistic to poetry, which it embraces in the compass of its analysis. A metaphysician like Kant is too knowing, too all-sided in knowledge, to despise poetry as a mere mathematician does. Plato's sentence upon poetry in the "Republic" has probably been misunderstood. Chemistry seems akin to poetry, from the brilliant shows and curious combinations which it deals with and produces: it is full of sensuous matter for poetic thought. Davy poetized, though he was not a *poet*. I have heard Mr. Wordsworth say he might have been; but I think my father, though he overflowed with love and admiration of Davy, would not have subscribed to that opinion. He thought Wordsworth too lavish in his attributions of poetic power in some directions, as he was generally considered too slow to allow it in others. When, in my girlhood, I visited my

————

* Remark of General Wolfe on Gray's "Elegy in a Country Churchyard."—E. C.

brother Derwent at St. John's College, Cambridge, with my dear mother, Professor Sedgwick showed me the statue of Newton by Roubiliac; and I remember his expressing an opinion, from which my young mind strongly dissented, that he was a far greater man than Milton. He knew far more of Newton's merits than I did; but even then I *felt* Milton as many able, intelligent men can never do. And I doubt whether the power and services of a philosopher like Newton can not be far better estimated by one unlearned in mathematics and astronomy, than those of the author of "Paradise Lost" by one who does not *understand* poetry. For the benefit of poetry is poetry itself: both to the composer and the reader, it is its own exceeding great reward.

2. Eminent men, especially in literature, have often—that is, many eminent men have owed more to their mother than their father, both for nature and education. It was so with Cowper, and with my Uncle Southey. But the truth, no doubt, is, that the parent whose mental qualities are most powerful and excellent, most moulds the child that attains to eminence, whether it be father or mother; and when it happens to be the latter that is best endowed, we are struck to find that man has derived less from man than from woman. Seldom has a poet had so poetical a son as S. T. C. had in Hartley. Not one poet of this age besides has transmitted a spark of his fire to his offspring; but it is curious that Hartley excelled most in the sonnet, in which my father excelled least of all the poetic forms that he attempted.

3. "A father's wrongs." Is not this a doubtful expression? But for what had gone before, we should suppose wrongs *suffered by a father* to be meant. A *wrong* is not a wrongful thing done, but undergone, I think, in common parlance. "Your injuries," is more ambiguous; perhaps this is a wrong of mine, my active wrong to your style.

4. All that you say in these pages about the enduring benefit of early happiness and tranquillity is well said, and to my mind most true. It is good for children to be happy and cheerful; early sorrow weakens the mind, if it does not harden it, as premature disproportionate labor injures the body. I know this by experience, and have carefully shielded my children's young minds from the trouble and constraints which so often came upon my own, like frosts and wintry blasts on the "darlings of the spring."

5. "Horace Walpole."—The oftener one meets Walpole in the region of literary biography, the more the impression is intensified that he was a respectable fribble, and a compact, solid mass of frivolity and littleness. Poets are men of feeling—*κατ' ἐξοχήν*. They are like soft rich peaches, and he was the crude, hard, winter pear, that leaves a dint in every one of the former with which it comes in contact.

6. I should think Gray could never have written a philosophic poem under any circumstances. I do not believe that Keats would ever have written any thing better or higher than he had already produced. The "Hyperion," so exalted by Shelley, is, to my mind, a falling off in felicitous originality. It is too Miltonic. Gray was a very sensible man, and self-knowing. His own remarks on the poetical habits which unfitted him for the production of a poem of large compass seem to me excellent, and are just what I have often heard in other words from W. Wordsworth and H. Taylor. There must be flat, rough spaces in an extensive domain, if it is to be traversed with pleasure, and Gray could not be flat and rough like Dante. He had not masculine force enough for that. His verse, if not neat and polished, would have been nothing. Elegance and tenderness are its very soul.

7. "Delicate handwriting."—It is remarkable what fine hands men of genius write, even when they are as awkward in all other uses of the hand as a cow with a musket.

8. Do you think "Ion" a work of poetic genius, or only of an admirer of poetic genius? There was a want of poetic judgment in putting such intense Wordsworthian *modernism* into an ancient form, I thought; like drinking Barclay's entire out of an antique drinking vessel, meant to hold Chian or Falernian wine. "Ion" was of the same kind as the Düsseldorf reproductions of Raphael.

9. Landor would be pleased at your compliment to his verse Latinity. I have been wont to hear scholars say that his Latin verse had merit, but not that of classicality. Last winter's number of the *Edinburgh Review* contains an article on Landor's poetry by my friend, Mr. Aubrey de Vere. The article contains an ingenious and eloquent comparison and contrast between the genius of ancient Greece and that of Catholic Christianity with reference to poetry and the arts. But it failed to inspire me with any warm admiration of the poetic produc-

tions of Landor. In him I had, as a girl, an implicit faith, induced upon me by my uncle's attributions to the great self-assertor, whose most amiable trait, I must think, is his cordial admiration of, and warm testimonies to, Robert Southey. Landor's criticism is very acute and refined; his dialogues I admire; but his poems appear to me cold and ineffective—the verse of a man too knowing and tasteful to write bad poetry, but without poetic genius to write well. At least, such was the impression on my mind. Some few passages of Landor's poetry are striking. I was a little disappointed that you did not notice here my father's notes on Gray's "Platonica." "Whatever might be expected from a scholar, a gentleman, a man of exquisite taste, as the quintessence of sane and sound good sense, Mr. Gray appears to me to have performed. The poet Plato, etc., etc. But Plato the philosopher was not to be comprehended within the field of vision, or to be commanded by the fixed immovable telescope of Mr. Locke's human understanding."

10. De Quincey ("the Opium Eater," as he undisguisedly calls himself) called Parr a coarse old savage; and, whatever his scholarship might be, would give him little credit, I believe, for any judgment on the internal merits of Plato.

11. "Ode to Eton College." My father criticises the stanza "Say, Father Thames," as the "only very objectionable one in point of diction;" the worst ten lines, he calls it, in all the works of Mr. Gray; "falsetto throughout, harsh and feeble." He also condemns—

    1, "And Envy wan," etc.
    2, "Grim visaged," etc.
    3, "And sorrow's piercing dart."

As, 1, bad in the first; 2, in the second; 3, in the last degree. How different the fate of poor "Christabel," when she did appear! Enemies so fierce that even old friends seemed afraid to admire and protect her. I have heard her sneered at, and Lord Byron's praise called flummery, by men who *now* would as soon think of sneering at Gray's "Elegy" as at the "wild and original poem." I wonder what Dodsley's "pinches" were? One would rather not have any particular locality for the "Elegy" than have one assigned, I think.

12. The strain of *thought* in the "Elegy" would not have made it popular without the strain of verse, the metrical accordance with the tone of feeling in the contents. But this metrical

accordance is surely but the *causa sine qua non* of its general acceptability. The efficient cause—the peculiar merit—I have ever supposed to be that inexpressible felicity and delightfulness of diction of which the line noticed by Sir E. Brydges—"The rude forefathers of the hamlet sleep"—is but one instance out of a host. Then the composition and combination of the sentiments and images—in *this* lies the charm, more than in the images themselves. These, indeed, were not new—scarce one but had been presented in poetry before. It has been the fashion with admirers of Shelley and Keats to disparage Gray. I remember coming out bluntly to my friend Mr. De Vere with the opinion that he looked coldly upon the author of the "Elegy" purely because he was simple and intelligible, and used the English language in the ordinary senses, not procuring for himself a *semblance* of the sublime by an easily assumed obscurity, and a mock magnificence by straining and inflection. For the same reason Crabbe is undervalued by devotees of Tennyson. Yet his "Tales of the Hall" display an acquaintance with the fine shades of human character, and the various phases and aspects of human sorrow—a vein of reflectiveness softened by poetic feeling, which render them a most interesting study to persons who have seen enough of life, as it is, in all its strangeness and sadness, to recognize the truth and worth of his representations. I believe that Crabbe, in his personal character, has all that sympathy with suffering humanity which appears in his poems; yesterday I read a private letter of his, in which he laments over the introduction of machinery—and yet allows for the necessity of the employers to use agents that "do not eat and drink." His sympathy with both parties is remarkable. I believe he was a gentle-hearted creature.

13. How stupid not to like the "Long Story!" Surely that might have been understood at once. "Not a wise remembrance." It is sometimes a relief thus to *objectize* our ailments. It seems to cast them *out* from us, and give us a sort of mastery over them. The dumb state of misery, when one dares not talk of it, is by far the worst. Then it seems to possess one's whole being. There is a comfort also in looking back, and seeing what miseries one has gone through before and got beyond.

14. "Tour to the Lakes." It is said that Gray set the fashion of touring to the English lakes in search of the picturesque. His horse-block is still shown near the vicarage of Keswick, on

a hill overlooking Crosthwaite church-yard, where my Uncle and Aunt Southey's remains lie buried, with Skiddaw in front.

15. Tintern Abbey. The "Lines on Tintern Abbey" is, in my opinion, one of the finest strains of verse which this age has produced.

16. This disquisition is very interesting. I think it is not sufficiently attended to, that "what a man does is the measure of what he can do," from one cause or another.

17. "High spirits take away mine."* The quiet gladness of children always cheers me; but the hilarity and vigor of grown persons depress the weak and tremulous spirits. We are hurt by the want of sympathy; and the comparison is odious.

XIX.

Character of a Friend.

To Professor REED:

Chester Place, 1850.—I have lived among poets a great deal, and have known *greater* poets than he is; but a more *entire* poet, one more a poet in his whole mind and temperament, I never knew or met with. He is most amiable, uniting a feminine gentleness and compassionateness with the most perfect manliness, both negative and positive. He is all simplicity, yet graceful, and so gracious; sportive and jestful, yet with a depth of seriousness in his nature ever present.

It is rather the habit of his mind to idealize *ad libitum*. But this, if a defect, is the defect of a large and beautiful intellect. His mind is like his face, which seems to be all eye and forehead; not that it is disproportioned in size, but that the eyes and forehead alone fix the attention, and seem to constitute the face.

XX.

The Lower Mastership of Eton School.—Moderation Acquired by Experience.—Speeches for and against the proposed Parliamentary Enactment Rejecting the Pope's Claim to Exercise Territorial Jurisdiction in England.—Such a Protest neither Intolerant nor Unpractical.

To the Rev. EDWARD COLERIDGE:

10 *Chester Place, December* 7, 1850.—My dear Edward, I heard yesterday from C—— with great delight of your having

---

* A saying of Gray's.—E. C.

obtained the Lower Mastership, and in a most satisfactory manner.

May it do you and your family all the good that your many friends desire it should, and may you do it and the school at large all the good you wish to do, and I suppose have long been meditating! You come to this really important post at the right time, both for yourself and for the advantage of Eton School, with abundant experience, and that practical power in the management of human minds which long practice, with much knowledge, always gives to the capable. "Moderation" expresses but one side of that mental quality which experience and the trials of life superinduce upon energy and zeal. It is a quickness in perceiving, as it were, intuitively, requirements on all sides, and adjusting forces at once to the occasion, which gives to the experienced man a character for sobriety, with more real command than he possessed at an early period.

But this is prosing, which, however, I have slipped into, while I was fixing my eye on your personal, private successes and advantages. I had in my mind how much better you will be able to manage this post than you, or any man of your age, could have managed it ten years ago. What experience, what lessons, has the whole country had in the course of that decade. Coley* (by the bye, what a delightful fellow he is grown, or, at least, how delightfully his frank, honest, kindly, sensible character has matured itself!)—I was going to say that Coley talked with us yesterday, after lamenting Mr. B——'s secession, about M——'s speech. Our view of its contents is pretty much alike. To argue that there ought to be no national protest at all from clergy or laity, because an irreligious movement is going on at the same time among the lower orders, who are but showing on the present occasion their want of piety, rather than gaining any fresh accession to it, seems to me not a little *non sequitur*-ish. So, again, it is not very apparent why the clergy should not resist Rome by strict attention to ordinary duty, and yet join in a national movement against the Papal aggression too.

I thought the Bishop of Oxford met the toleration argument very well, when he asked whether every Christian would not think it a glaring piece of sophistry if the Hindoo in England were to claim a right to burn his brother's widow at Charing

---

* Her nephew, Coleridge Patteson.

Cross, on the plea that all religions are to be tolerated in England.

It was said truly and pithily about the time of Catholic Emancipation, that "sincere Roman Catholics can not conscientiously be tolerant," and that, if such be the real character of Catholicism, the only security of toleration must be a certain degree of intolerance in regard to its enemies; "as prisons in the freest governments are necessary for the preservation of freedom."

But in the present case it really is in no sense a question of tolerating or not tolerating. The new Bishops can not be unmade, and, as "naught is never in danger," imaginary sees and jurisdictions can not be removed out of the imaginations in which they have been created. But it does not follow from this that there ought to be no Parliamentary enactment on the subject—at least, so I am led to believe, or that it will be a mere "dead letter" and "brutum fulmen," if not followed by an outward and corporeal penalty. It will exactly meet the exigencies of the case. It will be bull against bull, declaration against declaration. The Pope affirms and asserts that he can parcel out our country into sees, and grant territorial jurisdiction in the realm of England. The people of England, through the mouth of Parliament, shout aloud that he can not, and that shout is not to pass into the air, a passing ineffectual sound, but to be fixed, and as it were substantiated, by means of parchment and printer's ink. Just so much as Rome has done against the honor of our Church and State by the late act will be undone to all intents and purposes, as it seemeth to me, by a Parliamentary declaration that the new Bishoprics are contrary to the law of England.

J—— says that the Pope's act shows strength and consciousness of strength, and our stir against it only weakness. I doubt very much whether the Pope thinks by this time, or Wiseman either, that the national protest against Popery shows only that we are afraid of it, and know not how to keep it at bay. It is an evidence of the fact that Popery is unendurable to the mass of the people, high and low, high still more than low, in the end and at the bottom, in this land of strong hands and strong hearts and practical ways of thinking; that it is against the spirit of our domestic manners, of our social arrangements, and of our institutions, and never has been submitted to since the nation was in an adult state.

H H

XXI.

Essay on Baptism in the " Aids to Reflection" inadequately Expressed.—
   Distinction between Signs and Causes.—Action of the Will indispensable to an Inward Renewal.

To AUBREY DE VERE, Esq., Curragh Chase, Adare :

Chester Place, 1850.—How prove you what you averred, at
least as your opinion, that my father's view of Baptism, or his
objections to the ordinary High-Church view, are founded on
two or three sophisms easily refuted ?

I think, when you said this, you had in your eye the essay on
Baptism in the "Aids," which does not fully enunciate my father's objections to the High-Church argument on behalf of momentary infant regeneration.

And I also fancy you, in your own mind, triumph over the
turn of certain sentences which my father might easily have re-
cast, so as to render them impregnable, had'he reconsidered
the essay, rather than the main thoughts which underlie the
whole structure. Had my father to express these thoughts
again, he would not have laid his chief stress on the inadequacy
and trifling character of the means—the mere sprinkling of water on an infant's face. He well knew that our Anglican divines have described the outward signs of sacraments to be
mere arbitrary concomitants of the spiritual effect, not proper
instruments or real causes ; and that, although betwixt cause
and effect there must be a harmony and proportion, betwixt an
arbitrary condition or mere appointed adjunct and a spiritual
work annexed to it, there need be none at all. But then it remains true that God has given to man a certain spiritual constitution, and that, according to the law of that constitution
which He has framed, it can not be changed without a concur-
rent act of its own. Because the spiritual being of man is will
and intelligence, and will can not acquire a new character and
being, except by willing after a new manner under the influencive redemptive act of the Holy Spirit of God.

To this objection to momentary passive regeneration, an objection implying that the very statement involves an essential contradiction, I have never yet heard a reply even attempted. Men
write volumes about the High-Church modern theory, but they
always go dry-footed over this difficulty. They travel over miles
of ground, but still avoid this *pons asinorum*, which ought to be
passed before the ground of logical coherency can be obtained.

CHAPTER XXIV.

1851. — January – July.

LETTERS TO THE REV. HENRY MOORE, MRS. MOORE, MISS FEN-
WICK, MRS. FARRER, AUBREY DE VERE, ESQ., EDWARD
QUILLINAN, ESQ., PROFESSOR HENRY REED.

I.

Causes of the Indifference to the Papal Aggression displayed both by Ultra-
High-Churchmen and Ultra-Liberals.—Mixed Character of all National
Movements.—The Three Chief Religious Parties, and the Right of Each
to a Place in the English Church.—Inconsistency and Dogmatism
among the Bishops.—True View of the Royal Supremacy.—Roman Intolerance to be Resisted.

To Mrs. MOORE :

Chester Place, January 2, 1851. — My dear Mrs. Moore, I
should much like to know Mr. Moore's opinion on the present
crisis in the Church. I think you and he and Miss H—— generally agree on matters of this kind, your root principles and
sentiments being pretty much the same ; and therefore I mention only him—his being the masculine voice of the trio. We
in this house are very decided anti-papal-aggressionists, and I,
for my part, am too regular a " John Bulliana," as Sir F. Palgrave once called me, to give in to any of the new-fangled views
of toleration preached up by the Ultra-Church party on one
hand, and the Ultra-Liberal party on the other. I conceive that
a certain sympathy with Rome inspires these views in the former, secret hopes of a reunion of Christendom, and reluctance
to adopt any strong measure or use any strong language against
his Holiness ; and that, in the latter, they proceed from indifference both to Anglicanism and Romanism, an opinion that
the pretensions of the Vicar of Christ are not more nugatory
and chimerical, even if more extravagant, than those of our own
priests and bishops.

I can not help thinking that this indifference and scorn in

the latter party would shrink into a very small compass — I mean that few respectable and thoughtful men would entertain it—if the pretensions and claims of the clergy in our Church were put on a more rational, intelligible foundation, if they were moral rather than mystical, according to the spirit of the Reformation, and entirely purified from Romish and *dark-agish* superstitions. However that may be, I rejoice in the demonstration against Popery which is now making by the people of England, and I have been telling Mr. ——— that to style it a *no-Popery* row about the *royal supremacy* is more sarcastic than just. The movement has a thousand different grades and faces, but it is partaken by a very large proportion of the worthiest and most refined of the clergy and laity of this land. How could a national movement like this fail to include in its lower circles all that was low and abhorrent to the wise and well-educated? All the great movements to which we owe our present high place among the nations have carried along with them a mass of iniquity. Maurice, in his "Church a Family," observes that "when the words 'no Virgin Mary,' 'no forgiveness of sins,' are seen written upon our walls, clergymen should think a little before they fill whole sermons with specimens of Mariolatry, or with the perversions of the confessional."

I protest I can not see the logic of this. ("How should you?" Mr. Moore would say—"being of the illogical sex.") Ministers of the Gospel, a part of whose vocations is to drive away false doctrine and prevent schism, are to refrain from preaching against the corruptions of Popery, even when it is beleaguering us round about and thundering at our very gates, because idle, irreligious boys scribble thoughtless nonsense upon the walls! "No Virgin Mary" may be a good Protestant sentiment—it may mean *no Virgin Mary to be made an object of worship;* and "no forgiveness of sins" may mean *superstitiously by a priest.* If it is meant in the literal sense, it is a denial of revealed religion; and what have we to do with that?

The irreligion of these scribblers is not caused by controversial sermons, but arises from want and misery and spiritual destitution, and is to be met by positive remedies, if at all—not by abstinence from a particular line of preaching fitly addressed to any decent congregation.

I dare say you will agree with me on one point with respect to the present movement, and that is in detesting the silly, narrow, shabby way in which Tractarianism has been attacked in so many quarters, or rather Tractarians. This is sheer party spirit and overbearing intolerance. *Some* of the Tractarians are really disloyal to our Church; and it is too true that many do unintentionally, by the tenor and spirit of their preaching, send younger men to Rome, while they themselves are not prepared to go that length in honor of their principles. But the main body of the Anglo-Catholics have as much right to keep their places in our Church as the main body of the Evangelicals or the Philosophicals.

Tractarianism is as wide and vague a word as Rationalism or Germanism; every man so calls his neighbor who is more High Church than himself, and adopts more of those doctrines and practices which belong to Rome, and are not forbidden to us, than he thinks proper to do; and so, too, every man accuses every other man of Rationalism who doubts the truth or accuracy of any tenet or doctrinal formula which he holds sacred, on the score of its wanting reason.

The Tractarian party have shown such an intolerant spirit themselves on many occasions, that I own my feelings are more of contemptuous indignation against their adversaries than of sympathy with themselves. Even now how many of them are pining for a Convocation, which, as they flatter themselves, is to banish from the Church the school represented to their minds by Gorham. A decree of the assembled Synod is to drive away the whole multitude of those who will not declare positively before God and man that *all* infants are internally regenerate *in* baptism, and rendered secure of heaven *by* baptism—a belief not properly compatible with belief in election; for St. Augustine's *regeneration* of the non-elect was a mere term for baptism, implying no spiritual gift whatever, no forgiveness of sin, or possession by the Spirit.

Now this would be to banish a school which has existed in the Church ever since the Reformation, and is in reality quite as intolerant as the conduct of their adversaries in the present moment, though it may not have been manifested in so coarse and childish a form, simply because Anglo-Catholicism is not a popular mode of faith, and has never spread so wide nor gone so low in the mass of society as puritanical Protestantism.

The Bishop of L—— is much blamed by some parties for yielding to the popular voice and the *Times* newspaper. D——

holds his conduct inconsistent, because, on finding that his charge of 1844 could be carried out only on one side—that he has not power to require compliance with the rubric in regard to the prayer for the Church Militant and the preparation of the elements — against the Low-Church party, he leaves them alone, and is driven into making a strict inquisition into those churches which offend on the other side.

It should be remembered, on behalf of the Bishop's honesty or consistency with himself, that he has always been, on principle, what is commonly, though I believe improperly, called a practical character—which should rather be called an empirical one. He was always for going by authority and the voice of the existing influential majority, and acting upon what was already established, rather than upon speculative principle, and abstract views of what is in itself right or wrong, true or untrue. This practical mode of shaping his course brings him at last to be the executor of the sovereign will and orders of the *Times* newspaper. It does not signify appealing to rubrics, except as rubrics are backed up by some existing power. They become a dead letter when that fails. The Church party were the Bishop's authority when he began his course. This seemed dignified and ecclesiastical more than his present subserviency; but it contained no security a bit more than his present authority for truth and justice.

As for the Bishop of E——, his state of mind may be somewhat higher than the Bishop of L——'s, but I doubt whether there is more of heart in his doctrine, or whether he cares for any thing but carrying out an ecclesiastical system which is radically Romish, and opposed to the spirit and principles of the Reformation, however imperfectly that was understood at the time of the resettlement of our Church. His objections to the Bishop's address seem to me overstrained and captious, taking the matter every where by the wrong handle. He will not call the Queen *Head of the Church.* Why, she is not at all the Head in the sense that our Lord is such; but is there not a sense in which she may properly be called so (in which the Pope claims to be so over all Christendom together, together with another which does, to our Protestant mind, invade our Saviour's office)? May not she be called the Head of the Church, as having to assign the territorial sphere of jurisdiction to Bishops, to call councils when any are formed, and to be the source of all temporal powers and privileges by which the Church is enriched and strengthened?

Then he says that the Bishops have nothing to do with encroachment on the prerogative. But when such encroachment is bound up with spiritual claims and pretensions, surely the Bishops who sit as temporal Lords in the Council of the nation may not improperly petition the Queen on the subject.

But, after all, what can be done? I am one who think that already a good deal has been done by the demonstration that has been made of the anti-Popish mind of the nation; but I should hope that something more might be done in Parliament to fix and ratify that demonstration. Revival of disabilities no one thinks of for a moment. But without infringing the principles of toleration, I do think an act might be passed to prevent offensive ceremonies and imposing symbolisms importing that our Church is a nullity, and our orders null and void. This might come under the head of pure *self-defense*, and resistance of public indecorum. And it is idle to say that Romanists ought to be tolerated equally with all other Dissenters. When they claim no more than other Dissenters, and give no more offense to the National Church, they will be refused no more.

II.

Faith and Works.—Allowances to be Made on all Sides.—Insult offered to our Church by Rome in affecting to Ignore its Existence.—Anomalous Position of the Establishment in Ireland. — The Royal Supremacy as Representing the Lay Element of the Church.

To the Rev. H. MOORE:

10 *Chester Place, January* 29, 1851. — I am delighted with your address, and assent heartily to your whole letter, which seems to my poor understanding to display a right judgment in all things that pertain to this wily aggression.

Never in my life before did I feel so near (comparatively near, but absolutely far enough off) fraternizing with the Tractarians as on the recent agitation, when at meetings those shabby, shallow, intolerant addresses to put down the Tractarians were got up by ignorant vulgarians. The plain truth being this, that no thoughtful, earnest mind can embrace the natural sense of *all* the formularies and documents of our Church, and that each party needs toleration from the other. Certainly not a Tractarian in the land teaches justification by faith alone, in the genuine sense of the Article and Homily on Salvation. All teach Bull's view, and Bull does well enough with St. Paul, who, as you often say, was not thinking about the point at issue; but when he tries to harmonize his view with the Homily, he descends into a quibbler and sophisticator, just as he proves Tully and the other fellows to have sophisticated in his "Animadversiones."

And I do think that Chapter III. of Romans favors the Lutheran logic: grace were not grace if given to works as such. All works are a man's own works, whether they come of grace or no. All works are of God, whether done before the special grace of Christ or no, because God gives the power to work, and sustains it by His presence.

But faith first brings us to Christ, the real Justifier, and so justifies instrumentally—not as qualifying us for heaven. This formula all Tractarians reject with scorn. It certainly keeps the mind upon Christ more than the other, and it can never mislead, if taken with Luther's own repeated statement, that a good life must come of that saving faith, and that he whose deeds are evil must not believe himself by any other sign to have true faith.

The other party can not take, in the sense of the framers, or at least of those by whom the forms were originally devised, certain sentences in the Liturgy.

But no doubt there are Tractarians, who are Romanists in disguise, who act a dishonest part—proselytizing to Rome while they eat the bread of our Church; and there are, on the opposite side, no-Churchmen, who are utterly alienated from the spirit in which our Church services and articles were composed, and who in reality believe no more of the Church system than Quakers. Such are individuals who ought not to be confounded with the bodies to which they externally belong.

All you say about the Supremacy seems to me excellent. As I say to ———, you go on about the Supremacy; you say truly that the Queen's power over the loaves and fishes is not touched —but here is an insult offered and a wrong done to our *Church*, an insult to every Bishop of our Church and his diocesan flock. Dissenters have never done the like. They acknowledge not the Church in our sense. You do acknowledge it, and you proclaim openly by your ostentatious arrangements that you *cover the whole ground*, and that our Bishops and Bishoprics are nothing. Tell me that toleration requires us to endure this injury to the influence of our Church—for such it is, and will be, if unresisted! No one can maintain this but by a quibble, by setting up words against practical realities, for the hurt to our Protestant religion would be real, and we have a right to defend it.

Ultra-Liberals say this free country will never bear any restrictions on religious liberty, and so says the *Guardian* and the Ultra-High-Church. Let us see whether John Bull, who is a practical personage, and apt to go by *feel* in these matters rather than by tongue, does not bear very well the suppression of a development of the Romish Church organization—not necessary to the full exercise of the religion of Romanists, and only useful in *policy* as the means of aggrandizement.

Even if it were a necessary part of their religion, men can't be indulged in a religion injurious to the religion of the nation.

The example of Ireland in this, as in all such occasions, is in our way. The national religion there is robbed—maltreated. We feel it necessary to admit Bishops' titles to Romanists there, and then are called upon, in consistency, to allow them here in the face of the Establishment. The nation and the Established religion ought ever to be in unity, and to treat Ireland as a mere part of Great Britain is a practical falsehood.

I send you H. C. Robinson's paper. It has been greatly approved. It shows so clearly how the matter may be presented purely in a national point of view, since such are the thoughts and feelings of a *Unitarian*.

About the Supremacy, may we not say, that though, of course, there is nothing spiritual in it—directly—yet that there is an element that may be called Ecclesiastical. As entitled to convoke the clergy, and to assign the territorial sphere of jurisdiction, which surely is independent of emolument, our Sovereign owns a power which can not belong to Christ, but is something beyond mere headship in temporal things. It is quasi-spiritual, since it concerns spiritual matters. This power relates to the Church as visible. It must reside somewhere, and, when we deprived the Pope of it, we vested it in the Sovereign, as the head and representative of the nation. This is a true Protestant idea, because it assigns the authority of determining the general movements of the visible Church to the representative of the laity, that is, of the nation, lay as well as clerical—not to a priest or representative of priests.

* * * I should have been *cracky* if you had taken up any non-national coxcombical view on the present occasion.

III.

"Letter to Countess Ida Hahn-Hahn," by Oberken.—"Death's Jest-Book," and other Dramatic Works, by Mr. Beddoes.

To Mrs. FARRER, 3 Gloucester Terrace :

Chester Place, January, 1851.—I am much pleased at your concurrence of opinion with me about the letter to Countess Ida. It is by Oberken, a great friend of the Chevalier Bunsen. This little work sets forth the distinctive characters of Romanism and Protestantism more forcible, I should almost say *profoundly*, than any other work I have met with. The defense of the Reformation seems to me admirable. It mirrored to me all my own views with new force and distinctness.

Dearest Mrs. Farrer, you once kindly sent some dramatic poems of Beddoes here, which I declined reading, not liking my impression of the "Death's Jest-Book," in which I saw much to admire, to be interfered with, and hearing they were much inferior to that. Just before I went into Staffordshire, I received that drama from the author, and put it aside. After my return, I took it up, considering it a duty at least to look it through. I had been repelled by the first peep I took into it. Those were my days, or rather nights, of reading in bed, and so struck was I with the powerful original imagery, and some of the wild situations of the drama, that I did not lay it down till I had perused the whole. I was really thrilled with some parts, the effect, perhaps, being enhanced by the nightly gloom and silence. Well, I resolved to express my admiration to the author the very next day, and I was not the less inclined to be pleased, that on the blank leaf I found a gratifying inscription, and that the author was the son of an old Bristol friend of my father. But in the morning came a letter from Mr. Quillinan, expressing warm admiration of the drama I had just been reading, and at the same time announcing the death of the author in rapid decline. I thought mournfully of Gray's elegiac sentiment—

"Can flattery soothe the dull cold ear of death?"

It was not flattery, in the common acceptation of the word, that I meant to address to Mr. Beddoes, but a sincere tribute of praise, for as much as it was worth.

Yet, after all, dear Mrs. Farrer, I quite agree in your strictures on this same striking production. The plot is most extravagant, and some of the characters are so wicked for mere wickedness' sake that they are placed without the pale of humanity, and therefore out of reach of our human interests and sympathies. Still, with all these great faults, the play interested me greatly.

IV.

Inaccuracies of a Review in the *Quarterly* of the "Life of Southey."

To Miss FENWICK:

Chester Place, February 11, 1851.—Did you read the review of the Southey Life in the *Quarterly?* It has been answered in very hearty, gallant style by Forster in the *Examiner.* The summary of my uncle's literary merits at the end of Forster's paper is excellent. There are many inaccuracies in the review. How strange to call Lloyd "a pauper," and suitor to a fourth Miss Fricker! Lloyd was the son of a wealthy banker, and always well off, poor only in health and nervous sanity. He never proposed to one of my aunts, but married Miss Sophia Pemberton, a lady of great worth and sense, and some fortune. Lloyd left money to all of his eight children. Then I do not think it true that no congregation would elect my father on account of his unpunctuality. He might have remained as preacher at Shrewsbury, when he received Mr. Wedgwood's offer, and resolved not to tie himself up. He did not like the shackles of preachership to a body of religionists. "Hiring another division of Greta Hall," too, is incorrect enough; but these are minor matters.

V.

Mr. Carlyle's "Life of Sterling."—Autobiography of Leigh Hunt.—Epicureanism.

To Miss MORRIS:

March 12, 1851.—Did you read Carlyle's "Life of Sterling?" To me the work is fascinating, as far as the biographical part is concerned. Dr. Calvert (Sterling's dear friend) was a life-

long intimate friend of mine. The chapter on S. T. C. is ridiculous. Leigh Hunt's Autobiography is most entertaining.
What a Christianified epicureanism is his religion! Yet such
is the religion of a large portion of our amiable, refined, intelligent men. High Churchmen, Evangelical, Skeptical, Epicurean—such are the chief divisions of religious thought, I believe,
among the educated nowadays.

VI.

Early Reminiscences of the Character and Conversation of Mr. Wordsworth and Mr. Southey.—Youthful Impressions mostly Unconscious.—
The "Platonic Ode."—"The Triad" Compared with "Lycidas."—
"The Prelude."—Testimonies contained in it to the Friendship between her Father and Mr. Wordsworth.

To Professor HENRY REED, Philadelphia :

Chester Place, May 19, 1851.—I dare say that you and your
friend, Mr. Yarnall, have lately been dwelling a good deal on
the "Memoir of Wordsworth," which I finished, slowly perusing
last night in my hours of wakefulness. For, alas! I sleep but
every other night—the intervening one is now almost wholly
sleepless. Mr. H. C. Robinson requested that I would use the
pencil or pen freely on the margin of his copy : "the more notes,
the better." I fear he will be greatly disappointed by what I
have written, and I almost wish it rubbed out, it is so trifling,
and in some instances not to the purpose—as, I fear, the owner
of the book will think. I knew dear Mr. Wordsworth perhaps
as well as I have ever known any one in the world—more intimately than I knew my father, and as intimately as I knew
my Uncle Southey. There was much in him to know, and the
lines of his character were deep and strong—the whole they
formed, simple and impressive. His discourse, as compared
with my father's, was as the Latin language to the Greek, or, to
borrow a comparison which has been applied to Shakespeare
and Milton, as statuary to painting—it was intelligent, wise, and
easily remembered. But in my youth, when I enjoyed such
ample opportunities of taking in his mind, I listened to "enjoy
and not to understand," much less to report and inform others.
In our spring-time of life we are poetical, not literary, and often
absorb unconsciously the intellectual airs that blow or stilly
dwell around us, as our bodies do the fragrant atmosphere of

May—full of the breath of primroses and violets—and are nourished thereby without reflecting upon the matter, any more than we classify and systematize, after Linnæus or Jussieu, the vernal blossoms which delight our outward senses. I used to take long walks with Mr. Wordsworth about Rydal and Grasmere, and sometimes, though seldom, at Keswick, to his Applethwaite cottage, listening to his talk all the way; and for hours have I often listened when he conversed with my uncle, or, indoors at Rydal Mount, when he chatted or harangued to the inmates of his household or the neighbors. But I took no *notes* of his discourse either on the tablet of memory or on material paper; my mind and turn of thought were gradually moulded by his conversation, and the influences under which I was brought by his means in matters of intellect, while in those which concerned the heart and the moral being I was still more deeply and importantly indebted to the character and daily conduct of my admirable Uncle Southey. Yet I never adopted the opinions of either *en masse*, and, since I have come to years of secondary and more mature reflection, I have been unable to retain many which I received from them. The impression upon my feelings of their minds remains unabated in force; but the formal views and judgments which I received from their lips are greatly modified, though not more than they themselves modified and re-adjusted their own views and judgments from youth to age.

You express surprise at something I let fall in a former letter on what I consider the difference and inferiority in kind of Mr. Wordsworth's late poems from those of his youth and middle-age. I must own that I do see this very strongly, and should as little think of comparing that on the " Power of Sound" with the " Platonic Ode," or the " Song at the Feast of Brougham Castle," as—what shall I say?—the Crystal Palace with Windsor Castle, or the grand carved sideboard in the former with the broad oak of the forest when its majestic stem of strong and solid wood is robed in foliage of tender, mellow green. Those earlier odes seem to be *organic* wholes: the first of them is in some sort an image of the individual spirit of which it is an efflux. The energy and felicity of its language is so great that every passage and every line of it has been received into the poetical heart of this country, and has become the common expression of certain moods of mind and modes of thought which had hardly been developed before its appearance. The ode on the "Power of Sound," like "The Triad," is an elegant composition by a poetic artist—a poetical will-work—not as a whole, I should say, a piece of inspiration, though some lines in it are breathings of the poetic spirit.

I confess, at the risk of lowering my taste in your esteem, which I should be right sorry to do, yet not liking to retain it by mere suppression of a part of my mind—a serious and decided part, which has stood assaults of poetic reasoning of no small force and animation—I do confess that I have never been able to rank "The Triad" among Mr. Wordsworth's immortal works of genius. It is just what he came into the poetical world to condemn, and both by practice and theory to supplant. It is, to my mind, *artificial* and *unreal.* There is no truth in it as a whole, although bits of truth, glazed and magnified, are embodied in it, as in the lines, "Features to old ideal grace allied" —a most unintelligible allusion to a likeness discovered in dear Dora's contour of countenance to the great Memnon head in the British Museum, with its overflowing lips and width of mouth, which seems to be typical of the ocean. The poem always strikes me as a mongrel—an amphibious thing, neither portrait nor ideal, but an ambiguous cross between the two. Mr. De Vere, before he knew me, took it for a personification of Faith, Hope, and Charity, taken in inverse order—a sufficient proof, I think, that it is extravagant and unnatural as a description of three young ladies of the nineteenth century. In "Lycidas," poetic idealism is not brought so closely into contrast and conflict with familiar reality as in "The Triad," because it contains no description of the individual. The theme in reality is quite general and abstract—death by drowning of the friend of a great poet, in his bloom of youth, a minister of the Gospel. This theme is adorned with all the pomp and garniture of classic and Hebraic imagery that could be clustered and cumulated round it. After all, in theory, Milton's mixture of Pagan mythology with the spiritualities of the Gospel is not defensible. The best defense of "Lycidas" is not to defend the design of it at all, but to allege that the execution is perfect, the diction the *ne plus ultra* of grace and loveliness, and that the spirit of the whole is as original as if the poem contained no traces of the author's acquaintance with ancient pastoral poetry, from Theocritus downward. I am much pleased to see how highly

Mr. Wordsworth speaks of Virgil's style, and of his " Bucolics," which I have ever thought most graceful and tender. They are quite another thing from Theocritus, however they may be based upon Theocritus.

You invited me, in a former letter, to speak to you of "The Prelude ;" but this must be reserved for a future communication. I can only say, now, that I was deeply delighted in reading it, and think it a truly noble composition. It is not, perhaps, except in certain passages, which had been extracted and given to the public before the publication of the poem as a whole, effective and brilliant poetry ; but it is deeply interesting as the image of a great poetic mind : none but a mind on a great scale could have produced it. As a supplement to the poetic works of the author, it is of the highest value. You may imagine how I was affected and gladdened by the warm tributes which it contains to my father, and the proof it affords of their close intimacy and earnest friendship. . I think the history of literature hardly affords a parallel instance of entire union and unreserve between two poets. There may have been more co-operation between Beaumont and Fletcher ; but from the character of their lives, there could hardly have been such pure love and consonancy of thought and feeling on high themes, and accordance in high aims and endeavors. Mr. Yarnall's remembrances of the poet in his last year I thought highly interesting. I saw in them a touch of Wordsworth's own manner, a reverent tenderness and "solemn gloom." To judge from the notes of Mrs. Davy and Lady Richardson, Mr. Wordsworth must have been somewhat more like his old self in discourse when at his own home, surrounded by the natural objects in which he took such high interest, than when I was with him at Miss Fenwick's, at Bath, in the spring of that sad summer which deprived him of his beloved daughter. Then he seemed unable to talk, except in snatches and fragments ; and there was nothing fresh in what he said. His speech seemed to me but a feeble, mournful echo of his former utterances.

VII.

Visit to the Crystal Palace in Hyde Park.—Sculpture and Jewels.—The Royal Academy of 1851.—Portrait of Mr. Wordsworth by Pickersgill.—Supposed Tendency to Pantheism in the "Lines on Tintern Abbey."

To Miss FENWICK:

Chester Place, May 25, 1851.—Dearest Miss Fenwick, yesterday, for the first time, I visited the Crystal Palace, and ever since I have been longing for you to see it. Is it quite impossible for you to come up, to me first, and see this interesting assemblage of works of art? I saw so many Bath chairs, and invalids in them, so many, many degrees weaker than you or I. You could be wheeled about to every thing with perfect ease, and there are several gentlemen, either of whom would delight to devote time to going about with us and showing us every thing.

I had a perfect dread of the thing before I went, and would not have gone at all but to escape the perpetual question—"Have you seen the great wonder?" and "Do go with me. Do let me take you to see it." I would not go with any party, fearing that I should have to stay longer than my strength would allow. E—— went with her cousin S——, a very sweet girl, the image of her beloved papa—whose sudden death she so deeply mourned—both in face and the gentle affectionateness of her manner. I procured for them the escort of Mrs. P. E——. Yesterday E—— and I went under the care of Mr. D——, brother-in-law of Mrs. D. C——; we stayed *four hours,* and I came away far less fatigued than I have often felt after half an hour in the Royal Academy. The difference arises from the freedom in walking about, and the freshness of the atmosphere. In this great conservatory, or glass house, we are perfectly sheltered from all inclemency of weather—all *too muchness* of hot or cold, wind or sun—and under foot are smooth boards, which do not try the limbs like the inequalities of street or road; and yet there is an openness and space and free circulation of air such as were never enjoyed, I suppose, *under cover* before. I did not think to stay more than one hour, but four soon slipped away. We were lucky in meeting Lord Monteagle, who talked instructively to me on the works of art, and pointed out a most graceful and beautiful piece of sculpture by Gibson, which I afterward showed to friends whom I met, telling them at the same time of Lord M——'s criticism. * * * Lord M—— talked of little A——, and of his having enjoyed one of the greatest honors a mortal could obtain, in having been preferred to the hippopotamus! I dare say you may have heard the story of little A——'s choosing to see grandpapa rather than to visit the zoological favorite new-comer.

At first I felt mortified to see how British art, in the high line of sculpture, appeared to be outdone by foreign—all the striking pieces, and those which occupied the conspicuous places in the centre of the great middle aisle, being German, Italian, or French performances. The grandest thing in this way is an Amazon* on horseback, about to spear a lioness, who has leaped upon her horse, and is trying to throttle it. The huntress sits back upon her steed, the right leg drawn up, the left extended on the other side below the belly of the horse—a superb tomboy indeed. The piece is colossal. Then there are two fishing-girls by Monti, of Milan, most lovely, but quite *real-life-ish* —not like Gibson's piece, which would be almost taken for a Greek antique. And there are such beauteous little babes in marble, one little fellow strapped to his cot, from which he is trying to rear himself up. But among the most striking performances are two groups by Lequesne: 1. A dog protecting a boy, about four or five years old, from a serpent. 2. The dog, having bitten off the serpent's head, caressed by the child. The contrast in the face of the dog, when he is about to kill the serpent and when he has done the job, is most expressive; in the first group it is sharpened with anxiety—it looks almost like that of a wolf, full of horror and disgust at the noxious beast, and cautious determination. In the second, it is all abroad with comfortable, placid satisfaction, and affectionate good-nature. These, of course, are only a few in a crowd.

I was disappointed in the great diamond, even though I had heard that it disappointed every one. There is nothing *diamondy* in it that I can see—no multiplicity of sparkle—it looks only like a respectable piece of crystal. The two strings of large pearls of the East India Company are very fine; but I have some strings of large mock pearls which look almost as well, and they can be imitated still more nearly. The huge em-

---

* By Kiss, a German sculptor.—E. C.

I I

eralds, too, look rather glassy. Of all the works of art adapted
to the uses of domestic life, the most exquisite is the Gobelin
tapestry; in our noblemen's palaces and houses there is nothing like it. The bunches of flowers are more delicate and
brilliant than any painting I ever saw. The carved wood furniture is very fine; but in that department the English equal
the French, except in one sideboard, supported by four hounds,
which is the most elegantly magnificent thing I ever saw. The
grand beds, too, are very grand. * * * The crowd was far greater yesterday than it ever was before, and what it will be on
the shilling days I know not. It was fine to look down from
the galleries, and see such a vast mass of human beings all in
motion, enjoying themselves and animated. Every body looked
pleased and comfortable.

The picture exhibition, too, is worth seeing. I like Watts's
portrait of Mr. Taylor much, and there are beautiful portraits
of Gibson, the sculptor, and a lady by Boxall. Eastlake's "Hip-
polita" is very beautiful, but too pinky. Pickersgill's portrait
of our dear departed great poet is *insufferable* — velvet waist-
coat, neat shiny boots—just the sort of dress he would not have
worn if you could have hired him—and a sombre sentimental-
ism of countenance quite unlike his own look, which was either
elevated with high gladness or deep thought, or at times simply and childishly gruff; but never tender after that fashion, so
lackadaisical and mawkishly sentimental.

Dr. Wordsworth's apologizing in the "Life" for the "Lines
on Tintern Abbey" seems to me injudicious. Those great
works of the poet's vigorous mind must stand for themselves;
it is on them, I believe, that Wordsworth's fame will rest, and
by them he must be judged.

But why admit for a moment that they might be accused of
Pantheism, or that Wordsworth might, had he not written in a
different spirit late in life? If they had really proceeded from
a Pantheistic view, they ought to have been suppressed if possible. Their beauty and power ought not to have saved them;
this would give them influence — add wings to the poisoned
shaft. But there is no such thing as Pantheism truly imputable
to them.

VIII.

Intellectual Tuft-hunting.

To E. QUILLINAN, Esq. :

1851.—A parent can not say to a son, "You must never form an intimacy except with decidedly superior men." There would be a sort of intellectual tuft-hunting in this, which could not lead to good, for man is a very complex animal, and can not be determined in his movements and procedure by one part of his nature without regard to the rest, and our connections arise from many influences, all of which can not be given an exact account of.

IX.

The Bears of Literature.—Margate.—Bean-fields and Water Companies.—Hartley Coleridge's Lines to Dr. Arnold. — Eutychianism. — Liebnitz on the Nature of the Soul.—Materialism of the Early Fathers.—Great Metaphysical Work projected by Mr. Coleridge.—Historical Reading.—Scott's Novels.

To AUBREY DE VERE, Esq. :

3 Zion Place, East Cliff, Margate, June 20, 1851.—I have delayed writing to you more as reserving a pleasure than postponing a time-consuming task ; for the subjects which you invite me to investigate with you are so interesting to my mind that a letter to you is always a high entertainment to myself, whether or no to you it be a *treat* so far as it is a *treatise,* or only acceptable as a personal communication. I ought to have written sooner, however, to express my grateful delight in what you have undertaken on behalf of dear Hartley's poetry. It is painful to think of your composition being cut and slashed and squeezed and ground, and perhaps inlaid and vamped, by editorial interference. Still, in any shape, the article will be *very* acceptable, unless more tampered with than I can believe probable ; and, even if aught unforeseen should prevent its appearance altogether, it would always be most agreeable to me to think of your having written it. I should like to see your composition in its original virgin state, like the gadding vine or well-attired woodbine, free and luxuriant in kindly remark and beauty-finding criticism. An editor of a critical review ought

to be painted with a pruning-hook in his hand as big as himself, and an ax beside him, just ready to fall edge foremost
upon his own foot—only that it would tantalize one to see it always suspended. There's a piece of savagery! The foot ought
to be represented as rough as that of a bear, and clumsy as
the pedestal of an elephant, to denote the rough, clumsy way in
which these ursine editors go ramping and ravaging about the
fairest flower-gardens. Don't you remember how C——'s great
hoofs went plunging about in Tennyson's first volume, containing "Mariana," "The Miller's Daughter," and the "Ode to
Memory," and "The Dying Swan" and "Œnone," the loveliest
and most characteristic things, to my fancy, that he ever wrote?
Indeed, C——'s stamping down that pretty bed of heart's-ease,
Moxon's Sonnets, was shameful, and showed him fit to be
chained to a post, or shut up with the guests of Circe, in a sty
of tolerable accommodation and capacity, for the rest of his
bearish and Grilline existence. All this indignation streams
forth from me on the pressure of the mere thought of the treatment that your article is to receive. "But let them go, and be
you blithe and bonny," oh! products of poetic genius of every
degree, from the greatest to the least, in spite of the Bears of
Literature, remembering how Keats was treated, who now by
some critics is boldly styled the most poetical poet of the age.

My general health has derived as much benefit from my stay
here as it usually does from a sea-side visit. I walk an hour in
the morning, and in the evening an hour or fifty minutes. I
could do more than this in the way of exercise, but, though my
strength would allow of it, I fear that it might not be prudent.

The weather was quite wintry—a spring temperature, with the
squally look and sound of winter—during the first nine or ten
days of our stay. Now it begins to be Junish: the butterflies
are abroad, especially the azure ones, that seem to be animated
bits cut out of the sapphire of the still, blue sea; the corn-poppy
rears its head, that was hung down like that of an eastern slave
making a low obeisance, and discloses its scarlet head-gear;
while the blossomed beans look up and seem to *stare* at us with
their clear black eye, the jetty iris surrounded by a snowy cor-
nea. Have you ever observed this in the bean-blossom? it is
really pretty to behold. The sweet odors from the bean-fields,
and from little gardens full of stocks, carnations, roses, gilly-
flowers, pinks, and southernwood, which we pass on our cliff

walk, are an agreeable contrast to the vile ones which annoy us when we enter the town to post letters or get a book from one of the libraries. The whole way round the town, there are not many yards of ground free from this nuisance. Surely many summers will not pass ere Margate radically reforms her drainage, and every town and city in England adopts those better plans of water-supply and extrusion of uncleanness which are already before the public. How strange it seems that Government should in any degree admit the proposals of the water companies for consolidating them, and granting them a monopoly of this lucrative business! What can they say in answer to the allegations against the old system, and all that is advanced in support of another plan? I do think, in all matters of this kind, which concern the public health, Government ought to be paternal and governing; and I hope, in time, the country will support them in taking such businesses into their own hands, and conducting them on a plan having the advantage of unity. But you will see that I am talking after the article on centralization, etc., in the last *Quarterly*—an article which pleased me very much, because it both gave me new information and confirmed some of my old opinions that the Government on sanitary matters should act more boldly, and take more upon it than heretofore, and not suffer what is important to the health of the community to be *misguggled* by individual selfishness and caprice, or the rapacious dishonesty of companies.

To return to the Hartley poems. You told me that in the lines on the death of Dr. Arnold you could not make any thing of "His subject and his Lord." Now I can not help seeing that the commencing lines of this poem are awkward, ambiguous, and ill-expressed, but the meaning of "subject" in the third line I doubt not is *theme*, the subject-matter of discourse and preaching; the sense is not that which is directly opposed to *Lord*. The parenthesis I rather thought rightly placed. But it is a great pity that a good poem of the weightier sort should begin so carelessly and ineruditely.

I must soon bid you good-by and take my evening walk, and must not now enter upon theology, though your last leaves me charged with the heresy of Eutyches. Friend De Vere, does not Eutychianism consist in the denial of the two natures of our Lord? Is it not the Catholic faith that our Lord had but one person, with the human and divine natures, only adding that, if, as some divines, Aquinas and others, affirm, the personality of Christ is divine, not human, we must say the human personality is merged in the divine. Even if this is an inconvenient expression, I see not how it infers Eutychianism. Perhaps it would be better to say that the human nature distinctly appears in our Lord in every other attribute save this of personality, and that, in bare personality considered in itself, apart from every other attribute, the distinction between human and divine can not manifest itself. The Church, speaking in the Creed commonly called of Athanasius (if we are to consider that Creed as her voice, and I do not think it is the voice of Christ), but the Church, speaking through decrees of councils, has merely decided, I believe, that our Lord is one person having two natures. It is only individual schoolmen and divines who have declared Him not to have taken human personality. We are not obliged to any explicit doctrine on the point in question.

I have been reading Leibnitz on the origin and nature and composition of the soul, and found much in his teaching that is satisfactory. But of this more anon. He says, with a sage simplicity, that if his doctrine, as was objected to it, represents the souls of beasts as imperishable, it is much better to allow *them* immortality than to deny it to men. He thinks that the Anti-Platonism of some of the early Fathers (indeed, I believe, of all the orthodox ones)—which made the soul, in all finite beings, men and angels, to be material, not immortal *per se*, by its original conformation, but only made so, in particular cases, by the arbitrary determination of the Creator, keeping alive the good for reward and the evil for punishment—is a dangerous notion. And certainly, if Materialism, in any shape, is commended to the minds of men, however guarded it may be by the teachers of it within the Church, by a corollary framed in support of Revelation, it will be laid hold of by teachers without the Church, and easily separated from its pious appendix. The more agreement can be made out betwixt philosophy and religion, the better for the interests of the latter; the more foundation for the hopes to which Revelation points can be laid on the ground of reason, the better for the authority of the former. And yet some Christian teachers in all ages have manifested a jealousy of support to religious doctrine supplied by reason, as if the ally must needs prove a usurper. Such usurpation would be but a supplanting of herself.

I have been answering a letter from Sir John K——, inclosing one from a clerical friend of his, containing a most earnest inquiry about my father's great "metaphysical opus," a great profession of admiration of his mind, confidence in his powers, and value for his speculations, as throwing light on the truths of the Christian religion. This kind of inquiry is frequently made to me, and begins to embarrass me a good deal. At one time I hoped that Mr. Green would be able, in the course of a few years, to exhibit a scheme of Divine Philosophy, the ideas or substance whereof would be my father's—the composition, except in some portions where he was furnished with regular dictation of his master, his own. Now I scarce know what to say. Difficulties seem to unfold themselves as he proceeds in the execution of the work,* but it is best to refer such inquiries to Mr. Green himself. Meantime, this I think, and have ventured to suggest to Sir John K——'s friend, that the writings of my father already published, the latter volumes of the " Literary Remains," "Appendix to the Statesman's Manual," "Church and State," and its notes, and even the "Aids to Reflection," have never yet been made full use of, or *approfondis*, even by professed admirers of my father's mind, or thoroughly enucleated, digested, and applied.

My reading-books here are Leibnitz, Ranke, and the Scotch Novels, and of these the middle is the one to which alone I find it difficult to enchain my attention. History is always difficult to me, because taking in so much *fact* at once is like making a meal all of dry bread. As for Scott, I grieve to be nearing the end of his charming productions. They fill a place in literature which they have entirely to themselves. No other books combine the same qualities—so much humor, so much information, so high a tone, varying from the chivalrous to the gentlemanly, and such an out-of-door freshness, the scene being so much in the open air, or in mansions connected with nature or elevated by historic association, or rendered interesting by the way in which they show characteristics of the Scottish peasantry or townsfolk.

* " Spiritual Philosophy, founded on the Teaching of the late S. T. Coleridge," by the late T. H. Green. Edited by Dr. Simon. Macmillan & Co., 1865.—E. C.

X.

To AUBREY DE VERE, Esq.:

10 *Chester Place, July* 11, 1851.—My dear friend, I have just
finished reading your article on Hartley, and am even more
thankful for it than I expected to be.   It is the only essay on
the subject that has satisfied *my heart.*   Oh, how true it is
that charity is the best wisdom !   Your article seems to me far
truer and wiser than any of the rest.   There is so much more
of intuition in it, of insight into the good of Hartley's nature.
The article in the *Christian Remembrancer* is a brilliant essay,
eloquent and touching in parts, and, as every orator can be, pathetic—it is a part of his art.   It does justice to Hartley's intellect and genius, and to his amiability ; but the desire to show
up the subject as a moral lesson, to use it by way of illustrating
the peculiar or characteristic principles and sentiments of the
review, gives a dryness and heartlessness to the whole, and
makes even the tenderness seem artificial.   I do not lament
over the curtailment of your paper so much as I did in prospect, although I grudge losing what you have written.   Yet so
impatient are readers nowadays, and so fastidious from the
quantity of food always pouring in upon them, that I dare say
the *effect* of the article will be the greater from its having been
shortened.

That is a beautiful description at p. 5—"With a vague grace,
with feet that seemed almost unable to keep their hold of the
ground," etc.   That does so bring him before me !   As I read,
it was like a lightning flash revealing what long had lain amid
the shadows of memory.   I marked also the affecting paragraph at p. 15, 16, and that between p. 25, 26, and that sentence at p. 21 : "She interpreted between him and his neighbors, she sweetened the draught of an impoverished life, and
made atonement to a defrauded heart."   That is beautiful, and
my tears are flowing, as I read, at this and other passages.

That is a pretty fancy at p. 29, on the character of his love
poems—"The moonlight of a warm climate."

This is a point, too, on which your intuitive knowledge of
Hartley appears, which no other review brought forward.   The

impetuosity of manner in my brother gave to some a notion that he had strong passions. But I have been comparing him with my father lately in musing on the two, and feeling how much stronger were all the features of *his* character—his emotions more vehement.

I dwell thus upon those that have been long removed, while sorrow is in my heart at the unexpected departure of one for whom I had, what you had also, a warm regard. Another of my set of valued old friends is taken from me! Mr. Quillinan was one whom it was impossible to regard with indifference—striking and peculiar in character, and full of gifts as well as attractions.

Our new clergyman (I do like him *so much!*) had a little, or rather longish, talk with us the other day on the religious debates of this time and of the past, and in the course of it he asked if we knew Moehler's "Symbolik." He said that Manning considered the first 120 pages of Vol. II. as quite unanswerable; that he was enthusiastic about it, and was endeavoring to proselyte by means of it right and left; that he declares he has shown it to several of our Anglican doctors; that they are quite unable to answer it, and so forth. Now I thought all the argument of that book had been long ago reproduced to the English public by Newman, had been answered by Archer Butler, and other controversialists on their side, at least to the satisfaction of Anglicans and themselves. But I should like very much to see the book.

Your criticism on Hartley's poetry is by far the best, in every way, that I have seen; it presents the poems in their deepest and most dignified aspect, and the dear man's character along with them. Yet there is nothing that can be caviled at as exalting them too highly in the scale as compositions, nothing that seems violently partial and exaggerated. One review speaks more highly of the "Prometheus" than you speak of it. I certainly think the hymn fine at the conclusion. To that you allow all its merit.

CHAPTER XXV.

1851.—*July–December.*

LETTERS TO MR. ELLIS YARNALL, PROFESSOR HENRY REED, AUBREY
DE VERE, ESQ., THOMAS BLACKBURNE, ESQ., MISS FENWICK.

I.

Visit to the Zoological Gardens.—Dependence on Outward Conditions a
Characteristic of Animals in Contradistinction to Man.

To AUBREY DE VERE, Esq. :

10 *Chester Place, August* 18, 1851.—I was very sorry to find
that I had missed you on my return from the Zoological Gardens. You should visit the animals, if you have not been there
for some time. I never saw the creatures so well provided for
before—their dwellings so spacious, or their peculiar habits so
attended to in the arrangements : sham rocks and trees appropriately distributed, and careful directions every where to the
visitors what is *not* to be done to the annoyance and injury of
the unspeaking inhabitants.

There are two kitten jaguars, which alone are worth going to
see. Such darls ! I wish I had seen them when they were
still smaller. These are on the lion side. On the opposite,
one of the large dens holds six or seven lovely leopards, which
were lying about in a choice variety of easy, elegant attitudes,
the long tail of one special beauty depending carelessly over a
bough, the lithe limb stretched out opposite. She looked like
an eastern sultana, very young. Wordsworth might well choose
the "Panther in the Wilderness" as an emblem of beauty—
their forms, their motions, their exquisitely variegated coat, all
are so beautiful ; and they look both good-natured and playful.
The giraffes so remind one of a delirious dream, that I think if
I were to look at them long I should go off into a sort of trance.
Oh, how very hideous the orang-outang is ! Why *did* Nature
make such a hideous creature? And how the elephants look
like a first rude, clumsy formation of her "'prentice hand," and

yet I suppose their construction is not simpler or less refined than that of slenderer creatures. How one is struck, in these gardens, with the way in which the inferior animals are adapted and conformed, each to a certain habitat—monkeys and leopards and the sloth to trees, though each in a different way, great birds to rocks, giraffes to places where there are high trees, the hippopotamus to streams, etc.—while man is fitted to no habitation, but fits a habitation to himself, except that the constitutions of some peoples are suited to certain climates.

II.

Immortality.—Causes of Ancient and Modern Infidelity.—Comparative Advantages of America and Europe.—Copies from the Old Masters.—The Bridgewater Gallery. — The High-Church Movement. —The Central Truth of Christianity.—Merits of Anglicanism as Compared with Romanism, Quakerism, and Skepticism.—Danger of Staking the Faith on External Evidences. — Pre-eminence ascribed by Certain Fathers and Councils of the Church to the See of Rome.—The Protestant Ground of Faith.—The Theory of Development.—A Dinner-party at Mr. Kenyon's.—Interesting Appearance and High Poetic Gifts of Mrs. Browning.—Expression and Thought in Poetry.—Women's Novels.—Conclusion.

To Mr. ELLIS YARNALL,* Philadelphia, U. S. :

10 *Chester Place, Regent's Park, August* 28, 1851.—Dear Mr. Yarnall, I will begin an answer to your interesting letter at once, not waiting for more time, or aught else, to answer it suitably, and as I should like to do ; for I know how much better ever so brief an answer is than none, so that it be not short in friendly feelings. It was by no means necessary to apologize, as you do, for the personal accounts in your letter, which were to me remarkably interesting. A good and wise man, one who is enjoying life himself, and promoting the welfare and happiness of others, called away suddenly,

> " While those whose hearts are dry as summer dust
> Burn to the socket,"

is always a subject for serious meditation on the ways of God with man, and to religious minds an evidence that here we have *no abiding city*—that the best estate of frail mortals, so frail as

---

* A friend and fellow - townsman of Professor Reed's, from whom he brought an introduction to my mother, while on a visit to England in the summer of 1849.—E. C.

earthly beings, so strong in the heavenly part of their constitution, is when they feel themselves to be strangers and pilgrims here below. What a depth of consolation there is in some of those expressions in the eleventh chapter of Hebrews! How they articulate the voice of immortality within us, and countervail the melancholy oracle of Lucretius, with their calm and confident assurances! The atheism of Epicurus gained its power upon the mind from the irrationality and antimoralism, the sensuality and cruelty involved in the popular religion which it opposed. And just so it is, I think, in the present day; the deniers of Revelation, and doubters of a future state, the disbelievers even of a God and an immortality for man in His presence, acquire all their strength from the weakness of the mediæval ecclesiastical system, its audacious contradictions of Scripture and the moral sense, and the unscrupulous use it makes of the most corrupt human instrumentalities for the furtherance of its purposes and consolidation of its power. But I must not plunge into this large subject at present.

I looked out in the Diffusion of Useful Knowledge Society's maps for the places you mention, and found some of them, and ascertained their relation to New York. It is very interesting to think how a ready-made civilization is rapidly spreading around that vast westerly lake, Michigan. It seems to me that in your country you have a great deal of our refinement without our troublesome, tedious conventionality. You have books, and in them the main substance of cultivation, the best part of civilization; and you have a noble, beautiful nature around you, which would do nothing to elevate the mind *by itself*, but where intellectual education has laid a groundwork, becomes an exalting and refining influence, and a perpetual source of delight. I wish you had more pictures by the old imaginative masters, and some of the architectural and sculptorial works of past generations of men, whose circumstances enabled them to do what never can be done again, unless a new state of things comes in, of which there is now no prospect. But the facilities of intercourse with Europe will do something to make up for that deficiency, by enabling every man of taste and leisure (even occasional) in your country, to fill his memory with those noble and lovely forms. Surely all of you who visit Italy, or the galleries of France and England, or the palaces of Spain, enriched by the painters of that sunny land, ought to bring home some copies of the finer productions of art. I have seen copies of old pictures which, I do believe, have in them *almost* all that the originals possess—*almost* all those qualities which constitute their charm and salutary influence; and it is, fortunately, paintings of the higher order of merit, the merit of which is most adequately conveyed by copies, and even by prints. There is in them a grace and loftiness of design, which can not be absent from any attempt at translation. Whenever I see an original Raphael, I behold an infinite deal of beauty which no print can convey; a soft exquisiteness of outline, and a life-like elasticity in the flesh; and yet I greet it as an old acquaintance. Lately I visited Lord Ellesmere's noble collection of pictures, which used to be called the Stafford or the Bridgewater Gallery (Lord Ellesmere is brother to the Duke of Sutherland). I had seen this splendid assemblage twice in my life before, once when I was a girl, and saw little more in the Titians and Poussins and Raphaels than products of power which I could not understand. A year ago I saw them again with Mr. Quillinan, Mr. Wordsworth's son-in-law, whose death filled us with grief two months ago. In Lord Ellesmere's new house the pictures are not well lighted, and many of them are placed so high as to be quite lost to the eye in all but a general outline. Still I received a pleasure from them unfelt before. In the centre of the principal room are the four Raphaels: "La Vierge au Palmier," the Virgin seated under a palm-tree, presenting the infant Saviour to the kneeling Joseph. This is one of the loveliest pictures I ever beheld. To judge from the print, the "Virgin de la Maison d'Albe," seated on the ground, with the Child Jesus climbing into her lap, St. John smilingly adoring close by, must be of equal beauty. Both these paintings are in a circular form, which aids the effect of their soft symmetry and perfect grace. The next in beauty of the Raphaels is the standing Virgin,* with Jesus and John, as boys of seven or eight, close beside her. "La Vierge au Linge" is least interesting, the Babe being too young to display grace of form and motion. It is asleep, the mother lifting the veil from its face. The fourth is the "Blessed Mother," with her Babe stretching itself across her arms. The two large Titians—"Diana, Calisto, and Nymphs," "Diana, Actæon, and Nymphs"—form a part of this rich group. I feel their

---

* "La Belle Vierge."—E. C.

power, but can not properly appreciate these pictures; and they are out of harmony, in tone, with the main mass of the paintings around. The famous "Assumption of the Virgin," by Guido, is at the end of the room, a large painting in a sort of alcove. It was one of the first pictures that ever awakened pictorial enthusiasm in me, or rather excited poetical enthusiasm by means of the pictorial art, when I saw it at the British Institution. The Maid Mother, robed in pink, with a blue scarf fluttering over her rich, graceful form, floats upward through a sky of aerial gold. The face is round and fair, and exquisitely delicate, with soft, yellow hair, and upturned hazel eyes. The " Michael Triumphing over Satan," in another apartment, is to my imagination quite as delightful as this more admired production of the same master. In the Archangel there is the same rich, full form as in the ascending Madonna, the same round, almost infantine face, surmounted with a natural glory of light golden hair; the beauty is womanish, as if Venus had been transformed into Apollo, for one day's festival in heaven, with an expectation of going back into her original state of goddesshood the day after. By comparing this picture with some of Murillo's, we obtain a notion of the superiority in the latter of religious depth and seriousness. For Murillo is always *serious*, though never quite sublime; evangelical more than ecclesiastical, which latter may be Christian, and yet will admit of Paganized conceptions of divine things, and these accompanied with a Pagan air of luxurious and voluptuous earthiness. I was led to this remark by thinking of the Angels or Divine Persons who appear to Abraham in Murillo's great picture, companion to the still finer " Prodigal Son " by the same great artist (both are in the possession of Lord Ellesmere's brother, the Duke of Sutherland, and are in his palatial town-house), they are so much more spiritual in their beauty.

You speak of the Movement in our Church, originated by Newman and other writers of the " Tracts for the Times," and I can entirely agree with you in thinking that it has awakened a loftier spirit than before was prevailing. I believe, too, that the discussions it has occasioned must be in the main for good, and at any rate were inevitable. The particular Tractarian movement, indeed, is itself but the offspring of a deeper one, which is common to all Europe, and has been produced by such a complex cause of circumstances, states, and relations as ever brings about the great general changes in the public condition of things, and social arrangements at large. Matters pertaining to religion could not remain as they were left by the Reformation; as thought advanced, and when this nation was no longer occupied with foreign wars or internal commotions, and began to think seriously of setting its house in order, the discrepancies and incoherencies, intellectual and moral, discoverable to the searching eye in various departments of Church and State, must be revealed in a clear light, and call for remedy. Tractarianism was a stage in the progress of newly awakened thought; but how men who *go on* thinking can suppose that it set forth a coherent religious system, with which a serious mind could rest satisfied, or settled religious matters on a firm basis, I can not imagine for a moment. On the contrary, of all forms of the Christian faith that ever have found favor with respectable bodies of men, Anglo-Catholicism seems to me the most baseless and inconsistent. My friend, Mr. H. Crabb Robinson, says that its inconsistency is its merit, as compared, he means, with Romanism, on the one hand, or Straussism on the other. Differing as I do materially from Mr. Robinson respecting the great central truth of Christianity, the Divinity of our Lord (for I believe the Redeemer to be God himself, and he holds Jesus Christ to be a Being empowered by God to save the world—no mere man, and yet not very God), I do agree with him in this, and believe Anglo-Catholicism a far better religion than Romanism, Quakerism, or general skepticism, though more inconsistent than either.

I think it far better than Romanism, because it rejects that impious supplementary gospel, those blasphemous pretensions, heathenish figments, demoralizing principles, and debasing practices which the Church of Rome keeps up for the benefit of the clergy, together with those doctrines of Papal authority, which, if unresisted (providentially it has always been kept in check), must soon destroy all national independence, and introduce a despotism inimical to the progress and best interests of the human race.

I think it better than Quakerism, which rejects the whole Visible Church system, because I see in that system, so far as it is maintained on sound principles, for the educating of mankind in spirituals, not for blinding and enchaining them, immense utility. All temporal governments require a Church to work in alliance with them; and the Anglican form, retaining the Episcopate, is an excellent institution, which may be placed on a firm basis of reason and morality. On this foundation it has been standing all along, amid the various theories of men hovering around it, and supposed to be the foundation by mystified beholders, who can not distinguish between cloudage and *terra firma.*

I need not say why Anglo-Catholicism is better than such doctrine as that of the rejectors of Revelation, who think that St. John confounded his own dreams, engendered of human philosophies, with the teaching of the Spirit, and deprive those whom they seduce of all solid ground of hope in a better life to come. Such views appear to be the immediate result, in some minds, of the High-Church externalism and dogmatism, which denies the inward revelation to be the true ultimate assurance of faith. They examine that external authority to which they have been commanded to bow, and find it wanting in the material of conviction; and they have never been led to think and feel that the Christian religion, so far as it answers any true purpose of a religion in purifying and elevating our nature, *is its own evidence;* that the Bible attests its own divineness, as the sun reveals itself by its own light. These skeptics, equally with the externalizing Romanist, are ever seen to be deficient in a sense and perception of *moral evidence;* they are blind to the traces of God, both in the course of the world and in the volume of Revelation; equally with the Romanist, the Infidel fails to see that religion is a spirit, a power or principle, not a certain set of formal beliefs bound up together in a frame, so that a man must take it all up at once, or leave it all. The Romanist urges that if the ideas of reason (or aught in the mind within) are the criterion of truth, a man's creed will be always varying; he does not understand that we may perceive truth in a thousand different ways and degrees, but that we can really perceive none at all except by the mirror of heaven within us. Just so the skeptic finds out certain incoherencies, or thinks he finds them, in the scriptural accounts of our Lord's course upon earth, and thereupon concludes that the Word of God can not be *contained* in the Bible, because he finds it in part to be the mistaken word of man.

The inconsistency of the Anglo-Catholic position seems to me to be this: The Anglican, who firmly maintains the doctrine of Apostolical Succession, as absolutely essential to the being of the Christian Church, and boasts that our hierarchy, by means of regular ordination, descends in an unbroken line from the Apostles ; who insists upon the absolving powers of the clergy, and founds them upon Scripture, by transferring the promise of our Lord to His faithful followers (the chosen Twelve) that they should have the power of binding and loosing, to all their successors ordained in due form, whatever their personal qualifications may happen to be ; when it is objected that the language of the New Testament itself authorizes no such application, that it is an arbitrary extension of the sense, and supposes a thing in its own nature unreasonable, because the mission and the promise are obviously adapted to the personal qualifications of those to whom they were originally addressed—their supernatural powers, which ceased with them—their burning faith and zeal, which can not be conveyed by ordination, or any other ceremony ; the Anglican, I say, constantly replies (and certainly no other reply can be given) that all sound members of the Catholic Church submit to the judgment of the Church, which is to be ascertained by the decrees and acts of general councils and the consent of ancient bishops and doctors. But on all the same grounds of Scripture, and application of Scripture by Councils and Fathers, we ought to believe in the primacy of the Pope, that he is the supreme judge in all controversies, and the determiner of doctrine, whence it follows that we ought to accept the whole Romish system, with its deification of the Virgin, doctrine of the Mass, adoration of saints (for such it practically is), with all those religious institutes and practices which the English mind so revolts from and contemns—the mockery of indulgences, the corruption of the confessional, monasticism with all its social mischiefs, loosening the bonds of family life, intrusion and domination of the priesthood. For all these things and more are contained within that dark womb— so simple without, so labyrinthine within—the Papal Supremacy and Infallibility ; for though the latter article is not called *de fide*, yet it so obviously follows from the former that exalters of the Papacy may very well afford to leave it to take care of itself when the Supremacy has been established. Here the Anglican interposes, taking exception at the term *Supremacy*. He tells you the primacy acknowledged by the Church of the first six centuries is a widely different thing from the headship now claimed for the Pope; it may be proved by overwhelming evidence that bishops of old, the very same men who used high language concerning the Chair of Peter, did hold their own against this most exalted and venerable Chair, whenever they thought it necessary to assert their independence, and defend their proceedings and their doctrine against an adverse decision of the Holy See; nay, that some of them openly disclaimed a Bishop of Bishops, alleging that the Apostles were heads of their several charges, and declaring that there is no Head of the whole Church but Christ. To this answer the modern Romanist replies that the doctrine was as yet not fully *developed*, which is a plain fact; but, without admitting his pretension that an article not known or understood in the first ages can be a divine truth, necessary to be admitted by all Christians on peril of salvation, I must concede to the Romanist that the Fathers generally, and by a sort of consent, attributed a pre-eminence to the See and Bishop of Rome, which properly involve the Supremacy even in the modern sense, and their words and actions, repudiating the paramount authority of the latter, are really inconsistent with their attributions to the successor of the Fisherman, when no particular interest or influence induces them to diminish his claims. I have lately examined this question in debates with Mr. ———, who has satisfied himself that the Romish Church theory is the only tenable one, and although unable myself to receive or admire any mystico-ecclesiastical system, Roman or Anglican, yet with a strong desire to find the Romanist pretensions to patristic testimony in favor of the Papacy wholly vain. But in this I have been disappointed. The language of Cyprian, Ambrose, and very many other Fathers, as well as of councils venerated by Anglo-Catholics, is unmeaning and self-contradictory, if understood so as to exclude the Supremacy. It imports that the Bishop of Rome is the centre and *origin* of unity; his See the Rock on which the Church is built; himself the successor of Peter, from whom the "Apostolate and Episcopate in Christ took its beginning;" that "where Peter is, there is the Church;" that to be out of communion with Rome is to be cut off from Christ; that from the See of Peter "*the full grace of all Pontiffs is derived;*" that the Roman Church is the "foundation and mould of the Churches;" that the Holy See *transmits its rights* to the universal Church;" that "the Pope is the head of the Church, other bishops the members." In the Third General Council he was acknowledged to be the "*Head* of the whole Faith." Now surely this language, and it is quite as general as any which can be cited from the Fatherhood on the Consubstantiality of Christ with the Father, or the three Persons in the Godhead, is senseless babble, if it does not mean that the Pope is the source of jurisdiction and the ultimate decider of controversy in the Church. The ancient Fathers, with scarce a dissentient voice, ascribe a pre-eminence and authority to Peter over the other Apostles; and as *all* the Apostles had supernatural powers, what could St. Peter have beyond them, except what is now ascribed to the Pope as his successor, namely, to be their earthly head, the channel of grace and episcopal power from Christ to them, consequently to be the ultimate judge of questions concerning the faith?

I fully admit that the Fathers and Bishops often contradict this doctrine, as I have already said (though Tertullian's language proves that the Papal supremacy was asserted in the second century), and the Canons of Sardica are strong evidence that it was not a " Law and Tradition of the Church " acknowledged from the beginning, as well as the silence of the earliest Christian writers, especially St. Ignatius, who exalts the Episcopate, and says naught of any Bishop of Bishops. But surely this incoherent and conflicting testimony, of which it seems impossible to make a harmonious whole, and which keeps up the controversy between the churches, contains ample vindication of the attitude assumed by genuine Scriptural Protestantism, which acknowledges no positive divine ground of faith but the Bible, acknowledged to be divine by its own internal character, and corresponding to the image of the divine within us, not by any external testimony of the visible Church. Surely it shows those to have reason on their side who refuse to be absolutely determined, in all the articles of their belief, by majorities of ancient Bishops and Doctors, or even by their consentient voice. It begins to be generally felt that no consistent scheme of doctrine can be obtained from the ancient Fathers; and that the principle of development must be freely acted on, in order to the maintenance of any Church system founded in the Christian Revelation, and connected with it by unbroken tradition. But this principle of development is contradictory to the general mind of the Ancient Church, which always appeals to Scripture and the continuous teaching of the Church authorities; it is incongruous with the root-principles of a system of externalism and uniformity of doctrine in its intellectual aspect, which ought to be supported by outward and historic testimony. Hereafter a Head Bishop, or a General Council, may decide that Arianism is, after all, the right doctrine of the Godhead, and who could disprove the assertion that it was the proper development of the original belief, always acknowledged by a part of the Church, held in germ, and so forth. Development is too large a key for the lock to which it is deceptively applied. The lock it really fits is one which opens into the illimitable Court of Anarchy, not into the area of the existing Visible Church system. There is no conceivable corruption or transmutation of doctrine and practice which may not be called a true development, if there is no rule or standard by which the legitimacy of the extension is to be judged; and all depends on the judgment of an irresponsible Head, presumed to be the oracle through which Christ speaks to His Church.

* * * My daughter and I lately met at the house of my excellent old friend, Mr. Kenyon, that poetical pair, Mr. and Mrs. Browning. You probably know her as Elizabeth Barrett, author of the " Seraphim," " Drama of Exile," and many ballads and minor poems, among which " Cowper's Grave " is of special excellence. She has lately published " Casa Guidi Windows," a meditative political poem of considerable merit; Mazzini admires it, and it has been translated into Italian. Mrs. Browning is in weak health, and can not remain in this foggy clime; they are to reside in Paris. She is little, hard-featured, with long, dark ringlets, a pale face, and plaintive voice—something very impressive in her dark eyes and her brow. Her general aspect puts me in mind of Mignon—what Mignon might be in maturity and maternity. She has more poetic genius than any other woman living—perhaps more than any woman ever showed before, except Sappho. Still there is an imperfectness in what she produces; in many passages the expressions are very faulty, the images forced and untrue, the sentiments exaggerated, and the situations unnatural and unpleasant. Another pervading fault of Mrs. Browning's poetry is rugged, harsh versification, with imperfect rhymes, and altogether that want of art in the department of metre which prevents the language from being an unobstructive medium for the thought. Verse and diction are the bodily organism of poetry; this body ought to be soft, bright, lovely, carrying with it an influence and impression of delightfulness, yet not challenging attention by itself. These defects in poetical organism are inimical to the enduring life of the poetry; the same or similar thoughts will re-appear in better form, and so supersede the earlier version; whereas, if poetic thoughts are once bodied to perfection, they will remain and exclude all future rivals. There is fear with regard to many of our present producers of poetry, lest the good that is in them should be swamped by the inferior matter, which gives a grotesque air to their compositions at large.

It has been ever a favorite saying with me that there is one line of literature, and only one, in which women can do something that men can not do, and do better; and that is a certain style of novel. I warmly admire the better novels produced by women during the last seventy or eighty years—the writings of Inchbald, Burney, Edgeworth, Jane Austen, Miss Ferrier, and those interesting productions of the present day from the pens of Mrs. Marsh and Miss Brontë. Mrs. Gore's novels are full of talent, and display a most extensive acquaintance both with modern books and modern things; but there is a most unpleasant tone about them. "Jane Eyre" and "Shirley," by Miss Brontë, are full of genius. There is a spirit, a glow and fire about them, a masculine energy of satire and of picturesque description, which have delighted me; but they also abound in proofs of a certain hardness of feeling and plebeian coarseness of taste. The novels of Mrs. Marsh, upon the whole, please me better than any that are now forthcoming. They are thoroughly feminine; and though often too diffuse, their diffuseness may be skimmed over without leaving any unpleasant impression on the mind. "The Wilmingtons," with its sequel, "Time the Avenger," is to my feelings an interesting book.

If you happen to have any communication with Newburyport, Massachusetts—but this is a vain thought. I was thinking of my unseen friends and correspondents, Mr. and Mrs. Tracey, of that place. My last to them spoke of my weakened health, and they are anxious to know how I am going on. I can not give a good report of myself, and from several causes must not attempt more letter-writing at present. My kindest wishes attend them. I have already sent kind regards and thanks to Mr. and Mrs. Reed. Accept the same yourself, dear sir, and may you

long have health and strength to enjoy the infinite delights of
literature, and the loveliness of "this bright, breathing world,"
which the poets teach us to admire, and the Gospel makes us
hope to find again in that unseen world whither we are all going.—Believe me truly your friend,   SARA COLERIDGE.

III.

Prayer for Temporal and Spiritual Benefits.

To Miss FENWICK:

September 4, 1851.—Your friendship, dear friend, has been
one great blessing of these last years of my life, and I trust not
only a comfort and happiness, but a lasting benefit, which will
survive all the worsening and decay of our poor, frail, earthly
tabernacle.   My gratitude to you is one of my deepest feelings.
God bless you, and bestow upon you all whatsoever He knows
to be best for you.   I must still pray for temporal comforts to
be granted you.   We are to pray ever, and He will set our prayers straight.   But still more earnestly, and with more confidence
for you and for myself, I ask for that *peace which passes understanding.*—Ever most affectionately your friend,

SARA COLERIDGE.

IV.

Increase of Illness.—Fancied Wishes.—Trial and Effects of Mesmerism.
  —Editorial Duties still Fulfilled.—Derwent Isle and Keswick Vale.—
  Visit of the Archdukes to General Peachey in 1815.—Old Letters.—
  Death, and the Life beyond it.

To AUBREY DE VERE, Esq.:

10 *Chester Place, October* 1, 1851.—My dear friend, you will
regret very much to learn how much worse and weaker I am
than when you saw me last.   I can not now walk more than
half an hour at a time, when I am at the best.   At Margate an
hour or hour and twenty minutes did not fatigue me.   I still
take short walks twice a day, but how long my power of doing
this will last I can not say.

You can hardly imagine how my mind hovers about that old
well-known church-yard, with Skiddaw and the Bassenthwaite

hills in sight; how I long to take away mamma's remains from the place where they are now deposited, and when my own time comes, to repose beside her, as to what now *seems* myself, in that grassy burial-ground, with the Southeys reposing close by. My husband I hope to meet in heaven. But there is a different feeling in regard to earlier ties: Hartley and Mr. Wordsworth I would have where they are, in that Grasmere church-yard, within an easy distance of Keswick, as it used to be in old times.

These are strong *feelings*, translated into fancied *wishes*—not sober earnest. When we are withdrawn from society and the bustle of life, in some measure, and our thoughts are from any cause fixed on the grave, how does the early life rise up into glow and prominence, and, as it were, call one back into itself! Yet during that early life how I looked forward, imagining better things here below than I had yet experienced, and going beyond this world altogether into the realms above!

A few weeks ago, my old friend C. H. Townshend* came to town for a short time on business from Lausanne. He reproached me for not trying mesmerism, and, on my yielding to his representations on the subject, brought Dr. Elliotson to give me advice. My house-maid willingly undertook the business, was instructed, and now mesmerizes regularly twice a day. The effect on me is not strong, sophisticated as my nerves have been by morphine; but there is a perceptible *peculiar* sensation produced by the passes. They soothe me at the time, and make me drowsy, and I think there is some beneficial influence exerted on the constitution. From what I feel, I am much inclined to believe that some agent in the physical frame is called into action by the passes; that the mesmeric influence of the operator *excites* this principle in the patient, as heat kindles heat upon communication. Neuralgic pains are soon relieved by the passes. They return after a while, but are quieted for the time. An article on Electro-biology in the last *Westminster*, reducing all the phenomena under ordinary causes, I think shallow, and know to be mistaken.

I have not yet opened the book of new poetry you have sent

---

* The name of Mr. Chauncy Hare Townshend will be familiar to all visitors at the South Kensington Museum, where the fine collection of pictures and jewels bequeathed by him to that institution is now exhibited. He was the author of "Facts in Mesmerism," and of several volumes of poetry, and was, besides, an accomplished amateur artist and musician.—E. C.

me to read, but hope to do so ere we meet. I have a great many books on hand, and Derwent keeps me busy in matters which he is concerned in, as far as my weak strength will allow. He wants some new editions of the Esteesian Marginalia prepared for the press, and this can not be done at present, as I have so long been the Esteesian *housekeeper*, without my superintendence.

We have seen a good deal lately of Mr. Blackburne, a poetical friend of my brother Hartley, a charming converser, but very much in want of a steady, regular profession. He has always some new poem or poemet to recite whenever he comes. His poetry is graceful, abounding in sweet images, but lacks *bone*. He is too fond, I think, of the boneless Keatsian sort of poetry, which is all marrow, and wearies one at last with its want of fibre. Indeed, I say the other extreme is better in the end.

October 2.—Sweet Derwent Isle! how many, many scenes of my youth arise in my mind in connection with thee! I had a personal and a second-hand association with that lovely spot; for mamma used to tell me much of Emma, the first young wife of General Peachey, youngest daughter of Mr. Charter, of Taunton, whom my Uncle Southey so beautifully described in those epitaph lines, which present her as she appeared, " like a dream of old romance, skimming along in her little boat ; and how she was laid, before her youth had ripened into full summer, amid Maderia's orange-groves to rest.". She was tall—a man's height—five feet eight at least, but so feminine—a slender, blue-eyed blonde.

I can not remember that fair Emma ; but what pleasant visits have I paid to the island—in summer, autumn, icy winter— in the second lady's time! There I was when the Archdukes came to visit the island, and lunched there after the entrance of the Allied Kings into Paris. Oh, the fussiness of the general on that occasion! How their Serenities *Russianly* absorbed the preservative butter of the potted char! What a beautiful Prussian Count they had with them, with whom I fancied myself in love for two or three days!—tried hard to be, I believe, though the cement was wanting of advances on his part toward me, without which Apollo himself would soon have slipped away from my heart and fancy. Sometimes we were detained in the island by stress of weather, and once were prevented from a visit to it by the same cause.

I wonder whether the feathery fern I transplanted from the Cardingmill Field, the part among trees beside the river, is yet living, and the beech-tree, which I used to climb, with its copper foliage, at the foot of which, in spring, a few crocuses grew.

I was quite sorry to say farewell to C. H. Townshend. He was more agreeable, more clever in talk, than ever; and we have such interesting common Greta Hall and Keswick remembrances.

A sweet and affecting set of verses from Blackburne, on receiving back old letters of Hartley's:

> "There they lie, a frozen ocean,
>   Running on without a shore,
> But the ardor and the motion
>   Of the heart beats there no more.
> And *thou?* art thou grown brighter
>   Since I saw thee then so bright?
> Thinner are thy hands, and whiter,
>   And thy hair like autumn light."

Oh, Keswick vale! and shall I really die, and never, never see thee again? Surely there will be another Keswick—all the loveliness transfused, the hope, the joy of youth! How wholly was that joy the work of imagination!

Oh, this life is very dear to me! The outward beauty of earth, and the love and sympathy of fellow-creatures, make it, to my feelings, a sort of heaven half ruined—an Elysium into which a dark tumultuous ocean is perpetually rushing in to agitate and destroy, to lay low the blooming bowers of tranquil bliss, and drown the rich harvests. Love is the sun of this lower world; and we know from the beloved disciple that it will be the bliss of heaven. God is Love; and whatever there may be that we can not now conceive, love will surely be contained in it. It will be Love sublimed, and incorporated in Beauty infinite and perfect.

I am very faint and weak to-day—more so than I have yet been; but I have been as low in nerves often formerly, otherwise I might think that I had entered into the dark valley, and was approaching the river of Death. How kind of Bunyan— what a beneficent imagination—to shadow out death as a *river*, which is so pleasant to the mind, and carries it on into regions bright and fair beyond that boundary stream.

Miss Fenwick is to me an angel upon earth. Her being near me now has seemed a special providence. God bless her, and spare her to us and her many friends. She is a noble creature, all tenderness and strength. When I first became acquainted with her, I saw at once that her heart was of the very finest, richest quality; and her wisdom and insight are, as ever must be in such a case, exactly correspondent.

V.

Leave-taking.—Value of a Profession.—A Lily and a Poem.—Flowers.—Beauty and Use.

To Thomas Blackburne, Esq.:

10 *Chester Place, October* 13, 1851. — I feel much in saying farewell to you, dear friend of my ever-lamented brother. You have known me in a sad, shaded stage of my existence, yet have greeted my poor autumn as brightly and genially as if it were spring or summer. Hitherto my head has been " above water;" ere you return to this busy town, *the waves may have gone over my head.* My great endeavor is not to foreshape the future in particulars, but, knowing that my strength always has been equal to my day, when the day is come, to feel that it ever will be so on to the end, come what may, and that all things, except a reproaching conscience, are "less dreadful than they seem."

God bless you! Cultivate your poetical talent, which will ever be a delight to you, but still, as I used to say to my friend Mr. ———, have a profession—a broad beam of the house of life, around which the bright occasional garland may be woven from time to time. Believe me, dear Mr. Blackburne, yours with much regard, SARA COLERIDGE.

> "Espouse thy doom at once, and cleave
> To fortitude without reprieve,"*

are words that often sound in my ear.

Wordsworth was more to my opening mind in the way of religious consolation than all books put together, except the Bible.

Regent's Park, September 28.——Thank you, dear Mr. Blackburne, for that beauteous flower and lovely poem. Two lines I specially admire—

---

* "White Doe of Rylstone," Canto II.—E. C.

> "And like a poet tell it with a blossom
> To each new sun."

The corolla of flowers is intended to protect the fructifying system in its tender state. But this purpose might have been served by something unsightly. Nature has provided exquisite beauty both in the stamina and pistils (which give all the grace and spirit to many blossoms, or, expanding into petals, form the richness of the *rosa centifolia,* and numberless other double flowers), and in their guard, which exceeds the robes of Solomon, and rivals the butterfly, which "flutters with free wings above it."

How stupid are those people who reduce all beauty to the sense of usefulness—early association! I have heard a very clever man insist that children may be taught to admire toads and spiders, and think them as beautiful as butterflies, birds of paradise, or such a lily as you have sent me.

VI.

Proposal to Visit the South of France.—Climate and Society of Lausanne.—The Spasmodic School of Poetry.—Article on Immortality in the *Westminster Review.*—Outward Means a Part of the Christian Scheme.—The "Evil Heart of Unbelief."—The Foundations of Religion.

To AUBREY DE VERE, Esq.:

Chester Place, October 19, 1851.—My dear friend, are you still at that dear Derwent Island? I must direct a few lines thither for the chance of their finding you there. Since your last most kind letter, I have been longing to thank you for its most soothing contents.

I am sure you would have a pleasure in giving up your own favorite project of visiting Rome—postponing it in order to guard the poor invalid on her way to a better clime than this. Alas! it is but a pleasant vision, the thought of my journeying to the south of France. Yet I believe a foreign climate, more bracing, less damp and unsettled than this, might afford me as much advantage as I could receive from external things. C. H. Townshend talked to me of the effect of Lausanne air upon his relaxed and ailing frame, till he inspired me with a great wish, unfelt by me before, that I could live abroad with my E——. The discourse of other friends, William and Emma G——, who are delicate people, goes strongly the same way. Mrs. Browning feels life abroad to be life indeed.

Then Chauncy Townshend says that he prefers the state of society around him at Mon Loisir to London excitement and bustle. "There," he says, "I may be sad if sorrow comes, but I am *always calm.*" The way in which he uttered these words was calming to my spirit; and certainly never did I see our old friend in better mood, more quietly gladsome, free, and variously eloquent. He tells me that he has a most agreeable, refined, intellectual set of acquaintances at Lausanne, whom he visits without London formality and expense. He provides himself with a store of books for the winter, and is as independent and happy as a man can be in this life. "But why did you furnish this fine house in Norfolk Street, Park Lane," said I, "and fill it with beautiful works of art, only to enter it at long intervals, and then for a few weeks?" He declared he had as much pleasure in thinking of it, and roaming all over it in imagination, as if he were actually occupying its space, and beholding its adornments. This is, perhaps, rather fantastical. An imagination so pliant might go a step farther, and imagine the house and contents, without keeping money locked up in it.

I read through the dramatic poem you were so kind as to send me, and found it full of passion and energy, but, on the whole, painful and unsatisfactory—a production which shoots its bolt at once, and then has no more that it can do. I was reminded of the Preface to the "Virgin Widow" in reading it. One most powerful passage is a vision of the death of an ancient gladiator; but then it is utterly extravagant and untrue. Such things could not be—such horrid combinations of incompatible terrors and sufferings and ecstasies of enjoyment, and power and weakness, could not exist together. There are no lines and expressions, lovely and felicitous, which take place among the treasures of the mind, and are revisited ever and anon. Mr. Taylor has not written a great deal, but the proportion of such satisfactory passages to the total quantity of his compositions is considerable, and will give him a place, I think, finally, above all the other spasmodists of the present day.

Did you read Helps's "Companions of my Solitude?" There is a great charm in Helps, and he does give some help to reflection, though rather butterflyish in his movements.

Last night I read an article on Immortality in the *West-*

minster. What a shallow sciolist that A—— seems to be! This life would be a gorgeous vestibule to no edifice, only a darksome cavern, if there were naught for man beyond it. How disproportionate our intellectual and spiritual education! " Few of us seem fit for heaven. What human goodness is commensurate to perfect, endless felicity—what human frailty to eternal woe ?" Thus men argue against a future state. But we know not how heaven hereafter will be apportioned, and how the soul may expand in heaven-worthiness. If man be destined for the dust in a few years, he is a strange riddle. This life has ever seemed a mere transitional state, and tolerable only on that supposition, to the most elevated and cultivated men.

Viewing the Romish system as you do, my dear friend, a bright ideal, I can not regret that you think as you do of the compatibility of my father's scheme of philosophy therewith, assured as I feel that he had done that papal system too much justice to believe in it as a divine institution. Do not think I am ever worried by what you call your "rough notes" on Romanism, however surprised I may sometimes be at your views in all their eloquence.

I do verily think no pious Romanist can suppose that faith does not involve a spiritual intuition and internal revelation of the truth. But the question was, which is the *ultimate ground of belief*, that which underlies and supports all the rest, this discernment of divine things which Christ himself by his Spirit works in the heart, or the teaching of the Church? Is the latter necessary to assure us that the very work of God in the soul of man is really and truly His work?

An external system for teaching Christianity, for initiating men into it, leading them to Christ, I believe to be a part of God's providence; and such a system, in so far as it is conformed to reason and moral truth, will have the blessing of the Spirit. But I can not think it necessary, or even desirable for the right religious education of mankind—the education of the higher faculties and nobler feelings—that this system should be infallible. I admit that sin is not the only obstacle or impediment by which divine truth may be kept from the minds of men. The African savage can not make himself religious wholly from within. There must be a preacher and outward instrumentalities. I only meant to say that when the deep spiritual verities, which are the substance of the faith, are presented to the mind, it is *sin*, and not any imperfection in our faculties, which can alone prevent it from being clearly perceived. This seems to be plainly intimated by our Lord, when He shows why the Jews did not receive Him, and in His discourse to Philip. Upon the whole, we have as good means of knowing the Saviour, and all that concerns our peace, as our Lord's disciples had. We can not know Him at all, except by an inward revelation of the Spirit. It is by knowledge of the truth—that is, information of it from without—that this communion with the enlightening Spirit comes about. But where it is, surely it is an absolute, independent certainty.

The term "private judgment" is ambiguous. It may be interpreted in a bad sense, in which I do not see that it is fairly chargeable on Reformed Christianity. But it is confounded with *individual intuition*, and in that sense it is not easily convicted of error. But I do not pretend to maintain any particular reformed system as the very truth. I believe we have but approximations to absolute truth.

I own, too, that there are to my mind far more interesting considerations concerning religion than those which we have been discussing. It is the foundations of religion, those problems and difficulties that belong to every system, or underlie them all, which engage my serious thoughts. I care not so much about the difference between Romish and Anglican, though I confess the views of the Blessed Virgin in the Church of Rome do seem to me to make modern Romanism an essentially different faith and system from that of the Bible and of early Christianity.

VII.

Gradual Loss of Strength.—Credulity of Unbelievers.—Spiritual Peace.—
Thoughts of Past Years.

To Aubrey de Vere, Esq.:

10 *Chester Place, October* 27, 1851.—My dear friend, I was sorry not to see you yesterday, and the more so lest I should be too weak when you come again,

"For I'm wearing awa, Friend,
Like snaw when it's thaw, Friend,"

and I feel as if I should not be long here. There is a torpor ever hanging over me, like a cloud overspreading the sky, only rent here and there by some special force; and my eyes have a heavy, deathy look. I am decidedly worse since I saw you, and I begin to wish to get rid of the mesmerism, which is producing no good effect.

Thank you for the "Valley of Lilies."* I have been looking at that strange book of A—— and M——. In all the volume of Humanity, as far as I have opened it, this is the very strangest, saddest page, as far as relates to states of thought and opinion. Is it not astonishing that, in a Christian country, there can have been such a one-sided intellectual development? The *condition* constantly throughout the book confounded with the efficient cause. I now feel as if I had never seen arrogance and shallowness before these Letters came before me. The monstrous credulity, on the one hand, and utter faithlessness on the other, is truly frightful.

Do you remember how beautifully Hooker shows how our spiritual peace may be smothered for a time by bodily clouds? But, as my father says, there is a mind *within the mind*, and we must try to draw out and strengthen that.

I dwell on the Southey Letters. My mind is ever going back to my brighter days of youth, and all its dear people and things of other days.

VIII.

Congratulations on a Friend's Recovery from Illness.—Her own State of Health and of Mind.—Wilkie's Portrait of her Brother Hartley at Ten Years of Age.—"The Northern Worthies."—A Farewell.

To Professor HENRY REED:

10 *Chester Place, December* 22, 1851. — My dear Professor Reed, many weeks ago I heard from Mr. Yarnall with deep concern of your severe, lingering illness — lingering, though transitory, I trust, in its nature. A week since I received from your friend another long and very interesting letter, which conveyed to me the welcome news that, though still confined to your bed, you were in a fair way of recovery. It may be premature to congratulate you on positive recovery, and Mrs. Reed with you; but I may say how hopefully I look forward to it,

---

* A devotional work by Thomas à Kempis.—E. C.

and how rejoiced I should be to hear of your restoration to your family and all your various activities, literary and professional. Would that *my* health prospect were as yours—as hopeful! I am now an invalid, confined to my own room and the adjoining apartment, with little prospect of restoration, though I am not entirely hopeless. My malady, which had been threatening me ever since the summer before last, did not come into activity till a few months ago. What my course and the event may be perhaps no physician can tell to a certainty. I endeavor not to speculate, to make the most of each day as it comes, making use of what powers remain to me, and feeling assured that strength will be supplied, if it be sought from above, to bear any trial which my Father in heaven may think fit to send. I do not suffer pain. My principal suffering is the sense of sinking and depression. Of course all literary exertion and extensive correspondence are out of the question for me in my present condition. New editions of my father's works are in contemplation, and I can still be of use to my brother Derwent in helping to arrange them. But any work that I do now is of a very slight and slow description.

Mr. Herbert Taylor kindly offers to send to Philadelphia any book or packet for me, and I take the opportunity of sending you an enlarged engraving of Wilkie's sketch of my brother Hartley, in which you were so much interested, and the more from a likeness you discerned in it to your son. My brother's biographical work, "The Northern Worthies," is in the press, and great pleasure I have in reading the proof-sheets, and perceiving how much more merit there is in these lives than I ever knew them to possess before. Their chief interest consists in the accompanying criticisms and reflections. I feel sure you will like them exceedingly, though, of course, you may dissent from many of the opinions and sentiments expressed.

Farewell, my dear sir; you have my sincere wishes and prayers for your entire restoration. I *may* not be able to answer any more letters from America—a land in which I shall never cease to take an interest—but I shall ever hear with pleasure of you and yours, as long as my powers of thought remain.

Give my kind regards to Mrs. Reed, and believe me yours, with much esteem and sympathy, SARA COLERIDGE.

THE END.

VALUABLE & INTERESTING WORKS

FOR PUBLIC AND PRIVATE LIBRARIES,

PUBLISHED BY HARPER & BROTHERS, NEW YORK.

FLAMMARION'S ATMOSPHERE. The Atmosphere. Translated from the French of CAMILLE FLAMMARION. Edited by JAMES GLAISHER, F.R.S., Superintendent of the Magnetical and Meteorological Department of the Royal Observatory at Greenwich. With 10 Chromo-Lithographs and 86 Woodcuts. 8vo, Cloth, $6 00.

HUDSON'S HISTORY OF JOURNALISM. Journalism in the United States, from 1690 to 1872. By FREDERICK HUDSON. Crown 8vo, Cloth, $5 00.

PIKE'S SUB-TROPICAL RAMBLES. Sub-Tropical Rambles in the Land of the Aphanapteryx. By NICHOLAS PIKE, U. S. Consul, Port Louis, Mauritius. Profusely Illustrated from the Author's own Sketches; containing also Maps and Valuable Meteorological Charts. 8vo, Cloth, $3 50.

TYERMAN'S OXFORD METHODISTS. The Oxford Methodists: Memoirs of the Rev. Messrs. Clayton, Ingham, Gambold, Hervey, and Broughton, with Biographical Notices of others. By the Rev. L. TYERMAN, Author of "Life and Times of the Rev. John Wesley," &c. Crown 8vo, Cloth, $2 50.

TRISTRAM'S THE LAND OF MOAB. The Result of Travels and Discoveries on the East Side of the Dead Sea and the Jordan. By H. B. TRISTRAM, M.A., LL.D., F.R.S., Master of the Greatham Hospital, and Honorary Canon of Durham. With New Map and Illustrations. Crown 8vo, Cloth, $2 50.

SANTO DOMINGO, Past and Present; with a Glance at Hayti. By SAMUEL HAZARD. Maps and Illustrations. Crown 8vo, Cloth, $3 50.

LIFE OF ALFRED COOKMAN. The Life of the Rev. Alfred Cookman; with some Account of his Father, the Rev. George Grimston Cookman. By HENRY B. RIDGAWAY, D.D. With an Introduction by Bishop FOSTER, LL.D. Portrait on Steel. 12mo, Cloth, $2 00.

HERVEY'S CHRISTIAN RHETORIC. A System of Christian Rhetoric, for the Use of Preachers and Other Speakers. By GEORGE WINFRED HERVEY, M.A., Author of "Rhetoric of Conversation," &c. 8vo, Cloth, $3 50.

CASTELAR'S OLD ROME AND NEW ITALY. Old Rome and New Italy. By EMILIO CASTELAR. Translated by Mrs. ARTHUR ARNOLD. 12mo, Cloth, $1 75.

THE TREATY OF WASHINGTON: Its Negotiation, Execution, and the Discussions Relating Thereto. By CALEB CUSHING. Crown 8vo, Cloth, $2 00.

PRIME'S I GO A-FISHING. I Go a-Fishing. By W. C. PRIME. Crown 8vo, Cloth, $2 50.

HALLOCK'S FISHING TOURIST. The Fishing Tourist: Angler's Guide and Reference Book. By CHARLES HALLOCK, Secretary of the "Blooming-Grove Park Association." Illustrations. Crown 8vo, Cloth, $2 00.

SCOTT'S AMERICAN FISHING. Fishing in American Waters. By GENIO C. SCOTT. With 170 Illustrations. Crown 8vo, Cloth, $3 50.

ANNUAL RECORD OF SCIENCE AND INDUSTRY FOR 1872. Edited by Prof. SPENCER F. BAIRD, of the Smithsonian Institution, with the Assistance of Eminent Men of Science. 12mo, over 700 pp., Cloth, $2 00. (Uniform with the *Annual Record of Science and Industry for* 1871. 12mo, Cloth, $2 00.)

COL. FORNEY'S ANECDOTES OF PUBLIC MEN. Anecdotes of Public Men. By JOHN W. FORNEY. 12mo, Cloth, $2 00.

MISS BEECHER'S HOUSEKEEPER AND HEALTHKEEPER: Containing Five Hundred Recipes for Economical and Healthful Cooking; also, many Directions for securing Health and Happiness. Approved by Physicians of all Classes. Illustrations. 12mo, Cloth, $1 50.

FARM BALLADS. By WILL CARLETON. Handsomely Illustrated. Square 8vo, Ornamental Cloth, $2 00; Gilt Edges, $2 50.

POETS OF THE NINETEENTH CENTURY. The Poets of the Nineteenth Century. Selected and Edited by the Rev. Robert Aris Willmott. With English and American Additions, arranged by Evert A. Duyckinck, Editor of "Cyclopædia of American Literature." Comprising Selections from the Greatest Authors of the Age. Superbly Illustrated with 141 Engravings from Designs by the most Eminent Artists. In elegant small 4to form, printed on Superfine Tinted Paper, richly bound in extra Cloth, Beveled, Gilt Edges, $5 00; Half Calf, $5 50; Full Turkey Morocco, $9 00.

THE REVISION OF THE ENGLISH VERSION OF THE NEW TESTAMENT. With an Introduction by the Rev. P. Schaff, D.D. 618 pp., Crown 8vo, Cloth, $3 00. This work embraces in one volume:
    I. ON A FRESH REVISION OF THE ENGLISH NEW TESTAMENT. By J. B. Lightfoot, D.D., Canon of St. Paul's, and Hulsean Professor of Divinity, Cambridge. Second Edition, Revised. 196 pp.
    II. ON THE AUTHORIZED VERSION OF THE NEW TESTAMENT in Connection with some Recent Proposals for its Revision. By Richard Chenevix Trench, D.D., Archbishop of Dublin. 194 pp.
    III. CONSIDERATIONS ON THE REVISION OF THE ENGLISH VERSION OF THE NEW TESTAMENT. By J. C. Ellicott, D.D., Bishop of Gloucester and Bristol. 178 pp.

NORDHOFF'S CALIFORNIA. California: For Health, Pleasure, and Residence. A Book for Travelers and Settlers. Illustrated. 8vo, Paper, $2 00; Cloth, $2 50.

MOTLEY'S DUTCH REPUBLIC. The Rise of the Dutch Republic. By John Lothrop Motley, LL.D., D.C.L. With a Portrait of William of Orange. 3 vols., 8vo, Cloth, $10 50.

MOTLEY'S UNITED NETHERLANDS. History of the United Netherlands: from the Death of William the Silent to the Twelve Years' Truce—1609. With a full View of the English-Dutch Struggle against Spain, and of the Origin and Destruction of the Spanish Armada. By John Lothrop Motley, LL.D., D.C.L. Portraits. 4 vols., 8vo, Cloth, $14 00.

NAPOLEON'S LIFE OF CÆSAR. The History of Julius Cæsar. By His late Imperial Majesty Napoleon III. Two Volumes ready. Library Edition, 8vo, Cloth, $3 50 per vol. *Maps to Vols. I. and II. sold separately. Price $1 50 each, NET.*

HAYDN'S DICTIONARY OF DATES, relating to all Ages and Nations. For Universal Reference. Edited by Benjamin Vincent, Assistant Secretary and Keeper of the Library of the Royal Institution of Great Britain; and Revised for the Use of American Readers. 8vo, Cloth, $5 00; Sheep, $6 00.

MACGREGOR'S ROB ROY ON THE JORDAN. The Rob Roy on the Jordan, Nile, Red Sea, and Gennesareth, &c. A Canoe Cruise in Palestine and Egypt, and the Waters of Damascus. By J. Macgregor, M.A. With Maps and Illustrations. Crown 8vo, Cloth, $2 50.

WALLACE'S MALAY ARCHIPELAGO. The Malay Archipelago: the Land of the Orang-Utan and the Bird of Paradise. A Narrative of Travel, 1854–1862. With Studies of Man and Nature. By Alfred Russel Wallace. With Ten Maps and Fifty-one Elegant Illustrations. Crown 8vo, Cloth, $2 50.

WHYMPER'S ALASKA. Travel and Adventure in the Territory of Alaska, formerly Russian America—now Ceded to the United States—and in various other parts of the North Pacific. By Frederick Whymper. With Map and Illustrations. Crown 8vo, Cloth, $2 50.

ORTON'S ANDES AND THE AMAZON. The Andes and the Amazon; or, Across the Continent of South America. By James Orton, M.A., Professor of Natural History in Vassar College, Poughkeepsie, N. Y., and Corresponding Member of the Academy of Natural Sciences, Philadelphia. With a New Map of Equatorial America and numerous Illustrations. Crown 8vo, Cloth, $2 00.

WINCHELL'S SKETCHES OF CREATION. Sketches of Creation: a Popular View of some of the Grand Conclusions of the Sciences in reference to the History of Matter and of Life. Together with a Statement of the Intimations of Science respecting the Primordial Condition and the Ultimate Destiny of the Earth and the Solar System. By Alexander Winchell, LL.D., Professor of Geology, Zoology, and Botany in the University of Michigan, and Director of the State Geological Survey. With Illustrations. 12mo, Cloth, $2 00.

WHITE'S MASSACRE OF ST. BARTHOLOMEW. The Massacre of St. Bartholomew: Preceded by a History of the Religious Wars in the Reign of Charles IX. By Henry White, M.A. With Illustrations. 8vo, Cloth, $1 75.

LOSSING'S FIELD-BOOK OF THE REVOLUTION. Pictorial Field-Book of the Revolution; or, Illustrations, by Pen and Pencil, of the History, Biography, Scenery, Relics, and Traditions of the War for Independence. By BENSON J. LOSSING. 2 vols., 8vo, Cloth, $14 00; Sheep, $15 00; Half Calf, $18 00; Full Turkey Morocco, $22 00.

LOSSING'S FIELD-BOOK OF THE WAR OF 1812. Pictorial Field-Book of the War of 1812; or, Illustrations, by Pen and Pencil, of the History, Biography, Scenery, Relics, and Traditions of the Last War for American Independence. By BENSON J. LOSSING. With several hundred Engravings on Wood, by Lossing and Barritt, chiefly from Original Sketches by the Author. 1088 pages, 8vo, Cloth, $7 00; Sheep, $8 50; Half Calf, $10 00.

ALFORD'S GREEK TESTAMENT. The Greek Testament: with a critically revised Text; a Digest of Various Readings; Marginal References to Verbal and Idiomatic Usage; Prolegomena; and a Critical and Exegetical Commentary. For the Use of Theological Students and Ministers. By HENRY ALFORD, D.D., Dean of Canterbury. Vol. I., containing the Four Gospels. 944 pages, 8vo, Cloth, $6 00; Sheep, $6 50.

ABBOTT'S FREDERICK THE GREAT. The History of Frederick the Second, called Frederick the Great. By JOHN S. C. ABBOTT. Elegantly Illustrated. 8vo, Cloth, $5 00.

ABBOTT'S HISTORY OF THE FRENCH REVOLUTION. The French Revolution of 1789, as viewed in the Light of Republican Institutions. By JOHN S. C. ABBOTT. With 100 Engravings. 8vo, Cloth, $5 00.

ABBOTT'S NAPOLEON BONAPARTE. The History of Napoleon Bonaparte. By JOHN S. C. ABBOTT. With Maps, Woodcuts, and Portraits on Steel. 2 vols., 8vo, Cloth, $10 00.

ABBOTT'S NAPOLEON AT ST. HELENA; or, Interesting Anecdotes and Remarkable Conversations of the Emperor during the Five and a Half Years of his Captivity. Collected from the Memorials of Las Casas, O'Meara, Montholon, Antommarchi, and others. By JOHN S. C. ABBOTT. With Illustrations. 8vo, Cloth, $5 00.

ADDISON'S COMPLETE WORKS. The Works of Joseph Addison, embracing the whole of the "Spectator." Complete in 3 vols., 8vo, Cloth, $6 00.

ALCOCK'S JAPAN. The Capital of the Tycoon: a Narrative of a Three Years' Residence in Japan. By Sir RUTHERFORD ALCOCK, K.C.B., Her Majesty's Envoy Extraordinary and Minister Plenipotentiary in Japan. With Maps and Engravings. 2 vols., 12mo, Cloth, $3 50.

ALISON'S HISTORY OF EUROPE. FIRST SERIES: From the Commencement of the French Revolution, in 1789, to the Restoration of the Bourbons, in 1815. [In addition to the Notes on Chapter LXXVI., which correct the errors of the original work concerning the United States, a copious Analytical Index has been appended to this American edition.] SECOND SERIES: From the Fall of Napoleon, in 1815, to the Accession of Louis Napoleon, in 1852. 8 vols., 8vo, Cloth, $16 00.

BALDWIN'S PRE-HISTORIC NATIONS. Pre-Historic Nations; or, Inquiries concerning some of the Great Peoples and Civilizations of Antiquity, and their Probable Relation to a still Older Civilization of the Ethiopians or Cushites of Arabia. By JOHN D. BALDWIN, Member of the American Oriental Society. 12mo, Cloth, $1 75.

BARTH'S NORTH AND CENTRAL AFRICA. Travels and Discoveries in North and Central Africa: being a Journal of an Expedition undertaken under the Auspices of H. B. M.'s Government, in the Years 1849-1855. By HENRY BARTH, Ph.D., D.C.L. Illustrated. 3 vols., 8vo, Cloth, $12 00.

HENRY WARD BEECHER'S SERMONS. Sermons by HENRY WARD BEECHER, Plymouth Church, Brooklyn. Selected from Published and Unpublished Discourses, and Revised by their Author. With Steel Portrait. Complete in 2 vols., 8vo, Cloth, $5 00.

LYMAN BEECHER'S AUTOBIOGRAPHY, &c. Autobiography, Correspondence, &c., of Lyman Beecher, D.D. Edited by his Son, CHARLES BEECHER. With Three Steel Portraits, and Engravings on Wood. In 2 vols., 12mo, Cloth, $5 00.

BOSWELL'S JOHNSON. The Life of Samuel Johnson, LL.D. Including a Journey to the Hebrides. By JAMES BOSWELL, Esq. A New Edition, with numerous Additions and Notes. By JOHN WILSON CROKER, LL.D., F.R.S. Portrait of Boswell. 2 vols., 8vo, Cloth, $4 00.

COMPLETE WORKS

OF

SAMUEL TAYLOR COLERIDGE,

WITH AN INTRODUCTORY ESSAY UPON HIS PHILOSOPHICAL
AND THEOLOGICAL OPINIONS.

EDITED BY REV. W. G. T. SHEDD, D.D.

PORTRAIT.

In sets, 7 vols., Crown 8vo, Cloth, $12 00.

VOL. I. AIDS TO REFLECTION—STATESMAN'S MANUAL. II. THE FRIEND. III.
BIOGRAPHIA LITERARIA. IV. LECTURES ON SHAKESPEARE AND OTHER
DRAMATISTS. V. LITERARY REMAINS. VI. SECOND LAY SERMON
AND TABLE-TALK. VII. POETICAL AND DRAMATIC WORKS.

The Volumes sold separately, in 12mo, at $1 75 each.

These seven volumes, edited by Professor Shedd, comprise the only complete edition of Coleridge's works, and are an important and valuable memorial to the rare gifts of one of the most profound thinkers of the present century. Prof. Shedd's essay is considered one of the most intelligent, profound, and discriminating discussions of a philosophical theme to be found in American literature. It is singularly lucid in thought, consecutive in argument, and chaste and appropriate in expression ; and is well worthy of the place which it occupies at the side of President Marsh's Preliminary Essay.

This illustrious man ; the largest and most spacious intellect, the subtlest and most comprehensive, in my judgment, that has yet existed among men. —DE QUINCEY.

His mind contains an astonishing map of all sorts of knowledge, while in his power and manner of putting it to use, he displays more of what we mean by the term genius, than any mortal I ever saw, or ever expect to see.—JOHN FOSTER.

I think, with all his faults, old Sam was more of a great man than any one that has lived within the four seas, in my memory.—Dr. ARNOLD.

PUBLISHED BY HARPER & BROTHERS, NEW YORK.

Any of the above Volumes will be sent by mail, postage prepaid, to any part of the United States, on receipt of the price.